SECOND EDITION

PREVENTIVE MEDICINE

Principles of Prevention in the
Occurrence and Progression of Disease

edited by

HERMAN E. HILLEBOE, M.D.

PROFESSOR OF PUBLIC HEALTH PRACTICE,
COLUMBIA UNIVERSITY, SCHOOL OF PUBLIC
HEALTH AND ADMINISTRATIVE MEDICINE

and

GRANVILLE W. LARIMORE, M.D.

FIRST DEPUTY COMMISSIONER OF HEALTH,
STATE OF NEW YORK,
DEPARTMENT OF HEALTH, ALBANY

W. B. SAUNDERS COMPANY
Philadelphia and London

W. B. Saunders Company: West Washington Square
Philadelphia, Pa.   19105

12 Dyott Street
London WC1A   1DB

833 Oxford Street
Toronto 18, Ontario

Listed here is the latest translated edition of this
book together with the language of the translation
and the publisher.

Portuguese (*1st Edition*)—Serpel (**O** Medico Moderno), Sao Paulo, Brazil

Spanish (*2nd Edition*)—Nueva Editorial Interamericana, S.A., de C.V.,
Mexico City

Preventive Medicine   ISBN   0-7216-4681-6

Print No.:   9   8   7   6   5

Dedication

This book is affectionately
dedicated to

Eda and Lee

and to the wives
of medical students and physicians everywhere

CONTRIBUTORS

FRANKLYN B. AMOS, M.D., M.P.H., F.A.C.P.M. *Continuing Education for Physicians—Vital Statistics*
Director, Office of Professional Education, New York State Department of Health, Albany; Associate Professor of Community Health, Albany Medical College, Albany; Lecturer, School of Public Health and Administrative Medicine, Columbia University, New York; Adjunct Professor of Environmental Engineering, Rensselaer Polytechnic Institute, Troy, New York; Formerly, Instructor, Harvard School of Public Health, Boston.

DAVID B. AST, D.D.S., M.P.H., F.A.C.D. *Dental Health*
Director, Bureau of Dental Health, New York State Department of Health, Albany; Instructor in Community Health, Albany Medical College, Albany; Lecturer, School of Public Health and Administrative Medicine, Columbia University, New York.

JOHN J. BOURKE, M.D., M.P.H., F.A.C.P.M. *The Role of the Hospital in Preventive Medicine*
Assistant Commissioner, Division of Hospital Review and Planning, New York State Department of Health, Albany; Assistant Professor of Community Health, Albany Medical College, Albany.

I. JAY BRIGHTMAN, M.D., D.Med.Sc., M.S.P.M., F.A.C.P., F.A.C.P.M. *Follow-up of Screening and Diagnostic Examinations—Alcoholism*
Assistant Commissioner, Division of Chronic Disease Services, New York State Department of Health, Albany;

Associate Professor of Community Health, Albany Medical College, Albany.

HENRY BRILL, M.D., F.A.P.A. *Mental Health—Narcotic Addiction*
Director, Pilgrim State Hospital, Brentwood, New York; Clinical Professor of Psychiatry, Albany Medical College, Albany; Lecturer, State University of New York, Upstate Medical Center, Syracuse; Lecturer, College of Physicians and Surgeons, Columbia University, New York; Vice-chairman, New York State Narcotic Control Commission; Formerly, First Deputy Commissioner, New York State Department of Mental Hygiene, Albany.

JOHN H. BROWE, M.D., M.P.H. Cert. Am. Brd. Nutrition. *Provision of Suitable and Sufficient Nutrition—Obesity*
Director, Bureau of Nutrition, New York State Department of Health, Albany; Instructor in Community Health, Albany Medical College, Albany.

CLAUDE H. COLVIN, B.S. *Milk-borne Illness—Food-borne Illness*
Chief, Sanitation Services Section, New York State Department of Health, Albany; Formerly, Bacteriologist, Borden Farm Products Company.

ANDREW C. FLECK, JR., M.D., M.P.H., LL.B., F.A.C.P.M. *Food-borne Illness*
Deputy Commissioner, New York State Department of Health, Albany; Assistant Professor of Community Health (Epidemiology), Albany Medical College, Albany; Formerly, Associate Commissioner, Community Health Service, New

York State Department of Health, Albany.

JULIA L. FREITAG, M.D., M.P.H. *Immunization*

Assistant Director, Office of Epidemiology, New York State Department of Health, Albany; Lecturer in Environmental Engineering, Rensselaer Polytechnic Institute, Troy, New York.

ANNA C. GELMAN, A.B., M.P.H. *Bacterial Disease—Viral Disease—Rickettsial Disease —Fungal Disease—Parasitic Disease*

Assistant Professor of Epidemiology, Division of Epidemiology, School of Public Health and Administrative Medicine of the Faculty of Medicine, Columbia University, New York.

JOHN T. GENTRY, M.D., M.P.H., F.A.C.P.M. *Hygiene of Housing*

Assistant Dean for Program Development and Associate Professor of Public Health Administration, University of North Carolina School of Public Health, Chapel Hill; Formerly, Clinical Associate Professor, Department of Preventive Medicine, State University of New York, Upstate Medical Center, Syracuse; Regional Director, New York State Department of Health, Syracuse.

WM. D. MORTIMER HARRIS, M.D., M.P.H., F.A.P.H.A. *Venereal Disease*

Chief, Division of Social Hygiene, New York City Department of Health, New York; Special Consultant, United States Public Health Service, Venereal Disease Branch, Washington, D.C.; Formerly, Professor of Dermatology and Venereology, Faculty of Medicine of Haiti; and Senior Advisor, Venereal Disease and Treponematoses, World Health Organization.

ROBERT D. HENNIGAN, P.E., M.A., DIP., A.A.S.E. *Water Supply—Hygiene of Housing*

Principal Engineer, New York State Office for Local Government, Albany; Formerly, Chief, Water Pollution Control Section, New York State Department of Health, Albany.

HERMAN E. HILLEBOE, M.D., M.P.H., F.A.C.P.M. *Preventive Medicine, Public Health and the Physician—Ionizing Radiation—Medical Defense Against Atomic Attack or Natural Disaster—Bacterial Disease —Viral Disease—Rickettsial Disease—Fungal* *Disease—Parasitic Disease—Screening Methods for Heart Disease—Rehabilitation— Official Health Agencies*

DeLamar Professor of Public Health Practice, School of Public Health and Administrative Medicine, Columbia University, New York; Formerly, Professor of Community Health, Albany Medical College, Albany; Assistant Surgeon General, United States Public Health Service, and Commissioner of Health, New York State Department of Health, Albany.

HOLLIS S. INGRAHAM, M.D., M.P.H. *Milkborne Illness—Official Health Agencies*

Commissioner of Health, New York State Department of Health, Albany; Professor of Community Health, Albany Medical College, Albany; Adjunct Associate Professor of Public Health Practice, School of Public Health and Administrative Medicine, Columbia University, New York; Formerly, First Deputy Commissioner, New York State Department of Health, Albany; and Lecturer in Epidemiology, Johns Hopkins School of Public Health, Baltimore.

SANDRA H. KINCH, B.A., M.A., M.S. *Vital Statistics*

Principal Biostatistician, Office of Biostatistics, New York State Department of Health, Albany.

MORRIS KLEINFELD, M.D., F.A.C.P., F.A.C.P.M. *Occupational Health*

Director, Division of Industrial Hygiene, New York State Department of Labor, New York; Adjunct Assistant Professor of Occupational Medicine, Columbia University, New York; Clinical Associate Professor of Medicine, State University of New York, Downstate Medical Center, Brooklyn.

JAMES H. LADE, M.D. *Medical Defense Against Atomic Attack or Natural Disaster*

Director of Medical Defense, New York State Department of Health, Albany; Associate Lecturer in Community Health, Albany Medical College, Albany; Formerly, Director of Syphilis Control, New York State Department of Health, Albany; and Venereal Disease Consultant, World Health Organization.

GRANVILLE W. LARIMORE, M.D., M.P.H., F.A.C.P.M. *Accident Hazards—Narcotic Addiction—Health Education and the Social Sciences—Patient Education and Communication*

First Deputy Commissioner, New York

State Department of Health, Albany; Associate Professor of Community Health, Albany Medical College, Albany; Lecturer, School of Public Health and Administrative Medicine, Columbia University, New York; Formerly, Deputy Commissioner, New York State Department of Health, Albany.

MORTON L. LEVIN, M.D., DR. P.H., F.A.C.P.M. *Cancer Detection and Screening*
Chief, Department of Epidemiology, Roswell Park Memorial Institute, New York State Department of Health, Buffalo.

ABRAHAM M. LILIENFELD, M.D., M.P.H. *Epidemiologic Methods and Inferences*
Professor of Chronic Diseases and Chairman, Department of Chronic Diseases, Johns Hopkins School of Hygiene and Public Health, Baltimore; Associate Professor of Medicine, Johns Hopkins School of Medicine, Baltimore; Formerly, Chief, Department of Statistics and Epidemiology, Roswell Park Memorial Institute, New York State Department of Health, Buffalo.

BERWYN F. MATTISON, M.A., M.D., C.M., M.P.H. *Voluntary Health Agencies*
Executive Director, American Public Health Association, New York; Lecturer, School of Public Health and Administrative Medicine, Columbia University, New York; Formerly, Secretary of Health, Commonwealth of Pennsylvania; and Secretary of National Health Council.

RUSSELL H. MORGAN, B.A., M.D. *Ionizing Radiation*
Professor of Radiological Science and Chairman, Department of Radiological Science, Johns Hopkins School of Hygiene and Public Health, Baltimore; Professor of Radiology and Chairman of Department of Radiology, Johns Hopkins School of Medicine; Radiologist-in-Chief, Johns Hopkins Hospital, Baltimore.

MARY E. PARKER, B.S., R.N., M.S.P.H. *Public Health Nursing*
Director, Office of Public Health Nursing, New York State Department of Health, Albany; Formerly, Instructor in Public Health Nursing, University of Minnesota, Minneapolis.

KURT REICHERT, M.A., Ph.D. *Social Work*
Associate Professor, Department of Social Work and Social Research, Bryn Mawr College, Pennsylvania; Formerly, Director of Public Health Social Work, New York State Department of Health, Albany; Assistant Professor and Chief Psychiatric Social Worker, University of Minnesota Medical School and Hospitals; Instructor, University of Minnesota School of Social Work, Minneapolis; Social Work Consultant, United States High Commission, Germany.

FRANK W. REYNOLDS, M.D., M.P.H., F.A.C.P. *Periodic Health Inventories — Screening Methods for Diabetes Mellitus*
Director, Division of Adult Health, Massachusetts Department of Public Health, Boston.

ALEXANDER RIHM, JR., P.E., B.S., M.S. *Air Pollution*
Director, Bureau of Air Pollution Control Services, New York State Department of Health, Albany; Executive Secretary, New York State Air Pollution Control Board, Albany; Lecturer in Community Health, Albany Medical College, Albany; Lecturer in Environmental Health Engineering, Rensselaer Polytechnic Institute, Troy, New York; Formerly, Chief, Radiological Health and Air Sanitation Section, Bureau of Environmental Sanitation, New York State Department of Health, Albany.

ARTHUR B. ROBINS, M.D., Dr. P.H., D. Med. Sc., F.A.C.P. *Tuberculosis*
Director, Bureau of Tuberculosis, New York City Department of Health, New York; Clinical Professor of Preventive Medicine, New York University College of Medicine; Lecturer, Department of Community Health and Environmental Medicine, State University of New York, Downstate Medical Center, New York.

IRWIN M. ROSENSTOCK, Ph.D. *Health Education and the Social Sciences*
Associate Professor of Public Health Administration and Co-Director, Research Program in Public Health Practices, School of Public Health, University of Michigan, Ann Arbor; Formerly, Chief, Behavioral Studies Section, Bureau of State Services, Public Health Service.

HOWARD A. RUSK, M.D., F.A.C.P. *Rehabilitation*
Professor and Chairman, Department of Physical Medicine and Rehabilitation, New York University School of Medicine, New York.

JOSEPH A. SALVATO, JR., P.E., B.S., M.C.E. *Food-borne Illness—Milk-borne Illness*
Director, Bureau of General Engineering and Sanitation Services, New York State Department of Health, Albany; Lecturer, Rensselaer Polytechnic Institute, Troy, New York; Formerly, Director, Division of Environmental Hygiene, Rensselaer County Health Department, Troy, New York.

MORRIS SCHAEFFER, A.B., M.A., Ph.D., M.D. *Mechanism of Infections and Resistance*
Director, Bureau of Laboratories, Department of Health, City of New York; Member, Public Health Research Institute of the City of New York; Professor of Medicine, New York University School of Medicine; Formerly, Medical Director in charge of Virus and Rickettsial Section, Communicable Disease Center, Public Health Service.

EDWARD R. SCHLESINGER, M.D., M.P.H., F.A.A.P. *The Maternity Cycle and the Newborn Period—Preventive Health Services in Childhood—Screening Methods*

for Hearing Defects and Visual Defects
Assistant Commissioner, Division of Special Health Services, New York State Department of Health, Albany; Assistant Professor of Community Health, Albany Medical College, Albany; Formerly, Director of Maternal and Child Health, New York State Department of Health, Albany.

MEREDITH H. THOMPSON, Dr. Eng., P.E. *Waste Disposal*
Assistant Commissioner, Division of Environmental Health Services, New York State Department of Health, Albany; Adjunct Professor of Environmental Engineering, Rensselaer Polytechnic Institute, Troy, New York; Formerly, Director of Environmental Hygiene, Rensselaer County Health Department, Troy, New York.

VICTOR N. TOMPKINS, M.D. *Insect Vectors*
Assistant Commissioner, Division of Laboratories and Research, New York State Department of Health, Albany; Professor of Pathology, Albany Medical College, Albany.

ACKNOWLEDGMENTS

Sincere appreciation is expressed to our colleagues in medicine and the other health professions for the favorable reception which they accorded the first edition of PREVENTIVE MEDICINE. We hope that they will find this second edition, embracing as it does a number of new features, of even greater interest and value.

To our contributors we say many, many thanks for taking time from their busy schedules to provide, from the wealth of their specialized knowledge, the many valuable contributions which this book contains.

We should also like to express our deep appreciation to the staff of the W. B. Saunders Company, particularly to Mr. Robert B. Rowan and to Mr. James P. Hughes, for their encouragement, patience, understanding and support, without which this book would not have been possible.

Finally we should like to indicate our gratitude to Mrs. Nancy N. Fey and to Miss Judith I. Terko for their most helpful assistance in the editing and processing of the manuscript and proofs.

HERMAN E. HILLEBOE, M.D.

GRANVILLE W. LARIMORE, M.D.

CONTENTS

Section B.   Prophylactic Measures Against
              Disease

Appendix to Section B

Section C.   Provision of Proper and Adequate
Nutrition

Section D.   Elimination of Predisease
Conditions

Section E.   Preventive Dentistry

PART TWO.   PREVENTION OF
PROGRESSION

Section A.   Periodic Health Inventories

Section B.   Early Detection of Disease

Section B.   Services Aiding the Practice
of Preventive Medicine

INTRODUCTION

The purpose of this book is to help medical students, physicians and others in the health field understand better how to practice preventive medicine.

Public health physicians see prevention in two major phases—preventing the occurrence of disease and disability and, when that is not possible, preventing their progression.

These two phases interlock in practice. A middle-aged father may come to his doctor complaining of a cold and harsh cough. The physician who is not prevention-minded might respond with a cursory auscultation of the chest, then write out a prescription for cough medicine and advise the father to return if there is further trouble.

The prevention-conscious physician is not satisfied until he has recorded a detailed family history and taken a chest roentgenogram, made a tuberculin test and ordered some laboratory tests. For his extra pains, this physician may be rewarded with the discovery of an active tuberculous lesion in the lungs at an early stage. Chances are good that prompt use of drugs will prevent progression of the lesion and arrest the disease. Thus, the physician is practicing prevention of progression, because the disease is already present.

However, the job is still unfinished. The next step is to bring in family contacts, try to find the primary source of the infection, then distinguish the uninfected family members from the infected. If the children of this father, for example, are tuberculin negative and the father is kept away from them until his disease is no longer communicable, the physician has prevented new cases of tuberculosis. This is prevention of occurrence.

Throughout this book, outstanding specialists in their field have spelled out ways the physician can apply the double-barreled concept of prevention. They have tried to present the knowledge learned by generations of physicians who have practiced preventive medicine and public health. Their sole aim is to help medical students, physicians and others in the health field see how the principles of preventive medicine can be put to work. Their approach is to present in concise form and with realistic examples, the two-phased but interlocking practice of preventive medicine.

The approaches described can be used equally by family physicians and specialists. The places where these methods can be put to use are anywhere the physician works—the office, the patient's home, the clinic, the nursing home, the hospital.

Opportunities for prevention literally surround us. The physician who seizes them gains the admiration of his patients and the respect of his colleagues. He realizes, in short, the dreams of personal and professional fulfillment that first drew him into the practice of medicine.

PART ONE

PREVENTION OF OCCURRENCE

1

1   Preventive Medicine, Public Health and the Physician

Many workers in medicine are puzzled over the distinction between the terms "preventive medicine" and "public health." Often, the terms are used interchangeably. They are related but have distinguishing characteristics.

Preventive medicine is that aspect of the physician's practice in which he applies to *individual patients* the knowledge and techniques from medical, social and behavioral science to prevent disease or its progression.

Public health is the science and art of applying knowledge and skills from medical and allied sciences in an organized *community* effort to maintain and improve the health of *groups of individuals*.

PRACTICING PREVENTIVE MEDICINE

The prevention-minded physician is alert for chances to prevent the occurrence and progression of diseases among patients and their families, an alertness which must usually be acquired. Once it is, it becomes second nature for the physician to be on the lookout for congenital defects in the newborn, for rehabilitation needs among stroke victims, for opportunities to improve the immunization status of his patients, for cautioning against the dangers of poisons left around the home within reach of toddlers, for malnutrition among his aged patients, for polluted wells on the farms of rural patients, for emotional danger signals among his teen-age patients and for the early signs of mental disorder among young and old married couples.

Often the preventive approach is suggested by patients themselves. This generation has seen the emergence of a lay public that is well aware of the wonders modern medical science offers. Mass communications have created, as never before, an urgent and persisting demand by patients for a brand of medical care that promises continued health. The extension of prepaid medi-

3

cal and health services has further accelerated the demand for preventive medicine.

Swamped by these requests for preventive medical services, the physician may feel beleaguered. The preventive approach to medicine does, after all, take more time, and time is always of the essence in the practice of medicine. However, the physician has vast resources at his command. He is backed up, first of all, by his colleagues in public health. They can help in many ways. Public health nurses, physical therapists and medical social workers in the health department are available to visit homebound patients. Public health laboratories manned by skilled personnel can perform a host of diagnostic tests.

The physician and the health officer can collaborate effectively on health education campaigns among families in rural areas, schoolchildren, factory workers or in the community as a whole.

Most state health departments today stock a wide variety of pamphlets, leaflets, films and exhibits produced for the lay public. Physicians may have most of these for the asking. Among them are colorful and well-illustrated materials on subjects ranging from heart disease, obesity, lung cancer and diabetes to poison ivy and infant care. All impress upon their readers the importance of seeing their physician early and regularly. Each is most effective if complemented by a personal reminder from the physician himself.

Health departments are giving increased attention to the problems of the chronically ill. Some have launched early case-finding efforts against such diseases as cervical cancer, diabetes and glaucoma, with those patients found to be "positive" referred to their physicians for care. Public health nurses are devoting more time to giving home bedside nursing care to the chronically ill. Physical therapist services to persons in their homes have increased.

Many communities are also exploring new ways to help the private practitioner care for his patient either in long-term care facilities or in the patient's home. These services range from bedside nursing service to comprehensive home-care programs, and include homemaker services and the use of nurses to help plan the early discharge and follow-up care of hospitalized patients.

Health departments also offer a wide range of advisory services to help the physician practice preventive medicine. A state health department with a nutrition bureau may offer, as a regular service, assistance to general practitioners who have patients with the special nutritional problems that accompany obesity, heart disease and diabetes.

Consultation services are also sometimes available through a state or local health department's medical rehabilitation program. Clinics for handicapped children are held throughout most states, and general practitioners are able to refer patients to these clinics, provided the condition indicates the need for specialist consultation. Recommendations of the clinic physician are returned to the referring physician through the local health officer.

In the communicable disease field, the private practitioner has a host of public health services at his command. It is the health department's job to keep track of communicable diseases on a community basis. Patients and their contacts are investigated and sometimes restricted. Family members are advised how to prevent spread of the disease.

Tuberculosis diagnostic and treatment clinics are usually operated by local health departments because of the contagious nature of the disease. Specially trained venereal disease investigators seek out persons with early infectious disease and help to arrange for the examination of contacts.

Many health departments provide (or cooperate with other community agencies in providing) prenatal and postnatal care via well-child and pre-school clinics. General practitioners and pediatricians participating in these clinics help to teach families the importance of seeing the family doctor regularly. Public health nurses also provide health supervision of well infants, expectant mothers and others; their services are available at the physician's request.

Immunization clinics and community-wide immunization campaigns are carried out by health departments. These prevent many diseases that could easily overwhelm the physician and consume much of his time. Many health departments make vaccines available to practicing physicians.

Recording and analyzing of statistics on births, causes of death and disease incidence by health departments also ease the work of the prevention-minded physician since this information is always available, providing a useful diagnostic tool.

Follow-up work on environmental conditions relating to illness are available to physicians for the asking. Health departments supervise water supplies, waste treatment facilities, milk production, food processors and restaurants, places of public accommodation, and x-ray installations and are on the alert for vectors of disease and disability.

Health department services available to the physician vary with time, place and local custom. Not all the services mentioned will be available in some places; others not mentioned will be. The point is that a range of complementing public health services is at the ready call of any physician. By finding out what services are available in his locality, and using them, the physician significantly extends the preventive services to his patients. By tapping health department resources, the physician saves precious time while at the same time he brings into play a skilled group of specialists to assist him in the practice of preventive medicine.

Despite the range of help available from health departments, the physician still needs to involve himself directly in the practice of preventive medicine. There can be no question that practicing preventive medicine does take extra time. The physician, busy most of his waking hours with diagnostic and treatment problems, may balk at devoting more of his energies to prevention. He may ask: "How can I possibly do more work than I'm already doing?"

One answer lies in reorganizing his activities, his office arrangements, his priorities and his appointments. This requires that he truly run his practice and not let his practice run him. Around him he will find colleagues who have done just that and who are more than willing to pass on their know-how. A well-run practice that actually permits a physician to apply preventive medicine does not just happen. It must be forged from the physician's own experiences and tempered by his own determination to build a practice that meets his highest ideals. He must give priority to his patient's needs and not just their demands. He will begin thinking how he may serve some of the emotional and mental needs of his patients as well as their physical ones.

By improving and applying preventive techniques, the physician can serve his patients better, enlarge the scope of his practice and contribute effectively to his community's health. He will find the combined practice of preventive and therapeutic medicine deeply rewarding.

The Role of the Specialist

Preventive medicine is not solely the province of the general practitioner; it is equally the responsibility of the specialist.

The pediatrician practices preventive medicine on every patient and parent he sees in his office, in the clinic, in the hospital, in the school. He prevents the occurrence of countless numbers of cases of communicable disease by his immunization procedures. He encourages mothers to bring their apparently healthy children into his office for detection of early disease and advice on normal growth and development. He anticipates social and psychological problems among children and their parents and tries to correct these conditions before they become serious or irreversible. The pediatrician is truly a clinical practitioner of preventive medicine.

The specialist in internal medicine also realizes that his main chance, often the only one, to help his patients avoid permanent impairment and premature death is by preventive action. Cigarette smoking and the toxic air pollutants associated with certain occupations are classic examples of the manner in which removal of the cause makes possible subsequent avoidance of future disability. The internist looks at the whole body and not just at one organ or disease. Accordingly, he has the opportunity to be a leading exponent of both preventive and therapeutic medicine.

The obstetrician practices preventive medicine in his insistence that his patients come in early and regularly for prenatal examinations. Usually he arranges that a pediatrician be on hand to take whatever preventive action may be indicated at the birth of the child and during the critical first week of life. He insists on postnatal examinations of the mother to prevent future gynecological difficulties.

The industrial physician practices preventive medicine in most of its phases. He makes pre-employment and periodic examinations to detect disease early or in a minimal stage and follows through to make certain that treatment is given. He is concerned with providing a healthy working environment and in keeping workers fit so that they will have low absenteeism and high productivity rates. In some instances he helps to maintain the health of the worker's family.

The psychiatrist explores the mind to seek out hidden threats to mental health. He cannot always cure, but early detection often enables him to arrest progression and avoid deterioration.

The modern surgeon practices preventive medicine by making certain that his patient is truly prepared for surgery and by anticipating biochemical as well as bacteriological complications that may follow operative procedures.

The pathologist is becoming a strong exponent of the importance in medical teaching and practice of the complementary aspects of etiology and prevention. He points out the stages of progression of disease at which changes are still reversible and promotes concepts of prevention by retracing the complete evolution of lesions for his colleagues and students.

From these examples it should be apparent that every specialist can reap significant benefits for the recipients of his services by the systematic and continuing application of the knowledge and skills of prevention.

THE PRACTICE OF PUBLIC HEALTH

We have said that the practice of preventive medicine is conducted on a physician-to-patient basis. The practice of public health is conducted primarily on a public health physician-to-community basis. Some public health functions may be conducted on a one-to-one basis—the work of the public health physician in the tuberculosis clinic, for example; and some of the private physician's work may be conducted on a community-wide basis as, for example, when he takes on the job of school health physician or part-time health officer. In the main, however, the distinction and its attendant responsibilities hold clear.

The areas in which the public health physician operates elude precise identification for the simple reason that the range of public health activities varies in each locality. The reasons for this variation are not difficult to understand: The health problems of a locality depend on the natural and social environment of that locality. Every place is different in its soil, water, climate and topography. Each locality also has a distinctive profile of cultural and subcultural modes, ethnic makeup, political structure and historical heritage.

Because of this unique character of a locality's health problems—and the people's response to them—public health often turns out to be a compromise between what the people of a community want it to be and what the public health officer proposes it should be. The success of the compromise is a measure of the statesmanship of the health officer, and his ability to persuade people to adopt health services that truly reflect the needs of the community often depends upon the support given him by the practicing physicians in the area.

PROBLEM AREAS OF PUBLIC HEALTH

Despite the local shifts in emphasis that public health practice must reflect, there are, in general, four main areas of concern today.

In the *developed* nations of the world, these main concerns can be grouped under certain broad headings. So broad are these concerns that, when the health officer gets down to the fundamental techniques of solving them, he finds that problems and solutions often overlap.

Chronic Disease and Disabilities.   These would include heart disease, cancer, cerebrovascular diseases, mental disorders, chronic alcoholism, and the diseases of the aging, the degenerative processes. The primary victims of these diseases, the aging, also face severe social and economic problems.

Acute Medical and Surgical Conditions.   These usually require hospital and other medical services. The viral diseases are becoming more important in this area and demand special attention.

Child Health and the Care of Pregnant Women.   The obstetrician, pediatrician and general practitioner share these responsibilities. Special problems include physically and mentally handicapped children, the preschool and school-age child and the adolescent. Preventive mental health services have a great potential among children because early diagnosis is easier and therapy more successful.

Environmental Hazards to Health.   These include accidental injuries and disabilities occurring at home, at work, at play and on the road; contamination of water, food, air and soil by the organic and inorganic wastes of communities and industry; the effects of ionizing radiation; and industrial, recreational and housing hazards to health, especially in large cities.

These four categories are about equally important.

In overcrowded urban areas, poverty and lack of education often make solution of health problems difficult. Cultural patterns and customs associated with illness among the heterogeneous populations of a city often add to this complexity. Health and social problems are inseparable.

In *developing* countries, the major problem areas are grouped differently because of the morbidity and mortality patterns associated with depressed social and economic conditions. These are the four main areas:

Acute Communicable Diseases.   These often lead to chronic illnesses in all age groups and produce marked debilitating effects on large population groups.

Environmental Health Hazards.   These include especially water and food supplies contaminated by human excreta; infection and infestation spread by a variety of animal and insect vectors; poor housing; accidents at home and at work, mostly in rural areas.

Child and Maternal Morbidity and Mortality.   These have an adverse social and economic effect on family life.

Malnutrition.   This is often due to frank poverty; it is frequently complicated by infections and infestations, disabling entire families and whole communities.

In many developing countries, the task of improving health is made exceedingly difficult because of the shortages of food, pure water, adequate housing, education and work opportunities and the lack of health personnel and facilities. Poverty is the great enemy of health in all such countries. Other retarding influences are the general attitudes, cultural characteristics and customs of the people when illness is present.

THE METHODS OF PUBLIC HEALTH

The objectives of all health programs, public or private, are to reduce the prevalence, incidence, mortality and debility from diseases and disabilities and to promote the general health of the people.

Methods and resources for this task vary with the community. Priorities must be locally determined and are based upon two main considerations: the social, cultural and economic complexion of the area; and the distribution of diseases, injuries and disabilities by age, sex, occupation, educational status and other epidemiological factors.

Ideally, periodic health surveys provide the medical and public health leaders with the data upon which to base types and amounts of work to be done by medical practitioners and public health personnel. Practically speaking, planning usually proceeds from gross estimates based on vital statistics, hospital admission records, morbidity reports to health departments and inventories of professional personnel and medical facilities. In planning, data from other countries may be used for comparative purposes only if one makes allowances for social, cultural and economic differences.

The Binding Link—Enough Trained Manpower

In Developed Countries. The key resource in meeting the health problems of a community is professional personnel of high quality and in adequate numbers. One cannot provide adequate health services without qualified personnel, including nonprofessional workers. There can be no compromise on this principle, which is applicable in all countries.

In fact, the World Health Organization (WHO) since its beginning has given special attention to preventive medicine and has recognized the unique relevance of prevention to every aspect of medical care. Without preventive services the financial burden of medical care would soon become unbearable even in developed countries. Accordingly, WHO has stressed the need for teaching preventive medicine in the undergraduate curricula of medical schools and in the postgraduate education of medical practitioners, so that prevention will become an indispensable part of everyday practice. The WHO Technical Report on the Promotion of Medical Practitioner's Interest in Preventive Medicine[1] provides a comprehensive view of the subject from the standpoint of both the family physician and the medical student.

An adequate number of qualified educational and training centers for basic and postgraduate medical education and auxiliary technical training is also important. Teachers of adequate number and training are equally essential. Health personnel require adequate facilities in which to work—hospitals, health centers, clinics, laboratories, nursing homes, rehabilitation centers, and medical practitioners' offices (for solo or group practice).

We need fully qualified professors of preventive medicine in medical schools to give this specialty the status and attention it deserves among the faculty members and medical students. We need well-supported departments of preventive medicine to enable departmental staff to teach, to do research, and to collaborate with their colleagues in private practice and public health in their communities. Teachers of preventive medicine can emphasize to students the social and economic implications of illness and disability to the individual, the family and the community.

We need teachers of preventive medicine to bring to the attention of other faculty specialists, in both the basic sciences and in the clinical fields, the contributions that biostatistics and epidemiology, the social and the behavioral sciences can make to all specialties. We need preventive medicine teachers to work closely with health departments and medical associations in postgraduate education programs for medical practitioners, especially in suburban and rural areas.

Our primary hope of solving the major health problems in the years ahead is to help future physicians to understand and to apply the broad concepts of the preventive aspects of medical care.

For this reason, it is highly desirable for medical students to participate in community health activities under the competent supervision of family physicians. It is in the home that social and psychological problems develop insidiously and complicate the medical treatment ordered by the physician or by some distant hospital or clinic. It is here that the student can learn to appreciate and use the services of the public health nurse and the social worker. This recommendation stems from the principle that the best place to practice prevention is at the source—where the people live.

Certainly every student before he finishes medical school should have had the responsibility of a family case study. Here he can observe over a two- or three-year period the evolution of disease as illness affects the mental, physical and social well-being of all members of the household. Here he can learn to apply preventive measures before damage is done and to apply ameliorative measures in those inevitable conditions whose occurrence we have not learned how to avoid. This kind of teaching and learning experience in the home is available under the guidance of prevention-minded practitioners assisted by their local health officers.

In developed countries, governments and medical societies are bringing increasing numbers of postgraduate courses in general medicine and its preventive aspects to general practitioners in their own communities. Teaching groups go out from teaching hospitals and medical centers to meet with family physicians at mutually agreeable locations. Case studies are presented and actual consultations are held for teaching purposes. Experts from health departments and schools of public health are added to the teaching groups to emphasize the preventive approach to practice. All this is to the common good and is deficient only in coverage and continuity.

In Developing Countries. In developing countries, the picture is quite different. There is a scarcity of physicians, medical schools, health departments and hospitals. The practitioner is often isolated from his colleagues, receives small pay for his work, treats everything from diaper rash to skull fractures, and competes with unlicensed and ignorant native healers. He has little time for the social and psychological aspects of medicine. These major obstacles to practicing preventive medicine are likely to continue unless central governmental health agencies join hands with the local physicians to overcome these difficulties. General practitioners have a role to play in national campaigns of disease control such as malaria, tuberculosis and trachoma; they should be included in planning any such campaigns and not be brought in as an afterthought.

Stark poverty prevents many people in developing countries from obtaining adequate nutrition and from preserving their health. Yet these same people live to reproduce their kind in overwhelming numbers. Overpopulation threatens the future welfare of a number of nations in the developing areas of the world. Population control offers the only feasible solution. It is another example of prevention of occurrence of a health and welfare problem at its source. The many methods of family planning, although none is perfect or acceptable to all, offer a diversity of approaches for use by the physicians and health departments of the developing countries.

In fact, as Baumgartner[2] noted at the 1964 Johns Hopkins International Conference on Population: "It is recognized that the decisions as to population policies and their implementation in other countries are to be made by individual countries and families in accord with their own needs and values. This is true in our own country, too. There is an ever wider recognition of both artificial and natural methods of regulating pregnancy and they are increasingly being made freely available to all segments of the population. The U. S. Government feels it desirable that all health facilities supported by public funds shall provide such freedom of choice so that persons of all faiths are given equal opportunities to exercise their choice without offense to their consciences." This is a problem of prevention that demands a mass attack if its benefits are to accrue in the present and succeeding generations.

In all phases of planning and execution of health and medical services the family physician has a key position in both preventive and therapeutic medicine, but he should be paid for preventive services as well as for diagnosis and treatment. He should be paid for mass prophylaxis and screening, for family counseling, for services in community hospital work. He should receive support for postgraduate education if his income is insufficient to permit participation otherwise.

In developing countries, governmental health leaders can improve preventive services by providing the methods and the resources to extend postgraduate education for its medical practitioners, no matter how isolated. Meeting the therapeutic needs of the people is not enough. Only by a combination of preventive and therapeutic medicine is there hope of solving the problem of adequate medical care.

PUBLIC HEALTH TODAY

In this book, the authors have tried to blend the preventive aspects of family medical practice with the preventive aspects of public health. The two are interdependent and essential in improving the health of all persons in the community. Today's broad concept of public health did not always exist. The twentieth century concept had its origin when people realized that organized community action with public funds was the only way to control communicable diseases and unsanitary surroundings.

The community's leaders met the need by creating and then directing health agencies to diagnose, treat and prevent diseases of public concern, which when uncontrolled caused intolerable social and economic drains on families. As time went on and public benefits became clearly evident, communities supplied hospitals and medical care for the tuberculous, the physically handicapped and the mentally disordered.

Public concern over children as helpless victims of disease and disability led to health protection programs for mothers and babies at public expense. There has developed a strong public conviction that no child should be denied his birthright to good health because of economic barriers. Maternal and child health services have become a permanent part of the services of official health agencies.

In the United States and other developed countries, official health agencies, with the support of voluntary health agencies, have added each year to their responsibilities for the care of those suffering from cancer, heart disease and other chronic illnesses. They have extended their efforts to reduce or eliminate environmental hazards in the air, water, food and surroundings in which people live, work and pursue leisure activity.

The list of public health interests and responsibilities is still growing, stimulated by the people's interest in health problems. In the United States hundreds of millions of national tax dollars have gone to state health agencies for service, research and education, to help local communities solve their complex health problems. The stimulus for these expenditures came from the elected representatives of the people and not solely from the demands of the health agencies. The needs of the people have been translated into militant attitudes toward unsolved health problems. Increased resources to fight disease have been the inevitable result.

The official health agencies in the United States have not attempted to assume an all-inclusive role in public health activities. They have shared responsibilities with voluntary health agencies, medical societies, urban medical teaching centers and schools of public health. The voluntary health agencies have demonstrated strong leadership in research, in health education of the people and in demonstrations of mass campaigns to control disease and disability.

Today the specialist in public health has the education and experience to give health leadership in the community. He possesses knowledge and skills in organization and administration, in group processes, and in the social and economic structures of his community in addition to his basic training and experience in epidemiology, public health practice and bio-statistics. This new generation of public health physicians, specialty board qualified and dedicated to their public responsibilities, merits the respect of its medical colleagues in hospital and private practice. The public health physician does not compete with the family physician in preventive services but complements him and assists him in practicing a quality of preventive medicine otherwise impossible.

Through the mutual confidence which comes from working together on a common problem, private practitioners and public health physicians, both general practitioner and specialist, can provide the community with the high quality of preventive and therapeutic services that neither could provide so well alone.

HERMAN E. HILLEBOE, M.D.

REFERENCES

1. Promotion of Medical Practitioners' Interest in Preventive Medicine, WHO Technical Report Series No. 269, 1964. Geneva, World Health Organization.
2. Baumgartner, Leona: Address before the International Conference on Population, Baltimore, Md., May 27, 1964. Washington 25, D.C., Agency for International Development, State Department.

2   Accident Hazards

INTRODUCTION

In 1963 there were 101,000 accidental deaths in this country.[1] Accidents rank fourth as a cause of death, exceeded only by heart disease, malignant neoplasms and cerebrovascular lesions. Accidents are the leading cause of death between the ages of 1 and 24, dropping to second in the 25 to 44 age group, fourth in the 45 to 64 age group, fifth in the 65 to 74 age group and sixth in the group over 75. Accidental death rates by age groups range from 18 per 100,000 for the 5 to 14 age group to 276 for those over 75. The fact that accidents are only the sixth cause of death for the oldest group, in spite of the higher rate, is accounted for by the high death rates from heart disease and other chronic illnesses among the elderly. Quantitatively, the group contributing most to the accidental death total is the 15 to 34 age group, among whom 25 per cent of all accidental deaths occur.

Accidents are not only a major cause of death, but contribute greatly to morbidity as well. The National Health Survey conducted by the United States Public Health Service reports that annually during the period from July 1959 to June 1962, inclusive, about 10,800,000 persons suffered "bed-disabling" injuries* as the result of accidents.[2] That accidents have an appreciable impact on medical care facilities is shown by the survey made by the Bureau of Medical Economic Research of the American Medical Association,[3] which indicated that nearly one out of every three hospital emergency room patients is an accident victim and that approximately 7 per cent of the nation's general hospital resources are devoted to caring for those injured in accidents.

Accidents also result in a severe economic loss. The National Safety Council estimates that the total cost of accidents in 1963 was 16.1 billion dollars, which includes such items as wage losses, hospital and medical expenses and property damage and destruction.[1]

In spite of the fact that accidents are obviously not only an economic

---

* A "bed-disabling" injury is one which confines a person to bed for more than half of the daylight hours (on the day of the accident or on some following day).

but also a major health problem, their prevention has received relatively little attention from the medical profession and from health agencies. Although Godfrey,[4] in 1937, categorized accident prevention as a public health problem, it is only within recent years that papers devoted to accident prevention have become fairly common in medical journals. Yet the medical profession, particularly in the area of preventive medicine, has much to contribute toward a solution of the accident problem. It may be predicted that with the developing public concern about accidents, particularly motor vehicle accidents, there will be increasing demands upon physicians for greater participation in accident prevention.

There are ample opportunities for such participation. The physician may take a moment to caution the mother about the hazards of household poisons to the exploring toddler. When making a house call, he may notice insecure throw rugs on waxed floors in a home where elderly people are living. The physician should be on the lookout for disturbances in gait, especially in the elderly, a condition conducive to disastrous falls. The physician should be cautious in prescribing barbiturates or other potent drugs and should order only enough to meet the immediate need. This, and a precautionary warning, may help to eliminate the hazard of such medicines falling into the inquisitive hands of small children. The physician can emphasize the use of safety devices, such as bathtub rails, in homes where there are elderly patients. He can assure himself that his community has an adequate and workable plan for providing good emergency medical care for accident victims; he can support research activities aimed at finding better ways of coping with the accident problem. Finally, he can keep himself informed so that he can help to promote accident prevention measures which are carefully conceived and can aid in the defeat of unsound measures.

Health agencies also have an opportunity to contribute toward a lessening of the accident toll. The epidemiologic approach to the accident problem holds great promise. The accident syndrome may be dissected into virtually the same components as any disease: agent, host and environment. In the epidemiologic approach, accidents are first grouped by causation and then studied as to the factors associated with the victim or host, the agent which produced the accident and finally the contributing circumstances in the environment. Just as with any disease problem, this approach enables the investigator to bring into sharp focus the relevant etiologic factors and separate them from the nonessential. In this presentation, the accident problem will be approached in these terms.

The number of deaths from accidents has remained fairly constant for about 30 years. In 1928 there were 95,000 accidental deaths, a figure only somewhat less than that in 1963. The relative stability of the number of accidental deaths tends to obscure the fact that there has been considerable improvement over the years. The death rate per 100,000 population, which was 83.1 during the period from 1908 to 1912, dropped to 52 in 1963. Expressed another way, the total deaths in 1963 would have been about 160,000 (instead of 101,000) had the 1908 to 1912 rates prevailed. When these crude accident death rates are adjusted for age distribution, the differences become even more pronounced and indicate a drop of nearly 40 per cent in the rates over the past 50 years. The improvement has, however, been spotty among age groups. While there has been a 56 per cent improvement in the group 0 to 5 years of age and 31 per cent in those over 65, there has been no improvement in the 15 to 24 age group, whose accidental death rate is essentially the same now as it was 50 years ago. In interpreting the figures, it must be remembered that the improvements are not due entirely to fewer accidents, but are also the result of better medical care which saves the lives of many accident victims who 50 years ago would have been numbered among the fatalities.

In considering accidents from the standpoint of host-agent-environment, it is convenient to group them by the major environments in which they occur: motor vehicles, home, public places and on the job. This last category may be broken down into industrial (work) accidents and farm accidents. Of these environments, the motor vehicle is the largest accidental killer and maimer. Of the 101,000 accidental deaths in 1963, 43,600 were the result of motor vehicle accidents. Next in point of danger was the home, where accidents caused 29,000 deaths. Work accidents resulted in 14,200 deaths, including 2600 in agriculture; and in public places accidents numbered 17,500.*

Sex and age are important factors in the accident picture. Males have a far higher accidental death rate than females, except at ages over 85. In fact, 70 per cent of all accidental deaths occur to males, and the ratio of male to female accidental deaths is 4 to 1 at ages 15 to 24. There are also differences according to race; for most ages under 75, rates for nonwhites are higher than for whites.

The epidemiologic picture of accidents presents seasonal variations. December generally has the highest number of accidental deaths, with July second. The peak in December is due primarily to the high mortality from motor vehicle accidents, but the nonmotor vehicle accident incidence is also high. In July the peak is due to a rise in the number of nonmotor vehicle deaths from warm weather causes such as drowning, water transport accidents and excessive heat. Some accidental death causes, such as poisoning, show little seasonal variation.

There are also marked regional variations within the United States. In 1963 the accidental death rate for the Mountain States (Nevada, Arizona, Montana, Wyoming, New Mexico, Idaho, Colorado and Utah) was the highest of any group of states, 70.6 per 100,000, as compared to 40.1 for the Middle Atlantic States (New York, Pennsylvania and New Jersey). The highest accidental death rate among all of the states was that of Alaska, 115.3; the lowest was Rhode Island, 36.0. Other regions and their death rates were: New England, 43.9; Middle Atlantic, 40.1; East North Central, 48.3; West North Central, 59.3; South Atlantic, 57.8; East South Central, 63.4; West South Central, 58.9; Mountain, 70.6; Pacific, 46.8. These regional variations are due mainly to differences in motor vehicle accident death rates, although it is of interest to note that death rates from falls are highest in the North Central and Northeast Regions and in the South the rates from fires are highest.

While statistical data from different nations must be compared with caution because of differences in reporting and other factors, it is interesting to note that in the latest tabulation the United States had the 13th highest

---

* Because of certain statistical duplication in classification of accidents, these figures total more than 101,000. Figures quoted are for the United States.

death rate among the 49 countries reporting their experience to the World Health Organization.

Although this chapter on accidents has been placed in the section dealing with prevention of occurrence, some of the textual treatment also deals with prevention of progression. The change has been made in this instance to assure a more integrated result and also because the twin aspects of prevention of occurrence and prevention of progression are inextricably bound together in any discussion of accidents.

ACCIDENTS IN THE HOME

Home accidents cause more injuries than any other category of accidents, and as a cause of accidental death rank second only to motor vehicle accidents in the United States. There were 4,400,000 injuries (persons disabled one or more days) and 29,000 deaths from home accidents in 1963. These figures represent 44 and 29 per cent, respectively, of the total accidental injuries and deaths recorded in 1963. In the past 35 years, total deaths from home accidents have decreased only slightly although the rate has dropped 40 per cent, this being accounted for by the growth of population during this period. Home accidents ranked ninth among the causes of death in 1963.

In spite of these decreases the toll from home accidents is still a cause for concern, and every physician should be aware of potential accident hazards when he visits the home of a patient. He should also be alert to conditions among his patients which increase the likelihood of accidents. While home accidents may affect any age group, the persons most susceptible are those under 5 and over 65. Among the very young, 7 out of 10 accidents occur at home. Aged persons are involved in well over half of all deaths from home accidents.

The primary accident hazard conditions in the home that the physician should caution his patients about are those which predispose its occupants to falls, since this is the largest single cause of accidental death, accounting for almost half of the total. Ranking second are fire burns, followed in order by suffocation, poisoning by liquids or solids, firearms and gas poisoning. The balance of accidental home deaths is due to a miscellany of causes which include drowning, electrocution and burns from hot substances.

The area in the home where the physician is most apt to find accident hazards is one that he is most likely to observe when caring for a patient—the bedroom. Falls in the bedroom account for almost 90 per cent of home accident deaths among persons over 65. Following the bedroom in accident hazard potential are the kitchen, stairways, living room and basement, in that order. Of the total accidents caused in the home, about 80 per cent occur inside the home, with the remainder occurring in areas immediately adjacent, such as the yard.

Another factor of increasing importance in the home accident pattern is the increasing amount of leisure time, with the resultant mushrooming interest in do-it-yourself home repairs. The number of accidents resulting from activity in the home workshop has jumped upward, and injuries from workshop power tools (virtually an unknown category 30 years ago) are now significant. The trend toward suburban living has increased the use of power lawn mowers. While no comprehensive figures on power mower accidents are as yet available, a study of 67 such accidents by the Pennsylvania Department of Health[5] points up certain of the factors involved: one injury in seven was an amputation, one in ten a puncture or perforation, most of the remainder were cuts or lacerations; toe, fingers and legs were the body parts most frequently injured; objects thrown by the mower caused nearly half of the injuries; 12 per cent of the operators had less than one month's experience with the mower and more than half the injuries occurred during the first 2 months of the lawn-care season. This suggests the need to build more adequate safeguards into power mowing equipment, and to educate homeowners and others in the use of caution in operating mowers, with emphasis on the danger of flying objects and forbidding the use of mowers by children.

The same need for safety engineering exists among other items of household equipment and home appliances, for there is little the homeowner himself can do to increase such safety. Engineering disregard for electric shock hazards, unprotected moving parts and inadequately shielded hot areas contributes to the rate of accidents caused by household equipment. About the only protection that the consumer or householder has against fire and electrical hazards is to purchase equipment rated by the Underwriters Laboratories, whose UL symbol of approval should be on every piece of electrical goods purchased. Consumer protective groups, such as the Consumers Union, also serve by recommending safe household equipment and appliances.

PREVENTION OF OCCURRENCE

Since many falls in the home occur among the elderly, the physician can contribute a great deal toward their prevention by seeing to the adequate nutrition of his elderly patients and by prescribing activity in keeping with an aging person's physical capacities and requirements. Proper nutrition aids in the maintenance of strength, and moderate physical activity helps to maintain muscle tone—important factors both in giving persons maximal ability to evade accidents and in minimizing the effect of injuries. The physician should be on the lookout for erratic gait or imbalance among his patients, since these conditions predispose to accidental falls. Osteoporosis is also a factor of importance in the greater susceptibility to fractures among the elderly. Aged patients should be cautioned about the greater hazard of falls due to muscle and joint stiffness immediately after they arise from sleep or after a period of inactivity. Certain drugs may also contribute to this hazard, particularly in the elderly. The physician, as health counselor to his elderly patients, should also caution about the use of ladders and the need to leave one hand free for grasping the handrail when using stairs.

The physician should note accident hazards when visiting the homes of patients and bring them to the attention of household occupants whenever he sees unsafe conditions which might predispose to falls.

Fire

Fire burns are particularly hazardous for children and the elderly, since both are relatively helpless in fleeing from fires that have already started. This points to the need for providing adequate protection in the home for the very young and very old. The physician should caution mothers with small babies and those who have an elderly person in their home to avoid leaving such persons alone. In addition, young children are frequently tempted to experiment with matches and fires and, when they are left unattended, this becomes critically hazardous.

Suffocation

In 1963 suffocation due to ingested objects resulted in 1400 deaths and suffocation due to mechanical causes, e.g., thin plastic materials, confinement in closed places and mechanical strangulation in 1300 deaths. Together these represent about 9 per cent of the total of deaths from accidents in the home. The ingested objects producing suffocation ranged from small toys, hard candy, nuts and similar materials in the case of young children to a bolus of food, especially meat, in adults. Mothers should be cautioned about the propensity of the small child for conveying any object within reach to the mouth where it may be either swallowed or aspirated. In adults, poor dentition, or hasty or faulty eating habits may contribute to aspiration of food masses.

Many deaths from mechanical suffocation could be prevented if thin plastic materials were kept out of the reach of small children, if discarded refrigerators had their door-locks or doors removed and if small children were more closely watched at play to avoid cave-ins from juvenile digging and sometimes too realistically carried out games.

Solid or Liquid Poisons

More than four-fifths of all fatal accidental poisonings occur in the home. Barbituric acid derivatives are the most common offenders, with aspirin and kerosene ranking first among children. Accidental deaths by poisoning are a particularly tragic category since about one-third occur in children under 5, thus representing carelessness, not of the victims, but of the adults in the home. Like firearm accidents, poisonings are almost without exception completely preventable.

The most important factor in the prevention of poisonings is that of protecting the young child who cannot be expected to know the hazards presented. As the child grows older, protection must be supplemented by education, which is again the responsibility of the adults in the home. Those in the home who may have impaired vision, such as the elderly, also need protection to avoid their misreading poison warnings on bottles and cans, or the labels on drug containers.

The prevention of poisoning in the home concerns not only the sub stances generally recognized as having toxic properties but also the group of potential poisons, such as bleaches, soaps, detergents, cleansers and similar household products which may cause poisoning, especially when ingested.

Firearms

Half of all fatal firearm accidents take place in the home (1100 out of 2200 firearm accidental deaths in 1963). There has been an increase of about 10 per cent in the number of such accidents during the past few years. In all likelihood this reflects the increased interest in hunting and other sports involving the use of guns, which has paralleled the increase in leisure time. To no other class of accidents can the statement that all accidents are preventable be applied with more authority. Almost without exception, such accidents are caused by human error, reflected in carelessness in handling a loaded weapon.

The physician should keep in mind that one-third of the fatal firearm accidents in the home involve children in the 5 to 14 age group. Firearms should be stored so that they are inaccessible to younger children. Older children should be allowed to handle or use firearms only after detailed instruction from and with proper supervision by informed adults. Firearms should never be handled by anyone who is intoxicated, for the possession of sound judgment is necessary at all times where firearms are involved.

Poison Gases

There has been a considerable drop in recent years in the number of accidental deaths from gas poisoning in the home. In 1950 there were 1250 deaths from this cause; by 1963 this number had dropped to 1000. By far the most important agent in home accident gas poisonings is carbon monoxide. In 1945 approximately 1000 deaths from gas poisoning were due to inhalation of manufactured gas used for heating and cooking in the home. In 1961 there were 302 such deaths. Manufactured gas contains carbon monoxide. Natural gas, which is rapidly replacing manufactured gas in many of the large population centers, does not, in its pure state, although it may contain very small amounts in the mixture that is supplied to homes (natural gas to which a gas is added to provide odor to the finished product). This decrease in the use of manufactured gas has brought about the major reduction in deaths from gas poisoning. Both natural and manufactured gas can, however, give off carbon monoxide if improperly burned. Other sources of carbon monoxide are defective flues, improperly operating heating devices and automobile exhaust fumes.

Most accidental deaths from gas poisoning can be traced to poor judgment or the lack of protection of the helpless, such as small children or the elderly. Over half of these accidental deaths occur in the older age groups, where faulty memory, mental confusion and other factors play a substantial role. Preventive measures addressed to the individual must take into account these factors and provide the necessary protective devices to minimize the hazard involved. One effective way to do this is to suggest that debilitated patients install cooking devices other than those which burn manufactured gas. This is especially important when the patients are elderly, for such persons may become confused in lighting an oven, or are likely to forget the pot of liquid which may boil over and extinguish the flame, allowing gas to escape in its toxic, unburned form.

MISCELLANEOUS CAUSES OF HOME ACCIDENTS

In addition to the six major categories of home accidents just described, there were a variety of causes which accounted for about 12 per cent of home accident deaths in 1963. Among these were drowning within the home, burns from hot substances and electrocution. In this group of miscellaneous causes, children under 5 were the major victims, with about 40 per cent of the deaths occurring in this age group. An additional 30 per cent occurred among persons 65 or over. There is one factor which is common to nearly all these accidents and that is the necessity for providing protection in the home for the very young and the very old to minimize for them the hazards of accidental injury and death.

PREVENTION OF PROGRESSION OF INJURIES AND THEIR SEQUELAE

After the ultimate has been done to prevent accidents from occurring, efforts must then be directed toward preventing the more serious accidents from ending in death and to minimize the disability from the less serious. In this area, physicians have a major and direct responsibility, both individually and as the medical members of the community to whom the rest of the citizens look for guidance and direction. Among the medical resources which will minimize the injury potential of accidents are these:

Training Courses in First Aid

Since the very life of the accident victim may depend on what is done in the important minutes before expert medical care is available, every community should make available to its citizens organized courses in first aid, such as those given by the American Red Cross. Physicians should encourage the development of such courses in the community and should urge patients and their families to participate.

Establishment of Poison Control Centers

Every community should have as available as the nearest telephone a center to which questions regarding poisons or suspected poisons can be immediately referred for expert answers. The rapid increase in the number of chemical compounds for use in the home makes it virtually impossible for the practicing physician to keep up with the nature and toxicity of each new compound that may be sold under a trade name that gives no hint as to its contents. To meet this need, poison control centers, first established in Chicago, are now being developed in other areas of the country. In New York State, for example, poison control centers under Health Department sponsorship are now located in Buffalo, Rochester, Syracuse, Albany and New York City. These centers, which are readily accessible by telephone to all physicians and hospitals in the state, provide information regarding the toxicity of the common household compounds as well as detailed information on antidotal measures. They are located in medical centers, equipped with extensive files of data supplied (often on a confidential basis) by manufacturers of household products and are manned on a 24-hour schedule. Every physician should check locally to see if such a center is available to him, and if it isn't he should approach the local or state health department for assistance in having one established.

Provision of Inhalator and Rescue Squads

Trained inhalator and rescue squads can be lifesaving in the case of gas poisonings. Many utility firms and fire departments have such squads, trained and suitably equipped, which are available on 24-hour call. Again, the physician should check to be sure that his community has such facilities, and if it doesn't he should take the leadership in seeing that they are provided. The result could well be the saving of many lives.

Availability of Emergency Medical Facilities

As discussed later under motor vehicle accidents, each community should have its own plan for emergency medical care which can be immediately mobilized in case of disaster or accident. The availability of blood, the presence of an emergency surgical team and some provision for prompt procurement of specialized medical or surgical skills can save the lives of many injured in accidents.

WORK ACCIDENTS*

In 1963 there were 14,200 deaths due to work accidents and 2,000,000 disabling work injuries in the United States. Of these the largest category were accidents among agricultural workers, which resulted in 3300 deaths and 280,000 injuries; 2400 deaths, and about 400,000 disabling injuries occurred in industry. The other deaths and injuries occurred in such work as government and service, construction, transportation, and public utilities, trade, and mining (see Figure 1, page 24 for death rates in different types of work). The total cost of all work accidents was estimated at 5 billion dollars. This includes such indirect costs as damaged machinery and materials as well as interrupted production schedules. While these figures are large, they are not so great as the deaths, injuries and costs of motor vehicle accidents (43,600 deaths; 1,600,000 injuries; 7.7 billion dollar cost), nor as the deaths and injuries from home accidents (29,000 deaths and 4,400,000 injuries).

While one cannot minimize the tragedy inherent in the 14,200 deaths which resulted from on-the-job accidents in 1963, yet the picture does represent a most significant improvement compared with previous years. In 1933 there was a total of 14,500 fatal on-the-job accidents to workers, with far fewer workers. If accidental deaths had occurred in 1963 at the same rate as in 1933, there would have been approximately 26,000 deaths, so this reflects close to a 50 per cent improvement.

The leading cause of work injuries is the lifting, carrying, moving or placing of various materials, machine parts or other objects. This manual handling of objects accounts for 22.6 per cent of all work injuries. Falls account for 20.4 per cent, with falling objects and machinery responsible for about 10 per cent each. When viewed from the standpoint of seriousness, the etiology changes: vehicular accidents caused 20.7 per cent of the accidents which resulted in a fatality or permanent disability. Handling of objects, which caused 25 per cent of all injuries, accounted for only 13.9 per cent of fatalities or permanent disabilities.

In an analysis of accident data supplied by individual industrial establishments, the National Safety Council[6] groups the etiologic factors into three categories: an unsafe act by the workers, a "personal cause" inherent in the worker himself, and mechanical causes due to equipment failure or unsafe working conditions. In the first category are listed unnecessary exposure to danger, unsafe or improper use of equipment, working on moving or dangerous equipment, neglecting to use personal protective equipment,

---

* See also Chapter 12.

improper starting or stopping, overloading, poor arranging, making safety devices inoperative, and operating at unsafe speed.

Listed in the personal cause category are improper attitude on the part of the employee, lack of knowledge or skill and bodily defects. Under mechanical causes the following are judged the major factors: hazardous arrangement or procedure, improper guarding, defective equipment, unsafe dress or apparel, and improper illumination or ventilation.

Apparently fatigue is also a factor in causing accidents. Studies by the Bureau of Labor Statistics have shown that injuries increase disproportionately as daily work hours are extended to 9, 10 or 11, and also with an increase in weekly hours above 40.[7] With some exceptions, frequency rates (the number of disabling injuries per million man hours of exposure) were sharply higher with longer hours. One plant had a frequency rate for all work injuries (most requiring only first aid) of 1000 when the work week totaled 48 hours. The rate rose to 2727 when the work week was extended to 60 hours.

During a normal working day of 8 hours, the most common period for accidental injury was the first 4 hours on the job, when more than half of the injuries occurred. The peak periods occurred during the second and third hours with improvement taking place during the fourth.

PREVENTION OF OCCURRENCE

Many industrial safety researchers feel that probably the most important factor in the prevention of industrial accidents is the attitude of management. If management exhibits a safety-conscious attitude and backs it up with an active safety program, most plants can reduce work accidents. Such a program involves not only continuous attention to safety education, but insistence upon the utilization of safety equipment and the employment of safe on-the-job procedures, even to the point of discharge or suspension for noncooperation. Because of the ever-increasing costs for workmen's compensation arising from on-the-job accidents, management has of necessity become more and more safety conscious.

Next in importance is the attitude of labor. Workers who are safety conscious are more likely to use protective devices and safety equipment. Safety education programs promoted by both management and unions are an effective way to influence worker attitudes and behavior.

Adequate training programs are also a factor in accident prevention. Before any worker is allowed to use a complex piece of equipment he should undergo a thorough and detailed training program to ensure that he has accumulated the necessary knowledge and skill required to operate the equipment safely.

Safety equipment should be provided whenever necessary. This includes personal equipment such as protective goggles, safety shoes, protective helmets, protective clothing against heat and chemical splashing and masks against gas hazards.

Other plant safety features include the following:

1. Provision of built-in safety devices on all hazardous machinery and equipment, including guards, shut-off devices and fail-safe mechanisms.

2. Adequate guarding of hazardous areas with protective railings, grills and other barriers.

3. Proper ventilation, particularly in those areas where the air is dusty or contaminated with toxic pollutants.

4. Sufficient illumination to minimize the hazards of misjudging distances or failing to see an oncoming danger.

5. Provision of safe equipment for handling materials to minimize the movement by hand of materials, machinery or other objects within the plant or in the plant yard. Hand movement is expensive not only in terms of manpower but also in the production of compensable work injuries.

In all aspects of the prevention of accidents the full- or part-time industrial physician can play an important role. He should take every opportunity to participate in the safety education of workers, and he should seek management participation in a plant safety inventory in which he would take part along with safety engineers. Small plants which cannot afford the full-time services of a safety engineer can often obtain assistance from state departments of labor and health and from local safety councils.

PREVENTION OF PROGRESSION OF INJURY

Once an accident has occurred with resulting injury, much can still be done to minimize the ultimate effect in causing death or permanent disability. Here, as in the prevention of accidents themselves, physicians have a major responsibility.

Workers need to be trained as to what steps to take if an accident occurs, how to shut off machinery, turn off electrical current or take any other measures necessary to prevent further injury. On each shift in each area of the plant there should be a worker trained to direct first-aid measures.

Directions as to whom to call and the address and telephone number of the physician or hospital where the injured are to be referred should be prominently posted if the plant does not provide a round-the-clock first-aid suite. Every plant whose size permits should have a well-equipped, conveniently located first-aid suite, a full-time industrial nurse and physician.

The first-aid facilities should be backed up by a well-planned program of emergency medical care, involving local physicians and local hospitals. Every plant should consider the possibility of a major fire, explosion or other disaster and plan in advance how it will meet such an emergency to minimize the loss from injury and death.

Every industrial plant should see that the services of a well-equipped, adequately staffed medical rehabilitation center are available to its employees. Just as soon as his condition will permit, the victim of an accident should be referred to the rehabilitation center. Through the techniques of modern physiatrics the worker's period of disability can be shortened and his return to gainful employment hastened.

FARM ACCIDENTS

Agriculture has more accidental work deaths than any other major industry. Of the 14,200 workers killed on the job in 1963, 3300 were killed in farm work. Death rates for farm work accidents are not, however, as high

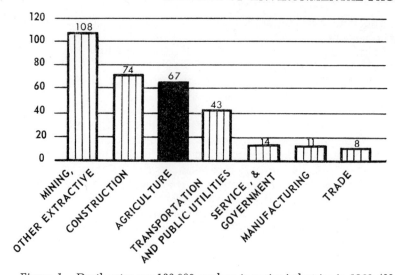

Figure 1. Death rates per 100,000 workers in major industries in 1963 (National Safety Council).

as those for mining and construction industries. The 1963 rates were 108, 74 and 67 per 100,000 workers for mining, construction and agriculture, respectively (Fig. 1). Comparison of rates must, however, be made cautiously since it is difficult to procure accurate exposure data for farm workers. Rates are based on the number of farm residents, which is likely to be considerably higher than the number of workers actually involved. If accurate figures for population-at-risk were available, the farm work death rates might well be much higher.

In addition to the deaths chargeable to farm work per se, there were in 1963 an additional 6100 accidental deaths among farm residents. These included deaths from accidents which occurred during the performance of ordinary household duties or farm chores, deaths resulting from motor vehicle accidents, and those from a variety of other causes, including drowning, firearms, burns and falls.

The trend in total accidental deaths among farm residents has shown a significant drop since 1950. Farm resident deaths in 1950 totaled 15,500 as compared to 8400 in 1963. This drop in farm resident deaths must, of course, be viewed in the light of the nation's steadily decreasing farm population. In 1950 the United States farm population totaled 25.1 million; in 1963 it had dropped to 13.4 million. Although the number of deaths has decreased, the rates (61.9 per 100,000 in 1950 and 62.8 in 1963) have remained essentially unchanged. It should be noted, however, that there has undoubtedly been an increase in the accident hazards for farm workers concomitant with the ever-increasing mechanization of farming.

Counterbalancing the increased hazard there have been several factors which may have contributed to preventing an increased accident toll. The first of these is the long-term educational efforts of farm cooperative groups, safety councils and insurance companies aimed at making farm workers and farm families more safety conscious; second is the effort of farm machinery manufacturers to build protective devices and other safety features into farm machinery; and third has been the gradual shift in the agricultural economy from small one-family farms to large agricultural operations in which work is more specialized and workers have an opportunity to become more skilled in the safe operation of a particular piece of equipment.

PREVENTION OF OCCURRENCE

The principles in the prevention of farm accidents which involve firearms, falls, poisonings and drowning are, in general, the same as those which apply to nonfarm populations. Physicians practicing in rural areas have a superb opportunity to promote farm safety in their practice among farm families. There is also great need for better coordination between agricultural and health agencies at all levels. The outstanding program of the Iowa Institute of Agricultural Medicine of the University of Iowa Medical School is an illustration of what physicians working together with others can accomplish in an epidemiologic study of accidents and which, in turn, can lead to the development of more effective farm accident control programs.

Farm workers should always have an adequate period of supervised training before beginning the operation of any piece of farm machinery. No industrial worker would be permitted to operate a piece of complicated, high-speed machinery without undergoing such a training period.

Farm workers should be taught not to operate machinery when overly fatigued, since fatigue, which dulls sensory stimuli and promotes carelessness, tends to increase accidents.

Children, the very old or those with neurologic disturbances in gait or balance should not operate farm machinery. Child labor laws prevent children from exposure to mechanical hazards in industry, and motor vehicle laws prevent children from operating automobiles, yet nothing other than the conscience and watchfulness of parents of farm families prevents children from operating or riding on tractors and other farm machinery. That there are deficiencies here is apparent from the fact that one-fourth of all farm accident deaths in those under 19 involve machinery.

Much has been done and much obviously remains to be done in the area of educating farm workers in matters of safety. Adequate training in safety education should be a part of the curriculum in every agricultural high school. Farm workers must be taught to make use of protective devices built into machinery and not to remove or inactivate guards or other devices. Farm buildings should also be of a safe design which will permit their use with a minimum of hazard.

PREVENTION OF PROGRESSION OF INJURY

Once an injury occurs on a farm, the factors which reduce its severity are not too dissimilar from those which lessen the impact of accidental injuries elsewhere, with several notable exceptions.

Among these is the relatively greater need for adequate first-aid measures. Since farm families are more likely to be farther removed from medical facilities, the care that the accident victim receives in the first minutes or hours assumes greater importance. It is essential that at least one person in each farm family be trained in first aid. Physicians practicing in rural areas can do much to encourage the presentation of first-aid courses for farm families. Each farm should also have an adequate stock of simple first-aid needs. The remoteness of farms from medical facilities may mean that the farm accident victim must travel many miles to obtain medical care. To keep the shock and hazard of such a trip at a minimum, farm communities should be encouraged to develop cooperative ambulance services. Hospitals serving rural areas must be equipped, just as hospitals elsewhere, with an emergency plan for the handling of accident victims. Physicians have a primary responsibility for the development of such facilities in the hospitals serving the area where they practice. Practicing physicians and health agencies serving rural areas should diligently promote active immunization against tetanus among all farm residents. Rehabilitation is equally as important for the injured farm worker as for the industrial worker, and the principles set forth in Chapter 33 need to be applied with equal vigor in rural areas.

MOTOR VEHICLE ACCIDENTS

In recent years there has been an increasing awareness of the seriousness of the motor vehicle accident problem. In 1963 motor vehicle accidents in the United States resulted in 43,600 deaths and 1,600,000 injuries (disabling beyond day of accident). Economic losses from motor vehicle accidents in 1963 were estimated to be 7.7 billion dollars. These totals far exceed the deaths, disability and economic loss from many of the diseases which are of national concern. While public interest in motor vehicle accidents has had its greatest expression in the past few years, the problem itself is not a new one.

Except for the war years, 1942 to 1945, the absolute numbers of deaths from motor vehicle accidents have been relatively stable since 1934, when 36,101 were killed.* The death rate per vehicle mile has, however, shown a marked decline over the years. In 1963 there were about 20 times as many motor vehicle accident deaths as in 1912, but there were over 80 times as many vehicles on the road, with corresponding increases in the number of miles driven. The number of deaths per hundred million miles driven has shown a drop from nearly 20 in 1924 to approximately 6 in 1964. It is of interest to note, too, that the rates in recent years in the United States are believed to be substantially lower than those in Western Europe, the Near East, South America and Asia.

While the drop in rates is encouraging, and while there is comfort of a sort in the realization that the United States is no worse in this regard than other countries, the losses are still staggering. Concern for these losses must be shared by physicians; in fact, no group should have a greater interest in reducing motor vehicle accidents since their daily professional activities bring them face to face with the carnage from the nation's highways. Physicians can assist in the reduction of motor vehicle injuries and

---

* Preliminary figures for 1964 indicate that there may be significant increases in the absolute numbers of deaths.

deaths, both directly and indirectly: directly, for example, through the development of effective emergency services for accident victims, and indirectly through contributing to the prevention of automobile accidents and to the lessening of the injuries produced.

Since all accidents do not occur within ambulance reach of the nation's top medical centers, each community and the physicians who serve it have an opportunity and an obligation to develop a workable operating procedure for the handling of accident victims. This must make full use of the professional skills and medical facilities available and provide for, on an emergency basis, skills such as neurosurgery that may not ordinarily be available in the community. All too often the fate of the accident victim, in terms of life itself as well as of the immediate and ultimate disability produced, depends upon the quality of the medical care received in the initial minutes and hours after the accident.

In addition to physicians' obvious concern for the quality of emergency medical care in the community, they also have an obligation to see that adequate facilities are available for the transportation of those injured in motor vehicle and other types of accidents. Attention is called to the measures adopted in Flint, Michigan, and in other cities for the improvement of emergency transportation and handling services through city ordinances. These measures include requirements regarding the training of ambulance drivers and attendants, the regulation of ambulance speed, the use of the siren, and other similar provisions. Medical societies can take the leadership in developing good community programs in this area.

Physicians also need to cooperate fully with designated governmental authorities in the operation of programs aimed at the removal of hazardous drivers from the highways. One of the most important involves the determination of blood alcohol levels of individuals arrested for drunken driving and related offenses. Since it has been repeatedly demonstrated that drivers with high blood alcohol levels have substantially increased accident potentialities, the physician has a professional obligation to aid in the apprehension and removal of such drivers from the highways.

Indirectly, physicians can use their professional influence to make certain that efforts to reduce the toll from motor vehicle accidents are exerted from a base of scientific fact, a base to which physicians can add by participating in those research programs directed at unraveling the complexities of the motor vehicle problem. Physicians, both individually and through medical society groups, can discourage overenthusiastic efforts aimed at keeping groups of individuals off the road simply because they are suffering from some physical condition which has been singled out as hazardous by lay people or by poorly informed members of the medical profession. No one has yet succeeded in showing through a scientifically controlled study that any disease per se, including deafness, color blindness, diabetes, cardiac pathology or musculoskeletal handicaps, results in a higher accident rate than among "normal" individuals. Yet, continuous efforts are made to prevent people with heart disease, for instance, from driving, and in some states application forms for a driver's license contain questions regarding a number of medical entities.

It must be pointed out, however, that the absence of statistical data from adequately controlled group studies in this area should not be interpreted as a prohibition against physicians exercising their responsibilities for the welfare of individual patients under their care. If it is a physician's professional judgment, after carefully assessing all the factors involved, that a particular patient, in the interest of his own welfare and that of others, should not be driving, then the physician has an obligation to so advise that patient.

In approaching a solution to the over-all motor vehicle accident problem, physicians need to maintain an attitude of scientific objectivity. The motor vehicle accident problem is multifaceted and its solution will not come from a concentration on one etiologic factor to the exclusion of all others. Yet, this panacea approach has plagued those working in the area of motor vehicle accident research and prevention and has handicapped efforts to apply epidemiologic skills to the problem. Both from the press and rostrum have come statements by prominent individuals, some in the medical profession, who would solve the whole motor vehicle accident problem in a manner reminiscent of the nostrum purveyor of an earlier era.

There are those who would eliminate the accident problem simply by requiring all automobiles to travel under some given speed. There are others who see the solution solely as the necessity for increased law enforcement. Still others, for example, would prevent all over 60 years of age from driving or would apply psychological tests to driver-licensing procedures. Studies and experience clearly indicate that no one of these is the whole answer, and the time wasted in expounding them would be better devoted to a more critical and meaningful approach to the problem.

The premise, for example, that speed is the sine qua non of all motor vehicle accidents immediately breaks down when one examines data from such studies as those of John O. Moore and his associates in the Crash Injury Research Program of Cornell University.[8] In studying a sample of urban accidents, this group found that only 6 per cent of the cars involved were traveling in excess of 50 miles per hour at the time of the accident, and that 52 per cent of fatal accidents involved vehicles which had been traveling at less than 30 miles per hour. In studying rural accidents, the same group found that 45 per cent involved speeds of less than 50 miles per hour. While it is true that speed is an important factor in the severity of an accident, these data and the safety records of modern high-speed highways clearly demonstrate that it is only one factor in the over-all problem.

Increased or tightened-up law enforcement is another popular "complete" remedy for the motor vehicle accident problem. The experience of those jurisdictions that have tried to apply the maximum law enforcement, that is possible under practical conditions has been that, while the number of accidents does show a substantial drop, continued intensive enforcement is required to prevent a return to the original levels. Although intensive law enforcement has been effective in producing reductions in motor vehicle accidents, it cannot by itself, completely eliminate motor vehicle accident injuries and deaths.

The premise that accidents are due to some particular group or groups in the population and that the problem would be solved if only these were kept off the road also breaks down when it is examined objectively. One of the groups most often cited for elimination from the highways is the elderly. The dubiousness of such a move becomes promptly evident when the accident rates of older drivers, both per capita and per mile, show themselves to be lower than those of younger individuals.

The fallacy of such panaceas becomes readily evident when accidents are separated into categories composed of those occurring under similar circumstances. Furthermore, in considering prevention in terms of the over-all accident problem, it is essential to recognize that there are two basically discrete approaches: first, the prevention of the accident itself, and second, the prevention or minimization of injuries once the accident has been initiated. In addition, the preventive aspects can be further broken down in each instance into those factors involving the individual, the vehicle and the environment.

PREVENTION OF OCCURRENCE

Accidents Involving Pedestrians

Nationally, pedestrian accident fatalities in 1963 represented approximately 20 per cent of the total of motor vehicle accidental deaths. This figure varies widely, however, from rural to urban areas, being lower in rural areas. In New York City, for example, about 70 per cent of traffic fatalities are among pedestrians.

The most important preventive measure that has yet been developed for lessening pedestrian accidents has been the segregation of the vehicular traffic stream from the pedestrian stream by the construction of thruways, freeways, turnpikes and similar roads. Accidents involving pedestrians have been reduced almost to zero on these well-engineered roadways. In cities, at least in the business areas, it may eventually become necessary to build grade separations that will place vehicular traffic on one level and pedestrian traffic on another. In fact, this is already being done in a number of communities.

Next in importance to separation of vehicular from pedestrian traffic is better traffic control, especially in congested areas. Reduced speed, for example, provides a better opportunity for the driver to take the proper evasive action in order to avoid striking a pedestrian. Prevention of jay walking, education of children on the hazards of street play, as well as the education of adults regarding such common sense factors as walking against the traffic stream at the side of the road and wearing light-colored clothing at night for greater visibility, are all sound preventive measures. It is interesting to note that there is a significant incidence of intoxication among pedestrians involved in traffic accidents. In a controlled investigation of adult pedestrians killed by motor vehicles in New York City, McCarroll and Haddon[9] found that only 26 per cent had no alcohol content in their blood and that in 47 per cent the level was 50 mg. per cent or higher.

Accidents Involving the Driver and Occupants

The driver's judgment, skill, ability to take the proper evasive action and even his emotional attitudes all bear upon the accident picture. As is readily apparent, anything that will lessen the acuteness of the driver's faculties will be likely to have an adverse effect on his ability to avoid an accident. Foremost among these is the consumption of alcohol or drugs. Haddon and Bradess[10] have reported in a study of 83 drivers killed in single vehicle, non-pedestrian accidents in Westchester County, New York, that one-half of the drivers were legally drunk at the time of death (i.e., they had blood alcohol levels of at least 0.15 per cent by weight) and that another 20 per cent had blood alcohol levels between 0.05 and 0.15 per cent, a range in which many individuals have markedly decreased reflexes. These authors presented similar data from a study made in the state of Delaware. It is essential that physicians cooperate in drawing blood from drivers for alcohol content determination when requested to do so by law enforcement officials.

Research by Loomis and West[11] has shown that barbiturates and certain tranquilizers in doses commonly employed have an adverse effect on driving ability, and it is probable that many other pharmacologic agents in common use have similarly undesirable effects.

As pointed out earlier, the relationship of disease and disability to motor vehicle accident causation has not been scientifically established. Even if it were shown that individuals suffering from a given disease had a slightly higher accident rate than the balance of the population, restrictions on private motor vehicle operators would not be feasible, because of the huge number of persons who would have to be forbidden to drive in order to prevent even one accident occurring as a result of the condition in question. In the instance, however, of commercial motor vehicle operators, where it is feasible to choose a small number of individuals from among a large number of applicants, it is both possible and desirable to establish effective screening programs because of the possible serious consequences of accidents involving such drivers and because of the high mileages driven by this group. Such screening programs, as well as all other medical aspects of driver licensure, should be under the direct and continuing supervision of qualified physicians. Where this has not been done, lay persons have repeatedly tried to practice their own erroneous ideas of medicine, with the result that grave injustices have occurred. It is suggested that physicians and medical groups who plan to supply medical information to Departments of Motor Vehicles should first ascertain whether the handling of such information is restricted to physicians. They should determine also the precautions taken to keep as confidential those data which represent privileged communications between the physician and his patient.

There are distinct differences on a sex and age basis for drivers as to accident experience. Accident rates are higher among male adolescents and young adults. Conversely, truck drivers and intercity bus operators have distinctly lower accident rates.

The whole subject centering around the question "who is competent to drive," needs carefully controlled scientific study. There is little to indicate at this time that there is a type of individual, other than on the sex and age basis noted above, who is inherently and consistently a poor risk driver. What studies have been done suggest that most individuals use bad judgment or behave in a manner likely to produce an accident at one time or another. When that bad judgment or negative behavior combines with other adverse factors, an accident is more likely to result.

Driver education training courses for students are included in increasing numbers of high school curricula. In fact, in some areas such courses are compulsory for teen-age drivers. Some insurance companies offer lower rates for young drivers who have taken these courses.

Efforts aimed at making the automobile safer to drive have involved two major factors. The first of these may be termed human engineering, the other mechanical reliability. Human engineering aims at the production of man-machine systems in which the device to be operated becomes an integrated extension of its human operator, rather than the reverse. It is an area of technology which has repeatedly demonstrated its utility, particularly during the past two decades. The automobile industry has been criticized in recent years for designing a product in which an attempt is made to fit the driver to the vehicle rather than starting with the needs of the driver and building the vehicle around them. That some manufacturers have succeeded better than others on this score is shown by a carefully controlled study of the experience of one company with a large nationwide fleet of cars in which, with all other factors equal, "there was an increase in accident rate of more than 50 per cent from make A to make B that was attributable to automobile design properties."

Mechanically, the car should be reliable and free from such defects as brake and steering failures, blowouts, and other shortcomings that can produce accidents. The car should also have aerodynamic stability at high speed, signaling devices and lighting systems that are of appropriate size and position to function with maximum effectiveness. For example, tail lights and stop lights which are placed too low are not visible to the driver behind when cars are closely spaced in heavy traffic.

It is the belief of many in the field of motor vehicle accident prevention that much can be accomplished in the development of safer cars and that manufacturers have an obligation to give greater attention to safety in automotive design, both in the prevention of accidents themselves and in the "packaging" of the occupants, so that injuries and deaths are avoided or reduced.

MINIMIZATION OF INJURY

Accidents Involving Pedestrians

The gadgetry that abounds on the front ends of today's automobiles carries a special hazard for pedestrians. Although the once popular winged hood ornament with its sharp frontal prominence has been eliminated from recent models, other hazardous structures have taken its place. Indeed, if one were to attempt to produce a pedestrian-injuring mechanism, one of the most theoretically efficient designs which might be developed would closely approach that of the front of some present-day automobiles. It is fundamental to the production of trauma that the more localized the area which receives the force of a blow, the more severe is the injury produced. Needless sharp projections located in the primary area of pedestrian impact, are tragic examples of unnecessarily dangerous design, the results of which are seen daily on surgical wards and autopsy tables.

Accidents Involving the Driver and Occupants

Epidemiologically, in considering the factors involved in minimizing injury, it is necessary to consider the following components involved: the driver, the vehicle and the highway.

Driver Component. While many of the factors in this category involve the car itself, there is much that can be done to prevent the progression of an injury to a fatal termination, or to a condition that results in severe or permanent disability. This applies both to the driver and occupants and involves the immediate and continuous availability of skilled emergency medical services and facilities. This is an area in which physicians have the primary responsibility and one in which there is considerable room for improvement.

Vehicle Component. Once an accident has occurred, the design of the car has a major bearing on the extent and severity of injuries that will be sustained by the occupants. Generally speaking, the objective in this instance is to slow down the abruptness of deceleration of the driver and occupants, and to spread out the force of the impact in terms of the area involved. Unfortunately, the occupant of the modern vehicle, as one worker so aptly phrased it, is like a china teacup in an empty barrel. When the barrel is dropped, the cup continues in free flight until it crashes abruptly against the hard surroundings, which by that time not only have acquired a substantially different velocity from the cup, but which may actually be moving in the opposite direction, thus further increasing the energy of impact. Since the threshold velocity required to produce fracture in the adult human head colliding with a hard heavy structure is only about 15 miles per hour, it is readily apparent how essential is both the reduction of the possibility of impact and the modification of impact areas, such as instrument panels, steering wheels and windshields.

If the occupants can be tied in with the structure of the car, they will have the advantage of sharing in the ability of the car to absorb progressively the impact of the crash and thus spread out its effect in time and space. Among the devices which aid in this are safety door locks and seat belts. Competent investigators have concluded that effective door locks will reduce the probability of serious to fatal grades of injury by about 20 per cent, since they will help to prevent the occupants from being thrown from the car, thus absorbing with their own bodies the effects of a high speed impact. Safety seat belts have been found to be very effective. By restraining the occupant in a crash, the belt provides a controlled deceleration and further minimizes the occupant's impact on the structure of the car. This restraining effect has been well documented by comparing the impact energies on the heads of instrumented dummies placed in crashes with and without seat belts. Another factor which has been shown to reduce injuries to the driver is the use of a steering wheel which can aid in slowing down his forward movement. Substantial progress has been achieved recently in the design of steering wheels. As a result, fatal injuries to the chest, caused by broken spokes, horn rings and steering shafts, are being increasingly prevented.

If the localization of impact forces can be avoided, the resultant trauma is thus reduced. This is best accomplished by the elimination from the car's interior of all projecting knobs and sharp edges against which the body might be thrown. By striking against the sharp edge of an instrument panel or windshield frames, the head can easily suffer a fatal blow. The full force of an impact being absorbed by the sharp point of the steering column can and frequently does result in severe to fatal injury to vital structures in the thorax. In addition to the elimination of projections and sharp edges, much can be done to lessen the force of crash impacts by the design of structures within the car which progressively and smoothly deform as they absorb the energies of impacts, thus permitting slower and more gradual deceleration of the body areas which strike them. Designs should be such that they will translate the kinetic energies of the impacting body tissues into appropriately engineered deformations of the impacted structures. Such designs may be achieved with a great variety of materials, including metals, the behavior of the materials on impact being the crucial consideration.

Highway Component. Highway engineering has continued to make very substantial contributions to highway safety. This is most spectacularly seen in the records of the New York State Thruway, the Ohio State Turnpike and similar roads whose fatal accident rates in 1963 were 2.4 per 100 million miles driven, as compared to a nationwide figure of 7.2 per 100 million miles driven on rural roads. Furthermore, facts apart from highway design accounted for sizeable fractions of this residue. In 1963 in nearly 40 per cent of fatal accidents on turnpikes the condition of the driver was a contributing factor, e.g., asleep or under the influence of alcohol or drugs. Improper driving accounted for another 40 per cent; vehicle factors and miscellaneous causes each contributed 10 per cent of the fatal accidents.

Among the basic principles whose application has contributed to these low rates, has been the use of grade separations with their elimination of intersections; the use of wide center strips to separate opposing streams of traffic; the elimination of low radius curves and steep grades which cause unevenness of traffic flow; the provision of acceleration and deceleration lanes; the development of more legible and easily understood signs and signals and the provision of wider lanes, repair strips and shoulders. Although the costs of such highways are usually justified on the basis of the traffic loads which they carry, there are considerable indirect savings in life and property damage which should be included in assessing the reasonableness of their construction.

A number of other environmental variables are also of importance. It has been repeatedly shown that accident rates increase with adverse changes in the weather and with decreases in visibility, whether due to fog, snow, rain or the time of day. Ice or snow render traction unsatisfactory and result in poor braking and steering ability and make control of the vehicle difficult. At least a portion of the increased hazard of such driving conditions may, however, be assigned to the failure of drivers to modify their actions to the dangerous conditions. The time of day has a definite effect on the accident risk; as visibility decreases with the coming of darkness, the rate of accidents goes up. Much can be done to lessen problems of this type through proper lighting of highways. It is probable, too, that at least part of the increase in the evening accident rates is the direct result of such factors as driver fatigue coupled with an undue haste to reach destinations. Field studies have shown that the percentage of drivers who have been drinking heavily increases markedly during the evening hours, particularly on weekends.

Adequate patrolling of roads so that there is prompt discovery of accident victims helps to minimize the effects of injuries that result from an accident. All too often accident victims who could have been saved by prompt medical attention have died because their plight was discovered too late. Sometimes this very vital function of highway policing is not appreciated or understood by the public.

In summary, preventive techniques have a major contribution to make in reducing the injury and loss of life that result from motor vehicle accidents. Physicians have an important responsibility in this area and should inform themselves of the facts involved and direct their efforts, first, toward those measures aimed at the prevention of accidents themselves and, second, toward the reduction of injuries or fatalities that result from those accidents which occur in spite of preventive efforts.

PUBLIC ACCIDENTS

In addition to those accidents occuring in the home, at work, on the farm and as a result of motor vehicles, there is an accident category that the National Safety Council designates as public accidents.[1] This covers such nontransport causes of accidental death and injury as drowning, firearms, explosives, falls, fires, excessive heat, cataclysms, therapeutic misadventures in medical or surgical procedures, lightning and snake bites. It also covers those accidents occurring outside the home, farm or industry and includes accidents associated with all forms of transport, except motor vehicles.

In 1963, deaths charged to public accidents totaled 17,500, somewhat less than a fifth of all accidental deaths in that year. Public accidents ranked third as a cause of accidental deaths, being preceded only by motor vehicle and home accident deaths. Injuries due to public accidents totaled approximately 2,200,000.

Of the 17,500 total deaths from public accidents, 3000 occurred in rail, air, water and other forms of transportation exclusive of motor vehicles, while drownings and falls each accounted for about one-fourth of the total. The other causes mentioned above accounted for the balance.

NONTRANSPORT ACCIDENTS

Drowning

The incidence of deaths from drowning in this country follows a definite seasonal pattern. From a low level during the winter and early spring, deaths from drowning rise rapidly in May, reach a peak in July, remain high during August, then decline in September and October as cooler weather brings an end to outdoor swimming and water sports in many parts of the country.

Deaths from drowning are concentrated among children and young adults. Since slightly more than a fourth occur in the 5 to 14 age group, and a fourth more are among the 15 to 24 age bracket, nearly half involve children and young adults.

A significant reduction in deaths from drowning could be achieved if more preventive measures were undertaken. Included in these are efforts in each community to see that children are taught to swim and to appreciate the importance of water safety practices, that swimming pools are adequately protected and equipped and that swimming areas are effectively staffed with trained lifeguards.

Once a water accident has occurred, the victim's chance of avoiding permanent injury or death depends on a number of factors. Some of these include the presence of trained lifeguards who are able to apply lifesaving measures. Other factors involve the provision of good emergency medical care facilities, such as would be needed in accidents involving head or neck injuries.

Whenever a physician is called for emergency care after an apparent drowning, his first instruction should be that artificial respiration be begun, and continued until his arrival. While mechanical resuscitators have certain advantages over manual methods, they are often not immediately available and valuable moments, which can mean the difference between life and death, may be lost while they are being brought to the scene.

For complete instructions on artificial respiration techniques the reader is urged to refer to the *American Red Cross First-Aid Textbook* and to its manuals on swimming and lifesaving. Physicians should also become familiar with closed chest cardiac massage, which can be lifesaving under certain circumstances.

Water accidents in which injuries other than drowning are involved require the same careful handling as do injuries due to other causes. Since head, neck and back injuries are not uncommon as a result of diving, lifeguards, ambulance personnel, hospital emergency room staffs and others must be trained in the proper handling of victims with such injuries. The medical literature is replete with case histories of neck and back fractures that resulted in death or permanent paralysis because of careless handling. Every physician must be on guard in injuries involving the neck or back to see that the victims are cared for properly and that personnel under his direction exercise the necessary precautions.

Falls

Falls are the second most important cause of death resulting from public nontransport accidents. This category excludes falls from moving vehicles, but represents falls from one level to another, e.g., a fall down the stairs of a public building, or falls on the same level, such as may occur on a slippery or icy pavement. In 1963 there were 3900 deaths due to such falls, about 75 per cent of which occurred in persons 65 or over. This latter fact suggests that preventive measures to reduce deaths and injury from this cause need to be directed primarily toward the older age groups.

Disturbances in gait, slowed reflexes and deficiencies in vision and hearing all contribute to the occurrence of this type of accident among the older age group. Physicians need to be on the alert for such disturbances in their elderly patients, so that those in whom such handicaps develop can be cautioned about the hazard of falls and urged to take preventive steps, such as using a cane if necessary and holding onto stair banisters. Physicians should also caution their elderly patients on the importance of wearing well-fitted, flat, rubber-heeled shoes providing good ankle support.

Adequate handrails or stairs should always be provided. In buildings frequently used by the elderly, such as senior citizen centers, churches and medical office buildings, stairs should be supplemented by ramps with very gradual inclines also equipped with handrails. Experience has shown that the difficulty which many of the elderly experience in getting on and off moving stairways can be considerably reduced by placing waist-high handrails at both ends of such stairways. Stairwells or open areas in buildings above the ground floor should be properly guarded to lessen the risk of falling into them.

Sidewalks and streets should be promptly sanded or salted following snow or sleet to lessen the hazard of a slippery surface, and irregular or broken sidewalks should be corrected to eliminate hazards which promote falls.

Since in this category of accidents we are dealing chiefly with the older age group, the type of medical care following injury assumes even greater importance. Shock must be especially guarded against immediately following the injury. As soon as possible the injured patient should be made mobile to lessen the inevitable risks of prolonged bed rest. Here again, community facilities for prompt and efficient handling and subsequent rehabilitation of the accident victim are most essential.

Firearms

As has been noted earlier, about half of all deaths from firearms accidents occur in the home. The remainder are classified in the public accident category and these include accidents that occur during hunting and target practice, as well as other uses of guns. In 1963 there were 1000 deaths from firearms accidents outside the home. The number of deaths from this cause has shown some decline over the years, the comparable figure for 1950, for example, being 1150. The largest proportion of deaths from firearms accidents, about 40 per cent, occurs among those in the 15 to 24 age group.

Instruction in firearms safety should accompany the teaching of marksmanship. As soon as a young person is able to shoot a gun he should be taught the proper handling of guns. An excellent set of guiding principles for the safe use of firearms has been developed by the Sporting Arms and Ammunition Manufacturers' Institute.

Manufacturers of firearms, quite like other equipment manufacturers, have an important and continuing responsibility to build ever greater safety into their product and to see that safety devices and other protective mechanisms are made as effective as possible. Purchasers can encourage this by buying only firearms which have built-in safety devices. Sportsmen must also take care to use the proper type of ammunition in each gun. Clothing of a bright red or other vivid color is a vital factor of environmental safety for hunters.

Since many firearms accidents, particularly those resulting from hunting, take place in remote areas, the possession of at least the rudiments of first-aid knowledge is a must for every hunter. Application of basic knowledge about the control of bleeding and the splinting of fractures can help to save a life or prevent permanent injury. Sportsmen's clubs, with the cooperation of physicians, could well take the lead in seeing that their members obtain such knowledge. Once an accident victim reaches medical aid, it is essential that adequate emergency care be immediately available to him.

OTHER CAUSES OF PUBLIC ACCIDENTS

Of the other miscellaneous causes in the public accident category, some, such as fire burns and injuries in conflagrations, are touched on in other parts of this chapter. Causes such as therapeutic misadventure are more properly the concern of texts on medicine and surgery. Of the remaining causes, two, snake bites and accidents involving sports participation, do come within the purview of a book on preventive medicine. Many snake bites are preventable, and for those that do occur, proper handling greatly minimizes the extent of tissue destruction and death. Accidents involving sports can also, in the main, be prevented or their effects minimized.

Snake Bite

As a cause of death, snake bite is relatively minor in the United States. Worldwide, the number of deaths is estimated to be between 30,000 and 40,000 annually, but it is estimated that no more than 20 deaths a year occur in this country from this cause. There are no reliable figures, but a good estimate would be around several thousand bites annually. In many of the cases in which death does not occur, considerable tissue destruction results from the proteolytic, hemorrhagic, hemolytic and antibactericidal reactions of the snake venom deposited in the tissues. These reactions may result in dysfunction or loss of a finger, hand or other limb. Add to this the pain, loss of income and cost of medical care, and it is apparent that the problem, even in this country, is larger than the small number of deaths might suggest.

Poisonous snakes of the United States are of two main groups: the pit vipers (Solenoglypha) and the coral snakes (Proteoglypha). Few areas are entirely free from poisonous snakes, although specific types may be found exclusively only in certain areas. Pit vipers are the most widely distributed group. There are three types of pit vipers native to the United States: copperheads, water moccasins and rattlesnakes.

The copperhead (*Ancistrodon contortrix*) is found in the eastern and south central parts of the country. The habitat of the water moccasin (*A. piscivorus*) extends from Virginia to the Rio Grande and it is usually found in swamps or near water. There are a number of types of rattlesnakes and these are found as follows: the Massauga (*Sistrurus catenatus*) from western New York to Kansas and from Kansas to Mexico; the pygmy rattler (*S. miliarus*) from Virginia to the Rio Grande; the timber rattler (*Crotalus horridus*) across the plains from Canada to Mexico; the diamondback rattler, eastern type (*C. adamenteus*), from Florida to North Carolina and west to Louisiana; the western type (*C. atrox*), from Louisiana to California. The pit vipers derive their name from a small deep pit or depression between the nares and the eye on each side of the head. The head is arrow shaped; the body is thick and tapered to a smaller tail and neck, and the pupils of the eyes are vertical ellipses. The pit vipers, particularly the rattlers, grow quite large.

The coral snakes are of two types: the eastern coral snake (*Micrurus fulvius*), found from North Carolina to Florida and through southern Louisiana to Texas; and the western coral snake (*Micrurus euryxanthus*), found in western Colorado and Utah, southwestward to Mexico and Southern California.

Most venomous snake bites in the United States are inflicted by the pit vipers. This is due partly to their greater abundance and wider distribution, and also to the fact that their habits and habitats are more likely to conflict with the activities of man. Pit vipers have a pair of self-erecting hollow fangs attached to the upper jaw which are connected to a small sac containing the venom. As the snake strikes, it opens its mouth wide and makes a wound with the sharp fangs, injecting venom at the same time. The snake then lets go, recoils itself quickly and is soon ready to strike again. The amount of venom injected depends to some extent on whether the snake has recently emptied its sac on some other prey. Snake bites early in the spring may be more serious since snakes are just resuming activity after the winter dormant period. The amount of venom injected is an important factor in gauging the possibility of a fatal outcome, but serious tissue destruction can also result from the bite of even the youngest pit viper.

Coral snakes are small compared to pit vipers. They are characterized by their brilliant markings, which consist of colored bands of red, yellow and black, the red and black bands being separated by narrow bands of yellow. The coral snake bites only when provoked. Because its mouth is small, it has difficulty in fixing itself to larger parts of the body and most bites of the coral snake are on the hand. When it bites it hangs on, injecting its venom as it bites. The fang marks are small and relatively inconspicuous, and may later be almost completely obscured by the swelling that occurs at the site of the bite. The venom is extremely potent.

It is well to bear in mind the necessity of differentiating between the wounds inflicted by poisonous and nonpoisonous snakes. This is important, since the patient often cannot identify the type of snake that has bitten him. Some nonpoisonous snakes have bodies shaped like pit vipers. While no North American nonpoisonous snakes have the pit of the pit vipers on each side of the head, some snakes do have coloring somewhat similar to the coral snake, although the coloring bands are not in the same sequence. Since these differences are not easy to detect in a rapidly moving snake, the victim may not always know whether the snake was poisonous. The nonpoisonous snake leaves no fang marks; instead there may be two U-shaped rows of teeth marks. In comparison, the bite of a poisonous snake will usually appear as paired fang marks, although it may leave only one mark if the snake failed to score a direct hit. The marks may also be rather quickly obscured by swelling. If there is doubt and the killed snake is available, it should be examined by someone familiar with the reptiles of the area. If the snake was not killed and the question of whether it was poisonous is in doubt, the victim should be watched carefully and treatment instituted as developments dictate.

Prevention of Occurrence. Awareness of the possibility of snake bite and the necessity to take precautions are factors in prevention. Hunters or woodsmen in areas where there are likely to be snakes should walk carefully through obscuring underbrush. Carrying a walking staff to probe the areas of brush just ahead is a sound preventive measure. Similarly, it is wise to look before placing the hands where they may be exposed to a bite. Many have been bitten as they reached down to pick a flower or reached up to grasp a rocky ledge or sat down without looking.

Protective clothing is the best device for preventing snake bites. Since two-thirds of all snake bites occur on the feet and legs, snakeproof boots or heavy high-topped shoes and leggings give an excellent degree of protection. When it is necessary to reach into brush or otherwise expose the hands in snake country, gloves thick enough to turn back snake fangs should be worn.

Minimization of Injury. The prompt application of a ligature above a bite, limitation of activity, and use of antivenin and the institution of supportive therapy tailored to the individual case are steps which, if applied quickly after the bite, minimize the risk of death and lessen tissue destruction. If antivenin is not immediately available, the generally recommended tourniquet-cut-and-suction method may be employed. In deciding whether or not to incise the area the physician should remember that such an incision, when superimposed upon the local effects of the venom, has frequently led to infections and other complications of considerable severity. Instructions for this method are contained in standard first-aid texts and, when followed, sterile precautions should be employed to the extent possible. Stahnke and others[12] of the Poisonous Animals Research Laboratory at Arizona State College have advocated, in lieu of the tourniquet-cut-and-suction method, a technique they call the L-C method (from ligature and cryotherapy). This technique, while not generally accepted, involves the immediate application of a ligature between the site of the bite and the body of the victim and the placing of the injured limb in iced water and later in finely crushed ice. The cryotherapy is continued for a minimum of 24 hours. The objective of both the tourniquet-cut-suction and L-C methods is to slow down the rate of absorption of the venom and, in the case of the former, to remove some of the venom through multiple incisions around the site of the bite, followed by suction of the incisions. The only specific method of neutralizing the venom is through the prompt use of antivenin.

SPORTS ACCIDENTS

While the death toll from sports accidents is not high in terms of the whole accident picture, it nonetheless represents a cause for concern, since most such deaths and injuries are preventable. While comprehensive figures are not available on the number of deaths and injuries resulting from participation in all athletic events, a measure of their extent can be gauged from figures supplied to the National Safety Council.[1] These show that 1.4 million student accidents occurred in the 1962–63 school year among the total enrollment of the nation's schools. (Accidents were defined, in this instance, as any mishap which required a physician's care, or which resulted in absence from school for one or more days.) About 40 per cent of these accidents occurred during participation in sports and games.

Physicians who serve as consultants, advisors or examiners to athletic teams need to keep in mind at all times the necessity to take every possible positive step to make the sport with which they are concerned safe for the participants.

Prevention of Occurrence

One of the most important accident preventive measures is that of adequate training, which leads to proper conditioning of the participants.

It is a generally accepted axiom in athletic circles that the well-trained, well-conditioned athlete is less likely to have an accident. This means that there should be ample training periods, including sufficient conditioning exercises, before athletes are permitted to enter competition. Similarly, in sports played during winter it is important that an adequate warm-up period be provided before an athlete is allowed to go into a contest. Muscles must be "warmed up" if they are to respond promptly and enable the athlete to take the proper evasive action that will prevent an accident. Skilled officials can also be a positive factor in accident prevention, particularly in the body contact sports. Officials should make it plain that they will tolerate no conduct which might contribute to an accident and should be on the lookout for the participant who shows excessive fatigue and either remove him from the game or, in the case of boxing, promptly stop the contest.

Age is also a factor of importance. For example, there is increasing professional opinion that children under high school age should not be permitted to participate in body contact sports such as football.

Considerable strides have been made in recent years in the development of protective equipment for sports. Shock-absorbing football helmets, better uniform padding, the plastic helmet for the batsman in baseball and energy-absorbing plastic covering for boxing ring floors are among such items. Every player should, of course, have the advantage of such equipment and every physician serving in any capacity in athletics should familiarize himself with the types of protective equipment available for the particular sport and insist that it be provided and used on every occasion. In choosing such equipment, particularly helmets, it should be remembered that their efficacy often depends upon their quality, and this may vary widely.

Minimization of Injury

Medical care should be promptly available for all athletic injuries. This involves the presence of physicians during athletic contests wherever possible. It also involves the education of coaches and trainers in the early signs of injury, so that they can recognize an injured player and obtain immediate medical attention for him if the injury occurs during a practice session or when a physician is not at hand. The potential seriousness of any head injury needs to be particularly stressed to coaches and trainers. Any participant who has suffered a head injury—whether or not there was loss of consciousness—should be removed from the game and examined by a physician before being allowed to play again.

Once an injury has occurred, prompt medical attention followed by rehabilitation will do much to minimize ill effects. The professional sports are a great testimonial to the benefits that can be derived from physiatrics. The period that a player is out of the game following an injury has been greatly lessened, and the active playing years for participants in many sports have been lengthened by rehabilitation.

TRANSPORTATION ACCIDENTS

Of the 3000 deaths in 1963 due to accidents associated with transportation (excluding motor vehicle deaths and deaths of transportation workers), about a third each were due to water and aircraft accidents. Of the balance, about a fourth were the result of railroad accidents and the remainder were due to miscellaneous causes, including deaths from accidents on subways, elevators, buses, street cars and bicycles. The 1963 total represents a considerable drop over the preceding decade. In 1953 there were 3800 such deaths. The biggest decline during the period was in deaths from railroad accidents, from 1100 in 1952 to 600 in 1963. Aircraft accident deaths also dropped from 1350 to 1100, despite great increases in air travel. Only deaths from water transport accidents showed an increase.

AIRCRAFT AND RAILROAD ACCIDENTS

Prevention of Occurrence

Since in some 80 per cent of aircraft accidents pilot error is a contributory factor, it is obvious that this area needs further exploration. Considerable progress was made by the U. S. Air Force during World War II in minimizing factors contributing to pilot error. Many air safety authorities believe that federal agencies concerned with the regulation of aircraft should expand their research into causes of pilot errors. Possibly, railroads too could profitably study problems relating to errors of locomotive engineers and other operating personnel.

While many of the environmental factors in transportation accident prevention are not of direct concern to them, physicians can, nonetheless, lend their support as informed, alert citizens to measures designed to reduce accident hazards on the country's airways and railroads. Physicians working with engineers can make a contribution in improving the environment of the operator. Aircraft pilots particularly are confronted with a complex of instruments whose readings must be accurately interpreted and translated. Apparently the maximum number of instruments which can be comprehended efficiently has been reached, and therefore efforts must be made to minimize the instrument problems of the pilot. Further, it is apparent that in situations in which evasive action must be taken to prevent the collision of high-speed aircraft the limits of human reaction time have been reached. Automatic instruments and prevention through ground control must come to the aid of the pilot under such circumstances.

The field of aviation medicine, recognized as a specialty branch of preventive medicine, has made great contributions to air safety and deserves the support of all physicians in its continuing programs.

Minimization of Injury

Two major factors in minimizing accident injuries are the development of rescue services which can be called into immediate action and the provision of organized emergency medical care facilities to back up the rescue operation. Accidents such as train wrecks provide a severe test for the emergency medical care facilities of all but the largest communities, yet every community should, in its disaster planning (Chapter 10), take into account the possibility of such a catastrophe and prepare in advance the steps that can be taken to cope with it.

WATER TRANSPORT ACCIDENTS

Included in the category of water transport accidents are all those involving regularly chartered passenger ships, as well as those resulting from the operation of small craft. Of the 1100 deaths from accidents involving water craft in 1963, three-fourths of the drownings involved boats with a capacity of less than 10 persons. The number of deaths from water transport accidents has climbed sharply since 1945, when 600 deaths were recorded. The increase may be attributed in a large measure to the tremendous upsurge in the nation's small boat population since World War II. Along with the increase in numbers of boats has also come more powerful and more efficient motors, which mean higher operating speeds. The current popularity of water skiing is considered by some to be a factor also, especially since water skiing requires relatively high boat speeds.

The increased number of deaths and injuries and the continuing increase in the number of boats of all types has been a cause for concern by many state governments and by Congress, which in 1958 passed the Federal Boating Act. Its provisions are summarized in the U. S. Coast Guard Publication, CG-29D.

Prevention of Occurrence

In addition to general safety precautions, some government and voluntary agencies concerned with boat safety believe that two areas need further study. These are the operator's qualifications and the policing of boat speed limits, particularly on crowded waterways. The solution to the former problem may lie in the testing and licensing of motor boat operators; the solution to the second may require the development of a constabulary for navigable waters similar to that now patrolling highways.

Minimization of Injury

Since boating accidents may well take place at a considerable distance from medical care, the importance of first-aid training for boat operators is evident, as is the availability of a suitable first-aid kit on the boat. Proper first-aid measures must be backed up, as in all accidental injuries, with adequate emergency medical services.

GRANVILLE W. LARIMORE, M.D.

REFERENCES

1. Accident Facts, 1964. Chicago, National Safety Council.
2. National Health Survey, National Center for Health Statistics. Washington, D.C., U.S. Department of Health, Education, and Welfare.
3. Bureau of Medical Economic Research, American Medical Association. Reported in Accident Facts, 1958. Chicago, National Safety Council.
4. Godfrey, Edward S., Jr.: Role of the health department in the prevention of accidents. American Journal of Public Health, 27:152, February, 1937.
5. Pennsylvania Department of Health: A study of power lawn mower accidents. Reported in Accident Facts, 1963. Chicago, National Safety Council.
6. Accident Facts, 1956. Chicago, National Safety Council.

7. Bureau of Labor Statistics, United States Government, Washington, D.C. Reported in Accident Facts, 1953. Chicago, National Safety Council.
8. Moore, John O.: A study of speed in injury-producing accidents: A preliminary report. American Journal of Public Health, 48:1516, November, 1958.
9. McCarroll, J. R., and Haddon, W., Jr.: A controlled study of fatal automobile accidents in New York City. Journal of Chronic Diseases, 15:811-826, 1962.
10. Haddon, William, Jr., and Bradess, Victoria A.: Alcohol in the single vehicle fatal accident: The experience of Westchester County, New York. Journal of the American Medical Association, 169:1587-1593, April, 1959.
11. Loomis, T. A., and West, T. C.: Comparative sedative effects of a barbiturate and some tranquilizer drugs on normal subjects. Journal of Pharmacology and Experimental Therapeutics, 122:525, April, 1958.
12. Stahnke, Herbert L., Allen, Frederick M., Horan, Robert V., and Tenery, John H.: The treatment of snake bite. American Journal of Tropical Medicine and Hygiene, 6:323, March, 1957.
13. Larimore, Granville W.: Home Health Emergencies. 1956. New York, Equitable Life Assurance Society.
14. McFarland, Ross A., Moore, Roland C., and Warren, A. Bertrand: Human Variables in Motor Vehicle Accidents. Boston, Harvard School of Public Health, 1955.
15. McFarland, Ross A.: Health and safety in transportation. Public Health Reports, 73:663, August, 1958.

3   Ionizing Radiation

GENERAL CONSIDERATIONS

The protection of the public against the effects of excessive exposure to ionizing radiation is the concern of all practicing physicians and health departments. Because of the increasing use of radiation in industry and medicine in recent years, as well as the exposure of whole populations to significant amounts of radioactivity dispersed throughout the world as a result of nuclear weapons testing, radiation safety has become one of the nation's most important public health problems.

Furthermore, increasing knowledge of the effects of radiation on biological systems and discussions of the problems connected with radiation safety by the mass media have produced a marked awareness of the situation, not only among professional users of radiation, but also among the lay public. Physicians, other licensed practitioners and x-ray technicians must be prepared to cope with radiation hazards and to be able to allay the fears of laymen regarding the use of radiation.

Ionizing radiation may occur in several forms. When produced by x-ray tubes, such radiation consists of myriads of small bundles of energy called photons. Photonic radiation may also be produced by the disintegration of radioactive materials. For convenience, photons produced from radioactive nuclei are called gamma rays whereas those produced by extranuclear processes are called x-rays.

In addition to gamma rays, a number of high-speed particles may be emitted from radioactive materials. Among the more common of these are electrons and the nuclei of helium atoms. Collections of electrons emitted during nuclear disintegration have been given the name beta rays; collections of helium nuclei are called alpha rays.

In general, x-rays and gamma rays are very penetrating. Since they are pure radiant energy they move with the speed of light. Beta rays move more slowly and are less penetrating. They are usually stopped by a few mm. of tissue. Alpha rays, being large particles, are strongly ionizing but penetrate only the thinnest of materials; under most circumstances, a few layers of paper are sufficient to stop them.

44

BIOMEDICAL EFFECTS

The biomedical effects of human exposure to ionizing radiation fall into two broad categories: the effects of repeated exposures to relatively small does of radiation, and the effects of exposure to single large doses.[2, 5, 25, 26, 35, 36] The small-dose effects may be further classified into genetic and somatic.

Small Dose Effects

Genetic effects, caused by irradiation of the reproductive organs, are marked by the appearance of mutations in succeeding generations.[23, 24] Their significance is that an inapparent injury to the present generation may be conveyed to many generations still unborn. Furthermore, the genetic changes induced by a given dose of radiation appear to be irreversible; hence, the genetic effects of small doses of radiation delivered over a period of time are cumulative. Also, the changes in the genes appear to be proportional to the dose, becoming more severe as the dose increases. Recent experiments in mice have shown that the genetic effects produced by a single dose of radiation may be greater by a factor of several times than the effects produced by the same dose given in multiple exposures over a period of time.[28]

The somatic effects of small doses of radiation are produced by the irradiation of certain critical organs and may lead to the development, after the lapse of a variable amount of time, to a number of neoplastic states including leukemia (blood-forming organs), skin cancer and bone cancer.[4, 19, 31-33] In general, the somatic effects may be expected to be greater when the dose of radiation is high than when it is small. However, it is not at all certain that the magnitude of somatic damage is entirely proportional to the radiation dose. It is quite possible that extremely small doses create little or no somatic damage; that is, there may be a threshold dose below which no somatic effects may be expected. However, the scientific data on this point are so uncertain that one must assume the existence of no somatic threshold dose until conclusive evidence to the contrary is forthcoming.

In addition to the specific effects of ionizing radiation on critical organs, radiation exposure may produce a more generalized effect on the individual such as early aging and premature death.[15, 40] The basis of this phenomenon is not understood. When death comes, it is usually due to a cause quite unrelated to identifiable exposure to radiation.

The quantitative relationships between low doses of radiation and their biomedical effects have not been established with satisfactory precision. Indeed, almost every value which has been suggested for a particular dose-effect relationship has been challenged. However, as a guide, it may be worthwhile to cite at this time a few data to give some impression of the magnitude of the damage which may be produced by various dosage levels. It must be emphasized that the data given below are not based upon well-controlled comprehensive experimental investigation and some may well be proved incorrect by an order of one magnitude or more.

Genetic Effects. It has been estimated that an exposure of about 200 roentgens to the gonads of an individual prior to reproduction is required to double the probability that a mutation will occur in the individual's children. Since the spontaneous mutation rate of the population is of the order of 2 per cent, an exposure of about 200 roentgens to the prereproductive segment of the population may be expected to increase the mutation rate to 4 per cent.

Somatic Effects. It has been estimated that the probability of one's developing leukemia after a radiation exposure is one to two parts per million per roentgen of whole-body exposure for each year of survival after the exposure takes place.[19] The probabilities for the development of most other neoplastic states appear to be smaller although this is not at all certain. In the phenomenon of the shortening of life by radiation exposure, the data are particularly inconclusive. Quantitative estimates of this dose-effect relationship vary through a wide range. One of the more widely quoted values is a life shortening of one week per roentgen of whole-body exposure.[15, 40]

The foregoing data indicate that the most important hazards of ionizing radiation for persons who are in the reproductive or prereproductive age group are genetic. Current estimates of the exposure received by the reproductive organs of the population in the United States indicate that the contribution from medical x-ray sources probably lies between 0.2 and 5.0 roentgens prior to and during the family formation period of an average individual.[18, 20, 22] This dose may be expected to increase the mutation rate of the population by 0.1 to 2.5 per cent over the spontaneous level.

LARGE DOSE EFFECTS

In the discussion of the effects of small doses of radiation, it was noted that a considerable period of time usually elapses following an exposure before changes of any kind appear; that is, there are no immediate clinical manifestations of disease. When the whole-body dose exceeds 100 rads, however, clinical changes are likely to appear within a few hours to a few days.[8, 12, 29, 34] Indeed, a characteristic syndrome is produced whose severity is a gauge of the dose received and the sensitivity of the irradiated individual. This syndrome, often called the acute radiation syndrome, should be fully understood by anyone working in the field of radiology since the success of treatment often depends upon early recognition of the condition.[9, 11]

One of the most important problems which a physician faces when called upon to care for persons who have received acute large doses of radiation is the evaluation of the magnitude of the biomedical problems at the accident site. Reliable data on the exposure fields which prevailed during the accident are often absent or incomplete. No single laboratory examination is available with which an exposed individual may be examined for a precise determination of the radiation exposure he has received. Much rests upon the clinical skill of the physician to judge the seriousness of the situation from early clinical signs. Such judgments often are made more difficult by an air of panic which frequently develops when radiation accidents have occurred. It is the responsibility of the physician to restore order, to make a calm appraisal of the extent of the accidental exposure, and to proceed with the clinical care of the irradiated individuals.

One cannot overemphasize the value of the carefully-trained physician in such a situation, for this is an opportunity for public health action at its best. By working closely with the radiological engineer, the physician is better able to determine how serious the particular accident may be. If careful evaluation indicates that the damage is not great, the physician may do much to eliminate unnecessary apprehension. On the other hand, if the exposures have been high, a good physician will be able to move with confidence to take care of the injured and to give assurance to both the injured and their associates that the situation is well in hand.

The procedures to be carried out by the public health physician when a radiation accident occurs are relatively simple and are based principally on common sense. These procedures include: (a) evacuation of all exposed individuals to a nearby uncontaminated area where the injured may be isolated from one another and given first aid, (b) survey of the exposed persons for surface contamination by radioactive materials, (c) simple decontamination of body surfaces, (d) estimation of the radiation dose received, (e) saving of clothes, urine, feces, vomitus, and blood samples of the irradiated individuals for dosimetric study, (f) taking of a careful history of the accident, and (g) transfer of the irradiated persons to hospitals for careful evaluation and clinical study when the whole-body dose is suspected to be in excess of 100 rads.

Those who exhibit the acute radiation syndrome may be conveniently divided into five broad groups according to the whole-body dose of radiation received and the clinical manifestations exhibited. The first group includes individuals whose dose has been under 200 rads. These individuals usually are asymptomatic or at most exhibit mild nonspecific prodromal symptoms. The second group includes those persons who have received a whole-body dose ranging from 200 to 400 rads. The acute radiation syndrome here is mild, with transient prodromal nausea and vomiting and minimal laboratory and clinical evidence of hematopoietic damage. The third group consists of those who have received a dose ranging from 400 to 600 rads. Here, the course is more serious with hematopoietic damage and gastrointestinal disorders manifested relatively early. The fourth group includes those who have received doses ranging from 600 to 1400 rads. The acute radiation syndrome under these circumstances is accelerated, with gastrointestinal damage dominating from the beginning. The final group includes those receiving doses in excess of 1400 rads. The individuals in this category suffer a fulminating course, with marked damage to the central nervous system arising within a short time after exposure.

The acute radiation syndrome may be divided into four stages: a prodromal stage, 8 to 48 hours in length; a latent stage of 2 to 3 weeks' duration; an overt illness stage lasting from the second or third week to about the sixth week after irradiation; and a recovery stage ranging to 15 weeks or more in length.

The prodromal symptoms include anorexia, nausea, vomiting, prostration, fatigue and sweating. If these symptoms begin within a few minutes after exposure, one may expect a fulminating course. This is particularly true if these symptoms become progressively worse in a short period of time. If improvement occurs soon after the onset of the initial symptoms, a more benign course may be anticipated. The physician often finds it difficult to evaluate many of these symptoms because they may be produced by anxiety and apprehension as well as by radiation exposure. It is therefore important that calm and order at the accident scene be restored as quickly as possible after the accident occurs. Isolation of the injured from one another may be helpful in the prevention of fear.

Diarrhea in the prodromal stage is an indication that the individual has received a serious radiation dose, probably in excess of 600 rads. Oliguria also indicates that serious exposure has occurred.

Evidence of damage to the central nervous system is the most ominous of the many clinical symptoms. Ataxia, disorientation and autonomic collapse are three such manifestations which are followed uniformly by death within a few hours or days.

During the latent stage of the acute radiation syndrome, symptoms often regress to the point where the individual is asymptomatic. The length of the latent period varies from 2 to 3 weeks and is usually shorter when larger doses have been received.

During the stage of overt illness, the patient may exhibit a variety of symptoms. The principal findings, however, include fever, infection and purpura as manifestations of hematopoietic damage; diarrhea and paralytic ileus as evidence of gastrointestinal derangement; and paresthesia, motor disorders, and autonomic collapse as evidence of injury to the central nervous system. Epilation, lethargy and weakness also may prevail. The extent of these clinical symptoms will depend upon the radiation dose.

The laboratory findings of acute radiation syndrome are particularly valuable in assessing the injury. Studies of blood and bone marrow permit determination with some quantitation of the extent of damage. If neutron* exposure has occurred, examination of the sodium-24 levels of the blood gives valuable information regarding the magnitude of the dose received.

Treatment for the acute radiation syndrome includes strong supportive care with the use of antibiotics to control infection. Bone marrow transplants with cells from a homologous donor, matched in sex and major and minor subgroups, have been used by some in the hope that they will restore the hematopoietic systems of patients exposed to severe doses. The value of such therapy is not yet entirely clear.[1, 21] When considerable inhalation or ingestion of radionuclides has occurred, colloidal ion exchange carriers and chelating agents may be employed to increase the excretion of some of these radioactive materials.[17, 27]

RADIATION STANDARDS

Historically, the need for a system of radiation standards or exposure guides for the control of ionizing radiation was first recognized by radiologists and physicians soon after the discovery of the x-ray. Such standards are needed to protect patient and physician alike against the hazards of excessive exposure. In the late 1920's the Advisory Committee on X-ray and Radium Protection (now known as the National Council on Radiation Protection and Measurements or NCRP) was established to make recommendations concerning safe operating practices in the field of radiology. Through the years, this body, composed of outstanding members of the radiological and associated sciences, has made a large number of

* See glossary of radiological terms, page 58.

recommendations which, as applications of radiation techniques have affected increasingly large groups of people, have been extended to fields of activity well beyond medical radiology.

One of the first recommendations by the committee concerned what has become known as the maximum permissible dose (MPD) or the weekly dose which individuals working with ionizing radiation may be expected to receive without the development of serious biological damage. In the beginning, the maximum permissible dose was set at a rate of approximately 1 roentgen per week. Over the years, this value has been reduced until now the maximum permissible dose for workers in most situations is only 0.1 roentgen per week.

It is interesting to observe the methods which have been used in setting this standard. Although the members of the NCRP were of scientific discipline, scientific data were by no means their only consideration. Practical factors have had a profound influence as well. For example, the maximum permissible dose for radiation workers has been reduced over the years not because new information has come to hand which indicates radiation to be substantially more dangerous than it was once thought to be, but because it has been found that, with reasonable operating skill, radiologists and their technicians could easily limit exposure well below 0.1 roentgen per week. Furthermore, such a limit could be obtained without added expenditures of time and money. This point is emphasized because it is frequently felt that scientific factors alone have determined the limits specified in radiation protection standards. Actually, practical considerations have often played an equally important role.

Since it is prudent to assume that there is no threshold dose of radiation below which biological damage may be avoided, it follows that there is a large philosophical element in the development of radiation protection standards. The specification of a permitted radiation dose in a given standard carries with it the possibility that some biological damage will result when the standard is applied. Hence, those who are charged with the formulation of radiation standards must continually balance biological risk against radiation benefit. If the dosage level is set too high, human damage may outweigh socioeconomic, medical, or other benefits; if the dose is set too low, developments in nuclear science and medicine may be curtailed. These judgments are not without their difficulties because it is necessary to compare unlike quantities when the balance between risk and benefit is evaluated. For example, in occupational exposure, the risks are biological whereas the benefits may be economic. Certainly, an evaluation of these two factors requires careful judgment by men not only with a sound scientific background, but with broad philosophical insight as well.

As noted earlier, the biological damage produced by ionizing radiation increases progressively as the dose increases. That is, when the dose is small the probability of damage is small, but as the dose becomes larger the probability of damage becomes greater. It therefore follows that when a radiation protection standard covering a given set of occupational or environmental conditions sets forth a maximum permissible dose, the standard does not mean that there is complete safety when the dosage levels are below the MPD or that there is great danger when the MPD is exceeded. It does mean that those formulating the standard considered the probability of damage at the maximum permissible level to be so small as to be inconsequential.

In the past, the maximum permissible levels have been set sufficiently low that the probabilities of serious damage either to an individual or to the population at large are small even at dosage levels several times the MPD. It is important that the public and those working in the field of public health appreciate this fact, for it will permit a better understanding of radiation protective measures wherever they may be required. Many times the lay public has become quite apprehensive when, under certain circumstances, the maximum permissible levels have been approached or exceeded. Such a reaction has not often been consistent with the risks.

The manner in which biological risk increases progressively with radiation dose makes questionable the continuation of radiation protection standards which are expressed in terms of maximum permissible dose. It seems wise that standards in the future should be formulated in a framework in which measures to control radiation exposure would become increasingly stringent as radiation dosage levels rise; that is, standards should be based on a concept of graded action to meet increasing risk. Specifically, protective standards should establish a set of guiding principles which include, in each case, the specification of a lower dosage limit below which biological risk is negligible. Above this limit, the standard should specify a series of dosage levels, each one of which would call for the application of a set of specific public health measures to meet effectively the problems the dose level imposes. These measures could be expected to become more extensive as dosage levels increase. Radiation protection standards developed in this manner would not only do much to erase confusion which has resulted from misunderstanding of the term "maximum permissible dose" but would also set the stage for effective public health action.

As an example of how standards based on the "graded action" principle might operate, consider the problem which presented itself in 1960 in several communities because of extensive nuclear testing during the preceding year. At that time the strontium-90 levels in milk rose to substantial fractions of the maximum permissible concentration established by the NCRP. The rise was rapid and it appeared that the maximum permissible concentration might be exceeded. The prospect of such an event alarmed many people. Although this situation should be and was of concern to public health authorities, it need not have caused public apprehension. Contrary to some points of view, the risk to the population would not have suddenly worsened if the maximum permissible concentration for strontium-90 had been exceeded. Indeed, these risks would have been only slightly greater than those which had prevailed at the levels actually reached.

Nevertheless, with the protective standard for strontium-90 based on the concept of a permissible maximum, a substantial number of people feared that the danger to the population was sufficiently serious that milk supplies should be confiscated. That such a viewpoint was quite unjustified may be illustrated by the fact that intake of milk products containing strontium-90 at the maximum permissible concentration would be required for a period of several decades for an individual to receive a dose to bone approaching the whole-body dose received by properly protected radiation workers during their daily work. Since no case of bone cancer has been found in such workers in the past, the public danger from the temporary rise in strontium-90 concentration in milk certainly did not call for the heroic measures suggested.

Radiation protection problems like that just cited have occurred with increasing frequency since the early 1950's. The concern of the lay public with social as well as scientific matters made it increasingly evident that there should be an official governmental body for the formulation and promulgation of radiation protection standards. As a result, in 1959, the Federal Radiation Council (FRC) was created by public law 86-373 to advise the President with respect to radiation matters directly or indirectly affecting public health. The Council currently includes the Secretary of the Department of Health, Education, and Welfare (presently the Chairman), the Secretaries of the Departments of Defense, Commerce, Labor and Agriculture and the Chairman of the Atomic Energy Commission or their designees. It uses a working group of government scientists as well as outside consultants to aid in the formulation of its policies and in the preparation of its reports. It also relies heavily on related federal agencies for data on the biological effects of ionizing radiation. The National Committee on Radiation Protection and Measurements has considerable impact on Council action.

To date the Council has issued a number of reports, the first two of which provide the basic framework of radiation protection standards in the United States.[6, 7] Many of the recommendations contained within these reports have important public health implications. The most pertinent are summarized in the paragraphs which follow:

1. As a basis for its recommendations, the Council has introduced the concept, radiation protection guide. The RPG is defined as "the radiation dose which should not be exceeded without careful consideration of the reasons for doing so; every effort should be made to encourage the maintenance of radiation doses as far below this guide as practicable."

2. The RPG for whole-body exposure of individuals in the general population is 0.5 rem (roentgen-equivalent-man) per year; the suggested guide for whole-body exposure of population groups is an average of 0.17 rem per year.

3. The RPG for thyroid and bone tissues is 1.5 rems per year for individuals in the general population and an average of 0.5 rem per year for population groups. For bone marrow, the corresponding RPG's are 0.5 and 0.17 rem per year, respectively. All values take cognizance of the special problems posed by the most sensitive elements of the population, that is, infants and children, insofar as scientific information is available.

4. Specific ranges for daily intake have been established for I^{131}, S^{89}, Sr^{90} and Ra^{226} in conformity with the following criteria:

    a. Daily intakes in range I are not expected under normal conditions to result in any appreciable number of individuals in the population reaching a large fraction of the RPG.

    b. Daily intakes in range II would be expected to result in average exposures to population groups not exceeding the RPG, and

    c. Daily intakes in range III would be presumed to result in exposures exceeding the RPG if continued for a sufficient period of time.

The daily intake ranges averaged over one year for each of the four radionuclides are:

Iodine-131
  Range I: 0-10 picocuries/day
  Range II: 10-100 picocuries/day
  Range III: 100-1000 picocuries/day
Strontium-89
  Range I: 0-200 picocuries/day
  Range II: 200-2000 picocuries/day
  Range III: 2000-20,000 picocuries/day
Strontium-90
  Range I: 0-20 picocuries/day
  Range II:20-200 picocuries/day
  Range III: 200-2000 picocuries/day
Radium-226
  Range I: 0-2 picograms/day
  Range II: 2-20 picograms/day
  Range III: 20-200 picograms/day

Although knowledge of the biological effects of ionizing radiation is incomplete, current recommendations of the FRC provide a generally sound basis for public health action when radiocontamination occurs as a result of peace-time uses of atomic energy. The Federal Radiation Council currently is at work developing similar standards for application when radiocontamination of the environment occurs from nuclear weapons testing.

Over the years Council recommendations may be expected to become continuously more valuable as additional radiobiological data become available. It is to be noted that the Council has expressed its guidance on radioactive contamination in terms of human daily intake values. In doing so, it points out that an individual approaches the limits of his radiation protection guide only when his daily intake of a radionuclide is continued indefinitely at the nuclide's maximum range II guidance level. The practical significance of this is that the daily values of radioactive contamination in such environmental components as the food supply should not be regarded as the only determinant of public health policy in the application of countermeasures. Projections of future values must be developed, and from these estimates, a determination made of the likelihood that the total radionuclide intake of the population will cause exposures in excess of the RPG.

SOURCES OF PUBLIC EXPOSURE AND THEIR CONTROL

The radiation hazards which currently are of primary concern to public health fall into two categories. The first is the fallout of radionuclides from the testing of nuclear weapons or from accidental reactor releases;[9-11, 16, 37, 38] the second is the not inconsiderable number of x-ray exposures performed by careless and sometimes poorly trained physicians and technicians in diagnostic medical practice.

ENVIRONMENTAL CONTAMINATION

One of the principal radioactive contaminants of the environment is radioiodine or I^{131}. This radionuclide is produced in relatively large amounts in the detonation of nuclear weapons of both the fission and fusion types.

Ordinarily, one might not expect to find sizeable amounts of radioiodine following the explosion of a fusion bomb since this weapon depends upon the fusion of elements of low atomic number to produce its explosive energy. However, fusion bombs can be triggered only by the large quantities of heat generated characteristically by fission weapons. Hence, every fusion bomb has a fission-type trigger, and it is the firing of this trigger which causes the production of radioiodine. The yield of radioiodine from a nuclear weapon is sufficiently high that considerable contamination of the environment takes place.

Radioiodine is interesting because of its relatively short half-life of approximately 8 days. Also, taken into the body it is concentrated within the thyroid gland and, hence, essentially all the radiation dose delivered by an ingested quantity of radioiodine is received by the thyroid.

In general, the hazards of radioiodine from fallout, as far as the general population is concerned, become greatest when the weapon is detonated at low altitude. Under these circumstances the radioiodine enters the troposphere or the lower reaches of the atmosphere and, hence, returns to ground in a relatively short time. High altitude tests, on the other hand, distribute their radioiodine in the stratosphere and the time for its return to earth is quite long.

The preventive measures which are required to control environmental contamination due to I^{131} are almost entirely related to the supply of fluid milk. Since radioiodine has a relatively short half-life, almost the entire intake of this radioisotope is through food products, fluid milk in particular. Small quantities may enter the body through the ingestion of fresh vegetables which have not been thoroughly washed, since little time elapses between the picking of such foods and their consumption. Almost all other foods, with the exception of fluid milk, have relatively long processing times between harvest and consumption and hence contain little or no radioiodine by the time they are eaten.

Since fluid milk reaches the consumer's table within a few days of the time dairy herds have eaten contaminated pasture grasses, fluid milk supplies deliver the great bulk of radioiodine to the population. It therefore becomes the duty of public health officials to institute those measures which will prevent highly contaminated milk from reaching the public. Little or no radioiodine is taken into the body by inhalation or from drinking water. In most areas air and water concentrations do not rise sufficiently high, probably due to dilution effects, for these vectors to pose important health problems.

Preventive measures against radiation must fulfill certain requirements if they are to be useful in the control of public health problems. First, the measure must be effective; that is, it must substantially reduce population exposures below those which would prevail if the measures were not used. Second, it must be safe; that is, the health risks associated with its use must be considerably less than the contaminant at the level at which the preventive measure is applied. Third, it must be practical. The logistics of its application must be well worked out and its cost must be reasonable. All legal problems associated with its use must be resolved before it is applied. Next, responsibility and authority for its application must be well identified. There must be no indecision due to jurisdictional misunderstandings between health and other agencies concerned with radiation control. Finally, careful attention must be given to such additional considerations as its impact on the public, industry, agriculture, and the government.

One of the preventive measures which has recently been used for the control of radioiodine contamination in milk is the feeding of dairy cows with uncontaminated feeds or with feeds which have been stored long enough for their radioactivity to decay. This, of course, requires the availability of large feed storage capacity the year round unless ways and means can be found to produce feed under conditions in which contamination cannot take place. The latter possibility seems unlikely in the near future although experimental methods of feed production to achieve this goal are currently under study.

Other control measures concerning the milk supply which have been considered include (1) the placing of all children of early age, lactating mothers, and pregnant women on evaporated or powdered milk, and (2) the use of refrigerated fluid milk, frozen fluid milk, frozen whole-milk concentrate, and canned, sterile whole milk, each of which has been stored an appropriate time. Although such preventive measures would be effective in reducing population exposures to I^{131}, the milk industry does not at the present time have the production, storage, refrigeration, or processing capacity to make them applicable for the entire population. However, a combination of these measures may be helpful in reducing exposure to a portion of the population.

The decontamination of I^{131} from milk by the ion-exchange method is another preventive measure which has been studied, but none of the processes is, as yet, wholly satisfactory.

The addition of stable iodine to the diet and the medical administration of thyroid extract are two preventive measures which have received considerable study in recent years. Evidence is at hand which indicates that relatively small amounts of stable iodine (1.0 mg. in children and 5.0 mg. in adults) taken daily will induce over a period of a few days a reduction of about 80 per cent in radioiodine accumulation by the thyroid gland.[3] Greater and more rapid reduction can be achieved by larger doses. The medical administration of thyroid extract also prevents radioiodine uptake when doses sufficient to suppress the function of the thyroid gland are given. In spite of the ability of both methods to reduce radioiodine accumulation, their use as preventive measures should usually be reserved for limited application because of the dangers inherent in the administration of food additives and medicants to large population groups.

Other radioactive contaminants of the environment include strontium-90 and cesium-137. These radionuclides are also produced in the detonation of nuclear weapons. Both have relatively long physical half-lives (approximately 28 and 33 years, respectively). Hence, they may enter the body through many elements of the food chain. Strontium-90 is perhaps the more important public health hazard because its biological half-life is also very long. This radionuclide is concentrated in bone where it stays for lengthy periods. Cesium-137, on the other hand, has a relatively short biological half-life and therefore poses few public health problems except in those locations where unusual dietary habits may exist in the population (e.g., the Eskimo).

So far, no useful countermeasures have been developed for Sr^{90}. It is possible to remove this radionuclide from milk, but milk and dairy products account for only a small fraction of the Sr^{90} intake and, hence, this counter-measure has only limited value.

MEDICAL X-RAY HAZARDS

The radiation hazard created by the unwise use of x-rays in diagnostic medical practice is an entirely different problem from that posed by radio-contamination of the environment. In medical practice one has, theoretically, some control of the radiation sources involved and of the individuals who use these sources. Furthermore, the radiation is applied externally and does not involve the ingestion of materials which cause exposure to the individual over a prolonged period of time.

The problems of medical exposure may be divided into two general types. First are the problems created by the use of unsafe x-ray equipment; second are the problems caused by the careless or imprudent use of x-ray equipment by physicians and technicians who have received inadequate training or who are unwilling to employ safe operating principles in practice.

The control of the first problem involves the removal of unsafe x-ray equipment wherever it may be in use. To achieve this objective it is necessary to employ in the local or state health department a competent group of radiation technicians and radiation advisory consultants who can be given authority to inspect on a systematic basis the various x-ray installations operated by the members of the healing arts. Certified radiologists tend to use safer techniques than those who have received relatively little training in the use of x-ray apparatus. However, any inspection program should include the equipment of all practitioners of the healing arts regardless of background.

The problem of preventing imprudent use of diagnostic x-ray equipment is much more difficult than preventing the use of unsafe apparatus. Here one deals with the working habits of the physician and the technician and, since careless and imprudent use of radiation does not result in any immediate deleterious effect, the correction of undesirable habit patterns is extremely difficult.

The best solution to this problem can probably be found in the field of education. At the present time students in the healing arts receive insufficient training in the use of x-ray apparatus, both fluoroscopic and radiographic. It is therefore perhaps not surprising that many individuals using x-ray equipment do so with little concern for the radiation hazards involved. Now that such hazards have been well demonstrated, there is little excuse for a medical curriculum which does not include extensive instruction on the use of x-rays in medical practice, with particular attention given to discussions of the methods by which diagnostic information can be gained with the least possible radiation.

The matter of technician education is also important. Efforts should be made to establish high standards of training and practice for all technician training schools.

RADIOACTIVE ISOTOPES

All personnel working with radioactive isotopes used for medical purposes should be familiar with and be on guard against the external and internal hazards of such materials. Shielding, time and distance are the cardinal points that must guide operators handling these materials. Physicians and their co-workers who use radioisotopes should conform to the tenets of safe practice set forth in the series of handbooks on radiation safety of the National Bureau of Standards and in state sanitary codes or public health regulations on use of ionizing radiation.[13, 14, 42] The maximum permissible daily dose for operators is presently 100 mrem per 40 hour week for 50 weeks of a work year.

Internal radiation hazards from radioactive isotopes are, generally, greater than the external, because of the continuous absorption of radiation at very close range by the internal tissues exposed. This may possibly continue for a long time because many isotopes are eliminated very slowly from the body.

RESPONSIBILITY OF GOVERNMENTAL AGENCIES

Virtually all of the man-made ionizing radiation that United States residents are exposed to is subject to control by state health departments and state labor departments. The United States Atomic Energy Commission exerts primary control over the relatively small levels of public exposure to radiation emanating from by-product materials or nuclear reactors. The authority of the Commission is outlined in the McMahon Act of 1946 and in the 1954 extension of that Act. However, as the volume of by-product materials increases, a more active role will be played by the guardians of public health in protecting the public from this source of radiation exposure.

The United States Public Health Service has helped to develop a nation-wide program of radiological health by: conducting basic research in the biological effects of radiation, training federal, state and local workers, providing limited funds to states initiating control programs and demonstrating preventive measures and the use of modern instruments for detecting ionizing radiation. However, the primary responsibility for public control of radiation hazards rests with the state health departments which work through the county, city and district health units.

The goal of a state health department's radiological health program[13] is to prevent unnecessary exposures to ionizing radiation and to keep the exposure to humans at a minimum wherever people live, work and play. To accomplish this, three major functions are involved:

1. Determination of the extent and character of radiation problems as they now exist and as new ones appear.

2. Supervision of radiation installations either directly or by utilization of local health units which have qualified personnel available for this exacting type of work.

3. Procurement of new information and development of better methods of control through basic and applied research and by the evaluation of programs under way.

To perform these functions, state health departments work with other groups concerned with radiation problems. One such problem requiring cooperative effort is the ultimate disposal of all atomic wastes. These wastes from industrial, medical, research and allied sources will continue to accumulate in our environment to pollute the air, water and soil. Health authorities must work with industry and the Atomic Energy Commission to make sure that the accumulation of radioactive waste materials is not detrimental to human welfare.

These materials accumulate wherever nuclear fission occurs. Thus, whether it be the detonation of an atom bomb or the operation of a nuclear reactor, the results are energy and material fission products. In the case of a bomb, the energy is produced so rapidly that an explosion occurs; in the case of a reactor, the heat is drained away almost as fast as it is produced.

When a bomb explodes, the fission products are violently dispersed into the environment; in the operation of a reactor, an attempt is made to contain all the fission products produced. However, this containment cannot go on indefinitely because fission products tend to "poison" the fuel elements of a reactor. Even if the reactor works perfectly, the reactor must be separated periodically (or, in some reactor designs, continually) from its accumulation of fission products. Today's reactors produce so much fission product between cleansings of the fuel elements that even if one reactor cleansing were safely contained and kept from dispersing into the atmosphere for 1000 years, the product would still decay after all that time and constitute a continuing public health problem. Reactors are, therefore, potential sources of danger because they accumulate hazardous waste products which require safe disposal. The research and sanitary engineering aspects of radioactive waste measurement, transport and disposal are mentioned briefly only to draw attention to their importance.[30, 39]

Another problem for labor and health departments is the extensive use of radiation in industry to detect imperfections in metal products. Industrial engineers and public health personnel are developing programs to protect both industrial workers and the people living in the areas surrounding such industries.

Health and labor departments also work closely with appropriate professional societies in planning and developing statewide programs of radiological health. Special advisory committees from the societies of the medical and physical sciences help in educational campaigns and give technical advice in programs to reduce radiation hazards. State radiological societies can be especially valuable in the latter type of program.

Health departments are encouraging self-discipline among professional persons in the use of ionizing radiation. Many of the larger medical institutions, in addition to appointing radiation safety committees, are employing full-time safety officers to provide protection for such activities.[13]

Hospitals and institutions that desire detailed information on the establishment of rules and regulations for control of the use of ionizing radiation are referred to the Guide of the Johns Hopkins Medical Institution.[14] This guide, when used with the series of handbooks on radiation safety, constitutes a comprehensive manual for the control of all radiation sources used in hospitals.

Health Departments in many areas are encouraging all medical centers to develop radiation safety programs and offer advice and services from their staffs and advisory consultants. The teaching centers have special problems in the use, transport, storage and disposal of radioactive isotopes. Suppliers of such isotopes usually provide detailed instructions on their use. Nevertheless, health departments must survey the use of these products to assure uniformity of control and maximum safety.

Another concern of health departments is the food and pharmaceutical processors who use radiation to destroy bacteria. Radiation techniques are being developed to sterilize foods and pharmaceuticals to keep them marketable for prolonged periods. Many other commercial applications of radiation techniques are appearing, and hundreds of industrial plants currently use a variety of radiation sources. All of these installations require monitoring, inspection and rigid surveillance to control radiation exposure. We must know what radiation hazards exist, where they exist, whom they affect and to what degree. As new uses for radiation appear and as known uses are expanded, the government's responsibility for measurement and control of this hazard will grow. We can keep abreast of developments by directing basic and applied research to the problems of control as they appear. We can keep our public health programs up to date only by means of periodic re-evaluations of these programs in the light of the newest concepts and developments.

GLOSSARY OF RADIOLOGICAL TERMS

The following glossary of radiological terms and units is included in this chapter to provide the student with a readily available set of definitions covering many of the concepts encountered in the field of radiological health.

Absorbed Dose.   The quantity of energy imparted by ionizing particles to unit mass of material when the material is exposed to any ionizing radiation.

Curie.   Unit of radioactivity. It is the radioactivity of a material disintegrating at a rate of 3.7×10^{10} atoms/sec.

Dyne.   Cgs (centimeter-gram-second system) unit of force. A dyne is the force which imparts an acceleration of 1 cm./sec./sec. to a mass of 1 gm.

Electron-volt.   Unit of energy, equal to the energy imparted to an electron when it is moved through an electrical potential of 1 volt. It is equal to 1.6×10^{-12} erg.

Erg.   Cgs unit of energy. The erg is the work or energy expended by a force of 1 dyne acting through a distance of 1 cm.

Exposure.   The quantity of x- or gamma radiation measured in terms of the ionization such radiation produces in air. Unit: the roentgen.

Gram-rad.   Unit of integral dose; the gram-rad is equal to an absorbed energy of 100 ergs.

Integral Dose.   The absorbed dose received by a structure multiplied by the weight of the structure in grams. Since the absorbed dose is never uniform throughout a structure, integral dose must be determined by the division of the structure into a large number of incremental volumes. For each incremental volume, the absorbed dose is calculated from appropriate depth dose data and the product of absorbed dose by mass determined. Finally, these products are summed or integrated over the entire structure. The resulting summation gives the integral dose.

Intensity.   The quantity of radiant energy flowing perpendicularly through a surface of unit area per second and expressed in ergs/sq. cm./sec.

Microcurie.   Unit of radioactivity equal to one-millionth of a curie.

Millicurie.   Unit of radioactivity equal to one-thousandths of a curie.

Neutron.   An elementary particle of nature having a rest (or stationary) mass of 1.00894 atomic mass units. (One atomic mass unit equals 1.66 × 10^{-24} gm.) The neutron does not carry any electrical charge; it is one of the constituents of all atomic nuclei except hydrogen.

Photon. Quantum of electromagnetic radiation equal to the product of the frequency of the radiation in cycles per second and Planck's constant ($6.62 × 10^{-27}$ erg-sec.).

Picocurie. Unit of radioactivity equal to one millionth, millionth of a curie.

Rad. Unit of absorbed dose equal to 100 ergs/gm.

Radiation. The process in which energy is emitted by a body in the form of quanta, each quantum having associated with it an electromagnetic wave possessing a frequency v (and wavelength, λ). In a looser sense, radiation includes also energy emitted in the form of particles such as alpha rays and beta rays.

Radioactivity. The spontaneous disintegration of atomic nuclei, with a concurrent emission of radiant energy (gamma rays) and a number of high speed particles of matter, including electrons and helium nuclei.

Relative Biological Effectiveness (RBE). The biological change produced in tissue by a dose of one type of radiation compared to the change produced by a similar dose of another type of radiation. Relative biological effectiveness is measured as the inverse radio of the absorbed doses of the two types of radiation to produce a particular biological effect under otherwise identical conditions.

RHM. Indirect unit of radioactivity, defined as the quantity of radioactive material which yields an exposure of 1 roentgen per hour measured at a distance of 1 meter from the material.

Roentgen. Unit of exposure, defined as the quantity of x- or gamma radiation such that the associated corpuscular emission per 0.001293 gm. of air produces in air, ions carrying 1 electrostatic unit of electrical charge of either sign. The mass of air referred to in this definition is equal to 1 cc. of dry air at 0° C. and 760 mm. of Hg barometric pressure. One electrostatic unit of charge is the charge carried by $2.083 × 10^{9}$ ions of either sign.

Roentgen-Equivalent-Man (rem). Unit of dose, useful in protection, equal to relative biological effectiveness × absorbed dose in rads.

RUSSELL H. MORGAN, M.D.
HERMAN E. HILLEBOE, M.D.

REFERENCES

1. Andrews, G. A.: Criticality accidents in Vinca, Yugoslavia, and Oak Ridge, Tennessee (and editorial). Journal of the American Medical Association, *179*:191-197, 1962.
2. Auerbach, C.: Effects of atomic radiation. Nature, *198*:343, 1963.
3. Cooper, J. A. D.: Radioisotope toxicity: As related to the thyroid in radioisotopes in the biosphere. Editors: R. S. Caldecott and L. A. Snyder, University of Minnesota Symposium, 1960, p. 449.
4. Court-Brown, W. M., and Doll, R.: Leukemia and aplastic anemia in patients irradiated for ankylosing spondylitis. London, Medical Research Council, Special Report Series No. 295, 1957.
5. Cronkite, E. P., Bond, V. P., and Dunham, C. L. (ed.): Some effects of ionizing

radiation on human beings. TID-5358. Washington, D.C., U.S. Government Printing Office, 1956.

6. Federal Radiation Council: Report #1, Background material for development of radiation protection standards. Washington, D.C., U.S. Government Printing Office, 1960.

7. Federal Radiation Council: Report #2, Background material for development of radiation protection standards. Washington, D.C., U.S. Government Printing Office, 1961.

8. Finkel, A. J., and Hathaway, E. A.: Medical care of wounds contaminated with radioactive materials. Journal of the American Medical Association, 161:121-126, 1956.

9. Great Britain, Atomic Energy Office: Accident at Windscale No. 1 Pile on 10 October 1957. London, Her Majesty's Stationery Office, 1957.

10. Hayes, D. F.: Summary of accidents and incidents involving radiation in atomic energy activities, June 1945 through December 1955. TID-5360. Oak Ridge, Tenn., Atomic Energy Commission, 1956.

11. Hayes, D. F.: Summary of incidents involving radioactive materials in atomic energy activities, January-December 1956. TID-5360 (supp.). Oak Ridge, Tenn., Atomic Energy Commission, 1957.

12. Hempelmann, L. H., Lisco, H., and Hoffman, J. G.: Acute radiation syndrome: study of nine cases and review of problem. Annals of Internal Medicine, 36:279-510, 1952.

13. Hilleboe, H. E., and Rihm, Alexander: Program planning for radiological health. American Journal of Public Health, 48:965-970, 1958.

14. Johns Hopkins Medical Institutions: Committee on Radiation Control, Rules and Regulations. Baltimore, Feb. 1, 1957.

15. Jones, H.: Life-span studies. In Curtis, H. J., and Quastler, H. (ed.): Mammalian aspects of basic mechanisms in radiobiology. Nuclear Science Series Report No. 21. Washington, D.C., National Academy of Sciences-National Research Council Publication No. 513, 1957, p. 102.

16. Knapp, H. A.: Gamma ray exposure dose to non-urban populations from the surface deposition of nuclear test fallout. U.S. AEC Report TID-16457. 50 pp., 1962.

17. Kroll, H., et al.: Excretion of yttrium and lanthanum chelates of cyclohexane 1, 2 transdiamine tetra-acetic acid and diethylene-trianmine pentacetic acid in man. Nature, 180:919-920, 1957.

18. Laughlin, J. S., Meurk, M. L., Pullman, I., and Sherman, R. S.: Bone, skin and gonadal doses in routine diagnostic procedures. American Journal of Roentgenology, Radium Therapy and Nuclear Medicine, 78:961-982, 1957.

19. Lewis, E. B.: Leukemia and ionizing radiation. Science, 125:965, 1957.

20. Lincoln, T. A., and Gupton, E. D.: Radiation dose to gonads from diagnostic x-ray exposure. Journal of the American Medical Association, 166:233-239, 1958.

21. Mathe, G., et al.: Transfusions et greffes de moelle osseuse homologue chez des humains irradies a haute dose accidentellement. Revue francaise d'études cliniques et biologiques, 4:226-238, 1959.

22. Ministry of Health: Radiological Hazards to Patients: second report of the Committee. London, 1960.

23. Muller, H. J.: The production of mutations by x-rays. Washington, D.C., Proceedings of the National Academy of Sciences, 1928, pp. 714-726.

24. Muller, H. J.: An analysis of the process of structural change in chromosomes of drosophila. Journal of Genetics, 40:1-66, 1940.

25. National Academy of Sciences-National Research Council: Biological effects of atomic radiation. Washington, D.C., 1956.

26. National Academy of Sciences-National Research Council: Pathological effects of thyroid irradiation. A report of panel of experts. Washington, Federal Radiation Council, 1962, 8 pp.

27. Norwood, W. D.: DTPA-effectiveness in removing internally deposited plutonium from humans. Journal of Occupational Medicine, 2:371-376, 1960.

28. Russell, W. L.: Genetic hazards of radiation. Proceedings of the American Philosophical Society, 107:11-17, 1963.

29. Saenger, E. L.: Radiation accidents. American Journal of Roentgenology, 84:715-728, 1960.

30. Sax, N. I.: Dangerous properties of industrial materials. New York, Reinhold Publishing Co., 1957.
31. Simpson, C. L.: Leukemia and radiation. Lancet, 2:999-1000, 1958.
32. Stewart, A., Pennybacker, W., and Barber, R.: Adult leukemias and diagnostic x-rays. British Medical Journal, 2:882-890, 1962.
33. Stewart, A., Webb, J., and Hewitt, D.: A survey of childhood malignancies. British Medical Journal, 1:1495-1508, 1958.
34. Thoma, G. S., and Wald, N.: Diagnosis and management of accidental radiation injury. Journal of Occupational Medicine, 1:420-447, 1959.
35. United Nations Scientific Committee on the Effects of Radiation: Report. General Assembly Official Records, 13th session, supp. 17(A/3838). New York, 1958.
36. United Nations Scientific Committee on the Effects of Atomic Radiation: Report. General Assembly Official Records, 17th session, supp. 16 (A/5216) New York, 1962. This report includes an excellent bibliography of pertinent work in the field of diagnostic x-ray dosimetry.
37. U.S. Atomic Energy Commission: Fallout from USSR 1961 nuclear tests. TID-14377, 1962.
38. U.S. Congress, Joint Committee on Atomic Energy, Subcommittee on Research Development and Radiation: Hearings on fallout, radiation standards and countermeasures. Washington, D.C., U.S. Government Printing Office, 1963.
39. U.S. Congress, Joint Committee on Atomic Energy, Subcommittee on Research and Development: Public hearings on employee radiation hazards and workmen's compensation. Washington, D.C., U.S. Government Printing Office, 1959.
40. Upton, A. C.: Ionizing radiation and the aging process. Journal of Gerontology, 12:306-313, 1957.
41. Upton, A. C., et al.: Some delayed effects of atom-bomb radiations in mice. Cancer Research 20:1, 1960.
42. U.S. Department of Commerce: National Bureau of Standards Handbooks. Washington 25, D.C., Supt. of Documents.

4   Air Pollution*

HISTORY

The roots of medical concern about unhealthy air reach down at least to the practice of ancient Greek medicine, when consideration of the winds and what they bore for man and man's environment was considered vital. However, a systematic consideration of the problem, its source and remedy, probably can be traced back only as far as John Evelyn and his pamphlet "Fumifugium" published in 1661. Evelyn's work was primarily a reaction to the large-scale use of bituminous coal and peat for heating in London. Even a law invoking the death penalty, decreed three centuries earlier and forbidding the use of soft coal, had failed to deter the production of sulfurous fumes and smoke. Evelyn advocated the use of better fuels as a means of reducing air pollution and more effective urban planning to prevent effects on health, property and vegetation by consideration of such factors as weather, topography and proper source location.

Air pollution became a widespread problem with the development of the steam engine and the resulting industrial revolution. Associated with the technological and economic changes of that period were a population explosion and an increased population concentration in urban centers. Burgeoning industrial activity and the increasing number and density of domestic sources of smoke in these centers rapidly reduced the ability of the atmosphere to absorb and dilute either the ever-familiar smoke or the growing number of less apparent contaminants.

In the late nineteenth century, a number of European studies were made of air pollution. Then, as now, concern was centered on the most obvious contaminant, smoke. An English commission in 1881, and German and French commissions in 1894, were formed to study the problem. A Smoke Abatement Society was founded in Leeds in 1890 to evaluate air pollution caused by coal smoke, to consider coal consumption in boilers, furnaces and fireplaces and to examine existing control systems.[1]

---

* Sincere appreciation is given to Mr. Sheldon W. Samuels for his collaboration in the preparation of this chapter.

In the United States, smoke was first declared a nuisance in 1864 as the result of a lawsuit filed in St. Louis, Missouri. But the first smoke control ordinance in this country was adopted by Chicago in 1881. Similar ordinances were passed shortly afterward in Cincinnati and St. Louis. By 1912 in the United States 23 of 28 cities with populations of more than 200,000 had smoke abatement programs.

St. Louis and Pittsburgh, when they banned the use of soft coal, demonstrated that the smoke nuisances could be controlled. In Pittsburgh[2] a smoke problem existed for many years, but no organized movement was initiated to control it until 1911. Legislation was passed by the state permitting the city to institute smoke control measures, but efforts made through education and reliance on individual action were ineffective. The first comprehensive control program began in 1941, but World War II intervened and little could be accomplished. However, during the war the Civic Club of Allegheny County formed the United Smoke Council and smoke control leaders prepared to continue their efforts in the postwar period.

The city ordinance in Pittsburgh was partially enforced in 1946. In 1947 it was extended to control smoke from all sources, including one and two family home units. It required all consumers to use either smokeless fuel or to employ a stoker or other equipment which would prevent the production of smoke. By the winters of 1947 and 1948, gains in smoke control were already apparent; day-long smogs were eliminated. Weather bureau visibility records, on which the progress report was based, are shown in Table 1.

Table 1. *1956 Annual Report of the Hours of Smoke in Pittsburgh*

INTENSITY	YEAR										
	1946	1947	1948	1949	1950	1951	1952	1953	1954	1955	1956
Moderate	707	400	375	437	393	256	263	303	139	103	122
Heavy	298	236	132	162	56	51	21	16	4	10	0
Total	1005	636	507	599	449	307	284	319	143	113	122

Other indications of substantial progress were noted. During this period decreases in soot and dustfall ranged from 3.2 to 28.2 per cent in various sections of the city.

The pioneering efforts in air pollution control did not take place in public health agencies, despite the problem's traditional public health aspect. The term "smog" was coined at a London Public Health Congress in 1905,[3] but not until after the Donora, Pennsylvania, disaster of 1948 did federal, state and municipal public health agencies become seriously aware of their responsibilities. Today the federal, all state and a growing number of municipal programs are under the control of public health agencies.

AIR CONTAMINANTS AND SOURCES

Contaminants discharged into the atmosphere fall into two general classifications: aerosols and gases.

Aerosol particles may be either solid or liquid. Liquid particles tend to be spherical; solid particles, because of their small size, generally behave as spheres.[4] Aerosols disappear from the atmosphere by evaporation, precipitation, diffusion or settling. Larger particles tend to settle; smaller ones disperse by diffusion.

An aerosol's stability is chiefly affected by brownian oscillations and gravity settling. Liquid particles collide and adhere or coalesce to form larger droplets, while solid particles come together into loose aggregates which are roughly spherical or filamentous in shape. The more particles present in a given unit of air, the greater the coagulation rate.

Organic and inorganic solid and liquid aerosols present in the community atmosphere include carbon black, fly ash, soot, smoke, metallurgical dust and fumes, silica and silicates, sulfuric acid mist, pollens, bacteria, viruses, molds and fungi. More than 20 metallic elements have been found in aerosol samples.[5] Most aerosols, which vary in size from a fraction of a micron upward, result from combustion processes.

Aerosol sizes are shown in Figure 2. Fumes generally range from a diameter of 0.1 micron to 1.0 micron (a micron is one-millionth of a meter), while individual smoke particles usually are smaller than 0.3 micron in diameter.

Aerosol contaminants vary more widely in concentration than in particle size. In community air, concentrations of 100 to 125 micrograms per cubic meter are common. Wide variations may occur among neighborhoods in the same community, and within the same neighborhood at various times. The variations are influenced by meteorologic conditions and human habits. Well-defined cycles of concentration with distinct diurnal rhythms have been noted. The aerosol concentration is often used as an index of urban air pollution.

An important aerosol property is its ability to scatter light, which makes it readily visible. Aerosols of small particle diameter (0.3 to 0.5 microns) near the lower wavelength range of visible light are usually responsible for the blue haze characteristic of a polluted atmosphere.

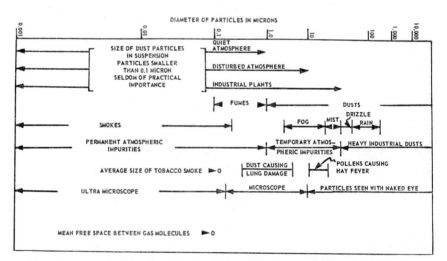

Figure 2. Scale of atmospheric impurities. (From Size and Characteristics of Air-Borne Solids, compiled by W. G. Frank. Copyrighted in 1931 and 1937 by American Air Filter Co., Inc., Louisville, Kentucky.)

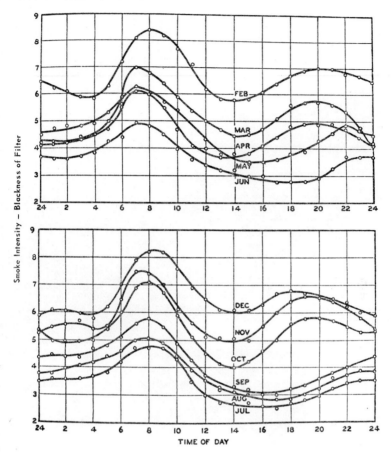

Figure 3. Daily cycles of aerosol concentrations. (Davidson, W. F.: A study of atmospheric pollution. Monthly Weather Review, 70:10, October, 1942.)

The smaller sized particles (less than 1 or 2 microns) of smoke make only a minor contribution to the total weight of air-borne particulate matter. Nevertheless, because they travel long distances, have a high ability to diffuse light and therefore can be seen easily, they are highly significant in community air pollution.

It is not surprising that air pollution is usually identified with dust clouds and smoke palls; to most people the noticeable effects of aerosol contamination are visibility limitations and deposition of particles on clean surfaces.

One of the earliest and still one of the cheapest air pollution evaluation techniques is measurement of aerosol solids that settle from the air. Deposit gauges or dust-fall jars collect particles greater than 20 to 40 microns in size. While the samples do not truly represent the total material present in the air, the gauges are used successfully in specific source problems and to indicate areas of high and low pollution. In coal-burning areas, solids collected by fallout often indicate a deposition rate of 50 to 100 tons, or more, per square mile per month.

In the atmosphere, aerosol particles often adsorb atmospheric gases or

Figure 4. Power plant smoke stacks are an obvious source of air pollution, but less conspicuous sources of air pollution are often more important.

adhere to other aerosol particles. Such combinations may increase the physiologic effects on the human body, or have an effect different from their separate effects.

Unlike aerosols, gaseous contaminants show no tendency to mass or agglomerate. Generally, they do not settle out because of brownian movement and they tend to diffuse. A pocket of gas will rise or fall depending on its relative density to air, but once the gas has been dispersed in a turbulent atmosphere it shows no such tendency.

Sources of air pollution are many: home and factory heating; power-producing operations; industrial and commercial processes; incinerators; pesticide spraying; open fires for disposing of garden and construction debris and commercial wastes; motor vehicles; nuclear weapons; and natural sources (trees, grass and plant pollens, road dust, ocean salt water spray, fog and forest fires).

Although a host of new sources has been introduced since 1900, decreasing the relative importance of smoke as an air contaminant, the indications are that home heating plants and automobiles produce about half of all air pollutants. The remainder comes from industrial, commercial and natural sources.

In Los Angeles in 1955 it was estimated that the petroleum industry discharged only 305 tons of gasoline vapors into the air daily, while the discharge from motor vehicles amounted to 1050 tons.[6] Almost 65 per cent by weight of all aerosols spewed into the Los Angeles atmosphere came from backyard incinerators before laws were enacted banning them. Rubbish burning alone contributed some 6000 tons of wastes to the atmosphere daily.[7]

In Greater Elmira, New York, 60 per cent of the air contamination comes from the public and public-owned sources; 40 per cent comes from industrial and commercial activities.[8]

Industry does, however, discharge large amounts of air pollutants. It produces smoke, sulfur oxides, nitrogen oxides and fly ash when it burns fuel to generate heat and power.

Hydrogen fluoride, hydrochloric acid and organic halides are emitted by plants which make aluminum, phosphate fertilizer, chemicals and petroleum. Many industries discharge carbon monoxide, carbon dioxide and ozone. Ozone may also be generated by photochemical reactions. Carbon monoxide

Figure 5. Smoldering and flaming dumps, both private and public, contribute enormous quantities of foreign material to the air we breathe. (N.Y.S. Health Photo by M. Dixson).

is a serious problem in some vehicular tunnels and poorly ventilated urban areas.

Hydrogen sulfide is a highly toxic, malodorous compound given off by petroleum refineries, pulp mills, sewage disposal and gas plants.

Sulfur dioxide, sulfur trioxide, hydrogen sulfide and mercaptans are common atmospheric contaminants. They are produced when solid, liquid and gaseous fuels containing sulfur impurities are burned by incinerators, refineries, paper, and chemical plants. Sulfur dioxide, sulfur trioxide, nitrogen oxides, arsenic, zinc, iron and other metallic contaminants result from smelting operations, particularly those involving the processing of sulfide ores.

Sulfur dioxide is such a common pollutant that it is sometimes used as a contamination index. However, a community's atmosphere can be heavily polluted even when its sulfur dioxide concentration is low. Oxidation of sulfur and sulfur compounds to sulfur trioxide, followed by hydration, forms sulfuric acid aerosols—a common cause of the familiar blue haze often seen near the top of smokestacks.

Organic compounds in high concentration characterize the urban atmosphere. This group of compounds, in addition to hydrocarbons, includes aldehydes, ketones, organic acids and many others. These come mainly from oil refineries, automobile exhausts, dry cleaning establishments, garages and service stations, and industrial processes which employ solvents or burn organic substances.

Domestic and foreign nuclear weapons tests have generated large quantities of radioactive particles which are suspended in the stratosphere and will return to the earth over a long period of time. Some of these isotopes will decay to innocuous levels before re-entering the troposphere, but others with a long half-life such as strontium-90 will contaminate the environment for long periods.

Radioactive compounds in the atmosphere can also come from natural sources, industrial, medical and commercial establishments and from educational and research institutions using radioactive materials.

Nature's contribution to air pollution includes dust, fungi, pollens, molds, bacteria and other organic and inorganic materials, all of which can be wind borne over great distances.

Any specific pollution problem, however, is the result of a specific complex of contaminant sources. For instance, in the central and eastern portions of the United States, where coal is a major fuel, emissions from heat and power plants differ from those in the west, where the use of oil and gas predominates. Contaminants in an industrial community differ greatly from those of a predominantly residential or rural area.

FACTORS OF AIR POLLUTION POTENTIAL

Many factors are responsible for changes in air quality, not the least of which are seasonal cycles of air polluting activities, such as the home heating season; economic cycles, illustrated by diminished pollutant levels during periods of low industrial production; and technological efficiency, illustrated by greater atmospheric loading from improperly operating automobiles, buses and trucks.

The three critical factors, however, are population density, topography and weather. The persistent smog of the Los Angeles basin is largely the result of these three. Yet, to some degree, most communities with a population of 2500 or greater share the same problem regardless of location.

Population density is an important accumulation factor because air contamination is the product of people at work and play. The more closely people, and the activities of people, are packed into a given area, the greater the resulting air pollution.

The effects of topography and weather are inseparable. Unequal solar heat in different latitudes creates thermal imbalance and causes movement of large, homogenous air masses. They rapidly change the weather along their route and are modified slowly by surfaces which they encounter.

Large low and high pressure areas accompany the movement of air masses. Low pressure areas are normally accompanied by moderate wind speeds, small diurnal temperature changes, widespread cloudiness and precipitation.

High pressure areas are characterized by light surface winds, clear skies and large diurnal temperature and humidity changes.

Within a high pressure area the air is dense and tends to flow downward and outward, while in a low pressure area, the air is lighter and flows upward and outward, creating an air flow pattern between adjacent high and low pressure areas. Since low pressure air rises, there is good dispersion of air pollutants. The converse is true within a high pressure area.

Heating of the earth by the sun and nighttime cooling cause a corresponding heating and cooling of layers of the earth's atmosphere adjacent to its surface. Those air layers immediately above the surface are heated or cooled by conduction, so that the vertical air temperature profile at night differs from that during the day. In the daytime, surface air temperatures are higher and the air tends to rise; after sundown, the ground cools rapidly. The lowest air layers also cool rapidly and, being denser than the warmer layers above, tend to remain in place, forming a temperature "inversion" or temperature pattern opposite to that of the daytime pattern. Unless it is modified by other weather factors, such as strong winds, cloudiness and frontal movements, this change in air stability occurs daily.

In summertime days are longer and normally provide more solar heat than in winter. Long winter nights increase nighttime cooling and decrease the intensity of surface heating during the day. Thus a larger number of inversions persisting through the daytime hours occur in the fall and winter than in spring or summer, despite the fact that winter wind speeds generally are stronger and there is usually more cloudiness, which reduces the radiational cooling of the earth during the night.

Most recorded smog episodes took place in weather that included the inversion factor and other conditions such as the presence of a high pressure air mass. Greenburg et al. noted that during the 1953 incident in New York City, "the lower few hundred feet of the atmosphere remained colder than the air mass immediately above. The warmer, lighter air above formed a lid, trapping the cooler, dense air near the ground. This prevented the contaminants from rising and being dispersed."[9] The presence of the stagnant air mass was confirmed by the smoke, haze and fog which were widespread during the period.

Based upon the analysis of weather factors such as these, it is possible

INVERSION

Figure 6. Ventilation resulting from unstable meteorological conditions increases dispersion and decreases concentrations of air contaminants. Stable conditions, shown above, characterized by temperature inversions, lead to air stagnation and the creation of smog.

to forecast with great accuracy stagnant air conditions or high air pollution potential. But the analysis is complex and for many reasons regional forecasts often do not precisely reflect local variations.

There are significant localized differences in the ability of the earth's surface to gain or lose heat by radiation. These properties can strongly affect surface atmospheric temperatures and, therefore, the vertical temperature profile. Bare ground absorbs and loses heat rapidly, but vegetation modifies the transfer of heat. Snow is an exceptionally good radiator. A cloud top or fog layer will reflect sunlight in the daytime and act as a radiator at night. When clouds or fog occur beneath an inversion layer, the temperature drop associated with radiation may intensify the inversion. This effect of fog or low clouds on the temperature profile is important to air pollution; when it combines with stagnant air conditions, the combination increases pollution concentrations.

Local topography, in addition to modifying wind speed and direction, influences the temperature profile through air drainage and radiation. Valleys have greater diurnal temperature variation than surrounding hills. Cold air tends to drain away from hilltops and settle in valleys. Heating and cooling of a valley may occur more rapidly on one side than on the other.

The integrated roles of the factors of air pollution potential are depicted by the frequent occurrence of smog formation over urban areas in the fall and early winter. This is the time of the year when temperature inversions are most frequent and persist for the longest periods of time and is also the time when the home heating season begins in most parts of the United States and commercial activities are accelerated. The concurrence of these and other factors results in the heavy concentration of pollutants in a blanket of stagnant air we call smog.

ATMOSPHERIC CONTAMINATION: A DETERMINANT IN HUMAN ECOLOGY

The size of a population, human or otherwise, is determined by the ability of the environment to support it. Increases in the potential capacity of our urban environment to support life have taken place over the years through solutions to problems of food supply, water, waste disposal, transportation and housing. It is probable that future increases will depend in part on our ability to solve the problem of air pollution.

Just prior to 1920 the population of the United States was almost equally divided between rural and urban residence; today only about one-third of this country's population remains rural. The consequent rising levels of air pollution could make further urban development undesirable and eventually impossible if new controls are not developed.

Great segments of the eastern seaboard as far inland as the Great Lakes are becoming a gigantic urban tract and, consequently, present an inter-related complex of air pollution problems. The wilderness associated with the Appalachian chain of mountains is being reduced to the same relative significance that Central Park has to the rest of Manhattan island.

The air over many cities of the world fosters growing intra-urban deserts where human habitation is undesirable, vegetation is sparse and scrubby, and property is in a state of deterioration. The bulging suburbs provide no escape. The ex-urbanite's automobile, his leaf and trash burning, the nearby smoking dump, and the bus- and truck-choked arterial roads that keep his community alive are creating serious problems in the most countrified developments.

The precise effect of air pollution on urban environments is obscured by the immensity and complexity of the relationship involved. But the general ill effect is well established.[10]

Any change in natural ground coverage has significant effects on local climate. Every farm and village and even every road produces a new micro-climate. This new climate is the result of surface alterations which affect the aerodynamic and moisture systems, heat production, and changes in atmospheric composition. But even when the topography favors good ventilation, and therefore the rapid dispersion of pollutants, as in New York City, other factors create a poor microclimate. Pollutants serve as nuclei on which moisture can condense, thus increasing precipitation. Rough surfaces and dark colored objects allow absorption of more solar heat, thus increasing temperature. The cooling effect of winds is decreased by structures which lessen the wind speed. In New York City wind speed is approximately 19 per cent slower in Central Park than at LaGuardia Field.

Natural topography, arterial orientation, building height and contours, construction materials and the location of major sources of pollution in the wind field are important factors in the air pollution of urban areas. Thus it is often true that the sources of pollution are most concentrated where the ventilation possibility is the poorest.

Cities, in general, have fewer clear days; they have less illumination and ultraviolet radiation than rural environs. As a result, a wide range of plant life, from lichens to trees, has fared badly in urban centers.

In addition, many chemicals in gaseous form induce characteristic local or systemic injury to vegetation. In fact, plants are excellent instruments for measuring pollution levels in the atmosphere. Plant damage frequently is a more sensitive indicator of the degree of air pollution than chemical or physical tests. Since plant species differ in susceptibility to gases, they are often used to identify specific pollutants.

Plant tolerances are sometimes suggested as standards in justifying air quality controls for given areas because of the considerable cost of damage to ornamental and agriculturally valuable plants, such as white pine, gladioli, spinach and alfalfa. But the total costs of air pollution, including plant damage, are considerably greater. Total economic losses in the United States range in the billions of dollars each year. Although impossible to accurately estimate, they include proportionate costs of the following: fuel waste; lost raw materials and by-products from manufacturing and commercial processes; damage to vegetation and livestock; medical care for humans and veterinary care for animals; increased structural maintenance, painting, cleaning, renovation and replacement; property depreciation; damage to manufactured products and foodstuffs; increased wear on machinery; increased laundering and frequent replacement of clothing and other materials; increased use of artificial light because of reduction of natural light intensity; air filtration for delicate manufacturing processes; decreased shelf life of goods in stores and inventories; maintenance and operation of navigational aids when visibility is restricted by smog; decreased use of transport vehicles; expensive delays of air travelers; and the cost of traffic accidents resulting from air pollution.

The direct annual loss from air pollution in the United States is grossly estimated to be about $65 per capita. The economic losses due to atmospheric contamination are a reflection of our society's failure to control man-made environmental changes. From this point of view, these losses represent more than dollars and cents; they become an index of a uniquely destructive waste of human energy.

HEALTH EFFECTS

Foremost among the potential effects of polluted air on human ecology are the health effects. These are also the most immediate. To live, man must ingest about 30 pounds of air daily compared to about 4½ pounds of water and 2¾ pounds of food. Without a constant renewal of his air intake, death is only a few minutes away. Less clear-cut is the effect of an intake laden with noxious impurities.

The evidence that air pollution contributes to the pathogenesis of a number of diseases is overwhelming and continues to mount. Yet the kind of evidence necessary to determine reasonable levels of air quality for control purposes is virtually nonexistent.

The analysis of air pollution as a pathogen is complicated by a number of factors, including the fact that composition of the air constantly changes; the human receptor is rarely, if ever, exposed to one pollutant at a time; and pollutants may combine to produce a different effect from their effect singly.

The data are further obscured by differences in disease nomenclature, instrumentation, statistical methods and insufficient documentation.[11] Chronic bronchitis in Great Britain, for example, does not generally denote the same disease entity that it does in the United States. The condition of intense, general air pollution popularly known as smog varies greatly according to the kinds and quantities of pollutants in the air and current meteorological conditions. Research on the effects of smog is hampered because in most areas knowledge of the substances contributing to it and subsequent relationships and changes in the atmosphere is either vague or nonexistent.

Several spectacular air pollution disasters have provided some valuable information. These episodes took place during weather conditions characterized by high pressure and temperature inversion systems accompanied by fog. Great masses of stagnant, heavily polluted air remained over small areas for relatively long periods of time.

The immediate effects were similar: healthy persons experienced stinging and burning of the eyes, nasal irritation, heavy coughing, shortness of breath, wheezing, chest constriction and even nausea and vomiting. Those who were already ill were made more ill and in some cases died, especially patients with chronic lung and heart diseases. At Donora, Pennsylvania, in 1948, some 6000 persons out of a total population of 13,000 were made ill.[12] A relatively small number, 20, died. Under similar conditions, thousands died in London in 1952,[13] 1956 and 1962. The total number of those made ill has never been determined. The reports on morbidity and mortality in New York City associated with two smog incidents which covered a large portion of the Eastern United States are particularly enlightening.[9, 14] No deaths were reported in 1962 under meteorological conditions similar to those in 1953 when approximately 200 deaths in New York City alone were attributed to a 10-day smog. Soot fall in 1962 was reported to be lower; sulfur dioxide was reported higher.

This varying effect of different pollutant mixtures emphasizes the importance of studying the chemical significance of these mixtures as well as of individual pollutants.

As Table 2 indicates, a number of pathogenic substances are contained in motor vehicle exhaust. These contaminants and others contained in the exhaust under conditions favorable to the formation of photochemical smog produce peroxyacetyl nitrate (PAN) and other intermediate compounds known to be pathogenic.

The effect of repeated exposures to pollutant mixtures at low concentration that produce no immediately discernible effect is considered by many authorities as a greater, if less dramatic, public health problem than the occurrence of acute air pollution incidents.[15] These incidents usually accelerate among the chronically ill a process begun years before. The multiple diseases from which they suffered initially may well have been aggravated by constant intake of polluted air over long periods of time. Such patients are unable to adapt themselves easily to sudden increases or high levels of pollution, and chronic conditions become extremely aggravated and may result in death.

Table 2. *Established Pathogens Found in Motor Vehicle Exhausts**
(Partial List)

POLLUTANT	POTENTIAL EFFECTS
Aldehydes	Respiratory stress in infants; extreme dermal hypersensitivity; eye irritation.
Carbon Monoxide	Anoxia; chronic optic neuritis; hearing impairment; vestibular disturbances.
Chrysene Benz (a) anthracene Benzo (a) pyrene Benzo (e) pyrene Benzo (j) fluoranthene 1,1 H-Benzo (b) fluoranthene Dibenzo (a,h) anthracene Dibenzo (a,e) pyrene Dibenzo (a,l) pyrene	Carcinogenic.
Nitrogen Oxides	Anoxia; central nervous system depression; asphyxial convulsions; central paralysis; respiratory irritation; pulmonary edema; bronchopneumonia; bronchiolitis; pneumonitis.
Ozone	Eye irritation; decreased cold resistance; partial paralysis of respiratory organs; chest pains; headaches.
Sulfates	(Associated with air pollution disasters in London, New York City, Meuse Valley, Germany, and Donora, Pennsylvania.) Alters rate and depth of breathing; chest pains; coughing; bronchial restriction; pulmonary flow resistance; aggravates bronchial asthma.
Lead	Body burden significantly increases with exposure to vehicular traffic.

* Adapted from a report of the Surgeon General, U.S.P.H.S., to the U. S. Congress, June, 1962.

Heart disease, bronchopneumonia, emphysema, asthma, lung cancer, hayfever and even the common cold are the diseases most often associated with constant low-concentrated exposure.[16, 17] In the absence of extreme air pollution incidents, the appearance of these diseases is merely delayed.

Heart Disease

Sulfates in areas of high population density are found in concentrations known to make breathing more difficult. Ozone, by scarring the linings of the respiratory tract can also make breathing difficult.[18] These breathing difficulties can lead to dangerous overburdening of the heart. It is not surprising that the immediate cause of death during air pollution episodes is usually heart failure. Deaths from heart disease trebled during the London smog disaster of 1952.

Lung Cancer

Concentrates of urban smog, as well as a host of individual pollutants, are known carcinogens. The role of general air pollution in increasing the risk of lung cancer, is considered by most authorities as less than the role of personal air pollution, i.e., cigarette smoking.[19] But the highest incidence of lung cancer usually occurs in areas of high atmospheric pollution. In London, for example, the highest incidence is in the northeast sector where the prevailing winds bring pollution from the central and southern sectors.[11] Lung cancer rates in Dublin and Belfast are compatible with the hypothesis that among men one-third of the lung cancer deaths in Dublin and one-quarter in Belfast result from air pollution.[31]

The greater incidence of lung cancer in cities coincides with the greater concentrations of carcinogens, such as benzo (a) pyrene, known to characterize the urban atmosphere. Ozonized gasoline (artificial smog) containing this carcinogen has been demonstrated to cause lung cancer in mice previously infected with virus influenza in about the same male to female ratio experienced in the human population.[32, 33]

Respiratory Allergies

As of 1963 almost 12 million Americans were reported to suffer from respiratory allergy in the form of asthma and hayfever, resulting in 33 million bed disability days annually.[34] The relationship of these disorders to air contamination is well established. Ragweed pollen, a natural pollutant ignored by most air pollution control agencies, is considered the primary cause of hayfever. Asthma has been linked to man-made air pollution in Nashville, Tennessee, and Pasadena, California. New Orleans, Louisiana, reported an asthma epidemic clearly related to combustion in the city dumps. Air pollution-induced asthma epidemics in Yokahama, Japan, have resulted in an increased percentage of permanent impairment of pulmonary function, disability and death among those affected.[20] Respiratory allergies are considered by many investigators as potentially the most fruitful area for studies relating air pollution to morbidity.

Respiratory Infections

"Colds" and respiratory diseases in general have been associated with air pollution levels indicated by dust-fall and sulfate concentration. In at least one instance employee absenteeism is known to have decreased when air pollution levels decreased. Pneumonia deaths, chiefly from bronchopneumonia, occur at a greater rate in areas of New York State where levels of suspended particulate matter are greatest. During the 1962 smog episode in New York City, upper respiratory infections increased significantly among inmates of homes for the aged.

Chronic Respiratory Disease

A number of studies are in progress to establish the degree to which respiratory function is impaired by exposure to air pollution. That such a relationship exists has already been accepted by many authorities. For example, short-term impaired lung function among schoolchildren in polluted areas of Japan has been noted during periods of heavy air contamination. Study of the effect of long-term exposure to pollutants in less than episodic concentration may turn out to be of great importance. Some studies have been obscured by inconsistent terminology. In Great Britain, where chronic bronchitis is the third leading cause of death and the leading cause of disability, it is often found combined with bronchial asthma and emphysema and often directly associated with air pollution.[21] In this country the presence of bronchitis is often ignored and the presence of emphysema is noted exclusively or considered a more important diagnosis.

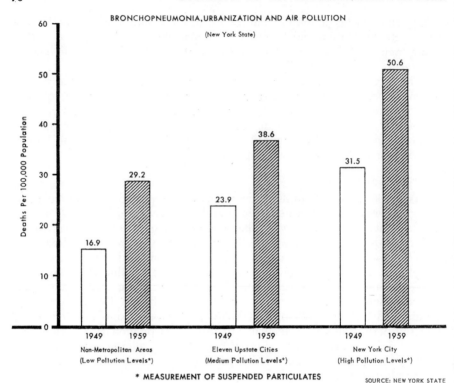

SOURCE: NEW YORK STATE
HEALTH DEPARTMENT

Figure 7. Rising bronchopneumonia death rates are associated with an urban factor of which air pollution is probably a part.

In one study, emphysema seemed to develop first in small localized areas of the lungs where soot deposits were usually trapped.[22] Whether the soot caused the damage or previous lung damage favored the deposit of soot is unknown. Cases of increased susceptibility to respiratory infections that can lead to emphysema have been noted after exposure to air pollutants.

The sevenfold increase of deaths in the United States since 1950 attributed to emphysema has been described as alarming. The age-adjusted urban rate of this disease, double the rural rate, clearly indicates a causative factor inherent in city residence.

THE CONTROL PROGRAM

A comprehensive air pollution control program has two general objectives: prevention of the occurrence of pollution and reduction when it is present. The program's specific objectives are control of health hazards, reduction of economic loss and control of esthetic nuisances. The basis for such a program is comprehensive and accurate information, since not every contaminant need be eliminated from a community's atmosphere for satisfactory air purity. Air pollution control seeks to reduce harmful and obnoxious contaminants to safe, comfortable levels. Two common approaches used by control agencies for reaching their objectives are the management of total air resources by establishing and enforcing community air quality standards and the adoption of design criteria to limit source emissions. Most programs in the past have utilized the latter approach, but currently the establishment of air quality standards is receiving much greater emphasis.

To be effective, a control program should incorporate in its structure means by which those interested in air pollution control are fairly represented in the making of policy and its implementation. Boards, technical councils and other advisory groups, operating within the smallest political jurisdiction able to cope with the problem, have been found effective provided their decisions are given due importance in the problem-solving process.

DETERMINING SOURCES, TYPES AND QUANTITIES

One must determine sources of air pollution, types of emissions and quantities of contaminants discharged into the atmosphere. This information is obtained from inventories of contaminant sources supplemented, when necessary, by area-wide sampling.[23] Laboratory facilities are an essential part of this activity.

Sampling industrial effluents and the general atmosphere is complex and presents problems in obtaining representative samples. Atmospheric studies require sampling of relatively dense stack effluents as well as sampling of urban and suburban atmospheres containing only minute amounts of contaminants. Frequently, indoor sampling equipment has been adapted for sampling the outdoor atmosphere with dubious results. In workroom atmospheres the investigator is concerned generally with one highly concentrated contaminant; outdoors, the investigator deals with many contaminants in low concentrations.

Primitive and sometimes inaccurate devices continue to be used for sampling air pollution.[24] One example is the Ringelmann Chart, used for grading smoke density. The chart grades the relative blackness of smoke, but supplies no quantitative information about the amount of particulate material being discharged. The dust-fall jar, which collects heavier settleable particulates, is another example of inadequate equipment. The results are expressed in tons per square mile, predicted from a gauge usually less than 12 inches in diameter. This method leaves considerable margin for error.

Basic to the collection of particulate matter from the air is efficient separation of material in quantities sufficient for accurate physical and chemical analysis and accurate measurement of sampled air volume.

Stack sampling usually presents only minor problems in collecting sufficient material for analysis, but the effluent volume being sampled may be hard to measure accurately.

Collection of gaseous samples is difficult and involves two broadly classified techniques: those used to collect highly concentrated gases found in stack effluents, and those used to collect low concentrations in the outdoor atmosphere.

Automatic, continuously recording equipment sometimes reduces the man hours required for sampling and analysis, but this equipment is very expensive. One of its advantages is the recording of momentary changes in pollutant intensities. It also records peak concentrations that might otherwise escape attention but are important in evaluating the efficiency of air-cleaning equipment and the adverse effects of polluted atmosphere.

In sampling outdoor atmosphere, it is virtually impossible to obtain a single sample which is representative of a city or community. Representative sampling can be achieved only by use of many sampling instruments and repeated analysis of the same contaminant throughout the area.

Wind velocity and direction further complicate representative sampling. Pollutant concentration at ground level depends largely on micrometeorological conditions at any particular moment.

In order to evaluate samples, factors which contribute to dispersion should be measured continuously. In addition to wind direction and velocity, air turbulence, air temperature and velocity gradients with height, coefficients of dispersion in vertical and horizontal directions and relative humidity are considered. Instruments are available for recording or collecting the needed information but are usually expensive.

Continuous research and study of the detection, causes and effects of air pollution are necessary components of any control program. New sources and types of pollutants—and new combinations of old ones—are continually arising, creating a need for changing investigative techniques. This makes necessary the availability of adequately trained professional and technical staffs with a high level of laboratory and equipment support.

VOLUNTARY CONTROLS

Community involvement is essential in every phase of the program, especially in the dissemination of public information. An organized public information activity can lead to control without recourse to legal action. Public information activities are most effective if they create two-way channels of communication between the agency and the public. This results in a high degree of involvement and therefore identification with the program.

The ultimate goal of an effective public education program is action based upon a realistic awareness of both the problem and possible solutions. Much of the program's content must be in concrete, everyday terms that leave little question as to what must be done and who should do it. Information should be continually addressed to the individual in his capacity as a private citizen, as a participant in government and as an agent of commerce and industry. Public education carried on by a number of agencies working in unison can significantly increase voluntary control of industrial emissions, use of backyard incinerators, ragweed infestation, municipal refuse disposal, space heating and other sources of dirty air.[25]

INTEGRAL CONTROLS

Integral controls—modification, elimination and substitution—are the first means to consider for prevention of occurrence of atmospheric pollution.[26] Los Angeles, for example, has prohibited use of backyard incinerators to eliminate pollution from a particularly vexing source of atmospheric contamination. Substitution of fuel oil or gas for coal as a heating source reduces or eliminates smoke and fly ash.

In general, integral controls are more difficult to achieve but are more effective in the long run. Automobile engine modifications to reduce exhaust emissions through greater engine efficiency would be preferable to muffler and crankcase devices designed as afterthoughts, but such changes are still in a developmental stage.

Integral controls are not always process controls. In selecting industrial sites careful consideration should be given to factors such as topography, micrometeorology, point of contaminant emission, and existing and projected urban composition.

From the point of view of air pollution, consideration of urban composition is a key integral control method since it involves the air quality and land use objectives of the community. Control agencies should integrate their activities with those of urban planning groups.

When substitution or elimination is not possible, some means of treating effluents, i.e., supplementary controls, must be found.

Supplementary Controls

There are eight main types of air-cleaning methods:[27-29] gravitation, inertial separation, filtration, wet collection, electrostatic collection, adsorption and absorption, incineration and catalytic combustion, and sonic collection. (See Figures 8 to 15.)

By gravitation, dust-laden streams pass through a settling chamber where gas velocity is reduced to permit dust particles to settle out. This method is of most use when particles are large enough to settle readily.

Inertial separators depend on sudden changes in the gas flow direction or on centrifugal action. The impingement separator forces dust-laden gas around or through fixed elements interposed in the gas stream. The greater inertia of the suspended particles tends to deposit them on a collection element, around which the gas flows. The cyclone separator is one of the least expensive and most widely used. Gas enters a conical or cylindrical chamber tangentially and leaves axially at the top, and the dust discharges into a receiver at the bottom. Most cyclone separators work well for the removal of large-sized particles but are inefficient for removal of small particles.

Many filtering devices for removing dust from gas streams are on the market. They range from the small disposal type to the bag type filters used in large, dusty industrial operations. Fabric collectors are highly efficient even for submicron-sized particles, but are limited to air conditions dry enough to prevent condensation or deposition of free moisture. Maximum gas stream temperatures also are critical.

Wet collectors or scrubbers include all devices that use liquid to expedite removal of contaminants from a gas stream. They present no secondary dust problems during disposal of the collected material, can clean high temperature and moisture-laden gases, require little space, and efficiently remove particles greater than 10 microns in size.

The use of water, however, introduces secondary problems. Costly corrosion-resistant materials often are required and water used in the collector requires clarification before disposal or reuse. Wet collector effectiveness is dependent on many factors such as: (a) impaction or impingement efficiency—very small droplets must be created to collect small-sized aerosols, (b) diffusion—very small particles may behave as gases and collection effi-

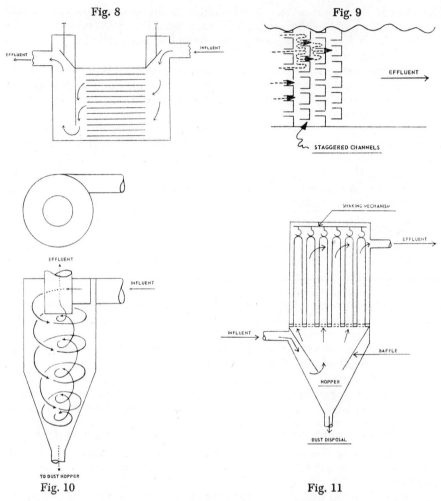

Fig. 8

Fig. 9

Fig. 10

Fig. 11

Figure 8. A settling chamber. The slow movement of air across the trays within the chamber, allows heavier particles to deposit and be retained. The trays are cleaned intermittently.

Figure 9. An impingement separator. Many types are available; all are dependent on inertial deposition of particles as the gas passes around an obstruction.

Figure 10. A cyclone separator. The dust is removed by centrifugal force.

Figure 11. A bag house collector. Accumulated dust is removed by intermittent shaking. In some types a reverse jet ring travels up and down the bag and removes collected material continuously. Many designs are available.

ciency increases because of diffusion, (c) electrostatic attraction—fragmentation of the liquid stream and high air flow velocity may create static charges which increase efficiency of aerosol capture, and (d) condensation—aerosols may serve as condensation nuclei to create removable droplets. Numerous scrubber types are available but generally units having high power consumption achieve the best degree of dust or mist collection.

In an electrostatic precipitator, dust or mist particles suspended in gas are ionized in an electrostatic field. Particles become electrically charged and are attracted to a collecting surface having an opposite charge. Although the electrostatic precipitator is expensive, its removal of small particles is very efficient.

Many industries remove toxic or obnoxious gases and vapors by adsorption to beds of special chemicals, such as activated carbon, silica gel, lithium chloride and activated alumina.

Absorption equipment can also be classified as wet collection. There are

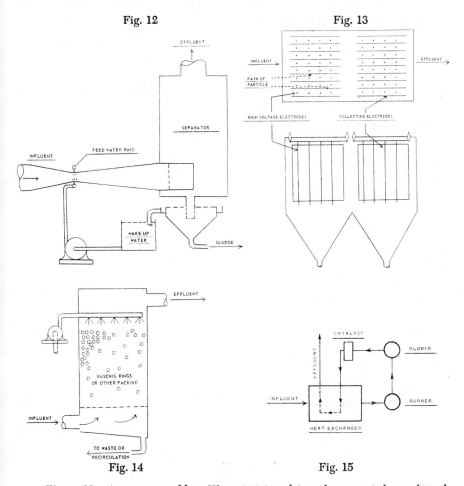

Figure 12.   A venturi scrubber. Water is injected into the venturi throat through the feed water ring. Atomized water and collected material are removed in the separator.

Figure 13.   A single stage electrostatic precipitator. Aerosols are ionized as they pass high voltage electrodes and migrate to the collecting electrodes.

Figure 14.   A packed tower. This has a tendency to become clogged when exhaust gases contain solids. It can handle a large volume with low pressure loss.

Figure 15.   Catalytic combustion. For combustible gases and vapors, the influent is heated to approximately 500° F. and then passed through the catalyst bed. In some cases the burner may be shut off after the start up, or may not be needed if gases are at a high enough temperature. Oxidation may also be accomplished by direct heating without catalysts. This process, called incineration, requires additional heat.

reactive and nonreactive absorbents. The reactive type absorbs gas or vapor by chemical reaction. A nonreactive absorbent is a liquid in which gas or vapor is soluble without chemical reaction. In one type, materials are packed in towers which help break liquids into small droplets to increase the absorbing surface.

Many industries rely on combustion for decomposition of malodorous or toxic gaseous effluents. Supplementary high temperature burners are used in the waste gas stream to oxidize gases into innocuous substances. The catalytic oxidation process uses special catalysts which allow substances to oxidize at lower than normal temperatures.

Coagulation of dust and mist by sound waves offers interesting possibilities. However, equipment is not yet available for widespread commercial applications.

Selection of treatment equipment for gases and vapors depends on many factors. The contaminants' characteristics, chemical nature, corrosiveness and flash point are important. The temperature of effluent gases has a bearing on the selection of equipment, particularly in catalytic oxidation. Solubility of gases and vapors is important in wet collection.

The many factors affecting pollution control often make final selection of treatment equipment a compromise. It is usually impracticable or impossible to remove and treat all contaminants of an effluent. Effluent treatment is usually expensive and in only a small percentage of cases can the recovered product pay for the installation and operation of removal equipment.

Supplementary controls applied to minimize the ill effects of pollutants are much less effective than integral controls which prevent the generation of pollutants. In many cases supplementary controls are stop-gap adaptations to inherently inefficient processes.

The problems of disposing of collected contaminants and undesirable secondary contaminants created by the initial control process are added disadvantages.

The consensus of expert investigators and practicing physicians[30] is that air pollution is a growing public health problem which warrants greater attention by the medical profession. Physicians must become sufficiently aware of the relation of atmospheric quality to health and participate in every effort by their own communities to reduce or eliminate air pollution for the benefit of their patients and the well-being of all community residents.

ALEXANDER RIHM, JR., P.E.

REFERENCES

1. Proceedings of a Seminar on Air Pollution Problems, September 20-21, 1955. Washington, D.C., U. S. Department of Health, Education, and Welfare, Public Health Service.
2. Annual Reports. City of Pittsburgh, Department of Health, Bureau of Smoke Prevention. (Now under Allegheny County Health Department.)
3. West, Wallace: Clearing the Air. American Petroleum Institute (pamphlet).
4. Handbook on Aerosols. Chapters from summary of Technical Report of Division 10, National Defense Research Committee. Washington, D.C., United States
5. Chambers, L. A., Tabor, E. C., and Foter, M. J.: The Characteristics and Distribution of Organic Substances in the Air of Some American Cities. Presented at the
Atomic Energy Commission. 1950.

48th Annual meeting of the Air Pollution Control Association, May, 1955, Detroit.

6. Los Angeles Air Pollution Control District: Smog Brief No. 4, Hydrocarbons. Smog Brief No. 12, The Disposal of Rubbish.
7. County of Los Angeles: Air Pollution Control District Report. July, 1956.
8. New York State Air Pollution Control Board: Air Pollution in Greater Elmira, 1960.
9. Greenburg, L., et al.: Report of an air pollution incident in New York City, November, 1953. Public Health Reports, 77:7, 1962.
10. Rihm, A., Jr.: Air pollution and urban planning. Health News, New York State Department of Health, November, 1962.
11. Lawther, P. J., et al.: Epidemiology of Air Pollution. World Health Organization, Public Health Paper No. 15.
12. Schrenk, H. H., Heiman, H., Clayton, G. D., and Gafafer, W. M.: Air Pollution in Donora, Pa.; Epidemiology of the Unusual Smog Episode of October 1948. Preliminary Report. Public Health Bulletin, No. 306, 1949. Washington, D.C., United States Government Printing Office.
13. Scott, J. A.: Fog and deaths in London. Public Health Reports, 68:5, 1953.
14. Greenburg, L., et al.: Intermittent air pollution episode in New York City, 1962. Public Health Reports, 78:1061, December, 1963.
15. Prindle, R. A., and Landau, E.: Health effects from repeated exposures to low concentrations of air pollutants. Public Health Reports, 77:901, October, 1962.
16. Spicer, W. S.: The Complexity of the Relationship Between Air Pollution and Respiratory Health. Proceedings of the National Conference on Air Pollution, p. 126. Washington, D.C., U. S. Department of Health, Education, and Welfare, Public Health Service Publication No. 1022.
17. Dohan, F. C.: Prepared Discussion of the Complexity of the Relationship Between Air Pollution and Respiratory Health. Proceedings of the National Conference on Air Pollution, p. 137. Washington, D.C., U. S. Department of Health, Education, and Welfare, Public Health Service Publication No. 1022.
18. Motor Vehicles, Air Pollution and Health; A Report of the Surgeon General. Washington, D.C., U. S. Department of Health, Education, and Welfare, 1962.
19. Smoking and Health. Washington, D.C., U. S. Department of Health, Education, and Welfare, Public Health Service Publication No. 1103, 1964.
20. Goldsmith, J. R.: Air pollution and medical research. Science, 141:832, August 30, 1963.
21. Introduction to Respiratory Disease. 2nd ed. New York, National Tuberculosis Association, 1964.
22. Oderr, C. P.: Emphysema, soot, and pulmonary circulation—macroscopic studies of aging lungs. Journal of the American Medical Association, 172:1997, 1960.
23. Maneri, C. S.: Prepared Discussion of Program Development Through Applying Measurements and Monitoring Know-How. Proceedings of the National Conference on Air Pollution, p. 233. Washington, D.C., U. S. Department of Health, Education, and Welfare, Public Health Service Publication No. 1022.
24. Magill, P. L., Holden, F. R., and Ackley, C.: Air Pollution Handbook. New York, McGraw-Hill Book Co., 1956.
25. Rihm, A., Jr.: Air pollution control in New York State. Civil Engineering, 34:56, February, 1964.
26. Rihm, A., Jr.: Prepared Discussion of the Status of Engineering Knowledge for the Control of Air Pollution. Proceedings of the National Conference on Air Pollution, p. 272. Washington, D.C., U. S. Department of Health, Education, and Welfare, Public Health Service Publication No. 1022.
27. Johnson, H. F., and Roberts, M. H.: Deposition of aerosol particles from moving gas streams. Industrial and Engineering Chemistry, 41:11, 1949.
28. Lapple, C. A.: Dust and Mist Collection. Air Pollution Abatement Manual. Washington, D.C., Manufacturing Chemists Association, Inc., 1951.
29. Jenny, R. J.: Gas and Vapor Abatement. Air Pollution Abatement Manual. Washington, D.C., Manufacturing Chemists Association, Inc., 1953.
30. Weisburd, M. I.: Physician's guide to air pollution. Journal of the American Medical Association, 186:605, November, 1963.
31. Stocks, P.: A Study of Tobacco Smoking, Air Pollution, Residential and Occupational

Histories and Mortality from Cancer of the Lung in Two Cities. Inter-regional Symposium on Criteria for Air Quality and Methods of Measurement. Geneva, Switzerland, WHO.

32. Wiseley, D. V., Kotin, P., Fowler, P. R., and Trivedi, J.: The combined effect of repeated viral infection on pulmonary tumor induction in C57 black mice. Proceedings of the American Association for Cancer Research, 3:278, 1961.

33. Kotin, P.: Combination of stimuli in experimental lung cancer. Presented at the Fifth Air Pollution Medical Research Conference, Los Angeles, Calif., December 4-7, 1961.

34. Bulletin—Research and Statistical Division, National Tuberculosis Association, October, 1963.

5　Water Supply

INTRODUCTION

Water is a major environmental factor in man's physical well-being. An ample supply of potable water is needed for social, economic, and health purposes. This is an age of accelerating urbanization, which, in turn, places greater demands on available sources and complicates problems of allocation, development, and quality control.

Man's dependency on water is all encompassing. It is used to wash the land, the city, and the people; to put out fires; to carry away waste materials; to grow feed grain and fiber; to manufacture goods; to produce food and beverages; to provide recreation; to transport people and goods; and, most important, to sustain life itself.

Primary water use is for drinking and food preparation. Since water quality cannot be separated from quantity, a sufficient amount of water with satisfactory physical, bacteriological, chemical, microscopic and radiological characteristics is required. Insufficient quantity disrupts routines, leads to insanitary practices, and encourages the use of water of questionable quality.

Direct health concern focuses initially on water-borne disease, then on the other quality characteristics important in potable water. This concern is met by the proper development, protection and treatment of individual and municipal water supplies.

Bacterial, viral and parasitic disease can be water-borne. Control methods have been developed which can minimize and all but eliminate the danger of water-borne outbreaks of disease. However, the possibility of such outbreaks always exists. Epidemics due to water contamination continue to occur, even in developed countries.

The physiological and toxic effects of the chemical and radiological constituents of water vary. Some are well-known, such as nitrates, sodium, strontium-90, and arsenic. Research on new contaminants to determine their effects and methods of control is being carried out continuously.

Public acceptance and usage requires a clear water with no taste, odor, or color. Present treatment techniques make this possible.

The great dependence on private wells in some areas and the ever-growing ground and surface water contamination affecting water supplies make it imperative that every practicing physician be familiar with the technology of water supply, water quality determinants, evaluation tests and techniques, and the proven methods of protection and treatment.

MEDICAL CONCERN

Water quality is of real and continuing interest to every physician, not in terms of the old typhoid problem, which in developed countries is practically nonexistent, but in terms of other water-borne diseases, present water needs, the physiological effect of water constituents, and the complex contaminants now found in both public and individual supplies.

As a responsible member of the community concerned with the general health and a wholesome environment, the physician can be a powerful force in insuring the proper selection of water sources, effective development and treatment, and efficient operation and maintenance of the system. He can give counsel or make referrals to experts concerning the proper selection, development, and treatment of private supplies.

Background information on water quality can be of great assistance in choosing the right course of action in diagnosis and treatment. Examples are bacterial contamination, the effects of fluorides in mottling and dental caries, calcium and nitrates in infant feeding, and sodium in hypertension.

Water is even more important than food to man. The physician who knows the value of high quality water, its sources, treatment and safe distribution, can serve his patients and the community by protecting this indispensable natural resource at every opportunity.

HISTORICAL BACKGROUND

In the United States urban water supply became an increasingly major concern in the late 1790's and early 1800's. Water was needed for domestic purposes, for street flushing and cleaning, and for fire fighting. Neighborhood or individual wells could not fill these needs.

The major stimuli for action were conflagrations and cholera and typhoid epidemics. These led to the development and construction of urban water supply systems. However, because of the lack of understanding of the transmission of disease, many of the systems used water from contaminated sources and water-borne outbreaks of disease were common.

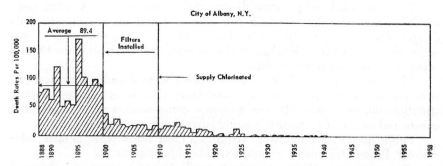

Figure 16. The effect of water treatment on the typhoid fever death rate of the city of Albany, N. Y. (Prepared by the New York State Department of Health.)

The need for treating raw water before use was gradually recognized. The first treatment provided was filtration through sand, followed later by disinfection using chlorine compounds. The first filter system in the United States was put into use in 1872 in Poughkeepsie, New York. The first attempt to disinfect a public water supply was in Jersey City in 1908, when equipment was installed to apply a chlorine solution. In 1912 commercial equipment was developed for the application of chlorine gas.

The dramatic drop in the typhoid fever death rate in the New York state city of Albany after filtration and chlorination of water was instituted is shown by Figure 16. This is a typical example of the experience of cities throughout the United States.

Water works technology has developed effective design and control standards and procedures which insure a bacteriologically safe, potable water. The present challenge is to keep the gains made by application of modern technology and to meet effectively the problems of water quality control posed by increasing population, water re-use, and new and complex contaminants.

HYDROLOGY AND GEOLOGY

Water Cycle

Water precipitates to earth as rain and snow. Some is held by trees and vegetation; some infiltrates into the ground to be used by growing plants or

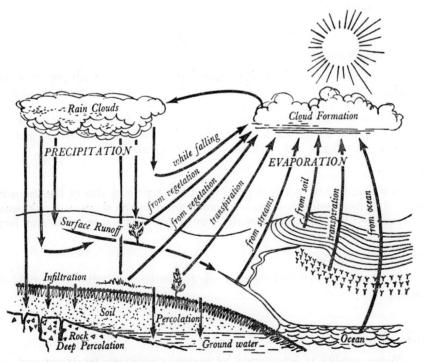

Figure 17. The hydrologic cycle. (Reprinted from the Yearbook of Agriculture. 1955. United States Department of Agriculture.)

becomes ground water to feed into lakes, streams or the ocean; some runs over the surface of the ground directly into the streams, lakes, and the ocean.

Water returns to the atmosphere by evaporation from the earth, lakes, streams, and vegetation, and by transpiration from plants and trees. This water forms clouds and eventually precipitates back to the earth (Fig. 17). Availability of water as represented by the water cycle is subject to extreme variation. This variation is seasonal, periodic, and geographic. There are areas of water plenty and areas of water scarcity; there are wet seasons and dry seasons; there are radical changes from day to day, month to month, and year to year.

Subsurface Geology

Subsurface material is divided into three general classifications: consolidated, unconsolidated, and top soil.

Consolidated material includes hard solids, such as limestone, sandstone, granite, shale, salt, and similar material. Unconsolidated material varies from sand to gravel to clay to mixtures commonly called till. The surface or top soil is the relatively shallow, enriched organic, aerated material found at the ground air interface.

The character and depth of the subsurface material will vary from place to place on both a vertical and horizontal plane. Unconsolidated deposits can be very deep—200 to 1000 feet—or nonexistent where the consolidated material outcrops through the surface of the ground.

All of these materials, consolidated and unconsolidated, have differing abilities to store and transmit water.

WATER QUANTITY

Increasing Demands

Man's basic need for drinking water can be satisfied with one quart per day. However, other water needs increase as water becomes readily available and water fixtures and appliances are used.

As living standards rise, there is a perceptible increase in use of water. This is typified in the modern household by multiple bathrooms, garbage disposers, automatic dishwashers, and washing machines.

Industry

Industrial water needs depend upon the type and size of the industry. Some industries, such as assembly plants and machine shops, use only small amounts; others, such as canneries, breweries, and paper mills, use large quantities of water.

Water Consumption

Table 3 shows typical water needs for various activities and establishments.

WATER QUALITY

Determinants

Water quality is determined by natural conditions, treatment and use of land, sewage discharges, and industrial waste discharges.

Table 3. *The Range of Water Requirements for Various Potable Water Supply Uses**

Domestic public water supply sources	35 to 250 per person
Domestic private sources	35 to 50 per person
Temporary residence camps	25 to 75 per person
Hotels	75 to 100 per person
Schools	15 to 20 per person
Farms, milk herd	7½ to 20 per head
Milk receiving stations	150 to 175 per 100 lbs. of milk received
Milk pasteurizing plants	175 to 250 per 100 lbs. of milk processed
Nursing homes	75 to 125 per person
Child care centers	15 to 20 per child
Hospitals	150 to 250 per bed
Restaurants	5 per meal served
Picnic areas	5 to 15 per person

* Numbers are given in gallons per day except where otherwise indicated.

Natural Conditions. Water quality is greatly affected by natural conditions. Rain water has the general quality characteristics of distilled water as contrasted with the water found in lakes, streams, and in the ground, which contains a great variety of chemical and physical characteristics. As rain falls, seeps into the ground, and runs off into streams and lakes, the quality of the water is greatly changed.

Runoff water from rocky cleared areas is usually clear, alkaline, and hard, whereas that from forests and woodlands is acid, highly colored, and usually contains dissolved iron and manganese.

Ground water quality varies with the type of minerals found in the area. From shallow strata it is moderately hard and without special quality characteristics. Deeper strata may produce water that is extremely hard or contains various salts, such as sodium chloride.

Within lakes and streams, quality changes take place due to biological and physical action, the most common being temperature rises in shallow bodies of water and the growth of microorganisms, such as algae.

Land Use and Treatment. Land use relates to the methods used in producing food, grain, fibers and wood products and to recreational, residential and industrial development. Poor land use leads to heavy runoff, erosion, and the carrying of excessive sediment into the streams.

Land treatment refers to the use of fertilizers, insecticides, herbicides, and pesticides. Use of such chemicals has greatly increased in the past few years, resulting in deleterious effects on water quality in lakes and streams.

Use of toxic materials for weed and fish control can also adversely affect water quality.

Sewage Discharges. The discharge of the inadequately treated sewage into surface waters results in floating and settleable solids, consumption of oxygen with attendant nuisances, and bacterial contamination. This renders the water unsatisfactory for many uses, especially for domestic use, recreation, and food processing. Detergents in sanitary sewage adversely affect both ground and surface waters, and produce taste, odor, and foaming.

Industrial Waste Discharges. Industry uses water for processing, for cooling, and for general purposes. The waste produced includes ordinary sewage, processing waste which can have a variety of forms, and cooling water. Most municipal sewage contains some industrial waste, which may include toxic substances, radioactive material, oxygen-consuming material, petro-chemicals, and a wide variety of other chemical substances.

CHARACTERISTICS AND STANDARDS

Water quality is measured by physical, bacteriological, chemical, microscopic and radiological characteristics.

Standards have been established to insure that water will not be a hazard to the health of the consumers and will have other acceptable characteristics. The standards formulated by the U. S. Public Health Service represent the consensus of the best technical and scientific knowledge available.

Physical

Turbidity, color, taste, odor, and temperature constitute the physical characteristics of water.

The presence of suspended material such as clay, silt, and other inorganic material, finely divided organic material and plankton causes turbidity. Turbidity and color are measured by comparison with known standards and reported as units.

Taste and odor determinations are purely subjective. They are reported by threshold number, which is the maximum dilution of the sample still producing the taste and odor.

The most desirable drinking waters are consistently cool and do not have temperature fluctuations of more than a few degrees. Ground and surface water from mountainous areas generally meet these criteria. Most individuals find that water having a temperature between 50 and 60° F. is most palatable.

The limits on physical characteristics are set at the point where most people object to using the water for esthetic reasons.

Bacteriological

Coliform Organisms. Bacteriological testing of water for domestic drinking purposes is based upon the presence or absence of coliform organisms and their concentration. Coliforms include all of the aerobic facultative and anaerobic gram-negative, non-spore forming, rod-shaped bacilli which ferment lactose, with gas formation within 48 hours at 35° Centigrade. Some of the coliform group are characteristically found in human and animal intestines; others are found in the soil and on various types of vegetation and materials used in pipes and valves.

Coliform organisms are not all pathogenic. They serve mostly as indicators of contamination. Two laboratory procedures are commonly used in estimating the presence of coliforms.

1. The most commonly used is a geometric series of multiple dilutions with an estimate made as the "most probable number" (MPN) which would produce the given results. This method is time consuming and takes 48 or more hours to complete. The results are not definite because of the random distribution of bacteria. The greater the number of samples, the more valid the results.

A single sample has questionable reliability. An MPN of 240/100 ml. has a possible range of 12 to 3700 with 95 per cent confidence limits.

2. In recent years the membrane filter technique has been accepted as a standard method. This is based on filtering 100 ml. of the water to be tested through a membrane filter containing a differential medium for coliforms. The filter is then incubated and the number of colonies formed reported per 100 ml. This has the advantage of being simple and producing definite results in 18 to 20 hours. The major disadvantage is inability to handle turbid waters.

The presence of coliform organisms in treated drinking water suggests either inadequate treatment or contamination of the water after treatment. The concentration of coliforms in untreated water is an indication of the degree of sewage pollution. The presence of coliforms calls for definitive action to eliminate them.

There are procedures which can be used for differentiating coliform subgroups to better identify source and to identify streptococci, but they are relatively complicated and time consuming and are not ordinarily needed for effective quality control. There is no routine procedure for virus identification and enumeration.

Chemical

Chemical characteristics of water determine corrosiveness, tendency to deposit solids, taste, toxicity, degree of sewage and industrial waste contamination, method and ease of treatment, and physiological effect.

Some chemical elements are found naturally in surface and ground waters. Others are added by waste water disposal and other activities of man.

Chemical elements found in natural waters include sodium, chloride, sulfates, fluoride, iron, manganese, nitrates, copper, and zinc. The type and concentration depend mainly on natural environmental conditions. Sodium, chlorides, nitrates, and fluorides may be increased by waste water disposal practices or other activities.

Contamination by phenols, alky-benzene-sulfonate (detergent), arsenic, cyanide, lead, barium, cadmium, chromium, carbon chloroform extract (undifferentiated hydrocarbons), selenium, and silver result from industrial and residential waste disposal and use of fertilizers, herbicides and insecticides.

Other chemically related characteristics of interest are pH, alkalinity and hardness.

The pH of water in its natural state varies from 5.5 to 9.0. Determination of the pH value assists in the control of corrosion, the determination of proper chemical dosages, and adequate control of disinfection.

Alkalinity is imparted to water by bicarbonate, carbonate, or hydroxide components. Knowledge of the alkalinity components is useful in the treatment of water supplies.

Hard water contains carbonates and bicarbonates which retard the cleaning action of soaps and detergents. Furthermore, when hard water is heated, it deposits a carbonate scale (as in a kettle, heating coils, or on cooking utensils) with a consequent waste of fuel.

The chemical characteristics of water supplies vary widely, as does the ability to control these characteristics by treatment. Water supply quality based on the chemical constituents can be broadly characterized as desirable, acceptable, and unacceptable.

Desirable water contains no contaminants, but does have optimum amounts of chemical elements which result in a water which is clear, odorless, tasteless, noncorrosive, does not result in the deposition of solids, and does not produce undesirable physiological effects.

Acceptable water may contain some contaminants or have excessive amounts of some natural constituents. However, the concentration of these elements is sufficiently low that it does not constitute a health hazard and the water is generally acceptable for use.

Unacceptable water will contain contaminants in such concentration as to constitute a real hazard to the user. In some instances, the concentrations will fall between the limits established for acceptable and unacceptable waters, and in such cases judgment must be exercised based upon known toxicity and the availability of more acceptable supplies.

Microscopic

Microscopic organisms found in water supplies include plants, such as algae, and animals, such as ameba and roundworms. Algae presents a common surface water supply problem in the United States, causing unpleasant taste, odor, and color. Ameba and roundworms are a serious problem in semitropical and tropical countries.

Radiological

Radium-223, iodine-131, strontium-90 are some of the radioactive isotopes that are of concern when present in water in high concentration. (See Chapters 3 and 10.) The main sources are weapons testing and waste disposal from nuclear reactors.

SANITARY SURVEY

Evaluating and drawing conclusions concerning water quality on the basis of laboratory tests alone is subject to great error. The purpose of collection of samples and analysis of water is to aid in the evaluation of water supply sources and water treatment performance.

Proper evaluation of quality requires a detailed, complete background which can come only from a sanitary survey made by a qualified person. The survey should include the sources of water, all possible sources of pollution that may affect the raw water supply, the type of development and treatment needed and provided, the adequacy of the distribution system, the presence or absence of cross or interconnections with other water sources, and the level of competence of water system operation.

With the background provided by such a comprehensive sanitary survey, the indicated laboratory determinations can be made, and results will aid in proper evaluation and indicate any corrective action needed.

WATER SUPPLY DEVELOPMENT AND PROTECTION

MULTIPLE BARRIERS

Desirable standards of quality are maintained by proper development, protection of the source, adequate treatment and safeguarding of the water from the point of treatment to the point of consumption.

The underlying philosophy is prevention of occurrence of pollution. The basis of the prevention, as with all public health practice, is the establishment of multiple barriers between sources of contamination and the consumers. This principle of multiple barriers is exemplified by selection of the best possible source of supply, development of the source, protection of the source of supply from contamination, provision of necessary treatment, protection of the supply in the distribution system, sampling and inspection to insure quality control at all steps.

MUNICIPAL—INDIVIDUAL

Municipal supplies of water are under the control of health department standards and are usually treated by filtration and/or disinfection, and are under regular supervision.

The development, protection and treatment of individual supplies are usually the owner's responsibility. Such supplies are usually wells, with an occasional spring or surface source. Many are incorrectly developed and poorly protected, with limited or no treatment and no regular supervision. Consequently, individual supplies can become contaminated without warning and produce water of unsatisfactory quality.

WATER SUPPLY SOURCES

Sources of water include the air, ground water, and surface waters.

AIR

Cisterns. Directly intercepting rainfall and storing it in cisterns was a common practice among rural families years ago when the ground water was extremely hard and soft rain water was needed for laundry and washing purposes.

More elaborate methods of collecting rainfall directly by the construction of large catchment areas are used in certain areas of the world where the only water otherwise available is saline. In the United States, the direct collection of rain water is no longer widely practiced.

GROUND AND SURFACE WATERS

The ordinary sources for water supply development are ground and surface waters. The choice depends upon the quality, the quantity available to meet foreseeable needs, and the cost of development.

Dependence on ground or surface water varies considerably throughout the world. In the United States, for example, in the water-rich Northeast bordering on the Great Lakes, surface sources supply 92 to 97 per cent of all water used, with 3 to 8 per cent being supplied by ground water. In the Texas-Oklahoma-New Mexico area, 52 to 63 per cent of all water used is from ground water sources, with 37 to 48 per cent being surface waters. The percentages vary in other regions of the country, with major ground water development located in the central plains states and in the South and Southwest border area.

Ground Water

Ground water is the water stored in the interstices of consolidated and unconsolidated subsurface material. In withdrawing water from the ground water reservoir, the important factor is that over a time cycle the amount of water withdrawn should not consistently exceed the replenishment by rainfall. Otherwise, the ground water reservoir will become depleted. Ground water can be developed for use from wells or springs.

Springs. Springs are places on the earth's surface where ground water comes to the surface and flows freely under natural pressure. Springs can be shallow, deep, or of limestone origin.

A *shallow spring* results when containment of the downward movement of water by an impervious layer occurs. The outflow appears at the point where the impervious layer breaks through the surface of the ground. This spring is characterized by a temperature which varies with air temperature. It is easily subject to contamination, and the flow from the spring will vary with precipitation in the immediate area. During dry weather the spring will dry up quickly.

The *deep spring* results from the containment of a water-bearing stratum, by impervious layers of material both above and below. As with the shallow spring, the outflow of water occurs at the point where the impervious containing layers break through the surface of the ground. The temperature of the water from the deep spring tends to be constant, around 50 to 60° Fahrenheit. The fluctuations of flow are not so pronounced since the spring frequently draws from a wide area which levels out local variation.

Limestone springs are the outflow from solution channels in limestone. These solution channels collect water and deliver it to a point much the same way that a surface drainage system would work. The area tributary to a limestone spring is practically impossible to determine.

Springs must be protected from superficial contamination. This may be done by the construction of a watertight spring basin with a screened overflow pipe and with diversion ditches to carry surface water away from the spring basin. Severe restrictions or prohibitions for the discharge of sewage or industrial wastes in the tributary area are necessary. Further treatment, particularly disinfection, may be needed to insure satisfactory water quality at all times.

Since it is impossible to determine the tributary area to a limestone spring, and pollutants can be carried many miles through limestone channels, all limestone springs must be disinfected continuously and water samples collected periodically for testing in order to insure a water of satisfactory quality.

Wells. Well supplies can be shallow or deep and may come from con-solidated or unconsolidated material. The waters available will depend on the storage and transmitting properties of the water-bearing stratum as well as rainfall and infiltration rates. Limestone wells or wells in creviced material obtain water from solution channels the same as limestone springs.

There are three common types of wells, depending on the manner of development—dug, driven, and drilled.

Dug wells are hand or machine dug. Such wells are relatively shallow.

One form is the bored well, constructed with a hand or machine auger. It obtains water from the upper layers of the unconsolidated material.

Driven wells are developed by driving a well point and pipe through the ground to reach the water level. This type of well is restricted to use in sandy areas where the ground water is located 12 to 20 feet below the surface of the ground. A driven well can also be developed at the bottom of a dug well.

Drilled wells are used to develop supplies when it is necessary to go through resistant material or to great depths to develop a satisfactory supply.

The ground water must be free from contamination. Widespread use of the ground waters for disposal of sewage and industrial wastes can result in contamination of ground water. This is particularly true in highly porous, unconsolidated deposits, such as sand and gravel, and when fractured crevices occur in consolidated material. These conditions encourage disposal of waste into the ground water.

High levels of nitrates, detergents and cyanide and heavy metals have made the use of ground water unacceptable in some areas. In highly populated suburban areas the detergent problem is becoming common and serious.

The well itself must be protected from surface drainage and surface contamination. A watertight seal should be provided around the top of the well casing. The well casing should be watertight for at least the top 10 feet in order to prevent superficial contamination by surface water or by water draining from the well itself. This requires a concrete platform and drain troughs to carry away excess or spilled water from the well itself. The principles of surface sealing by a cover slab and grouting apply equally to dug, driven and drilled wells.

Cases of direct contamination of well supplies by nearby location of a sewage disposal system are innumerable. All sewers and sewage disposal systems must be located away from the well a sufficient distance to prevent contamination. For household systems this would mean at least 100 feet. For municipal systems the distance should be 500 to 1000 feet or more.

Water drawn from a well may be highly mineralized, and it may be desirable to provide softening and, in some instances, removal of iron and manganese.

Disinfection of the well water by chlorination may be necessary. Disinfection is desirable in municipal supplies in order that a chlorine residual can be carried throughout the distribution system. For wells of limestone origin, continuous chlorination is necessary because of the impossibility of protecting the source.

Surface Water

Surface water is available from lakes and ponds, which provide natural storage for water supply purposes, and from streams and rivers.

Lakes and Ponds. Water quality in lakes and ponds will vary considerably depending upon the size and depth of the body of water. Shallow lakes tend to be weedy, to have extensive algae blooms, and to become extremely turbid with wind and wave action, requiring extensive treatment. Extremely large lakes make it possible to locate water supply intake to minimize such conditions. Lakes of great depth will usually produce a water which is clear, cold, less likely to become turbid, and with minor or nonexistent weed and algae problems.

In a large lake, control of raw water quality by regulation is difficult; consequently, greater dependency is placed on treatment processes.

Streams and Impoundments.   Upland streams draining rural areas are a major source of water supply. Such streams can usually provide a sufficient supply of water over a water year or years, but during periods of low flow would be deficient without storage. It then becomes necessary to construct dams and to impound the water during times of plenty for use during times of deficiency.

This is a situation in which effective control is simplest because of the relatively small watershed areas. Rules and regulations can be enacted to control the discharge of any waste effluents on the watershed. The use of fertilizers, herbicides, insecticides, and pesticides can be controlled.

Rivers.   The term "river" is used in the sense of the large, flowing water systems which can provide a sufficient quantity of water even at low stages without storage. Water supplies can be developed from such rivers with proper intakes. Raw water may be highly turbid, contain toxic elements from industrial wastes and runoff and be of poor bacteriological quality due to sewage and industrial waste discharged. In this instance, the treatment process becomes the single barrier between the pollutant and the consumers. The treatment problem is complicated by the variable quality of the raw water. Safety of the water rests completely on the treatment process because of the unavoidably poor water quality.

SALT WATER

Use of salt water for water supply purposes requires treatment to reduce the salt content.

Experimental programs are now underway because of ever-increasing needs for more water. Procedures have always existed for the production of fresh water from salt water on a small scale basis. Many different types of processes to remove salt are now undergoing full scale operational tests. However, the production is still experimental and, though technically feasible, very expensive.

Further development and use will depend upon the scarcity of available fresh water and the cost of the processes.

WATER TREATMENT

Water treatment is provided by physical, mechanical, chemical, and bacteriological means.

Treatment for removal of turbidity, color, taste and odor, and disinfection is provided by filtration and chlorination.

Aeration, pH adjustment, ion exchange, chemical stabilization, chemical precipitation and filtration through carbon (anthrafilt, activated carbon) are other processes used for taste and odor control, removal of iron or manganese, corrosion control, softening, and removal of excess fluoride.

Some treatment is afforded by natural processes.

Nature provides some of its own purification for water polluted by drainage, sewage, or industrial wastes, the degree depending upon the nature and amount of polluting material as well as the physical, chemical, and biological characteristics of the water itself.

Time is the important factor, together with such conditions as temperature, sunlight, velocity of flow and other complex chemical, physical and biological characteristics. Quiescent sedimentation in a reservoir for about a month may serve as well as filtration. Sluggish flow in a stream for a long period of time may accomplish the same results.

Disinfection

The purpose of disinfection is to prevent the transmission of pathogens to man. Effective disinfection provides a water of safe, sanitary quality.

Emergencies

Emergency disinfection of small amounts of drinking water can be accomplished by boiling for one minute, by adding 2 to 4 drops of 5 per cent chlorine bleach per quart of water, or by adding 5 to 10 drops of 2 per cent tincture of iodine per quart of water. After treatment, with chlorine or iodine, let stand for 30 minutes. Tablets containing chlorine or iodine for disinfecting water are commercially available.

Chlorination

The element chlorine is used practically exclusively as the disinfecting agent for water supplies because of its effectiveness, ease of application, general availability, and low cost. The term "chlorination" is used synonymously with disinfection in water works practice.

Under conditions of normal temperature and pressure, chlorine exists as a gas. It readily combines to form compounds, such as chloride of lime or sodium hypochlorite. It is used for disinfecting both as the pure gas and in compound form. In either case, the active disinfectant is chlorine.

Special apparatus has been developed to feed chlorine as a gas or as a hypochlorite solution into a water supply. Chlorine is a lethal gas, and extreme care must be used in storing and handling.

Chlorine Disinfecting Action. Chlorine is a strong, oxidizing agent. As it is added to water, it reacts with the reducing substances in the water to produce a chlorine demand.

The chlorine demand is the difference between the original chlorine applied and the amount of chlorine present in the water after the contact time. The chlorine demand of a water supply is not constant, particularly with surface supplies.

Water completely free of organic and inorganic reducing substances has a zero chlorine demand. This is sometimes true of well waters. However, all surface waters contain some reducing substances. This means that as the chlorine is added, a certain amount is used up in side reactions. It then combines with free ammonia or organic nitrogen in the water to form chloramines. When these reactions are completed by the addition of sufficient chlorine, chlorine will then be present in the water as hypochlorous acid and as the hypochlorite ion.

Chlorine residual in the form of chloramine is known as a combined available chlorine residual. In the form of hypochlorous acid or hypochlorite ion, it is known as free available chlorine residual.

Free available chlorine is a strong disinfectant, while combined available chlorine is a relatively weak disinfectant. *Because of this, it is important that sufficient chlorine be added to produce a free available chlorine residual.*

The relative disinfecting properties of free and combined chlorine are shown in Table 4.

Table 4. *Minimum Chlorine Residuals for Drinking Water at 20° C.*[*]

pH value	6 to 7	7 to 8	8 to 9	9 to 10	10 to 11
Free avail. chlorine mg./L. after 10 min.	0.2	0.2	0.4	0.8	0.8
Combined avail. chlorine mg./L. after 60 min.	1.0	1.5	1.8	1.8	

[*] C. T. Butterfield, et al.: "Influence of pH and temperature on the survival of coliforms and enteric pathogens when exposed to free chlorine." U.S. Public Health Reports, 58:1837, 1943.

The disinfecting action of free chlorine is affected only slightly by changes in pH and temperature, whereas the disinfecting action of combined chlorine is drastically affected by such changes. This presents difficult control problems when combined chlorine is used as the disinfecting agent. There is a distinct improvement in taste and odor control with the use of free residual chlorination.

If a free chlorine residual is carried throughout a distributive system, it keeps the water mains clean, the water sweet, and is additional protection against any contaminating substance introduced into the distribution system.

FILTRATION

In order for disinfection to be effective, it is necessary to have a clear, nonturbid water. Most water uses also require a clear, nonturbid water.

Filtration may be either mechanical or biological, depending upon the type of filtration used. Filters commonly used in municipal water treatment are the slow and rapid sand filters, the designation depending upon the volume of water filtered per unit area of filter surface per day. The volume filtered by a rapid sand filter is about 50 times greater than for a slow sand filter. The major characteristics for each type of filter are shown in Table 5.

Coagulation and sedimentation *must* be provided before a rapid sand filtration; it may be provided before use of a slow sand filter.

Coagulation and Sedimentation

Coagulation is the process of changing soluble constituents of water into nonsoluble ones. This is done by adding a coagulant, such as aluminum sulfate (alum). This reacts with the natural alkali in the water, forming crystals of aluminum hydroxide.

The coagulant is added to the raw water and distributed by a rapid

Table 5. *Water Supply Filtration*

TYPE OF FILTER	FUNCTION	RATES OF FLOW	CLEANING	PRETREATMENT REQUIRED	CHLORINATION	TREATABLE RAW WATER	OPERATION
Rapid Sand	Mechanical	200-300 m/g/a/d•	Automatic reverse flow	Coagulation Sedimentation	Before and after filtration	Poor—highly turbid	Demands highly skilled operator
Slow Sand	Mechanical & Biological	2-10 m/g/a/d•	Manual	None usually	After filtration	Limited turbidity only	Almost foolproof —limited attention required

• m/g/a/d—Million gallons per acre per day.

mixing device. The water then flows through a flocculation basin which provides slow mixing and permits the reactions to take place. The water next flows into a sedimentation tank where the floc masses consisting of coagulant particles, bacteria, and suspended solids settle out. The water is then filtered, and remaining suspended floc forms a mat on top of the filter and further strains the water as it is filtered. Control tests are carried out to determine optimum coagulant dosages.

Slow Sand Filter

A slow sand filter is a bed of sand and gravel about 36 inches in depth. On the bottom there is an underdrain system to collect the filtered water. On top of this is a gravel layer 12 to 18 inches in depth. Above this gravel layer is 30 to 36 inches of relatively fine, high quality sand. The filter operates under a positive head of water at all times.

A water depth of 3 to 5 feet is maintained over the surface of the sand. The rate of flow through the filter, controlled by valves on the outlet line from the filter, is 2 to 10 million gallons per acre of surface area per day, the rates depending on the quality of the raw water—the better the quality, the higher the rate. A filter will remove 98 to 99 per cent of all bacteria, practically all suspended solids, and reduce color up to 40 per cent.

Suspended matter is strained out from the water as it passes through the filter. In addition, a film of biological life develops in the upper part of the filter which increases the efficiency of solid removal and removes organic matter and bacteria from the raw water. The filter gradually accumulates solids, becomes more resistant to flow, and starts to clog.

Cleaning of the filter is a manual operation. The water is drawn down, and the top inch or two of sand is removed from the top of the filter, washed, and stored for later use. When the sand in the bed has been reduced to a depth of 24 inches, the cleaned sand is added to bring it back to its original depth.

The slow sand filter is limited to treatment of water in which the turbidity is not too great, unless some type of pretreatment for removal of solids is placed ahead of the filter unit. The advantages of slow sand filtration are many, and its use should always receive consideration. Chlorine is applied after filtration.

Rapid Sand Filter

The rapid sand filter is also a bed of sand and gravel. The filter has a porous bottom. On top of this is a 12- to 24-inch layer of gravel, and on top of this a layer of sand, 24 to 30 inches deep. The sand is much coarser than that used in a slow sand filter. The rate of flow through the filter is 200 to 300 million gallons per acre of surface area per day. The filtration rate is controlled by valves on the discharge lines from the filter. The water is at a depth of about 30 inches over the top of the sand during filtration. The principal elements of the filter are shown in Figure 18.

The rapid sand filter mechanically strains the previously coagulated and settled raw water. There is no biological activity in a rapid sand filter. When the filter starts to clog, it is cleaned by draining the filter and reversing the flow of water through the filter, causing the sand to expand and washing the dirt from the stand. When the backwash water runs clean, the filter is

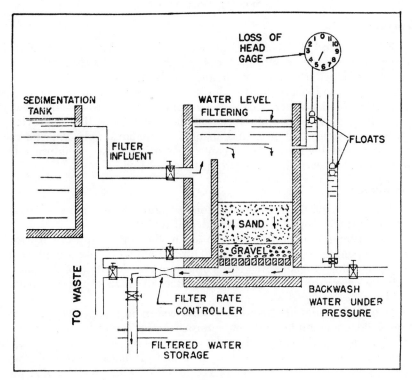

Figure 18. Schematic diagram of a rapid sand filter. (New York State Department of Health Water-training Manual.)

put back into operation. Filtered water is wasted until the filter is settled back down and producing a good effluent.

Frequently, additional alum or activated carbon for odor and taste control is added directly to the incoming water when a filter is being started up. Pre- and postchlorination are usually practiced with rapid sand filtration. The big advantage of rapid sand filtration is the relatively small space required and its ability to handle poor quality water.

There are two other types of filters that have some application in the water works field, the pressure filter and the diatomite filter.

Pressure and Diatomite Filters

A pressure filter is similar to an ordinary rapid sand filter except that it is completely enclosed in a steel tank and the unit is operated under pressure rather than under gravity. The main use of pressure filters has been in filtering swimming pool waters. Some are in use in small municipal water plants, but their use is not recommended for this purpose.

The diatomite filter consists of central pores or tubes on which a thin layer of porous diatomaceous earth is supported and through which the raw water passes. Its use as a permanent treatment device for public water supplies has been very limited. The main use for this unit is in emergency situations and where portable units are needed.

General

Filtration and disinfection eliminate turbidity, taste, odor, and color and produce a water of safe bacterial quality. It may be desirable to take other steps, depending upon the quality of the raw water.

For taste and odors control due to algae, a program of microscopic examination of the water, followed by copper sulfate treatment of water impoundments will be found effective. Other common quality improvement includes softening, and iron and manganese removal. pH adjustment is sometimes desirable for corrosion control. Aeration is used to improve taste and odor and to encourage the precipitation of iron.

Fluoridation

Adjustment of the fluoride ion concentration is becoming common in municipal water supplies to prevent dental caries.

The optimum amount of fluoride ion in the water supply is 0.6 to 1.2 mg./L., depending upon temperature. This amount will prevent dental caries with no mottling of enamel. To reach optimum concentration of fluoride ion, it may be necessary to remove excessive fluoride or to supplement natural fluoride.

Natural fluorides are found in ground waters in practically every state. Some 2300 communities, serving approximately 7 million people in the United States, have natural fluoride concentrations of 0.7 to 1.5 mg./L. Of these communities, 52 per cent are in Illinois, Indiana, Iowa, Ohio, South Dakota, and Texas. The number of communities with excessive fluoride is very small; only 13 have reported levels in excess of 5.0 mg./L.

Approximately 2600 communities, serving approximately 47 million persons now have fluoride added to water supplies to bring it up to optimum concentration to improve dental health by preventing tooth decay.

Any fluoride medication prescribed by physicians or dentists should take into account the fluoride concentration, either natural or augmented, in the water supply serving the patient.

Compounds generally used are sodium fluoride, sodium silicofluoride, and ammonium silicofluoride. These compounds are applied either with a dry feeder into a solution tank or by a solution pump using a prepared solution. Powdered fluoride compounds are toxic, and handling precautions are necessary. Exact laboratory control with frequent determinations of fluoride concentrations in raw and finished water is an essential part of the treatment process.

OPERATION AND MAINTENANCE

The responsibility for water quality does not end at the treatment plant. It is possible for the water to become polluted in the distribution system. This may result from open reservoirs, which are fairly common, or cross connections with other water sources or with sewage and industrial waste lines. Chlorination of the outlet water from an open reservoir is desirable. An active program of inspection and control is essential to eliminate all undesirable cross connections. Factors which are frequently overlooked are the competence and interest of those who operate the water works. It is essential to operate the system on a highly professional basis, to keep appropriate records, and to collect samples regularly to determine the quality of the water and insure that the treatment provided is effective.

ROBERT D. HENNIGAN, P.E.

REFERENCES

1 Fair, Gordon M., and Geyer, John C.: Water Supply and Waste Water Disposal. New York, John Wiley & Sons, Inc., 1951.
2. Smillie, Wilson G.: Preventive Medicine and Public Health. Ed. 2. New York, The Macmillan Co., 1952.
3 Standard Methods for the Examination of Water and Wastewater. Ed. 11. New York, American Public Health Association, American Water Works Association, Water Pollution Control Federation, 1960.
4. Steel, Ernest W.: Water Supply and Sewerage. Ed. 3. New York, McGraw-Hill Book Co., 1953.
5. The Yearbook of Agriculture. Washington, D.C., United States Department of Agriculture, 1955.
6. Water Quality and Treatment. Ed. 2. New York, American Water Works Association, 1950.
7. Phelps, Earle B., and Velz, Clarence J.: Public Health Engineering. New York, John Wiley & Sons, Inc., 1948.
8. Annual Report. Washington, D.C., United States Department of Health, Education, and Welfare, 1961-62.
9. Water Treatment Plant Design. New York, The Committee of the Sanitary Engineering Division on Water Treatment Plant Design, American Society of Civil Engineers, 1939.
10. Water Supply and Plumbing Cross-Connections. Washington, D.C., United States Department of Health, Education, and Welfare, Public Health Service, 1963.
11. Drinking Water Standards. Washington, D.C., United States Department of Health, Education, and Welfare, Public Health Service, 1962.
12. Manual of Individual Water Supply Systems. Washington, D.C., United States Department of Health, Education, and Welfare, Public Health Service, in cooperation with Joint Committee on Rural Sanitation, 1963.
13. Civil Engineering Handbook. Ed. 4. New York, McGraw-Hill Book Company, Inc., 1959.
14. Seelye, Elwyn E.: Data Book for Civil Engineers, Design. Ed. 3. New York, John Wiley & Sons, Inc., 1960.
15. Water Atlas of the United States. Port Washington, N. Y., Water Information Center, 1963.

6 Waste Disposal

This chapter is intended to give the practicing physician a basic knowledge of waste disposal methods, since improper waste disposal is a menace to health. The physician may apply the knowledge directly in seeking causes of disease among his patients. In addition, his ability to gauge the potential danger of improper disposal methods that come to his attention will be of assistance to his local public health department. Finally, intelligent solutions to waste disposal problems will be helped if he is aware of the solutions to these problems offered by sanitary engineering.

Disposal of wastes has been a problem of man since he inhabited the earth. The Bible notes its importance in Deuteronomy, 23:12-13:

> Thou shalt have a place also without the camp, whither thou shalt go forth abroad:
> And thou shalt have a paddle upon thy weapon; and it shall be when thou wilt ease
> thyself abroad, thou shalt dig therewith, and shalt turn back and cover that which
> cometh from thee.

Although this was a satisfactory method of waste disposal and, if followed by all, prevented the transmission of disease, the public health significance of the act was not recognized. However, as families and communities developed and certain diseases became more prevalent, illness was associated with human wastes, without the actual relationship being known. It is now known that without safe and adequate disposal of human wastes, many diseases have been and can be transmitted to man, such as typhoid fever, cholera, bacillary and amebic dysentery, hepatitis, ancylostomiasis (hookworm infestation), ascariasis and trichinosis. Diseases, such as ancylostomiasis, typhoid fever and cholera, have been controlled on a family basis by the simple expedient of building individual privies and locating satisfactory water supplies. The dramatic control of such diseases as typhoid fever and cholera on a communitywide basis was accomplished by the complicated and costly processes of filtration and chlorination of municipal water supplies.

Water treatment facilities are limited as to the amount of polluting material they can be depended upon to remove from water sources. Such facilities are dependent upon chemical, physical, biological and mechanical operations. There is no individual process or combination of processes which is 100 per cent dependable or 100 per cent efficient. Therefore, adequate treatment of community wastes discharged to watercourses is necessary, so that the water will not be unfit for use as a community water supply, for recreation, wild life, agriculture or industry.

The public health objective of waste disposal is to collect, treat and dispose of wastes in a manner that will protect health, preserve our natural resources and prevent nuisance conditions. The methods of acomplishing this objective are varied, but are definite and important to the growth of communities. The practicing physician should possess knowledge of the basic problems and the principles of waste disposal methods, since they have a direct bearing on disease control and prevention.

Wastes include both liquid and solid materials produced from household, commercial and industrial activities of the community. Liquid wastes include human and animal wastes, household wastes, such as those of the laundry and kitchen, street and land washings and commercial and industrial wastes. Solid wastes include garbage, ashes and rubbish.

WATER POLLUTION—PREVENTION AND CONTROL

Wastes, especially liquid wastes, have been discharged uncontrolled into waters (surface and ground) of many nations for so long that safe reuse of the waters for municipal, industrial, commercial and recreational purposes has been reduced materially. The control of pollution of these waters is a major activity of the federal, state and local governments in the United States, and in other countries. Continued expansion and growth of industry and communities depends on pollution control. This is a costly operation and must be commensurate with the use of the water. If a watercourse is to be used as a source for a public water supply it must be maintained in a higher degree of purity than one used for industrial purposes, which means more complete treatment of the wastes discharged and, consequently, a higher cost for installation and operation of treatment facilities.

Therefore, a generally accepted procedure in water pollution control is to set classifications and standards of purity for all waters (surface and ground) based on the best present and future use of such waters. These standards then determine the degree of waste treatment required for their maintenance. The higher the degree of treatment, the higher the construction and operation cost to community and industry.

In order to determine that watercourse standards are being met, a surveillance network of some type is usually established. This is a method of sampling and analyzing the watercourse at statistically sufficient locations and times to evaluate the effectiveness of existing treatment and the need for additional future treatment. Sampling can be done manually or by automatic equipment. Automatic monitors take a water sample from a water course and automatically analyze it at the site. The results are recorded on a chart. The results may be telemetered to a central location where the information may be automatically typed out and at the same time be put on magnetic tape for future use.

Water pollution will become increasingly important as more and different types of wastes are discharged and as these same waters must be reused many times to furnish all the needs for community and industrial growth.

DISPOSAL OF LIQUID WASTES

INDIVIDUAL HOME DISPOSAL SYSTEMS

Privies

The earth pit privy (Fig. 19) still offers a safe and satisfactory method of excreta disposal for rural homes, recreational areas and other units where water carriage systems of disposal cannot be provided. The location, construction and maintenance of the privy is important.

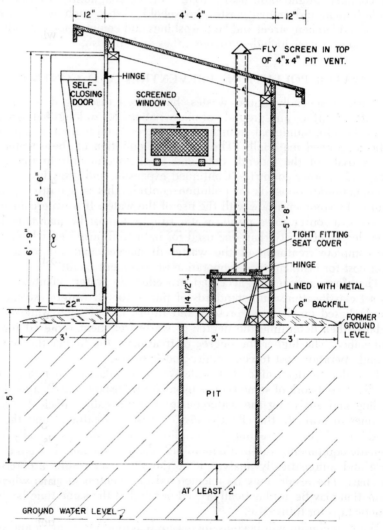

Figure 19. A sanitary pit privy.

Generally, the privy should be at least 100 feet from any source of ground water supply, at a lower elevation than the source of water supply and not on a direct line of drainage to the water supply to provide protection from sewage contamination. The pit should have a minimum capacity of 50 cubic feet (4′ × 4′ × 3′) for the average family. The bottom of the pit should be at least 2 feet above ground water to prevent ground water pollution. The structure should have a self-closing door and self-closing seat to prevent contact between flies and the excreta in the pit. Earth should be mounded about the base of the structure and sloped away from the structure for a distance of approximately 36 inches to make the vault insect and rodent proof and to assist in carrying away surface drainage. When excreta is within 18 inches of the top of the pit, the pit should be cleaned or the superstructure moved to another pit. When moved, the old pit should be filled with soil and tightly tamped. For convenience, the privy should be located between 50 and 150 feet from the building to be served. The modern earth pit privy may consist of a concrete platform with a concrete or metal riser and regular toilet seat cover.

A water-tight concrete pit privy is used where complete protection of a water source is required, such as near the shores of a public water supply reservoir or where soil is unsuitable for subsurface methods of disposal.

The pail or can privy is the replacement of the pit with a pail located directly under the seat of the privy. This privy serves temporary installations such as camps. Provision must be made for daily disposal of the contents by burial or by scavenger service, with ultimate disposal preferably to a public sewer system.

The Chemical Toilet

The chemical toilet is used where it is desirable to have toilet facilities in or near a building, but where running water under pressure is not available or where soil conditions are unsatisfactory for subsurface disposal. The commode type consists of a pail directly beneath the seat containing a chemical solution. The tank type holds the chemical solution in a large metal tank in the ground directly beneath the seat. The tank is emptied by draining to a subsurface seepage pit. The contents of the pail type are buried. Sodium hydroxide is the chemical generally used, in the proportion of ¼ pound of sodium hydroxide for each cubic foot of tank volume. Odor elimination is possible if the sodium hydroxide is maintained at full strength and if the contents are agitated each time the toilet is used.

The Modern Bathroom

Rural homes are replacing privies and chemical toilets with modern bathrooms. The most commonly accepted method for disposal of this large volume of liquid waste is by discharge to a septic tank and then to a tile field or seepage pit, or by discharge to a cesspool. This same method is also used for suburban homes beyond the reach of existing sewers. The satisfactory design and installation of home sewage treatment facilities require engineering knowledge and should be referred to the sanitary engineer of the local health department.

A *home septic tank* (Fig. 20, A) is a watertight unit usually of concrete or steel for receiving household wastes. It should have a minimum

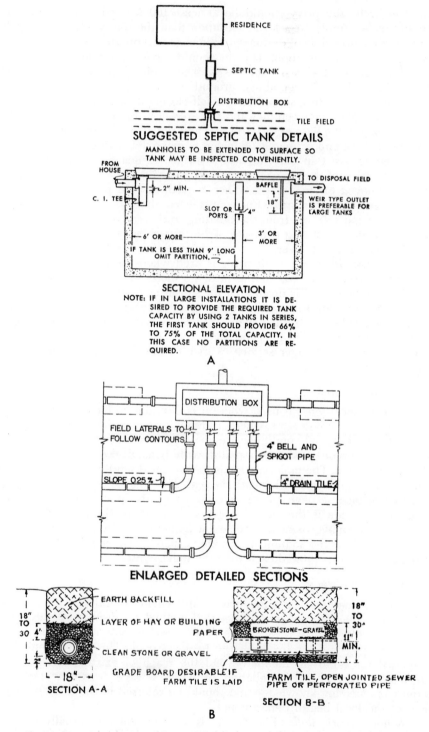

Figure 20. **A, A** septic tank. *B,* Subsurface disposal of septic tank effluent by a disposal field.

volume of 600 gallons. The tank holds the sewage for approximately 24 hours to provide separation of the wastes into solids and liquids. The liquid is discharged from the tank by displacement by incoming wastes and is disposed of by subsurface means. The solids settle to the bottom of the tank. Some solids accumulate on the surface of the liquid, forming scum. The solids at the bottom of the tank are decomposed by anaerobic bacterial action into a compact mass called sludge. Since the primary purpose of septic tanks is to collect solids, they build up in the tank. Unless periodically removed, the solids will eventually fill the tank, discharge with the effluent to the subsurface disposal unit and clog these units. When the scum on the surface of the liquid in the tank and the sludge on the bottom reach a combined depth of approximately 18 inches, the tank should be cleaned. Therefore, every 2 to 3 years a septic tank should be checked for sludge deposits and scum and cleaned out if necessary. The sludge is removed by pumping into commercial tank trucks and trucked to an approved place of disposal. This can be a municipal sewage treatment plant or an approved isolated site.

Septic tank effluent cannot be depended upon to be free of pathogenic organisms and should not be discharged directly to the ground surface or to a watercourse and in no case to old abandoned dug wells. The ground water in the dug well may be the same source of ground water furnishing the new drilled well. The effluent should be discharged to a subsurface disposal system designed specifically for the soil and ground water conditions of each individual site. The normal methods of subsurface disposal of septic tank effluent are by disposal field or seepage pit. The method chosen depends upon local topographic and soil conditions.

A *disposal field* (Fig. 20, *B*) is a series of open-pointed or perforated pipes placed in trenches 18 to 30 inches deep and 18 inches to 3 feet wide. The tiles are laid in gravel from a distribution box into which the septic tank effluent discharges and from which the sewage enters the individual subsurface disposal lines in equal amounts and seeps into the surrounding soil.

Another method of subsurface disposal of septic tank effluent is by *seepage pits* (Fig. 21). A seepage pit is similar to a dug well but operates in reverse. A seepage pit is normally used when the upper soil strata are not satisfactory for disposal by tile fields, but where satisfactory soil is available below this depth. The ground water table should be at least 4 feet below the bottom of the trench or pit so that ground waters used for water supplies will be protected.

The size of the seepage pit or the length and width of tile trenches is determined from the quantity of waste to be handled and the absorptive capacity of the soil. The absorptive capacity is determined from a soil test made on the site of the proposed disposal facility.

A method of direct household waste disposal is the *cesspool*. This is a unit similar to the seepage pit, except that it receives raw sewage and wastes directly from the home. Its use is not generally recommended since sewage solids clog the openings in the lining. They are frequently used when soil conditions are satisfactory and when it is planned to install public sewers within a reasonable period of time.

A dry well is similar to a seepage pit, but receives drainage from roofs and basements.

The location and construction of subsurface disposal systems is primarily important so that they do not pollute individual water supplies, such as wells and springs. In general, they should be located 100 feet (Fig. 22) from any potable water supply, at a lower elevation than the water supply and not on a direct line of drainage to the water supply. The figure of 100 feet is only a guide. If limestone areas are encountered, 10,000 feet may not be satisfactory. On the other hand, soil and geological conditions may make 50 feet safe.

Individual sewage disposal facilities, such as septic tanks and tile fields, meet the needs of truly rural areas where soil conditions are satisfactory for subsurface disposal. However, as the numbers of homes increase in rural areas, it becomes more difficult to satisfactorily discharge sewage into the ground and at the same time take an individual, safe water supply from the same property, unless the lots are exceptionally large. Growth into a community necessitates the development of a municipal water supply and a municipal sewer system.

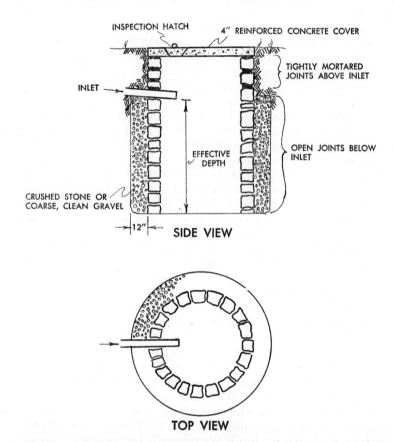

SIDE VIEW

TOP VIEW

Figure 21. Subsurface disposal of septic tank effluents by a seepage pit. The cesspool and dry well are similar in construction, but differ in the type of waste disposed: the seepage pit receives sewage effluents from the septic tank; the cesspool receives raw sewage directly; and the dry well receives nonsewage waste, such as footing drainage and roof water.

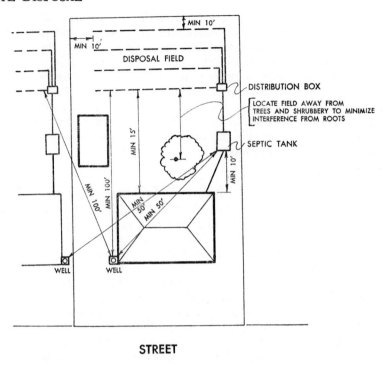

MIN 10'

MIN 10'

DISPOSAL FIELD

DISTRIBUTION BOX

LOCATE FIELD AWAY FROM
TREES AND SHRUBBERY TO MINIMIZE
INTERFERENCE FROM ROOTS

MIN 15'

SEPTIC TANK

MIN 10'

MIN 100'

MIN 100'

MIN 50'

MIN 50'

WELL   WELL

STREET

Figure 22. A typical lot layout, showing the relationship between individual wells and sewage disposal systems, and their minimum desirable separations.

COMMUNITY DISPOSAL SYSTEMS

The municipal sewer system is a necessity for the growing community. Sewer systems are referred to as separate, storm or combined. A separate or sanitary sewer system collects only domestic and industrial wastes. A storm sewer collects only runoff water from roofs, streets and similar facilities. A combined sewer system collects domestic and industrial wastes and storm water. A sewerage system consists of the sewer system, a method of collecting the wastes from residences and industry and a plant to treat the wastes.

Some communities do not provide for the treatment of wastes, but discharge them raw (untreated) from the collecting system directly into a watercourse. This practice generally is illegal. A public health hazard is created when such watercourses are used as sources of water for potable and culinary purposes, requiring additional and costly water treatment processes. Some industries need water for process purposes of higher chemical purity than that required for drinking purposes. Pollution of watercourses, which means a higher cost of water treatment for industrial uses, may be the difference between an industry locating or not locating in a community. An economic burden is also placed upon the downstream property owners since property values along the stream banks will depreciate. Recreational use of the water (becoming more important in our way of life as populations increase and people have more leisure time) will be restricted.

It is necessary to maintain a reasonable degree of purity of our various waters for public health, public enjoyment, propagation and protection of fish and wild life and for industrial and agricultural development. This does not mean that streams are to be returned to or maintained in their original virgin condition. However, in order to maintain reasonable watercourse conditions, it is necessary that varying degrees of treatment be provided for domestic and industrial wastes. The federal government and most states have laws to safeguard the waters of the states by preventing new pollution and abating existing pollution; this generally means the provision of some degree of treatment of sewage and waste.

Sewage Treatment Plant

The purpose of a sewage treatment plant is to remove a determined portion of the organic, inorganic and bacterial load, so that ultimate disposal of the liquids and solids can be accomplished without jeopardizing public health and the propagation of fish and wild life or creating a nuisance and without unnecessarily restricting recreational, industrial and agricultural use. The degree of treatment provided depends upon the strength and volume of sewage or waste to be treated and the volume of flow, existing pollution and normal use of the watercourse into which the treated effluent will discharge. The basic types of treatment are preliminary, primary or mechanical treatment and secondary or biological treatment. The combination of preliminary, primary and secondary treatment is called complete treatment (Fig. 23).

Preliminary Treatment. The preliminary units consist of screens, comminutor and grit chamber. Primary or mechanical treatment units consist of sedimentation, sludge digestion and drying. The sewers bring the sewage from the community to the plant where the raw sewage may first pass through *bar screens.* The purpose of bar screens is to remove large solids, such as rags and sticks, which may clog pumps or interfere with the operation of devices for treatment. The screen is made of iron bars placed 1 to 1½ inches apart and at an angle with the horizontal of 30 to 60° inclined in the direction of the flow of the sewage. The screens may be cleaned by hand raking or by mechanical means. Screenings may amount to as much as 2 cubic feet per million gallons of sewage. Disposal of screenings is difficult since they contain from 90 to 95 per cent moisture, are offensive and tend to decompose quickly. Burial and incineration are the most satisfactory methods.

Frequently, a *comminutor* replaces the bar screen. The comminutor is a mechanical grinder which cuts the large solid particles into particles small enough to pass through a ¼ to ½ inch screen opening on the comminutor. This unit eliminates the problem of disposing of the screenings from a bar screen. After passing through the screens or comminutor, the sewage enters the grit chamber.

The purpose of the *grit chamber* is to remove grit from the sewage. Grit is the heavy mineral and inorganic material in wastes. It is largely sand, gravel and cinders and includes such objects as bits of glass, bottle caps and fruit stones. This material, if allowed to remain in the sewage, causes excessive wear on pumps, grinders, sludge collectors, valves and other equipment. The grit chamber is constructed in the form of a long narrow, deep channel. Sewage flows through the channel from one end to the other. Grit settles to the bottom of the channel while the lighter, decomposable solids are carried

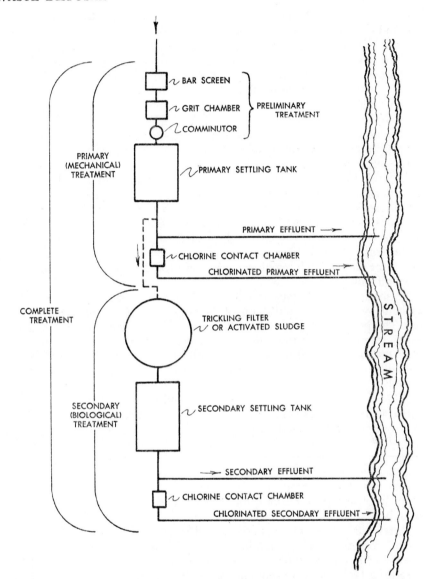

Figure 23.   Complete treatment processes, preliminary, primary and secondary, in a sewage plant.

on with the sewage. The size of the channel and its slope are such that the sewage moves about 1 foot per second. Grit chambers are cleaned by hand (shovel and bucket) or automatically by a mechanical cleaning device. Disposal of grit is usually by use as land fill.

The volume of flow through a sewage plant varies widely. Normally, peak flow is reached in the late morning or early afternoon, and a very minimum flow is reached about 5:00 A.M. Extreme high flows at odd hours frequently result from rainstorms. Because of these variations, it is not possible in most cases to build a grit channel that will provide the desired velocity of flow under all conditions. Therefore, special devices are usually needed to regulate the flow rate of the sewage through the grit chamber. The two regulating devices in most common use are proportional flow weirs and control flumes. Either may be used as flow-measuring devices as well as for velocity control, but in order to do this, it is necessary to provide a means of recording the depth of flow at some given point with respect to the regulating device. The sewage then flows to the primary treatment units.

Primary Treatment. The first primary treatment unit is a *settling tank.* The purpose of the settling tank is to reduce the rate of flow of the sewage so that settling of solids will take place. Sewage solids settling to the bottom of the tank form sludge, while those rising to and floating on the liquid surface of the tank form scum. Basins used for this purpose have been given such names as "clarifiers," "sedimentation basins" or "settling basins."

Many years ago, when little was known about sewage treatment, settling tanks were operated by the fill and draw method. Sewage was allowed to flow into an empty tank until it was full, then the flow was diverted to another tank. After the full tank remained quiet for a few hours, all of the liquid was drawn off slowly.

In modern settling tanks reliance is placed on good design of inlets, outlets, baffles and the size and shape of the tank to provide good settling conditions. The purpose of the baffle at the inlet end is to help spread the flow of sewage evenly through the tank. If the sewage moves through the tank uniformly and only in the direction of the outlet, settling conditions will be good. The baffle at the outlet serves mainly to prevent floating solids from leaving the tank.

There are two general methods for collecting sludge. The simplest method is used only in small tanks. In these the entire bottom of the tank is steeply sloped and the settled sludge slides down the slope to the point of draw-off. Most treatment plants use mechanical sludge collectors in tanks having a gently sloping bottom. The sludge collectors move settled sludge along the bottom in the opposite direction from that of the sewage flow to hoppers near the inlet. At the same time, the returning scrapers or flights sweep the floating scum along the surface in the direction of flow toward a trough near the outlet.

After settled sludge has been moved to the sludge hopper, it must be removed from the tank. The method of removal may affect the sludge digester more than the settling tanks. All the sludge must not only be removed from the settling tanks but also must be concentrated into the least possible volume. The problem is to pump the sludge with as little liquid as possible.

The most marked change in passing sewage through a settling tank of proper design is in the solids content of the sewage. Settleable solids are nearly all removed; suspended solids are usually reduced about 40 to 50 per cent. Most of the biochemical oxygen demand (B.O.D.) in sewage is caused by smaller particles in suspension and solution which will not settle. The biochemical oxygen demand is the weight of oxygen necessary to oxidize the organic matter in the waste. Usually, the B.O.D. will be reduced about 35 per cent in a primary settling tank. These removals will vary from one plant to another and, especially, with different characteristics of sewage.

An *Imhoff tank* (Fig. 24) is another primary treatment unit. It differs from a sedimentation unit in that it is a two-story affair with the sedimentation unit located directly over and an integral part of the sludge compartment The tank is named after Dr. Karl Imhoff, its inventor. Its purpose and operation are similar to those of the plain primary sedimentation tank, except that the settling solids in an Imhoff tank pass down through the settling compartment of the tank through an overlapping slot in the bottom of the tank to the sludge compartment beneath. The overlapping edges prevent gas and rising sludge from entering the settling compartment. Sludge is permitted to settle and collect in the sludge compartment to a depth approximately 18 inches below the slot. It remains in the digestion compartment until it decomposes to a reasonably stable material. The period for digestion depends upon the nature of the solids and the temperature. At 40° F. about 2½ months are required for good digestion, while at 80° F., similar results will be obtained in 1 month. Most of the solids settle near the inlet end of the tank, filling up that portion of the sludge compartment first. For even distribution of the sludge, the inlet and outlet channels are usually arranged so that the flow through the tank may be periodically reversed. Digested sludge is drawn by gravity or pumping to sludge beds through a pipe extending to the bottom of the digestion section. The sludge compartment is not heated artificially as in some separate sludge digesters. Consequently, in the winter months little digestion takes place and sufficient storage space must be provided for the accumulation of solids.

The effluent from primary treatment units (the sedimentation tank or Imhoff tank) is now either discharged to a watercourse, chlorinated or further treated. The method followed depends upon the volume of water in the stream, the pollution load of the stream, the possible use of the water and the strength and volume of the effluent from the plant. If stream conditions and uses are such that the effluent from primary treatment or primary treatment plus chlorination cannot be safely discharged, then additional treatment called secondary treatment must be provided.

Secondary Treatment. Secondary treatment units may consist of trickling filters and secondary settling or an activated sludge unit and secondary settling. Variations of these methods are used, depending upon the degree of treatment needed. These units may be followed by chlorination.

The primary sedimentation tank effluent is conducted to the trickling

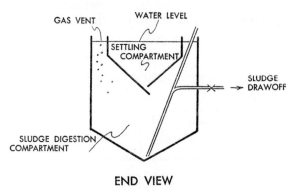

END VIEW

Figure 24. Imhoff tank.

filter or activated sludge unit, the effluent of which discharges to the secondary settling basin and is followed by chlorination, if needed. Final disposal is to a watercourse. Secondary treatment is by biological action and utilizes the natural fact that the ultimate destruction of organic wastes is brought about by the life activities of bacteria and other organisms. These organisms, searching for food, break down complex organic materials into simple and more stable substances. Bacteria and other organisms associated with them in biological treatment of sewage require continuous food supplies, need no rest, but do need some medium in or on which to live.

The basic principles of secondary treatment include setting up aerobic environmental conditions where saprophytic organisms may multiply and be contained. The organic material is made available in suspension and dilution as a food under times and conditions conducive to maximum use of the food.

Secondary treatment is often referred to as an oxidation process, since it depends on the stabilization of nitrogenous and carbonaceous material. The effectiveness of secondary treatment processes is usually measured by the reduction in oxygen demand secured through the use of the processes. As a rough measure of the rates of activity that might be expected, the B.O.D. reduction in properly designed and operated biological contact processes will approach 90 per cent. This can be accomplished in activated sludge tanks with 4 to 8 hours of detention and possibly 1 to 2 hours of contact through sand beds or trickling filters as balanced against 10 days or more of stream flows at normal summer temperatures where dilution is used.

Dosing tanks or pumps receive the flow of settled sewage from the primary settling tanks at sewage treatment works which employ trickling or sand filters. One or more automatic dosing siphons are installed in a dosing tank for the purpose of collecting a certain volume of flow and discharging it at optimum rates to the filter units.

A trickling filter's function (Fig. 25) is to reduce the stream pollutional effect of organic matter in sewage and wastes that cannot be removed by primary treatment. The primary treatment process removes and treats that portion of the organic matter in sewage which will readily settle. A trickling filter, in some respects, also functions as a settling tank. Some of the suspended matter in sewage, which remains because it was too fine to be removed by the primary tank, is retained in the filter by sedimentation action. The flow of sewage over the stone in the filter is at a much reduced velocity and the suspended material has a relatively short distance to fall. However, most of the suspended matter is retained in the filter by the action of the

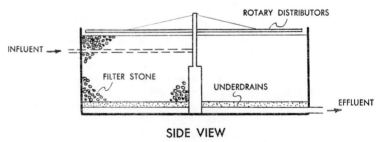

SIDE VIEW

Figure 25. Trickling filter.

biological mass, which also removes, retains, and works upon dissolved material in the sewage. The biological action of a trickling filter also removes much of the bacteria and other microorganisms that were originally in the sewage.

A trickling filter does not permanently remove organic matter from sewage and wastes.

Practically all of the organic material which is introduced upon a filter is still present in the effluent or outflow from a filter. However, the form of the organic material is changed by biological action to suspended matter that will settle out in a final settling tank or to relatively stable matter that will not be a source of pollution to the receiving stream. A *trickling filter* that is normal and functioning properly is very much alive. It contains billions of biological organisms which do the work of treating sewage and wastes. The organisms consist of bacteria, protozoa, various other kinds of small animals such as worms and bugs, as well as molds and plants. Their food is the organic matter in sewage and wastes and each other. The biological life forms the slimy mass that coats the surfaces on and in the medium. The biological organisms in a filter are largely aerobic; therefore, a trickling filter must be designed and operated to provide the organisms on the medium with sufficient air throughout the entire unit.

The distribution system of a filter, in addition to providing for the uniform spreading of the sewage upon the surface of the media, is designed to introduce oxygen from the air into the sewage. The sewage is sprayed on the rock medium in a thin sheet, which breaks up into droplets, particularly when it splashes upon the medium. The falling and splashing sewage picks up air from the atmosphere and holds it in the solution to be used by the organisms. Oxygen is also provided the biological life by the flow of air through the open spaces in a filter. The medium for a filter is selected and placed to provide the most favorable environment for the function and activity of the biological life. The depth of medium in the newer filters, usually between 5 and 7 feet, provides for adequate contact between the sewage and the biological life to obtain sufficient breakdown of the organic matter.

Filters are classified as standard rate or high rate units, on a basis of volume of flow per unit of surface area and biochemical oxygen demand loading per unit of medium volume. Generally, standard rate filters are dosed at less than 4 million gallons per acre per day with an applied biochemical oxygen demand of less than 15 pounds per 1000 cubic feet per day. High rate filters are dosed at 10 to 30 million gallons per acre per day with biochemical oxygen demand loading generally in excess of 15 pounds per 1000 cubic feet per day. High rate filters do not break down the organic matter in sewage so completely as standard rate units. They are employed, therefore, where less complete treatment is required and where the receiving stream provides sufficient dilution of the final effluent of the sewage treatment works to prevent detrimental pollution of the stream.

A number of chemicals that may be received at a treatment plant, particularly some industrial wastes such as plating materials, when in an appreciable concentration in the sewage, are toxic to biological life. It is essential that those toxic chemicals which will interfere and hinder, or even completely kill off the biological organisms, be entirely eliminated from the sewage, or that they be neutralized or reduced in concentration sufficiently to prevent their detrimental effect on the biological life of the filter. A filter can effectively treat organic industrial wastes, such as cannery and milk plant wastes, in combination with domestic sewage. The biological activity in a filter may even reduce some chemical wastes which may be present in sewage. An advantage of a properly functioning filter is that it may take a considerable shock load of organic or chemical loading without greatly reducing its efficiency.

Recirculation of final or filter effluent to the primary tank or to the filter influent is essential in the operation of some trickling filter plants. It is employed for various purposes and performs a number of functions. Recirculation may be necessary to provide for continuous dosing of the filter, to dilute or reduce the concentration of exceptionally strong sewage, to obtain more over-all efficiency or breakdown of organic material, or to prevent odor nuisances or freezing.

Activated sludge is another biological method utilized for secondary treatment. This is a process of treating the effluent from a primary settling tank with sludge from the secondary settling tank, which has been activated. Such sludge is initially prepared by mixing untreated sewage and sludge for several weeks in the presence of oxygen. The process of developing the special forms of bacteria is called activation and the biologically active sludge containing them is called activated sludge.

The sewage entering the aeration tank is mixed with approximately 25 per cent of activated sludge and agitated by oxygen added by compressed air. The aeration period varies from 4 to 8 hours, depending upon the degree of treatment needed. The organic solids in the sewage are rapidly oxidized while the suspended and colloidal matter tends to coagulate and form a precipitate that is readily settleable. The resultant effluent should be clean, sparkling and low in organic matter. From the aeration tank, the sewage flows to a secondary settling tank in which the coagulated material is permitted to settle. This settled sludge is biologically active and part is returned to the incoming sewage of the aeration tank as activated sludge to inoculate it. The effluent from this secondary settling tank is discharged directly into a watercourse or receives chlorination before discharge to the watercourse.

Secondary settling tanks, which are similar to primary settling tanks, follow treatment of wastes by trickling filters or activated sludge. The filter and activated sludge units change suspended and colloidal material to a form which will settle out. The purpose of the secondary settling basin is to settle out those oxidized materials.

Disinfection. If required for control of pathogenic organisms, the sewage effluent from a primary or a secondary treatment plant will be chlorinated just prior to discharge to the watercourse. Chlorination may be undertaken for several reasons, but the most important is for the destruction of pathogenic microorganisms. The total number of microorganisms in raw sewage is in the order of millions per milliliter. Most of them are beneficial, as they live on dead organic matter causing it to decompose into forms which are inoffensive and available to plants as fertilizer. These organisms, called saprophytes, are essential for the processes of sewage treatment. However, sewage contains the discharges from a whole community and in any community there are always persons suffering from disease. Therefore, sewage always contains disease-producing organisms which, if brought into contact with healthy individuals, may cause disease. Laboratory studies and experience with plants have demonstrated that pathogenic organisms are more easily killed by chlorine than are most of the saprophytic organisms. Thus, in disinfection the pathogenic organisms are killed and, incidentally, many but not all of the saprophytic organisms are destroyed. Chlorination as practiced does not sterilize. To accomplish disinfection, sufficient chlorine must be added to satisfy the chlorine demand of the sewage and leave a residual chlorine that will destroy bacteria.

A fairly complete laboratory is necessary to measure the destruction of bacteria and the tests require several days to complete. Thus, bacteriologic examinations are not practical for the day-to-day control of the operation of a chlorinator. Laboratory experiments and actual experience with plants have shown that disinfection will be accomplished if sufficient chlorine is added to sewage so that 15 minutes after the chlorine has been added a residual chlorine concentration of 0.5 ppm is present. Thus, disinfection of sewage is arbitrarily defined as the addition of sufficient chlorine so that a chlorine residual of 0.5 ppm is present 15 minutes after the chlorine is applied. The control of chlorination for disinfection is by measurement of the residual chlorine using the orthotolidine test. Results can be obtained in a few minutes and the chlorinator adjusted to the proper feed.

Disinfection must be a continuous process as it would be hazardous to discharge untreated effluent even for a short period of time.

The object of disinfection is destruction of bacteria, and the ultimate measure of effectiveness is the bacteriologic result. The measurement of residual chlorine does apply a tool for practical control. If the residual chlorine value commonly effective in most sewage plants does not yield satisfactory bacteriologic kills in a particular plant, then the residual chlorine that does must be determined and used as control. In other words, the 0.5 ppm residual chlorine, while generally effective, is not a rigid standard but a guide that may be changed to meet local requirements.

Other Treatment Units. Sludge digesters and sludge beds are additional treatment units in a primary or secondary treatment plant.

In discussing primary and secondary treatment, it was pointed out that sludge settled out in the primary and secondary settling tanks. This sludge is pumped, or run by gravity flow, to a *sludge digester* (Fig. 26). Sludge is digested to produce an inoffensive material for disposal, to reduce the amount of sludge to be handled for disposal and to produce a sludge that will dry readily. Digesters are circular, enclosed metal tanks approximately 20 feet deep and varying in diameter, depending upon the volume of storage needed. Some are provided with additional heat for better and more consistent digestion. Here the organic matter in the sludge is broken down. Certain of the solids in the sludge become liquid, some become a burnable gas and others are changed so they compact more readily, thus reducing the quantity of sludge to be handled for disposal. When sewage solids are added to this process, they pass through four stages: (a) a period of intensive acid production (acidification) (pH *drops* from 6.8 to 5.1); (b) a period of acid digestion (liquefaction) (pH *raises* from 5.1 to 6.8); (c) a period of intensive digestion and stabilization (gasification) (pH is 6.8 to 7.2); and (d) a period of humification—decreased gas production (increase in pH).

In a properly operating digester, all of these periods of digestion are

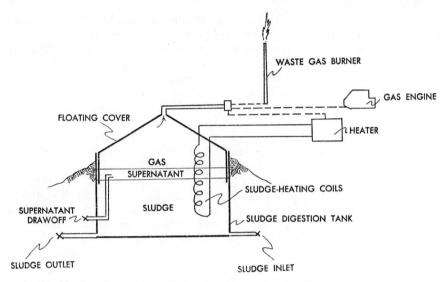

Figure 26. Sludge digestion with gas collection.

taking place at the same time, unless the process is divided into several stages by several tanks. The digester liquor (supernatant), the product of the lique-faction and mechanical separation of the sludge and liquid, is removed frequently and gas is removed continuously.

The liquid discharge from the digesters is normally discharged to the primary settling tank, to the sludge beds or to a lagoon. Difficulties have been experienced in some instances with the supernatant causing the primary tank to become septic and, as a result, disposal to sludge beds or lagoons has been practiced. Some plants have found it advantageous to discharge supernatant directly to the aeration tanks or trickling filters.

The type of digester, sludge-drying facilities and the season of the year normally govern the withdrawal of digested sludge. It is important in all instances to leave enough digested sludge in the tank to seed the raw sludge and to maintain a balanced alkaline digestion. Only well-digested sludge should be withdrawn from the tank. This is usually granular in appearance, dark in color and has a tarry odor. Gray or light brown streaks in the sludge are signs of less well digested material. It has a solids content of 6 to 10 per cent. If air is drawn into a digester during sludge withdrawal, it is pos-sible to have an explosive mixture of air and digester gas present in the digester. Sludge from the digester is dewatered by sludge-drying beds or by a mechanical method—generally vacuum filters.

Sludge-drying beds (Fig. 27) are the most widely used units for air drying of the sludge from separate digesters or Imhoff tanks. A sludge-drying bed is really a sand filter. Commonly, the bed is built of a layer of 9 inches of sand on top of 12 inches of gravel or crushed rock. Lines of tile are laid in the bottom of the gravel about 10 feet apart to drain the water given up by the sludge. Sludge beds are either glass enclosed or open. Even the smallest plant should have at least two beds. Sludge drawn onto beds floats on the thin film of water which separates from it. Sludge is applied to the

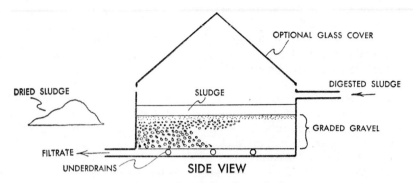

Figure 27.   Sludge-drying bed.

bed to a depth of 9 to 12 inches. With enclosed beds, approximately 10 days are required before the sludge is dry enough for removal. With open beds and under favorable weather conditions 10 days may be sufficient. But, under unfavorable weather conditions, 3 to 4 weeks may be required. The sludge, at the time of removal, normally has a moisture content of 70 per cent.

Mechanical dewatering is usually used in the larger plants and may be accomplished by the use of presses, centrifuges or vacuum filters. The vacuum filter, the only one that is used extensively, consists of a cloth-covered rotating drum, a portion of which is in the sludge and upon which a vacuum is applied during part of the rotation period. The vacuum draws the sludge upon the filter and dewaters it while a blower aids in the removal of the dewatered sludge from the filter. Successful operation is dependent upon the use of chemicals to flocculate the wet sludge. When chemicals, such as alum, ferric chloride or ferric sulfate, are added to the sludge, large flocs form. This allows the water to be more readily removed from the sludge by the filter. If chemicals are not added, the water-binding properties (the ammonium compounds formed during digestion) are not lowered and the water is not so readily separated.

Elutriation is another method of lowering the water-binding properties of sludge. The sludge is mixed with water or sewage plant effluent. The ammonium compounds tend to disperse in the water and the sludge settles out. A minimum amount of chemicals is used.

A good practice for getting the final sludge into a more suitable condition is to stockpile it over winter or for several months. Weathering the sludge takes the heat from it and it falls apart into smooth, small particles, very much like soft earth. In this condition it is quite suitable as a conditioner, not fertilizer, for lawns and crops. There is often local demand for the sludge if it is in good condition and free from industrial wastes. Sludge in some communities is incinerated or dumped at sea. There is not much proof that year-old sludges are particularly likely to pass on diseases, but public health authorities warn users not to put air-dried sludge on gardens where root or low-growing leaf crops are cultivated, especially when these crops may be eaten raw, such as carrots or lettuce. Sludge is conditioned with other fertilizing chemicals and sold as a fertilizer. Also, sludge is a commercial source of vitamin B_{12}.

Production of Sludge Gas.   Gas produced by digestion may be used as a source of fuel for the heating of sludge in digesters, for the heating of buildings, to dry or burn sewage sludge and to furnish power. The use of sludge gas as a source of fuel can result in considerable saving in the operation of a sewage treatment plant, provided that the gas produced is of such a nature that it can be readily burned.

Under normal operation, when alkaline conditions are maintained in the digestion process, the burnable gases will be mostly methane gas which is similar to and has a heating value about the same as most bottle gases. Methane will ordinarily total between 65 to 80 per cent of the gas produced. The remaining gases, which are mostly carbon dioxide, nitrogen and oxygen, will not burn. Other burnable gases which may be produced are hydrogen and hydrogen sulfide. These gases are collected either in the dome of the sludge digester itself or in a separate gas holder.

Digesters may be equipped with fixed covers or floating covers. If a separate gas holder is provided, a fixed cover digester is used. A floating cover may be compared to a kitchen pan turned upside down in a larger pan filled with water, so that the edges of the smaller pan are sealed by the water. Floating covers are free to move up and down with respect to the volume of gas produced, just as the inverted pan would move up and down as air is removed from or forced into the air space under the pan, or as water is added to or removed from the larger pan. As floating covers are free to move up and down for a considerable distance, it is not necessary to remove liquid from the tanks each time fresh sludge is added.

Sludge gas is usually odorless and its presence in the atmosphere is not readily detectable unless it contains hydrogen sulfide, a gas which is toxic in concentrations of .001 per cent or more. Because of the corrosiveness of hydrogen sulfide to metals in the presence of moisture, some plants have been provided with scrubbers to remove the hydrogen sulfide from the sludge gas. Sludge gas will burn and is highly explosive over a range of 1 part of gas with from 10 to 15 parts of air. As the methane constituent of the gas is lighter than air and the hydrogn sulfide and carbon dioxide content heavier than air, ventilation should be provided at high and low points in areas where the gas might be expected to collect because of leaks and other unusual operating conditions. There is also a danger of suffocation from lack of oxygen in areas containing excessive amounts of sewage gas.

Pressure relief valves protected by flame traps must be installed on gas collectors. These valves and traps are exposed to severe corrosive conditions and should be inspected and cleaned periodically. In those areas where there is a possibility of gas accumulating, *all* parts of the electrical installation, including light switches, should be explosion proof and care should be taken by operators to assure that the explosive proof features of an installation are not eliminated by improper maintenance and repair.

Other Treatment Methods

When favorable soil, climate and location are present, raw or settled sewage can be given biological treatment by means of sewage stabilization basins or *oxidation ponds*. The process employs atmospheric oxygen as well as the oxygen produced by the photo-synthetic activity of algae to keep the ponds aerobic, and hence, nuisance free. Loadings of 0.5 pounds of B.O.D. per 1000 sq. ft. are commonly employed. Multiple units, careful construction of embankments, control of seepage and an overflow structure that allows control of depth from 2 to 5 feet are important design details.

Package plants can be defined as prefabricated treatment units manufactured in standard sizes by modern production methods for those designers who choose to use them as a means of reducing both equipment and construction costs to their clients. Package plants usually employ the biological processes of trickling filtration or activated sludge; the extended aeration and contact stabilization modifications of the activated sludge process are two such examples. Preliminary treatment by screening or comminution is usually employed. Primary sedimentation is not generally used for the activated sludge processes. Package plants, being biological treatment units, require competent, trained operating personnel who will employ the results from laboratory tests for process control.

A method of sludge disposal recently applied in the sewage field is a form of wet combustion known commercially as the Zimmermann Process. Preheated liquid sludge is pumped at high pressure through heat exchangers and thence to a reactor where at a temperature of about 500° F. and pressures of 500 to 1800 psi the oxygen in the air introduced into the system combines with the organic matter in the sludge to produce an end-product which is biologically stable. Depending on the heat value and the moisture content of the sludge being introduced, the process may or may not be self-sustaining.

Many modifications of the activated sludge process have been developed in recent years. *Tapered aeration* utilizes the principle of supplying maximum air to the inlet of the aeration tank with gradual reduction toward the outlet end. *Step aeration* developed by Gould in New York City provides for reaeration of the return sludge and introduction of the incoming sewage at various points in the aeration tank. *Contact stabilization* or "biosorption," first developed in Austin, Texas, employs a system of sludge reaeration of 4 to 6 hours with the stabilized sludge being introduced into the incoming raw or settled sewage and then aerated for about 30 minutes to 2 hours prior to settling. Completely mixed systems refer to aeration tanks in which the incoming sewage is mixed throughout the tank. *Extended aeration* is a type of completely mixed system usually found in package plants in which an aeration period of 24 hours is usually employed. The *modified* or *high-grade* activated sludge process developed at New York City uses a small amount of return sludge to inoculate the incoming sewage in order to take advantage of the log growth phase of bacterial reproduction. The B.O.D. removal efficiency of this process usually ranges from 57 to 76 per cent. Loading rates for this process are considerably higher than conventional activated sludge processes.

Contact aeration, sometimes called the *Hays process,* employs closely spaced vertical plates upon which biological growths occur. Compressed air is introduced below the plates by diffusers. Settling tanks are used before and after the contact aeration tanks.

DISPOSAL OF LIQUID INDUSTRIAL WASTES

Industrial wastes, resulting from manufacturing and industrial processes, have not been specifically discussed but we have mentioned them as part of the community wastes. The strength, composition and character of industrial wastes vary greatly for different industries and often for different plants manufacturing the same product. Each problem involving the treatment of industrial wastes must be considered on an individual basis. Before plans for the treatment of wastes are considered, it is desirable to make a complete investigation of the individual processes to study methods of reducing the pollutional load and increasing the possibility of satisfactorily treating the waste. Most industrial wastes can, with adequate controls, be treated with sewage in the municipal sewage treatment plant. When industrial wastes are toxic, biological methods of treatment cannot be used. Other processes used to treat or condition industrial wastes are lagooning, use of fine screens, ion exchange, centrifuging, absorption, flotation and the control of acidity and alkalinity. Industrial wastes discharged to watercourses have public health significance but not the same as that associated with sewage, since pathogenic organisms are not generally associated with industrial wastes. However, industrial wastes have many other detrimental effects on watercourses.

TESTING SEWAGE TREATMENT UNITS

Sewage and waste treatment units require competent operating personnel conducting necessary control tests and maintaining adequate records for continuous and adequate operation. In order that plants may be operated efficiently and effectively, certain operating regulations and laboratory tests are stipulated by most state and local departments of health. Some of the basic laboratory control tests are settleable solids, methylene blue or putrescibility test, residual chlorine, sludge solids, biochemical oxygen demand and pH. In order that the tests may have significance, the samples for testing must be collected with concern for desired results. The object of sampling is to collect a portion of sewage small enough in volume to be conveniently handled in the laboratory and still be representative. The sample must be collected in such a manner that nothing is added or lost in the portion taken and no material change occurs during the time between collection and laboratory examination. In collecting samples, certain general principles apply: (a) the sample should be taken where the sewage is well mixed; (b) large particles should be excluded; (c) no deposits, growths or floating material that have accumulated at the sampling point should be included; (d) samples should be examined as soon as possible—if held for more than 1 hour, they should be cooled by immersion of the sample bottle in ice water, because after this period the changes due to bacterial decomposition are appreciable; (e) the collection of samples should be made as easy as possible—sampling points should be readily accessible, proper equipment should be at hand, safety precautions established and protection of personnel from inclement weather provided.

Two types of samples are collected, depending on the time available, the tests to be made and the object of the tests. One is a catch or grab sample and consists of a single portion of sewage. The other is an integrated sample which consists of many portions of sewage taken at regular time intervals, the volume of each portion being proportional to the sewage flow at the time it is collected. All portions collected are mixed to produce a final sample representative of the sewage over a time interval and integrated according to flow. Catch samples are not representative of the average sewage since they reflect only the condition at the instant of sampling. However, in many plants the time available for sampling is so limited that catch samples must be used. The samples should be collected at that hour of the day when the treatment plant is operating under maximum load. This usually coincides with the period of maximum flow and occurs at most plants between 9 A.M. and 12 noon. If good operating efficiency is indicated at this time, it is reasonable to assume that plant efficiency will be satisfactory during other periods. When catch samples are used to determine the efficiency of a treatment process, the effluent sample should be collected after a period of time corresponding to the flowing through period of the unit, so that approximately the same sewage is sampled at inlet and outlet. For some tests, catch samples must be used: thus, for residual chlorine and pH value, if two portions are mixed, reactions would occur and the result would not be an average but the result of interaction and have no relation to the sewage sampled. Sometimes the object is to determine the effect of a substance in sewage on the treatment process. It can happen that the substance is present in high concentration for only a short period of time. If individual portions were integrated, an average concentration would be obtained. Thus, to determine the high concentration, catch samples should be examined.

Integrated samples indicate the character of the sewage over a period of time. The effects of intermittent changes in strength and flow are eliminated. The portion used should be collected with sufficient frequency to obtain average results. If the strength and flow do not fluctuate rapidly, hourly portions over a 24-hour period are satisfactory. If the fluctuations are rapid, half-hourly or quarter-hourly samples may be required. Generally, integrated samples are used to determine the character of the sewage.

Settleable solid tests indicate the volume of solids which settle from the sewage in a given time. The results of tests made upon tank influent and effluent provide a means of measuring the efficiency of the settling tank.

Methylene blue tests measure the tendency of sewage to become septic. It is a valuable test for the control of plant operation and should be made at least weekly, especially on effluent samples. If the color remains without change for 10 days, the sewage may be considered stable. If it decolorizes in 5 days, it has been stabilized to about 70 per cent and is suitable for discharge into a stream providing dilution of at least 10 to 1. If the color disappears within 1 day or less, sufficient putrescible material is present to cause a nuisance if discharged into a small volume of diluting water.

Residual chlorine tests indicate the amount of chlorine remaining in the sewage after the organic matter present has absorbed a portion of that applied. More specific information on other important tests and their significance can be secured from the many texts covering this subject.

Operators are generally required to have minimum education and experience, to maintain daily records of their prescribed routine plant tests and to submit the results of such daily tests to the municipal officials and the health department on a monthly basis on forms prescribed and furnished by the health department.

DISPOSAL OF SOLID WASTES

Solid wastes include garbage, ashes and rubbish. Disposal of such wastes from the truly rural home is generally different from disposal of community refuse. The collection and disposal of this material in the city is normally the function of the department of public works or corresponding agency, but for many years was one of the major activities of local health departments. This philosophy was based on the theory that accumulations of filth in and of themselves were important in the production of disease. In *Public Health— Its Promise For the Future* we read that Dr. Benjamin Rush in 1815 stated in his book, *Medical Inquiries and Observations,* that the great yellow fever epidemic of Philadelphia in 1793 was initiated by a pile of rotting coffee at Ball's wharf. Dr. Rush was quite specific about the dangers of various accumulations of wastes such as rotten cabbage, rotten hemp, bilge water, dead fish and similar wastes. Dr. Rush's ideas were representative of those of the educated people of that time.

Refuse disposal is one of economy, convenience and general cleanliness. There are indirect relations of refuse disposal to public health. The sanitary disposal, especially of garbage, is of concern to the physician and health department. Methods of disposing of refuse are dumping, disposal at sea, trenching, hog feeding, reduction, incineration, treatment with sewage and sanitary land fill. The oldest and least acceptable method of disposing of community refuse is by dumping. This is the uncontrolled discharge of refuse to the open ground surface without covering. Dumps are unsightly and conducive to fires, odors, rat infestation, fly breeding and human scavengering. Disposal by sea, practiced by some communities, is the transporting and discharging of refuse into open waters. Many times the refuse is not carried out of the immediate vicinity of the shore and, even when carried out to deeper water, may be washed back by the tides or storms at sea. Hog feeding has been practiced for a long time. Unavoidable nuisances, together with the frequency of animal diseases and incidence of trichinosis among hogs fed on uncooked garbage, provide concern about this method of disposal. Interstate quarantine regulations require garbage shipped interstate for hog feeding to be cooked for 30 minutes at 212° F. Reduction is cooking garbage under steam pressure with recovery of melted fats and a dry residue. Incineration is the destruction of garbage and rubbish by burning at high temperature. The essential feature in satisfactory operation is high temperature (1800° F. to 2000° F.) combustion. Ashes and clean fill are separately disposed of by land fill. Although with careful separation the combustibles may support combustion, auxiliary fuel is provided and used. Incineration is probably the best method for many communities, especially when land is not available for a sanitary land fill.

The sanitary land fill process consists of controlled dumping in depth, together with compacting and continuous covering with earth. Dumping operations are completely covered each day with earth with a final compacted 2-foot cover of earth. The sanitary land fill, if planned and handled satisfactorily, will not cause nuisance problems. It has the advantage of recovering land for playground sites and other municipal uses.

Some consideration has been given to the disposal of community garbage by grinding it and discharging it to the municipal sewage treatment plant. A variation of this treatment is provided at Jasper, Indiana, where the city installed individual garbage grinders in each home which discharge to the municipal sewer system. Individual home grinders are becoming common in the rural home with discharge to the private sewage disposal system. The rural home without such home grinders must resort to individual burial or burning of garbage or disposal in a public dump area.

MEREDITH H. THOMPSON, D.Eng.

REFERENCES

1. Hardenbergh, W. A.: Sewerage and Sewage Treatment. Scranton, Pennsylvania, International Textbook Company, 1956.
2. Individual Sewage Disposal System. Washington, D.C., United States Department of Health, Education, and Welfare, Public Health Service. Reprint No. 2461.
3. Manual of Septic Tank Practice. Washington, D.C., United States Department of Health, Education, and Welfare, Public Health Service. Publication No. 526.
4. Minimum Requirements for Individual Water Supply and Sewage Disposal Systems. Albany, New York, Federal Housing Administration. Issued yearly.
5. Phelps, Earle B.: Public Health Engineering. Vol. 1. New York, John Wiley & Sons, Inc., 1948.
6. Preventive Medicine in World War II. Vol. 11. Washington, D.C., Office of the Surgeon General, United States Army, 1955, pp. 131-179.
7. Rosenau, Maxcy: Preventive Medicine and Hygiene. New York, Appleton-Century-Crofts, Inc., 1956.
8. Smillie, Wilson G.: Preventive Medicine and Public Health. New York, The Macmillan Co., 1952.
9. Smillie, Wilson G.: Public Health—Its Promise for the Future. New York, The Macmillan Co., 1955.
10. The Sewerage Manual and Catalog File. Ridgewood, New Jersey, Public Works Magazine, 1963.
11. Thompson, Meredith H.: Training Manual for Sewage Treatment Plant Operators. Albany, New York State Department of Health, 1955.
12. Salvato, Joseph A., Jr.: Environmental Sanitation. New York, John Wiley & Sons, Inc., 1958.
13. Babbitt, H. E., and Baumann, Robert E.: Sewerage and Sewage Treatment. Ed. 8. New York, John Wiley & Sons, Inc., 1958.
14. Fair, Gordon M., and Geyer, John C.: Water Supply and Waste—Water Disposal. New York, John Wiley & Sons, Inc., 1954.
15. Sawyer, C. N.: Journal of the Water Pollution Control Federation, 32(3): 232, March, 1960.
16. Torpey, W. N., and Chasick, A. H.: Sewage and Industrial Wastes, 27(11):1217, November, 1955.
17. Porges, R., et al.: Journal of the Water Pollution Control Federation, 33(12):1260, December, 1961.

7   Milk-borne Illness

Milk is one of the most important items in the human diet and is almost irreplaceable for modern man. Milk has many valuable ingredients, including high quality protein and riboflavin. It is unique in its calcium content, which is present in abundance in a readily assimilable form. Herbivorous animals are able to obtain this element from the vegetation which they consume. Carnivorous animals receive their supply largely from ingesting the bones of their victims. Since man rarely consumes sufficient vegetation to supply his needs and has largely given up eating the bones of animals, it is difficult for him to obtain the recommended daily allowance of calcium without the use of milk or milk products.

Practically all milk in this country is derived from cows. The same sanitary precautions should, however, be taken with goat's milk which is available in limited amounts in a few areas. Milk from goats infected with brucellosis is apparently much more likely to cause human illness than milk from infected cows. In other parts of the world various animals are used for milk. The gamoose is the milch animal of Egypt; sheep are milked in some areas, as are mares, yaks and reindeer in others.

DISEASES CAUSED BY MILK CONTAMINATION

It was long suspected that milk could transmit disease, but apparently one of the first carefully studied and published reports on the subject was made in 1857. In that year, Dr. Michael Taylor of Penrith, England, studied an epidemic of typhoid fever and traced its transmission through milk. In 1867 he showed that scarlet fever could also be milk-borne. By the year 1881 more than 70 outbreaks had been traced to contaminated milk.

An illustration of the frequency of illness due to contaminated milk in the days before pasteurization was universal is found in the records of the New York State Health Department. In the 25-year period from 1917 to 1941, a total of 168 outbreaks of milk-borne disease were investigated. These outbreaks were of typhoid and paratyphoid fever, streptococcal infections, "gastroenteritis," bacillary dysentery, diphtheria and poliomyelitis. A total

128

of 10,000 persons were affected. A study of the situation in New York State suggests that dozens of other milk-borne outbreaks may have occurred in the same territory during this period but were not brought to the attention of the Health Department.

Because of the effective job done by health departments generally and the dairy industry, and the improved equipment developed, the number of illnesses associated with milk has been dramatically reduced throughout the United States. For example, since 1949 there have been no milk-borne disease outbreaks reported in New York State. However, dairy farms and processing plants have been getting larger, and smaller farms and plants have been going out of business. Since raw milk is still potentially dangerous, any breakdown in equipment or control can involve large numbers of people.

Because of the manner in which it is produced and distributed, its extensive handling and its contact with many individuals prior to the time it reaches the consumer, milk offers unusual opportunities for the development and wide distribution of disease organisms. Any fluid food handled in the same manner as milk would be a frequent source of infection. In addition, milk serves as a medium of growth for some pathogenic bacteria and, therefore, is doubly dangerous. Milk has been implicated in the conveyance of a great variety of human diseases. The known list includes typhoid fever; streptococcal infections; bacillary dysentery; tuberculosis, bovine and (rarely) human; brucellosis, bovine, porcine and caprine; salmonella infections; diphtheria; infectious hepatitis; poliomyelitis; Q fever; staphylococcal toxin poisoning; and milk sickness or "trembles."

Other diseases may, on occasion, be milk borne. There have been numerous outbreaks of diarrhea of undetermined etiology spread by milk. It is possible that some of these incidents are the result of a mixed flora of bacteria in extremely high numbers, and it is also conceivable that some are due to enteric viruses. These outbreaks have occurred most frequently in infants or young children. Leptospira, nocardiosis organisms and rabies viruses have been found in milk, although this is uncommon.

SOURCES OF MILK CONTAMINATION

Milk is contaminated by direct contact, through polluted water or by other agents such as flies. In some disease conditions the cow may be infected and become part of the cycle. Streptococci may be directly introduced into milk, but the usual course is for the cow to develop streptococcal mastitis from human contact and then pour myriads of cocci into the milk. It is almost certain that all extensive epidemics of streptococcal infection have been thus caused. Cattle may rarely be infected with human tubercle bacilli, but they are unlikely to excrete such bacilli in their milk. The milk may be contaminated by human excreta, which may be introduced into the milk by careless handling, carrying the tubercle bacilli, typhoid and other microorganisms along with it. Diphtheritic infection of the teats and udder has frequently occurred.

Rodents may introduce certain salmonella and the organisms of Haverhill fever. It is therefore important to protect milk supplies from contamination by mice and rats. Incidents have occurred in which paper cartons of milk ready for delivery and the caps from milk bottles in storage have been gnawed by mice or rats in their attempt to get the milk from the containers.

Incorrect storage temperatures may also result in large numbers of pathogens developing in milk or milk products.

Bovine tuberculosis was once a very important cause of severe and fatal human bone and joint disease as well as of pulmonary, meningeal and other types of tuberculosis. Cattle are subject to all three types of brucellosis, and milk from diseased cows has infected large numbers of human beings. In certain areas Q fever is a common bovine disease, with resulting heavy contamination of the milk. Milk sickness, or "trembles," is caused by the cow ingesting either the rayless goldenrod or snakeroot, both of which contain tremetol, which is secreted in the milk. This substance is poisonous to both animals and man and formerly caused numerous deaths in parts of the United States.

EPIDEMIOLOGY OF MILK-BORNE ILLNESS

Clinically, individual cases of disease which are transmitted through milk can in no way be distinguished from illness spread by other means. Epidemiologically, however, there may be differences which are obvious in some outbreaks and less so in others. Extensive milk-borne outbreaks tend to be more or less explosive in their onset with large numbers of persons being infected within the distribution area of the milk route within a few days' time. There also tends to be some variation in the age distribution of cases. This is sufficiently marked to be immediately obvious only in the case of streptococcal disease. In streptococcal milk-borne disease, whether with rash or without, there are relatively larger numbers of adults affected than there are under the ordinary method of contact spread. The reason for this is not obvious, but repeated experience has shown that attack rates are directly proportional to milk consumption and quite independent of age or sex. Thus, in any outbreak in which there is the simultaneous occurrence of large numbers of cases of streptococcal disease with a high proportion of adults infected, milk should be immediately considered as the likely vehicle of infection.

Most of the illness spread by fluid milk can also be effectively transmitted by milk products. Cream and ice cream from raw milk are fully as dangerous as the milk from which they come. Butter and cheese in various forms made from raw milk have frequently been implicated. Even powdered milk has caused disease, usually from contamination after dehydration. There are, however, indications that staphylococci may survive heating and dehydration and cause illness in those drinking reconstituted powdered milk.

PREVENTION OF MILK-BORNE ILLNESS

In theory, the prevention of milk-borne disease is relatively simple. From a practical standpoint it took many years of trial and error and research, together with much acrimonious discussion, for the development of the modern system of safe milk handling. If milk could be drawn from healthy cows, handled carefully by healthy men and packaged carefully before delivery to the consumer, there should be no milk-borne disease. This was the approach tried by the certified milk commissions. Certified milk might well be termed a noble experiment. Practically, however, it was found that on a large scale it was impossible consistently to deliver raw milk free of pathogens. There are many reasons for this; among them are the inherent difficulties in producing and handling milk, and the fact that milk is a good bacterial medium. The commercial instinct, moreover, repeatedly prevented the disposal of diseased cows and the destruction of dirty or mishandled milk. Human carriers or cases of disease among handlers are difficult of detection under practical conditions. Also, clean milk is not the full answer to preventing disease transmission.

There is a distinct possibility that clean milk is a better bacterial medium for pathogens than dirty milk, and it appears that clean milk was as often implicated in outbreaks of disease as was dirty milk. This seemed to be particularly true for the streptococcal diseases. The probable reason for this is that pathogens in a low count milk supply may have little competition from other types of organisms. Also, the growth of large numbers of nonpathogenic organisms, especially the lactic acid producers, lowers the pH to such an extent that the conditions for growth of the pathogens are not so ideal as in clean, low count milk, where they may multiply rapidly if incubation temperatures are eventually provided. It is probable that other waste materials from the growth of nonpathogens may discourage the growth of the disease producers, as well as develop acidity in the product. It is interesting to note that the literature contains very few instances where acid milk products, such as cultured buttermilk, sour cream, or cottage cheese, have been involved in the propagation of milk-borne disease.

PASTEURIZATION

Only one method has been demonstrated by long years of experience to be successful in controlling all types of milk-borne infection; this is pasteurization. Pasteurization consists of heating milk to a sufficient temperature and maintaining that heat for a long enough time to destroy pathogenic bacteria without appreciably altering the taste or appearance of the milk. The milk must further be kept free of contamination in a closed circuit from the time of heating until delivery to the consumer.

The first fully successful and satisfactory method of pasteurization consisted of placing milk in a large metal vat, heating it to a temperature of 143 to 145° F., holding at that heat for not less than 30 minutes and then cooling rapidly. More rapid methods of pasteurization were tried earlier and, because of mechanical difficulties, were not too successful. More recently, with the perfection of better automatic controls, the rapid methods of pasteurization are swiftly replacing the vat-holding method, especially in the larger installations. For some years, the standard time and temperature for rapid pasteurization has been set at 160° F. continuously for not less than 15 seconds. The milk is quickly brought to this temperature and then rapidly cooled. The milk is in continuous motion and this permits large quantities to be handled in a modestly sized plant. Machinery is now available which will allow even higher temperatures for shorter periods of time. Either the batch or so-called HTST (high-temperature, short-time) method of pasteurization has proven highly successful in preventing milk-borne disease. The organisms of Q fever, although greatly reduced in frequency by earlier pasteurizing temperatures and times, can survive in small numbers, but are reduced to the point at which they apparently do not cause disease. Recently, most milk-control agencies have changed their regulations by elevating the pasteurization temperature from 143 to 145° F. in the batch method and from 160 to 161° F. in the HTST method to be sure that the Q fever organisms are inactivated. All other common pathogens but staphylococcal toxin are destroyed by pasteurization as it has been prescribed for many years.

It is imperative that from the time of heating the milk be handled entirely in a closed circuit with no opportunity for recontamination by human hands or other means. This involves cooling automatically and capping mechanically. It is also necessary that all pasteurizing equipment shall be so designed that it can be disassembled and thoroughly cleaned to remove all deposits and be capable of being sterilized after reassembly and before the next batch of milk is run through.

The development of equipment meeting these requirements has required trial and error through the years, and its proper maintenance necessitates continuous vigilance by health departments. It is most important that the health department be certain all milk is adequately pasteurized. This involves repeated inspection of equipment to ascertain that it is working properly. One of the most obvious things for an inspector to observe is whether the plant is actually capable of processing the number of quarts of pasteurized milk that are being produced. In the early years it was repeatedly found that pasteurizing plants with a capacity of 1000 quarts a day were selling 2000 or 3000 quarts of milk per day.

Pasteurization has little effect on the nutritional value of milk. Vitamin C is reduced fractionally by the process, but since milk is not a good source of this vitamin the reduction is not of significance.

Tests on Pasteurized Milk

Phosphatase Test. In recent years, the phosphatase test has proven an invaluable tool in the determination of the safety of pasteurized milk. Phosphatase is a natural enzyme found in all milk which is inactivated at almost precisely the time and temperature required for pasteurization. Phosphatase or phosphomonoesterase is capable of hydrolyzing the monoesters of phosphoric acid. To test for the presence of phosphatase the sample of milk is incubated with a standard amount of buffered disodiumphenylphosphate solution. In the presence of phosphatase, free phenol is produced. The phenol can be detected in a cleared solution by a simple color test using Folin's or Gibb's reagent. The test is highly sensitive and will reveal as little as 1 part raw milk in 1000 parts of pasteurized milk. Milk found to contain the enzyme phosphatase has not been adequately pasteurized, or has been contaminated with raw milk. Therefore, the phosphatase test is routinely performed by health departments to test the efficiency of pasteurization.

The newer very high pasteurization temperatures have an adverse effect on the reliability of the phosphatase test. Positive tests may occur in milk adequately pasteurized at these temperatures. This also sometimes occurs in cream pasteurized at high temperature.

Coliform Test. Although pasteurization will destroy the organisms originating in the cow or added to the milk prior to pasteurization, any disease agents added subsequent to pasteurization may be fully as dangerous.

The coliform test in conjunction with pasteurized milk supplies is designed to reveal such recontamination. Normal pasteurizing temperatures destroy the coliform organisms so that if they again appear in the pasteurized product, the most probable answer is that the milk was recontaminated after the pasteurization process had been completed. Practically every department of health requires the application of this test to pasteurized milk supplies to guard against practices that result in such recontamination.

Standard Plate Count. This test is an estimation of the total viable bacterial population per milliliter of sample. Pasteurization will reduce the normal bacterial flora by 99+ per cent. However, raw milk for pasteurization having very high numbers of bacteria, thermoduric bacteria or other abnormal varieties, will still have high bacterial counts after pasteurization. A high standard plate count is normally associated with unclean milking practices, poor cooling and dirty equipment.

Tests on Prepasteurized Milk

Platform Tests. Odor, temperature and appearance are physical tests usually made on producers' milk at the receiving deck. The sediment test should be run on a monthly basis. These tests are readily made and are a time-saving screening technique to show which farms need inspection.

Tests for Abnormal Milk. The direct microscopic examination is a screening test providing information on the bacterial population and udder abnormalities. If, in the direct microscopic examination of milk, leukocytes are found that have engulfed bacteria, especially of the streptococcal variety, mastitis is almost certain to exist in the producing herd. Just what is an excess number of leukocytes in milk has been debated for years. The numbers of these cells in milk produced shortly after calving or near the end of the lactation period are considerably more than occur from normal udders in other stages of the lactation period. It is generally considered that a mixed milk supply with more than 500,000 leukocytes per milliliter of milk indicates that there may be udder infection in sufficient amount to require investigation. Such investigation normally should include a physical examination of the herd by a competent veterinarian. When treatment of infected animals is not effective, they are routed to slaughter or, if pure bred, may be segregated for breeding purposes only.

Other screening tests that may be used are the Modified Whiteside Test (MWT), the California Mastitis Test (CMT) and the Catalase Test (CT). These are relatively simple chemical tests which detect the presence of abnormal numbers of leukocytes in milk.

These tests can profitably replace the routine herd physical examinations for mastitis detection and help to direct attention to the dairy farms having animal health problems.

Tests for Antibiotics and Pesticides. The treatment of animal diseases with antibiotics may result in trace amounts appearing in the milk supply. Some individuals are sensitive to antibiotics and may experience an allergic reaction from their presence in milk. Pesticides have been demonstrated in milk following the consumption of contaminated feed or water. Since pesticides may be dangerous to human health, and particularly since their long-term effects have not yet been adequately determined, it is important to exclude these chemicals from the milk supply.

In view of the hazards associated with antibiotics and pesticides in the human diet, it is necessary to maintain surveillance of the presence and amounts of these chemicals in milk as well as in food and water supplies.

MAINTENANCE OF HEALTHY CATTLE

Attention should be paid to the health of cattle. In the case of two chronic diseases, tuberculosis and brucellosis, routine testing with the elimination of positive reactors is of great value.

Bovine tuberculosis, once widely prevalent, has now been largely eliminated in many areas of the country. The conquest of bovine tuberculosis in this country was a remarkable achievement. It was accomplished by nationwide tuberculin testing of herds and the slaughter of reacting animals.

Brucellosis in cattle, widely distributed in this country and of considerable economic importance, can also be controlled through a program of testing and slaughter, particularly if combined with calfhood immunization. Brucellosis in cattle can be readily detected by means of a serum agglutination test. A simple but highly sensitive colored ring test on milk has been developed which makes it possible to screen whole herds quickly by means of a single examination, eliminating the need for blood testing on ring-test negative herds. The ring test depends on the presence of brucella agglutinins in whole milk. Calfhood vaccination is accomplished between the ages of 4 and 8 months, using a special living strain of *Brucella abortus*. This leads to good protection, and a significant agglutinin titer does not usually persist long enough to interfere with testing when the animal reaches maturity.

Treatment of udder infection (mastitis) by infusion of antibiotic materials has proven very effective in recent years. Many animals so treated have been returned to a normal healthy condition and their useful milk production life extended. Treatment of udders in this way presents some problems. Unless milk from an animal so treated is discarded until all of the antibiotic has been eliminated, small traces will reach the consuming public and may cause reactions in sensitive individuals. If milk containing penicillin preparations from treated animals is used to make cheese, it is found that the curd of such milk cannot be precipitated due to the growth-inhibiting effect of the antibiotic on the acid-producing bacteria. Resulting economic losses may be considerable.

DAIRY FARM SANITATION

In the production of satisfactory milk it is necessary to require all dairy farms to have a clean and adequate supply of water. Farmers must also hold the fly population under control, use clean milking methods, keep the milking equipment clean and maintain the cattle in a healthy and clean condition. It is necessary to cool milk promptly and thoroughly after milking and hold it at a low temperature until delivered to the pasteurizing plant.

In recent years, the development of many new production methods and of new types of milk-handling equipment for use on dairy farms has played a major role in the improvement of prepasteurized milk supplies. Although there is still considerable room for improvement, much of the prepasteurized milk delivered to pasteurizing plants today is of considerably better sanitary quality than such milk was formerly. Dairy herds are, because of economic pressures, increasing in size. The small dairyman is finding it increasingly difficult to operate profitably because of increased labor and equipment costs. The dairymen of today, therefore, tend to be more efficient and better informed. With increased labor costs have come needs for new equipment that will permit reduction in the expense of operating personnel.

To meet current needs, equipment manufacturers have developed the bulk milk farm coolers and pipeline milking machines. These machines, however, have resulted in additional problems for the health departments. Since cleanliness of equipment is of major importance, the design of these machines must be passed upon by the inspection personnel. Once the design and method of cleaning are accepted, the net result is an improved prepasteurized milk supply from the standpoint of sanitary quality. The bulk farm cooler and the pipeline milker properly maintained have inherent characteristics that tend to facilitate the production of clean milk with a low bacterial count.

The Bulk Farm Cooler

A bulk farm cooler is a milk storage tank of sanitary design provided with built-in refrigeration facilities. It may be obtained in different sizes to fit the milk production capacity of any dairy farm. Previously, the small dairyman operated with cooling systems that were primitive, such as suspending the cans of milk in a dug well or an open spring. The temperature of the cooling medium was, in many instances, not much below the temperature at which the milk was required by regulation to be cooled. It was even possible, in many installations, to flood the cans with the cooling water, and such cooling water was not always of sanitary quality. Later, the development of mechanically cooled wet storage boxes improved the situation considerably. The bulk farm cooler, so-called cold wall tank or refrigerated bulk milk storage tank, was another big step forward. Milk stored in these tanks of proper design is quickly cooled to a low temperature (38 to 40° F.), effectively inhibiting bacterial growth. These bulk coolers are also tightly covered, which prevents the entrance of extraneous materials as well as preventing the farmstead's cat and dog population from helping themselves to the uncovered milk can or milk pail. Further, the need of cans is eliminated since the milk is collected from each of the producing farms in large tank trucks properly designed and effectively sanitized, that add little to the bacterial population. Milk cans have always been a source of contamination since the cans themselves are often of poor construction, with open seams which make cleaning very difficult. The elimination of the milk can also obviates the need for can-washing and receiving room equipment at the processing plant. This further saves on investment in labor and equipment. The cleaning of a bulk cold wall tank is more effective than the cleaning of several milk cans. The net result, therefore, is an improved product at a reduced cost.

The Pipeline Milker

The pipeline milker is, as the name implies, a mechanical milking machine connected by sanitary piping to the farm milk storage system— preferably a bulk farm cooler.

The use of pipeline milking equipment also reduces the possibility of contamination of the milk on the farm, since the milk is in a closed system of piping from the animal to the bulk milk cooler. Such milk is not exposed to the environment of the cow stable and is protected from flies, dust and other stable contaminants. This apparatus must be designed so that it is suitable for the purpose intended and constructed so that it can be easily and effectively cleaned. To save labor, methods for cleaning the pipelines without complete disassembly have been developed. Pipelines which may be in lengths of 500 feet or more cannot be brush washed without taking them apart. Suitable detergents flowing at rapid velocities will do an effective job of cleaning if the pipelines are properly constructed. By trial and error methods, with considerable research by the agricultural colleges, by the industry and by health department personnel, methods have been developed that are doing the cleaning-in-place job effectively.

INFANT FORMULA CONTROL

Diarrhea of the newborn, responsible for many deaths in hospital nurseries, has been associated with poor sanitation in formula preparation rooms. The knowledge and techniques successful in milk sanitation can be applied to hospital formula preparation. The same is true of companies preparing infant formula on a commercial basis. A new development is the mass production of sterilized infant formulas which are distributed to hospitals, grocery stores and supermarkets. In addition to having a long shelf-life, the sterilized formula is placed in single service containers, thereby eliminating the problems associated with the preparation, handling, cleansing and sterilization of bottles and nipples in the home and hospital.

ROLE OF THE HEALTH DEPARTMENT

The policing of the herd's health and the attention to dairy farm sanitation, while of minor public health importance as compared with pasteurization, are essential in order to produce satisfactory as well as safe milk. Long experience has shown that without competent supervision, milk becomes a dirty and contaminated product. Without a system of inspection, anything that is white and fluid will be sold as milk, regardless of its content of pus, manure, water, antibiotics, pesticides, or other extraneous matter. The collective needs and desires of the public weigh as nothing against the commercial pressures on farmers and dealers, unless such needs and desires are implemented by a competent health department. The health department, to be effective, must be adequately staffed with inspection personnel. Professional training and experience are essential in maintaining adequate supervision of milk production and processing. This is even more true today, with complicated mechanization both on the farm and in the processing plant, than in earlier years.

New developments in processing equipment have kept pace with or exceeded the mechanization of the producing farm. Although the previously mentioned pasteurization processes have effectively controlled milk-borne diseases, the industry continues to develop new methods. Currently, new types of ultrahigh temperature pasteurizers are being offered that will further increase the efficiency of milk pasteurization and also reduce labor costs. Ultrahigh temperature, UHT, pasteurization is the heating of milk to 190 to 270° F. with holding times shorter than 2 seconds. UHT pasteurization will require the development of sufficiently sensitive control systems and flow-diversion valves. It will require suitable field-testing procedures, and experiments with milk seeded with actual pathogens, or organisms equivalent in heat resistance, before health departments can accept these new processes. Proposed changes in equipment and processing methods require the continuous attention of health departments. Health departments, therefore, must maintain a staff of well trained, experienced milk sanitation experts to control the complicated processes and to test the new techniques used all the way from production to consumption of milk and milk products.

ROLE OF THE DAIRY INDUSTRY

Many health departments are moving to place greater responsibility upon the industry for policing its own product, especially in the production and handling of the milk on dairy farms. This will, of course, allow health department personnel to spend a greater portion of their time on the pasteurizing plants' operations, where the most effective public health work can be performed. There must be continuing supervision by health departments of milk production, but routine farm inspection can well be borne by the industry itself. The milk control program should be based on adequate rules and regulations and enforced by technically sound inspection and supervision procedures. Continuous effort leading to the substitution of pasteurized for raw milk must be exerted to provide a safe and clean milk supply for all people.

ROLE OF THE FAMILY PHYSICIAN

The family physician has a central part to play in the prevention and control of milk-borne illness. He may be the first to see evidence of illness due to a breakdown in the system of safeguarding milk, and by prompt reporting will give the health department an opportunity to initiate an investigation. His is an authoritative voice in developing and maintaining community awareness of the continuing need for pasteurization of milk and milk products, and of effective health department supervision and inspection.

HOLLIS S. INGRAHAM, M.D., M.P.H.
CLAUDE H. COLVIN, B.S.
JOSEPH A. SALVATO, P.E.

REFERENCES

1. North, C. E.: Commercial Pasteurization. Public Health Bulletin No. 147. Washington, D.C., Superintendent of Documents, 1925.
2. Hull, T. G.: Diseases Transmitted from Animals to Man. Ed. 4. Springfield, Ill., Charles C Thomas, 1955.
3. Standard Methods for the Examination of Dairy Products. Ed. 11. American Public Health Association, 1790 Broadway, New York, 1960.
4. Stebbins, Ernest L., Ingraham, Hollis S., and Reed, Elizabeth A.: Milk-borne streptococcic infections. American Journal of Public Health, 27:1259-66, 1937.
5. Armigo, R., et al.: Food poisoning outbreaks associated with spray-dried milk—An epidemiological study. American Journal of Public Health, 47:1093, 1957.
6. World Health Organization: Milk Hygiene. New York, Columbia University Press. International Document Service, 1962.

8   Food-borne Illness

Food poisoning is a general term, including some illnesses for which the natural history is not well known. The features which are common to all of them are a food-borne route of transmission for the etiologic agent, an acute onset of gastrointestinal symptoms and relatively short incubation period following the ingestion of a food containing the deleterious substance. It includes food infection and food intoxication.

The food poisoning syndrome of nausea, vomiting and diarrhea is part of every physician's daily practice. Diagnostic signs and symptoms may also include fever, sweating, muscle pain, skin eruptions, edema around the eyes, dizziness, headache, disturbances of vision and even coma. The differential diagnosis includes a wide variety of illnesses unrelated to food poisoning. The alert practitioner of preventive medicine must take an adequate history of his patient's food and drink ingestion to avoid missing the diagnosis of food poisoning. On the other hand, he should not overlook the possibility of mistaking the symptoms of such entities as carbon monoxide poisoning for food poisoning.

The history should not be confined to the obvious items, such as the consumption of foods of an unwholesome nature or foods obviously contaminated with disease-producing substances. There should be an appreciation that there is no sharp borderline between food, food adulterant and drug. Some foods have specific effects depending on quality and quantity. Figs are food but are prescribed as mild purgatives. Citrus fruit is a common breakfast item and also a specific for scurvy. The diagnostician must be alert to the effects of food on his patient in terms of quantity, methods of handling food and individual idiosyncrasies. He must have a knowledge of the more common clinical manifestations associated with known food poisoning agents. If he has this basic understanding, it is possible to make early presumptive etiologic diagnoses, to intelligently select food and laboratory tests for confirmation and to plan immediate treatment of his patient.

Knowledge of the natural history of the known food poisons enables the physician to instruct the patient on how he can avoid future episodes of poisoning. In the case of an outbreak, preventive measures can be instituted to prevent recurrences. This is an important part of preventive medicine since food poisoning is easier to avoid than to treat.

The practice of preventive medicine based on clinical observation and knowledge also needs to be supplemented by clinical research, since not all causes of food poisoning are known, and by better reporting of illnesses which might be due to food poisoning.

The history of food-borne disease is replete with instances of individual practitioners making significant contributions based on careful observations. William Budd (1811-1880), a country practitioner, elucidated the epidemiology of typhoid. George Baker (1767), confronted with "endemial colic in Devonshire," took accurate food and drink ingestion histories. He found the cause to be the lead content in cider which had been stored in lead cisterns or prepared in presses covered with lead. A more recent example of original investigation initiated by a private physician is the description of nicotinic acid poisoning caused by the ingestion of hamburger and producing similar symptoms in two separate families.[1] The cause was a proprietary preparation containing nicotinic acid and sold to meat markets to preserve the red coloration of ground meat.

This type of clinical research depends on the development of careful individual case histories. These case histories may reveal a number of common factors which will lead to the discovery of a previously unknown cause of disease.

Small outbreaks of gastrointestinal disease occurring in family groups quite often come to the attention of the family physician. The most distinctive characteristic, if such an outbreak has been caused by food poisoning, is the sudden illness of several persons following the ingestion of a common dietary item. This may occur at a common meal, or a common food may be ingested at different times or in different places. In searching for the cause, the investigator must not be misled by the fact that some individuals who have eaten the suspected item are not made ill. Nor should he be misled by his observation that some persons in the group who are ill did not eat the suspected food. This may be the result of psychological factors, individual resistance or the quantity of other foods eaten. The discovery of the causative relationship depends on carefully interviewing persons who are not ill, as well as those who are. If the suspected food caused the illness, the majority of those not eating the item will not be ill. The physician may find that demonstrating the statistical validity of his tentative conclusion is of little value in a small outbreak, since a larger number of observations are usually necessary for most statistical tests. Nevertheless, by looking for the presence or absence of such association, on the basis of attack rates, valuable leads may be obtained and many possible causes may be eliminated as unworthy of further investigation.[15]

To confirm the physician's suspicions, foods should undergo laboratory examination. But, frequently, if the physician compares his experience with that of his colleagues he may find that they are having similar episodes in their practices. The local health officer may also have useful information concerning episodes of a similar nature which have occurred in the area. The information obtained from these other sources may enable the physician to make more reliable inferences about specific causes. The search for epidemiologic case information frequently provides more clues as to causative factors than will be obtained by the laboratory examination of food specimens. The results of bacteriological and chemical examinations are sometimes equivocal or fruitless. Laboratory results should be used to confirm or rule out suspicions developed on the basis of the epidemiological information.

The more common use of processed packaged food including frozen dinners has increased the potential food poisoning hazard to individuals and small groups consuming such foods. The general practitioner is in a position to detect such isolated episodes and report them to the health department for determination of possible causal relationship with other apparently isolated incidents. Table 6 shows what has been happening in England and

Table 6. *Food Poisoning in England and Wales, 1949-1960*[*]

YEAR	ALL INCIDENTS	GENERAL OUTBREAKS		FAMILY OUTBREAKS		SPORADIC CASES	
		NUMBER	PERCENTAGE OF TOTAL	NUMBER	PERCENTAGE OF TOTAL	NUMBER	PERCENTAGE OF TOTAL
1949	2428	410	17	265	11	1753	72
1950	3977	538	14	452	11	2987	75
1951	3345	343	10	285	9	2717	81
1952	3518	371	10	340	10	2807	80
1953	5277	492	9	422	8	4363	83
1954	6014	504	8	630	11	4880	81
1955	8957	609	7	722	8	7626	85
1956	7710	560	7	616	8	6534	85
1957	7070	473	7	500	7	6097	86
1958	7300	285	4	601	8	6414	88
1959	7846	295	4	666	8	6885	88
1960	6427	261	4	616	10	5550	86
	69,869	5141	7	6115	9	58,613	84

[*] Number of incidents reported annually, excluding chemical outbreaks.

Wales during the years 1949 to 1960, where the reporting system is considered good.[16] An increase in the number of family related outbreaks and in the number of unrelated sporadic cases can also be expected in those countries where convenience foods are popular.

There are many disease-producing substances which are food-borne. They can be classified in three groups on the basis of their mode of action on the host. Salmonella, *Streptococcus faecalis* and some other bacteria are agents which produce food poisoning by infection, invading and multiplying in the host. Certain staphylococci and *Clostridia botulinum* produce toxins in food which produce toxemias when ingested. Included in the third group are the naturally occurring toxic substances in plants or animal life, which are usually consumed in ignorance, and chemical poisons, such as arsenic and fluorides, which are introduced into foods accidentally.

FOOD POISONING PRODUCED BY INFECTION

SALMONELLOSIS

Salmonellosis as a cause of food poisoning is a term applied to human infection by a large group of serologically similar species and types of bacteria which are capable of being propagated and transmitted in food. The human disease is produced by infection, which distinguishes it from staphylococcal food poisoning and botulism, both of which are due to toxemias. The salmonellae are classified on the basis of morphology, nutritional requirements and serological characteristics. The commonest species incriminated in food poisoning is the *Salmonella typhimurium*, although others such as *Salmonella enteritidis* are also common.

The clinical picture of salmonellosis is similar to that seen in staphylococcal disease, except for two features which are of great value in differential diagnosis. The onset for the majority of food-borne salmonellosis cases is about 12 hours after ingestion of the food, with a range of from 4 to 48 hours occurring in a few cases. This compares with a mean incubation period for staphylococcal poisoning of 3 hours. The other distinguishing feature is that salmonellosis is a febrile disease, whereas staphylococcal poisoning is characteristically afebrile.

Salmonellosis starts with the sudden onset of nausea, vomiting, diarrhea, chills and fever. The diarrhea tends to be copious, foul smelling and may cause severe dehydration, weight loss and oliguria. The stools frequently contain mucus and occasionally blood. Physical examination may reveal nothing but signs of dehydration. A pure culture may be obtained from the stool during the acute illness. Recovery takes place in 48 hours in mild cases, but the disease may last 8 to 10 days in severe cases.

The acute gastroenteritic form associated with food poisoning is probably the result of the ingestion of large numbers of salmonella, the symptoms being produced by an endotoxin as well as infection. The typhoid type has an incubation period of from 3 to 10 days, with fever the most prominent feature. Fever may not be followed by the triad of nausea, vomiting and diarrhea. The typhoid variety of salmonellosis is usually not associated with the food route of transmission. Food may serve as a vehicle of transmission but propagation in food has not taken place; it has been acquired by more direct contact with a carrier or other primary source.

The sources of salmonella are human carriers, clinical cases, fowl, or domestic animals used as pets or food sources. Salmonella have been isolated from the intestinal tracts of cats, dogs, poultry, swine, cattle and rodents. They have been isolated from fresh and dried poultry eggs. However, many of these sources which have been bacteriologically identified are not necessarily effective sources. The demonstrated sources which should be considered are clinical cases and carriers who handle food and those meat or poultry products which are eaten without being cooked to the thermal death point of salmonella.

When the physician is confronted with a group of suspected food-borne salmonellosis cases, the best proof of a common food cause of the epidemic is the finding of the same species, serotype and phage-type salmonella in the food consumed and in the patients' stools.[2] This proof is hard to obtain in practice since samples of food are not always available. The investigator must rely on histories of food intake and time of onset of symptoms in all members of the group eating the suspect foods. Association of illness with the consumption of one particular food will provide circumstantial evidence of the cause.

The isolated case of salmonellosis of the typhoid type is not properly a case of food poisoning, even though a food route of transmission may be suspected. The typhoid type of case, diagnosed on the basis of fever and vague general symptoms plus isolation of salmonella in the stool, should prompt the physician to search for a carrier or case among the household and family contacts. The physician who takes the trouble to survey family contacts by taking stool specimens for examination is frequently rewarded with the discovery of a carrier source.

Prevention of salmonellosis outbreaks is best accomplished by instructing food handlers how to cook and refrigerate food properly. The present food-handling and cooking practices in the United States seem to be effective in preventing large salmonellosis outbreaks, but the number of reported individual cases and small outbreaks occurring sporadically is quite large, and many more undiagnosed cases probably occur.

The elimination of salmonella from foods sold for human consumption by the manufacturer or distributor is difficult. Most meat and poultry inspection service is designed to prevent the sale of obviously diseased meat or to control sanitary conditions in abattoirs. In spite of these efforts, the salmonella group is frequently found in food purchased for the table. The practicing physician should impress on his patients the necessity of maintaining the line of defense in the kitchen—adequate cooking. Cooking procedures which reach 162° F. for at least 2 minutes throughout the food item will destroy salmonella.

Streptococcus Faecalis

Streptococcus faecalis has been incriminated as a cause of food poisoning. Nausea, vomiting, diarrhea and colicky pain occur 4 to 5 hours after eating. The slightly longer incubation period and bacteriologic findings are the major features which distinguish the *Streptococcus faecalis* outbreak from the staphylococcal enterotoxin outbreak.

Other Bacteria

Bacillus cereus, Proteus vulgaris, Escherichia coli, and the paracolon group of organisms are associated with outbreaks of food poisoning, but evidence of their causative role is not conclusive.[3] Large numbers of microorganisms seem to be required to produce symptoms. Paracolon organisms of the Arizona group have been classified and identified as being pathogenic for animals.

FOOD POISONING PRODUCED BY TOXEMIAS

Staphylococcal Enterotoxin Poisoning

Staphylococcal food poisoning is probably the most common form of food poisoning that will confront the practitioner.[4] It is caused by the ingestion of an enterotoxin produced by alpha and beta hemolytic staphylococci growing in foods.

Clinically, the picture is quite variable, depending on the dosage of toxin ingested and host resistance factors. The usual picture is a sudden onset of nausea, vomiting, diarrhea and cramps about 3 hours after the ingestion of food containing the enterotoxin. In some cases the incubation period is as long as 6 hours but it may be as short as ½ hour. In mild cases there may be only slight abdominal discomfort or nausea. Severe cases may have mucus and blood in the stools and experience collapse. Almost all cases are afebrile, but the more severe cases may experience either a rise in temperature or subnormal temperatures acompanied by decreased pulse rate and blood pressure.

Staphylococci capable of producing enterotoxin are ubiquitous, and laboratory proof of the presence of enterotoxin in suspected foods is difficult to obtain. Human volunteers or laboratory animals may be utilized, but give equivocal results. Frequently, all of the suspected foods have been eaten or are otherwise unobtainable. Agar diffusion tests for the identification of enterotoxins may prove of value.[5]

In spite of the limitations of laboratory testing, the physician can develop circumstantial evidence of etiology if he knows the natural history of enterotoxin production. The enterotoxin-producing staphylococci are always available for inadvertent food inoculation. They are frequently present in nasal discharges, skin lesions and on the hands of food handlers. They grow well in most foods except those which have a low pH. Many foods, including ham, chicken, sausage, potato salad, custard, turkey, gravy, dried skim milk, ice cream, cheese made from raw milk, and beef, have been incriminated. Since the first two conditions—source of organisms and culture media—are so frequently available, the clinician may find it more fruitful to query the patient about the time and temperature conditions of food handling, factors which are important for enterotoxin production. If prepared contaminated food is unrefrigerated, the period of time required for enterotoxin production may be as short as 5 hours, depending on how close the room temperature is to the optimum staphylococcal growth temperature of 82.4 to 98.6° F. If food is heated and the thermal death point for the organism is not reached, incubation temperatures, which considerably shorten the period of time necessary for enterotoxin production, may be produced in the center of larger food masses. The likelihood of a food being a toxic source depends primarily on how it has been handled.

The prevention of staphylococcal enterotoxin outbreaks depends on the elimination of the abuses in food handling, that cause the production of enterotoxin. In most situations, the initial dosing of food with staphylococci cannot be eliminated, but it can be minimized. The patient can be advised to wash his hands before preparing foods, and to abstain from food handling when lesions are present on the hands or other exposed skin surfaces. The most important measure is to impress on the family and in food service establishments, especially on the owner or manager, the necessity of refrigerating prepared foods and the need to use adequate heat for a sufficient period of time in preparation since the toxin is not destroyed by the usual warming of foods.

This disease is frequently associated with group eating of foods prepared at multiple points and transported by amateur cooks or food handlers. The egg salad sandwiches eaten at a picnic may have been transported in a warm car trunk. The covered dish supper or the banquet in a commercial eating establishment which overtaxes the refrigeration facilities are both typical social settings for the staphylococcal outbreak. Most of these group activities are characterized by: (1) a lack of adequate refrigeration facilities, (2) persons preparing foods in larger quantities than they are accustomed to handling, and (3) inexperience in the methods of protecting food during transportation from the place of preparation to the place of consumption.

The treatment of staphylococcal food poisoning is supportive. No specific drug or serum therapy is of value. In most cases, the disease is self-limited. If the patient is dehydrated or debilitated, the treatment is directed at the complication rather than the enterotoxin. Prevention of occurrence is the best medical management.

Clostridium welchii FOOD POISONING

Certain strains of *Clostridium perfringens* (*Cl. welchii*) are common causes of food poisoning where detection is attempted and results are reported. Since *Clostridium perfringens* is widely distributed, being found in human, animal and fly feces, on cutting boards and raw meat, and in soil dust and clothing, the organism can be assumed to be present in almost all kitchens. It is a spore-former which is resistant to heat and withstands boiling and normal cooking. The symptoms of the illness include abdominal pains, diarrhea, nausea, but seldom vomiting. It is explosive but there is rapid recovery. The incubation period is 12 to 20 hours, with an average of 15 hours. To prevent the illness prepared foods should be cooled within 1½ hours, which would require that meat cuts be limited to 6 pounds or less, refrigerated immediately or held at a temperature above 140° F. until served. Foods should never be allowed to cool slowly overnight at room temperature.

BOTULISM

Botulism is a severe neurologic disease caused by ingesting neurotoxin produced by the growth of *Clostridium botulinum* in underprocessed preserved foods or improperly packaged foods. Modern commercial food processing is capable of eliminating the heat-resistant botulinum spores in foods. As a consequence, the disease is no longer common, but every physician should be familiar with this entity. The most serious food-poisoning sources of toxin at present are anaerobically packaged low acid foods with high protein content, such as meat, beans and fish. Home-canned food, even low protein foods, and nonsterile foods in plastic anaerobic packages should be suspect. The most recently reported deaths from botulism have been caused by the eating of improperly tinned tuna fish and smoked fish packaged and marketed in anaerobic plastic containers without benefit of refrigeration.

The typical symptoms of botulism appear within 12 to 36 hours. The incubation period may be as short as 4 hours or as long as 3 days, depending on dosage and conditions of eating. The patient is afebrile in the absence of complications such as bronchopneumonia. Epigastric distress and burning may be present, accompanied by constipation following an initial period of slight diarrhea. Neurologic signs consist of disturbances of vision as a result of paralysis of extraocular muscles producing diplopia, mydriasis, blepharoptosis and loss of reflex to light stimulation. Other cranial nerve involvements produce difficulty in swallowing, speech impairment and, in severe cases, regurgitation of fluids through the nose and paralysis of neck muscles causing drooping of the head. Once the typical neurotoxic symptoms appear, the patient is likely to die. Death occurs within 3 to 7 days in about two-thirds of the patients as the result of cardiac and respiratory paralysis.

To prevent the occurrence of this disease, the practicing physician should concern himself with educating housewives and others involved with home canning of foods. They should be instructed not to take chances with food from home-packed jars or anaerobically packaged nonsterile foods. The absence of signs of spoilage cannot be relied upon as a safety guarantee. The concentration of toxin may be high enough to produce disease in the housewife who even tastes a small amount of the supernatant liquor from the jar before cooking. Spoilage and toxin production may be accompanied by leakage over the rubber ring, by gas formation or by the presence of a rancid musty smell. Since the neurotoxin is destructible by heating, home-canned foods should always be mixed thoroughly and boiled for at least 5 minutes.

FOOD POISONING FROM NATURAL SUBSTANCES AND CHEMICALS

PLANT AND ANIMAL FOOD POISONS

The differential diagnosis of the food-poisoning outbreak includes the specific effects of toxic animal and plant foods. Most of the commonly incriminated foods are not available commercially. A history of amateur gathering of unusual foods should suggest the possibility of food poisoning. The amateur mushroom picker is the prototype. Mussels, noncommercial varieties of fish, wild carrots or water hemlock, rhubarb leaves, fava beans and tung nuts are toxic foods which can also produce poisoning.

Mushroom Poisoning

Mycetism, or mushroom poisoning, occurs often enough to constitute a distinct public health hazard. Amateur mycophagy is a common practice among persons of recent European extraction, particularly among Slavic peoples. There is no uniform agreement among expert mycologists as to the toxicity of certain varieties of mushrooms. What is identified as an edible variety by European experts will frequently be labeled as poisonous by American mycologists. This may be a reflection of habitat or other ecological variations, which make a single species toxic in one area and nontoxic in another.

An example is the *Gyromitra esculenta* mushroom which is eaten in Russia but has been the cause of illness in this country.[6] Confusion as to the edibility of mushrooms does not deter the mycophagist, who will frequently gather mushrooms in this country on the basis of experience gained halfway around the world and then invite his friends to share the risks of a wild mushroom meal.

There are three types of toxins found in mushrooms: muscarine, the hepatotoxins and the hemolysins. These toxins may be present singly or in combination. All three are found in the commonly involved Amanita genus.[7] There is no single test for the identification of edible or poison mushrooms other than expert botanical knowledge which includes attention to such details as microscopic spore examination. Rarely, commercial mushroom beds will be invaded by a toxic species resembling the commercial variety, *Agaricus campestris*. A history of the ingestion of mushrooms from any source preceding the onset of gastrointestinal symptoms in a group of persons should alert the investigator to the possibility of mycetism.

Symptoms often appear within 15 minutes after eating. Even when toxin absorption is delayed, this interval is seldom longer than 3 hours. The incubation period in most cases is longer than that in chemical food poisoning, but shorter than that in staphylococcal enterotoxin poisoning. The muscarine effect produces salivation, excessive perspiration, tearing, nausea and increased intestinal movement. Hepatotoxins may produce central necrosis of the liver and signs of liver failure. Choreiform symptoms may also be present.

The treatment of mycetism should consist of induced emesis or gastric lavage with the concomitant administration of subcutaneous atropine as a specific antidote to muscarine. There are no readily available specific remedies. Supportive treatment of liver failure should be the same as that used for any other form of acute hepatitis.

Water Hemlock Poisoning

Water hemlock poisoning occurs when the *Cicuta maculata* is mistaken for wild white parsnips or carrots, usually by children. Gompertz has described a typical outbreak and reviews the literature.[8]

Symptoms occur within 30 minutes. Nausea and vomiting are followed by convulsions. Twitching of the eyes and facial muscles, dilated pupils and cyanosis sometimes appear. The treatment consists of gastric lavage and large doses of atropine.

Snakeroot Poisoning

Snakeroot poisoning, or milk poisoning, occurs from ingesting the milk of cows which have eaten the leaves of the white snakeroot (*Eupatorium urticaefolium*), a common weed in the central United States. The active principle is tremetol, an unsaturated alcohol found in many native uncultivated plants in the United States. Other plants which contain tremetol include deerwort, rayless goldenrod, witchweed and squawweed.

Ingestion of contaminated milk causes weakness, vomiting and abdominal distress. The urine and breath may have an acetone odor. Pasteurization does not inactivate the toxin. The onset is gradual, with the gastrointestinal symptoms developing 24 to 36 hours after ingestion.

The treatment consists of the administration of sodium bicarbonate by mouth followed by gastric lavage, magnesium sulfate, 30 gm., by mouth and 500 to 1000 ml. of 5 per cent glucose in saline intravenously.

Convalescence is slow and the mortality rate is 50 per cent.[9]

Fish and Mussel Poisoning

Fish and mussel poisonings are almost exclusively confined to persons who gather these foods on an amateur basis.

Mussel poisoning has caused large epidemics in the San Francisco coastal area and in the Bay of Fundy area in eastern North America. Rarely is a commercial variety involved, since commercial supplies are routinely tested for the presence of the toxin and strict controls are maintained. The toxin has been isolated from plankton on which shell fish feed. The presence in mussels of the heat stabile toxin, which belongs to the same class of alkaloids as strychnine and muscarine, follows a seasonal pattern. It is present in the late summer and fall on the East Coast. On the West Coast, mussel-poisoning epidemics have been reported from the middle of May to the end of October.

The poisonous qualities of fish seem to be related to feeding habits, since species are frequently poisonous only at certain times of the year. Several species of shark, roe from fresh water minnows, members of the genera Euthynnus and Katsuwonus and the Moray eel (Gymnothorax) have been incriminated. However, much more information is needed about the distribution and identification of toxic fish. As a general rule, fish which are common commercial varieties are safe for human consumption.

The symptomatology of fish and mussel poisoning are similar. Seasonal variation and a common clinical picture lend support to the proposition that plankton food sources are the common causative agent.

The symptoms occur within 5 to 30 minutes. Nausea, vomiting, numbness and a prickling sensation about the mouth appear early, followed by abdominal cramps, muscle weakness and paralysis. In fatal cases respiratory paralysis occurs.

The emergency treatment consists of induced emesis and gastric lavage if persistent vomiting has not already occurred. Apomorphine as an emetic should be given carefully and only once since it may aggravate respiratory depression. Magnesium sulfate or another purgative may be administered. Since death occurs from respiratory paralysis, the administration of oxygen and the use of a respirator may be lifesaving if continued until recovery from paralysis has taken place.

CHEMICAL FOOD POISONING

Food poisoning from the ingestion of chemicals usually results from the accidental contamination of food with cleaning and insecticidal preparations. The more common examples are sodium fluoride and arsenic in insecticides and cyanide-containing silver polishes. Lead, in cooking vessel solder, copper vessels or tubing and cadmium plating in contact with acid foods have also been incriminated.

The physician should think of chemical food poisoning if a group of persons becomes ill a half hour after eating. The lapse of time between ingestion and onset of symptoms may vary from 10 to 30 minutes. In rare instances, the incubation period may be as long as 2 hours. If the dosage is large, symptoms of gastroenteritis will be present, with nausea and vomiting more prominent than diarrhea. Other symptoms vary with the type of chemical ingested. Antimony poisoning produces vomiting within a few minutes. Arsenic acts within 10 to 20 minutes, with vomiting and painful but ineffectual efforts to defecate. Heavy metal poisoning should be suspected when patients give a common history of metallic taste and salivation.

The prevention of chemical food poisoning is based on an awareness of potentially toxic substances in common household use. The number of chemical preparations used increases daily, and labels often do not carry a chemical description of the active ingredients. When the physician suspects a particular chemical contaminant in food he may need immediate expert toxicological advice. In many states, the health departments maintain Poison Information Control Centers at strategic points. The centers operate on a 24-hour basis and provide up-to-date information on the chemical com-

Table 7. *Chemical Poisons Reported as Causing Food Poisoning and Their Common Source*

ACTIVE PRINCIPLE	SOURCE INCRIMINATED
Antimony	Occasionally used in the preparation of inexpensive cooking vessels.
Arsenic	Insecticides, fruit sprays, rodenticides.
Cadmium	Cadmium plated vessels in which acid food or drink is served.
Copper	Carbonated water back flow into copper tubing and acid foods or liquids stored in copper pots.
Cyanide	Food accidentally contaminated with silver polish containing cyanide.
Fluorides	Sodium fluoride used for insecticidal purposes, mistaken for baking powder.
Lead	Lead-containing cooking vessels and pipes, lead-containing solders, lead arsenate used as a fruit spray.
Nicotinic acid	Preparations added to raw meat to preserve red color.
Nitrates	Usually in well water, producing methemoglobinemia, particularly in infants. Water content above 0.04 gm. of nitrate per liter.
Zinc	Acid foods, such as apples, cooked in galvanized iron containers.

position of common household articles and recommended antidotes. Such centers on a nationwide basis are of great service to the medical profession.

The treatment of chemical food poisoning should be specific if the active principle is known. In the absence of such information, general supportive measures including induced emesis or gastric washing should be carried out immediately.

TRICHINOSIS

Outbreaks of acute trichinosis may resemble food poisoning. In the acute phase the patient will show diarrhea, nausea and vomiting. During the invasive stage, the larvae cause considerable irritation of the intestinal mucosa. When gastroenteritis follows the ingestion of a meal of pork, bear or other meat from an omnivorous or garbage-eating animal the physician should suspect trichinosis. Other features of this disease are described in the chapter on parasitic diseases, page 258.

Families involved in these outbreaks uniformly state that they have adequately cooked the meal. The investigator should inquire into the actual details of cooking and form his own conclusion.

Since the acute cases manifest themselves only after large dosages of larvae, the consumption of cuts of meat which have the largest populations of *Trichinella spiralis* should increase the investigator's suspicion. Generally, these cuts include the animal muscles of most activity, the muscles of respiration (intercostals and diaphragm) and the neck muscles.

Prevention consists of protecting meat animals from infestation. Other methods of prevention are requiring that all garbage fed to hogs be boiled, and cooking meat to at least 140° F. using a meat thermometer or storing it at 5° F. for 20 days.

FOOD TECHNOLOGY

Gastroenteritis, staphylococcal food poisoning, salmonellosis and shigellosis head the list of food-borne illnesses in the United States. Although the number of cases reported by state health departments has been averaging between 10,000 and 11,000 annually in the United States, the Public Health Service estimates that one million cases occur annually. For recent years the number of cases reported is about ten times the number of illnesses associated with water and thirty times the number associated with milk and milk products. Whereas the number of outbreaks associated with water, milk and milk products has been going down, the number of outbreaks associated with food has been going up.

Food poisoning is preventable if food producers, processors, handlers and consumers are aware of certain precautions which are the basis of the science of food technology. All physicians cannot be experts in food technology. Consequently, the services of a good technologist should be utilized when the physician has a responsibility for insuring a safe food supply for a population in an army camp, a children's institution, a hospital or similar setting. The administrative heads of such installations frequently turn to physicians for advice on food-handling practices and their associated disease hazards.

There are a number of authoritative texts on food technology which covers a wide area, encompassing milk, other dairy products, meat, beverages, food additives and preservatives, as well as food preparations.[3, 10-12, 14] Many economic factors, as well as preventive medicine principles, are involved in this science.

The basic preventive objectives of food technology are to minimize food adulteration and bacterial and chemical contamination; to prevent the growth of pathogens in food; and to remove or avoid the health hazards associated with food processing—proper preservation and minimum handling immediately prior to consumption.

Food technology is not static. The economics and methods of food preparation and distribution are changing constantly. Every innovation brings with it a new set of problems for the food technologist. The invention and wide use of the home storage freezer has decreased the opportunity for incubating pathogens during food storage, but it has also made possible the use of frozen prepared meals by just warming and serving. Ordinary cooking of raw foods involves temperatures which reach the thermal death point for pathogens, but inadequate heating of precooked frozen foods can produce incubation temperatures and result in the multiplication of pathogens to effective dosage levels. Under such circumstances, prepared turkey dinners must be absolutely free of salmonella if disease is to be prevented.

The father of food technology was Louis Pasteur, whose pioneer efforts to prevent spoilage of wine by heating also laid the basis for the antiseptic techniques developed by Lister and the pasteurization of milk. Pasteur's work on this and other problems of immediate economic interest was the groundwork for the prevention of food-borne disease by food technologists.[13]

PREVENTION OF FOOD-BORNE DISEASE

The basic principles of food-poisoning prevention are prevention of occurrence of bacterial and chemical contamination of food and utensils;

adequate refrigerated storage of raw and processed foods; and use of adequate temperatures for food preparation and utensil cleaning.[14]

Since many forms of food-borne illness are yet to be described, we strive for good food sanitation as well as the elimination from food of specific etiologic agents, such as the staphylococci and the salmonellae.

Prevention of Food Contamination

Prevention of food contamination is the first principle. Proper cleaning and handling of equipment and food will accomplish the desired results. Any restaurant operator or food handler can understand and properly execute soap and water cleanliness rules. In principle this is the easiest to understand, but sometimes the hardest to put in practice.

Routine searching for carriers of specific pathogens need not be done. Such efforts are of little value and create a false sense of security. It is more important to teach the food handler to exclude himself from the kitchen when ill or when he has a lesion on his hands or another exposed skin surface. If a person is a known chronic carrier of pathogens or practices poor personal hygiene, he should not work as a food handler. Yet, almost every person is a carrier of staphylococci and may also be a temporary carrier of other pathogens. Handwashing and personal hygiene are the best defenses against contamination by carriers. The food preparation area should have the hot water, soap and clean towels necessary for handwashing available in it and near the toilet areas.

Clean floors, impermeable work surfaces which are easily cleaned, wet mopping and the liberal use of soap and water in cleaning will decrease opportunities for contamination of food.

Equipment should be easily dismantled for cleaning and be cleaned after use. Food choppers, chopping blocks, dispensing devices and knives stored in inaccessible slots between counters are common sources of food-contaminating pathogens.

Food preparation areas should be kept free of rats and insects. Cats and dogs should not be allowed in the kitchen. Urine from these animals may carry infectious agents, such as *Leptospira icterohaemorrhagiae*. Insecticides, rat poisons and toxic substances should be kept away from food storage and preparation areas to prevent accidental contamination of food.

New developments in food processing have introduced a number of food additives, and new ones may be expected. Hormones and antibiotics are commonly added to feeds to increase the growth of cattle and poultry. The significance of these additives is not yet clear. The prevention of food contamination by new additives is subject to governmental control. The prevention of food poisoning by such controls requires considerable knowledge of food technology. The physician who suspects such a problem should ask for expert advice from his local health department.

Food Storage

Since cold has a bacteriostatic action, refrigerated space functioning at an adequate temperature (usually below 45° F.) and of sufficient volume to handle peak storage loads is a necessity in every kitchen. Dry foods should be stored in a cool, dry space inaccessible to vermin. All storage spaces should have covers to prevent dust contamination of foods. Food should not be stored in uncovered containers on counters or other places where it is accessible to droplets from coughing and sneezing.

Serving milk which is unpasteurized or dipped from bulk containers has caused streptococcal outbreaks. Commercial milk dispensers of sanitary design or individual service bottles are the only acceptable methods for serving milk.

The striking increase in frozen food storage has introduced new problems (p. 149). If this technique is used, temperatures should be maintained in the freezer at or below 0° F. Food stored at this temperature will not deteriorate for months, but conditions of thawing prior to use should be checked. Frozen foods, particularly poultry, should be thawed in the icebox at 45° F., since some strains of salmonella grow at 50° F. Refrigerators should be clean and dry.

Food Preparation and Utensil Cleaning

The final line of defense is the heating process in cooking. Most human pathogens are destroyed at boiling temperatures if the food is thoroughly mixed. A number of factors determine the thermal death point of pathogens in food. Consistency of the food, mixing, pH, time and temperature are major controlling factors, the most important of which are time and temperature. Heating or freezing under proper circumstances may be used. The greatest opportunity for error is relying on oven temperature or other recording devices without checking to see that the safe temperature is reached in all parts of the food. Cooking thermometers which are inserted into the food mass, but not touching bone, are useful tools to control this process. They are acceptable to housewives since they help in reaching the desired degree of palatability in meat cooking. Table 8 shows the temperature and time relationships required to kill pathogens, allowing for a safety margin.

Table 8. *Time and Temperature Relationships Required for the Destruction of Selected Pathogens by Freezing or Cooking*

PATHOGENIC AGENT	REQUIRED TEMPERATURE	REQUIRED TIME
Botulinum toxin	162° F.	10 minutes
Botulinum spores	248° F.	10 minutes
Taenia saginata	15° F.	6 days
Trichinella spiralis	5° F.	20 days
	131° F.	10 minutes
Mycobacterium tuberculosis	142° F.	30 minutes
	160° F.	12 seconds
Streptococci	135° F.	30 minutes
Diphtheria	132° F.	30 minutes
Salmonella	137° F.	10 minutes
	162° F.	2 minutes
Staphylococcus aureus	160° F.	15 seconds

In general, cooking temperatures above 162° F. for 2 minutes or more in all parts of the food will destroy food-borne pathogens.

After foods are cooked they are sometimes placed in steam tables. If incubating temperatures are to be avoided, steam tables should be kept at a temperature of 150 to 155° F. at all times.

Instruction on food preparation temperatures can be simplified by advising food handlers that there are two critical temperatures to be watched: 150° F. or more when cooking, and 45° F. or less when refrigerating. In between is a "no-man's land" for food.

The correct method of washing utensils and dishes consists of the following steps: scraping, prerinsing, washing, rinsing and sanitizing. Washing requires a good detergent. Sanitizing requires that dishes be submerged for 30 seconds in water of at least 170° F., or in an approved chemical solution.

In the kitchen, some of the important items to check are: cooking temperatures, steam table temperatures, adequate refrigeration of foods immediately after cooking (especially poultry), clean meat grinders, cutting boards and utensils, general cleanliness, all foods under cover and protected from flies, avoidance of vermin infestation, handwashing facilities, and proper storage facilities for food, utensils, dishes and garbage.

LABORATORY CONTROLS

After all efforts have been made to see that food handling and preparation is satisfactory, there are laboratory controls in common usage which roughly measure the degree of safety attained. They are the examinations for total bacteria plate count and coliform count on samples of food, plate, glass and utensil swabs. Under specialized conditions, the investigator may wish to test samples of wash water, or swab such areas as food preparation counters or meat cutting blocks. The interpretation of laboratory tests depends on the observations made during the inspection of the facility and are of little value without such information.

Solid foods are examined by taking representative samples, weighing out a portion which is placed in water and then in a mechanical disintegrator. Decimal dilutions of the resulting suspension are then poured on agar media for total bacteria count and on selective media for coliform counts. Total bacteria count plates are incubated 48 hours and coliform count plates are incubated for 24 hours at 35° C. The counts are reported in terms of bacteria per gram of food.

Approximately the same procedure is followed with glasses and utensils, except that they are swabbed with a standardized applicator which is immersed in a buffered diluent and agitated. Decimal dilutions are then used for plating on culture media. The counts are reported in terms of coliform organisms per milliliter. Acceptable bacterial standards vary by food and source of the swabbed material.

ANDREW C. FLECK, M.D.
CLAUDE H. COLVIN, B.S.
JOSEPH A. SALVATO, P.E.

REFERENCES

1. Lyman, E. D., et al.: Food poisoning due to nicotinic acid in meat. Nebraska State Medical Journal, 42:243, May, 1957.
2. Anderson, E. S., and Williams, R. E. O.: Bacteriophage typing of enteric pathogens. Journal of Clinical Pathology, 9:94-110, May, 1956.

3. Dack, G. M.: Food Poisoning. Revised Edition. Chicago, University of Chicago Press, 1956.
4. Feig, M.: Diarrhea, dysentery, food poisoning and gastroenteritis: a study of 926 outbreaks. American Journal of Public Health, 40:1372, 1950.
5. Casman, E. D.: Serological studies of staphylococcal enterotoxin. Public Health Reports, 73:599-609, July, 1958.
6. Dearness, J.: Gyromitra poisoning. Mycologia, 16:199, 1924.
7. Krieger, L. C. C.: A Popular Guide to the Higher Fungi of New York State. Albany, University of the State of New York, State Education Department, 1935, pp. 134-149.
8. Gompertz, L. M.: Poisoning with water hemlock. Journal of the American Medical Association, 87:1277-78, 1926.
9. Flint, T.: Emergency Treatment and Management. Ed. 3. Philadelphia, W. B. Saunders Co., 1964.
10. Adams, H. S.: Milk and Food Sanitation Practice. New York, The Commonwealth Fund, 1947.
11. Parker, M. E.: Food Plant Sanitation. New York, McGraw-Hill Book Co., 1948.
12. Sanitary Food Handling. Albany, University of the State of New York. State Education Department, 1950.
13. Rosen, G.: A History of Public Health. New York, MD Publications, Inc., 1958, pp. 294-344.
14. Salvato, J. A.: Environmental Sanitation. New York, John Wiley & Sons, Inc., 1958.
15. Procedure for the Investigation of Foodborne Disease Outbreaks. Shelbyville, Indiana, International Association of Milk and Food Sanitarians, Inc., 1957.
16. Cockburn, W. C., Taylor, J., Anderson, E. S., and Hobbs, B. C.: Food Poisoning. London, The Royal Society of Health, 1962.

9 Insect Vectors

A striking burden of global illness is attributable to arthropod-borne (arbo) diseases. These are the great endemics which have limited the population of man, shaped history, decided battles and determined sites of habitation. These diseases have made quarantine and other community action imperative. Yet there is much to be done. One of the best reasons for acquiring knowledge in this field is the possibility of disrupted environmental control because of war or improved transportation. No one today is far from the rest of the world or its disease vectors.

Insects and related arthropods still dispute with man for control of the earth. They compete with him for food and annoy him in divers ways, but they are particularly troublesome as carriers of disease incitants. Carriage may be mechanical, as when the housefly transports bacteria from feces to food, or more complicated, as when a mite maintains St. Louis encephalitis virus in birds which infect a mosquito which takes the virus to man. Control of a particular disease is, therefore, dependent on an exact knowledge of the pathogen's reservoir as well as the vector's habitat, life cycle, sites and seasons of breeding and susceptibility to control measures. This knowledge, which is to some extent independent of human disease, comprises medical entomology. Vector control presupposes need and feasibility, which are matters of professional judgment. Control in practice involves desirability and cost, both matters of public interest.

TYPES OF INSECT VECTORS

Arthropod vectors of disease belong to many genera and species. They may be grouped as bugs, lice, gnats, flies, fleas, mosquitoes, ticks and mites. Each has special characteristics in producing disease.

The burrowing parasitic mite of scabies causes itching, which provokes scratching and abrasions of the skin. Infection by pyogenic bacteria is likely to follow. The association of impetigo with head lice is similar. One type of flea, *Tunga penetrans*, burrows beneath the toe nails to wait for her eggs to hatch. The resulting lesion disables and predisposes to tetanus.

154

Female ticks of certain species induce an ascending flaccid paralysis which can be fatal unless the tick is removed. Other poisonous arthropods are the tarantula and black widow spiders, scorpions, bees, wasps and many others. Repeated stings by venomous insects such as yellow jackets do not usually threaten life but can give rise to fatal anaphylaxis.

Body lice are borne with fortitude by many people, but the same arthropod becomes a dreadful vector in transmitting typhus and relapsing fever from man to man, the louse's only host. The rat flea prefers his usual host, but when that host dies of plague he transfers both allegiance and pathogens to man. In much the same way, rickettsial pox is transmitted from a mouse by Dermanyssus mites which take man as an alternative host. Most ticks live on the blood of wild animals but some will attach to man and transfer relapsing fever, rickettsioses, tularemia and virus diseases, such as Colorado tick fever. Ticks are especially dangerous because in all stages they are blood feeders. The longevity of adult ticks is great—2 to 6 years—and they pass on many disease agents to their offspring. Similar transmission from generation to generation occurs in the Trombicula bush mites, vectors of tsutsugamushi fever.

Mosquitoes, the females at least, are important because of their abundance, ubiquity, blood feeding and ability to adapt breeding habits and survive over the winter. They transmit malaria, epidemic yellow fever, elephantiasis and dengue from man to man. They feed on a wide range of animals besides man and they can interrupt zoonotic barriers and tap reservoirs, as they do in jungle yellow fever, St. Louis and equine encephalitis and in a growing number of arboviruses known locally all over the world.

Certain gnats, like the Simuliidae, carry the blinding agent of onchocerciasis from man to man; other gnats, like the Phlebotomus, transfer sandfly fever between men. Still other Phlebotomus species transmit bartonellosis and dermal and visceral leishmaniasis from animals to man. Reduviidae biting bugs (Triatoma) carry Chagas' trypanosomiasis from armadillo to man. Blood-sucking Muscoid flies of the genus Glossina are the dread tsetse flies, vectors of African trypanosomiasis, enzootic in big game.

The cosmopolitan housefly has revolting feeding habits that exploit sanitation lapses. It transmits enteric bacteria or viruses, such as those causing poliomyelitis, and transmits yaws by going from sore to sore.

CONTROL

Whatever the special attributes of the vector, control consists of breaking the infection cycle. There are two quite different ecologic scenes. One is man to man transmission by a vector typified by the Anopheles mosquito in malaria. In contrast there is animal to man transmission by ticks from wild rodents, such as in Rocky Mountain spotted fever, or by tsetse fly, as in African trypanosomiasis. In the man to man cycle, combinations of isolation and medication of the man and environmental attacks on the vector are appropriate. In the animal to man cycle, it is sometimes possible to control the alternate host, the reservoir of infection dangerous to man.

The control action is divided into avoiding, repelling, killing and, finally, reducing the numbers of breeding vectors. This last seeks especially to interrupt the vector's life cycle at the most vulnerable point and at lowest cost. Even so, it can involve huge engineering ventures. Combinations of these actions are the rule.

Avoidance

Avoidance is practiced on a grand scale, although unconsciously. The city dweller in the temperate zone has highly systematized paving, drainage, waste disposal and medical care. He would hesitate to assign the cost of such things to arthropod control, but flies, mosquitoes, fleas, mites, bugs and gnats are generally reduced as a result. When the city dweller stays home or confines his wanderings to other cities, even those of other countries, he avoids many vectors. When he leaves the cities in temperate climates, he encounters many vectors of potential importance; however, he will encounter practically no malaria, because, owing to medical care, reservoirs of that disease have been dried up. More specific examples of avoidance are seen in folk customs, such as taking to the roofs at sundown to avoid low flying mosquitoes. Other avoidance schemes of established value are netting and screening beds against mosquitoes, since most mosquitoes are night biters. In contrast, most black flies are day biters, breeding in swift streams. In such areas, night travel is preferable. Tsetse fly districts are simply shunned, or head nets and protective clothing are worn to prevent bites. Often travelers and troops camp at a distance from human settlements where elephantiasis, espundia or kala-azar are known to occur. Both in the southern United States and in the Orient, bush mites or chiggers live in tall grass or cane, and such places are generally avoided.

Repellents

Repellents have logical use where avoidance is impracticable. Their importance was shown during World War II when troops were of necessity exposed to a variety of disease vectors. The most successful of the repellents are N, N-diethyl-m-toluamide and dimethyl phthalate; others of use are ethyl hexanediol, dimethyl carbate and butopyronoxyl. While there are certain differences among them according to the species they are used on, all have broad repellency and can be used to impregnate clothing. The duration of their effectiveness varies with the factors influencing vaporization, but it lies somewhere between 3 and 5 hours. The common formulations are well tolerated on human skin, even with prolonged use.

Insecticides

Insecticides are applied when dwellings are being treated for human use or when a limited area is being prepared for camp. The mist thrower or bug bomb, consisting of compressed freon gas with pyrethrum and DDT, is available in various sizes, especially for field use. They are used in debugging buildings where vectors are known to exist or where arthropod-borne diseases have occurred. Their use is somewhat subject to misunderstanding by untrained people who note their effectiveness and become lax in other precautions. It is entirely possible for a disease-bearing mosquito to fly freely in the treated zone once the mist has settled and to bite the man who forgets to use a bed net. DDT remains active for about 2 months and will continue to be lethal for insects which make contact. Cheaper and more versatile than the bombs are sprays of 5 to 10 per cent DDT in kerosene or water emulsions, which are suited to use in knapsack and wheeled pump sprayers or in more advanced power sprayers on trucks or airplanes. Large areas can be covered reasonably well, and nearly any setting can be attacked with one or another of these devices. Airplane spraying has recently been used in New York state in the Adirondacks on black flies. In habitations, one gallon of 5 per cent agent will treat 1000 to 2000 square feet. Combinations of organophosphates such as malathion increase residual killing power.

Powders of 5 to 10 per cent DDT in talc find special use in delousing people and clothing during epidemic typhus. This was conspicuously successful in the Italian epidemic of 1943. Similar powders can be used to treat rat runs, counting on the rat to pick up the agent by contact so that his own fleas are killed, as well as other fleas in his habitat.

Another killing agent of merit is benzene hexachloride (12 per cent gamma isomer), which can be used in dust or spray. Applied at the rate of 4 pounds per acre, it provides good control of Trombicula mites. This agent is also effective in killing Reduviidae bugs in dwellings.

There are a few specialized applications. Ships have been fumigated with the dangerous hydrocyanic acid gas which kills both rats and mice as well as arthropods. Methyl bromide gas, which is also dangerous to man, is often used for dispensaries and vehicles, including airplanes. Both these agents have been used to gas burrows of ground squirrels.

The advantages of insecticides are somewhat offset by the need to keep re-applying them and their danger to man. Repeated use sometimes causes resistant strains to emerge. The housefly has become resistant to DDT, chlordane and other insecticides. Many mosquitoes have shown the same resistance. The alternatives include new agents, but environmental changes may be the ultimate goal.

Reducing Breeding Vectors

Interfering with vector breeding, though rewarding and often gratifyingly permanent, requires the combined skills of physician, entomologist and engineer. The methods of breeding control are legion, since each vector, indeed each species, is a special case. Generally, Aedes breed on wet ground and tend to overwinter as eggs; Culex lay egg rafts; Anopheles lay single eggs; both Culex and Anopheles breed in water and both overwinter as adults in buildings, cellars or culverts. Drainage of puddles and pools and elimination of Aedes mosquitoes were successful in preventing epidemic yellow fever in Panama. Such a course in Trinidad had virtually no effect on malaria because there the anopheline vector breeds in bromeliads located in trees.

Notable success in malaria control has followed a relatively simple plan. Given an idea of incidence, the first abatement step is to spray domiciles with residual insecticides. This is repeated at intervals, and vegetation is cleared for a few hundred yards around the dwellings. Obvious breeding sites are treated with oil or larvicides. These steps can be taken by relatively unskilled people. Suppressive drugs and active treatment, even if not universal, result in greatly improved health and vigor of the inhabitants. Entomologists usually advise what steps to take in reducing the mosquito population. Resurveys of specific vectors and human disease are a good yardstick to measure the effectiveness of engineering efforts. The sequence has been often repeated in undeveloped regions with small, but very crucial, differences for each country or town. The emphasis is on initial mosquito control to reduce human disease, which, in turn, reduces the reservoir of mosquito infection. A healthy people can better help to keep the vector in check. This program involves very little landscape change and perhaps no more than local change in vector population.

The annals of malariology are rich in interesting exceptions to all rules. To review all the ways in which the landscape was changed would be to touch on hydraulics in all its nuances—tunnels, ditches, dikes, pumps, valves, gates and tide barriers. All are used to drain water, make it flow faster, salinify it or change its level.

Mosquitoes usually breed in water. Making the available water unsuitable is one way to reduce their population. Larvicides are applied to water where other control is not feasible, as in tree holes. In cases where neither method is suitable, natural enemies, such as top minnows, are introduced or encouraged. The best and usually the cheapest method is to attack the larval stages.

Field trials of an old agent, Paris green, formulated with vermiculite have shown it to be exceedingly practical in control of salt marsh mosquitoes in Pinellas County, Florida.[5] The agent is larvicidal and spreading may be by flotation as well as by airplane. Residual toxicity is low.

In epidemic plague a good long-range plan could include rat proofing. As mentioned, treatment of ships fits into this scheme. When plague occurs, traps, gas, poison baits and insecticides are all steps to control the spread.

It would be highly desirable to control the vector for animals as well as man. However, this is not entirely practicable if the habitat of the vector and reservoir is wild, unsettled and of vast dimensions. The tsetse fly is an example, since it breeds along rivers and waterholes in dense thickets, especially mangrove. These breeding conditions are found in large areas of Africa where wild game reservoirs complete the setting of the waterhole. Combinations of trapping, DDT mist and clearing of the bush seem tediously difficult for widespread practice, especially since several species of Glossina are involved. Agriculture and the wholesale elimination of big game are spreading into the territories daily, but progress is slow.

Major undertakings in pesticide control always carry the possibility of ecologic disturbance with unexpected and sometimes undesirable results.

New and selective compounds called attractants have high promise for wholesale control of insects.[6] These substances may summon both sexes or may lure males to traps. Attractants of field merit have been developed through studies of natural secretions with concomitant synthesis as well as by empirical trials of organic substances, chiefly esters, which can be vaporized and tested in the laboratory.

Chemosterilants may also have a place in vector control.[7] These are compounds which inactivate gametes. Roentgen rays have been used to sterilize captive males who on release mate and induce the deposit of sterile eggs. This has been notably successful in control of screwworm flies in Florida. Its success depends on a single cycle of egg-laying and a numerically superior corps of sterile males.

The Bitter Root Valley of Montana is another extensive stretch where rodents keep alive the reservoir for Rocky Mountain spotted fever, tularemia and relapsing fever. There are no ready methods for eliminating ticks and fleas on a square mile basis. Good personal hygiene, vaccination and studied elimination of reservoirs have had some success. The need for control is not so great where the human population is small. There is good reason, however, to keep watch in these regions, for new methods of elimination may yet be found.

VICTOR N. TOMPKINS, M.D.

REFERENCES

1. Glasgow, R. D., and Collins, D. L.: Control of the American dog tick, a vector of Rocky Mountain spotted fever: preliminary tests. Journal of Economic Entomology, 39:235, 1946.
2. Herms, W. B.: Medical Entomology, with Special Reference to the Health and Well-Being of Man and Animals. Ed. 4. New York, The Macmillan Co., 1950.
3. Jamnback, H., and Collins, D. L.: The control of blackflies (Diptera: Simuliidae) in New York. Albany, University of the State of New York, State Education Department, New York State Museum Bulletin, No. 350, August, 1955.
4. Russell, P. F., Manwell, R. D., and West, L. S.: Practical Malariology. Prepared under the auspices of the Division of Medical Sciences of the National Research Council. Philadelphia, W. B. Saunders Company, 1946.
5. Rogers, A. J., and Rathburn, C. B., Jr.: Tests with a new granular Paris green formulation against *Aedes, Anopheles,* and *Psorophora* larvae. Mosquito News, 18:89, 1958.
6. Jacobson, M., and Beroza, M.: Chemical insect attractants. Science, 140:1367, 1963.
7. Chang, S. C., Terry, P. H., and Borkovec, A. B.: Insect chemosterilants with low toxicity for mammals. Science, 144:57, 1964.

10 Medical Defense Against Atomic Attack or Natural Disaster

Medical defense against atomic attack or natural disaster is preventive medicine of vast magnitude. We can prevent the progression of disability and can certainly reduce the number of deaths if we prepare a medical defense program as part of the community's total civil defense. The general principles of medical defense against enemy attack are applicable to such natural disasters as tornadoes and hurricanes, or to man-made disasters such as explosions or wrecks. Our country is susceptible not only to attack that could bring ionizing radiation to every region, but to various types of civil disaster as well. The only intelligent action is to prepare, knowing that the chances for survival after attack or disaster depend upon the maintenance of strength, morale and health. The potential hazard to the people from atomic warfare or from severe natural disaster must be faced by the medical profession in every state. The complex nature of the anticipated injuries and the urgent need for prompt treatment at the periphery of the blast or disaster demand that all physicians know the federal, state and local organizations for defense against atomic bombs and existing plans for coping with disasters. Physicians also need to familiarize themselves with the latest methods for handling casualties in unprecedented numbers.

Medical services are vital to the morale of the population. Physicians, and indeed all health workers, who take time to learn about the medical effects of atomic radiation and the related injuries can help to inform the public of the problem and what can be done about it. A mysterious weapon is robbed of much of its terror when its effects are known and steps toward self-protection are learned.

The physician must prepare to help provide emergency medical services and also carry out additional activities in public health. Public health services must be maintained and, in certain respects, expanded to meet the exigencies of atomic and biological warfare. The challenges for survival stimulate group activity; physicians should lead in such activity because of their special competence. A community properly organized to meet the predictable demands of civil defense maintains its own morale and builds a capacity to meet any emergency.

It is unquestionable, however, that no mass casualty care would be feasible after a thermonuclear attack directed at most of our civil centers of population as well as our military bases. Blast and heat would disrupt communications, destroy medical facilities, and cause heavy losses of medical personnel. However, the potentialities of modern warfare being what they are, the probability is that an aggressor would commit his striking power to the destruction of his opponent's capacity to retaliate—which would mean that his attack would be directed mainly or solely to military bases. This assumption reduces the postattack medical problem to manageable size. It would result in heavy fallout of radioactivity, because of the necessity of surface bursts to destroy hardened military installations. This would make shelter stay for at least 48 hours mandatory for all survivors. This would mean that those with major burns and other serious traumatic injuries could not survive, except for those fortunate few who happened to be in a shelter with persons of medical competence and with medical supplies. The period of shelter stay would reduce the medical problem to (a) radiation illness, arising mainly from exposure to fallout, (b) those with injuries of such degree that survival without medical care for 48 hours or more would be possible without more than first aid, and (c) normal illnesses.

Nevertheless, this would amount to a tremendous casualty care problem, so the emergency medical service would not be limited to physicians. Anyone with training in the fields allied to medicine would give emergency treatment under the supervision of physicians. This would include dentists, nurses, veterinarians, pharmacists and medical students. To blend these resources and trained personnel into an organization that would function successfully in the days after attack has been the task of the medical leaders in public health and organized medicine since 1950.

MISSION OF MEDICAL SERVICE

Briefly stated, the mission of emergency medical services is to safeguard the health of the uninjured, to prevent the death of the injured, to reduce the amount and duration of disability and to relieve suffering resulting from an attack or disaster. The advent of the hydrogen bomb does not lessen the need for highly organized medical and public health services. Regardless of the size of the area of total destruction there will be peripheral areas of lesser damage where the survivors will require emergency services. Their number is unpredictable, but it certainly would be staggering. Nevertheless, efforts must be made to care for the injured within the limits of available resources.

In the early days of planning for medical defense against atomic bombs, figures were based upon the Hiroshima experience. Today, with the new types of weapons, this is no longer possible. In so massive an operation as now contemplated, peacetime methods will not suffice and the efforts of untrained persons will compound confusion unless trained leaders are available in great numbers. The movement of hundreds of tons of medical supplies and thousands of medical and nonmedical personnel requires a common understanding of lines of supply, methods of communication and the system of command. After attack, no city can care for its potential number of injured without the full support of surrounding communities.

Since attack or disaster may occur at any time, the personnel of the medical services will be pursuing their normal occupations. Accordingly, after shelter stay, every member of the medical services will proceed to his appointed post without awaiting orders. This is one reason why every physician should understand the general plan of medical and other civil defense operations.

It is important to make preattack preparations in all areas so that proper support can be given at the time of attack to the target areas. Recruitment and training are essential if full use is to be made of all professional personnel and their facilities. Provision will have to be made for the care of people who are ill from causes other than those associated with attack. Many communities will receive considerable numbers of the homeless, either by evacuation or by spontaneous movement of the population. There will be some who will have left the disaster area with injuries that had not been treated and others with injuries complicated by chronic and acute illnesses.

It is not practical for every physician to know the full details of all of the medical defense plans in an entire state. However, he should have general knowledge of the over-all plan and should have specific knowledge of the part he would play in his particular area, or what use would be made of his particular skills if he were called upon to serve in some disaster area other than his own. Of particular importance is knowing where to go and how to communicate to secure the help, supplies or equipment he would need for his work, since ordinary channels would be useless in the event of an attack or a widescale disaster.

CHARACTERISTICS OF THE MEDICAL PROBLEM

As a consequence of the assumption of a minimum shelter stay of 48 hours after the last bomb has been dropped, the medical problem would consist mainly of the following elements:

1. Mechanical injury not complicated by persistent shock.
2. Burns of less than major degree and extent.
3. Radiation illness.
4. Radioactive contamination of patients.
5. The necessity for limiting the radiation exposure of attending personnel to amounts compatible with continued usefulness.
6. Pregnancies and the usual illnesses of peacetime.
7. Epidemics of communicable disease arising after weeks or months as a consequence of poor nutrition, poor hygiene, and multiplication of rodents and insects.

CRITERIA FOR OPERATIONS IN A RADIOACTIVE AREA*

Most persons (9 out of 10) will be able to stand an accumulated exposure of 200 roentgens† without loss of effectiveness. Whole body exposure

---

* Based upon Report No. 29, Exposure to Radiation in an Emergency, National Committee on Radiation Protection and Measurements.

† Roentgen-unit of radiation exposure, see p. 59. Designated r./h., roentgens per hour, or mr./hr., milliroentgens per hour (1/1000 r./hr.).

during the first 4 days should be considered a single or instantaneous dose. If no further exposure occurs, recovery from the immediate effects (not including genetic and long-term, life-shortening effects) may be anticipated at the daily rate of 2.5 per cent of the remaining injury, up to an irreparable residual injury equivalent to 10 per cent of the original exposure. Such residual injury will increase the probability of leukemia, cataracts, cancer, and a reduction in life expectancy as a function of the acceleration of normal aging processes. Thus the injury due to an exposure to 200 r. in the first 4 days would be reduced by recovery to an injury equivalent to 100 r. in 1 month and to the equivalent of 20 r. in 3 months. The remaining injury at any given time in the recovery process or at the end of recovery is termed the Equivalent Residual Dose (ERD).

A useful criterion for medical operations is based upon this recovery rate. An exposure rate of 1.5 r./day (60 mr./hr.) for periods up to 1 year would lead to an Equivalent Residual Dose of less than 200 r. An exposure rate of 3 r./day (120 mr./hr.) would lead to an ERD in excess of 200 r. between 6 months and 1 year.

Since we have assumed that the greater part of the casualty load would be radiation illness, no medical facility for continued care should be established in an area with fallout radiation intensity greater than 3 r./day (120 mr./hr.) out of doors (which would be reduced by the shielding effect of any permanent building to 1.5 r./day or less). To attempt continued hospitalization at significantly higher levels of radioactivity would result in additional radiation injury at a rate greater than the rate of recovery.

An effect of this rule, the establishment of medical facilities for continued care only where the indoor level is 1.5 r./day or less, is that medical service personnel could report for duty without fear, regardless of exposure during the shelter and travel period, for recovery would be possible at these levels, provided that the original exposure had not been too great for recovery under any circumstances.

Medical operations in temporary facilities, such as aid stations, would be feasible with safety only if personnel were provided with self-reading personal dosimeters, worn during the shelter stay period as well as upon emergence for duty. With the knowledge of radiation exposure before reporting for duty, and the length of time which had elapsed after attack, a Radiation Safety Officer could readily calculate how many days at what levels of activity could be tolerated without exceeding an ERD of 200 r. Without measurement of exposure prior to duty, an estimate could be made only on the basis of area monitoring, a guess at the protection factor of the shelter in which each individual had spent the first 48 hours or more following attack, plus an estimate of exposure during travel from shelter to the post of duty.

Decontamination of patients, personnel and the medical facility would be essential in a fallout area. Here the criterion of 1.5 r./day or 60 mr./hr. is useful. If weather or other circumstances made it necessary, patients could be admitted to a hospital (in an area of less than 3 r./day) without decontamination until levels in the wards approached 60 mr./hr. Then spot monitoring with a survey instrument measuring radiation intensity (mr./hr.) should be used to identify patients so contaminated as to raise the general level. These patients would have to be decontaminated to a level of 60 mr./hr. or less or, if impossible, removed to a nearby facility, for their continued presence would doom patients with a chance for recovery.

Needless to say, all possible decontamination should be effected before admission to a hospital or other facility for continued care, for the sake of the contaminated patient as well as for the safety of other patients and personnel. Cleaning the face, hands and other unprotected skin surfaces, and the removal of hats, outer clothing and shoes will reduce the contamination of patients to less than 10 per cent of the original level. Even wiping the hands and face with a damp cloth or paper towel will remove most contamination. When no hat was worn during the period of contamination, it may be necessary to clip the hair and vigorously wash the scalp.

The foregoing generalizations have been based upon the gamma ray exposure from fission products in fallout, since it is this which constitutes the major hazard. To the contaminated patient himself, however, direct skin contact with beta emitters is important, for serious burns may result from beta exposure which is of no importance in the whole-body exposure of the patient. A level of 2 microcuries per square centimeter ($\mu c/cm.^2$) has been cited as a level of skin contamination which begins to be of concern. This is perhaps academic, however, since the patient should be decontaminated as much as possible under the circumstances. Perhaps the 60 mr./hr. rule remains the most practical operational guideline.

Inhalation and ingestion of radioactive materials would probably present a far lesser hazard during the first 3 months than external whole-body exposure. After this time, ingestion with food and water would become the greater hazard, though of a far lesser magnitude than the earlier whole-body exposure. One cannot repeat too often that all inhalation or ingestion is undesirable. Criteria of choice of sources of water and methods of decontamination of food will be discussed later.

NONCASUALTY MEDICAL CARE

In addition to a plan for casualty care, provisions must be made for ordinary illness and injuries among the population not affected by the attack or disaster. Overcrowding would be inevitable in some areas for some time. Sanitary facilities would become overtaxed and personal hygiene would deteriorate. Food supplies would be inadequate in kind and quantity. Outbreaks of communicable diseases, both natural and enemy caused, would threaten the usefulness of people essential to the survival and recovery of the nation. Difficult decisions would have to be made concerning the allocation of physicians to casualty care and to the protection of the surviving uninjured.

In event of the evacuation of an urban population, it seems certain that physicians assigned to their care would have to serve as their own epidemiologists. The number of public health people trained to investigate communicable diseases would be far too few. When an outbreak of a communicable disease threatens a population under postattack or postdisaster conditions, the physician on the scene must make his own survey of prevalence, determine the source and institute control measures. He might well utilize instructed laymen in the effort. Trained public health personnel should be available at local and state civil defense headquarters for consultation after the problem had been investigated and defined locally.

GENERAL ORGANIZATION

For purposes of emergency medical service, a city and its suburbs that have been subjected to an attack or a disaster are called a disaster area.

The city or county control center for civil defense is located at some distance outside the city and functions through several subdivisions of the area called zone headquarters. The control center has a medical section which coordinates medical and nonmedical services, and, through the medical staff in each zone headquarters, directs and controls medical affairs by establishing, staffing and supplying the various types of aid stations, hospitals and holding stations.

Supply and assignment depots are located near each zone headquarters as a source of personnel and supplies for medical installations set up within the zone. There are four types of facilities that are used by the medical staff in each zone to carry out emergency medical services and public health functions. These are the aid stations, the hospitals, the holding stations and the mortuaries.

Aid Stations

Without self-reading personal dosimeters, aid stations could be established only at functioning hospitals, or in areas of radiation intensity suitable for establishment of temporary hospitals (1.5 r./day or 120 mr./hr. out of doors, 60 mr. or less indoors).

A buffer aid station near the entrance to a hospital could treat, decontaminate and discharge the walking injured, screen patients for admission to the hospital or to a nearby facility for expectant care where minimal treatment could be given those whose survival seemed impossible. The criteria for expectant care only would vary according to patient load, medical supplies (including blood for transfusion) and presumed degree of prior radiation exposure. The buffer aid station would also decontaminate patients before admission to the hospital, when time and facilities permitted.

When personal dosimeters become available to all civil defense personnel, the location of aid stations in areas of higher radiation intensity for days or weeks would become feasible. A safe working rule for healthy adults during the early postattack (after 48 hours or more of shelter stay) is not to exceed a total exposure of 200 r., as measured by dosimeter. Upon approaching this limit, personnel should be sent to an area of 60 mr./hr. or less, where recovery from exposure without overt clinical illness might be expected. This would mean, for personnel with no prior exposure, the following periods of work in aid stations in areas of the following average intensities of radiation

Intensity of Radiation		Permissible Continuous
r./day	mr./hr.	Work Periods (days)
5	210	40
10	425	20
15	635	13
20	850	10
25	1060	8
30	1270	6

Personnel with known exposure in shelter can compute additional permissible work periods in areas of the above intensities by converting shelter dose to aid station days by dividing the average intensity in the aid station area into their known dose and deducting the result from the permissible work period in the above table.

Thus, a physician whose dosimeter reads 100 r. after emergence from shelter and travel to an aid station in an area of 5 r./day could work 20 days in that area ($100 \div 5 = 20; 40 - 20 = 20$). If average radiation intensity is not known and cannot be computed, the initial intensity in the aid station area can be taken as the average.

These rules will err on the conservative or safe side, for they do not take into account reduction in radiation intensity through radioactive decay, weathering, shielding, or physiological recovery. A radiation safety officer will be able to make more exact estimates.

The necessity of triage, or classification of the injured, has frequently been stressed. In a mass casualty situation, it must take into account not only the urgency of the patient's need for treatment, but his prospect for recovery and the potential available treatment. After an atomic attack or a major disaster, the patient load will most certainly exceed the capacity of available medical facilities. In such a situation, triage must be exercised at all medical installations by all medical and nursing personnel. This function cannot be reserved, as has often been advised, to the surgeon alone, even though he has had extensive experience in traumatic injury. Wherever priority must be determined for the patient who will next be moved to an aid station, receive primary medical care or receive transfusion or definitive surgical repair, the principles of triage must be exercised.

Here, then, is another principle of disaster medicine which indicates the necessity for early and orderly communication in a disaster area, so that knowledge of the total situation may be collected and disseminated to those who must make decisions concerning patient disposition. Indeed, one can readily visualize postattack or postdisaster situations in which patient load would so exceed treatment capacities that medical care would have to be limited to the ambulatory or to those who could be expected to become ambulatory in a week or so. It would be idle to begin treating thousands of seriously injured if the completion of their care were clearly beyond the capacities of available personnel, supplies or facilities. Yet such a decision, clearly a responsibility of higher medical headquarters, requires numerical reporting from the total field. This, in turn, assumes that medical and allied personnel in the field understand the principles of sorting and reporting.

Holding Stations

Holding stations would be set up at points in the periphery in which the noncritical litter cases could be sheltered or receive temporary care until they could be transported to a more distant hospital. These holding stations should be set up where transportation can be arranged by rail, ship, plane or motor vehicles.

Mortuaries

After care is given to the injured and the homeless, mortuary facilities can be set up and civil defense personnel can attend to the dead. Mortuary areas should be selected where bodies may be transported, identified and then buried, of necessity, on a mass basis. The personal effects would be collected as an aid to identification.

COMMUNICATIONS AND CONTROL

The control of postattack medical services in the various headquarters in disaster areas is as complex as it is vital. Sound methods, based upon the requests for personnel and supplies received from such field installations as aid stations and hospitals, have been developed in many states. While records are kept and decisions made in medical headquarters by medically supervised personnel, the effectiveness of the logistics depends upon the comprehension of the basic plan by the participating physicians. These methods have been tried out in actual civil defense exercises. These test exercises continue year after year and must do so as long as there is a possible threat of attack. For example, the success or failure of communications and transportation will often determine the success or failure of the medical activities. The major channel of communications obviously would be written messages from field installations by way of the trucks sent for supplies or personnel. As each aid station begins to function, using surviving local personnel, its stretcher bearers bring information to the station concerning concentrations of the injured beyond their range of activity. This information then goes forward to the zone headquarters and needs would be filled as soon as possible. Another example is the importance of up-to-date information on hospital admissions, in order to plan for definitive care within 6 hours of admission. Ideally, no more cases should be admitted in a period of time to any hospital than can be given definitive care within such a period. This means that the zone headquarters must have current information on hospital occupancy so that it can tell the aid stations which hospitals can receive critical cases and which hospitals can receive cases requiring only supportive care, such as uncomplicated burns and radiation illness.

In considering the flow of the injured away from the disaster areas, the ambulatory injured who are treated at aid stations should be discharged to their homes or to the nearest welfare center. Litter cases treated at aid stations should be tagged as to the urgency of their need for hospitalization and then transported by truck to a hospital in that priority (Fig. 28).

STAFFING PATTERNS

The personnel of a typical aid station consists of one physician, one medical associate (a dentist, veterinarian or medical student), three nurses, one executive officer, one supply officer, 40 medical aides, one messenger leader and eight messengers. The medical aides collect litter cases in the field and staff the aid stations. The stretcher team usually consists of four medical aides. Their equipment consists of a litter cot, a field kit, a blanket and, at the option of the physician in charge of the aid station, morphine syrettes. Equipment does not include blood or its substitutes. The duties of the medical aides are to control bleeding, treat shock, cover wounds and burns, apply splints, give morphine if directed, transport the injured, assist the walking wounded to aid stations and tag the injured.

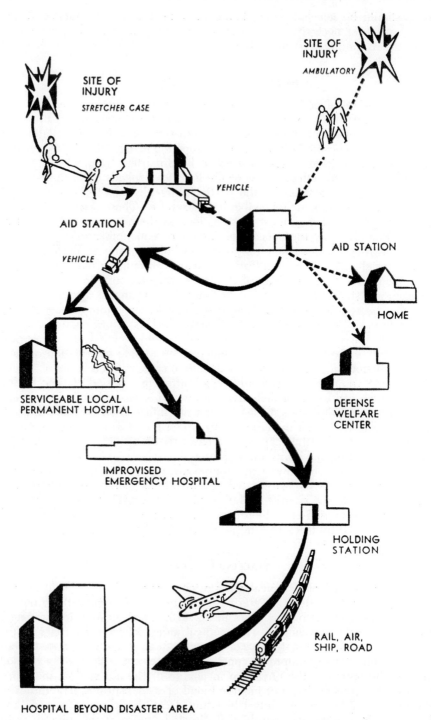

Figure 28. Flow of the injured away from the disaster area.

The staffing pattern of the aid stations is organized to relieve the physician of nonmedical duties. Consequently, training for laymen to assist the professional personnel is a continuing necessity in order to attain a corps of sufficient size and to provide replacements. Undoubtedly, some patients will suffer from inexpert or overhasty handling in the field, but the greatest number of lives will be saved by prompt transportation to the aid station for professional care. The medical associate is given maximum opportunity to treat the injured to the fullest extent of his knowledge and experience. When a physician becomes exhausted or when one is not available, the medical associate or nurse must be prepared to assume full responsibility regardless of background or experience, until a physician becomes available.

The aid station personnel will be expected to give first aid to the walking wounded, sort out the wounded, treat shock and direct the flow of injured to hospitals or their homes or to welfare centers, depending upon their condition.

Every hospital has a dual mission under medical defense. It may have to provide emergency medical care or, in some instances, shift its personnel, equipment and supplies to an adjacent community as directed by the civil defense authorities. Each hospital must have a disaster plan which would make it possible to double or triple the number of patients that can be given care if the hospital is fortunate enough to remain standing after disaster.[1] Furthermore, hospital personnel should receive aid station training in the event that the hospital is destroyed and they can no longer work there. It is assumed that permanent hospitals that remain usable and are functioning can continue to do so on their own supplies for the first 24 to 48 hours. After that, additional supplies can be made available from zone supply and assignment depots.

Mobile Hospital Outfits

In those areas where permanent hospitals are destroyed or insufficient, a mobile hospital outfit will be furnished from the nearest supply depot to set up an improvised hospital of 200 to 500 beds, complete except for litter cots which will arrive from the aid stations loaded with patients. The New York State mobile hospital unit consists of a basic outfit of 237 items, including emergency supplies sufficient for the first 12 hours and supplemental supplies sufficient for the care of 200 patients for 10 days. (The federal hospital mobile unit is similar, but has more items.) These mobile hospital units are stored in depots in rural areas throughout the state and can be transported rapidly on ordinary trucks to the periphery of an attacked city. Electric generators are included to supply light and power for roentgen equipment. A xeroradiographic unit is supplied; this employs a photoelectric process for recording roentgen images. No solutions, photographic film and darkroom are required in this process.[2]

These mobile hospital units are modifications of the mobile Army surgical hospital. They are packaged in fiberboard boxes that are waterproof and verminproof. They are so labeled that the equipment can be distributed rapidly for use in a school building or an empty warehouse (Fig. 29).

No firm prior assumptions can be made as to which communities will be

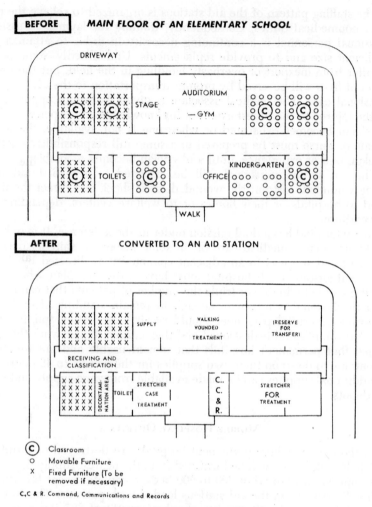

Ⓒ   Classroom
○   Movable Furniture
×   Fixed Furniture (To be removed if necessary)

C., C & R. Command, Communications and Records

Figure 29. Setting up an aid station.

used for hospitalization of casualties after attack or disaster. This designation will be the responsibility of the zone medical officer. He will designate hospitals and staff them in the appropriate areas according to the pattern of destruction and fallout and the concentrations of the injured. This same plan of designation can be used for massive civil disasters as well.

The complex problem of balancing personnel needs in aid stations and in hospitals adjacent to the disaster area can be solved only by a flexible plan that is understood by trained medical service personnel. Exercises must be carried out year after year to refresh personnel in the execution of the plan. When exercises are carried out in his community, each physician should offer his services, take part in the test exercises and give instruction to non-medical personnel. Only by such preparation can the medical profession be assured of the trained help it would need in a disaster situation.

The medical service of every area must prepare for ordinary care of the local population, to receive casualties, and also prepare to send aid to another city if requested. Flexibility of the plan is the only hope for the survival of any substantial proportion of the injured following an atomic attack or a large scale disaster.

The practicing physician can help recruit and train personnel for predisaster functions. Effective execution of postdisaster responsibilities cannot be accomplished without preorientation and training of personnel of all categories. The state health departments should have a uniform training program for the state as a whole. Duties should be set forth in specific terms; the subject matter must be concrete and practical in nature and as realistic as possible. After initial training is completed, intermittent training of a continuing nature must be conducted in order that skills and knowledge may be improved and kept current.

Medical supplies for training purposes are furnished by the state health department in the form of aid station outfits and improvised emergency hospitals. Supplies actually consumed in training are a necessary expenditure.

BLOOD COLLECTION

The blood collection program is one of the important parts of the medical defense operation. For example, during ordinary times there are no more than 3000 pints of whole blood in stock at any one time in upstate New York and approximately 4000 pints in New York City. It has been recommended by the medical defense advisory committee of the medical society of the state that only group O blood would be drawn and administered during the initial period of an attack, because facilities for cross matching would be meager in the disaster area.

In the immediate postdisaster period, blood will be collected from volunteers from the institutions of the Departments of Mental Hygiene and Correction. These institutions will be provided with radiation survey meters, so that the exposure of the potential donors can be accurately measured. Blood can be drawn if exposure rates have not exceeded an average of 1.5 r./day, or where the total dose has not exceeded 100 r.

Blood drawn at state mental hospitals or correctional institutions can be typed by the resident medical staff or adjacent local laboratories. Blood collected at these institutions will be held there until required in an installation treating casualties. Blood collection outfits stored at such institutions will be used for this purpose.

Both the mental hospitals and the local laboratories receiving blood will be considered blood depots, storing and shipping blood in containers in trucks capable of maintaining temperatures of 38 to 50° F. Such trucks are operated by distributors of ice cream, meat, and frozen foods. They are mechanically refrigerated (not cooled by water ice or carbon dioxide ice) by means of gasoline engines and compressors and may be readily adjusted within the desired temperature range. State mental hospitals, prisons and laboratories would have such trucks assigned to them by their local civil defense directors.

Blood depots would advise city and county control centers in their assigned areas when they had blood available. Control centers would, in turn, advise blood depots of medical installations in need of blood. The responsibility for delivery of the blood to the medical installation would rest upon the blood depot.

When there is a surplus of blood at a depot, it should so notify the state emergency operating center through the local control center. Blood depots unable to supply the need within their areas should request supplementary blood from the state emergency operating center through the local control center. The state emergency operating center would direct delivery of blood surpluses to blood depots requesting them.

Messages to the state emergency operating center (through the local control center) from blood depots should be limited to (a) major shortages of blood, not minor or temporary imbalances of requirements and supply, (b) surpluses of blood for which there is no foreseeable need, and (c) requests for supplies or personnel which are not available locally.

After the third postattack week, in areas with radiation intensities of 1.5 r./day or less, it should be possible to identify by the clinical picture those among the general population who have not received sufficient exposure to radiation to cause illness. (Since 99 per cent of fallout activity at 1 hour would have decayed away in the first 49 hours, 99.9 per cent in the first 2 weeks, there would have been more than 19 days following the major exposure to fallout radioactivity for clinical illness to develop.) It should be safe to draw blood of all types for transfusion from those without clinical symptoms 3 weeks after the disaster.

It is possible to collect 300 pints of whole blood per bleeding team every 6 hours. The number of teams in each area is decided by the quota of blood assigned to it. Blood collection outfits should be distributed throughout the state in strategic areas, where they will be readily available to the supply and assignment depots around each target city. Blood derivatives and substitutes can be stockpiled in considerable quantities throughout the state so that they will be quickly available to the supply depots.

Detailed instructions concerning the plan for bleeding in an emergency and methods of performing the laboratory tests are contained in the technical manuals for emergency blood services.[3]

ROLE OF HEALTH OFFICER

The health officer serving in the medical defense organization will be the principal advisor on public health problems and responsible for sanitary measures to be carried out through sanitary engineers and sanitarians. The problem of providing safe water, milk and food will be a tremendous one. Close liaison will be established by the health officer and his staff with the welfare services responsible for mass food preparation and distribution.

Although a special state radiation detection unit may be responsible for detecting and measuring radiation in the environment, the sanitary engineering staff of the health officer will collect specimens of water, milk and other foods suspected of radiological contamination.

Sanitary engineering personnel will give advice and counsel to the fire service and the public works services for emergency sources of water and advise on the degree and type of treatment necessary to produce safe potable water. Sanitarians will advise the welfare service on safe and effective ways of handling food and water in emergency situations.

The health officer will also be concerned with the over-all administration of the medical defense program because of his training and experience in these fields. Private physicians and public health physicians will work out local plans for the provision of medical services as soon as possible after attack or disaster depending upon local conditions. Plans will involve not only the medical profession but also the hospital groups, the welfare services and all professional groups concerned with the healing of the sick.

Water and Food

For emergency purposes following attack, no fixed standards of radioactive contamination of water should be applied. Since water is essential to life, and no one can survive more than a few days of total deprivation of water, the safest available water must be identified by the local sanitary engineer and made available for drinking purposes. Any water may be used for cleansing purposes, personal or otherwise, without concern for radioactivity.

Water from the following sources is listed in the order of its probable radiological safety.

1. Stored water (including that in covered reservoirs, tanks, and cisterns, hot water tanks, toilet reservoirs, provided that no rainfall or other water is permitted to enter such a cistern or reservoir after fallout has begun).

2. Deep wells.

3. Shallow covered wells.

4. Water supplies treated by coagulation, settling, and filtration, or any of these.

5. Streams, particularly rapid streams.

6. Deep open reservoirs with capacities of 100 days' supply at normal rates of use.

7. Shallow reservoirs with capacities of only a few days of normal rates of use.

Food stored in dust-free areas may be eaten with safety. Food which may have been contaminated with fallout dust may be eaten if coverings are removed without contamination of the contents. Washing solid food will reduce contamination from fallout to safe levels.[15] Nonperishable foods too contaminated for immediate consumption should be stored until radioactive decay has reduced activity to tolerable levels.

No practical defense against chemical or biologic agents directed against humans is considered possible. Chemical defense would require the distribution of gas masks to the entire population well in advance of attack or the provision of shelters with elaborate provision for air filtration. Neither of these safeguards exists. Defense against nerve gases would require distribution of syrettes of atropine or a synthetic congener to the general population, and training in self-diagnosis of nerve gas poisoning, a complex clinical syndrome which varies greatly with the degree of exposure.

Defense against biological warfare on a broad scale would seem to be limited to preattack immunization or the stockpiling of anti-sera or other therapeutic or preventive agents. Such measures would certainly lead an aggressor to choose a biologic agent for which no preparations had been or could be made.

RADIATION ILLNESS

Though a chief medical officer would not be concerned directly with the recognition or treatment of radiation illness, his logistical problems would be heavily influenced by the number of such cases and the requirements for their treatment. Furthermore, due to the rarity of such cases in ordinary practice, it is desirable for the physician to be familiar with the signs, symptoms and treatment of radiation illness. This clinical picture is described in the chapter on Ionizing Radiation, pp. 47 and 48.

Much will depend upon the availability of hospital beds, personnel, blood and supplies. Admissions should be based not only upon the availability of these resources within the hospital, but upon conditions within the area, such as the number of other hospitals functioning or to be set up. For this reason, the hospital executive officer should be in frequent communication with the local control center to provide information and to be advised of other resources available or anticipated.

OTHER CIVIL DEFENSE SERVICES

The chief medical officer of the civil defense organization works closely with the chief of the welfare services in referring walking wounded to welfare installations after medical treatment. Arrangements are made with the chief of the food distribution services to supply hospitals, holding stations and aid stations. The chief of public works is usually called upon to provide electric generators for permanent hospitals that have been deprived of their own power supply, and to supply water for installations cut off from normal sources. The police services are requested to supply auxiliary policemen to guard entrances of all hospital installations, particularly the permanent ones. These are just a few examples of the relationships that must exist for the whole civil defense action to function smoothly and to minimize the time lag in caring for the wounded.

The physician should remember, in considering medical defense against atomic bombs, that it has been necessary to plan in the light of limited experience with the atomic bomb and no experience with the hydrogen bomb combined with biological or chemical warfare. A tremendous number of persons may be injured simultaneously in many areas throughout the country. All medical defense personnel would have to move as soon as it is safe to predetermined points to assist in whatever way they can with whatever talents and tools are available. There will be no time to wait for orders, no time for consideration of the best route for movement and no time to sit down and work out a new plan. Hundreds of thousands of volunteers will drop their ordinary tasks and move according to predetermined orders that are understood and followed by all. The success of the operation is complicated by the necessity for relying upon volunteers, both professional and nonprofessional, many of whom will be unseasoned in caring for the sick and wounded and might be overcome by close contact with the dead and dying.

We can prepare successfully to meet the challenge of atomic attack or civil disaster if every physician will accept his share of the task, learn his role well and be ready to carry out his assigned job when called upon. The precision and speed with which physicians apply their knowledge and skill after a hydrogen bomb attack may well be the determining factor in our survival as a free nation.

HERMAN E. HILLEBOE, M.D.
JAMES H. LADE, M.D.

REFERENCES

1. Outlining a Hospital Disaster Plan. Albany, New York State Department of Health, 1961.
2. Roach, John Faunce, and Hilleboe, Herman E.: Xeroradiography. The American Journal of Roentgenology, Radium Therapy and Nuclear Medicine, Vol. LXXLI, No. 1, January, 1955.
3. Technical Manual for Emergency Blood Service. Albany, New York State Department of Health, 1951.
4. American Psychiatric Association Committee on Civil Defense: Psychological First Aid in Community Disasters. Washington, D.C., American Psychiatric Association, 1954.
5. Casberg, M. A.: Medical organization in national catastrophe. Journal of the American Medical Association, 154:501-505, June 21-25, 1954.
6. The Potentialities of Biological Warfare Against Man. Washington, D.C., Federal Civil Defense Administration, March, 1951.
7. Lade, James H.: The physician in civil defense operations. Journal of the American Medical Association, 155:209-213, May 8-12, 1954.
8. Langmuir, Alexander D., and Andrews, Justin M.: Biological warfare defense. American Journal of Public Health, 42:235, March, 1952.
9. Emergency Medical Services—Information Circular No. 10 (Revised). New York State Civil Defense Commission, December, 1963.
10. Guide for Medical Aides in Aid Stations. Albany, New York State Department of Health, 1964.
11. Manual on Establishing the Improvised Emergency Hospital. Albany, New York State Department of Health, 1961.
12. Medical Defense Committee, Medical Society of the State of New York and the Bureau of Medical Defense, New York State Department of Health: Will you know what to do? New York State Journal of Medicine, 56:1235, April 15, 1956.
13. Wedum, A. G.: Defensive aspects of biological warfare. Journal of the American Medical Association, 162:34-37, November 27-30, 1956.
14. Ziperman, Lieut. Col. H. H.: Sorting—The key to management of victims of disaster. Journal of the American Medical Association, 162:1438-1441, December 15, 1956.
15. Medical Self Help Training Kit. Available from the local director of civil defense or Division of Health Mobilization, Public Health Service, Communicable Disease Center, Atlanta, Georgia.
16. Ingraham, Hollis S.: Medical plans for civil defense. Health News, 39:12-19, June, 1962.
17. Medical Control Room. Albany, New York State Department of Health, 1961.
18. Medical Defense Committee, Medical Society of the State of New York and Bureau of Medical Defense, New York State Department of Health: Training Improvised Emergency Hospital Teams. New York State Journal of Medicine, May 15, 1958.
19. Family Guide Emergency Health Care. Revised 1963. Washington, D.C., U.S. Department of Defense, Office of Civil Defense, and U.S. Department of Health, Education, and Welfare, Public Health Service.
20. Exposure to Radiation in an Emergency. National Committee on Radiation Protection and Measurements, Report No. 29. Section on Nuclear Medicine, Department of Pharmacology. Chicago, University of Chicago, August, 1962.

11 Hygiene of Housing

HEALTH PROBLEMS ASSOCIATED WITH HOUSING

Approximately one-third of the 48,000,000 dwelling units in the United States are estimated to have major deficiencies. An even higher proportion of the housing for people in the developing countries of the world is also deficient.

These deficiencies include nonpotable water supplies, unsatisfactory sewage disposal, and asphyxiation, fire and other accident hazards. All of these have potential deleterious effects on the health or well-being of the occupants. Dampness, inadequate heat, darkness, poor ventilation, vermin and rodent infestation and overcrowding also characterize the unfavorable environment found in many of these units.

Housing problems are not limited to the deterioration of city housing into slums. The provision of safe water supplies and the adequate disposal of sewage are current and serious problems in many newly developed suburban communities. Widespread installation of septic tanks in these areas has resulted in threats to water supplies and the overflow of sewage into roadside ditches and onto the surface of the ground. Problems of disease control and safety hazards are also associated with many public and semi-public housing accommodations, such as hotels, motels, nursing homes, labor camps and children's camps.

There has been an increasing concern by health authorities with the contributions which poor housing may make to ill health, including social disability. In slum areas, the specific cause-effect significance of poor housing on the physical and mental health of occupants has been difficult to identify. Accompanying inadequacies in nutrition, medical care and similar items pertaining to a relatively low socioeconomic status may contribute to a family's health problems. A controlled study carried out by the Johns Hopkins University from 1954 to 1960 has provided some definitive answers to these problems.

Johns Hopkins Study

A study group was selected from families of the same socioeconomic and age level living in slum areas and divided into two equal portions. One

176

portion was moved into new public housing, and the other portion, the control group, remained in its present housing.

The entire group was evaluated in 10 different examinations made both before and after one portion had moved to new housing. The working hypothesis was that poor housing had a deleterious effect on the health and well-being of the residents.

Data for persons under 35 years of age revealed that those remaining in the slum area experienced more episodes of illness requiring either medical attention or resulting in one or more days of disability than those moving to the new housing project. The greatest differences were in the 5 to 9 age group and were associated with three illness categories: infections (mainly the communicable diseases of childhood) and parasitic conditions, digestive conditions, and accidents. Accident rates were one-third lower in the new housing project than in the slum homes.

Efforts to evaluate factors of social and psychological adjustment were generally supportive of a more satisfactory environment in the housing project. More women in the housing project liked their apartments and commented favorably on the safety of their children's play areas. The rehoused families underwent a marked increase in neighborly interaction of a mutually supportive nature and showed more pride in their immediate neighborhoods. The decreased morbidity in their children made possible an improved daily attendance at school and a better promotion record.

Public Health Service Study

Increased disease morbidity associated with residents in slum areas was reported by the United States Public Health Service in 1949 following a study of six major United States cities. Mortality and morbidity rates in the slum areas were much higher than the average city rates. These study data revealed that: (a) one-quarter of the cities' populations living in substandard housing accounted for more than one-half of the tuberculosis cases each year and 40 per cent of the mentally ill sent to state institutions; (b) communicable disease rates were 65 per cent higher in the slums; (c) the infant death rate in slum areas was five times greater, and juvenile delinquency twice as high; (d) venereal disease rates were 13 times higher in slums; (e) the infant mortality and communicable disease death rates were sometimes as high in the slums as they were nationally 50 years ago, in spite of the great advances in medicine and public health.

Financially, these blighted areas accounted for one-half of the cities' available medical and institutional care, one-half of the time of the police, one-third of the time of the fire department, most of the welfare benefits and more than 50 per cent of the sanitation complaints.

IMPROVING HOUSING CONDITIONS

Efforts to improve housing conditions are generally associated with seven major objectives: (a) elimination of grossly deteriorated housing, (b) rehabilitation of substandard housing, (c) prevention of the spread of blight, (d) control of new construction, (e) planning for the future development of communities, (f) protection of transients from health and safety hazards and (g) reduction of health and safety hazards.

Detailed objectives pertaining to physiological and psychological needs, as well as protection against contagion and accidents, have been recommended by the World Health Organization and by the American Public Health Association's Committee on the Hygiene of Housing.

World Health Organization

An expert committee of the World Health Organization has set forth the following objectives for satisfactory housing:

1. A safe and structurally sound, adequately maintained, separate, self-contained dwelling unit for each household, if so desired, with each dwelling unit providing at least:
    a. A sufficient number of rooms, usable floor area and volume of enclosed space to satisfy human requirements for health and for family life consistent with the prevailing cultural and social pattern of that region, and so utilized that there is neither overcrowding of living or sleeping rooms.
    b. At least a minimum degree of desired privacy, both: (1) among individual persons within the household; and (2) for the members of the household against undue disturbance by external factors.
    c. Suitable separation of rooms used for: (1) sleeping by adolescent and adult members of the opposite sex except husband and wife; and (2) housing of domestic animals apart from the living area of the dwelling unit.
    d. A potable and palatable water supply, piped by sanitary plumbing into the dwelling unit or in the courtyard, in quantities ample enough to provide for all the personal and household uses essential for sanitation, comfort and cleanliness.
    e. A safe and sanitary means for the disposal of sewage, garbage and other wastes.
    f. Sufficient facilities for washing and bathing.
    g. Appropriate facilities for cooking, dining and the storage of food, household goods and personal belongings.
    h. Appropriate protection against excess heat, cold, noise and dampness.
    i. Adequate ventilation and internal air free of toxic or noxious agents.
    j. Sufficient natural and artificial illumination.
2. A neighborhood or "micro-district" setting for the dwelling which conforms with sound town, country and regional planning practice and consists of:
    a. When economically feasible, a community water supply, sewage collection and treatment, collection and disposal of garbage and other wastes, and storm water drainage.
    b. An atmosphere which is free of toxic or noxious gases, odors, fumes or dusts.
    c. Protective facilities of police and fire services.
    d. Industrial, commercial, cultural, social, religious, educational, recreational and health and welfare facilities connected to the residential structures by a network of roads and public transportation and a system of footpaths.
    e. Freedom from hazards to health, welfare and public morals.

Methods of Achieving Objectives

There are at least seven elements of an effective housing program: analysis of specific neighborhoods, development of a comprehensive community plan, enactment of adequate codes and ordinances, provision of an adequate administrative organization, provision of adequate financing, development of a method for housing persons displaced by clearance projects and the obtaining of full citizen participation.

Analysis of Neighborhoods

It is necessary to determine objectively the local housing conditions. A standard technique often used is the housing appraisal method adopted by the Committee on the Hygiene of Housing of the American Public Health Association.* This method provides comprehensive and objective data on the conditions and adequacy of housing. By the use of this scheme, housing is evaluated from the viewpoints of health, safety and essential livability.

Comprehensive Community Plan

The external environment of a dwelling can be controlled only by the formulation and adoption of a comprehensive community plan.

This type of plan projects needs into the future and tries to provide orderly development to take care of the needs of the community. Such planning covers subdivision of land, roads, schools, water supply, recreation, refuse collection and disposal, sewers, land occupancy, population density, cultural needs and the other factors which contribute to a desirable community. The special needs of the elderly are increasingly being considered in community planning.

In slum clearance, the community plan should provide for the reuse of land areas cleared of substandard dwellings, plus revitalization and reorientation of city growth.

Adequate Codes and Ordinances

Structural standards for housing are usually contained in building codes. The elements covered in building codes relate basically to these points: structural protection against fire, building strength, plumbing, electrical wiring, heating and ventilation. Codes usually apply only to new or remodeled buildings.

The control of use of a structure is ordinarily covered by a housing code. This is generally applicable to all buildings new and old, but more particularly to old structures frequently built prior to the existence of building control, or to those in which radical changes in usage have taken place. A housing code will usually contain standards for basic equipment and facilities, natural and artificial light, ventilation, electrical requirements, common hallways and stairs, exterior stairs and porches, weather and water tightness, eaves, gutters and downspouts, freedom from infestation by insects and rodents, maintenance of structure, maintenance of supplied facilities, interior and exterior painting, means of egress, living space, sleeping space, room size, occupancy of basement and cellar space, rooming houses, motels

---

* The schedule used is obtainable from the American Public Health Association, 1790 Broadway, New York.

and hotels, duties and responsibilities of owners and duties and responsibilities of tenants.

Codes provide for inspection procedures, right of entry, appeal from regulations, penalties and other administrative details.

Unfortunately, most metropolitan communities are still using obsolete and unsatisfactory building codes; the use of strict housing codes is just beginning to gain acceptance. In suburban communities, codes are, for the most part, nonexistent.

Adequate Administrative Organizations

Provision of adequate administration is frequently difficult in a housing program. In many instances it has been almost impossible to integrate separate governmental activities pertaining to fire, health, building, welfare and the legal aspects of the program.

A trend in the management of slum areas is the establishment of a coordinating committee of the various agencies involved to secure uniformity of approach and to eliminate overlapping or neglected areas of interest. Ideally, a single agency should be established to provide inspection and enforcement services. This agency could work under a committee, board or commission which could provide professional direction and competence in the areas of special interest.

The effectiveness of a general housing office of inspection and enforcement depends primarily on the availability of staff, which in turn is dependent on an adequate budget. A part of the costs can be recovered from charges for permits, licenses, and penalties for violation.

In suburban areas, division of authority is not so much a problem as the lack of any responsible organization. This general abdication of their housing responsibilities by suburban areas has led to state and federal measures which attempt to provide some leadership. State interest is usually directed through the health department and aimed at the provision of an adequate water supply, sewage disposal, drainage and refuse disposal. Federal involvement is usually associated with Federal Housing Administration or Veterans Administration mortages, for the approval of which the agencies insist on certain standards.

Adequate Financing

Although some cities are carrying out slum clearance and housing programs, it would appear that practically all future activities in the U.S.A. will be based on federal urban renewal provisions, since slum clearance presents a financial burden that most communities cannot assume. This need was recognized by Congress in the Housing Act of 1949, which was expanded and improved under the Housing Act of 1954. This act provides federal aid for two-thirds of the cost of clearance and rehabilitation, providing the local community presents a workable program to the federal government. Most cities have seized upon the Federal Urban Renewal Program as the solution to their difficulties. Experience indicates, however, that this is no major solution. Desirable redevelopment of cleared land is a continuing problem.

Housing Persons Displaced by Land Clearance

The housing of persons displaced by urban renewal or other land clearance activities is a problem related to slum clearance programs. The common lack of adequate numbers of low rental housing units prior to slum clearance represents a serious handicap in adequately housing displaced families.

Citizen Participation

Active support of a housing program by the people of a community requires a well-developed educational campaign pointing out the hazards of uncontrolled housing construction and the spread of blighted areas.

Among lower income groups, education in good housekeeping and cleanliness has been a demonstrated need. Experience has shown that frequently good housing is turned into shambles by occupants of low social and moral standards. This has become a major concern of social scientists who are interested in stimulating change in attitudes and behavior.

APPLICATION IN THE COMMUNITY

In the past, housing activities have not been considered the sole concern of one regulatory agency. The elements of the house and its environment have usually been divided among a variety of agencies, despite newer concepts which have attempted to approach housing and community residents as an integral unit. In any one community as many as nine different agencies or departments may be concerned with housing. These include:

1. *Housing Authority.* Planning and construction of public housing.

2. *Planning Commission.* Determination of future land use, selection of areas for redevelopment and collaboration in establishment of policy.

3. *Social Welfare.* Assistance in development of adequate housing and raising the quality of housing of welfare recipients.

4. *Division of Buildings.* Review of plans for new buildings or remodeling of old. Inspection of all buildings for compliance, usually limited to structures, heating and electrical work.

5. *Fire Department.* Enforcement of regulations for fire prevention.

6. *Health Department.* Enforcement of compliance with health and sanitary requirements. Often administers plumbing code.

7. *Corporation Counsel.* Preparation of cases for prosecution of violators.

8. *Community Relations Council.* The prevention of social tensions caused by the housing shortage and substandard living conditions.

9. *Bureau of Urban Renewal.* Administration of projects involving slum clearance and rehabilitation of dwellings.

A major deficiency has been the absence of performance standards and methods of measuring the achievement of desirable goals.

ROLE OF PHYSICIAN

The practicing physician can make many valuable contributions in the initiation and management of community housing programs. As a member of a prominent and articulate professional group, he can use his influence in supporting or prodding local officials to take cognizance of housing problems and to institute community action. During his daily rounds a physician has many opportunities to observe and suggest corrections of undesirable housing conditions. Accident hazards may be pointed out to patients with recommendations for corrective action. Major housing problems beyond the immediate control of residents may be brought to the attention of appropriate agency personnel for their correction.

JOHN T. GENTRY, M.D.
ROBERT D. HENNIGAN, P.E.

REFERENCES

1. Wilner, D. M., Walkley, R. P., Pinkerton, T. C., and Tayback, M.: The Housing Environment and Family Life. Baltimore, The Johns Hopkins University, 1962.
2. Basic Principles of Healthful Housing. New York, American Public Health Association, Committee on the Hygiene of Housing, 1939.
3. WHO: Report Series No. 225, Expert Committee on the Public Health Aspects of Housing. World Health Organization, 1961.
4. An Appraisal Method for Measuring the Quality of Housing. Vol. 1: Nature and Uses of the Method. Vol. 2: Appraisal of Dwelling Conditions. Vol. 3: Appraisal of Neighborhood Environment. New York, American Public Health Association, Committee on the Hygiene of Housing, 1945-1950.
5. A Proposed Housing Ordinance. New York, American Public Health Association, Committee on the Hygiene of Housing, 1952.
6. Executive Office of the President, Office of Science and Technology: Better Housing for the Future. Washington, D.C., 1963.
7. City Planning and Urban Development. Washington, D.C., Chamber of Commerce of the United States, 1952.
8. Suggested Land Subdivision Regulations. Washington, D.C., United States Housing and Home Finance Agency, Housing Research Section, Government Printing Office, 1952.
9. Trichter, Jerome, and Halpern, Milton: Accidental Carbon Monoxide Poisoning Due to Domestic Gas Appliances and Gas Refrigerators: The Problem of New York City and its Control. Presented at the 79th Annual Meeting, American Public Health Association, San Francisco, 1951.
10. Standards for Healthful Housing. Vol. 1: Planning the Neighborhood, 1960. Vol. 2: Planning the Home for Occupancy. Vol. 3: Construction and Equipment of the Home, 1950. New York, American Public Health Association, Committee on the Hygiene of Housing, Public Administration Service.
11. Problems of Community Development—100 Selected References. New York, American Council to Improve Our Neighborhoods, Inc. (ACTION), 1955.

12   Occupational Health

Occupational medicine, in the broadest sense, embraces all phases of the practice of medicine involved with the health of the gainfully employed. Since the capacity to do work has always been a criterion of health and an objective of treatment, this is not a new field of medicine. Direct concern with the health of workers, as distinct from other groups, is a newer concept and is reflected in such terms as industrial medicine and industrial hygiene. Each term has a particular meaning for a group of specialists in accord with their special interests and backgrounds. The distinctions, however, are not sufficient to be meaningful and in most situations the three terms are used interchangeably.

RELATIONSHIP TO PUBLIC HEALTH AND GENERAL MEDICINE

Occupational medicine, like its parent discipline, public health, is primarily concerned with preventive and social medicine and other areas within the confines of health promotion. It is also concerned with the diagnosis and treatment of a specific group of diseases, the diseases of occupation. Its perimeter of interest is usually limited to the people employed in industry. However, its influence often extends beyond the plant gates. Occupational medicine differs from general medicine in that its emphasis is more on preventive and health promotion techniques and less on the treatment of disease.

OBJECTIVES AND SCOPE

The principal objectives of occupational medicine are: to prevent the occurrence of occupational diseases and injuries, to minimize the progression of any disease or injury and to utilize maximally residual capacities, and to promote the optimum health and well-being of the worker. To attain these objectives requires a well rounded, active and adequately administered occupational health program. The coordinated efforts of physicians, management, labor, the public, governmental agencies, insurance companies, universities and voluntary health agencies are essential prerequisites in any such program.

183

The importance of attaining these objectives is pointed up by the fact that about half of the adult population works in some form of industrial activity. Among these, significant numbers work in industries where dangerous or potentially hazardous materials are used or produced, although the exact number of workers exposed to these various hazardous agents is not known (Fig. 30).

The industrial medical department's main function is to evaluate existing disability and prevent further disability by fitting the individual to his occupational environment. The chief responsibility of the industrial hygiene and safety department is to adapt the environment to the individual by making it safe and healthful. While this division of responsibility is appropriate, it involves considerable overlapping on specific problems, and close integration of the two functions is essential.

Occupational medicine is concerned with all conditions which adversely

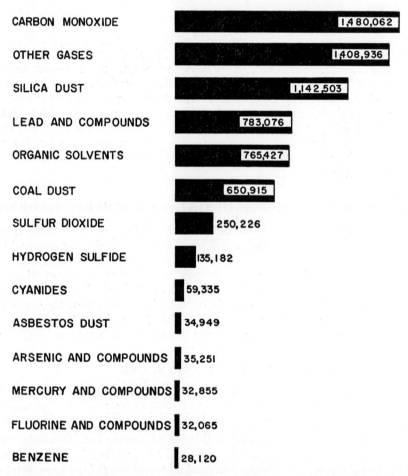

Figure 30. Health hazards in industry: a conservative estimate of the number of industrial workers exposed to toxins and other hazards. (Environment and Health. 1951. Public Health Service, U. S. Department of Health, Education, and Welfare, p. 93.)

influence the health and productivity of workers. While nonoccupational diseases, such as cardiovascular, common respiratory and gastrointestinal diseases and emotional disturbances, account for more disability than occupational diseases and injuries, interest and responsibility for the former is shared with all physicians. Occupational diseases—usually defined as diseases or injuries arising out of and occurring in the course of employment—are the unique concern of the industrial physician.

INDUSTRIAL ACCIDENTS

With due regard to the excellent accomplishments achieved by many national and local organizations active in the field of safety, it is not inappropriate to emphasize the equally important role of the medical profession in this area. As Hunter[1] has aptly stated: "Only doctors see the full consequences of accidents, with their wastage of life and working efficiency, the disruption of family life and the tragic effects on the individual. It is up to us as a profession to give more thought to the prevention of accidents and to make our views public." A statistical analysis of industrial (work) accidents has already been given in Chapter 2. An attempt will be made in this chapter to give some of the important views on industrial accidents which are generally held by the medical profession.

IMPORTANCE OF INDUSTRIAL ACCIDENTS

Claims paid for industrial accidents under Workmen's Compensation Laws account for 97 to 99 per cent of the amount paid for all occupational disabilities.[2] The low percentage cost associated with occupational diseases does not, however, reflect their true relative importance. Both play a significant part in sickness absenteeism. A realization of the human costs of industrial disease, in terms of prolonged discomfort from chronic industrial diseases and their frequently more permanent and totally disabling effects, must be considered. On the other hand, recent figures indicate that deaths and nonfatal injuries of occupational origin in the United States are significantly less than those attributed to the home and motor vehicles.[3] However, it is becoming increasingly evident that environmental safety is only a partial solution to the accident problem. A realization that human failure is the principal factor, or at least a major contributing one, in the majority of accidents emphasizes the responsibility and magnifies the role of the industrial physician in plant safety.

FACTORS INFLUENCING ACCIDENT RATES

The accident rate varies greatly among different occupations. The number and rates for deaths and injuries due to occupational accidents for the principal industrial groups are shown in Figure 31. The most dangerous is that listed as mining and quarrying. The comparatively low accident rates for many occupations are due to the excellent safety programs sponsored by the hazardous industries. The Workmen's Compensation Laws and especially the activities of the National Safety Council have been largely responsible for the excellent results in this field. Available figures suggest that absentee-

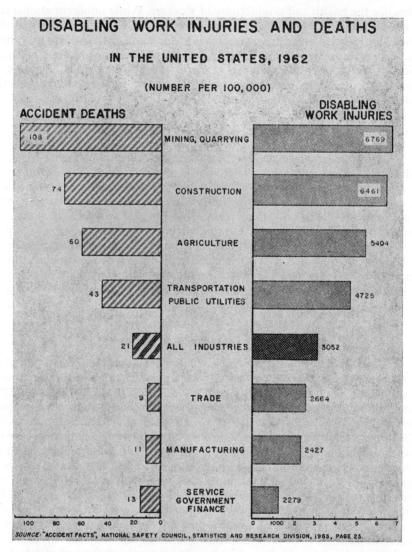

Figure 31. Disabling work injuries and deaths in the United States in 1962.

ism from work due to occupational injuries is appreciably less than that due to nonoccupational injuries.[4]

Certain data indicate that women have a lower rate of industrial accidents than men, but these differences may be due simply to differences in exposure. Industrial accidents are more frequent among young, inexperienced employees than among the more experienced workers.[5]

Fatigue also appears to be a factor. Studies show that the accident frequency rate increases significantly when the work hours are extended appreciably. This presented a real problem during World War II, since there was an urgent need to accelerate production in the face of a decreasing industrial population.

It has been shown that the majority of accidents occur among a relatively small group of people. Although this is not supported by all the available information, it has introduced the concept of accident-prone workers in industry. Industrial psychiatrists describe the personality of the accident-prone worker as one who is decisive or even impulsive, a person of action, and not of planning or deliberation.[5]

It is noteworthy that the term sickness-prone has also been introduced into industry, and this highlights the important part the personality factor plays in sicknesses and injuries within industry. Further data have shown that a close relationship exists between accident proneness and proneness to physical and emotional illness.[6]

PREVENTION OF ACCIDENTS

There is no simple solution to the accident problem in industry. However, accidents, like toxic hazards, are preventable. This can be achieved best by a properly oriented and adequately administered in-plant medical and safety program. A more complete discussion of this will be presented in the section dealing with the prevention and control of industrial diseases and injuries in industry.

DISEASES OF OCCUPATION

Since many of the agents producing occupational disease are found elsewhere, such as in the home and in laboratories, these diseases are not limited to the industrial environment. Household exposure to lead, carbon tetrachloride and hair dyes occurs often enough so that poisoning has been reported from inadvertent and improper household use of these agents.

Another significant point is that a nonoccupational disease may be aggravated by certain exposures in the industrial environment. A person who has anemia of nonoccupational etiology may develop a more severe anemia if his work exposes him to such hemopoietic toxins as benzol, aniline or ionizing radiation. As a result, a nonoccupational disease becomes an occupational disease.

From the foregoing, it is obvious that the practicing physician must be aware of the work exposures of his patients, the diseases they cause and the role they play in aggravating nonoccupational diseases. Due consideration to the clinical picture of industrial intoxication should facilitate the accurate diagnosis of nonoccupational poisonings.

It is beyond the scope of this chapter to discuss each, or even the major, occupational diseases. For this, the reader may refer to a number of comprehensive textbooks on occupational medicine and industrial hygiene. Table 9 presents a summary of the major symptoms, signs, organs and systems affected, and the biological tests indicated for the most common toxins encountered in industry.

CLASSIFICATION

The two classifications of occupational diseases which follow are given to demonstrate to the reader the diversity of this specialty. One is based on

Table 9. *Symptoms, Signs, Organs or Systems Affected by, and Diagnostic Laboratory Tests Relating to Some Commonly Used Toxic Substances*[7], *

SUBSTANCE	SYMPTOMS	SIGNS	ORGANS OR SYSTEM AFFECTED	INDICATED BIOLOGICAL TESTS
METALS				
Lead	Metallic taste Anorexia Weakness Abdominal discomfort Constipation Pains in muscles and joints Irritability	Pallor Blue line on gums Muscle weakness Tremors Abdominal tenderness	Gastro-intestinal Hemopoietic Nervous	Lead in blood or urine Porphyrins Blood cell counts, including stippled cells and reticulocytes Delta-amino, laevulinic acid
Mercury	Metallic taste Anorexia Salivation Sore gums Irritability Tremors Abdominal discomfort Insomnia	Stomatitis Gingivitis Fetid breath Tremors Erethism Dermatographia Pallor Psychic disturbances	Mucous membrane of oral cavity Gastro-intestinal Nervous Renal	Urinalysis Mercury in urine Renal function
Chromium	Irritation of upper respiratory tract	Characteristic skin ulcers Perforation of nasal septum	Skin Mucous membrane	Environmental analyses
Cadmium	Dryness and soreness of throat Metallic taste Cough Substernal pain Dyspnea	Pulmonary edema Tachycardia Tachypnea (Rales may not be noted until near death)	Respiratory	Blood cell count (leukocytosis, lymphocytosis)
HALOGENATED HYDROCAR-BONS				
Carbon tetra-chloride	Headache Nausea Vomiting Anorexia Fatigue	Jaundice Edema of face and ankles Hepatomegaly Oliguria	Gastro-intestinal Renal Hepatic	Routine urinalysis Liver function tests Blood nonprotein nitrogen Blood creatinine
Trichloro-ethylene	Dyspnea Headache Dizziness Disturbed gait Fatigue Anorexia Nausea Somnolence Numerous other	Tremors Abdominal tenderness Dermatitis Sluggish response to questions Diminished vision	Nervous Cardiac	Analysis of urine for trichloro-acetic acid

* Because of space limitations, certain portions of the original table have been omitted here.

Table 9—*Continued*

SUBSTANCE	SYMPTOMS	SIGNS	ORGANS OR SYSTEM AFFECTED	INDICATED BIOLOGICAL TESTS
	subjective complaints	Cardiac arrhythmia (Objective physical findings scant)		
AROMATIC HYDRO-CARBONS				
Benzol	Headache Dizziness Anorexia Insomnia Weakness Fatigue Muscle cramps	Purpura Bleeding from gums	Hemopoietic	Complete blood cell count (anemia, leukopenia) Urine sulfate ratio
Aniline	Headache Vertigo Weakness Unsteady gait	Cyanosis Weak pulse Muscular tremors Brown discoloration of urine	Blood	Methemoglobin Blood cell count
GASES				
Carbon monoxide	Headache Dizziness Nausea Vomiting Blurred vision	Tachycardia Peripheral vasodilation Cherry-red color of mucous membranes Weak, thready pulse	Blood (asphyxial phenomenon)	Determination of carboxyhemoglobin
Hydrogen sulfide	Irritation of eyes and respiratory tract	Reddened eyes Hyperpnea	Respiratory	Environmental analysis for hydrogen sulfide
Nitrogen dioxide	Cough Dyspnea Pains in chest	Pulmonary edema Peripheral vasodilation Respiratory paralysis Unconsciousness	Respiratory	Methemoglobin Chest roentgenogram
Organic phosphorus compounds	Tachypnea Ataxia Tremors Anorexia Nausea Vomiting Blurring of vision	Lacrimation Slurred speech Salivation Cyanosis Miosis Hypertension Tonic and clonic convulsions Hyperhidrosis	Nervous	Serum cholinesterase

Table 9—*Continued*

SUBSTANCE	SYMPTOMS	SIGNS	ORGANS OR SYSTEM AFFECTED	INDICATED BIOLOGICAL TESTS
DUSTS				
Silica	Dyspnea Cough Anorexia Fatigue	Cyanosis Reduction in vital capacity Clubbing of fingers	Respiratory Cardiac	Roentgenogram
Silicates (feldspar, talc, clay)	If present, similar to silica but much milder; may result from silica contamination	Generally very few; vital capacity reduced in advanced cases only	Respiratory Cardiac	Roentgenogram
RADIOACTIVE MATERIALS				
	Erythema Skin lesions Burns Malaise Nausea Vomiting Purpura	Capillary fragility Petechiae Ecchymoses Hematomas Gastrointestinal ulcers Anemia Loss of hair Cataracts Neoplasia	Hemopoietic Reproductive	Complete blood cell counts (anemia, leukopenia, lymphopenia) Bone marrow studies Biopsy, ionization chamber

etiology and the other on pharmacology. Both are presented with comments and examples. Each classification contains certain noteworthy features which will be of interest to the reader.

Etiologic

Chemical Agents. Since industrial chemical hazards are found in every phase of chemistry, it is impractical to classify them by their chemical formulas. A more convenient way is to group them according to the physical state in which they are usually harmful to exposed workers.

1. Dusts. Dusts are small particles of matter produced usually by disintegration of a solid. Dusts above a certain size and weight settle out of the air rapidly, but the dusts that remain in suspension for any length of time are those which are most important industrially since they may be inhaled. Dust particles larger than 10 micra are usually not inhaled into the deeper bronchioles. Dusts may be classified as:

a. Inorganic dusts, which are either mineral, e.g., silica and asbestos, or metallic, e.g., lead, arsenic and cadmium.

b. Organic dusts, which are either toxic organic compounds, e.g., trinitrotoluene and hexachlorethane, or allergic (containing foreign proteins), e.g., furs, grain and pollens.

2. Gases. A gas is a substance which exists as a free molecular dispersion

under normal conditions of temperature and pressure. Some of the most common etiologic agents in industrial disease are gases, e.g., carbon monoxide, ammonia, hydrogen sulfide and sulfur dioxide.

3. Vapors. Vapors are the gaseous components of substances which are liquids at ordinary temperature. Every liquid gives off a vapor and many are highly volatile. Solvent vapors are extremely important in industrial hygiene since they provide most of the poisonous substances. Examples include vapors of benzol, carbon tetrachloride and gasoline.

4. Fumes. Fumes are solid particles of matter dispersed in the air but usually derived from some physicochemical process, such as reaction of gases, combustion or sublimation. Among these are lead and zinc, which, when heated to a high enough temperature, give off fumes due to the reaction of the metallic component with the oxygen of the air. Fume particles are usually quite small, being less than one-fifth of a micron. Common in industrial poisoning are lead and zinc fumes and those produced in welding.

5. Mists. Mists are suspensions of small droplets of a liquid in the air. They are caused by the forceful dispersion of liquid into the air, e.g., by means of an atomizer or spray gun. They may also occur as the condensation of a vapor on a nucleus of solid matter, e.g., smog. A common industrial mist occurs in electroplating where escaping bubbles of gas entrap liquid chromic acid producing a mist.

Physical Agents. These agents are common causes of industrial disease.

1. Abnormalities of pressure. Some occupations require working in higher than atmospheric pressure, e.g., compressed-air workers and divers. If not protected, these workers develop decompression sickness (caisson disease, compressed air illness). An opposite condition—reduction in atmospheric pressure—occurs in high altitude flying and in mining operations at high altitudes. Physiologic changes are produced, notably anoxia, air embolism and middle ear disease.

2. Abnormalities of temperature and humidity. Many industrial processes require the use of great heat, as in the manufacture of glass and steel. Muscle cramps, heat exhaustion and heat stroke are frequent results of such exposure. Local heat, as well as sudden changes in temperature, abnormally low temperatures and dampness may also aggravate a pre-existing disease.

3. Abnormalities of sound. Noise often affects workers deleteriously. Audiometric studies show that workers in noisy environments (over 100 decibels) develop a definite type of nerve deafness.

4. Abnormalities of radiation.

a. Radioactivity. Exposure to radium is common since it is used industrially in radium dial painting and in industrial radiography. The effect on the body in radium dial painting is due to its accidental inhalation or ingestion and subsequent deposition in the bones. Exposure to roentgen rays sometimes occurs when high voltages are used to x-ray castings and welded parts. The effects are noted chiefly in the blood stream and genital organs but occasionally malignancy may be produced. For further details on effects of ionizing radiation see Chapter 3.

b. Ultraviolet rays. Workers are occasionally exposed to ultraviolet rays. The most serious effect of this is on the eyes, producing eye flash, e.g., in welding.

c. Infrared rays. Infrared rays are being used more often as a drying agent. Occasionally they produce conjunctivitis and dermatitis.

d. Microwaves. These are high frequency electromagnetic waves which are being used in communication and radar and for rapid cooking of foods. Excessive exposure may produce injury to the lens of the eye.

e. Lasers. These are devices which amplify the intensity of a beam of visible light. They are being used in medicine and in industry. In medicine, lasers are being used in the correction of retinal detachment. Industry is applying these devices in communications and in welding. Eye protection must be provided because of the danger of retinal burns.

f. Defective illumination. Miner's nystagmus rarely occurs in America, but defective illumination may produce eye strain and headaches.

5. Chronic friction. Mechanical effects of friction are quite common in industry and produce abrasions, callosities, bursitis and contracture. Strains may produce tenosynovitis and ganglions.

Infectious Agents. The diseases produced by these agents occur less frequently in the United States than in the less industrialized and less sanitary countries. Their etiology, treatment and prophylaxis are discussed in other chapters.

1. Bacterial. Anthrax, brucellosis, glanders, leptospirosis, septic infections and erysipeloid are all examples of bacterial disease that can result from occupation.

2. Fungi. Actinomycosis and blastomycosis are sometimes of occupational origin.

3. Parasites. Ankylostomiasis may be considered occupational in infected areas where workers are barefoot.

Pharmacologic

Some chemicals demonstrate a relationship between their composition and their pharmacologic action. However, it is practically impossible to anticipate the reaction of the body to any given chemical, since experience shows that chemicals do not necessarily excite a physiopathologic response in the body according to their formulas. For example, trichlorethylene (C_2HCl_3) is much less toxic than chloroform, although it has the same degree of chlorination.

Most chemicals initiate more than one response. The following classification is based on the predominant type of response.

Asphyxiants. These chemicals interfere with the supply or utilization of oxygen but do not injure the lungs.

1. Simple asphyxiants. These produce anoxia by decreasing the oxygen content of the air, e.g., nitrogen, helium, ethylene and methane.

2. Chemical asphyxiants. These accompany air which has a normal oxygen content, but they may prevent either the blood from carrying the oxygen or the cells from using it, e.g., carbon monoxide decreases the oxygen-carrying capacity of blood; the cyanogens (CN) interfere with cell metabolism, producing tissue anoxia.

Irritants. These produce an inflammation of the surface tissue, the respiratory tract and eyes.

1. Irritants which affect the upper respiratory tract, especially the nose and throat and also the eyes, usually produce such marked local effects that

these are in themselves a safeguard to dangerous exposure. Among these irritants are ammonia, acrolein, formaldehyde and hydrochloric acid.

2. Irritants to the upper respiratory tract which do not show an adequate margin between discomfort and harm include sulfur dioxide and the halogens, e.g., chlorine and bromine.

3. Irritants which affect the upper respiratory tract minimally but are severely harmful to the lower respiratory tract include ozone, phosgene and nitrous fumes.

Narcotics. These substances have a druglike action on the body. Practically all of them have some anesthetic properties, but also produce other effects. Among these substances are the alcohols, the ketones and the ethers.

Systemic Toxins. These substances produce changes in the visceral organs.

1. Protoplasmic toxins. These agents produce death of tissue, e.g., the heavy metals (mercury, lead and arsenic), phosphorus and phenols.

2. Neurotoxins. These chemicals have an affinity for nervous tissue, e.g., carbon disulfide and the aromatic nitro-compounds (trinitrotoluene, nitrobenzol and nitrophenol).

3. Hepatorenal toxins. These have an outstanding effect on the liver and kidneys, e.g., the chlorinated hydrocarbons (chloroform, carbon tetrachloride).

4. Hemopoietic toxins. These chemicals have an effect on the blood and/or blood-forming organs, e.g., benzol, chlorobenzol, aniline and radioactive substances.

5. Metabolic toxins. These have a general effect on the metabolism of the body, e.g., dinitrophenol.

Pneumoconiosis-producing Agents. These are dusts which produce various changes, primarily in the lungs.

1. Inert reaction, produced by carbon and iron.

2. Fibrotic reaction, produced by silica and asbestos.

3. Doubtful reaction, produced by talc and mica.

Dermatitis-producing Agents. Practically all chemicals if they come in sufficient contact with the skin may produce a dermatitis.

1. Primary irritants, e.g., acids, alkalies and solvents.

2. Allergens, which produce an allergic response, e.g., tetryl and poison ivy.

3. Combination of both irritant and allergens, e.g., chromic acid and formaldehyde.

Carcinogenic Agents. A number of exposures in industry produce malignancy; most notable are radium and roentgen ray. Betanaphthylamine produces bladder cancers. Asbestos can produce bronchogenic carcinoma.

INCIDENCE

Unfortunately, there are few reliable statistics on the incidence of occupational diseases for the general working population. Existing networks and techniques for reporting data on occupational diseases are ineffectual, despite the mandatory reporting requirements of most states. However, compensation records yield useful but limited information on the incidence of occupational diseases. A compilation based primarily on workmen's compensation records of 28 states showed that skin diseases lead in the frequency of the industrial diseases reported. Diseases due to chemical agents, physical agents and dusts follow respectively in the order of frequency.[8]

While actual incidence totals of various occupational diseases are important, the human and economic costs of certain of these diseases are of greater significance, as some recent compensation experience will illustrate. Figures released by the New York State Workmen's Compensation Board indicate that the percentage of costs for dermatitis was relatively low, as compared to the pneumoconioses, particularly silicosis, which amounted to almost 34 per cent for the period 1959 to 1962 (Fig. 32). This is no doubt due to the greater

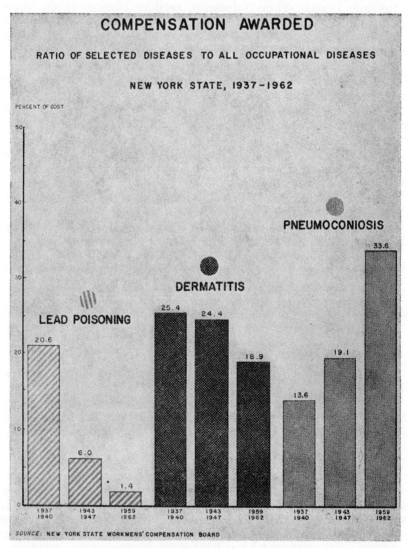

Figure 32. Compensation awarded—ratios of selected diseases to all occupational diseases (New York State, 1937-1962).

disability and mortality associated with the pneumoconioses. These accounted for 84.2 per cent of all permanent total disability cases and for 66.8 per cent of all death cases closed by the Workmen's Compensation Board during this same period.[9]

An improved system for more widespread and uniform reporting of occupational diseases is urgently needed, both for collecting data and for properly evaluating the extent and effectiveness of available occupational disease control methods. Uniform collection and tabulation of such data will identify areas most in need of further effort.

IMPORTANCE OF OCCUPATIONAL DISEASE DIAGNOSIS

The great variety of occupational diseases and their close resemblance to certain diseases of nonoccupational origin is apparent from the classification. There is a corresponding need for education and special training, particularly of the private physician, in the recognition and accurate diagnosis of occupational diseases. Often certain occupational diseases do not show their symptoms until the worker has left his industrial environment. This is true particularly in situations where he is exposed to certain solvents, such as trichlorethylene, and to lower respiratory tract irritants, such as phosgene, cadmium fumes, ozone and nitrous fumes. In the latter instance, pulmonary edema may follow 10 to 12 hours after the last exposure. This is indistinguishable from pulmonary edema of cardiac origin. Failure to associate the patient's clinical picture with his industrial environmental exposure may result in serious harm or death to the patient. Failure to correct or remove the environmental hazard may also bring about similar effects upon other workers.

In contrast to those disorders in which the effect is only delayed for 10 to 12 hours, there are other diseases of occupation, such as the pneumoconioses and certain blood diseases, which generally require a long incubation period and/or repeated exposure before symptoms and signs become evident. Silicosis and aplastic anemia are examples of such diseases. Sometimes the worker has left the hazardous environment for years when his symptoms develop. Only by familiarizing himself with the various agents and their characteristic effects can the physician develop a proper index of suspicion, in order to provide good therapy and institute preventive procedures.

On the other hand, knowing that an individual has been exposed to a harmful substance does not necessarily incriminate this substance in the etiology of his disease. An unqualified acceptance of such an association may result in needless effort and unjustifiable compensation claims. In most instances, the degree of exposure to the harmful substance should be ascertained, and this should then be related to existing knowledge of the disease.

The degree of exposure is primarily dependent on two factors: (a) the *duration* of exposure, and (b) the *concentration* of the air-borne contaminant. In determining concentration, certain values of air contamination by specific industrial substances have been established as standards by agencies in the field of industrial hygiene (American Conference of Governmental Industrial Hygienists and American Standards Association). These are called maximum allowable concentrations (MAC) or threshold limits. They are defined as the average concentration to which a worker may be exposed for 8 hours daily for an indefinite period without impairment of his health. However, these are not fixed standards and are subject to change on the basis of newer experience or research. Nonetheless, they are useful to the occupational health staff as guides in the environmental control and diagnosis of occupational diseases.

Fortunately, facilities for consultation and assistance in occupational disease diagnosis are becoming increasingly available through private consultants and through the agencies organized for this purpose. The private practitioner should be encouraged to use them more frequently.

NONOCCUPATIONAL DISEASES

As a group, the nonoccupational illnesses far outweigh both the occupational injuries and industrial diseases as a cause of lost time from work. Moreover, the relatively less serious short-term illnesses, such as the common cold and minor gastrointestinal disturbances, cause more lost time than major illnesses, such as pneumonia. Statistics show that each worker loses an average of a day and a half per year due to respiratory diseases (Fig. 33). Emotional disturbances are of increasing concern to occupational physicians, management and labor, since it has been shown that they play a significant role in one-third of all individual absences attributed to illness.

Industry is coming more and more to realize that the prevention of nonoccupational disease and the promotion of worker health is of equal benefit to the company and its employees. In addition to the huge direct cost of production loss because of sickness absenteeism, there is also the indirect cost of decreased productivity from workers who are on the job but are not optimally well. It has become a truism that healthy and contented workers are a company's most valuable asset.

Recognizing this, industry is increasingly assuming the burden of maintaining wages during illness and paying a major share of the incidental medical expenses. Sometimes this is assumed directly; more often it is covered by insurance plans which require a varying part of the premium to be paid by the worker. Medical care plans covering the nonoccupational disabilities now cost industry 5 to 10 times as much as workmen's compensation.[10] Industry is assuming this burden partly under pressure from organized labor and partly in recognition that security from fear of medical expenses makes for a healthy, well-adjusted and productive worker.

Appreciation of these facts is a cogent reason why industry needs, and is seeking, effective preventive medical programs. Such programs can reduce sickness absenteeism and on-the-job illness. In addition, they can detect early symptoms and, with the assurance provided by the fringe-benefit programs, refer the worker to his private physician for adequate care before a major illness develops. These programs coordinate preventive efforts, and include: (a) early detection and proper counseling within the plant, (b) consideration of the stresses at home and at work and (c) prompt referral. Particular attention is given when emotional factors are involved. Besides the immediate savings from preventive programs, a decreased incidence of disability can lower the premium on insurance programs and the savings from this

Kind of Illness

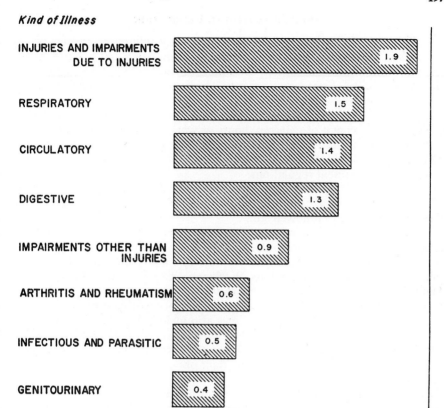

Figure 33. Average days lost from work because of illness, scaled according to the kind of condition, in the United States in 1957. The numbers shown are the days lost per person per year. (Health Statistics. Public Health Service, U. S. Department of Health, Education, and Welfare, Publication No. 584-B4, June, 1958, p. 18.)

can be used to broaden medical care for the worker. Since fringe benefits, once begun, are rarely curtailed, getting more for the money is often the only saving possible.

The preventive programs within industry and benefit programs to defray the cost of illness for large groups of people have obvious wider implications, since they affect also the home, community and nation. It is these broad implications which demonstrate the close relationship between occupational medicine and social medicine.

PREVENTION AND CONTROL OF INDUSTRIAL DISEASES AND INJURIES

The control of industrial diseases and injuries has been influenced chiefly by three lines of activity: industrial health legislation, services provided by governmental and nongovernmental organizations, and voluntary control measures provided by industry.

INDUSTRIAL HEALTH LEGISLATION

Although the federal government indirectly influences the control of diseases in industry by such means as taxation, education and research grants, the direct regulation of working conditions in the United States is primarily the responsibility of state governments. The programs and type of legislation vary from state to state.

The first laws which regulated the conditions of work were those dealing with the employment of children, hours of work for women and the prevention of accidents. The first child labor law was passed in Massachusetts in 1842. Progress in this type of legislation was slow, but today all states have some form of pertinent regulations.

Legislation directly relating to occupational diseases began in 1911, when California passed the first law requiring the reporting of occupational diseases. Other states followed suit.

The first major development was the passage of the Workmen's Compensation Laws. These govern the liability of the employer to his worker who may be killed or injured during his employ. The injury must be related to the job. New York state initiated its Workmen's Compensation Law in 1913. Within a decade, practically every state had adopted some form of workmen's compensation. At first it applied only to occupational injury, but later compensation for industrial disease was also included in the law. These acts have had a profound influence on the development of industrial hygiene and safety within industry. The periods beginning with 1910 and 1930 have been referred to as the beginning of the accident prevention and industrial hygiene phases, respectively.

In 1936 the Walsh-Healy Public Contract Act gave the federal government direct jurisdiction over working conditions in the states for the first time. It was given authority regarding the safety of the workers in industries which held government contracts above 10 thousand dollars for the manufacture or furnishing of materials and equipment. The act forbids giving or maintaining a contract where working conditions are unsanitary or dangerous to the health and safety of the employees.

Other federal laws were enacted which indirectly affect the health of the worker. Of particular interest is the Taft-Hartley Act (1947) which recognized that health and welfare provisions are a proper part of collective bargaining. The Atomic Energy Act of 1946, as amended in 1954, has provided the Atomic Energy Commission with the authority to issue licenses for the use of radioisotopes and to revoke a license if there is failure to comply with prescribed health and safety control procedures. This has made the atomic energy industry one of the healthiest and safest of the potentially hazardous occupations. The Atomic Energy Act was again amended in 1959 to provide for the establishment of the Federal Radiation Council. This Council advises the President on radiation matters affecting health, including guidance in the formulation of radiation standards and the establishment of programs of cooperation with states. The Longshoreman's Act was enacted in 1959 empowering the United States Department of Labor to establish safety standards for longshoremen and shipyard workers. This law requires that employers meet minimum requirements in maintaining safe equipment and healthful working conditions.

Not all of the labor legislation presently on the statutes has been mentioned. But it is important to bear in mind that there are direct, indirect and unknown variable effects brought about by all types of federal legislation. Among these was the passage in 1960 of the Federal Hazardous Substances Labeling Act, designed to protect consumers from the misbranding of hazardous substances used in industry and in the home. Often the indirect effects produce more potent results, and this is particularly true in occupational medicine.

The administration of laws relating to industrial hygiene is usually assigned to the state departments of labor. However, with three exceptions (Illinois, Massachusetts and New York), the divisions or bureaus of industrial hygiene function within the state health departments and provide, primarily, consultation and advice coupled with field and laboratory investigations. The state and local health and sanitary codes, the state labor laws and industrial codes usually provide the industrial hygiene agencies with effective instruments for administrative control.

AGENCIES ACTIVE IN INDUSTRIAL HEALTH

Particular attention is being given here to national organizations within the United States, although the positive influence of the International Labor Organization and World Health Organization in the field of industrial health in the United States should not be overlooked.

United States Public Health Service

The Division of Occupational Health of the United States Public Health Service is the official federal agency engaged in the promotion of occupational health. Its program includes field and laboratory studies of occupational diseases in cooperation with state industrial hygiene agencies. It provides field and laboratory assistance to state units. Through its extensive publication program, as well as through other educational media, it directly encourages industries to adopt corrective protective measures for the health and safety of the worker. It makes available occupational morbidity and mortality data on the extent of illness in the working population. The division has no law-enforcement powers.

United States Bureau of Mines

One of its functions is to promote the health and safety of miners. It has been actively concerned with the effects of harmful substances encountered in mining and in allied industries and with the control of underground exposures to these materials. The Bureau has made a real contribution in the control of silicosis and renders a valuable service in evaluating and providing standards for respirators used to protect against hazardous substances in industry.

The Armed Services

They maintain industrial hygiene personnel within their medical departments and are directly concerned with the health and environmental standards of civilians in their employ.

United States Department of Labor

The role of the United States Labor Department has been related chiefly to the promotion of sanitation, to the prevention of accidents, to the regulation of hours of work and to the control of types of work permissible for women and children. The department performs these functions by inspecting factories, collecting statistics and supporting labor legislation.

State and Local Health Agencies

The Social Security Act of 1935 made possible grants-in-aid to all states for the establishment of statewide industrial health programs. Whereas in 1935 few states had such services, within the past several years almost every state has established an active state industrial hygiene service.

State agencies are engaged in various types of services. These include field investigations of plants to evaluate control procedures. Where a hazard due to a chemical is suspected, air samples are taken both of the general air and of air at the breathing zone of the worker. If the chemical is found to be in hazardous concentrations, corrective procedures are advised. Follow-up visits are usually made to ensure compliance.

One very important function of the field personnel is to evaluate the adequacy and function of ventilation systems. Hazardous conditions often arise because of the inadequacy or breakdown of an exhaust system. The experience of industrial hygiene engineers is invaluable in locating the defect, recommending proper corrective procedures or in giving advice on design before equipment is installed. Industrial hygiene physicians evaluate the health status of workers in the plant by clinical examination of workers when necessary and by a study of the medical records for types of illnesses and the extent of absenteeism. Most state and local industrial health agencies spend considerable time helping individual plants to improve health services for their employees or encouraging their establishment. Some agencies have taken an active role in setting up cooperative medical services for small industries.

Many of the state agencies devote considerable time to educational activities through such means as on-the-spot teaching during plant visits. Some publish periodicals in which all subjects in the broad field of industrial health are covered, so that all interested parties are properly informed. Education also takes the form of papers for discussion at various association meetings, industrial health exhibits, teaching at universities and presenting seminars for interested groups.

Nongovernment Agencies

Many agencies are directly or indirectly concerned with the promotion of industrial health. Among these are industrial hygiene associations, medical societies, privately endowed foundations, insurance companies, health and welfare organizations, labor organizations and universities.

Many of these organizations cooperate with one another and coordinate their work with governmental agencies. A major share of the progress and advancement in industrial hygiene is due to participation of nongovernmental agencies.

HEALTH SERVICES PROVIDED BY INDUSTRY

The activity of private industry in the control of industrial diseases and injuries is motivated in part by the legislation mentioned, and enhanced by the services offered by the official and nonofficial agencies. In practice, it is the voluntary health program provided by industry that is the bulwark against these diseases.

Positive health promotion through the techniques of preventive medicine has been a major preoccupation of in-plant medical departments, in addition to their concern and responsibility for preventing industrial injury and disease. Indeed, historically, industrial health promotion grew out of the need to control these. However, the importance of nonoccupational disease to industry placed increasing emphasis on the preventive approach.

A discussion and evaluation of the essential elements for health maintenance provided by industry can best be considered from the standpoint of the large and small establishment. The objectives are the same; the differences lie in the facilities, the personnel and the methods which are available.

Medical Services in Larger Plants

In-plant medical services have been most elaborately developed in larger plants (over 1000 employees), and have reached the full extent of the program described below mainly in the very large corporations which operate many regional plants. This, however, is not exclusive, since a number of the smaller corporations provide even more than the basic elements of health maintenance to the worker. The functions of the medical program are categorized as curative, preventive and administrative.

Curative. Curative medicine in modern in-plant programs is the administration of first-aid treatment for occupational injuries and illnesses and first-aid and emergency treatment for nonoccupational illnesses. In the course of this work, many leads for preventive action can be found. Great care should be taken to adhere to medical ethics concerning the relationship between the medical department and the worker's personal physician. Although a few industries have extended full health services and even full medical care to employees and their families, this is unusual.

Preventive. Preventive medicine and health promotion are encompassed by the following activities.

1. *Selective placement of new employees* in jobs consistent with their intellectual, physical, social and emotional capacities. Suitability of a prospective worker for a specific job is evaluated by history, physical examination, chest roentgenogram and laboratory procedures such as urinalysis. Similar techniques are used to evaluate the health status of the worker at the time of his return from illness, contemplated transfer, termination of employment or retirement.

2. *Case finding* by means of dispensary visits, regular periodic evaluation and screening programs, such as those for tuberculosis, diabetes or cancer. Suspicion of disease may be followed by a diagnostic work-up, depending on the facilities available. In all cases the worker should be referred for treatment to his personal physician as soon as a positive diagnosis has been reached.

3. *Medical supervision of recuperating or handicapped workers.* Here

too, the treatment remains the responsibility of the private physician. The plant physician will evaluate the worker's current capacity and recommend the modification of the work situation accordingly.

4. *Health education* through individual counseling by the medical staff, leaflets and posters, movies on health and safety and talks by medical and safety personnel. All media, such as company and union magazines or newsletters, can be used. Special programs for special groups, such as nutrition education for the obese, may be initiated.

5. *Specific measures for health maintenance,* such as inspections of plant sanitation, supervision of food handlers and inoculation of employees against endemic and epidemic diseases.

6. *The elimination and control of specific occupational disease hazards.* The medical department in a large plant usually plays a vital role in this area. If it has been established that a potential health hazard exists, but there is uncertainty as to its severity or the adequacy of control measures, a plant survey is made. Whenever indicated, air analysis both of the general air of the workroom and at the specific work site is performed by a competent person. Assistance and advice can be obtained from state and local industrial hygiene divisions. In many instances, these agencies will not only perform these tests but will advise industry concerning proper exhaust ventilation and other protective measures. The medical department usually is and should be informed concerning changes in operations and the intended use of newer processes and materials.

7. *The prevention and control of industrial accidents.* These require an interdisciplinary approach, consisting of the physician, nurse, safety engineer, industrial hygiene engineer, foreman or supervisor and a member of top management. Accident prevention is a team responsibility inseparable from the total industrial operation. It cannot be delegated to specialists and then forgotten by individuals in the line of authority.

Since human failure is now recognized as such a large factor in accidents, it is the responsibility of the physician: to institute proper safety education; to evaluate the capacity of each worker to withstand stress through a medical history including off-the-job psychological factors and a physical examination; to know the stress of the job by environmental investigation, familiarity with other personnel and the medical records; to place the worker safely in terms of his capacity to withstand psychological and physical stress and the stresses of the particular job; to orient the worker's motivations and social attitudes toward safety; and to provide psychological guidance for the accident-prone worker, particularly by enabling him to verbalize his feelings and tensions.

The role of the safety engineer is equally important. The approach of the modern safety engineer involves planning, training and supervision. His planning includes the careful positioning of machinery, the adequacy of mechanical safeguards and provisions for personal protective devices and their maintenance.

The trained and experienced safety man recognizes that safety must be ingrained and taught; it is not innate. The attitude must be that the safe way is the right way. The aim of training is not only *how* but *why* such a procedure is being done, for there are no foolproof, built-in safety devices. The modern safety engineer also recognizes that proper supervision is vital to the safety program, for supervision ingrains the techniques and makes the safe way a habit.

Administration. Administration encompasses the organization and direct supervision of the medical department. This involves the planning of the space needed, the purchase of equipment, the procurement and training of medical, nursing, laboratory and clerical personnel, the establishment and supervision of all activities and the maintenance of accurate, systematic and efficient records.

All visits, observations and treatments should be recorded. They serve to evaluate the health status of the employees as a group, to measure the effectiveness of the preventive techniques in use, and to highlight areas for research and education of management. An important aspect of the medical record is that it constitutes documentary evidence for litigation.

Good administration also includes the maintenance of workmen's compensation records and advice to management and labor on human relation problems and auxiliary medical care or disability insurance.

Medical Services in Smaller Plants

These usually refer to establishments having less than 500 employees. Since the cost per employee tends to vary inversely with the number of employees serviced, smaller plants will usually be able to provide only a limited medical program.[11]

Although exact statistics are not available, it is probable that only a limited number of smaller plants maintain a good first-aid facility; an even lesser number have a program for the prevention of occupational disease and accidents, and rarely educate employees in matters pertaining to safety and health. Most often this depends upon the type of industrial operation, the product, and the hazard potential associated with the process and goods produced. For example, in such plants as radium dial painting, mercury battery or lead storage battery manufacturing, all three programs will usually be provided to a varying extent. At times the plant will have the services of a part-time nurse, particularly where a part-time nursing agency is available. Usually these nurses will work under the supervision of a physician who is on call. This is particularly worthwhile if the physician is familiar with the plant and its possible hazards, so that he can contribute to the development of a preventive program. In some plants these physicians will do preplacement examinations and other aspects of a more extensive program, but this is an unusual situation. In other instances, a few small industrial plants have pooled their resources for the establishment of a joint medical service. A central clinic reasonably accessible to all participants is set up. This clinic renders first-aid and emergency treatment and treatment of workmen's compensation cases. The staff personnel of this group occasionally visit the plant to evaluate control measures.

In general, many smaller plants can and should provide a good first-aid facility under the supervision of an employee trained in first-aid work, promote a minimum preventive program and educate their employees in health and safety.

In some states, particularly in the more hazardous industries, the type of first-aid equipment to be provided by the employer is prescribed by law. Legal requirements, however, are necessarily minimal and it is highly desir able that even small plants should go beyond these minimal requirements. Only the very small plant that is located in close proximity to a hospital, or has readily available to it the services of local medical practitioners, should limit its medical services to a first-aid kit.

Courses of training in first aid are easily available through all local chapters of the American Red Cross. In most plants one or two workers can be encouraged to take a regular course in first aid and be prepared to handle cases in accordance with accepted principles. The principles of first-aid care for the injured are authoritatively presented in two manuals, either of which may be used as a standard guide. They are the *American Red Cross First-Aid Textbook* and the *Manual of First-Aid Instruction of the United States Bureau of Mines*. There are certain general duties which the first-aid man should assume. He should: (a) be responsible for the first-aid supplies and equipment, (b) promote safety principles, such as the importance of first-aid treatment for all types of injuries, and (c) keep accurate records of first-aid treatments rendered. The injured person should be placed under the care of a physician at the earliest possible moment.

It is always desirable to secure the services of a part-time nurse and it is preferable that she work under the supervision of a physician who is on call, particularly one who is familiar with the plant and its possible health hazards.

As already mentioned, a cooperative group effort is one method of arranging for the services of physicians and other medical personnel for the smaller plant. However, there is a need for individual doctors interested in industrial work to provide this service to individual plants. Such physicians having a knowledge of industrial hygiene can offer their services to a group of plants of their choosing and so develop a satisfactory part-time medical service for a number of establishments. Physicians working for a group of plants should make periodic visits to the plants to examine employees there, institute measures for the control of health hazards and, in general, attempt to furnish or approach the same sort of medical service found in a large establishment. It cannot be stressed too strongly that the physician's familiarity with actual working conditions in the plant is a requisite for good and effective service.

Smaller plants must also recognize the need for positive efforts to prevent accidents and occupational diseases. The duties of the nurse and physician, whether part-time or from a cooperative medical service, should include a complete appraisal of hygiene and safety. Physicians offering service to the industrial groups should seek the assistance of the chemists and engineers of the plant whenever practicable.

There are a number of agencies, both governmental and private, to which a small plant may turn for help and advice on accident and occupational disease prevention. Among these are the state and local divisions of industrial hygiene, national and local safety councils, insurance companies, medical societies and industrial hygiene associations.

In the small plant—and this also holds true for the large plant—workers can best be educated to a feeling of responsibility for their own part in the safety program by personal contact, which acquaints them with the hows and whys of safety. Literature on the subject of health and safety is useful in conjunction with more personal efforts and can be obtained from such organizations as those already mentioned.

SPECIFIC INDUSTRIAL HEALTH PROBLEMS
OF CURRENT INTEREST

Examples of the types of medical problems encountered in industry are: standards of in-plant medical care, medical criteria for employment, the scope of preplacement and periodic examinations, the employment of elderly and hence presumably handicapped workers, the availability and quality of medical care in the community for workers and their dependents and the effect of insurance plans on the quality of medical care. Data relating to these should be gathered, defined, codified. standardized and then made available to the ultimate consumer, the worker. The following are some of the specific areas of special interest.

SMALLER PLANT PROBLEMS

It has been estimated by some that less than 5 per cent of smaller plants have any type of in-plant or on-the-job health service.[12] Yet they employ 70 per cent of the industrial population. Moreover, there are proportionately more lost time accidents in small plants than in large ones. It appears likely the incidence is similar for industrial diseases.

The need for the provision and extension of better-in-plant medical programs in small establishments is evident. An optimal in-plant program aids in the early detection of both occupational and nonoccupational diseases. Industrial workers, especially through the medium of labor organizations, have voiced a sincere interest in this area. Labor has supported the suggestion made by others that the problem of industrial safety and health in small enterprises can be approached most effectively by pooling community resources. The medical profession, governmental agencies active in this field, insurance companies and labor organizations can make progress in this area by coordinating their activities to permit such a pooling of community resources.

MEDICAL CARE PROGRAMS

In spite of the increasing costs and reimbursements for sickness and disability in industry, a wide segment of the industrial population is not adequately covered by voluntary sickness insurance benefits. Some organizations, particularly labor, have indicated that in most cases these plans do not offer anything like the complete answer to the medical care problem. The quantity and quality of benefits, the exclusions, the relationship to group practice and the free choice of physicians are not only varied but are largely incomprehensible to the average person. To meet the increased costs of voluntary sickness and accident insurance and to extend wider coverage for a larger segment of the industrial population, it is imperative that more widespread preventive medical programs be instituted. Since the cost of such insurance is based on experience, the cutting down of accidents and disabilities can provide additional funds for more extensive and varied insurance coverage.

REHABILITATION

One of the chief concerns of the industrial physician is the evaluation of disability. This is in contrast to the practice of diagnostic and therapeutic medicine in general practice. Of even greater concern is the prevention of disability and its mitigation. A way must be found to initiate early and to extend restorative training programs in order to provide the greatest benefit to the largest group. Our present inability to cope with this situation is reflected in the fact that some 250,000 persons each year reach a point of disability that requires rehabilitation, with an estimated reservoir of 2 million disabled. Even more significant is the fact that, on the average, 9 years elapse between the time of disability and the time that rehabilitation is started.[13] Too frequently disabled people are left to shift for themselves. There are many restorative training programs that should be extended and used to help bring the disabled worker back to productive work as quickly as possible. Here, again, there is need for coordination of the activities of management, labor, governmental agencies, the medical societies and hospitals with special knowledge, skill and activity in rehabilitation.

INDUSTRIAL HEALTH RESEARCH

At present there is a relative dearth of epidemiologic investigations in the field of industrial health, in spite of the availability of a fairly well-controlled industrial community. A real need exists to study the worker in relation to the various influences in his environment.

Mancuso and Coulter, through the use of statistics of the Federal Bureau of Old-Age and Survivors Insurance, have been able to select populations exposed to certain industrial conditions and match them with suitable cohort groups not similarly exposed.[14] Such data can indicate probable sources of industrial hazards and pinpoint the needs for more detailed epidemiologic research.

There is increasing emphasis on the importance of prepathogenetic tests to detect early evidence of intoxication. This is one aspect which should be accelerated, for there is need to correlate better the concentration of air contaminants in the breathing zone of the worker and the prepathogenetic indices found in man. The influence of motivation, the home environment and the worker's psychological reactions under stress must be carefully studied as part of the broad research program in safety.

No less important is the need for intensive studies of the biological effects of the physical energies, including ionizing radiation, microwaves, noise and lasers; and also the growing number of chemicals for which new industrial applications are being found almost daily.

STAFFING OF TRAINED INDUSTRIAL HEALTH PERSONNEL

The growth today of our industrial population and industry is far ahead of the influx of the various technical personnel so vitally needed in industrial health work. This is particularly true of physicians.

Kehoe has estimated that there is a need for 10 industrial physicians and industrial hygiene engineers for every one now employed.[15] A practical solution to this problem is urgent. It can be solved in large measure if universities and medical societies put more emphasis upon industrial medical programs for physicians interested in industrial medicine as a part-time or full-time career. Stimulating the medical community to appreciate the social significance of industrial health problems is also desirable. Universities and the government must expand their teaching facilities and laboratories to meet the demands of newer disciplines, such as radiation and air pollution. Specific training in these specialties is needed to provide proper control procedures and further development in this area.

THE OLDER WORKER IN INDUSTRY

The older worker, usually classified as 45 years of age or over, presently comprises about one-third of the labor force. The U. S. Department of Labor has predicted that by 1970 there will be 33.5 million workers in this category. Many of these people possess valuable skills and mature judgment based on years of experience. As such, they represent a valuable resource that must be conserved in order to meet the industrial production requirements of the 60's and 70's. The concerns of this group are primarily job security, health maintenance and economic security after retirement. The efforts of the industrial physician must be directed to the detection and control of the degenerative diseases. These diseases show a high severity rate and/or duration of absenteeism. Cardiovascular diseases, cancer and arthritis, for example, begin to increase in incidence and prevalence during these years, with a corresponding rise in nonoccupational absenteeism. By means of periodic medical examinations, health counseling, health education and, when necessary, job adjustments, the physician in industry contributes to the control of chronic diseases and helps to prolong the productive life of the individual. An important contribution by management towards health maintenance is the provision of adequate prepaid medical examinations. Such plans reduce the economic strain of hospitalization; prompt and adequate care reduces the degree of disability and permits earlier return to employment.

To provide for a smooth transition from work to retirement without the psychological concomitants which often accrue, certain prerequisites must be met. The first is the provision for relative economic security. Company financed or contributory retirement annuities, augmented by Social Security, have served in many instances to meet economic needs upon retirement. The second requisite for successful transition to retirement is preparation through counseling to minimize the emotional stresses which occur at that time. A number of retirement studies have shown that a good adjustment to retirement is much more likely to occur when retirement has been anticipated and planned for by both industry and the employee.[16]

There is growing appreciation that emotional and social deterioration are as important as physiological deterioration in determining the welfare of the retiree. The consequent effects of these three factors on the public health of the community are readily apparent to health authorities. In essence, pre-retirement planning by industry can aid materially in meeting some of the important needs of the aged in the community.

CONCLUSIONS

The objectives and scope of occupational medicine have been discussed. Particular emphasis has been given to the principles of prevention and control of industrial diseases and injuries, which are being achieved through such factors as legislation, education, research and implementation of industrial health programs. Certain specific industrial health problems which are of current interest have been mentioned. These include medical care programs especially for smaller plants, rehabilitation, the staffing of industrial health units and industrial health research.

The heart of occupational health is the in-plant medical program. Its backbone is the physical examination. Its senses are the personnel comprising the interdisciplinary team, which includes physicians, nurses and safety and industrial hygiene engineers. The spirit which vitalizes this program emanates from the coordinated interests and activities of management, labor, governmental and nongovernmental agencies, universities, insurance companies and other interested parties.

MORRIS KLEINFELD, M.D.

REFERENCES

1. Hunter, D.: The Diseases of Occupation. London, English Universities Press, Ltd., 1955, p. 942.
2. Dresser, W. C.: The problem of occupational disease. In Gafafer, W. M.: Manual of Industrial Hygiene. U. S. Department of Health, Education, and Welfare, National Institutes of Health, Division of Industrial Hygiene. Philadelphia, W. B. Saunders Co., 1943.
3. Accident Facts. 1963. Chicago, National Safety Council, Statistics Division, p. 3.
4. U. S. National Health Survey: Disability Days Due to Injury, United States, July 1959-June 1961. U. S. Public Health Service Publication No. 584, p. 21.
5. Baetjer, A. M.: Industrial health, diseases of occupation. In Maxcy, K. F.: Preventive Medicine and Public Health. Ed. 8. New York, Appleton-Century-Crofts, Inc., 1956, p. 1106.
6. Hinkle, L. E., Jr., of the Cornell University Medical Center: Personal communication.
7. Gross, P., Schrenk, H. H., and Walmer, C. R.: Importance of biological research in industrial medicine. Journal of the American Medical Association, *161*:571, June 16, 1956.
8. Trasko, V. M.: Occupational disease reporting. Washington, D.C., U. S. Department of Health, Education, and Welfare, 1953, Public Health Service Bulletin No. 288, p. 44.
9. Senior, Solomon, Chairman of the New York State Workmen's Compensation Board: Personal communication, 1963.
10. Seymour, W. H.: The problems of industrial health as seen by the industrialist. Journal of Medical Education, *31*:15, March, 1956.
11. Greenburg, L., Smith, A. R., and Mayers, M. R.: Essentials of Health Maintenance in Industrial Plants. New York State Department of Labor, Special Bulletin No. 213, 1942.
12. Golden, C. S.: The problems of health as seen by the industrial worker. Journal of Medical Education, *31*:27, March, 1956.

13. Magnuson, H. J.: Anticipating safety and health needs. Public Health Reports, 75:69, January, 1960.
14. Mancuso, T. F., and Coulter, E. J.: Methods of studying the relation of employment and long-term illness—cohort analysis. American Journal of Public Health, 49:1529, 1959.
15. Kehoe, R. A.: The need for industrial hygienists. Industrial Hygiene News Report, 1:3, December, 1958.
16. Goldstein, D. H.: Medical problems in employment continuity of senior citizens; from the viewpoint of the industrial physician. New York State Journal of Medicine, 61:2894, September, 1961.

13   Mental Health

INTRODUCTION

In spite of the lip service which has been rendered to preventive psychiatry many physicians will still wonder how one can speak of a prevention in this field where the illness is purely subjective in all but a minority of cases, where etiology is quite unclear, and where, at least by some standards, there is no quantitation and no objectivity.

Of the need for prevention no one can have any doubt. Population surveys quite regularly show that about a quarter of the entire general population suffers from a serious degree of psychiatric disability, another quarter has significant difficulty in this area and less than a quarter appears to be entirely free.[1, 2] This has been confirmed by military induction and morbidity figures from two World Wars,[3] and if one needs further proof it is to be found in an examination of medical practice, 50 per cent of which is generally acknowledged to be basically psychiatric in nature. If this last seems exaggerated we must consider the evidence of the prescription pad which shows that sedatives and tranquilizers make up a leading percentage of the medication dispensed to American patients. If we are inclined to lay this to the stress of modern living, to a recent decreased tolerance to discomfort or to some passing fad perhaps induced by intensive advertising, we still must explain why the sedatives are among our oldest medications; why in the mid- and late 1800's such vast quantities of bromides were used when these were alone in the market, and why almost a hundred years ago chloral sprang into such vast popularity, to be followed later by the barbiturates.

The extent and the permanence of the need for prevention seems incontrovertible and the evidence for this could be carried into many hundreds of pages of fascinating history of medicine and of demonology. But what of the possibility of meeting the need?

When we speak of positive programs of prevention and restrict ourselves to consideration of various educational methods and public health measures there is room for debate and question.[4-6] All of this may be reinforced by the unfortunate history of large-scale prevention theories of the past which will be described later. When, however, we bring the question close to daily practice it becomes abundantly clear that a considerable part of medical practice is and always has been aimed at controlling the harmful swings of human emotion, especially anxiety, which can threaten the life of a sick person. In addition, much effort has been expended in counseling, medicating, and arranging regimens of work, rest, and relaxation for patients suffering from all types and degrees of psychic disorder with the purpose of shortening attacks and preventing exacerbations or new attacks. Though some will doubt whether we can truly prevent functional illness, few experienced men will hesitate to accept the fact that unfavorable and preventable circumstances can in most cases make the situation worse, either precipitating or prolonging attacks or intensifying symptoms.

Since such a large proportion of the population is already affected to some degree and thus vulnerable, it would seem that we cannot underestimate the preventive value of medical procedures which tend to protect such persons from stresses that are dangerous to them. Thus it appears, in this sense at least, that preventive mental health procedures are a traditional part of medical practice. One can criticize the logic and question the purely empirical basis of the work but one cannot deny that it does exist or that it is important. In addition, it will also become clear from what follows that there is strong evidence that public health programs of prevention are also possible and that they have important implications for medical practice. Having seen that prevention is a reality in ordinary medical practice, this latter idea is easier to accept.

In writing on this subject it is possible to put the emphasis on either of two extremes. On the one hand, we could describe an imposing assemblage of specific, practical, professional considerations which guide the physician's daily work and which have preventive value for the mental health of individuals. On the other hand, we could restrict our discussion to broad programs of prevention which may potentially reach vast numbers but in which the physician's role is more general and where he acts as one of the forces which mold social organization and influence patterns of human relations. In this discussion we shall follow a middle course since the physician cannot afford to ignore the broader issues, yet the more specific material has a very direct importance in daily practice.

HISTORY OF PSYCHIATRIC PREVENTION—
UNFULFILLED PROMISES

The need for some form of prevention of mental and emotional disorders has long been intensely felt and this has led to a number of relatively unfortunate false starts which undoubtedly left behind a residue of medical skepticism as to the value of programs of prevention in this area.

Perhaps the earliest large-scale campaign was carried out by the famous Dorothea Linde Dix who in the mid-1800's promised that chronic mental illness could be prevented if only there were enough mental hospitals to permit early treatment. This was supported by professional optimism which has since come to be known by the name of "the cult of curability." This hope had no sooner failed than it was replaced by the promises of the eugenic school whose theories were later to find bizarre expression in the excesses of the Germans in World War II. Eugenics, too, has moved into the background and today it is recognized that even with modern advances we can expect only modest contributions from this direction. In the early 1900's came the mental hygiene movement which soon centered much of its attention on early treatment in the child guidance clinic as a preventive of mental illness in the adult. This idea, too, has had professional support but it has had to be abandoned as a theory. Child guidance clinics are now increasing their operations as never before, but this is purely on their immediate and demonstrable merits in the treatment of mentally sick and emotionally disturbed children and not for their preventive effect. Current medical attitudes still reflect the result of the discrediting of these major movements together with many minor ones such as the curious period of medical preoccupation with the mythological "degenerative" effects of masturbation and some later variants as to the preventive or curative value of gross sexual freedom in functional psychiatric disorder.

The history of failure of grand programs is discouraging but, when we descend from the level of broad generalizations and over-all promises to specific procedures, we find that prevention of psychiatric disorder and mental disability has been making advances steadily for many decades. There is even significant evidence that on a broader level we can begin to identify and measure harmful sociological influences which are subject to modification. Thus we stand today at a more hopeful point than ever before, with new data that ranges from the beginnings of a molecular biology as seen in the chromosome discoveries in mongolism to important and objective data in social psychiatry. These seem to form the clear outlines of a quantitative and objective approach with practical implications.

PREVENTION OF BRAIN DAMAGE

Prevention of brain damage involves almost every branch of medicine in some way and in this field technical advance has been steady and in some cases spectacular. Within a generation paresis has become a rare entity in our mental hospitals; pellagra has virtually disappeared from regions where it was once a common cause of psychosis and suicide. Cretinism has become a rarity and of only historical interest as a cause of mental deficiency. Mongolism has now been associated with a visible chromosomal abnormality and practical prevention may soon follow. In obstetrics we have learned of the importance of Rh factor, German measles, and oxygen deprivation as causes of mental defects. Now a broad national program[7] of maternal and child health promises to provide better care in that early period of life when the individual is most vulnerable to substandard and inadequate medical care. There is good evidence that this will have a powerful influence in reducing the disproportionate incidence of mental defects in the socioeconomically deprived. These elements comprise prevention of occurrence in the highest sense and taken together promise to reduce the amount of brain damage in the population.

We can add many more items to the above list: PKU as a source of mental defect; early and effective antibiotic treatment of the meningitides; protection against lead poisoning; greater awareness of the manifold types of asphyxia and their relation to brain damage; the dearly bought knowledge of the action of thalidomide and our better knowledge of the mycotic, viral and allergic encephalitides.[8] We can even add the newer knowledge about the reversible intoxications with drugs such as cortisone, iproniazid and others[8] as well as the control of convulsive disorders with drugs. Still it must be confessed that the bulk of mental and nervous disability remains untouched because only a minority of the cases bear a known relationship either to demonstrable brain damage or the various intoxications. It remains abundantly clear that if we are to pursue the question of prevention effectively in the present state of our knowledge we cannot confine ourselves to the realm of prevention of occurrence of demonstrable etiologies. We must move in a far more empirical direction and include psychogenesis and the use of drugs whose actions are only vaguely understood. Also, once brain damage has occurred, prevention of progression of clinical manifestations involves much the same considerations.

THE PSYCHOGENIC HYPOTHESIS AND ITS RELATION TO PREVENTION[9-11]

PERSONALITY DEVELOPMENT

No aspect of modern psychiatry has given rise to more discussion than the prevention of mental and nervous disorders as well as what is called mental retardation through the application of the hypothesis that these are basically the outcome of failures of adaptation to life requirements and that these failures are, in turn, the result of interaction of undue current environmental stress and weakness of development of personality. According to this view only the constitutional part of personality is genetically determined; all the rest, being the result of environmental influences, is subject to change from without.

Great emphasis is placed on the proper development of personality through the correct and adequate integration of the individual's life experiences, beginning in earliest infancy. This starts with the care and feeding of infants, proceeds on to toilet training and involves the various childhood problems such as thumbsucking, temper tantrums and the attention needs of the child, genital self-stimulation, the meaning of periods of negativism (that the child is on the way to making his own decisions), school experiences, problems of adolescence and young adulthood, mature life experiences with marriage, parenthood and work. The topics go on to include the personal, family and work experiences of middle life and of advanced age.

It is postulated that each individual will reach his best potential if he has been allowed to develop through all these phases free from overwhelming traumatic experiences that derive from the activities of poorly oriented parents and other authority figures. Trauma may come from exposure to a chaotic, insecure, unorganized social environment, economic deprivation, and disastrous situations in which the patient is unduly victimized at any stage in his life, including the most advanced years. The needs of each phase are different and quite specialized, and much documentation already exists on many aspects.[9, 12-14]

Taken as a whole this hypothesis opens a wide panorama of possibilities for public education which will supply a fuller and more correct understanding of those important and reasonable human needs which can be met by a practicable reorientation of public and personal attitudes. Among these we would number a more realistic set of criteria as to the limits of normalcy. It is hoped that in this way we shall arrive at a more flexible and realistic set of personal and public standards and overcome fully the outworn ideas that still control much judgment and action on human conduct. Such a reorientation would terminate identifiable activities which still needlessly disrupt development of personality, often in the name of mental health (such as bowel training, schedule rigidity, etc.).

Because he is a source of authoritative information on most of the questions that arise as to the proper and normal steps of personality development, the physician plays an important role in this public educational process. This has already brought about changes in attitudes and practices and led to the abandonment of many outworn concepts that once created turmoil in the lives of families and of individuals. In retrospective studies of mental and nervous disorders these were found to have left permanent weaknesses of personality structure, which later gave rise to clinical illness when the weakened personality was subjected to stress.[9] The rigid child feeding and care schedules of a few years ago have been largely abandoned by physicians, and the true importance of mothering in the development of even small infants has been better recognized.[15, 16] We have more realistic attitudes about bladder and bowel training. Excessive concern about thumb-sucking has been discarded and with it the harmful protective devices once prescribed against it. Alarm about genital manipulation and bed wetting, masturbation and nail biting is no longer reinforced by medical advice and cannot rouse the depth of counterreaction and anxiety once elicited in parents. These are but a few items in a broad program of education which hopefully will create in the general public a better awareness of what is normal in human personality development throughout life and what are its needs. Such a program will help to create a society where individual experiences will be more satisfying and acceptable and thus more capable of being integrated into the personality as they occur. Hopefully, these experiences will provide personalities with more resistance to stress. In this hypothesis we may find some hope for true prevention of occurrence on a scale which is commensurate with the vastness of the problem of mental disability in our society. It will be noted that the idea of personality as here presented is an intellectual construct quite alien to the more objective quantifiable elements with which medicine prefers to deal. Yet such constructs have proved to be of value even in theoretical physics and this one serves to explain a vast amount of clinical data which act "as if" this formulation were substantially correct.

The validity of these views on mental and emotional illness rests largely on retrospective accounts in which the psychiatric decompensation appears quite clearly related to experiences which were poorly assimilated, especially during the formative years. In mental retardation as it is identified in the community there are clinical and epidemiological data which indicate that a portion of the cases relate directly to social, economic and educational deprivation of various types.[17] It appears inevitable that the medical profession will be increasingly exposed to these views during the next few years and will be called upon to play its part in their dissemination and implementation.

THE STRESS FACTOR

The importance of current environmental stress[12] is a large part of the psychogenic hypothesis of mental disability, and the precipitation of such illness by external factors is a matter of common medical experience. The broadest application of this principle requires a social organization which would reduce group stress to the greatest practicable degree. Some of the elements required, such as better housing and control of poverty, represent areas of total national effort, but other important social stresses appear to arise from patterns of organization of human relationships and are quite independent of economics. During World War II it was repeatedly found that groups with high morale and strong cohesion among their members had lower rates of psychiatric morbidity in the field than did poor morale groups.[3] More recently, regional population surveys have shown that communities which are "disintegrated" and have poor cohesion and leadership have higher rates of psychiatric disorder than do those with better community organization.[2] It should be noted that even in the better communities of this study the majority of the population still showed psychiatric disorder. Yet this does seem to indicate that, within limits, environmental influences are reflected in prevalence of disorder. It also seems fair to assume that manipulation of such influences offers a hopeful approach to the prevention of occurrence of a significant amount of mental and nervous disorder.

PSYCHOPHARMACOLOGY—DRUG THERAPY AND REDUCTION OF PREVALENCE (PREVENTION OF PROGRESSION)

The psychotropic drugs are used on purely empirical grounds and are thus open to much controversy and wide differences of opinion. In recent years, for instance, the new tranquilizing drugs have been hailed as the dawn of a new day in treatment of mental and nervous disorder. Indeed, their appearance in the mid-1950's has been followed by a steady small annual diminution of the total population in mental hospitals, a decrease of true prevalence. On the other hand, these drugs have been condemned as grossly overpromoted, overpriced products of a greedy industry which seeks to profit from the human weakness for taking drugs that anesthetize our sensibilities and help us to evade our problems. The author feels that the truth lies between the two extreme positions and far closer to the more optimistic one. The practical fact is that the modern psychotropic medications are among the most widely used of all drugs in medical practice. Their sedative predecessors are among the oldest of all medicines, predating Hippocrates by as many years as Hippocrates predates our times. Furthermore, medications of this type have been among the most consistently employed during all the intervening time.

Sedatives and the minor tranquilizers can dampen the extent of emotional swings which, if uncontrolled, can turn a serious medical or surgical condition into a fatal one. They are also of proven value in controlling some of the tensions which find expression in the psychosomatic illnesses. It is somewhat less certain whether the timely use of such medications can prevent the outbreak of more serious psychiatric disorders. Some physicians feel that the new "minor tranquilizers" of the meprobamate class have less sedative and more antitension and anti-anxiety effect than do the barbiturates. In any event, for both, the technique of titration of drug against tension is similar. It is a fact that either drug without other psychotherapeutic effort is likely to be of very limited value. Used in doses several times the therapeutic level over a period of many weeks, these substances are in general fully addicting, and a knowledge of this fact is of importance in the prevention of addiction; persons who have already shown addictive tendencies, such as alcoholics, are particularly prone to such involvement.

The major tranquilizers, most of which are phenothiazines, are quite different from the minor ones in that they can cut short the duration of an attack of major mental illness or abort it when the prodromes are recognized in time. When used on a maintenance level they can prevent relapse. Side reactions from the major tranquilizers are in general of a far more serious nature than those from the minor group, but their use does not lead to habituation or addiction. The number of persons released from psychiatric hospitals on maintenance therapy with a major tranquilizer is increasing steadily. More and more of these are being supervised by physicians other than psychiatrists, a situation which has a very significant potential for future prevention of hospitalization. The initiation of treatment with the more powerful drugs requires considerable special skill and experience as well as adequate diagnosis. Maintenance therapy, however, is much simpler and only calls for some consultation to be available from time to time. In general, it is wise to limit oneself to a relatively few drugs with which one is very familiar and to avoid being persuaded to "try" every new drug that appears on the market. Most important is to know the patient and his reactions as thoroughly as possible.

The use and effects of the antidepressant drugs or so-called "energizers" is far less clear. The amphetamines have a minor activity and can be addicting. The more potent drugs such as imipramine (Tofranil) appear to have a greater degree of effect and are generally recognized as being able to cut short an attack in many cases. Where the pattern of reaction has been well established during previous attacks, these drugs may be used again in similar fashion but, in general, their use probably calls for psychiatric consultation.

Parenteral forms of many of the newer drugs are available but their use requires special caution. It may be said that most of the advantages claimed for them can be had from the use of oral preparations. Forms of somatic therapy other than drugs have lost most of their previous importance, but for severe depressions, electric shock remains the most rapid method and the one with the highest proportion of remissions.

THE INTERVIEW—BUILDING THE PHYSICIAN–PATIENT RELATIONSHIP

Work with psychiatric patients requires the use of various modalities such as counseling, psychotherapeutic sessions, drugs, and work with environmental factors. Regardless of what method or combination is used, any procedure within the mental hygiene field requires the ability to talk to patients and to listen carefully to them, all of which takes time, practice, and good will. It cannot be done hastily or with divided attention. Psychiatric patients more than others respond badly to irritation or impatience and are especially sensitive to the underlying attitude of the physician, especially if it is one of rejection. Even a brief contact skillfully conducted can be of value. During the first few contacts it is important to learn as much as possible about the patient from him and his family. If he has been a patient in a psychiatric hospital it is useful to secure an abstract of his record or at least to contact the hospital psychiatrist.

It should be particularly noted that the somatic therapies, including the drugs, have not in any way substituted for this important task of the doctor and the patient, namely, the building up of a useful doctor-patient relationship. This is a valuable preparation for future periods of stress and uncertainty. It is during this interchange that the physician gradually accumulates a knowledge of the patient in depth, a feeling for his reactions, and a knowledge of his past without which efforts at prevention would be only blind navigation without instruments.

One of the best ways to learn interview technique is to watch it being done by one who is skilled in the art, or even better to interview under the supervision of such a person. There are many styles and no two persons perform exactly alike, but there are many common denominators. As elsewhere in medicine, it helps greatly to know the nature of the experiences which the patient is trying to describe but it is equally important to be able to elicit this without influencing it. In the course of the discussion one must be able to identify points of sensitivity quickly and handle them with circumspection. Ill-chosen words, ill-timed questions and even unguarded flashes of facial expression can do considerable damage and can, on occasion, actually precipitate a reaction which one is trying to prevent. This sounds much more complex than it really is since it means only that the physician must expect the patient to be sensitive as any deeply dependent person is to his mentor. It is best to keep the conversation confined to relatively current problems. Active exploration of dreams, childhood memories and highly charged memories should not be undertaken without special training, a comment which incidentally applies also to hypnosis. A standard session often lasts about 50 minutes, although half-hour sessions may be made to suffice. Periods lasting well beyond an hour are best avoided. During a crisis period several visits a week may be necessary. In critical situations it is of great value for the patient to know that he can make telephone contact if needed.

The actual content of the psychiatric interview is far beyond the scope of a chapter on prevention and is extensively discussed in monographs and textbooks on psychotherapy and psychiatry.[10, 11] The purpose of this section has been served if it has left the impression that such interviews are important in preventive mental health work and that acquisition of a useful interview technique is well within the capacity of any physician who is able to devote a reasonable amount of effort to it.

PREVENTION OF SEQUELAE OF PSYCHIATRIC STATES

In many cases the expression of the psychiatric disorder is far out of proportion to the apparent intensity of the primary problem; a relatively small personality disorder can lead to profound alcoholism, narcotic addiction, sexual promiscuity, prostitution, social dependency or vagabondage, other asocial and antisocial behavior or some combination of these. Serious degrees of mental disorder can, of course, also give rise to similar effects.

Areas of prevention fall into several categories, some general and some specific; many of them are already dealt with elsewhere in this book (alcohol, narcotics). Public health education in the schools and in the public media to reach all levels of the population is a basic tool. It seems a favorable omen that even now only a small proportion of the population becomes involved in unfavorable behavior, although the great majority suffer from some demonstrable mental or emotional difficulty. Many causes other than psychiatric are also operating and each is open to separate attack. Among those outstanding is the big city slum with a clustering of multiple problem families, each afflicted by several types of social problems. Here one finds high rates of arrest, addiction, alcoholism, homicide, prostitution, illiteracy, mental deficiency, dependency, vagabondage, and hospitalization for mental illness. It is hard to escape the implication that theories of social organization can make a significant contribution here far greater than the once popular genetic approach which suffers from the fatal weakness that it can be applied only in cases of outspoken disorder where reproduction is already severely reduced. Here the role of the physician is that of an important social element in community organization.

When one comes to specific procedures, the physician is often called upon to treat such persons and much will depend on his attitudes and his techniques. In the past these patients were frequently rejected as difficult to treat, unreliable, unresponsive, manipulators of medical care and perhaps not really sick at all but only wicked. The fact that such disorders as alcoholism and addiction are illnesses is now recognized. This is opening various doors for emergency treatment to carry such patients through crises that threaten life or socioeconomic status or both. We are coming to see these conditions as chronic relapsing disorders where prolongation of useful life and reduction of morbidity is a worthwhile aim. We are discarding the idea that even a brief relapse constitutes "treatment failure."

Vagabondage and dependency occupy a special place among the long-term effects of mental disorder, and their prevention constitutes an unfinished chapter in public mental health practice. Much of this type of disability is the aftermath of schizophrenia. Prevention of progression begins with early diagnosis and active treatment. A second factor is early return to the community if the patient has been hospitalized. This is necessary to avoid his losing his place in society. Many patients, however, require long-term treatment, and rehabilitation becomes very important for them. Much of this is social and economic, and here the physician can play a significant role as counselor. In addition, most of these patients require permanent maintenance therapy with one or more of the major tranquilizers, and in this area the personal physician is coming to occupy a position of steadily increasing importance. The situation is somewhat analogous to that in epilepsy, although the pharmacology is more complex and the need for simple supportive psychotherapy renders personal contact with the patient even more important.

Direct psychiatric treatment of the underlying personality disorders and psychiatric illnesses and disabilities associated with the manifestations grouped under this title is ordinarily difficult. The statistics of response are meager even in the hands of the most expert. Many of the most distressing results, however, are preventable, and the medical contribution to prevention can be very large. First, the physician must be aware of the patient's need to live the fullest possible life and not be a prisoner of imagined limitations. On the other hand, the physician must be aware of the patient's limitations, because if he is driven beyond his capacities he may suffer psychiatric relapse or "act out" his conflict by exhibiting behavior of serious social significance.

In such situations one cannot operate by dead reckoning; an over-all estimate is useful only as a starting point. For the rest one must keep in touch with the patient and be in a position to revise judgment in the light of continuing performance. Most important of all, the physician must be able to recognize the early signs of rising emotional tension. Psychiatric distress signals are highly individual but have many common denominators, and these symptoms indicate that at some point the patient is under too much pressure. When this occurs, the available courses of action are quite familiar. One can attempt to identify the specific problem if this is possible, or one can move toward reducing general pressures on the patient since, within limits, reduction of pressure at any point tends to reduce the total load. If the patient is already receiving a maintenance dose of a major tranquilizer, it is necessary to be sure that he really has been taking his medication. Unauthorized suspension of therapy is one of the most frequent causes of impending relapse. It is often necessary to increase the dose for a period of time and in this event the patient may have to take time off from his work. The minor tranquilizers or the barbiturates may also be useful. Finally, depending on circumstances, psychiatric consultation may be necessary. However, unfavorable signs should not be ignored and the patient should not be allowed to continue without help until relapse or paradoxical behavior occurs. This is one of the preventable aspects of psychiatric illness.

Not all psychiatric disorders come to the physician labeled as such. In fact, it is probably fair to say that most of the psychopathology encountered will be associated with other conditions; yet the same basic principles of treatment apply. It is difficult to discuss this topic without a simple return to a description of the old-fashioned family doctor who knew all the family members, their environment, their personal histories, and remained in fairly intimate contact with them for long periods of time. This sort of relationship can be of the greatest value if one is to prevent some of the consequences of the stress of daily living among individuals of all grades and patterns of psychiatric vulnerability. Not all breaks with convention and not all criminal behavior is an expression of illness; most of it is probably not. Yet frequently one encounters such reactions so out of keeping with the person's previous record and under conditions that are so bizarre and lacking in logic that one cannot escape the conclusion that these are truly the product of a disordered personality reacting to the stress of environment, physical illness or both. Much of this is preventable and this task falls clearly into the area of medical practice.

MANAGEMENT OF CRISES AND PREVENTION OF SPECIFIC ACTS SUCH AS SUICIDE AND ANTISOCIAL BEHAVIOR

Prevention of suicide is one of the most important of medical responsibilities and calls for adequate diagnosis and a correct evaluation of the nature of each situation. Certainty is, of course, not to be had and even the most skillful and experienced psychiatrist may find himself in error, but some useful generalizations may be made.

It is not true that those who threaten suicide never go through with it; most successful suicides have made threats and many have actually made previous unsuccessful attempts. The incidence of suicide is higher in men than in women, greater in older persons than in younger. Alcohol is a predisposing factor, as is depression or schizophrenia. Continuous supervision is impossible and probably not even useful, but it is not desirable to leave a depressed person alone for long periods of time.

When there is serious concern about suicide it is desirable to get the patient under psychiatric consultation and observation as soon as possible. It should be kept in mind that even severe depressions can be reversed with electric shock therapy in a matter of days. In many instances adequate drug therapy with antidepressants can accomplish the same result although somewhat more slowly; also, the proportion of successful results will be smaller.

Suicide is by no means limited to obviously depressed persons. It occurs in schizophrenics, hysterics and psychopaths as well. Sometimes it occurs under circumstances which leave the impression that the patient was actually only "trying out" a procedure which miscarried and resulted in fatality without the full intent of the patient.

Where an adequate relationship has been built up between patient and physician it is often possible to reach an understanding that the patient will take no action for limited periods of time. During crisis periods it is important that the physician have frequent contacts with the patient and be readily available even by phone.

Antisocial or dangerous behavior may occasionally threaten and its prevention becomes an important issue. Estimate of risk is here a complex matter but is higher in men than in women. Alcoholism is an unfavorable element, a history of previous overt acts is also an indication of danger, as is specific training in techniques of combat (soldiers, police). When there is doubt, consultation should be obtained. When there is a good relationship of confidence with the physician the patient may be easily persuaded to enter a hospital, if for no other reason than to get the opinion of some disinterested authority as to his mental condition. Ordinarily such a person has some appreciation of the fact that he is ill and, if he is not swept away by hostility and suspicion, he can be brought to cooperate. The problem should be explained gently and circumspectly but with candor. In no case should one mislead the patient or deal with him as if he were not a reasonable man.

In some areas of the world, especially in England, this is all that is required for hospital admission except in rare cases. However, much depends on local custom and practice, and the physician will wish to be acquainted with the facilities and procedures for emergency care and treatment in his area of practice. He should be in a position to initiate a nonvoluntary form of admission if this is required. He will, of course, also wish to be informed as to the various facilities for outpatient psychiatric service, both public and private, in order that he may handle as many problems as possible on an outpatient basis. Where possible he should pay a personal visit to these installations to become familiar with such modern developments as the open hospital as well as newer treatment techniques and results, all of which will allow him to make his recommendations with fuller confidence. Certainly any judgments based on experiences dating back more than 6 to 8 years are now clearly outdated.

Prevention of hospitalization is still an important aim but now less than ever should it be an end in itself. There are times when hospitalization is urgently indicated for the mental patient. The physician's prompt and decisive action at such a juncture can prevent social damage to the patient and his family and may forestall a tragedy, although violent acts on the part of otherwise nonviolent types of persons are quite rare even in the presence of mental illness. When possible, hospitalization should be in a local psychiatric unit with psychiatric consultation in advance. The full consent and cooperation of responsible relatives should be secured and in the case of an involuntary admission one should carefully comply with the legal formalities.

PREVENTION OF PSYCHIATRIC DECOMPENSATION IN THE BRAIN DAMAGED

Prevention of decompensation in the brain damaged involves the same general considerations already outlined for the normal as well as those with minor or major underlying functional psychopathology. One needs to know the patient and his situation and to keep in touch with the interaction of the individual with his environment over a period of time. Signs of emotional tension are similar, and the means of dealing with intercurrent problems are analogous. However, there are a number of important special considerations to be kept in mind in each of several varieties of conditions.

By far the most important group is the aged who universally suffer from a certain amount of arteriosclerotic and senile change, usually in combination. The mental state of such persons is very sensitive to defects of nutrition, to fatigue, to intercurrent physical illness with its pain and anxiety, or any other disruption of the normal balanced round of daily activities, including work, recreation and rest. Even normal amounts of fatigue are clearly reflected in the memory capacity of otherwise normal older persons who become forgetful as they tire. All physical, mental and emotional stresses add up to play a cumulative role. Once decompensation sets in and the controls of the patient are weakened, a vicious circle of further deterioration is easily set off. The small degree of mental confusion that may be present is usually associated with irritability, anxiety, and depression which, in turn, lead to poor rest, decreased food intake, and poor general health. These quickly create further confusion and close the circle. The classical description of King Lear's delirium is an excellent example of such a reaction in very acute and transitory form supervening on excessive fatigue, exposure to the elements and profound anger at the treachery of his daughters. Unfortunately, chronic states frequently ensue and death is a common outcome.

Prevention here includes adequate diagnosis. Depression in the aged is far more frequent than usually realized because it is masked by secondary confusion. If this occurs, antidepressant drug therapy may produce excellent results, though electric shock is often required. In either case, psychiatric consultation and assistance are called for. Usually the picture is far more chronic and one can deal only with the restlessness and irritability. Drugs are of great potential value, but the unusual sensitivity of the older person to this type of medication must be kept in mind. Barbiturates easily produce intoxication by cumulative action and so also do the minor tranquilizers. The major ones must be used with caution because of the danger of hypotensive episodes and other side effects. Small doses of alcoholic drinks have much value. Many relatively minor points must be kept in mind in dealing with such persons. These include the need to maintain ambulation, to minimize bed care even when there are such indications as fracture and to combat their tendency to subsist on a carbohydrate-rich diet deficient in proteins and vitamins. In addition, it must be stressed that many of their needs are similar to those of others; a good relationship with the physician is of the utmost importance. It should not be forgotten that they have problems which are similar to those of younger persons, including problems in the sexual sphere. The physician as a "friendly listener" as well as a counselor can be of great help and can prevent much morbidity and mortality by surprisingly simple methods. In doing this sort of work, the volume of which promises to rise with the increased number of the aged in the population, one soon comes to realize the relatively large part which resentment and anger play in the psychic conflicts of the aged, their concern about loss of status and of capacity, and their anxieties about the future. This is in many ways a new field of medical activity and one in which prevention will remain in the foreground.

Incontinence, incidentally, is often a matter of the utmost importance, usually rendering institutional care necessary. It is probably best considered as a sort of index of the total physical and mental condition of the patient, and its prevention becomes a vital part of the health program for the aged. Chronic incontinence indicates a very grave prognosis as to life.

What has been said elsewhere about the importance of keeping the patient's activities up to his capacity and not driving him beyond them is especially important with the brain damaged, including the aged.

Similar principles hold true also for other types of brain-damaged persons although special features are characteristic of each type. Younger persons with gross brain injury are, for example, particularly sensitive to the effects of even small doses of alcohol and also to relatively minor bumps on the head. All react very poorly to physical restraint when in delirious confusion. This is particularly dangerous in the alcoholic, in whom sudden death can occur in spite of the apparently robust appearance of the patient. The adequate use of skilled, calm personnel and the judicious use of tranquilizers and sedatives can be lifesaving. Such patients are almost always aware of their surroundings in a restricted way and do respond to kindness and reassurance and to a well-lighted room. Darkness promotes delirium and anxiety. Intimidation and rough handling precipitate counteraggressions and excitement which may be fatal.

In the care of such patients one can see in operation a principle which has application throughout psychiatry, namely, the contagious nature of human emotions, both to the patient and persons around him. The physician is in an excellent position to set the emotional tone of the treatment setting, important whether in the home or in the hospital. Anxiety is a highly contagious emotion communicated quickly to the patient and his family. However, confidence is equally transmissible. This is a well-accepted fact in dealing with somatic illness but is often forgotten in dealing with the mentally ill or the retarded. It should be stressed that even when patients are apparently confused and in poor touch with their surroundings they respond to such emotions. Careless remarks in the presence of the semiconscious or even the apparently unconscious patient contribute profoundly to anxiety, tension, and excitement. Here one would do well to follow the practices of the anesthesiologists who guard their remarks in dealing with persons in a state of impaired consciousness.

A specific reaction of the brain damaged is the so-called "catastrophic reaction." Essentially it involves a state of confusion, often with excitement, when a brain-damaged individual is pressed to perform in areas beyond his capacity. The excitement states of the brain-damaged person are likely to be more disinhibited and for that reason more difficult to control than similar excitements in the functional disorders. The epileptic excitement or furor occurring often in the clouded period after a seizure belongs to the organic reaction type. To prevent injury their management calls for the type of care and tolerance already described for the alcoholic.

PREVENTION OF DECOMPENSATION IN THE EX-MENTAL PATIENT AND IN THE RETARDED

In many ways the onset of outspoken psychiatric disorder is analogous to the onset of cardiac decompensation. Exogenous factors of stress play an important role, as does the inherent resistance of the individual to life stresses. We cannot carry the analogy much further because the degree of physical pathology is little correlated with the intensity of the functional disorder in the mental patient. Most cases of mental retardation or mental illness show no demonstrable pathology. However, those who manifest signs of major disability or who have had previous attacks do represent a group whose vulnerability is greater than average. They require additional attention if exacerbations or new attacks are not to be precipitated.

The techniques available and the principles which are involved do not differ significantly from those already outlined in other areas. However, these cases require separate discussion since the nature of the clinical syndrome is such as to obscure the fact that the principles and procedures involved are basically familiar ones. This work can and is being done by physicians other than psychiatrists, a trend which is likely to increase in view of the rising number of such patients returned to their communities after being treated and rehabilitated in psychiatric hospitals.

Regardless of minor anomalies of expression and of conduct which many of these patients show, they still are sensitive to the same environmental influences which affect other persons. They are responsive to the same physician-patient relationships except that greater caution must be observed in exploring emotion-laden subjects. The danger signals of increasing tension may be quite specific and individual; for example: an increasing preoccupation with certain international or political questions, a sudden change of routine or a decrease of ability to follow any routine, a sudden loss of work efficiency, new physical preoccupations or paradoxical mood swings often with a tone of euphoria and exaltation. In addition, one may expect the more usual tension symptoms although these are far less regular in appearance than in other types of patient. However, there may be loss of appetite and of weight, insomnia, fatigue, tension headaches, irritability, etc.

To advise such a patient and to guide him with certainty it is necessary to be familiar with his past history of prodromal periods, since the symptom sequences tend to repeat themselves quite regularly and have a special meaning for the individual patient. For example, one patient needs additional chlorpromazine and reduction of work schedule when her Bible reading time increases beyond a half hour per day. It is necessary to be aware of the patient's point of view as to what is stressful to him. With these elements in mind and with some consultation available to him, a physician who has developed the necessary relationship with the patient and with the family may well carry such a patient indefinitely, warding off major attacks and incidentally developing considerable skill in this type of work. It should be noted that it is usually much easier to begin work in psychiatry with well-stabilized, well-studied cases (even schizophrenics) than to begin with less well-studied fresh cases of less serious diagnosis. In fact, diagnosis alone is a relatively poor guide as to the difficulties to be anticipated in a case.

The care of the mentally retarded is quite different and less complex although the principles which apply are somewhat similar. Ordinarily they are not under medical supervision unless there is a complicating convulsive disorder, difficulties in conduct, or a complicating psychiatric illness (which is not rare in higher grade cases). The type of problem to be anticipated will be apparent from the past history. The physician's aim will be to see that the patient is permitted to exercise his capacities to the full but is not driven beyond them. In the retardate this can provoke emotional episodes of various types and even full-blown psychotic attacks, though usually of brief duration. Drug uses are similar to those in other cases.

PREVENTION IN THE COURSE OF ORDINARY MEDICAL PRACTICE

When one considers that the physician presides to a large degree over the human experience of birth, illness and death and when one considers how heavily laden these are with anxiety and how much importance must attach to his actions at such times, it becomes clear that he must have a considerable opportunity to minimize the impact of these experiences on his patients. He can prevent a wide variety of subsequent emotional and mental problems, leaving completely open the question whether such experiences actually cause the subsequent reactions or whether they merely provoke reactions in already susceptible individuals.[12] Prevention of either occurrence or progression would seem to be well worthwhile.

The perinatal period is one of great stress for many women, and a considerable number actually experience various degrees of serious psychopathology. The recognition of such states is important because in some instances active psychiatric treatment is called for. In no instance should one ignore depression, agitation, and pathological thinking in such women; infanticide is far from rare under such circumstances. However, aside from the question of major mental illness there is a strong opinion that the mental health of the mother should be as much a cause of concern as her physical condition and normally requires no higher degree of sophistication or of attention. A full exposition of diagnostic and therapeutic procedures is beyond the scope of this discussion, but among the points often mentioned is one that the patient should be kept fully informed about her condition.

Some attention should be given to reassurance when this is called for and a degree of confidence in the physician should be developed. After delivery the mother should be allowed to see the child as soon as possible and she should see it as much as possible. Any abnormalities should be fully discussed and effort made to set her mind at rest. Following delivery and return home arrangements should be made for her to avoid excess physical stress.

A somewhat similar set of conditions is often outlined with respect to surgical operations or serious episodes of physical illness. Anxiety is often masked. The impersonal atmosphere of the hospital tends to accentuate it, especially for those who are strange to it, and the possible social and economic consequences of disability serve to sharpen the effect. Control of mental pain is in many ways as important as control of physical pain. Practical considerations play an important role here, too, and arrangements to ease physical stress during the period of recovery are of prime importance. The close relation between the mental state of the patient and his chances of recovery have been obscured by the miracle drugs and by the decisive advances in modern technology. Yet the literature is full of evidence as to the importance of the human side of medicine for the mental health of the patient. Our psychopharmacology is an important adjunct to this but only an adjunct.

Finally, the physician must face the mental and emotional problems involved in death, both in preparing the patient for its advent and in advising the family during the mourning which follows. Caplan[12] has outlined in a very clear-cut way the fact that mourning is a task which must be carried out and that it cannot be evaded by maintaining an imperturbable exterior.

The special relationship of the physician to his patient involves some very fundamental elements in human nature. This was recognized long ago in the Hippocratic Oath which even specifically provided adequate safeguards for handling the erotic expression which is occasionally stimulated in some patients, sometimes in a hypnoid reaction. Modern psychiatry has abundantly confirmed the fact that the physician has far greater power for good or for evil than is sometimes recognized. This is a force which can be forgotten under stress of busy practice, especially in these days of scientific medicine. For good or for ill, the physician retains in the eyes of the patient certain magical attributes. Translated into other terms this means that he still has vast powers for the promotion of mental health in his patients or, when his efforts miscarry, for the creation of important iatrogenic contributions to emotional disorder.

COLLABORATION WITH COMMUNITY AGENCIES

For the prevention of mental and nervous disorders the physician will often find himself involved in activities which involve schools, employers, social agencies and governmental bodies of various kinds. Many procedures such as retraining for new industry, relocation in better housing and solution of school problems require his cooperation with a group of such community agencies in close collaboration to an extent well beyond that required for most other aspects of medical practice. The role of the physician in such collective community effort is far from new and has much precedent in the field of contagious disease, maternal and child health and public health education. Nevertheless, it will require special effort and a willingness to become involved in public service in spite of other demands on his time.

CONCLUSION

In seeking to delimit the boundaries of preventive mental health the author tried a number of different formulas but none of them seemed to serve the purpose. Finally he turned to the index of this book and saw, somewhat to his amazement, that there were mental health implications in virtually all the chapter titles, with the possible exception of such items as sewage disposal and water supply. From allergy and aged to alcoholism, obesity and accidents the trail led to such words as addiction, housing, then to poisoning, polio, and pregnancy and finally ended with work accidents and workmen's compensation. Some of the terms are of mental health interest because they represent causes of brain damage; others are stresses which contribute to psychiatric problems; still others are in large part the expression of underlying psychic disorder, while many have to do with diagnostic, research and treatment methods that apply in the mental health field.

This was obviously a rediscovery of the well-known fact that the mental health field in addition to its interests in the major mental disorders represents only another way of looking at medical practice with emphasis on its human aspects. Any attempt to cover this topic completely could lead to an unfortunate rewriting of most of the material in the book. The author has accordingly restricted himself to presenting examples only of the entire possible range of ideas, hoping that this will be sufficient to convey a general point of view. Even this must be qualified with the statement that since opinion is far from uniform in mental health there is much room for differences with the opinions which have been set down.

HENRY BRILL, M.D.

REFERENCES

1. Srole, Leo, et al.: Mental Health in the Metropolis: The Midtown Manhattan Study. Vol. I. New York, McGraw-Hill Book Co., 1962.
2. Leighton, D. C., et al.: Psychiatric Findings of the Stirling County Study. Journal of the American Psychiatric Association, May, 1963, pp. 1021-1026.
3. Lewis, Nolan D., and Engle, Bernice: Wartime Psychiatry. New York, Oxford University Press, 1954.
4. Mental Health Education: A Critique. Philadelphia, Pennsylvania Mental Health, Inc., 1960.
5. Symposium on Preventive and Social Psychiatry, April 15-17, 1957. Washington 25, D.C., U. S. Government Printing Office, 1958.
6. Evaluation in Mental Health. U. S. Department of Health, Education, and Welfare P.H.S. Publication 413. Washington 25, D.C., U. S. Government Printing Office, 1955.
7. Message from the President of the United States Relative to Mental Illness and Mental Retardation. 88th Congress. House of Representatives Document No. 58, 1963.
8. Mackay, Ronald P., and Wortis, Sam Bernard (ed.): Year Books of Neurology, Psychiatry and Neurosurgery, 1950-1963, Inclusive. Chicago, Year Book Medical Publishers, 1950-1963, inclusive.

9. Lemkau, Paul: Mental Hygiene in Public Health. Ed. 2. New York, McGraw-Hill Book Company Series in Health Science, Blakiston Division, 1955.
10. Noyes, Arthur P., and Kolb, Lawrence C.: Modern Clinical Psychiatry. Philadelphia, W. B. Saunders Company, 1963.
11. Arieti, Sylvano (ed.): American Handbook of Psychiatry. New York, Basic Books, 1959.
12. Caplan, Gerald: Principles of Preventive Psychiatry. New York, Basic Books, 1964.
13. Migration and Socio-economic Differentials in Mental Disease: A Series of Three Articles Reprinted from the Milbank Memorial Fund Quarterly. New York, Milbank Memorial Fund, 1963.
14. Cumming, John and Elaine: Ego and Milieu. New York, Atherton Press, 1962.
15. Bowlby, John: Maternal Care and Mental Health. Geneva, WHO, Sixth Impression, 1953.
16. Keels, Harold S., et al.: A Study of Environmental Stimulation. University of Iowa Studies, Studies in Child Welfare, Vol. XV, No. 4. Iowa City, University of Iowa, 1938.
17. Masland, Richard L., Sarason, Seymour B., and Gladwin, Thomas: Mental Subnormality. New York, Basic Books, 1958.

PROPHYLACTIC MEASURES AGAINST DISEASE

14 Mechanisms of Infection and Resistance

PARASITISM

Man and the animals with which he is in contact are constantly exposed to large varieties of microorganisms that are present in the air, soil and water. Most microbes do not require a direct relationship with animals for their survival and are thus called *saprophytes*. Certain species, however, depend more or less upon some contribution from living tissues for their growth and reproduction. These are called *parasites*.

Some organisms, such as viruses and certain intracellular protozoa, are *obligatory* parasites. Others, which can periodically sustain themselves free in nature, are termed *facultative* parasites. When the parasitism is not disturbing to the host but represents merely a sharing of the food supply, the association is known as *commensalism*. If the relationship is of mutual benefit to the participants it is called *symbiosis*.

Successful parasitism is achieved when a biologic balance is established between the host and parasites which enables both to grow, propagate and flourish without harm. When the characteristics of the parasite are such as to favor the parasite and damage the host, the resultant impairment of function results in the production of *disease*.

INFECTION

A successive series of events are necessary for a parasite to produce infection. These include the entrance of the parasite into the host through a *portal of entry* which may occur via aerosols and dust particles through the respiratory tract or by contaminated food or water through the gastrointestinal tract. The superficial mucous membranes and skin are also accessible portals of entry for selected organisms which may be carried by *fomites*

228

or other vehicles. Certain parasites can penetrate the intact skin while others are introduced by *arthropod vectors*, some of which serve as *intermediary hosts*.

After entry, the parasite may spread directly through tissues or may be distributed by the lymphatic channels and the blood stream to tissues which favor its multiplication. To complete the cycle, it is necessary for the parasite to find a suitable *portal of exit* and there must further exist an efficient mechanism for its transmission to a new host. Infection can occur without necessarily producing disease and indeed this frequently takes place.

The characteristics of microorganisms which enable them to cause disease are known as their *pathogenicity*. To be pathogenic an organism must exhibit a certain degree of *virulence* which, in turn, is dependent upon its ability to enter, multiply and spread within the host. This property is termed *invasiveness*. The virulence of certain organisms may depend upon their ability to produce toxic substance, or their *toxigenicity*. Toxins are divided into two major groups. Those which are secreted into the environment, usually by gram positive bacteria, are named *exotoxins*. Toxic materials which are intimately associated with the cellular structures and liberated, mostly by gram negative bacteria, when the bacterial cells are lysed, are called *endotoxins*. Examples of diseases caused by exotoxins are botulism, tetanus, diphtheria and gas gangrene. Endotoxins produce local and systemic reactions and are frequently *pyrogenic*. They are produced, for example, by enteric bacillic (*Salmonella typhi*) and other gram negative bacteria.

In addition, certain bacteria may produce materials which are not true toxins but which indirectly enhance the infectious process. Examples of such substances are coagulase, hyaluronidase, streptokinase, hemolysins, leukocidins and proteolytic enzymes such as collagenase. These enzymes aid the bacteria in their spread through tissues and interfere with the destructive action of the natural host mechanisms.

HOST RESISTANCE

The various responses of the host to invasion by microorganisms may be divided into two major categories, specific and nonspecific. *Nonspecific factors* include the *skin* and *mucous membranes* which serve as physiologic barriers to most microorganisms at the portal of entry. Body fluids and blood contain antimicrobial substances such as lysozyme, hyaluronic acid, basic polypeptides, complement, properdin and certain enzymes which exert inhibitory influences on the multiplication of bacteria and viruses.

Microbes which have evaded these barriers are subsequently met by *phagocytes* and the other special cells of the *reticuloendothelial system* which are efficient in the engulfment and digestion of bacteria. Furthermore, when organisms begin to multiply in tissues, an *inflammatory reaction* may ensue which serves to suppress and limit the spread of the foreign invaders.

SPECIFIC IMMUNITY

The response of a host which renders it resistant to a specific infectious agent is called the immune response or *immunity*. *Natural immunity* is the inherent resistance exhibited by a species, a race or an individual toward a particular pathogenic agent which is not acquired by previous contact with that agent. *Acquired immunity* is that immunity which a susceptible animal develops against specific pathogenic microorganisms. This immunity may be *passive*, such as that obtained by a fetus in utero through the transfer of maternal antibodies, or by an individual who receives an inoculation of convalescent or immune serum which contain antibodies formed in another host. Passive immunity affords immediate protection, but the transferred antibodies are readily destroyed by the host. This immunity is therefore temporary, having a duration of several weeks to some months at the longest.

Active immunity is the state of resistance engendered in an individual following effective exposure to a specific microorganism. This may occur as a result of recovery from an overt, clinical infection, or following a covert, silent or inapparent infection or following the injection of living or inactivated microorganisms or their products. A successful response after entrance of the microbial antigen results in the active production of antibodies by the host. The host cells may, in addition, be sensitized to the foreign material and develop *immunological responses* to it. Active immunity develops over a period of days or weeks but it persists, usually for years.

In public health practice it is desirable to have some knowledge concerning the immunity of the total population as well as the levels of immunity in its various population segments. These data may be obtained by epidemiologic surveys and by obtaining periodic blood samplings from the various groups of individuals. The serum is then tested for the presence of antibodies with appropriate serologic assay techniques.

ANTIGENS AND ANTIBODIES

Antigens are substances such as bacteria, but may consist of any proteins, certain polysaccharides (or lipids, nucleic acids and other "haptenes" combined with proteins) which, when introduced into animal tissues, stimulate the formation of antibodies.

Antibodies are the hosts' modified serum proteins, mainly gamma globulins and some beta globulins which can combine specifically with the antigen that elicited the antibody formation. Generally, an animal will produce antibodies only against foreign proteins. However, an animal may produce antibodies against certain blood cell antigens called *iso-antigens*. Also, certain hormones and organ specific antigens from the kidney, brain and heart muscle may give rise to antibodies in the host from which they are derived and produce *iso-allergic phenomena*.

Antigen-antibody reactions occur when these substances are placed in contact with each other. The specific combination may be observed by a visible precipitation of the antigen-antibody complex. Red cells or bacterial cells clump or agglutinate in the presence of specific antiserum to form an *agglutination reaction*. Specific *toxin* is neutralized or detoxified by adding a specific *antitoxin* which is contained in immune serum prepared in animals inoculated with the homologous toxin. This effect may be measured by testing the toxicity of the *toxin-antitoxin* mixture by its inoculation into susceptible animals. Another specific reaction of antiserum may be noted by observing its bactericidal effect when in contact with the homologous organism. The lysing of bacterial cells or other foreign cells such as red blood cells by antisera prepared against them serves as the basis for the *complement fixation reaction*. This serologic test has found invaluable use as a means of detecting cases of syphilis and is currently one of the simplest and most effective laboratory tools employed in the diagnosis of certain viral and rickettsial infections.

Other serological reactions include the *protection* or *neutralization test* which measures the ability of an antibody in a serum to inactivate the infectivity of the microorganisms placed in contact with the serum and by the inoculation of the mixture into susceptible hosts. The ability of certain viruses to clump red blood cells from various animals has resulted in the development of a *hemagglutination test* for viruses. The ability of specific antibodies to prevent hemagglutination provides a serologic test known as the *hemagglutination-inhibition test*.

The most recent development in serology permits the visualization of antigen-antibody complex under the microscope. This involves a phenomenon known as *immunofluorescence*. When serum proteins containing specific antibodies are chemically coupled with fluorescein dye and this *fluorescent antibody* combines with its specific antigen, the resultant complex may be visualized in the darkfield microscope with ultraviolet light. Specific fluorescent antibody staining techniques are currently being employed in immunologic research as well as in the diagnostic laboratory.

IMMUNOLOGIC DISEASE

Not all immunological responses are of beneficial nature to the host. Indeed, exposure to certain antigens derived from microbes as well as non-microbial sources may induce *allergy* or *hypersensitvity* so that the host response to these antigens is essentially harmful to the host or injurious to specific tissues of the host.

In addition to *anaphylaxis* and various *allergic disorders*, there are other diseases considered to be of immunologic origin. These include rheumatic fever, rheumatoid arthritis, glomerulonephritis, disseminated lupus erythematosus, demyelinating encephalitis and sympathetic ophthalmia.

MORRIS SCHAEFFER, M.D.

REFERENCES

1. Raffel, S.: Immunity. Ed. 2. New York, Appleton-Century-Crofts, Inc., 1961.
2. Dubos, R. J.: Bacterial and Mycotic Infections of Man. Ed. 3. Philadelphia, J. B. Lippincott Co., 1961.
3. Horsfall, F. L.: Viral and Rickettsial Infections of Man. Ed. 4. Philadelphia, J. B. Lippincott Co., 1965.

15 Bacterial Diseases

INTRODUCTION

Material in this and the succeeding four chapters is designed to provide the reader with a ready reference for the preventive aspects of the more important communicable and infectious diseases. Disease entities are arranged under etiological groups of bacteria, viruses, rickettsiae, fungi and parasites and are listed alphabetically under each grouping. Information is provided on the etiology, epidemiology and prophylaxis of each entity. For information regarding diagnosis, treatment and pathology, the reader is referred to standard texts on general medicine or appropriate texts in specialized fields such as tropical medicine and parasitology.

ANTHRAX
ETIOLOGICAL AGENT: *Bacillus anthracis.*
EPIDEMIOLOGY: World-wide in distribution with cloven-hoofed animals, especially cattle, sheep and goats, serving as reservoirs of infection. Man is apparently relatively resistant to infection, and cases of human disease are sporadic and usually related to the handling of infected animals or products, such as hides, hair or wool. Shaving brushes, ivory in the piano industry and insect vectors have also served to transmit infection.
PREVENTION: Ultimate prevention of anthrax involves control of the disease in animals. Control is difficult to achieve because contaminated soil in many parts of the world cannot be eradicated. Human disease can be controlled through sterilization of potentially infected hides, wool and other animal products and by strict attention to personal hygiene among exposed agricultural and industrial workers. A cell-free antigen is under development for use in industrial situations.

BRUCELLOSIS
ETIOLOGICAL AGENT: *Brucella abortus* (bovine); *Brucella suis* (porcine); *Brucella melitensis* (caprine).
EPIDEMIOLOGY: World-wide in distribution; however, in a given area the reservoir of the Brucella organisms is directly related to the type of animal husbandry practiced: cattle (abortus), swine (suis) and goats (melitensis). Sporadic cases and rare common source outbreaks among humans have been related to the ingestion of raw milk or dairy products or direct contact with the infected animal or its organs. As a result there is a strong rural concentration of cases; men are more frequently infected than women.

232

PREVENTION: Ultimate control of the disease in humans depends upon the eradication of the disease in domestic animals by the most effective program for the community, namely: test and slaughter; segregation or vaccination of cattle and goats; slaughter of infected swine herds. Short of eradication of the animal reservoir, almost complete control of human disease can be achieved through boiling or pasteurization of milk or milk products and education of workers in meat handling occupations.

CHANCROID (soft chancre)
ETIOLOGICAL AGENT: *Hemophilus ducreyi.*
EPIDEMIOLOGY: World-wide occurrence, usually sporadic, although acute outbreaks have occurred. The third most frequent venereal disease, uncommon in some areas but relatively common in others. During the Second World War, there were approximately one third as many cases as syphilis and one eighth as many as gonorrhea in the United States Armed Forces. In addition to venereal infection, accidental infections on fingers of medical personnel in hospitals have occurred because of contact with infectious material. Susceptibility is general, no evidence of production of immunity. Hypersensitivity of variable duration demonstrated by a skin test.
PREVENTION: General measures for the prevention of the spread of venereal diseases. Cleanliness and care in the handling of infected material in hospitals. Epidemiologic investigation of the source of infection and treatment of exposed and infected contacts of cases.

CHOLERA
ETIOLOGICAL AGENT: *Vibrio cholerae,* including El Tor and other strains.
EPIDEMIOLOGY: Internationally quarantinable disease. Once widespread with extensive epidemics, now endemic in India, East Pakistan, Indonesia and Southeast Asia. Man is the only known reservoir and the source is feces or vomitus transmitted through contaminated water, person-to-person and any other mode of feces–mouth transfer of the organism including fomites, flies, food and utensils. Susceptibility is general, the case fatality ranging from 5 to 75 per cent. Recovery is accompanied by some degree of protection, duration not known. Diagnosis is undisputed in the presence of an epidemic, but sporadic or mild cases may be missed.
PREVENTION: Ultimate prevention, as has been achieved in many countries of the world where the disease has not been seen for more than 50 years, rests on completely interrupting the feces–mouth transmission. This can be accomplished only by general adherence to principles of good sanitation: proper sewage disposal, purification of water supplies, pasteurization of milk, fly control, good food handling procedures (individual and general), and the recognition and isolation of cases until no longer infectious. A vaccine is available for high risk individuals and travelers from endemic or epidemic areas to areas free of cholera. Investigation of outbreaks to determine source and compliance with International Sanitary Regulations will aid in preventing its spread.

DIARRHEA OF THE NEWBORN
Epidemic form
ETIOLOGICAL AGENT: Not a distinct entity. Enteropathogenic *Escherichia coli* types most often incriminated. Viruses and other bacterial species occasionally involved.
EPIDEMIOLOGY: A hospital associated disease usually limited to newborn infants up to 1 month of age, most often 8 to 9 days old, who have been kept in crowded hospital nurseries with poor standards of nursing care. Risk decreases with age; prematures most vulnerable. Outbreaks reported from North America and Europe.
PREVENTION: Prevention consists simply in the establishment of high standards of nursing care and complete adherence to these standards, the provision of adequate equipment for hospital nurseries and avoidance of overcrowding.

DIPHTHERIA
ETIOLOGICAL AGENT: *Corynebacterium diphtheriae.*
EPIDEMIOLOGY: World-wide in distribution with the reservoir in the human population. Infective discharges from cases or carriers serve as the source of infection through the

medium of person-to-person contact, contact with fomites or the ingestion of contaminated raw milk. Susceptibility is universal, one attack usually conferring long-lasting antitoxic immunity. Infants born of immune mothers retain passive immunity until about 6 months of age. The clinical disease is most common and severe in temperate climates, with the peak incidence in late summer or early autumn.

PREVENTION: Ultimate prevention of diphtheria depends upon the maintenance of a high level of immunity in the population by the artificial immunization of nearly all infants and children with toxoid, followed by periodic booster immunization of older children and adults. The carrier rate can be reduced by chemoprophylaxis of detected carriers in a poorly immunized community. Pasteurization of milk is another preventive measure.

GONORRHEA

ETIOLOGICAL AGENT: *Neisseria gonorrheae*.

EPIDEMIOLOGY: World-wide and widespread, most common of the venereal diseases. All ages susceptible but more frequent among persons within the ages of greatest sexual activity. Because of problems in diagnosis of chronic cases, especially in the female, reported cases represent only a small fraction of actual infections. Man is the only known reservoir. Transmission is almost entirely by sexual intercourse although ophthalmia in the adult may occur, and ophthalmia neonatorum may be contracted from the infected mother during birth. Occasionally, cases in institutions have resulted from the careless and indiscriminate use of rectal thermometers. Susceptibility is general and immunity does not develop.

PREVENTION: General measures for the prevention and spread of venereal diseases. Cleanliness and care in the handling of patients and infective discharges in hospitals. Epidemiologic investigation of the source of infection and prophylaxis and treatment of exposed or infected contacts. Avoidance of intercourse with untreated previous sexual partners to avoid reinfection. Diagnosis and treatment of disease in pregnant women and use of chemoprophylactic agents in the eyes of the newborn.

GRANULOMA INGUINALE

ETIOLOGICAL AGENT: *Donovania granulomatis*.

EPIDEMIOLOGY: Endemic throughout the world but of sporadic and infrequent occurrence, generally considered as a minor venereal disease. The majority of patients are in the 20 to 40 age group or the period of greatest sexual activity, and infection is more frequent among males than females. Susceptibility is variable and no immunity has been demonstrated.

PREVENTION: General measures for the prevention of the spread of venereal diseases. Cleanliness and care in the handling of infected material in hospitals. Epidemiologic investigation of the source of infection and prophylaxis or treatment of exposed and infected contacts of cases.

LEPROSY

ETIOLOGICAL AGENT: *Mycobacterium leprae*.

EPIDEMIOLOGY: Conservatively estimated that there are some 3 to 4 million infected individuals in the world. Prevalent in the tropics, subtropics and some temperate areas as well, usually among persons residing in a rural environment. No racial immunity has been noted and susceptibility appears greatest in infancy, decreasing through childhood. If adults have not been exposed as children they are susceptible. China and India estimated to have one-half of the world's cases, United States approximately 750 and South America 30,000, with Central and South Africa with the highest reported rates. Man is the only known reservoir of the organism and the source is the lesions of infected persons. Long incubation period and absence of laboratory methods for cultivation of the organism have hindered epidemiologic investigation.

PREVENTION: Children from leprous parents should be separated from them at birth. Cases should be treated until bacteriologically negative to prevent transmission to others. In areas of high endemicity patients should be treated as ambulatory patients in general clinics under trained medical personnel. Where the disease is not indigenous, home isolation and treatment and avoiding contact with young children are adequate.

LEPTOSPIROSIS
ETIOLOGICAL AGENT: Many species of Genus Leptospira: 21 groups and 59 serotypes to date.
EPIDEMIOLOGY: World-wide zoonosis infecting a wide array of wild animal hosts, rodents and domestic animals and causing sporadic and epidemic disease in man. The source of infection is the urine of infected animals and possibly infected tissues. Transmission is through contact with waters or wet soil contaminated with the organism and possibly through ingestion. An occupational disease among veterinarians, abattoir workers, dog owners, sewer workers, rice-field workers, farmers and others. Epidemics have occurred among persons swimming in contaminated waters. Susceptibility is general.
PREVENTION: Prevention in man depends primarily on avoiding contact with infected animal urine. Under occupational conditions this may be achieved through the use of protective clothing and strict sanitary conditions. Vaccines composed of dominant local strains have been of value for workers among whom the incidence of infection is high. Rodent control in human habitations, segregation of domestic animals, and avoidance of swimming or wading in potentially contaminated waters are recommended.

MENINGITIS, MENINGOCOCCAL
ETIOLOGICAL AGENT: *Neisseria meningitidis* (Meningococcus).
EPIDEMIOLOGY: Sporadic and occasional epidemic occurrence in most parts of the world with the reservoir in the human population. Meningitis is, in reality, a rare complication of a widely distributed inapparent infection of the nasopharynx, with spread by intimate person-to-person contact. Ratio of infection to disease in the general population estimated to be 1000:1. Epidemics usually caused by Group I organisms, interepidemic and sporadic cases by Group II. It has been suggested that crowding may have been the precipitating factor in United States epidemics.
PREVENTION: Prevention is primarily aimed at high risk groups such as in institutions and military camps where crowding occurs. Carrier rate can be reduced by chemoprophylaxis and person-to-person transmission by avoidance of overcrowding and improvement of ventilation in such places as sleeping quarters, work areas and public conveyances.

PERTUSSIS
ETIOLOGICAL AGENT: *Hemophilus pertussis.*
EPIDEMIOLOGY: World-wide distribution, with the reservoir in the human population. Susceptibility universal. It has been estimated that three-quarters of all persons in non-vaccinated populations acquire the clinical disease before attaining adulthood. Transmission by droplet spray or freshly contaminated articles from cases; no true carriers. Mortality universally higher in females than males and much higher in children under 1 year of age, especially under 6 months. Limited seasonal fluctuation.
PREVENTION: Ultimate prevention based on active immunization of all infants starting at 1 to 2 months of age. Prevention of exposure of young infants to cases and prophylactic use of hyperimmune or convalescent serum for unvaccinated exposed are also of value.

PLAGUE
ETIOLOGICAL AGENT: *Pasteurella pestis.*
EPIDEMIOLOGY: Internationally quarantinable disease. Human cases sporadic and limited to circumscribed foci where sylvatic reservoir in wild rodents is present. These enzootic areas in which the reservoir is always present are found in the Western Hemisphere, in western one-third of the United States, Mexico and South America. In Africa, chiefly central and south Africa, in Asia, chiefly Near East with a center in Iranian Kurdistan, also in the frontier area between Yemen and Saudi Arabia and Central Asia. Smaller foci also occur in other areas. Disease usually intermittent in the sylvatic rodents. When it builds up into an epizootic, the fleas transfer to domestic and urban rats, fleas then bite man (bubonic plague). Man-to-man transfer through the respiratory route results in pneumonic plague which may then reach epidemic proportions. Susceptibility is general. Untreated bubonic plague has a mortality of 25 to 50 per cent; primary septicemic and pneumonic plague usually fatal.
PREVENTION: Reduction of the sylvatic plague reservoir by trapping and destroying wild rodents and dusting harborages with insecticides to destroy fleas. Trapping and destruction of urban rats in homes, warehouses, harbors, and ships, together with the use of

insecticides. Continuing surveys of rodent and flea populations for evidence of plague infection. Chemotherapy of all plague cases and suspects as well as contacts. Strict isolation of all plague patients and careful handling of discharges. Active immunization with killed vaccines for persons at high risk, such as laboratory workers, troops, travelers, diplomats, foresters, is justifiable but not to be relied upon as the principle preventive measure. Instruction desirable for medical personnel including doctors in the recognition and handling of plague cases in countries where the disease is either indigenous in the sylvatic population like the United States or in danger of being imported.

PNEUMONIA, MYCOPLASMAL

ETIOLOGICAL AGENT: *Mycoplasma pneumoniae* (Eaton Agent, PPLO).

EPIDEMIOLOGY: Formerly classified as primary atypical pneumonia, world-wide in distribution, sporadic, endemic, sometimes epidemic in occurrence, not to be confused with virus pneumonia. Epidemics noted in institutions and among military personnel, incidence varies by geographic area from year to year and is greatest during the winter in the temperate climates. Man is the only known reservoir and transmission is through respiratory discharges. Susceptibility is general; only approximately 3 per cent of infections result in clinical disease. All ages can be infected but clinical disease noted more frequently among adolescents and young adults. Immunity produced and lasts for one or more years. Symptoms may range from common cold to severe pneumonia.

PREVENTION: Cleanliness and care in the handling of patients and disposal of soiled materials. Tetracycline antibiotics have been proven successful in treatment of this disease.

PNEUMONIA, PNEUMOCOCCAL

ETIOLOGICAL AGENT: *Diplococcus pneumoniae* (pneumococcus). (More than 75 distinct types.)

EPIDEMIOLOGY: World-wide, usually sporadic disease with its reservoir in the human population. Clinical cases represent only a small portion of the population harboring the organism; most individuals infected with it at one time or another. Epidemics have occurred in institutions, military camps and mines. Was the leading cause of death in many areas prior to advent of antibiotics and chemotherapy. Respiratory transmission facilitated by crowding and poor ventilation. Many nonspecific factors predispose to pneumonia including debilitating disease and influenza. Affects all ages but most severe in young and old. Most cases caused by the first 32 types, predominantly I, II and III.

PREVENTION: Prevention of pneumonia is directed primarily at high risk groups. There should be avoidance of crowding in existing epidemic foci such as army barracks, institutions and mines. Isolation of patients with known disease will prevent its spread in hospitals. Secondary pneumonia may be prevented by adequate attention to the primary condition. Active artificial immunization with bacterial vaccines or capsular polysaccharides of prevailing types is available for persons at high risk. Chemoprophylaxis may be used when warranted in an exposed population.

SHIGELLOSIS (bacillary dysentery)

ETIOLOGICAL AGENT: Shigella species.

EPIDEMIOLOGY: Fecal-borne disease of world-wide distribution with its reservoir in cases and carriers in the human population. Transmitted through the medium of fecally contaminated water, food, milk or fomites, flies and hand-to-mouth contact. Ranges from a mild subclinical infection to a severe, highly fatal disease, depending on the species of Shigella and condition of the host. Most severe in the very young, the elderly debilitated and institutional inmates. Institutional infections are common and much undiagnosed and unreported diarrhea may result from Shigella infections. Historically this has been a severe disease with exceptionally high mortality, especially among armies and crowded populations living in unsanitary environments.

PREVENTION: Ultimate prevention depends upon the elimination of the organism from the human reservoir and is based on preventing human ingestion of fecal material. This can be accomplished through the proper disposal and handling of feces, sanitary control of sewage, water, food and milk, fly control, food handler education and, in some areas, the treatment of "night soil." Patients should be isolated and treated adequately. Under special circumstances, mass chemoprophylaxis might be applied on a short-term basis.

STAPHYLOCOCCAL INFECTIONS (hospital acquired)

ETIOLOGICAL AGENT: *Micrococcus pyogenes*, var. *aureus*. (Variety of phage types.)

EPIDEMIOLOGY: Ubiquitous organism causing a wide range of clinical conditions in the general population. Almost everyone at some time harbors staphylococci. During the past decade, epidemics of staphylococcal disease due to antibiotic resistant specific phage types of these organisms reported from all over the world, with hospitals serving as the source of outbreaks within the community. Infected hospital personnel serve as the reservoir and the source is their infective discharges and contaminated environment. Newborn infants, their mothers, surgical patients and other debilitated patients, most susceptible.

PREVENTION: Prevention depends upon the strict adherence to aseptic techniques in hospitals. Usually necessary to establish a Hospital Infection Control Committee. More cautious utilization of antibiotics, surveillance of personnel for colonization with antibiotic-resistant, coagulase-positive, epidemic phage types and elimination of carriers will reduce the hazard of infection.

STREPTOCOCCAL INFECTION (hemolytic)

ETIOLOGICAL AGENT: *Streptococcus pyogenes* Group A. (At least 50 serologic types.)

EPIDEMIOLOGY: Endemic, epidemic or sporadic disease of wide distribution. Clinical disease more common in temperate zones, while inapparent infection more common in tropical and subtropical areas. Manifested as an extremely wide variety of conditions, including streptococcal sore throat, scarlet fever, erysipelas, puerperal fever, cellulitis among others. Any of the 50 types can produce these conditions, depending on portal of entry, host response and tissues involved. Reservoir is in the human population and transmission through contact with infective discharges, contaminated food and raw milk. One attack of streptococcal disease results in long-lasting immunity only to the specific type involved. One attack of scarlet fever usually results in lasting immunity to the erythrogenic toxin.

PREVENTION: Recognition of the widespread occurrence of the disease and its proper treatment with penicillin is the most adequate preventive measure available at this time. Chemoprophylaxis in areas of high incidence to prevent sequelae such as rheumatic fever and acute glomerulonephritis may be advisable. Pasteurization of milk and general hospital asepsis are also effective.

SYPHILIS

ETIOLOGICAL AGENT: *Treponema pallidum*.

EPIDEMIOLOGY: World-wide and widespread, one of the more frequent of the venereal diseases. All ages susceptible but most frequent among persons within the ages of greatest sexual activity. Man is the only reservoir and transmission is primarily through sexual intercourse or other intimate contact. Can be congenitally acquired from an infected mother and has been transmitted through blood transfusion and accidentally to nurses, midwives, dentists and physicians. Susceptibility is universal. Resistance to homologous strain and to heterologous strains such as *T. pertenue* is present during infection so that yaws and syphilis do not occur in the same individual at the same time. A nonvenereal syphilis caused by an organism indistinguishable from that causing venereal syphilis is common in localized areas with poor sanitary and socioeconomic conditions. Foci have been found in Africa, Turkey, Balkans and eastern Mediterranean countries. Transmission of nonvenereal form is by direct or indirect contact through common eating and drinking utensils and general unhygienic conditions.

PREVENTION: General measures for the prevention of the spread of venereal disease. Cleanliness and care in the handling of patients, discharges and blood in hospitals. Epidemiologic investigation of the source of infection and prophylaxis or treatment of exposed or infected contacts. Avoidance of intercourse with infected sex partners not under treatment. Control of blood donors. Prenatal serologic testing and treatment of mothers found infected. Prevention of the nonvenereal syphilis depends upon improving the educational, social and economic levels of the population with an emphasis on cleanliness and the finding and treating of infectious cases.

TETANUS

ETIOLOGICAL AGENT: *Clostridium tetani*.

EPIDEMIOLOGY: World-wide distribution, sporadic disease infrequent in occurrence in countries such as the United States, more often in tropical than temperate climates. Cases occur in rural and urban areas where sanitation is poor, population density high and medical services including immunization poor or absent. Rarely recovered from virgin soil, the organism is found in cultivated soil contaminated by feces of horse and cattle and enters the human host by puncture wounds, lacerations, splinters, contusions, vaccination and even insect bites. Insanitary midwifery during delivery may result in tetanus neonatorum. Important cause of death in many countries of Asia, Africa and Latin America, especially among agricultural workers and the newborn. During war a great hazard of military wounds among the unimmunized.

PREVENTION: Active immunization with toxoid is the most effective preventive measure and should be administered routinely to all infants, preferably together with diphtheria, pertussis and polio preventives. This should be followed by booster doses at prescribed intervals to maintain a high level of immunity, especially among persons at high risk. Passive immunization should be resorted to only in the absence of toxoid immunization since there is the danger of serum sickness if horse serum is used. Some antitoxic human serum now available. Appropriate local treatment and cleansing of all wounds is another integral part of prevention. Techniques of sterilization in hospitals should be carefully controlled. Licensing and control of midwives and education in aseptic techniques should reduce danger of tetanus to the mother and child following delivery.

TUBERCULOSIS

ETIOLOGICAL AGENT: *Mycobacterium tuberculosis*, var. *hominis*, var. *bovis*.

EPIDEMIOLOGY: World-wide distribution, but problem varies in different parts of the world. Range in mortality, which is declining, is from 5 to over 100 per 100,000, reflecting differences in socioeconomic levels in the different countries. In some areas like the United States, bovine tuberculosis is no problem. It still is in countries where boiling and pasteurization of milk are not practiced. The reservoir of the human species is man, that of the bovine, cattle. Transmission of the former is usually aerogenous from open cases. The latter is usually acquired through the consumption of raw milk from infected cattle. Susceptibility is general and almost all who have a primary infection with the organism develop hypersensitivity to its tuberculoprotein. The difference between infection and disease is usually determined by host and environmental factors.

PREVENTION: The bovine form can be prevented by tuberculin testing and slaughter programs for cattle. Pasteurization or boiling of milk is effective in killing the bacillus. Ultimate prevention of the pulmonary form rests upon finding and treating until non-infectious every case of open bacillary-positive tuberculosis. Case finding through tuberculin testing, chest x-ray films and sputum examinations is essential. This is still one of the most important problems and a leading cause of death and disability in many countries.

TULAREMIA

ETIOLOGICAL AGENT: *Pasteurella tularensis*.

EPIDEMIOLOGY: Limited geographically to those areas of the world in which the infection is present in a reservoir host, this fatal zoonosis of wild rodents can be transmitted to man through a great variety of arthropod vectors as well as through contact, indirect and aerogenous routes, and can also infect a remarkably wide range of animals. So far it has been isolated only in North America, continental Europe, Russia and Japan. Where it will next make its appearance is unpredictable. Usually endemic and sporadic, but extensive epidemics involving as many as 30,000 cases have occurred. In spite of the great variety of modes of transmission and reservoir animals, its occurrence is usually limited to trappers, hunters, fur processors, sheep herders, laboratory workers and individuals who consume flesh of wild animals such as rabbits.

PREVENTION: Epidemic waves usually preceded by epizootics in wild animals. In endemic areas precaution should be taken against arthropod bites, against the consumption of unboiled or untreated water, contact with the flesh and blood of freshly killed wild animals and the consumption of uncooked or inadequately cooked wild animal flesh. A vaccine is available for use in persons under risk such as laboratory workers. Education in the handling of carcasses of wild animals, the use of rubber gloves while handling such animals and the control of the sale of wild rabbits should also help to reduce danger of infection.

TYPHOID FEVER

ETIOLOGICAL AGENT: *Salmonella typhi*. (More than 30 phage types and subtypes.)

EPIDEMIOLOGY: World-wide distribution, sporadic and epidemic fecally transmitted disease with its reservoir in man. Spread by water, food, shellfish, milk and milk products contaminated with feces and occasionally urine of cases, convalescents or carriers. Approximately 2 to 5 per cent of cases ultimately become permanent carriers. Geographic distribution related to the state of environmental sanitation and practices of personal hygiene and food handling. Susceptibility is general but high degree of resistance follows recovery.

PREVENTION: Ultimate prevention would depend upon a high standard of environmental sanitation and the elimination of carriers. Provisions for adequate disposal of human wastes, chlorination or boiling of water, pasteurization or boiling of milk, refrigeration of food, use of treated water for ice, shellfish control, and the finding and control of carriers, primarily preventing them from handling food to be consumed by others. Fly control can greatly lessen the potential for transmission. Immunization of persons under risk is still recommended but under investigation as to its efficacy. Epidemiologic investigation of all cases to determine and eliminate source of infection is essential.

YAWS

ETIOLOGICAL AGENT: *Treponema pertenue*.

EPIDEMIOLOGY: Geographic distribution limited exclusively to tropical and subtropical countries with wet hot climates in which the disease is endemic and widespread. Intensive control activity has reduced incidence in many areas; however, estimates place the numbers still infected at about 100 million. Affects children before puberty predominantly, immunity developing as a result of infection, but adult cases also occur. Man is the only reservoir and transmission is by direct contact with open skin lesions containing viable treponemes. Flies and contaminated objects have also been suspected. No evidence of racial or natural resistance. Serologically indistinguishable from syphilis, bejel and pinta.

PREVENTION: Ultimate prevention would depend on the ideal state when all infected persons have been rendered noninfectious by chemotherapy and no more susceptibles become infected. Intensive control activities with this aim in view have been in effect in many areas with some degree of success but constant surveillance and provision for treatment must continue. Health promotional activities accompanied by improved sanitation and socioeconomic conditions are important. In the meantime, it should be stressed that all infected persons (cases active and latent) and their contacts should be treated. Intimate contact with patients should be avoided until lesions have healed. Cleanliness and care in the handling of lesions and discharges should be exercised. Furthermore, it is important to differentiate between endemic syphilis and yaws and to guard against an upsurge of venereal syphilis in areas in which yaws has been suppressed.

ANNA C. GELMAN, M.P.H.
HERMAN E. HILLEBOE, M.D.

16   Viral Diseases

ACUTE FEBRILE VIRAL RESPIRATORY INFECTIONS

ETIOLOGICAL AGENT: A variety of viruses, e.g., Para influenza, respiratory syncytial, rhinovirus, reovirus, and others.

EPIDEMIOLOGY: A large group of respiratory infections ranging from mild to severe and manifesting a great variety of clinical syndromes from pharyngitis to virus pneumonia are world-wide in distribution and endemic in almost all human communities. They may be sporadic, occur in small outbreaks, may be seasonal or continually present. Susceptibility is general and antibodies to a variety of viruses have been demonstrated. Man is the only known reservoir for most of these viruses (exception: reoviruses which have also been found in animals). Each has its distinctive epidemiology, including prevalence in a community and geographic distribution. Although morbidity is high, mortality is negligible.

PREVENTION: Since none of these respiratory infections responds to antibiotic or chemotherapeutic agents it is important to differentiate them from those with similar symptoms for which therapy is available such as Q fever and mycoplasmal pneumonia. It is also important to differentiate them from the epidemic communicable diseases, such as measles, which have respiratory symptoms. Crowding in schools, hospitals, nurseries, institutions and barracks should be avoided, especially in sleeping quarters.

ADENOVIRUS INFECTIONS

ETIOLOGICAL AGENT: Adenoviruses, 28 types.

EPIDEMIOLOGY: Since their first demonstration in 1953, more than 28 types of adenoviruses associated with human disease have been demonstrated, serologic evidence pointing to a world-wide distribution. They cause adenoidal, pharyngoconjunctival and acute respiratory diseases which occur in endemic or epidemic patterns. Epidemics have occurred in institutions or aggregations of individuals such as in military camps, children's camps and occupational groups. Epidemic keratoconjunctivitis or shipyard eye is most commonly associated with type 8; acute respiratory disease (ARD) of military recruits more commonly 3, 4, 7 and sometimes 14; pharyngoconjunctival fever, more commonly type 3, sometimes 7 and others. The endemic types are common in the population, the epidemic ones rare. Susceptibility is high. Immunity is demonstrable. (Types 7, 12 and 18 have been found to have oncogenic properties in hamsters.)

PREVENTION: Inactivated virus vaccines have been developed against the epidemic types 3, 4, and 7. They have been useful among military personnel but their mass use is unwarranted in the civilian population because of the small proportion of upper respiratory infections they cause. Avoidance of overcrowding and good personal hygiene can minimize spread of respiratory infections. Epidemic keratoconjunctivitis can be controlled by the use of safety goggles to protect the eye from predisposing trauma in industrial plants and shipyards, recognition of cases and institution of precautions against spread to others.

240

ARTHROPOD-BORNE VIRAL ENCEPHALITIDES
ETIOLOGICAL AGENT: Viruses of Groups A, B, C and others.
EPIDEMIOLOGY: A group of encephalitides occurring in different areas but classed together by mode of transmission and clinical features have been recognized since 1930. These include: (1) St. Louis encephalitis occurring in central and western United States, Trinidad and Panama; (2) western equine encephalitis in the western United States and Canada, scattered areas further east and in South America; (3) eastern equine encephalitis in the eastern United States and Canada, scattered areas of Central and South America and the Philippine Islands; (4) Venezuela equine encephalitis in South America and Panama; (5) Japanese B in the Far East; and (6) Murray Valley in parts of Australia and New Guinea. The reservoir of these infections, still under speculation, is probably birds. The source is an infective mosquito. The severity of infection is highest in infancy and old age. Immunity is conferred by each type but little if any cross immunity exists. The case fatality may be as low as 5 per cent in WEE and as high as 60 per cent in EEE. Permanent neurologic sequelae may occur in infants from EEE and to a much lesser extent from WEE and St. Louis. Other arthropod-borne encephalitides have been identified which are transmitted by ticks. These include Russian spring-summer, louping ill disease, and diphasic meningoencephalitis.
PREVENTION: Control of these infections depends upon elimination or suppression of mosquito or tick vectors and avoidance of bites in endemic areas. Recognition of the disease in horses and birds may be the first indication of its presence. There are experimental vaccines for protection of individuals at great risk. Formalinized virus vaccines have been used in the U.S.S.R. against the tick types with reported success.

CAT SCRATCH FEVER (benign inoculation lymphoreticulosis)
ETIOLOGICAL AGENT: Agent unidentified.
EPIDEMIOLOGY: Since 1935 when this disease was first described it has been reported sporadically from many areas of the world. The reservoir has not been identified. It is probably one of several animals including the cat. Most patients give a history of contact with a cat, although this is not always the case. It is assumed that the agent is introduced through bite, scratch or lick of the infected animal, also through minor trauma such as thorn scratches, insect bites or splinters. Susceptibility is unknown. It is usually not fatal although a few cases of meningoencephalitis have been described.
PREVENTION: Wounds due to bites or scratches, especially by cats, should be immediately cleansed and treated. Care should be exercised in the handling of suppurative discharges and contaminated dressings of patients.

CHICKENPOX (varicella)
ETIOLOGICAL AGENT: Varicella-zoster virus.
EPIDEMIOLOGY: Very widespread endemic and epidemic, highly communicable disease of childhood, occurring less frequently after 20 years of age. Frequency of epidemics depends upon concentration of susceptibles in the community. Man is the only known reservoir and transmission is by respiratory secretions. Susceptibility is almost universal and one attack usually confers lifelong immunity. Epidemiologic studies indicate that herpes zoster commonly known as shingles and affecting adults, middle-aged or older, is capable of initiating chickenpox in susceptible child contacts. It is believed that the virus is the same.
PREVENTION: Isolation for the incubation period of the disease is sometimes practiced but is of little value. There is no active immunization. It is important that all cases of chickenpox in persons over 15 years of age be considered as possible cases of smallpox, and care taken in differential diagnosis. Fatal chickenpox has been observed in patients receiving steroid therapy. If no history of chickenpox is obtainable it may be advisable among adults to prevent exposure to chickenpox. A case of shingles should be considered as a source of chickenpox and caution should be exercised accordingly.

COXSACKIE VIRUS INFECTIONS
ETIOLOGICAL AGENT: Coxsackie A virus, types 1 to 24; Coxsackie B virus, types 1 to 6.
EPIDEMIOLOGY: These viruses were first discovered in 1948. Since then two groups and 30 types have been found. They are world-wide in distribution, sporadic and epidemic in occurrence with their greatest incidence during summer and early autumn in temperate

climates, coincident with that of poliomyelitis. Clinical illnesses more frequent in children and young adults. Man is the reservoir, source pharyngeal secretions and feces. They are transmitted either through fecal-oral contact or by droplet. Sewage, flies, cockroaches and mice have been found contaminated but are not incriminated in spread. Susceptibility general. Many subclinical infections occur and antibodies can be demonstrated following both clinical and subclinical infections. Clinical syndromes associated with different types of these viruses include herpangina (Group A), epidemic pleurodynia (Group B), encephalomyocarditis and myocarditis neonatorum (Group B), common colds (Group A), acute febrile respiratory illness, and aseptic meningitis (Groups A and B).

PREVENTION: No method of prevention known except for the precautions normally taken with diseases spread through pharyngeal secretions and feces. When these illnesses are prevalent in the community, it is important for all physicians to be aware of their occurrence and their relationship to the differential diagnosis of poliomyelitis.

DENGUE FEVER

ETIOLOGICAL AGENT: Viruses of dengue fever, types 1, 2 and 4 (Group B arbo viruses).

EPIDEMIOLOGY: Endemic areas limited to parts of the world where the Aedes mosquito vectors thrive all year round. Epidemics in temperate climates terminate with arrival of cold weather. Large endemic areas found in Caribbean Islands, islands of the Southwest Pacific, Indo-China, India, Australia, etc. Has also occurred in other areas where the vectors are present. Susceptibility is high and immunity is produced so that perpetuation depends upon the presence of susceptibles such as newborns, immigrants, troops in transit. Classed with a large group of arthropod-borne viral fevers called dengue-like with a similar clinical picture and mode of transmission.

PREVENTION: Control depends upon elimination or suppression of the mosquito vector. Patients should be isolated to prevent mosquito bite. Attenuated live virus vaccines are under investigation.

ECHO VIRUS INFECTIONS

ETIOLOGICAL AGENT: ECHO viruses, types 1 to 30.

EPIDEMIOLOGY: In 1955 a committee was set up to study a group of viruses isolated during the search for polio and Coxsackie viruses and not known to be associated with clinical illness. These viruses, the so-called entero cytopathogenic human orphan viruses have since been found to be world-wide in distribution and associated with a number of clinical syndromes. These include acute febrile respiratory illness, aseptic meningitis (with or without a rash), maculopapular eruptions, especially in children, associated with types 4, 9 and 16 (the latter causing Boston exanthema), diarrhea neonatorum (type 18 and others) and common colds. Susceptibility is general. Clinical manifestations may differ with age of patient. They are spread from human reservoir as other enterovirus infections, through fecal and respiratory discharges.

PREVENTION: Prevention similar to that for other enteric viruses, with caution for several weeks after illness to prevent fecal contamination. Avoidance of contact with patients with fever and rash especially among prematures and very young infants. Investigate outbreaks of infant diarrhea for evidence of ECHO virus infection. Crowding and poor sanitation facilitate spread.

HEPATITIS, INFECTIOUS

ETIOLOGICAL AGENT: Virus of infectious hepatitis (presumed).

EPIDEMIOLOGY: World-wide distribution. Sporadic and epidemic. Prevalent all year round in the tropics but highest in autumn and winter in the temperate zones. Infecting agent present in stools of human host and presumed to be spread from person to person by the fecal–oral route. Transmission also possible through fecally contaminated water, food, milk and shellfish as well as through transfusion of infected blood and use of contaminated syringes, needles and other instruments. Susceptibility is general but the illness occurs more often in children and young adults. There are many unrecognized subclinical infections. Immunity accumulates in the population with advancing age. During the last two decades the numbers of reported cases of infectious hepatitis have increased considerably in all parts of the world.

PREVENTION: Prophylaxis against infection depends on good community sanitation and personal hygiene, with special attention to feces disposal. Shellfish beds should not be close to sewer outlets. Fecal contamination of food and drink should be avoided. Care should be exercised in selection of blood donors. The use of properly sterilized syringes or needles in any type of parenteral inoculation or blood examination procedure is essential. If the disease appears in epidemic form in schools or institutions or the military, mass prophylaxis with immune serum globulin may be indicated. In the search for missed cases among contacts nonicteric disease among children should be suspect. The occurrence of subclinical infections considerably complicates prevention.

HEPATITIS, SERUM (homologous serum jaundice)
ETIOLOGICAL AGENT: Virus of serum hepatitis (presumed).
EPIDEMIOLOGY: World-wide distribution occurring wherever inoculation with human blood plasma, serum thrombin or fibrinogen is practiced and wherever prophylactic or therapeutic agents are administered by injection. It has been reported among 2 to 5 per cent of the recipients of pooled blood products, though known batches of icterogenic plasma have caused hepatitis in as many as 60 per cent of the recipients. Man is the only known reservoir and the only known methods of transmission are through parenteral inoculation, or the use of infected needles, syringes and other instruments. Some known carriers of the virus have never experienced a clinically recognizable attack. Cases have occurred among drug addicts using nonsterile syringes and needles and among patrons of tattoo parlors.
PREVENTION: Since there is no other known method of transmission except through inoculation from infected person to susceptible, control should be aimed at preventing this. All instruments used for more than one individual should be thoroughly sterilized between procedures. Extreme caution should be exercised with known cases. The use of pooled blood should be limited. Storage of blood derivatives at room temperature for 6 months may reduce the hazard. Immune serum globulin does not transmit the virus. Donors should be carefully screened for a history of jaundice, although this is unreliable since no test is available. Those suspected of having transmitted the infection should not be used as blood donors. Epidemiologic investigation of cases is important to trace source and differentiate from infectious hepatitis. Drug addicts should be suspect as source.

HERPES SIMPLEX INFECTIONS
ETIOLOGICAL AGENT: Virus of herpes simplex.
EPIDEMIOLOGY: A very widespread viral infection. Once infected, man probably harbors the virus throughout life. An average of 70 to 90 per cent of adults demonstrate the presence of circulating antibodies which are not true protective antibodies but which indicate past subclinical or clinical infection. Wide symptom complex ranging from localized herpetic lesions (cold sores, fever blisters) on lips, face, cornea, genitalia, fingers and mouth, to an eczema herpeticum, herpetic meningoencephalitis, and a serious disseminated infection of prematures, infants and children. Man is the only reservoir and transmission is by discharges of lesions through kissing, sexual intercourse, towels, glasses, the process of being born, in general any contact with infected material. Crowding seems to facilitate transmission. Susceptibility is general. Immunity not protective against exacerbation by other illness or nonspecific stimuli such as fever, menstruation, sunburn, etc.
PREVENTION: There are no actual means of prevention. Repeated vaccination with smallpox vaccine has been recommended as a method for terminating infection with herpes simplex virus and preventing exacerbations.

INFECTIOUS MONONUCLEOSIS (glandular fever)
ETIOLOGICAL AGENT: Presumed to be a virus or viruses.
EPIDEMIOLOGY: Reported from many parts of the world, particularly United States and Japan, Great Britain, continental Europe and Australia. Occurs as sporadic or isolated cases and in localized outbreaks, the latter most often recognized in schools, institutions and hospitals. Man is presumed to be the reservoir and the source respiratory discharges transmitted by intimate contact, especially among young adults and children. Susceptibility is probably general. Mild unrecognized cases probably occur, conferring immunity. Greatest prevalence in temperate climates is from late autumn to early spring.

PREVENTION: Differentiate from infectious hepatitis and from syphilis if biologic false positive is reported. Cleanliness in the handling of articles soiled with nose or throat discharges is recommended.

INFLUENZA

ETIOLOGICAL AGENT: Virus of influenza, types A, B, and C.

EPIDEMIOLOGY: World-wide sporadic, localized epidemic and pandemic in occurrence. In epidemics the disease usually sweeps through the community within 3 to 4 weeks and may affect more than 70 per cent of the population within 4 to 6 weeks (ordinarily 15 to 40 per cent). Three types of serologically unrelated strains, A, B and C, have been identified. Types A and B have a number of variants which are antigenically distinct so that protection against one does not confer protection against the other. Type A appears in sizable epidemics at 2 to 3 year intervals; type B less extensive and less frequent at 4 to 5 year intervals. Type C is negligible. Susceptibility general but to varying degrees, depending upon previous exposure to related strains of the virus. A large epidemic presumably occurs when there is a change from the previously experienced antigenic pattern, e.g., A2 or Asian in 1957 world-wide pandemic. Clinical syndromes caused by influenza viruses include classic influenza, acute bronchitis, viral pneumonia, croup and common cold.

PREVENTION: Adequate control of influenza has yet to be achieved. Vaccines are available but may not protect against the prevailing strain. Protection must be employed in advance of anticipated epidemics. Frequent shifts in antigenic structure of the virus make this impractical. The vaccine has some side effects and duration of protection is short-lived. Efforts should be aimed at control of secondary infections. Influenza epidemics are associated with increased general mortality, especially among the more vulnerable.

LYMPHOCYTIC CHORIOMENINGITIS

ETIOLOGICAL AGENT: Virus of lymphocytic choriomeningitis.

EPIDEMIOLOGY: Endemic in lower animals, especially house mice, but sporadic in man. Transmitted from mouse reservoir through food and dust contaminated with dried mouse urine or feces. Infection perpetuated in some mouse colonies, occurrence in a community usually related to street or district in which infection is endemic. Serologic studies indicate that subclinical infections occur in man. Infections have been observed in dogs, monkeys, guinea pigs and swine.

PREVENTION: Cleanliness of home and place of work with elimination of mice in the environment is the only known prophylactic measure.

LYMPHOGRANULOMA VENEREUM (lymphogranuloma inguinale, lymphopathia venereum)

ETIOLOGICAL AGENT: Agent of lymphogranuloma venereum.

EPIDEMIOLOGY: World-wide endemic venereal disease. Actual occurrence not known since it is usually not reportable. Man is the only reservoir and transmission usually through sexual contact, homosexual and heterosexual. It may also be acquired through nonvenereal contact; medical personnel infected on the fingers during examination or treatment; contact with infected bedfellows or indirectly with items such as contaminated clothing, douche or enema nozzles. Susceptibility is believed to be general. Immunity does not develop but dermal sensitivity develops as indicated by a skin test.

PREVENTION: The same preventive procedures which apply to all venereally acquired diseases should be used. In addition, extreme care in the handling of infective discharges and avoidance of contact, sexual or otherwise, with lesions of patients. Investigation of source of infection and treatment of infected and exposed contact when possible. (These organisms, which hold a position between the rickettsiae and viruses, are susceptible to chemotherapeutic agents.)

MEASLES (rubeola)

ETIOLOGICAL AGENT: Virus of measles.

EPIDEMIOLOGY: World-wide, endemic and epidemic highly communicable disease of childhood. Eighty to 90 per cent of adults have had this disease by the time they reach 20. Major epidemics occur at intervals of 2 to 3 years in most countries or when a sufficient number of susceptibles has accumulated. Its introduction into an isolated community which has not experienced the disease for a long time results in widespread infection and increased case fatality. Deaths are usually uncommon but complications such as post-infectious encephalitis which may leave permanent neurologic or mental disability may occur. Man is the only reservoir and source is respiratory secretions of cases. Susceptibility is universal and highest incidence occurs in children under 5 years of age. Immunity is usual after an attack.

PREVENTION: Until recently the only preventive measure was to administer gamma glob-ulin to exposed contacts to avert or modify the attack. Recently two types of vaccine have been developed, a formalin-inactivated (killed) vaccine and an attenuated (live) vaccine. This is a great step forward but will require maintenance of a high level of immunity in the general population to avoid future hazards of severe epidemics. The duration of artificially induced immunity remains to be determined.

MUMPS (epidemic parotitis)

ETIOLOGICAL AGENT: Virus of mumps.

EPIDEMIOLOGY: World-wide distribution. Endemic, with sporadic and epidemic occur-rence approximately every 7 to 8 years. Man is only reservoir and source is saliva of infected individuals. Approximately 30 to 40 per cent of cases are subclinical, conferring immunity, and serving as source for others but masking actual incidence. Outbreaks occur in aggregations of young susceptibles, especially the military. Greatest prevalence during spring and winter. Susceptibility is considered to be general and immunity following clinical or subclinical attacks probably lifelong. Other manifestations of mumps virus infection are orchitis, meningoencephalitis, pancreatitis and oophoritis; these may occur with or without parotitis.

PREVENTION: Vaccines are available and may have limited usefulness among special groups of exposed susceptibles, as also may mumps hyperimmune serum globulin.

POLIOMYELITIS

ETIOLOGICAL AGENT: Virus of poliomyelitis (types 1, 2 and 3).

EPIDEMIOLOGY: World-wide in distribution, in epidemic form and at irregular intervals. Inapparent infections without illness probably outnumber clinical cases by several hundred to one. The highest reported incidence has been in the temperate zones in the more developed countries. Improved living conditions are correlated with recognition of epi-demic poliomyelitis. In highly congested areas of the world with poor sanitation, anti-bodies to all three types are usually present in children by the time they reach school age. In those countries with better sanitation and where artificial immunization has been widely used, paralytic cases occur primarily in the unvaccinated groups. Man is the only known reservoir and the virus multiplies in the alimentary tract. Type specific immunity follows recovery from both the apparent and inapparent disease.

PREVENTION: Cleanliness in the handling of the patient to prevent transmission of the infection to others should be the same as with bacterial and viral diseases transmitted through enteric or pharyngeal discharges. Active immunization with one of the available vaccines, Salk (killed) and Sabin (live), has been successful in bringing about a marked decrease in paralytic poliomyelitis.

PSITTACOSIS (ornithosis)

ETIOLOGICAL AGENT: Agent of psittacosis-ornithosis group.

EPIDEMIOLOGY: World-wide distribution, sporadic and epidemic in man, occurring all year round and usually contracted through contact with cloacal discharges of household psittacine bird pets, domestic fowl and probably other birds such as pigeons. Man-to-man transmission is rare, although cases have been reported and laboratory transmission is possible. Infection has been found in more than 100 species of domestic and wild birds, including parrots, parakeets, pigeons, ducks, turkeys, chickens, pheasants and sea gulls. An occupational disease of increasing importance in plants processing poultry, especially turkeys. Susceptibility is apparently general but the disease is more severe among older adults. Prior to broad spectrum antibiotic therapy the case fatality was as high as 20 per cent, primarily among adults or very young children.

PREVENTION: The incorporation of broad spectrum antibiotics in the feed of pet birds has been effective in reducing their infection. Regulations related to pet bird traffic, periodic testing for virus among commercially sold birds, test for infection in turkey flocks and epidemiologic investigation of infection in humans can aid in reducing infection from controllable sources. Wild birds and pigeons are more difficult to control. There is no vaccine available. Cleanliness around pet birds and thorough cleaning and disinfection of buildings housing infected birds are essential. When control by using antibiotic treated feed is not possible, infected birds should be destroyed or treated. (The lymphogranuloma-psittacosis group, which holds a position between the rickettsiae and viruses, is susceptible to chemotherapeutic agents.)

RABIES
ETIOLOGICAL AGENT: Virus of rabies.
EPIDEMIOLOGY: World-wide distribution among animals except for Australia, New Zealand, Hawaii and the other Pacific Islands, some of the West Indies, Great Britain, the Scandinavian Peninsula, Netherlands, Belgium and Sweden. Since these countries have no sylvatic reservoir the disease has been eliminated or kept out by a carefully supervised quarantine of imported dogs and other animals. Rabies is almost always a fatal zoonosis of warm-blooded animals and man. The only host which it does not usually kill is the bat. Live rabies virus has been found in the saliva of apparently healthy as well as sick bats. Foxes, coyotes, wolves, skunks, raccoons and other ground animals may be the source of infection for domestic animals and man. The disease is relatively uncommon in man but invariably fatal.
PREVENTION: Since most human infections are caused by the bite of a rabid animal, usually the dog, the most effective preventive measure which has been developed is the immunization of dogs against rabies. Stray dogs should be caught and pet dogs immunized. Persons at high risk such as veterinarians may be vaccinated with a live attenuated virus strain. In areas where cattle are frequently infected from vampire bats, immunization of cattle may be warranted. If man is bitten by an animal, the standard procedure for the handling of such cases (including vaccination if indicated) should be carefully followed.

RUBELLA (German measles)
ETIOLOGICAL AGENT: Virus of rubella.
EPIDEMIOLOGY: World-Wide common epidemic disease occurring mostly among children and most often in the winter and spring months. Less communicable than measles, therefore more common than measles among adults. Man is the only reservoir and source is respiratory secretions. Usually mild in childhood. May result in congenital malformations of the fetus if contracted by a pregnant woman during the first trimester of pregnancy. Immunity usually conferred by a single attack.
PREVENTION: There is no vaccine as yet. Due to evidence that it may cause congenital malformations in the fetus if contracted by the pregnant mother, it is not considered advisable to shield young healthy girls from infection. Some authorities advise deliberate exposure. Gamma globulin has been recommended for adult female contacts in the first four months of pregnancy who have no history of rubella; its use is now under discussion.

SMALLPOX (variola)
ETIOLOGICAL AGENT: Virus of variola.
EPIDEMIOLOGY: An internationally quarantinable disease with potential world-wide distribution. At present it still persists in parts of Africa, South America and Asia (especially the Indian subcontinent). These can serve as the foci for the introduction of the disease into those countries which have been free from it but where the level of immunity is now low. Man is the only reservoir. The sources are respiratory discharges of patients and lesions of the skin and mucous membranes as well as contaminated articles. Contact can be direct, but aerial transmission as well as contact with contaminated objects are also very important. Susceptibility is general in the absence of vaccination. Two types of the disease occur—variola major, the more severe form usually called Asiatic smallpox, with a 30 per cent fatality; and variola minor or alastrim which is much milder, with a 1 per cent fatality.
PREVENTION: Vaccination, revaccination and maintenance of a high level of immunity among persons at high risk, such as hospital employees. Strict enforcement of international quarantine regulations requiring immunization certificates and notification. Since

previous immunization modifies the clinical appearance of the disease, differentiation from severe chickenpox in the adult is important in order to be able to detect the reintroduction of the disease into a free area. Primary vaccination during pregnancy should be avoided unless directly exposed to hazard of smallpox. Caution to be exercised in the vaccination of a person with eczema or other dermatological condition. A new drug reported in 1964 appeared to prevent the occurrence of the disease in a high proportion of unvaccinated contacts. If confirmed by further trials the drug could become an important preventive measure.

TRACHOMA

ETIOLOGICAL AGENT: Agent of trachoma.

EPIDEMIOLOGY: Widespread chronic communicable disease still affecting large populations in the Middle East, Asia, Mediterranean littoral. Sporadic in many other areas including the Southwest United States. Different epidemiologic patterns occur in different regions. A low social and economic level of the population with its attendant poverty, crowding, malnutrition, poor sanitation and flies are generally associated with high prevalence. Man is the reservoir and the source is secretions from the eyes and nose of infected persons transmitted through direct contact with the discharges, indirect contact with soiled articles and flies. Irritation by sun, wind and sand in hot, dry dusty areas appears to contribute to susceptibility. Natural or acquired immunity has not been demonstrated.

PREVENTION: Tetracycline antibiotics and sulfonamides have been successful in treatment. Detect cases early to prevent transmission to others and to prevent blindness. Mass treatment of special groups under high risk. Special emphasis on finding cases among children and preschool children and instituting therapy. Education of the populace on the need for personal cleanliness as a means of preventing spread within families, need for sanitary practices to reduce fly populations, and availability of therapy. Vaccines are still under investigation. (The group of agents to which trachoma belongs holds a position between rickettsiae and viruses and is susceptible to chemotherapeutic agents.)

YELLOW FEVER

ETIOLOGICAL AGENT: Virus of yellow fever (a group B arbo virus).

EPIDEMIOLOGY: An internationally quarantinable disease. Occurrence depends on the distribution of Aedes mosquitoes and presence of cases to infect them. The urban form of this disease, depending on the man-mosquito-man cycle, has been largely suppressed and outbreaks are being reported only from Africa. The jungle form, animal-mosquito-animal is far more difficult to control and this can serve as a source for the urban form. Jungle fever occurs all the way from Mexico to Central and South America except for Uruguay and Chile where susceptible animals lack necessary conditions for transmission. It is also present in many areas of Africa. Although the vector and reservoir hosts are present in India, yellow fever has never been reported from there or from the Orient. Susceptibility is general. Mild inapparent infections occur and recovery from the disease results in lasting immunity. Among indigenous persons in endemic areas the fatality is approximately 5 per cent; however, among newcomers to the area, it can reach 30 to 40 per cent.

PREVENTION: The eradication of Aedes aegypti mosquitoes is necessary for the ultimate prevention of urban yellow fever. International control requires strict adherence to the International Sanitary Regulations regarding vaccination, spraying of airplanes and other carriers. The most effective method so far, for individuals who may be exposed, has been the use of a vaccine (attenuated 17 D strain). Protection of patients against the bite of Aedes mosquitoes is essential.

ANNA C. GELMAN, M.P.H.
HERMAN E. HILLEBOE, M.D.

17   Rickettsial Diseases

Q FEVER
ETIOLOGICAL AGENT: *Coxiella burneti.*

EPIDEMIOLOGY: Since first described in 1937 in Australia, this disease has achieved world-wide importance as a disease of livestock and man. So far cattle, sheep, goats, many tick species, domestic and migrating birds and wild animals (bandicoots) have been found infected. This disease differs from the other rickettsial diseases in not requiring the bite of an arthropod for its transmission, although cases have resulted from tick bites. The more common mode is through aerosols contaminated with rickettsiae from tick feces, dried milk, parturition discharges, contaminated soil and occasionally through ingestion of unpasteurized milk or direct contact with infected meat, or placenta during livestock parturition. An occupational disease of persons working with animals or their products, laboratory technicians or anyone else in contact with infected material. Susceptibility is general, one attack conferring immunity for at least one year. Transovarial transmission of the rickettsiae occurs in the tick.

PREVENTION: The control of this disease is dependent primarily upon its control in livestock. This can be approached through vaccination and regulating movements of infected animals. Persons working with the organisms in the laboratory or others exposed to high risk can be vaccinated with a killed vaccine. Milk should be either boiled or pasteurized at 145° F. for 30 minutes or 161° F. for 15 seconds to inactivate the organism.

ROCKY MOUNTAIN SPOTTED FEVER (prototype of tick-borne spotted fever group)
ETIOLOGICAL AGENT: *Rickettsia rickettsii,* including sub-species *R. conorii, R. pijperi, R. australis* and *R. sibiricas.*

EPIDEMIOLOGY: A group of clinically similar diseases, all with wild animal reservoirs, transmitted to man through infected ixodid and argasid ticks, widely spread throughout the world, each limited to its own geographic area and possessing its own immunologic and epidemiologic characteristics. The diseases are known as the spotted fever group and comprise: Rocky Mountain spotted fever (Western Hemisphere), boutonneuse fever (Africa, Mediterranean and India), Queensland tick typhus (Australia), North Asian tick-borne rickettsioses, etc. The epidemiology of Rocky Mountain spotted fever differs with the geographic area of occurrence within the Western Hemisphere due to differences in tick vectors involved. In the Rocky Mountain area the vector is a wood tick (*Dermacentor andersoni*) biting adults primarily and in the East it is the dog tick (*Dermacentor variabilis*) which may bite children. This may account for age and sex differences as well as case fatality since fatality increases with age. Transovarial passage in the tick maintains the agent even in the absence of infected reservoir animals.

PREVENTION: The most effective preventive measure is to avoid the bite of the tick through the use of tick repellents or protective clothing. If exposed, it is advisable to search for and remove ticks before their engorgement. In addition, in areas where they

248

occur, clear land and reduce small animal populations, detick dogs and livestock and educate children to look for ticks on pets and selves. Vaccines are available for persons at high risk but reinforcing doses are needed.

RICKETTSIALPOX
ETIOLOGICAL AGENT: *Rickettsia akari.*
EPIDEMIOLOGY: First recognized in New York City in 1946, and subsequently in other cities along the eastern seaboard of the United States and the U.S.S.R., this mild member of the spotted fever group of rickettsial diseases has its natural reservoir in the ordinary house mouse and is transmitted to man through the bite of infected rodent mites. The mite can also act as a true reservoir of the rickettsiae since transovarial transmission of the organisms occurs. Susceptibility appears to be general; the duration of immunity following the attack is undetermined.
PREVENTION: In view of the limited distribution and relative mildness of the disease, it is not feasible to develop a vaccine. Prophylaxis depends upon rodent and mite control in and around dwellings.

SCRUB TYPHUS
ETIOLOGICAL AGENT: *Rickettsia tsutsugamushi.*
EPIDEMIOLOGY: Limited to circumscribed areas of eastern and southeastern Asia, northern Australia, the Indian subcontinent and adjacent islands in which the rickettsiae, mite vectors and rodent reservoirs are present, this mite-borne disease has a fatality of from 1 to 40 per cent, depending on the locality and strain of rickettsia. Immunity to homologous agent strains may be of long duration but is transient for the heterologous strains so that a number of infections may occur in the same individual. Transmission to man is by the bite of infected larval mites of the *Trombicula akamushi* and related species. The cycle in nature is dependent upon transovarial transmission in the mite or mite-wild rodent-mite cycle and man is accidentally infected when bitten by the mite larvae.
PREVENTION: This disease can be completely prevented if man keeps out of the scrub in which the infected mite larvae are found or wears protective clothing impregnated with mite repellents. Bulldozing camp sites, burning of the scrub, using insecticides and killing the rodents may reduce the hazard of being bitten. Chemoprophylaxis with appropriate drugs for short periods of exposure may be used. A satisfactory and safe vaccine has not yet been developed.

TRENCH FEVER
ETIOLOGICAL AGENT: *Rickettsia quintana.*
EPIDEMIOLOGY: This disease, initially observed in Europe in 1915 during the First World War disappeared from view and then made a fresh appearance in epidemic foci during the Second World War in Yugoslavia and the Ukraine. During World War I it was, next to influenza, the most prevalent of the communicable diseases among the armed forces. There were no fatalities reported but extensive disability occurred. Transmission is through the louse *Pediculus humanus* just as epidemic typhus with the difference that the infection does not kill the louse. Susceptibility is universal and immunity does not develop.
PREVENTION: The only prevention consists in a suppression of pediculosis and the maintenance of good personal hygiene to prevent infestation.

TYPHUS FEVER, ENDEMIC FLEA-BORNE
ETIOLOGICAL AGENT: *Rickettsia mooseri.*
EPIDEMIOLOGY: World-wide, endemic or sporadic in areas where man and rats exist in close proximity. In the United States it has become primarily a rural disease. In other areas it may still occur in crowded port cities and where feed stores and granaries are to be found. The infection is maintained in nature by the rat-flea-rat cycle and man is an accidental host when infected with flea feces following a flea bite. Occasionally, dried tick feces may infect through aerosol transmission. Susceptibility is general, one attack usually conferring immunity though not always of a permanent nature. Transovarial transmission does not occur in the flea.
PREVENTION: Prevention is largely a matter of rodent control. However, it is always desir-

able to institute measures of flea control by dusting rodent burrows and harborages with insecticides prior to rodent destruction since fleas leave a dying rat and may bite man in their search for food. Vaccines are not recommended since specific therapy and mildness of the disease do not warrant their use.

TYPHUS FEVER, EPIDEMIC LOUSE-BORNE

ETIOLOGICAL AGENT: *Rickettsia prowazeki.*

EPIDEMIOLOGY: One of the internationally quarantinable diseases. Potentially world-wide in areas where people wear clothes and can become infested with lice. Most common in the colder months and has been prevalent in all parts of the world except the tropics. During wars, floods, earthquakes or other dislocations of people, with crowding and reduced opportunities for bathing, epidemics can be precipitated. The reservoir is man since the louse dies from the infection. Some persons, once infected, can suffer a recrudescence of typhus fever many years after the initial attack (Brill's disease), infect lice if present and initiate a new epidemic. Epidemic typhus has disappeared from the United States, Great Britain and Scandinavia. Endemic foci still exist in the Balkans, Eastern Europe, Asia, North Africa, mountainous areas of Central and South Africa, Middle East and mountainous regions of Central and South America. Susceptibility is general, an attack usually conferring permanent immunity.

PREVENTION: Prevention can be effected by the destruction of lice, bathing and changing of clothes, immunization of persons likely to be exposed and by prompt treatment of the sick individual to reduce the infected reservoir.

ANNA C. GELMAN, M.P.H.
HERMAN E. HILLEBOE, M.D.

18   Fungal Diseases

ACTINOMYCOSIS

ETIOLOGICAL AGENT: *Actinomyces israelii* and *Actinomyces bovis*.

EPIDEMIOLOGY: A rare chronic endogenous mycosis occurring sporadically throughout the world. It is suspected that the disease is the result of autoinoculation, following trauma, puncture wound or tooth extraction, of an organism which is part of the normal flora of the mouth. Man is believed to be the natural reservoir of this fungus and there is no evidence of communicability from man to man except as for all normal flora. A similar disease also occurs in cattle, swine, horses and other animals but there is no evidence of human infection from this source. Susceptibility considered low; immunity following disease has not been demonstrated.

PREVENTION: In the absence of definitive information the avoidance of the use of the organs of animals containing lesions for food and precautions in the handling of suppurative discharges and soiled dressings of patients are recommended. Good oral hygiene might prevent irritation.

BLASTOMYCOSIS, NORTH AMERICAN

ETIOLOGICAL AGENT: *Blastomyces dermatitidis*.

EPIDEMIOLOGY: A rare, highly fatal, chronic granulomatous mycosis of exogenous origin primarily involving the lungs. It may spread from there to other organs and tissues. Cutaneous blastomycosis is almost always a manifestation of existing systemic disease. Sporadic in man, dogs and horses in certain circumscribed geographic areas of central and southeastern United States, in Central America and Canada. The reservoir is presumed to be the soil and transmission through the inhalation of spore-laden dust. Susceptibility is unknown, assumed to be low.

PREVENTION: Incomplete knowledge regarding transmission makes prevention difficult. Common sense dictates that care should be taken with infected patients, their discharges and contaminated dressings. Diseased animals should be destroyed to prevent environmental contamination, and dust control should be instituted as for the other exogenous mycoses.

BLASTOMYCOSIS, SOUTH AMERICAN

ETIOLOGICAL AGENT: *Blastomyces brasiliensis* (*Paracoccidioides brasiliensis*).

EPIDEMIOLOGY: A sporadic chronic mycosis of exogenous origin endemic in South America, chiefly rural Brazil. It occurs as either a mucocutaneous or systemic infection. The reservoir of the fungus is assumed to be soil and the source, wood, soil or spore-laden dust. The highest incidence is in young males probably as a result of farm occupational exposure. It also appears to be higher in the white and oriental populations than in the Negro. Susceptibility is unknown. The systemic form, once contracted, is highly fatal and no immunity seems to be produced.

251

PREVENTION: There is no known prevention. Since primary lesions are usually in the mouth it is possible that good oral hygiene and the avoidance of trauma by twigs or pieces of vegetation might prevent infection. Few other measures can be suggested beyond care in the handling and disposal of patients' discharges and contaminated dressings.

CHROMOBLASTOMYCOSIS

ETIOLOGICAL AGENT: *Hormodendrum pedrosoi* and *H. compactum*; *Phialophora verrucosa* and others.

EPIDEMIOLOGY: A sporadic chronic mycosis found in rural tropical regions in widely scattered areas of the world, mainly Central and South America, the West Indies, Australia and Asia. It occurs most commonly among barefooted farm laborers, following puncture wounds or other traumatic contact with infected wood or other materials. The reservoir of the organism is presumed to be wood, soil or vegetation. Man is thought to be fairly resistant. No animals have as yet been found naturally infected.

PREVENTION: In the absence of specific knowledge about the infection, prevention is empirical. Wearing shoes, covering the extremities and cleansing and treating puncture wounds should be of value. Care in the handling of patients with lesions and their discharges and contaminated dressings is recommended.

COCCIDIOIDOMYCOSIS

ETIOLOGICAL AGENT: *Coccidioides immitis.*

EPIDEMIOLOGY: A systemic mycosis of exogenous origin which may occur as (1) an asymptomatic infection resulting in a positive coccidioidin reaction, (2) an acute influenza-like illness with little or no sequelae, (3) erythema nodosum or valley fever in about 5 per cent of the primary infections, and (4) a rare, progressively fatal, disseminated granulomatous disease. The primary infections are quite common in scattered endemic arid and semi-arid areas in the southwestern United States, particularly in the San Joaquin valley of California and in areas of Arizona and Texas as well as in northern Argentina and Mexico. The organism is found in the soil and transmission is usually through the inhalation of spore-laden dust. A variety of animals including rodents and livestock can be infected. Susceptibility to primary infection is general; recovery apparently results in immunity. Disseminated form found to be more frequent among dark-skinned individuals. An important occupational disease among military personnel and workers exposed to spore-laden dust.

PREVENTION: Prevention of primary infection is based mainly on dust control through wetting or oiling stripped soil, paving roads and airplane runways, and planting grass. Susceptibles should not be recruited for outdoor work. Animals who have died from the disease should be incinerated to prevent soil contamination. Care should be exercised in the handling of patients' discharges and soiled dressings and fomites. There should be a high level of suspicion among temporary or transient residents.

CRYPTOCOCCOSIS

ETIOLOGICAL AGENT: *Cryptococcus neoformans.*

EPIDEMIOLOGY: World-wide sporadic mycosis occurring as a primary pulmonary infection which may heal without progression or may progress to a chronic, usually fatal meningitis or brain abscess. Other manifestations including a cutaneous form and an acute pneumonitis have been described, sometimes occurring in small group outbreaks. The causative fungus has been isolated from old pigeon nests, pigeon droppings under roosts as well as soil contaminated with pigeon droppings. The frequency of the organism in the environment causes speculation that either subclinical infections may be widespread or that man is fairly resistant. In a number of cases serious debilitating pre-existing illness has been present. Cattle, horses, monkeys, dogs and cats as well as other mammals have been found naturally infected.

PREVENTION: Increasing suspicion about relationship of organism to pigeon droppings indicates a need to reduce or eliminate pigeons and pigeon roosts and to protect occupationally exposed persons by mask. Destruction of diseased animals has been recommended. Research is required to determine the true extent of infection in the human population. This should be facilitated by the perfection of a skin test.

HISTOPLASMOSIS
ETIOLOGICAL AGENT: *Histoplasma capsulatum.*

EPIDEMIOLOGY: An unusually widespread exogenous mycosis of man and some animals resulting from the inhalation of infective spores from soil around old chicken houses, silos, basements, starling roosts, caves, houses sheltering the common brown bat and in other soils with a high acid content. It has been reported from many countries, showing geographic variations within these countries. These include the Americas, Europe, Africa, Thailand, Japan, Indonesia, and the Philippine Islands. Five clinical forms have been identified, ranging in severity from an inapparent widespread infection of a large segment of the population detected only by hypersensitivity to histoplasmin, to a chronic, disseminated, usually fatal form which is relatively rare, but more common in infants and in adults over 40. Clinical disease apparently results from excessive exposure, and is usually sporadic, but outbreaks have occurred among individuals with a common exposure to a large number of air-borne spores either in families or as a result of occupation or recreation.

PREVENTION: Prevention consists primarily in preventing the inhalation of large numbers of spores and may be accomplished by masks or by spraying the contaminated area with water or disinfectant to reduce the dust. It is recommended to disinfect discharges from skin lesions, sputum and articles soiled with discharges and to practice good personal and environmental hygiene. Group outbreaks should be carefully investigated and suspicion directed to chicken houses, barns, silos, caves, starling roosts and other known reservoirs of the spores in order to prevent further infection.

MONILIASIS (candidiasis)
ETIOLOGICAL AGENT: *Candida albicans.*

EPIDEMIOLOGY: World-wide, sporadic, occasionally epidemic, mycosis of the skin, nails, lungs, vagina, oropharynx, esophagus, intestinal tract, meninges, etc. Occasionally endocarditis and generalized infections occur. The clinical reaction depends upon a number of factors including age, allergic state of patient, predisposing illness such as diabetes and cancer, general disability, nutritional debility or upset in microbial flora following prolonged antibiotic therapy. The outcome depends upon the location of the infection. Skin and local infections are usually benign; generalized systemic infections may be fatal. The organism is usually endogenous in origin since it is frequently found in the normal mouth, vagina and intestinal tract but can also derive from an exogenous source such as from mother to infant during delivery or through contaminated objects in a newborn nursery. Venereal transmission has also occurred.

PREVENTION: Prevention of the development of clinical disease from endogenous organisms is dependent upon a number of factors including: treating the predisposing condition such as diabetes; correction of ill-fitting dentures to prevent oral infection; the use of rubber gloves to prevent intertriginous moniliasis of the fingers; and caution in the prolonged use of antibiotics to prevent upset in normal microbial flora. Prevention of exogenous infection includes detection and treatment of vaginal infection in the pregnant woman prior to delivery and careful supervision of the cleanliness of nurseries to prevent occurrence or spread.

SPOROTRICHOSIS
ETIOLOGICAL AGENT: *Sporotrichum schenckii.*

EPIDEMIOLOGY: World-wide chronic mycosis of exogenous origin usually sporadic and relatively uncommon. Occurs among persons manually handling vegetable matter containing the fungus spores such as florists, agricultural workers, packers and miners exposed to thorn, barb or splinter pricks. The reservoir is soil, vegetation and wood and the source the same in the form of timber, thorny plants, packing straw or spore-laden dust. Occasional epidemics have occurred such as among mine workers handling infected timbers. Animals such as horses, dogs, mules and rats have also been found naturally infected. Susceptibility is general.

PREVENTION: Prevention can be accomplished by the use of protective clothing and gloves when handling plants, straw and timber and avoidance of trauma. The treatment of lumber with fungicides is recommended in industries where the disease has occurred. Care in the handling of patients with lesions and in the disposal of patients' discharges and contaminated dressings is recommended.

SUPERFICIAL MYCOSES (dermatophytoses)

ETIOLOGICAL AGENT: Trichophyton and Microsporum species; *Epidermophyton floccosum.*
EPIDEMIOLOGY: A group of superficial mycotic infections of the hair, skin and nails are
caused by various genera and species of fungi. They are world-wide in distribution, usually
sporadic and varying in incidence in different geographic areas. Some of the fungi infect
livestock and domestic animals such as the cat and dog, which in some cases serve as the
source of the infection for man. Many cases are the result of direct or indirect contact
with infected individuals or infected hairs and desquamated skin. Children are especially
susceptible to the ringworm of the scalp caused by *M. audouinii* before the age of puberty
but, following puberty infections usually clear up without treatment. (This form appears in
epidemics.) Ringworm of the feet may be asymptomatic and chronic but may be seriously
activated by excessive heat, moisture or unsuitable footwear. Susceptibility general.
PREVENTION: Good personal hygiene and caution in the handling of infected animals.
Supervision of children with ringworm of the scalp to prevent epidemics. Supervision of
barbershop and hairdressing establishments to prevent spread. Cleanliness of gymnasiums
and showers and thorough drying between toes following bathing may protect against
ringworm of the feet or body.

ANNA C. GELMAN, M.P.H.
HERMAN E. HILLEBOE, M.D.

19   Parasitic Diseases

AMEBIASIS

ETIOLOGICAL AGENT: *Entamoeba histolytica.*

EPIDEMIOLOGY: World-wide in distribution, and spread through the medium of fresh fecal contamination of food, vegetables, and water. This disease ranges from a mild subclinical infection to an acute dysentery, the former more common in temperate, the latter in the tropical and subtropical zones. It occurs in sporadic, endemic or epidemic forms, the latter sometimes water-borne or person-to-person, as in mental institutions. Estimates of prevalence of carriers of viable organisms vary from 50 per cent or higher in areas with poor sanitation, to 5 per cent or less in cities with good sanitation. Susceptibility is general.

PREVENTION: Prevention is based primarily on the sanitary disposal of human feces, the protection and treatment of water supplies with the added step of filtering to remove the cysts. Proper supervision and education of food handlers, protection of food against flies and, if necessary, the boiling of water, cooking of vegetables or dipping those to be eaten raw in boiling water for a brief time. Treatment of cases and carriers and barring them from food handling until well can prevent transmission from this source.

ANCYLOSTOMIASIS (hookworm disease)

ETIOLOGICAL AGENT: *Necator americanus* and *Ancylostoma duodenale.*

EPIDEMIOLOGY: Distribution limited to those areas of tropical and subtropical countries where human feces disposal is inadequate, people walk barefoot and conditions of soil, humidity, moisture and temperature favor the development of infective larvae. Estimates place infection at one-quarter of the world's population. In southeastern United States and tropical West Africa, *N. americanus* predominates, whereas in the Mediterranean countries and Nile Valley, *A. duodenale* is chiefly found. Both species coexist in these areas as well as the West Indies, Latin America and parts of Asia. Man is the only known reservoir of these helminths and the source is soil containing infective larvae. These may either penetrate the skin or be ingested (rare). The size of the infecting dose and nutritional status of the host appear to influence the severity of the disease. Very small doses do not appear to have a clinical effect. Susceptibility is general. Another form of ancylostomiasis in man, cutaneous larva migrans, is caused by *A. braziliense* from cats and dogs.

PREVENTION: Ultimate prevention depends upon the elimination of the disease from the infected human host by finding and treating the infected individual and the sanitary disposal of human feces. Education of the population in an endemic area about personal prophylaxis such as washing hands before eating, wearing shoes, and proper disposal of feces is important. Use of night soil for fertilizer should be proscribed or regulated.

CHAGAS' DISEASE (American trypanosomiasis, chagasiasis)

ETIOLOGICAL AGENT: *Trypanosoma cruzi.*

EPIDEMIOLOGY: Although its occurrence is limited to the Western Hemisphere with the

255

exception of Canada and possibly Cuba, it has been estimated that at least 7 million persons in Latin American countries are infected, with at least 35 million exposed to risk. Occurs primarily in rural areas and small towns but cases have been contracted in peripheral zones of cities. More than a dozen different animal species as well as man have been found infected and several species of triatomid bugs have been identified as vectors. Domestic animals are considered to be the most important reservoirs for man. The triatomid bugs live in human habitations, bite humans and infect them through contamination of bite wound, abrasions, conjunctiva or mucous membranes with contents of infected crushed bug or bug feces. Transmission has also occurred during blood transfusion. Infants and young children under 2 years of age as well as recent arrivals into an endemic area are particularly vulnerable to the acute form, with mortality sometimes approximating 10 per cent. In the chronic form the symptoms are very varied and may be misdiagnosed; among these are cardiac, alimentary and possibly neurologic symptoms. Sudden death from these forms may be incorrectly recorded.

PREVENTION: Prevention of this disease rests primarily in improvement in housing and promotion of hygienic habits. Dwellings should be so constructed as to eliminate animal harborages and hiding places of vectors. Infected domestic animals should be eliminated and wild animal hosts in the vicinity of human habitations should be destroyed. Contact with such animals in their natural habitat should be avoided. Bed nets should be used and insects controlled with residual insecticides wherever possible. Complement fixation tests to determine infection should be performed on donors who come from endemic areas. Experimental vaccines are under investigation.

MALARIA

ETIOLOGICAL AGENT: *Plasmodium vivax; P. malariae; P. falciparum* and *P. ovale.*

EPIDEMIOLOGY: Although endemic malaria has been virtually eliminated from the United States and many other countries where it was a serious problem a number of years ago, and some of the tropical countries with a high incidence of hyperendemic malaria have been successful in greatly reducing its incidence, it still remains a problem in parts of Asia, the southwest Pacific, Africa and Central and South America. The danger of its reintroduction into the free areas still remains since the Anopheles mosquito has not been eradicated. Transmission is traditionally through the bite of the infected female Anopheles mosquito but it is also transmissible through the injection or transfusion of blood from infected individuals and the use of contaminated syringes, e.g., by drug addicts. Susceptibility is general.

PREVENTION: Constant surveillance in malaria-free countries where the anopheline mosquitoes are present is required in order to prevent the reintroduction of the infection. Rigid adherence to laws requiring disinsectization of aircraft, ships or other vehicles which travel from an infected to a free area is necessary. The administration of antimalarial drugs to groups of individuals, such as migrant workers, coming from infected to free areas is recommended. Measures to suppress the species of Anopheles mosquitoes responsible for transmission in each locality, measures to prevent mosquito bites of infected and noninfected individuals and suppressive drugs are also recommended.

PEDICULOSIS

ETIOLOGICAL AGENT: *Pediculus humanus* var. *capitis* and *corporis; Phthirus pubis* (crab louse).

EPIDEMIOLOGY: Infestation with lice is a disease in itself. It has been found from the tropics to the arctic wherever man has clothed himself and has lived under insanitary conditions. Transmission is facilitated by crowding so that it becomes especially prevalent during population upheavals (wars, floods, earthquakes). The head louse occasionally occurs in epidemic form in children's institutions, camps and schools. *Pediculus humanus* can also serve as the vector of other disease agents such as those causing epidemic typhus, trench fever and relapsing fever. The crab louse cannot. Transmission of *Pediculus humanus* can be direct through contact or in clothing, beds, furniture, etc. *Phthirus pubis*, which favors the pubic area and occasionally the eyebrows or axillae, is transmitted either through sexual contact or infested toilet seats. Susceptibility to lice is general.

PREVENTION: To avoid outbreaks among children in schools, institutions and camps, there should be periodic inspection for lice and nits and treatment if found. Cleanliness of the body and hair and frequent changes and laundering of clothing and bedclothes as well as use of dusting powders and residual insecticides in cases following exposure to lice will reduce hazard of infestation. Good sex hygiene and avoidance of public toilet seats or other insanitary places will prevent crab louse infections.

SCABIES
ETIOLOGICAL AGENT: *Sarcoptes scabiei* (itch mite).
EPIDEMIOLOGY: A widespread, nonfatal skin infection, independent of climate. It is commonly associated with overcrowding and lack of cleanliness and although varieties of this mite affect animals (sarcoptic mange) the human infections are contracted only from other humans and can be transmitted through direct contact with skin of infested persons, or to a limited extent by contact with underclothing and linen. Most commonly transmitted by sleeping with an infested person or prolonged hand holding, such as in children's games. Susceptibility is general.
PREVENTION: Cleanliness of body and proper laundering of underwear and bed covering are prophylactic measures. Close contact with overcrowded and infested populations should be avoided. Cases and contacts should be treated and children should be excluded from school until treated. Infested persons should be denied use of public recreation and bathing facilities.

SCHISTOSOMIASIS (bilharziasis)
ETIOLOGICAL AGENT: *Schistosoma mansoni; S. haematobium; S. japonicum.*
EPIDEMIOLOGY: The geographic distribution of this disease is influenced by the availability of the fresh water snail necessary for the life cycle of the schistosomes. In some endemic areas it has been estimated that more than half the population is infected. *S. mansoni* occurs in the Caribbean area, South America, the Arabian Peninsula and Africa; *S. hematobium* in Africa, parts of the Middle East, Portugal and a small focus in India; *S. japonicum* in the Orient. Continental North America is free from indigenous infection. Man is the chief reservoir of *S. mansoni* and *S. hematobium*; dogs, pigs, cattle, water buffalo, horses, field mice and wild rats are animal hosts of *S. japonicum*. The snails become infected following the pollution of canals, pools and streams with urine and feces containing schistosome ova. Susceptibility is general. Man becomes infected by coming in direct contact with water in which schistosome cercaria are present.
PREVENTION: Ultimate prevention depends upon the interruption of the life cycle of the schistosomes either by eradicating the snail with molluscicides or else instituting such rigid sanitary practices that infected urine and feces are not discharged into waters used by the populace for washing, drinking and bathing.

TAENIASIS SAGINATA (beef tapeworm infection)
ETIOLOGICAL AGENT: *Taenia saginata.*
EPIDEMIOLOGY: Widespread, especially where raw or poorly cooked beef is consumed. More common in the United States than *T. solium*. Man is the only known host of the adult worm; cattle the only important intermediate host although other herbivors are sometimes infected. Susceptibility to infection is general. Where both *T. solium* and *T. saginata* are present, *T. saginata* is the more common.
PREVENTION: Proper disposal of human feces is the best means of prevention, especially in rural areas. Meat inspection is of limited value since cysticercosis in cattle is usually a light infection and may be missed. Adequate freezing or salting as well as thorough cooking of the meat are effective. The use of sewage effluents for pasture irrigation should be proscribed.

TAENIASIS SOLIUM (pork tapeworm infection)
ETIOLOGICAL AGENT: *Taenia solium.*
EPIDEMIOLOGY: Widespread, especially where poorly cooked pork is consumed. Rare in western Europe, England, Canada and the United States, high in the Slavic countries, Asia and Latin America. Man is the only known host of the adult worm although swine and occasionally other primates, dogs and sheep may also harbor the larvae. Two forms of the disease occur, depending upon the stage at which the organisms are ingested. In the event of consumption of the larvae in poorly cooked pork, intestinal infection with tapeworm results; if the ova themselves are consumed by the human host a serious infec-

tion with the larval forms or cysticercosis may result. An individual may infect himself either through fecal-oral transfer of his own ova or contaminate food and drink of others. Susceptibility to infection is general; resistance following infection has not been observed. PREVENTION: Ultimate prevention will rest on treatment of the infection in the human host since man is the only known reservoir of the adult worm. Proper disposal of human feces to prevent contamination of soil and food and drink of man and animals is extremely important. Thorough cooking of pork and prevention of food handling by infected individuals are also useful.

TOXOPLASMOSIS
ETIOLOGICAL AGENT: *Toxoplasma gondii.*
EPIDEMIOLOGY: Information concerning the epidemiology of this disease is incomplete; however, it is increasingly being recognized as the cause of severe sporadic disease in man. The infection is world-wide in distribution in man and a wide variety of animals and birds. It has been speculated that the reservoir is animal, except for the actively infected pregnant woman who then becomes the reservoir of the infection for the fetus; this organism is capable of passing the placental barrier and infecting the fetus, with resultant death or subsequent serious disease. In acquired infection upper respiratory, arthropod, and conjunctival routes have been speculated but not established. Also suspected to be by ingestion of infected flesh.
PREVENTION: Since so little is known about the disease, prevention can only be suggested. It is important to determine the extent of infection in man and in animals in contact with man and to elaborate the disease syndromes associated with such infection. Animal or avian sources of infection in local concentrations of cases should be investigated and the reservoir removed if possible. Contact with sick animals and birds and arthropod bites should be avoided and the premises kept free from rodents.

TRICHINOSIS
ETIOLOGICAL AGENT: *Trichinella spiralis.*
EPIDEMIOLOGY: World-wide, sporadic, occasionally epidemic parasitic infection limited to individuals who have consumed insufficiently cooked pork or occasionally bear or marine animals containing viable larvae. It is rare or absent in the tropics or in countries such as France where pigs are fed on root vegetables. In the United States where many of the pigs are garbage fed, the infection is especially common. Omnivorous and carnivorous animals including swine, rats, bear, fox, wolf and marine animals have been found to be reservoirs of the larvae. Susceptibility is general.
PREVENTION: Ultimate prevention depends upon eliminating the disease from swine by cooking all garbage fed to pigs or by limiting feeding to corn or root vegetables. Adequate cooking of fresh pork either at home or in restaurants, processing of pork by properly curing, holding, freezing, drying, salting and smoking under rigid specified conditions can prevent transmission to humans. Irradiation of meats is effective but has not yet been widely used commercially.

TRICHOMONIASIS
ETIOLOGICAL AGENT: *Trichomonas vaginalis.*
EPIDEMIOLOGY: Geographically a widespread and commonly occurring parasitic infection of females and males. Infection rates among population groups appear to reflect the socioeconomic conditions of these groups, including opportunities for washing and the quality of feminine hygiene practiced. The usual mode of transmission is through sexual intercourse but it has been transmitted through soiled fomites such as towels, douche nozzles, examination instruments, as well as at birth. Infections are usually asymptomatic or mild in both males and females, with clinical disease more common in the female. The reservoir is the human host and infective genital discharges are the source of infection.
PREVENTION: Strict personal and sex hygiene are important as well as avoidance of sexual intercourse with infected individuals. The sex partner should be examined or treated at he same time as the known case in order to prevent recurrent infections.

ANNA C. GELMAN, M.P.H.
HERMAN E. HILLEBOE, M.D.

REFERENCES

1. American Public Health Association: Control of Communicable Diseases in Man, Ed. 10. New York, 1965.
2. Jawetz, E., Melnick, J. L., and Adelberg, E. A.: Review of Medical Microbiology, Ed. 6. Los Altos, California, Lange Medical Publications, 1964.
3. Loosli, C. G. (ed.): Conference on Newer Respiratory Disease Viruses, October 3-5, 1962. The American Review of Respiratory Diseases. Journal of American Thoracic Society, Medical Section of the National Tuberculosis Society.
4. Rhodes, A. J., and van Rooyen, C. E.: Textbook of Virology. Ed. 4. Baltimore, The Williams & Wilkins Company, 1962.
5. St. Whitelock, O. V. (Editor-in-chief): Animal Disease and Human Health. Annals of the New York Academy of Sciences, Vol. 70, Art. 3:277-762, June 3, 1958.
6. World Health Organization Chronicles and Technical Reports (Selected).

20   Venereal Diseases

Venereal diseases (VD) are infections acquired chiefly by sexual contact. In this category are syphilis, gonorrhea, chancroid, lymphopathia venereum and granuloma inguinale.

SYPHILIS

Definition

Syphilis in its usual form is an acute and chronic relapsing treponematosis* transmitted venereally and of world-wide occurrence. The organisms are deposited on the skin or mucous membrane, usually during sexual contact, penetrate and reproduce themselves at the site of penetration. Generally within hours some are carried by means of the blood stream to other parts of the body where they too start to multiply.

After an incubation period of about 3 weeks (range 10 to 90 days) the primary lesion (chancre) develops at the initial site of infection. The chancre usually occurs on or around the genital organs, the anal region and lips, but may frequently pass unnoticed when in the anorectal area, on the cervix of the uterus or within the pleats and folds of the vulva. The chancre is often quite atypical or minimal, possibly because of the widespread use of antibiotics; even when noticed it often is misdiagnosed.

The chancre heals with or without treatment in days or weeks. Before the healing process is completed, or soon thereafter, other lesions of syphilis called secondary lesions may appear wherever spirochetes have localized in the body. The skin and mucous membranes are favorite sites. Secondary manifestations may include sore throat, muscle and joint pains, moth-eaten alopecia, headaches and mild constitutional symptoms. In the skin the lesions consist chiefly of macules and papules that are usually symmetrically distributed. They may be sparse or heavily disseminated over the entire body. The mucous membrane lesions are usually eroded patches or moist papules.

---

* There are other treponematoses besides venereal syphilis. These are all nonvenereal and confined to areas of the world where socioeconomic and climatic conditions as well as the habits and customs of the people favor their development, e.g., nonvenereal syphilis, bejel, yaws, pinta.

These lesions are usually nondestructive and always self-limiting. Healing occurs within days or, at the most, months.

The usual nonspecific serologic tests in use today become positive about a week or two after the appearance of the chancre and without treatment will remain positive, in the majority of cases, for the rest of the patient's life. The sooner treatment is completed, the sooner will the positive serology tend to revert to negativity (from weeks to months to years). In some long-standing cases a positive serology will persist for the remainder of a patient's life even after adequate therapy.

Early Syphilis. Syphilis is considered "early" for the first 2 to 4 years, depending on the country or the syphilologist concerned. Early syphilis is potentially communicable. The lesions are usually teeming with spirochetes because at this stage relatively little immunity has developed in the patient. During this stage the treponemata may pass from the blood of the pregnant woman to her unborn child after the 4th month of pregnancy (congenital syphilis). Adequate treatment prior to or during pregnancy assures a new-born free of syphilis. As the disease progresses, fewer and fewer spirochetes are in evidence, so that toward the end of this period spirochetes are rarely demonstrable in the lesions.

Late Syphilis. Late syphilis is associated with no demonstrable lesions in 60 to 70 per cent of cases (late latent syphilis). When demonstrable lesions develop they are chronic and destructive, always healing with scar tissue. Late lesions may be (a) gummatous reactions, relatively explosive inflammations of sensitized tissues that occur most often in the skin, mucous membranes and bone, more rarely in the other organs or tissues of the body; (b) diffuse granulomatous infiltrations and atrophies without obvious inflammation that occur most often in the aorta and central nervous system. This may lead to serious syphilitic cardiovascular disease, general paralysis with insanity, blindness and other disabilities. Here immunity is at the maximum, and treponema are not demonstrable in lesions except in the cerebral cortex in active general paresis. Following cure of late syphilis, reinfection is unlikely because of enhanced immunity.

Etiologic Agent

The infectious agent of syphilis is the *Treponema pallidum*, also called *Spirocheta pallida*. It has not been cultured in a virulent form on artificial media, though such claims have occasionally been made. Man is its only natural host.

Diagnosis

Syphilis is diagnosed by:

1. Clinical examination confirmed by finding the *T. pallidum* in serum from early lesions by the darkfield microscope.

2. Positive reactions of serologic tests for syphilis. Conventional Standard Tests for Syphilis (S.T.S.) are complement fixation and flocculation tests that employ a lipoidal antigen (extract of beef heart, cardiolipin) to demonstrate a presumed antibody known as reagin. Tests for more specific antibodies than reagin are available. The Treponema Pallidum Immobilization Test (TPI), the Fluorescent Treponemal Antigen (FTA), and the Reiter Protein Complement Fixation Test (RPCF), using as antigen a protein extract of the Reiter strain of treponema, are now being used. The TPI

and FTA seem more reliable. A recently developed FTA "absorption" procedure shows great promise.

3. Spinal fluid examinations for neurosyphilis. These consist of a serologic test for syphilis, cell count, total protein determination and colloidal gold test.

4. Fluoroscopy or roentgenogram of heart and aorta for the diagnosis of cardiovascular syphilis.

5. X-ray of other parts of the body and other technical procedures such as ophthalmoscopy are sometimes useful.

Serologic results should be carefully evaluated in terms of the clinical findings and the patient's medical history. There are many nontreponemal conditions which may give a positive serology for syphilis (false biologic positive). Not to be forgotten are the negative serologic results obtained in the first days or weeks of infection.

Epidemiology

Syphilis is acquired by contact with moist infectious lesions or with infectious body fluids. The *T. pallidum* is quite fragile, dies on drying and does not survive long outside the human body. The spirochetes have to be deposited, therefore, by direct contact, preferably on a moist skin or mucous membrane area.

Syphilis is world-wide in distribution, attacks all socioeconomic groups, both sexes, all ages. Since 1957 there has been a tremendous increase in VD incidence in most parts of the world. After an initial drop in the reported cases of early syphilis which began after the Second World War and ended about 1955, the rates of early syphilis have been increasing. A look at the data of reported cases of early syphilis from 1957 to the present shows an increase of up to about 600 per cent, depending on the area. About 128,000 cases of syphilis were reported in 1963 in the United States. More than 22,000 of these were in the primary and secondary stages, the highest since 1950. Syphilis is greatly undiagnosed and underreported, and the actual incidence is believed to be many times this figure. This increase is found in nearly all areas and is more marked in larger urban centers. Though this increase is observed in all age groups it has been particularly marked among teen-agers and young adults. It is important to note also that among primary and secondary cases interviewed, more and more often one gets a history of homosexuality.

This increase in early syphilis has been attributed to a multiplicity of factors, among which must be noted a diminished knowledge and fear of the disease; a decrease in the percentage of diagnosed cases reported, interviewed and followed-up by contact tracing and case finding; an increase in undesirable activities such as promiscuity and homosexuality, themselves often the result of frustration and conflict in family and community life.

Although syphilis is found in all socioeconomic levels, a higher reported incidence is found, however, in the poorer sections of the population, in the less educated, and in areas where community living conditions create stresses and tensions which may lead to undesirable behavior.

Treatment

Penicillin is the treatment of choice. Developed resistance of the treponema to penicillin has not been documented. Populations where penicillin has been used for years and for many ailments, however, show an increasing incidence of allergy to the drug. In early syphilis a blood level of about 0.03 to 0.2 units per ml. of blood must be maintained for about 8 to 10 days. In late syphilis this duration should be extended to 10 to 18 days, longer in the presence of certain complications. This level may be accomplished by daily injections of 600,000 or more units of aqueous procaine penicillin G; or by injections every 2 to 4 days of 1,200,000 units of procaine penicillin in oil with aluminum monostearate (PAM); or by an injection of 2,400,000 units of benzathine penicillin to be repeated in 7 to 14 days if necessary. Total dosages of approximately 2.4 to 10 million units are recommended, depending on the type of penicillin and the stage of disease. In penicillin allergy the tetracyclines are effective. Erythromycin, Declomycin and other similar products may also be given. These drugs are administered orally in dosages of 2 to 4 gm. daily for a total of about 25 to 50 gm., depending on the product used and the stage of the disease.

Prevention

To prevent occurrence of the disease, general and specific health promotion measures should emphasize: health and sex education; preparation for marriage; recreational, cultural and vocational training facilities for youth; community relations and improvement of social and economic situations. Premarital, prenatal and other selective examinations and serologic testing are recommended. Mechanical and local chemical prophylaxis as well as immediate personal hygiene have some effectiveness. Even more effective is prophylactic treatment after exposure.

To prevent progression of the disease and possible complications, early case finding is essential. This necessitates an interested and informed public so that medical care will be sought by the patient at the slightest suspicion. Also needed is a well-trained professional corps with a high level of awareness in venereal disease matters so that cases will not be missed and will be reported. Interview of all early cases followed by contact tracing is a sine qua non in a venereal disease control program, so that the source as well as the victims of the patient's infection may be found and treated. There must also be adequate facilities and personnel for diagnosis, treatment and follow-up of cases.

The Cluster procedure has proved its usefulness. It is the technique used to extend testing procedures to include persons other than the sex contacts of the patient. The cluster group includes persons the patient may know who have (or have had) lesions similar to his, other suspects in the patient's circle of friends, the associates and sex contacts of the suspect.

Prevention requires complete cooperation between the private physician and the health authorities and the involvement of the total community.

GONORRHEA

Definition

Gonorrhea is an acute venereal disease, with an average incubation period of 3 to 5 days (range 1 to 10 days), which is confined chiefly to the mucous membranes of the genitourinary tract, the rectum and, occasionally, the eye. The gonococcus is quite sensitive to conditions outside the human body and infection, therefore, usually requires direct deposit of the organism on or about the susceptible tissues. Hematogenous spread to serous and synovial membranes in other parts of the body is possible. Arthritis, the most common of these extragenital manifestations, as well as iritis, endocarditis, meningitis and skin lesions are rare since the advent of antibiotics.

In the male, gonorrhea causes an inflammation of the anterior urethra productive of a purulent discharge and accompanied by a burning sensation on urination. Ascending infection may involve the posterior urethra, prostate and epididymis. Urethral strictures may occur in chronic or poorly treated cases. A purulent proctitis occurs when the rectum is infected. Here symptoms are sometimes quite minimal and may pass unnoticed or undiagnosed.

In the adult female, gonorrhea may be asymptomatic and not suspected until complications occur or a sexual partner is infected. The female infection starts in the urethra or the cervix. A purulent discharge may or may not be noted. Some redness and pouting of the urethral meatus may be present. Skene's ducts in the urethra often are a hidden site of infection. Bartholin's glands may be infected with resulting pain and swelling. From the cervix where it is usually asymptomatic, infection may ascend through the uterus to involve the fallopian tubes and surrounding tissues, including the peritoneum. Here low abdominal pain is a prominent symptom. Infection of the tubes may cause sterility.

In female infants and children, gonorrhea causes an acute inflammation of the vulva and of the mucous membranes of the vagina. Prior to the advent of the sulfonamides and the antibiotics, vaginitis, presumed to be gonorrheal, spread rapidly in children who were institutionalized. The mode of spread was often difficult to determine. Indiscriminate use of rectal thermometers was sometimes incriminated.

Eye Infections. Infection of the eyes (gonorrheal ophthalmia) is serious. Untreated, it causes blindness. The eyes of an infant can be infected in the birth canal. Gonorrheal ophthalmia in children and adults is rare.

Etiologic Agent

The infectious agent of gonorrhea is the *Neisseria gonorrhoeae,* a gram negative diplococcus.

Diagnosis

Gonorrhea is diagnosed by clinical signs and symptoms confirmed by finding the gonococcus in smears and in the culture of a purulent discharge. Since other diplococci may resemble the gonococcus in smears, cultures confirmed by fermentation and other tests are frequently necessary, particularly in the female. Fluorescent-tagged antibody methods are also being used.

Epidemiology

Gonorrhea is an extremely common disease, present in all parts of the world. Its incidence is unknown because of self-treatment, undiagnosed cases mainly in females, and very deficient case reporting, more so than in syphilis. All ages and both sexes are susceptible, although some individuals appear to be peculiarly resistant to infection. Gonorrhea is found in all socioeconomic levels. The young and the promiscuous show the highest incidence. A high reported incidence is also found in the male, in the poorer sections of the population, among the less educated and among those living under conditions of stress and tension.

Gonorrhea has followed the increasing incidence trend of syphilis in recent years, but the true incidence of this disease is generally considered to be higher than that of syphilis. No appreciable immunity develops during a gonorrheal infection; hence, reinfections are common.

Treatment

The gonococcus is sensitive to most antibiotics. A single injection of 1,200,000 units of slowly absorbed penicillin is considered sufficient in most cases in the male. There is evidence, however, that some strains of gonococci require relatively high blood concentrations of penicillin and these relatively penicillin-resistant strains seem to be increasing. It is difficult to reach the blood levels sometimes needed with the use of PAM or benzathine penicillin.

Serologic follow-up for syphilis is essential among those who have gonorrhea. Because of the increasing prevalence of allergy to penicillin a careful allergic history is essential before instituting penicillin treatment.

Other drugs effective in the treatment of gonorrhea are any of the various forms of the tetracyclines, erythromycin and chloramphenicol, in dosages of about 2 to 4 gm. given in a single dose or within a 24-hour period. Streptomycin in a dosage of 1 to 2 gm. in one intramuscular injection is also effective.

There is increasing evidence that cures in the female are more difficult. For women, larger total doses of antibiotics and other drugs and more prolonged treatment seem to be necessary.

Prevention

Preventive measures should aim at the host, agent and environment. Almost all the measures mentioned for syphilis should be employed to prevent occurrence and progression of gonorrhea. Health education, personality development, vocational training, recreational facilities, job opportunities, community relations and attitudes are all integral factors in the control of the disease. Mechanical as well as local and general chemical prophylaxis are of value. Gonorrheal ophthalmia of the newborn is prevented by instillation into the eyes following delivery of penicillin or one per cent solution of silver nitrate.

Once the disease has occurred, all effort must be made to find the source and the victims of the patient's infection. Asymptomatic female carriers of the gonococcus provide a continuing source of infection. In view of the almost total absence of immunity and the great frequency of reinfection it is important that the patient and his spouse or other sexual partner be treated simultaneously to prevent repeated occurrence or "ping-pong" reinfection.

CHANCROID

Definition

Chancroid is an acute localized venereal disease characterized clinically by an ulceration at the site of infection and in many cases by an acute inflammatory reaction of the regional lymph nodes. The incubation period is 3 to 5 days, sometimes a few days longer. The ulcers are autoinoculable, with ragged undermined edges; if untreated they may become phagedenic, causing rapid local destruction of tissue. Genital lesions occur in about 50 per cent of cases, quickly followed by fluctuant, soft and tender lymph nodes in the area which drains the ulcer.

Etiologic Agent

The infectious agent of chancroid is the *Hemophilus ducreyi*, Ducrey bacillus. It is a streptobacillus generally seen under the microscope in short chains.

Diagnosis

Chancroid is diagnosed by its clinical picture and confirmed by finding the Ducrey bacillus (a) on microscopic examination of stained smears of exudate taken from the edge of lesions, (b) from culture of pus taken from bubos. Also of diagnostic value are the intradermal skin tests: (a) the Ito-Reenstierna test which uses killed bacilli and which may remain positive for many years after cure of the disease, and (b) autoinoculation using the exudate from an ulcer.

Epidemiology

Chancroid is endemic in most parts of the world. It is especially common, however, in Asia and in tropical and subtropical areas. It is more frequent in seaport and urban than in rural areas. Chancroid is primarily a disease of the unhygienic and the underprivileged. Both sexes are susceptible. Since the introduction of the sulfonamides, it has become less frequent in America.

Treatment

The sulfonamides are the treatment of choice. They should be given in doses of 1 gm. four times daily for about 1 week. The tetracycline antibiotics and chloramphenicol are also effective but may mask an incubating syphilis. These latter drugs should be given in doses of 2 or more gm. daily for 2 or more weeks. A chancroid bubo should never be incised but may be aspirated. Local cleanliness is of great importance and a treated case of chancroid should be followed by serologic tests for syphilis.

Prevention

Most of the preventive measures suggested for syphilis and gonorrhea are applicable. General hygiene and liberal soap and water washing of the genitals immediately after exposure have prophylactic value.

LYMPHOGRANULOMA VENEREUM (LYMPHOGRANULOMA INGUINALE, LYMPHOPATHIA VENEREUM)

Definition

Lymphogranuloma is a viral infection acquired venereally and affecting lymph channels and nodes which quickly become red and tender, adhere into groups and fluctuate, thus forming bubos. The incubation period varies from 5 to 21 days. The primary lesion is a small painless erosion or papule which may be so transitory as to escape notice. The lesions are often first brought to the attention of the physician after the formation of bubos or after multiple suppurating foci and fistulae have occurred. In the male these are most frequently seen in the inguinal region either unilaterally or bilaterally. In the female and the homosexual the rectum and the anal region are the sites of drainage or infection. Chronic proctitis and anal strictures are the frequent complications.

Generalized symptoms, including chills, fever, headache, anorexia and abdominal or joint pains, may accompany the bubo. Disability may be great due to the development of elephantiasis of the genitals, called esthiomene in the female. Infection of the axillary glands and glands in other areas of the body is occasionally seen.

Etiologic Agent

The virus of lymphogranuloma venereum, one of the lymphogranuloma-psittacosis group of large viruses, is the etiologic agent.

Diagnosis

The diagnosis of this disease is based on the clinical findings which may be confirmed by a positive Frei test, an intradermal skin test performed with the virus grown on the yolk sac of the chicken embryo and then inactivated. The complement fixation test is also useful but will not differentiate from other diseases caused by any of the psittacosis group of viruses. These tests may remain positive for variable periods after cure.

Epidemiology

The disease is world-wide in distribution but is more prevalent in tropical and subtropical areas. It is endemic in the southern part of the United States, particularly among the lower socioeconomic groups, though of relatively low incidence at present. The age preponderance is that of greater sexual activity. Both sexes are susceptible. Based on complement fixation test surveys it would seem that subclinical lymphogranuloma infections may be quite frequent in some areas.

Treatment

Many infections heal spontaneously. Sulfonamides in doses of 1 gm. four times daily for 1 to 2 weeks and the tetracyclines and most of the other antibiotics in doses of 2 to 4 gm. daily for a similar period are usually effective. A combination of these two drugs may be necessary in chronic proctitis and some other complications. Surgical procedures may be indicated in cases of stricture or other far advanced complications.

Prevention

Most of the preventive measures suggested for syphilis and gonorrhea are applicable. Cleanliness and good personal hygiene are helpful.

GRANULOMA INGUINALE

Definition

Granuloma inguinale is a chronic, locally progressive infection of the skin, subcutaneous and mucous membrane tissues. It usually affects the external genitalia but occasionally is seen on the lips, in the oral cavity and other extragenital areas. On occasion the regional lymphatics may be involved. After an incubation period estimated to be between 8 days and 12 weeks the disease starts as a small nodule, vesicle or papule or as an excoriation. This initial lesion progresses peripherally, often along the folds, following a creeping, ulcerative and cicatricial process. New lesions may occur by autoinoculation and later may coalesce with older ones. The ulcers may be raised or depressed, usually with a beefy red granular base which bleeds easily and with characteristic rolled edges. If neglected the disease may spread over large areas, causing serious destruction of genital organs. In the area of the vulva elephantiasis may develop causing great deformity (esthiomene). Granuloma inguinale though generally believed to be venereal is only mildly infectious. The spouse of an infected person often remains uninfected.

Etiologic Agent

Granuloma inguinale is caused by *Donovania granulomatis*, often called the Donovan body.

Diagnosis

The diagnosis is based on the clinical appearance. Laboratory confirmation is made by demonstrating the etiologic agent in smears made from granulation tissue taken from the edge of lesions. Wright or Giemsa stain are most frequently used to color the short oval-shaped rods found singly or grouped within the cytoplasm of large mononuclear cells, the Donovan bodies. Histologic examination of biopsy specimens is often helpful.

Epidemiology

The disease is usually associated with unhygienic conditions and habits. Those infected usually neglect it for weeks and months until the ulceration has spread over large areas, often exuding a foul odor. Granuloma inguinale is most common in tropical and subtropical areas but has been reported from all countries. In the United States it is endemic in the south, particularly among the low socioeconomic groups. Exact data on its incidence and prevalence are not available but it is undoubtedly the least common of the venereal diseases. Both sexes are susceptible. It is rarely seen in children before the age of puberty.

Treatment

One to 3 gm. of streptomycin daily over a period of 5 to 10 days, or 2 to 4 gm. daily of one of the tetracycline antibiotics or chloramphenicol over a period of 2 to 3 weeks, have been successfully used. The larger the area involved and the older the lesion the longer the duration and the greater the intensity of treatment.

Prevention

Most of the preventive measures suggested for the other venereal diseases are applicable. Cleanliness and good personal hygiene are important.

WM. D. MORTIMER HARRIS, M.D.

21   Tuberculosis

The key to the prevention of tuberculosis is the prevention of infection by the *Mycobacterium tuberculosis* (tubercle bacillus), for without the organism there can be no disease. The tubercle bacillus is not the sole factor in the development of tuberculosis, however, for under similar conditions of exposure the disease occurs with varying frequency in different individuals and species of animals. It is therefore necessary to consider factors in the host as well as the exciting agent in the development of tuberculosis.

Although the tubercle bacillus was first identified in 1882, surprisingly little is known about variations in its infectivity or virulence in vivo. Specific types of organisms pathogenic for certain animal species and also strains which differ in virulence on culture have been distinguished for many years. The behavior of the bacilli in the human body, however, has generally been regarded as relatively fixed. Two recent developments in the bacteriology of tuberculosis have altered this concept. The widespread prevalence of so-called atypical, acid-fast mycobacteria responsible for low grade tuberculin sensitivity in many areas, and for a number of instances of clinical pulmonary disease, has been recognized. The use of isoniazid in the treatment of tuberculosis has led to the frequent emergence of isoniazid-resistant strains of tubercle bacilli which are of a low order of virulence for animals and possibly for man as well.

Much more is known about factors which affect the response of the human host to tuberculous infection. One of the most important is age. Infancy is the period of greatest susceptibility, childhood the period of highest resistance. Pulmonary tuberculosis is more frequent in young females and older males. A close correlation exists between poverty and the prevalence of tuberculosis, and the former may almost entirely account for the relationship between race and tuberculosis so commonly observed.

The risk of a latent tuberculosis becoming active when prolonged steroid therapy is given is considerable, and it is sound practice to administer anti-tuberculosis drugs under such circumstances. Poorly controlled diabetes may have a bad effect on tuberculosis and must be treated vigorously. The influence of pregnancy on tuberculosis is not clearly defined but the prevalent opinion is that pregnancy itself is not deleterious. The most important factor in activation is probably the increased physical demands on the mother in the postpartum period.

Tuberculous infection is spread almost exclusively through the respiratory tract. (Tuberculin testing of cattle and pasteurization of milk has made bovine infection uncommon in humans.) Entry of the organism into the body by other routes is extremely rare. Although the air-borne transmission of the tubercle bacilli at considerable distance has been demonstrated experimentally, person-to-person contact is probably the most frequent method of dissemination. The likelihood of this will be strongly affected by amount, frequency and intimacy of exposure. It is believed that intimate and repeated contact in the household is more significant than casual massive exposure.

Diagnosis

The rapid decline in the proportion of infected individuals in the population in developed countries has made the tuberculin test increasingly valuable as a diagnostic tool. The test serves four main purposes; differential diagnosis of tuberculosis from other pulmonary conditions, preliminary screening in case finding, identification of infected and noninfected persons in need of preventive measures, and determination of infection rates as an epidemiologic index. The accepted techniques for tuberculin testing are the intracutaneous Mantoux, and the Heaf,[1, 2] and Tine[3, 4] multiple puncture methods. The Vollmer patch test is not recommended. The Mantoux test is the recognized standard and should be used in differential diagnosis and epidemiological studies. The multiple puncture methods are of value in screening individuals for x-ray examination, and for decision as to application of BCG or chemoprophylaxis. They are particularly useful in young children who do not accept intracutaneous tests readily.

The tuberculin test has its greatest applicability in private medical practice. Here the less frequent need for x-rays can be a major financial consideration, and the increase in personnel time and number of patient's visits are not serious drawbacks. In public health programs lack of available personnel and patient cooperation can be deterrents, and tuberculin testing has been largely confined to readily mobilized school groups. Its use in the general adult population, though widely recommended, has been limited.

The most important method for the diagnosis of tuberculosis is still the chest x-ray examination. It is the responsibility of the physician to see that one is taken when a positive tuberculin test is obtained, and at 3 to 6 month intervals for at least 2 years after a recent conversion from negative to positive tuberculin reaction. The chest film forms the basis of most case-finding programs carried out by public and private agencies. The concentration of tuberculosis among the highly infected segments of the population, and among older people, makes chest films by far the most productive screening method. Routine x-ray examination is particularly applicable to admissions to general hospitals, inmates of prisons and shelters, welfare recipients, residents in areas of high tuberculosis prevalence, and employees of heavy industries. The characteristics of the population examined rather than the way in which surveys are organized are responsible for the high yield in these situations.

The other essential diagnostic aid is the bacteriological examination of sputum and gastric contents. The identification of tubercle bacilli on concentrated smear, followed by culture, is conclusive evidence of tuberculosis. Cultural studies are important in differentiating tubercle bacilli from the unclassified acid-fast mycobacteria widely prevalent in certain areas. Facilities for determination of the sensitivity of the organisms to antituberculosis drugs must also be available as a guide to proper treatment.

These three procedures, tuberculin test, chest films, and sputum examination, are the keys to our most important preventive measures, the prompt diagnosis and adequate treatment of individuals with infectious tuberculosis. In susceptible groups the disease is apt to be explosive in onset and early diagnosis is frequently dependent on routine chest films at the time of hospital admission or in a community survey. The private physician can contribute significantly by developing a high level of suspicion toward tuberculosis and referring his patients for x-ray examination promptly. When such a referral is not practicable, examination of the patient's sputum may establish the diagnosis of tuberculosis.

The tuberculosis case-finding rate is higher among contacts than any other group and there is strong correlation between intimacy of exposure and frequency of disease. The first examination of contacts should receive special emphasis since the majority of the cases of tuberculosis are found among contacts at this examination. In communities in which the prevalence of tuberculosis is low, the examination of members of households of young children discovered to have positive tuberculin reactions has been recommended as a method of uncovering previously unknown sources of infection. This technique has not, however, proven productive in large cities with well-developed general case-finding programs.

Treatment

Effective treatment is as important as early diagnosis in the prevention of the spread of tuberculous infection. The adequate use of antituberculosis drugs is the essence of the modern treatment of the disease. Bed rest, once the mainstay of the management of tuberculosis, is now confined to situations in which the patient's symptoms demand it. Collapse therapy, temporary or permanent, is rarely recommended as a primary procedure. Resection of a lobe or lung is usually reserved for the relatively few patients with persistent cavitation and positive sputum in whom the usual medical measures have failed. It is generally believed that this group should not constitute more than 10 per cent of all patients with newly diagnosed disease. Long-term chemotherapy is now the procedure of choice for patients with quiescent tuberculosis.

The question of where tuberculosis is best treated is of less current concern than how it is treated. Three broad indications for hospitalization are recognized: when symptoms of serious disease necessitate it, in the early stages of treatment while a suitable drug regimen is being established, and during the period of communicability among those patients who cannot be isolated properly otherwise. In other circumstances ambulatory therapy can be employed if the prescribed medication is regularly taken. The Tuberculosis Chemotherapy Centre in Madras, India, has demonstrated that sputum conversion occurs as frequently in ambulatory as in hospitalized patients if these conditions are met. The Centre has also shown that the spread of infection in the households of nonhospitalized patients is not significantly greater than in those of the hospitalized. It is doubtful, however, that similar results can be obtained in urban areas in developed countries where the activities of the patients are less well controlled.

The initial course of treatment in tuberculosis should include at least two drugs, one of which should be isoniazid (INH). The drug most commonly employed with isoniazid is para-aminosalicylic acid (PAS), since oral medication is the most acceptable regimen. Streptomycin (SM) is usually substituted in those patients who cannot tolerate or are resistant to INH or PAS. Acutely ill patients are frequently treated with both isoniazid and streptomycin simultaneously since this is the most powerful therapeutic combination. When streptomycin is prescribed it should be given daily for the first 2 or 3 months at least. Second line drugs such as cycloserine, ethionamide, pyrazinamide and viomycin are normally used only in the retreatment of tuberculosis when resistance to both isoniazid and streptomycin has developed. These agents are less effective, more toxic and considerably more expensive than isoniazid and streptomycin.

Prevention

The measures discussed so far have as their objective the prevention of tuberculous infection. The maintenance of this state, in which the individual fails to react to the tuberculin test, is true prevention of occurrence. Another method of achieving the same result is through administrtion of isoniazid to uninfected persons during their period of exposure, so-called chemoprophylaxis. Recent studies by the Public Health Service[5, 6] and by Dormer[7] in South Africa have shown that the frequency with which infection and disease occur can be strikingly reduced as long as the isoniazid is taken. Chemoprophylaxis unfortunately is limited in general application. The number of uninfected individuals at risk is large and the time of exposure rarely predictable. The administration of the drug for long periods of time, possibly indefinitely, is difficult for large numbers of people.

An alternative procedure which can be applied to individuals not yet infected is BCG vaccination. BCG vaccine, an attenuated strain of the bovine tubercle bacillus, has been used widely in all parts of the world since its introduction in 1922. A potent vaccine, liquid or freeze dried, given by the intracutaneous route, will produce a positive tuberculin reaction in almost 100 per cent of the individuals inoculated. Controlled studies by the Medical Research Council of England and others have demonstrated that this is attended by a reduction of 80 per cent or more in the rate at which new cases of tuberculosis develop, and that the protective effect lasts for at least 10 years. Vaccination with BCG may produce an unsightly local reaction of relatively brief duration but is free from serious complications. BCG vaccination has not been used widely in the United States because of the low incidence of the disease in many areas and the adequacy of other control measures.

Most of our efforts at the specific prevention of tuberculosis must be directed against the extension of the disease in already infected individuals, that is, prevention of progression. In some instances, particularly in children and young adults, disease develops as a direct and more or less continuous result of the initial infection and is characterized as exogenous in origin. Isoniazid has proven to be an effective preventive agent in these circumstances. The generalized forms of tuberculosis in infants (miliary and meningitic tuberculosis) can be virtually eliminated, and the occurrence of pulmonary tuberculosis in adults materially reduced, as long as the medication is being continued. Persistence of benefits after discontinuance of drug therapy has not been clearly established.

Clinically active tuberculosis usually manifests itself for the first time as a result of the flare-up of a latent infection contracted in the relatively remote past. This is called endogenous reinfection and is believed to be the mode of origin of most of the tuberculous disease observed in older individuals. It has been estimated that approximately 75 per cent of the new active cases of tuberculosis occurring annually in the United States are due to endogenous reinfection.

This stage of tuberculosis can only be prevented by increasing the resistance of the host, the infected individual. No specific method for accomplishing this is available currently. Increased resistance is dependent, among other things, on improvement in living standards, better general medical care, and prompt treatment of intercurrent infections. These measures are not primarily medical but are related to changes in the social and economic structure of the community, an extremely slow process.

The possibility has been suggested that isoniazid may exert specific action in the prevention of endogenous reinfection in tuberculosis and this is the subject of current research by a number of investigators.

In summary, the essential step in the prevention of tuberculosis is the prevention of initial infection by the tubercle bacillus. The latter usually occurs through the air-borne transmission of organisms from patients with tuberculosis in communicable form to individuals with whom they are in close contact. Early diagnosis of active tuberculosis and its prompt treatment with antimicrobial drugs are the most important measures in tuberculosis control. BCG vaccination and isoniazid chemoprophylaxis are of value in decreasing the frequency with which exogenous tuberculosis develops. Reduction in morbidity from endogenous reinfection, the most common mode of origin of tuberculosis at present, is largely dependent on improvements in the social and economic state of the community.

ARTHUR B. ROBINS, M.D.

REFERENCES

1. Heaf, F. R. G.: The multiple-puncture tuberculin test. Lancet, ii:151, 1951.
2. A report of the Tuberculin Sub-Committee of Research Committee of British Tuberculosis Association: A single tuberculin test for epidemiological use. Tubercle, 40:317, 1959.
3. Rosenthal, S. R.: The disk-tine tuberculin test. Journal of the American Medical Association, 177:152, 1961.
4. Badger, T. L., Breitwieser, E. R., and Muench, H.: Tuberculin tine test. American Review of Respiratory Diseases, 87:338, 1963.
5. Ferebee, S. H., and Mount, F. W.: Tuberculosis morbidity in a controlled trial of the prophylactic use of isoniazid among household contacts. American Review of Respiratory Diseases, 85:490, 1962.
6. Ferebee, S. H., and Mount, F. W.: Preventive effects of isoniazid in the treatment of primary tuberculosis in children. New England Journal of Medicine, 265:713, 1961.
7. Dormer, B. A., Swart, J. A., Harrison, I., and Vidor, S. R.: Prophylactic isoniazid. Lancet, 2:902, 1959.

Appendix to Section B

IMMUNIZATION

RECOMMENDED ROUTINE IMMUNIZATION SCHEDULE

AGE	AGENT
1½-2 months	DPT (diphtheria-pertussis-tetanus) 1st dose Salk vaccine (inactivated polio) *or* type II Sabin (oral modified live monovalent polio) *or* 1st dose oral trivalent polio vaccine
3 months	DPT 2nd dose Salk *or* type I Sabin vaccine* Smallpox vaccination
4 months	DPT 3rd dose Salk *or* type III Sabin* or 2nd dose oral trivalent polio vaccine
8 months	Measles vaccine (see text below)
12 months	DPT 4th dose Salk *or* dose oral trivalent vaccine if primary immunization was with either type of oral polio vaccine.
5-6 years	*DPT or DT* Booster of Salk if primary immunization was with Salk, or dose of trivalent oral polio vaccine if primary immunization was with either of the oral polio vaccines. Smallpox vaccination

* In other than infants, it is recommended that a minimum of 8 weeks elapse between feeding of type II and type I and not less than 6 weeks between type I and type III of oral polio vaccine and a minimum of 8 weeks between feedings of live trivalent polio vaccine. The U.S.P.H.S. Surgeon General's Advisory Committee[1] recommends the administration of oral polio vaccine to adults only in those situations in which unusual exposure might be anticipated.

The recommendations in the table above are minimal, and periodic booster doses are necessary to maintain immunity against most diseases. Other vaccines, e.g., typhoid or influenza, may be indicated in special circumstances.

An injection of quadruple antigen, consisting of diphtheria and tetanus toxoids and *H. pertussis* and killed polio virus vaccine may be substituted for each of the separate injections of triple antigen and poliomyelitis vaccine.

274

MEASLES VACCINE

If measles vaccine is to be included in the immunization program the following schedule is suggested:

AGE	AGENT
8 months	Attenuated live measles virus vaccine with simultaneous administration of *standardized* gamma globulin into another site, *or* 1st dose inactivated measles vaccine
9 months	2nd dose inactivated measles vaccine
10 months	3rd dose inactivated measles vaccine

IMMUNIZATIONS FOR FOREIGN TRAVEL

Most countries require visitors to have been vaccinated against certain diseases. The United States Public Health Service requires that Americans returning from foreign travel have certain immunizations. Failure to have these exposes one to the risk of the disease in question, as well as to the possibility of being quarantined at the frontier. The United States Public Health Service also recommends that travelers have certain additional immunizations for the protection of their own health.

Precise information as to the nature of the immunizations required cannot be specified here, because these requirements depend in part on the countries that the traveler has visited en route and whether or not epidemics, such as cholera or smallpox, have occurred. This information is found in the booklet Immunization Information for International Travel.* This is revised frequently, but the revision cannot keep pace with the development of outbreaks. Latest information may be obtained from branches of the United States Public Health Service, from state or local health departments, from shipping and airline offices or from the Epidemiology and Immunization Branch of the Division of Foreign Quarantine, United States Public Health Service, Department of Health, Education, and Welfare, Washington 25, D.C.

Immunizations Required

Smallpox. Most countries require evidence of vaccination against smallpox within 3 years, and the United States requires returning Americans to have it, except for persons returning from Canada, the Bahamas, Bermuda, the Panama Canal Zone, Greenland, Iceland, the islands of St. Pierre and Miquelon, the West Coast of Lower California, Aruba, Curaçao, the British Virgin Islands or Jamaica.

The smallpox vaccination certificate is valid for 3 years, beginning 8 days after a successful primary vaccination or on the date of revaccination.

Yellow Fever. Persons who, within 6 days of arrival, have been in a zone infected with yellow fever are required by the United States and many other countries to show evidence of vaccination against yellow fever. Yellow fever exists in Central America, parts of South America and Africa.

---

* This can be purchased for a small sum from the United States Public Health Service, U. S. Government Printing Office, Washington, D.C.

The certificate is valid for 6 years, beginning 10 or 12 days after vaccination. The standard course is one injection of yellow fever vaccine.

Children may be vaccinated against yellow fever from the age of 6 months.

Cholera.   Countries where cholera is present may require entrants to be vaccinated against the disease. Other countries, including the United States, require persons arriving from cholera areas to present evidence of vaccination. Cholera is present in Asia.

The cholera vaccination certificate is valid for 6 months, beginning 6 days after the first injection.

The standard course is two doses, 7 to 10 days apart. A booster dose should be obtained every 4 to 6 months as long as exposure continues.

Immunizations Recommended

Smallpox.   If one goes to a country where smallpox is endemic or epidemic, vaccination may be indicated as often as every 6 to 12 months.

Tetanus.   Tetanus toxoid is recommended for everyone. The standard course depends on the nature of the toxoid, and the recommendations for the product used should be followed.

Typhoid.   Vaccination against typhoid is recommended for everyone traveling outside the United States and Canada. Typhoid-paratyphoid vaccine is preferable to plain typhoid vaccine. Initial course 3 doses at least 7 days apart.

Typhus.   Vaccination against louse-borne typhus is recommended for persons going to Afghanistan, Korea, China, Ethiopia, Indo-China, Burma, Northern India, Northwestern Pakistan, Iran, the Near East, Iraq, Yugoslavia, Africa, Mexico, the Andes and Eastern Europe. The standard course is two doses, 7 to 10 days apart.

There are two vaccines, one for louse-borne and the other for murine typhus. Neither provides protection against scrub typhus.

Diphtheria.   Vaccination is recommended for persons traveling outside the United States and Canada. (See table for the recommended schedule.) The standard pediatric diphtheria-tetanus toxoid can be used for persons under 15 years of age. For older persons in whom reactions to toxoid are more frequent, a diphtheria-tetanus toxoid made especially for adults should be used. Follow the schedule recommended with the product used.

Plague.   Plague has been present in scattered areas of South America, Africa and the Far East. The period and degree of immunity provided by vaccination is uncertain. It is recommended that immunization be completed at least 2 weeks before departure to an infected area. Two injections are given 7 to 10 days apart. A booster dose should be given every 4 to 6 months for persons staying in the infected area.

Children may be vaccinated against plague from the age of 6 months.

Poliomyelitis.   All international travelers should be vaccinated against poliomyelitis. The recommended adult minimum schedule with inactivated (Salk) vaccine is two doses, 6 weeks apart and a third dose 6 to 12 months later and a fourth dose one year thereafter; or two doses of oral live trivalent vaccine or three doses of oral live monovalent vaccine, at 8 weeks' intervals.

Documents

The only acceptable documents for international travel are International Certificates of Vaccination, which can be obtained in the United States from passport agencies, travel agencies, local and state health departments and the Public Health Service. The clerk of the court will give one to a traveler, together with the application for the passport. Completed vaccination certificates must be validated by the seal of the state or local health department.

JULIA L. FREITAG, M.D.

REFERENCE

1. Report of Special Advisory Committee on Oral Poliomyelitis Vaccines to the Surgeon General of the Public Health Service. Journal of the American Medical Association, *190*:49, October 5, 1964.

22   Provision of Suitable and Sufficient Nutrition

WHAT FOOD MEANS TO PEOPLE

The food preferences and eating habits of people are influenced considerably by their social, cultural and physical environment. People view food, their own bodies and the world through what they have learned about human existence.[1] Knowledge of nutrition plays a relatively minor role in determining people's food habits, even though its importance increases as advances are made in nutritional studies. Actually, the role of food in the maintenance of health and in the prevention and treatment of disease has been studied from the beginning of history.[2]

Because of their training, many professional people find it difficult to see any merit in points of view or patterns of behavior differing from their own. Unless the professional person is able to understand food patterns in terms of the culture of a people, he cannot cope adequately with problems of nutrition. Attitudes and beliefs differing from ours are often termed "illogical, misinformed, wrong"; the people who hold these different concepts are often regarded as "ignorant, superstitious, stupid."

Occasionally, physicians are convinced that their own particular sets of beliefs, attitudes and practices are the only correct ones and should be followed by people of all cultures and social classes. This presumes to know what is good for all. It also presupposes that laymen have absolutely no knowledge or concept of nutrition.[2] Actually, sufficient and suitable nutrition can be provided through a variety of patterns of food selection.

There is no American way of eating which applies universally in the United States. There are infinite variations from high to low income, from city to farm and from region to region.[3] Available descriptions provide a composite, mythical picture which is not completely relevant to any individual person or family. There are dietary surveys in which the nationwide

278

average picture is broken down to show broad patterns.[4] In any given area there may be several subcultural groupings of food habits. Each group has different attitudes, beliefs, knowledge and practices in regard to food, and for different reasons, only a few of which may be based on knowledge of or interest in the nutritional value of foods. Therefore, one cannot assume that in this country a region, state, district or even county has a culture with a completely homogeneous outlook about food.[2]

People classify some foods as rarer, finer, more delicate, more desirable or more expensive than others. The distinctions of a social nature between individuals or groups are often expressed in terms of foods eaten or believed to be eaten by other groups. Certain foods which are inexpensive but adequate substitutes for more expensive foods are often rejected because they are linked with low social status. Many people stubbornly cling to white bread because it is a symbol of high social status. Similarly, white sugar and "meat every day" are symbols of higher social standing. If the socially approved food cannot be obtained, persons will often go to great lengths to conceal its absence from their diet. This class distinction pertains not only to the food itself, but also to the manner in which it is purchased, prepared and served.[5] Persons often learn the eating habits of a different social level from magazines, newspapers, movies, radio and television. They proudly claim these practices as their own, even though they may not consume any of these "desirable" foods. After a nutritional survey team had obtained information from schoolchildren living in a poor area in regard to what they had eaten for breakfast, the teacher began to wonder about the responses. Several days later she decided to give the children a questionnaire herself and make it anonymous. In doing this she discovered the children had not eaten a single grapefruit, whereas in the earlier survey many of them had listed grapefruit. What they had done the first time was to use their knowledge of social status in listing the foods; one could attain prestige and get the teacher's approval by eating a food such as grapefruit.

The close connection between food and physiological state has led to the classification of certain foods as fit only for certain groups of people. Examples of this are foods for babies, prenatal and postnatal food for mothers, foods appropriate for the sick and the convalescent, foods for the old and foods such as meat to give strength to the man doing heavy physical labor. Obviously, people not among these groups often show resistance to accepting food which they believe is appropriate only for infants, pregnant women or aged persons. Some older persons would rather starve than eat foods which they know to be commercially prepared baby foods. The more we learn of the scientific reasons for the need for particular foods or types of foods in different physiological states, the greater may become the conflict between foods chosen by folklore and foods chosen by science.[5] Occasionally, science shows that folklore is valid, and supplies the reason.

Certain foods are valued and others tabooed or reserved for special occasions when they are associated with particular holidays, religious observances, deaths and marriages, business transactions and the improvement or maintenance of social position. Failure to consider food customs may mean the difference between success or failure with the person or family to whom the physician may be suggesting dietary adaptations. It is easy to remember the importance of the Jewish dietary laws and the fact that most Catholics fast and abstain during Lent and on other holy days. It is equally important to realize the great variety of ways in which food is part of the ritual of social ceremony, modest though it may be. These factors complicate family and group feeding, to say nothing about generalized nutrition education.[5]

Progress up the social scale may increase the acceptance or rejection of certain foods and the way they are eaten. There is a great deal of rigidity in table manners. The more limited the educational, social and economic background, the narrower is apt to be the range of foods known and accepted. That the educational level is not all-important seems indicated by an inquiry into food habits in one general hospital where some of the more educationally privileged student nurses were found to have as narrow a range of food selection as most of the patients.[6] Emotional implications vary considerably and are not necessarily related to the manner of eating. The mere way in which food is served may cause its rejection, even though it would be otherwise very acceptable. The manner of serving food, the kind of tableware and the presence of small children at the table with adults may greatly affect the kinds and amounts of food eaten. It is important for physicians to have an awareness of these things when dealing with the sick person, persons receiving public assistance and those in various institutions.

In simpler societies and in times of food scarcity, or in very poor families, everything may hinge around food. Many people still do not have enough money for sufficient food for themselves and their families.[5] Although it is important not to neglect the problem of how to get food in situations of scarcity, the main problem is to select food for sustaining good health with whatever funds are available. This should be done for a nutritionally adequate and emotionally satisfying diet.

Attitudes about eating vary throughout the country.[5] In some areas, such as the far West, good health is a major interest. This is shown by the volume of "health foods" and foods of special types offered in regular markets. In other areas there is a great deal of concern with the personal satisfaction and enjoyment of good food served in pleasant surroundings. In still other areas food itself is not so important as the feeling that we must eat a certain number of times a day merely to keep up our strength for work or play. A person may look upon a good diet as a thing of enjoyment. On the other hand, he may consider that a good diet and enjoyment of his food are incompatible.

The table training of many children presents difficulties in teaching good food habits. Often foods which are essential for good growth and development are considered "duty" foods. The less beneficial foods, like some desserts, are used as "reward" foods for eating the "duty" foods. The child may later learn that the foods of most benefit to him are generally considered "good" foods, and reverse himself by calling the previously designated "reward" foods, such as candy and cake, "terrible," and consider fruits and vegetables highly desirable.

Scientific information about nutrition is often distorted and applied in contexts never originally intended. At the same time unreliable sources of information seductively advertise products with supposedly unusual properties. This, too, exerts influence, although the effect is perhaps more transient and evanescent.

Eating and food habits are intensely personal. Each person's knowledge about food may be accurate as far as it goes, or woefully inaccurate in terms of the principles of good nutrition. Resistance to change, whether it be active or passive, not only makes necessary the imparting of the physician's knowledge to an individual or family, but, more important, the discovery of the family's or individual's cultural beliefs about food. The physician can then suggest modifications acceptable to these persons.

It is important to know who makes the decisions in a family, and the roles played by other members of the family in making them. Several investigators report that in the majority of American homes all major food decisions are made by the housewife.[7] In another study, the role of the father was found to be essentially a passive one with preschool children, in that their choice of foods tends to be limited to the foods the mother provides.[8] This suggests that the homemaker or mother may often be the key person in nutrition education. The physician must consult with the mother or the father to get background information preliminary to any dietary education. He must also get their full cooperation to increase the likelihood of suggestions being followed.

WHAT NUTRIENTS MEAN TO PEOPLE

Man has associated disease with his food supply from time immemorial. Hippocrates recognized that all foods might not be suited to all people. But it was not until the eighteenth century, when Lavoisier began to study what happens to food after it is digested, that we find the beginnings of real progress. In the nineteenth century Florence Nightingale recognized that good nursing care required adequate food.

The need of good quality protein for animal growth was demonstrated in the twentieth century. Also recognized as important was the need for minerals and certain accessory food factors. Proteins were broken down into their constituent amino acids. Hormones, essential fatty acids, enzymes, chemical regulators and intermediary metabolism were studied. As differences between species of experimental animals were recognized, it was realized that research on man himself was the only way to understand human metabolism.

The transfer of many of the animal findings to man did, however, bear fruit in the numerous studies of growth and development in various states of nutrition. We now know much about what is needed to foster good growth and development in human beings, and not merely to prevent rickets, scurvy and other deficiency conditions in children. We know how to prevent deficiency diseases in adults, but we have yet to learn the diet best suited to attain the physiological ideal. This is defined as "a state of well-being such that no improvement could be effected by a change in the diet."[9] More is known about the positive functions of vitamins than is known of their role in preventing deficiency signs and symptoms. Some inkling has been given of the relationship of certain nutrients to common pathologic conditions but much remains to be learned. There is very little knowledge at this time for general application in the prevention of these conditions, except what can be extrapolated from growth and development studies for the maintenance of health in adults and its preservation as far as possible in old age.

IMPAIRMENT OF NUTRITION

The causes of the diseases of man can be understood only in relationship to his environment. The agent of nutritional disease is the relative lack of an essential nutrient, but the etiology of the disease includes host factors, which determine whether or not a given nutrient intake will be adequate, and environmental factors, which affect both agent and host.

The environment includes biological and social as well as physical factors. All three influence the availability of nutrients, the requirement of the host for specific nutrients and the consumption of nutrients. Determining the cause of a nutritional disease is a study in human ecology—of the interaction of host, agent and environment.[10]

Preclinical or subclinical conditions can be detected in screening programs, and findings of abnormality made before the person is aware of illness. This fact makes more acceptable the concept that physiological and biochemical changes occur before there is clinical or anatomical evidence of full-blown deficiency states. This also implies that a person may be in a less favorable state of health which may improve through a more suitable diet. Finally, in the preservation of health, this indicates that attention should be paid to meeting nutrient needs during illness of any duration to maintain as far as possible a good nutritional state and hasten recovery. Therefore, one must caution that modified diets should be adequate not only for normal needs, but also for the unusual demands of illness or trauma.

Nutrition is more than diet. Nutrition also includes the digestion of nutrients and their absorption, transport to the tissues and utilization by the cells. Impairment of cellular nutrition may result from any one of several factors. These may be grouped under the following headings.[11, 12]

Factors Interfering with Ingestion

1. The first and probably most important group of factors contributing to poor nutrition includes intellectual and economic poverty, emotional, social and cultural patterns affecting food intake.

2. The loss of appetite or an aberrant appetite such as may occur in pregnancy; the loss of appetite in infectious diseases and other illnesses, in congestive heart failure, after anesthesia and operations, during excessive use of alcohol, in thiamine deficiency and during severe pain.

3. Neuropsychiatric disorders, such as psychoses, migraine headaches, neurosis, spastic forms of cerebral palsy, neurasthenia and neurologic disorders interfering with self-feeding.

4. Handicapping conditions and treatment which render it difficult for a person to feed himself, such as injuries to arms and hands, rheumatoid arthritis and wired fractures of the jaw.

5. Loss of teeth or ill-fitting dentures.

6. Gastrointestinal disorders, such as peptic ulcer, diarrheal diseases, obstructive lesions of the gastrointestinal tract, gallbladder disease and acute gastroenteritis.

7. Therapy: diets restricting the ingestion of essential foods as in food allergy, and other modified diets which may be inadequate in certain essential nutrients.

Factors Interfering with Absorption

1. Interference with the absorption of fat in any disease such as diarrhea, ulcerative colitis, dysentery, intestinal obstruction, celiac disease, sprue, congenital atresia of the bile ducts and fibrocystic disease of the pancreas. The absorption of vitamin A and its precursors, the carotenoids, and vitamins D, E and K is, in general, impaired in such conditions.

2. Reduced absorbing surfaces; altered secretions; hypermotility; taking of alkalis, adsorbents and lubricants introduced by mouth, which would make anatomic, chemical or physiological changes in the gastrointestinal tract, interfere with the absorption of water-soluble vitamins.

3. With regard to minerals, the absorption of calcium is governed by vitamin D, by the degree of acidity of the intestine and by other substances in the diet which may impair its absorption, such as oxalic acid and excessive amounts of phosphorus, iron, magnesium or potassium. Phosphorus absorption is diminished when the poorly soluble salts of phosphoric acid are more readily formed, as is favored by the presence of such ions as those of calcium and iron. An increase in alkalinity of the duodenum and the absence of free hydrochloric acid and of bile hamper the absorption of iron.

Factors Causing Destruction or Inactivation of Vitamins

1. The gastrointestinal tract may inactivate several water-soluble vitamins prior to absorption. A high pH of the gastric juice will destroy thiamine as in achlorhydria. Rancid fats may inactivate vitamin E and carotene.

Factors Interfering with Utilization

Since malnutrition is a deficiency of essential nutrients in the cells, any factor interfering with the use of an essential nutrient may produce a deficiency despite its digestion or absorption.

1. The absence of a suitable specialized carrier, such as the appropriate lipid, phospholipid or protein, for the fat-soluble vitamins.

2. The failure of selective uptake may impair utilization, as, for example, iodine being inadequately picked up by the thyroid, vitamin C by the adrenals, vitamin A by the liver and riboflavin by the liver and kidneys.

3. Inadequate conversion of essential nutrients into biologically active forms. Cirrhosis of the liver or other reason for inadequate liver function may result in impaired conversion of carotene to vitamin A, thiamine to cocarboxylase, riboflavin to flavoprotein and nicotinic acid to coenzymes I or II.

Factors Increasing Excretion

1. An increased fluid output, as in forcing of fluids, excessive perspiration, polyuria and lactation may accentuate existing deficiencies.

2. Various drugs used as therapeutic agents may increase the excretion of vitamin C and certain foods may also have this effect.

3. Excessive protein loss may occur from hemorrhage, operations, injuries, gastrointestinal obstructions, burns, proteinuria and continuous drainage of pus.

Factors Increasing Body Requirements

1. The requirement for many dietary essentials is proportional to the metabolic rate. There would, therefore, be an increased need for these factors in such conditions as hyperthyroidism, fever and strenuous physical exertion.

2. Pregnancy and lactation reflect increased metabolism and utilization of nutrients in the formation of fetal and placental tissue and milk.

3. Certain toxic effects of drugs and other agents may be alleviated by increased amounts of specific nutrients, such as methionine, although the specific mechanisms involved are obscure.

4. Thiamine, riboflavin and niacin may be of help in the treatment of shock and anoxia.

5. Carbohydrate consumption influences the thiamine requirement. The skin changes of niacin deficiency may be precipitated by trauma, as may be the corneal vascularization of riboflavin deficiency.

It is easy to see that a person may have subclinical or clinical deficiencies in certain nutrients even though his diet is adequate by any of several arbitrary standards.

Nutritional status tends to be favorable when tissues receive a sufficient amount of the biologically active form of the nutrients essential to their proper function.[13] Conversely, it tends to be less favorable when nutrients are supplied in amounts less than the tissues require. The ratio between nutrient supply and tissue requirements is the factor which determines the direction in which the body's nutritional process is heading at any moment. The sum total of the effect of the ratio in the past and at present determines present nutritional status.

An unfavorable ratio between nutrient supplies and requirements is the immediate cause of poor nutritional status. This ratio can be altered by an increase in supply or a decrease in requirements. The reverse can also occur, or both members of the ratio can proceed in the same direction.

There are many conditions which influence the ratio, foremost among which is an inadequate diet. Other conditions of importance which, as noted above, contribute to a smaller supply of nutrients available to tissues are those which interfere with ingestion, absorption or utilization of nutrients, and those which may increase their excretion or destruction. Still other conditions can increase the nutrient requirement of tissues. Prominent among these are growth, pregnancy and lactation, physical activity and those pathologic conditions which increase metabolism.

The ratio is dynamic. It is constantly influenced by environmental conditions, both internal and external. The degree of influence exerted by any one of these conditions changes from time to time in relation to other conditions. The ratio exhibits various rates of speed as it proceeds in one direction or the other.

During the period of an unfavorable ratio, biochemical and physiological changes may occur in tissues. Later microscopic anatomic changes take place and these may eventually be manifested grossly. Such anatomic changes when observed over a period of time also exhibit velocity, intensity and evidence of duration. In velocity, the lesion may be acute or chronic; in intensity, mild, moderate or severe; in duration it may be early, intermediate or advanced in the stage of the process. An acute process is faster and more intense than the chronic form from which it arises and into which it may subside. As these changes progress, secondary infection may supervene.

Stress is as important as time in the development of gross anatomic change. A guinea pig may be made scorbutic and present subperiosteal hemorrhages in its extremities from normal activity. If one leg is splinted, it will not show the typical changes of acute scurvy, although they are grossly apparent in the other extremities. Thus it appears that removal or diminution of stress may relieve signs and symptoms without affecting the underlying cause. These signs and symptoms recur almost inevitably when the same stress is reapplied or another stress of similar intensity occurs.

Therefore, inadequate diet alone may not be enough to show up poor nutritional status. Clinically detectable malnutrition needs the operation of other effective conditions in addition to inadequate diet.

From all this, it should be apparent that individual health factors are as important to nutritional status as information on the dietary habits of a person. He may be malnourished in spite of a diet ordinarily considered adequate. The usual history and physical examination must be considered, and laboratory findings consulted.

A person's individual eating habits may well conform to any of the authoritative lists of foods which are the basis for a sufficient diet. On the other hand, the diets of persons very often show considerable variation from this supposedly common pattern, so that the physician must know food values to determine the adequacy of a person's diet. Mere nonconformity to a particular set of rules is not enough to label a diet inadequate. It is also important to remember food's role in the person's daily living pattern before arbitrarily prescribing a diet.

NUTRITION IN THE LIFE CYCLE

The nutritional state of both parents is important at the time of conception. The best time for teaching this is during adolescence, but interest is naturally greater during pregnancy. The clearly demonstrated influence of the nutritional state of the mother on the health of her offspring makes nutrition an essential aspect of prenatal care,[14] especially during the early weeks of fetal development.

Adolescence

The onset of sexual maturity, the hallmark of beginning adolescence, is preceded by a marked acceleration of growth. This happens earlier in the female than in the male, and occurs during the 2 or 3 years just preceding sexual maturity. Tremendous physiological changes also are in process. Physiological and psychological adaptations may play a role in the very frequent development of the insatiable appetite that occurs in adolescence. Nutritional needs are greater at this time than at any preceding age, and they may be greater for most persons in this country during adolescence than at any later time. It is generally true that the consumption of a large number of calories during adolescence increases the chance that needed nutrients are present in the diet in sufficient variety and amounts. Nevertheless, adolescence is the time when poor eating habits may be greatly exaggerated. This is also the time when being as much as possible like the crowd or persons adolescents admire is very important. For this reason, it is not very likely that a good diet will be consumed if current practices and beliefs of adolescents are not consistent with a sufficient intake of nutrients. For girls, there is an added danger at this time; their quest for a conventionally fashionable figure may limit their caloric intake drastically and without much regard for the consumption of essential nutrients.

There are two reasons for concern about the nutritional status of our teen-agers.[16]

1. Young people in their late teens are establishing habits and attitudes that often remain the rest of their lives and may be passed on to future generations. Studies of family nutrition and research involving school groups at different ages indicate older girls and boys have the poorest food habits and the least satisfactory nutritional status, the diet of girls tending to be less satisfactory than that of boys.

2. One out of every 4 mothers bearing a first child in the United States today is less than 20 years old. Six per cent of the deaths among 18 to 19 year old girls result from complications of pregnancy and childbirth. If the dietary intake of the expectant mother was inadequate during an extended period of time prior to conception, her body will have difficulty responding to the new requirements imposed by the growing fetus. In addition, it must also make up for existing nutritional deficits. Accordingly, poorly nourished teen-agers frequently are poor obstetrical risks.

Pregnancy

Several studies have shown that the complications of pregnancy are fewer and the condition of the infant at birth is better among women on suitable and sufficient diets, as compared with those on poor diets. A woman entering pregnancy in a good nutritional state and consuming an appropriate diet should continue this diet throughout pregnancy. The mother does gain a reasonable amount in weight, about 20 to 22 pounds, as the fetus grows and develops. In the later months of pregnancy, basal metabolic rate increases by about 10 per cent. At this time, however, there is usually a decrease in physical activity which is ordinarily sufficient to cover the additional basal caloric requirements, so that there may be little need to increase the intake of calories. An enhanced appetite, a sense of well-being and an actual craving for foods make pregnancy a time when new patterns of eating may become established. These may result in an excessive gain in weight and ultimate obesity. On the other hand, there is an advantage in this increased consumption for the woman who enters pregnancy underweight; it may help her to achieve a better nutritional state calorically and otherwise. However, pregnancy is not the time to institute a weight control regimen for obese women. This has been done successfully by restricting weight gain to zero during pregnancy without danger to the child, but only under strictly controlled experimental conditions which insured an adequate intake of all essential nutrients. It is particularly important that the diet of the pregnant woman, no matter how adequate it was prior to pregnancy, be planned so that it provides the additional nutrients required for the development of the fetus. This calls for a sufficient intake of protein, calcium, iron and vitamins in particular. As pregnancy advances, "it takes approximately 2000 calories of very carefully selected foods to meet the daily increased needs for nutrients other than calories."[15]

"There is no evidence in this country that nutrient intakes superior to the National Research Council allowances will provide beneficial obstetric or pediatric results. Excessive amounts of nutrients have not lowered the frequency of obstetric complications or produced superior offspring."[17]

Lactation

The period of lactation is also very important nutritionally. It is one exception to the earlier general statement that adolescence is the time when nutritional needs may be greatest. Women in apparently good nutritional state throughout their pregnancy have become deficient during lactation. Therefore, in order to provide the highly nutritious food needed by the infant and to protect her own state of health, the nursing mother should have a diet adjusted for these added requirements.

Early Life

There is rapid growth and development of the body during the early phases of life. There are greater requirements proportionate to body size in infants than in adults for water, calories, protein, vitamins and minerals. These requirements decline proportionately as the child grows but continue in ever-increasing increments up to and through adolescence. The infant's diet, which consists largely or entirely of milk, is less likely to contain sufficient ascorbic acid, vitamins A and D and iron, so that special consideration may be needed to ensure provision of these essential nutrients.

The natural advantages of breast feeding are not limited to a lessened likelihood of error and contamination. So long as the mother's milk supply is adequate, children in poorly nourished areas grow as rapidly as those in well-nourished areas. It is after weaning that growth and maturation are markedly slowed down in the former.[18] However, it is entirely possible to feed young infants adequately on artificial mixtures which include cow's milk and still provide emotional and psychological satisfactions to both mother and child.

There are subtle indications that overnutrition in infants and children may be a harmful factor.[19] The greater retention of nitrogen and minerals by the baby fed cow's milk has intrigued the metabolic experts for the past 50 years. While the interpretation of available data comparing trends in weight gain between nursing and bottle fed babies is difficult, the suggestion that weight gains in the nursing infant are not so great as those of the bottle fed baby raises the question about the desirability of too great a gain in weight.

Childhood obesity is in many ways more of a therapeutic problem than is malnutrition. "Because of the prevalent practice of food fortification in the United States and Canada, there is now a definite possibility that the individual, even the young infant, may ingest considerably more than the recommended vitamin D allowance, and intakes of 2000 to 3500 I.U. per day are possible, particularly beyond infancy. Although there has been no specific evidence that intakes of this order produce deleterious effects beyond infancy, it is pointed out that the long term consequences of this new nutritional situation on older children or adults are entirely unknown."[20]

Throughout the period of growth it is important to assess periodically the progress of the child, judging him in terms of his own performance. Although children grow and develop in a generally well-recognized pattern, the time when various achievements occur tends to be unique for each child.

Adult Life

Some rather interesting parallels can be drawn between adults and children by examining the needs of the "reference" person described in the Recommended Daily Dietary Allowances of the Food and Nutrition Board.[21] The caloric needs of a 25 year old man compare closely with those of a 13 year old boy, about 2900 calories. As we increase in age, basal caloric requirements decrease and usually so does physical activity. Thus at age 45 the man of the same weight uses only 2600 calories. This is about the amount an 11½ year old boy consumes. When a man is 65, the number of calories needed may decrease to 2200. This is about what an 8½ year old boy needs.

It is even more interesting to compare adult women and young girls. On the same basis of comparison, the 25 year old woman needs 2100 calories, which is about the same as a 7½ year old girl. A 45 year old woman needs about 1900 calories, which compares with the caloric needs of a 6½ year old girl. At age 65, the 1600 calories that a woman might consume are sufficient for a girl of 4½ years of age.

The important point in maintaining good nutritional status among adults in the ordinary way of life is this general principle: as caloric consumption decreases, food must be selected with increasing discrimination to assure the intake of essential nutrients. This should be done as much as possible within the individual's culturally derived pattern of food selection. It is more difficult to select a diet adequate in essential nutrients at the 1800 calorie level than it is at the 3600 level. A corollary is that as we grow older there is less and less room in our diets for calories unaccompanied by essential nutrients. This means that there must be a judicious use of such sources of calories as sugars, syrups and fats.

Old Age

Health in old age has its origins in health during youth and maturity, and in favorable hereditary characteristics. Aging changes vary widely in different persons, and biologic age can vary from organ system to organ system. Basic nutritional needs in metabolism are not altered fundamentally throughout the life span, but the older person is an individual who reflects the total of everything that has happened to him. He does not suddenly assume certain characteristics at the age of 50, 60 or 70, even though broad generalizations may be made about such age groups. The ability to maintain the "steady state" of the organism by complex physiologic processes decreases with age. The accumulated effects of previous disease may further decrease this ability. These effects may be considerable; they are often insidious. Metabolic activity decreases with physical activity. If the needed caloric intake is as low as 1200 or 1000 calories, the aged individual needs to consume only about the amount of food required by a 1 year old infant.

There is still the need for essential nutrients as there is for any adult.

Protein, calcium and water intake are more critical. It is therefore of great importance that the diet of the aged be selected with the utmost care. He does better with frequent small feedings. He is very apt to have strong preferences. An adequate diet will aid the health of the aged person, but the true prevention of nutritional deficiencies starts with sound nutritional practices during youth and maturity.

THE PHYSICIAN'S RESPONSIBILITY

It is relatively simple to determine whether or not a person has been immunized against a particular disease or group of diseases by questioning him or looking at his record. The recommendation for a needed immunization and the patient's compliance are relatively easy to obtain. It is a generally accepted procedure and one to which the majority of people readily submit.

It is somewhat more difficult and requires more care and knowledge to assess nutritional state. The frank deficiency diseases, underweight or overweight are obvious. On the other hand, it may appear to be somewhat esoteric to inquire into the habits of a person who is healthy and yet may have food habits which are not conducive to good health. Nonadherence to some particular guide for eating is no guarantee that nonconformity will lead to malnourishment, but on the other hand adherence to such guides is no guarantee of good nutrition. This is not to belittle the usefulness of these guides, but they must be placed in a proper perspective. These are general educational tools which do not always apply when judging the quality of an individual diet. *Knowledge of food composition is essential because our concern is for the kinds and amounts of nutrients being consumed and not so much with the names of foods which contain them.* Nutrient intake, then, must be related to estimated needs for age, sex, activity and physiological and pathological states. Laboratory and clinical findings are also considered. Based upon all these factors, a decision is made as to whether or not the individual should alter his food habits to meet his needs. *Rules of thumb and short cuts are available, but these are not a substitute for a good general background of knowledge about the composition of foods.*

Once the decision is made that nutrient intake needs to be changed, the important problem is how to help the individual accomplish this. Food and food habits are inextricably bound up with the life of the individual and people are normally reluctant to change their ways for some vague benefit. Recognition of the various influences which may affect a person's way of eating should bring greater success in dietary management.

Public health nutritionists and qualified dietitians, equipped by training and experience, have a knowledge of practical nutrition, an understanding of racial, religious and psychological factors that influence food habits. They have a working knowledge of food economics including costs of food, standards of public assistance, and planning low cost meals. They possess special competence in the best methods of preparation and service of attractive meals for groups of people, families and individuals. Nutritionists, qualified dietitians and well-trained public health nurses can provide valuable assistance to the practicing physician in the dietary guidance of his patients.[22]

While the problem is fundamentally an individual one, mass approach has been used successfully. The enrichment program for bread and flour is an example. Leaders of the group involved are persuaded that the addition to staple foods of nutrients known to be low in the diets of a large percentage of the population will generally increase the consumption of those nutrients. It is relatively simple to effect this program through the action of a few key individuals.

In improving diets of individuals, however, we enter into a person's own life and suggest that he change in some way his everyday way of living. This is much more difficult and the individual needs help in learning how to change. It is unrealistic to tell a person to eat more vegetables, or to hand him a printed diet list. Although this may work occasionally, it fails in the great majority of cases. Where compliance is reported, it may often be that the patient learns what the appropriate answer should be and, rather than offend his physician, replies to his subsequent queries in the affirmative. Sometimes the patient is reluctant to inquire about details from a busy physician, and either does not follow the physician's recommendations or misinterprets them. Often the unfortunate result for the conscientious patient is a radical change in his way of living without accomplishment of the purpose of the dietary recommendations.

It is important to remember how insidious is the beginning of inadequate nutritional status and the time required for its manifestation. It is also important not to predict more from treatment than can reasonably be expected. The need for such advice by a great number of people is evident. Large sums of money are spent for special foods and food preparations whose purveyors claim their products have unusual qualities to enhance health and physical well-being. This certainly points to a need for authoritative advice in dietary matters. It means also that the medical profession should assume more leadership in advising individuals, agencies and institutions, commercial interests and the general public on adequate and suitable nutrition.

The first factor to consider in discussing dietary changes for the patient is money. Studies show that as incomes rise, people are more apt to be well fed. This does not deny the well-known fact that poor diets have been observed at all income levels (wealthy people have died of malnutrition), even though less frequently among persons of higher income. Total income itself, or obvious high standard of living, is not a satisfactory gauge of the adequacy of the food budget. Food purchases may be made to effect economies, or the kind of food eaten is considered less important than other goods, services and benefits that money can buy. A physician need not be a food-budgeting expert, but he should know how much his patient can spend for food and for living in general before he makes dietary recommendations. Too frequently diets are recommended without practical knowledge of food costs, so that one often finds a poor family attempting to feed itself with foods which the family cannot afford. This also applies to suggested supplements, whether they be specially prepared foods or pharmaceutical products. It makes little sense to recommend expensive vitamin capsules and other supplements for a pregnant woman if the money to pay for them must come out of the family food budget. It is pertinent to point out here that nonfat dry milk is the cheapest form of animal protein obtainable, but at the same time one cannot expect the family members to use it if they do not ordinarily use milk. In this sort of a situation, education should begin with the incorporation of milk in the diet before such food supplements as dried skimmed milk are suggested.

Despite obvious benefits, the tremendous variety of processed foods makes the selection of an adequate diet somewhat more difficult, particularly for persons on limited food budgets. Many of these foods are all or partly prepared for the table. It should be suggested that the patient compare prices so that she may decide whether it is better to buy these services or perform them herself.

The proposed money allowances for food are based realistically in most welfare departments on prevailing prices for foods which meet standards, such as the Recommended Daily Dietary Allowances of the Food and Nutrition Board. The actual money allowances may not keep pace with rising food costs. These food budgets are planned by persons trained to do so, and they leave little leeway for the welfare recipient who is uninformed about food matters to exercise any of his preferences, or for errors in food selection or preparation. Also there are many persons who are not welfare recipients who get along on no more money than is available to the welfare client, and frequently on less.

There are economic, intellectual and emotional levels below which an adequate diet is impossible of attainment and where survival itself seems a minor miracle. There are situations in which ordinary demands cannot be met and expectations of results have to be scaled down to a dangerous minimum. In many metropolitan areas in the United States there are hundreds of such families involving thousands of children.[23]

In general, the quality of diet tends to improve with the educational level of the population. But again, as with income, there are many exceptions. The possession of one or more college degrees does not assure that one's family will be well fed, nor does an uncompleted elementary school education indicate a person will be poorly fed. However, one may say generally that with higher income and educational level, a family is more likely to be well nourished.

Deficiency Disease

This entire chapter on the provision of suitable and sufficient nutrition is devoted to the prevention of malnutrition by correct diet. Evidences of malnutrition in the form of deficiency diseases such as pellagra, scurvy, beriberi and rickets are covered in standard medical texts and are not within the scope of this presentation.

The study of food consumption figures over the years shows that the average American diet is adequate. Many persons consume more than the necessary amounts of nutrients. However, the average consumption of several of the nutrients is adequate only by a narrow margin. There are many persons whose diet does not attain these averages. Changes in food practices and changes in food processing may at times combine to create dietary inadequacies in individuals.[24]

The physician in developed countries must be constantly on the alert for evidences of deficiency states, even though rickets, scurvy, beriberi and pellagra are considered to have virtually disappeared. Spies states that "... today the so-called classic case is the rare case and the so-called atypical or mild case is the usual one."[25] Multiple deficiencies are frequent and make the diagnosis of mild, chronic deficiency states difficult. The pattern of signs and symptoms may vary from person to person and even among family members who share a table. The existence of a deficiency state does not exclude the presence of other disorders. Nutritional problems may complicate an illness or may cause it.

The prevention of deficiency states is a fundamental responsibility of the physician. This is accomplished by the individual's consuming a diet adequate for his needs and by dietary modifications and nutrient supplements when cellular nutrition is impaired by any nondietary factors. The detection of deficiency states as early as possible, when their manifestations are barely observable, will often prevent minor complaints from developing into chronic ill health, major illness and even death itself.

Recognition of the role food and nutrients play in the enjoyment of life and their contribution to health should help the physician to practice a high quality of preventive and therapeutic medicine.

JOHN H. BROWE, M.D.

REFERENCES

1. Wellin, E.: Cultural factors in nutrition. Nutrition Reviews, *13*:129, May, 1955.
2. Casel, J.: Social and cultural implications of food and food habits. American Journal of Public Health, *47*:732, June, 1957.
3. Clark, F.: Family Diets Today. Proceedings of Nutrition Education Conference, United States Department of Agriculture Miscellaneous Publication No. 745, 2, 1957.
4. Household Food Consumption Survey. Reports 1-10. United States Department of Agriculture, 1955.
5. Manual for the Study of Food Habits. Report of the Committee on Food Habits. Bulletin of the National Research Council No. 111, January, 1945.
6. Anderson, L.: Personal communication.
7. Cussler, M., and de Give, M. L.: 'Twixt the Cup and the Lip. New York, Twayne Publishers, 1952.
8. Bryan, M. S., and Lowenburg, M. E.: The father's influence on young children's food preferences. Journal of the American Dietetic Association, *34*:30, January, 1958.
9. Orr, J. B.: Food, Health and Income. Ed. 2. London, Macmillan and Co., Limited, 1937.
10. Scrimshaw, N. S.: Ecological factors in nutritional disease. American Journal of Clinical Nutrition, *14*:112, February, 1964.
11. Jolliffe, N.: Handbook of nutrition: conditioned malnutrition. Journal of the American Medical Association, *122*:299, May 29, 1943.
12. Ershoff, B.: Conditioning factors in nutritional disease. Physiological Reviews, *28*:107, January, 1948.
13. Kruse, H. D.: A concept of deficiency states. Milbank Memorial Fund Quarterly, *20*:245, July, 1942.
14. Burke, B. S., and Stuart, H. C.: Nutritional requirements during pregnancy and lactation. Journal of the American Medical Association, *137*:2, 119, May 8, 1948.
15. Burke, B. S.: Diet during pregnancy. American Journal of Clinical Nutrition, *2*:425, November-December, 1954.
16. Peckos, P. S., and Heald, F. P.: Nutrition of adolescents. Children, *11*:27, January-February, 1964.
17. McGanity, W. J.: Nutrition in pregnancy. Modern Medicine, *28*:108, August 1, 1960.

18. Cuthbertson, D. P.: Nutritional problems in infancy and childhood: chairman's opening remarks. Proceedings of the Nutrition Society, 22:119, March 16, 1963.
19. Forbes, G. B.: Overnutrition for the child: blessing or curse. Nutrition Reviews, 15:193, July, 1957.
20. Committee on Nutrition, American Academy of Pediatrics: The prophylactic requirement and toxicity of vitamin D. Pediatrics, 31:512, March, 1963.
21. Food and Nutrition Board: Recommended Dietary Allowances. Washington, D.C., National Academy of Sciences–National Research Council Publication No. 1146, 1964.
22. Browe, J. H.: Health department nutrition services and the physician. Postgraduate Medicine, 30:351, October, 1961.
23. Scholz, B. W.: Medicine in the slums. Clinical Proceedings of Children's Hospital, of the District of Columbia, XVIII:345, December, 1962.
24. Woodruff, C.: Infantile scurvy—the increasing incidence of scurvy in the Nashville area, a report to the Council on Foods and Nutrition. Journal of the American Medical Association, 161:448, June 2, 1956.
25. Spies, T. D.: Some recent advances in nutrition. Journal of the American Medical Association, 167:675, June 7, 1958.
    Anderson, L., and Browe, J. H.: Nutrition and Family Health Service. Philadelphia, W. B. Saunders Company, 1960.
    György, P.: Nutrition: current advances with clinical applications. Modern Medicine, 28:67, August 1, 1960.
    Wohl, M. G., and Goodhart, R. S.: Modern Nutrition in Health and Disease. Philadelphia, Lea & Febiger, 1964.

23   Obesity

Obesity and its prevention and treatment are popular topics of conversation in the general population and of great concern to the medical profession. Methods of treatment of obesity are legion. In spite of the consistent experience of therapeutic failure, the commonly accepted explanation that overeating is the cause of obesity has resulted in our neglecting research into primary causes.

Definition

Obesity may be defined as an excess of fat in relation to other bodily components. A very obese person is recognized as such from his appearance alone. A moderate amount of obesity is easily identified by pinching skin and subcutaneous fat. However, the definition of lesser amounts of obesity is subject to considerable debate. The studies that created the great interest in the relationship of obesity to health, disease and increased mortality all define obesity in terms of actual weight in excess of a height-weight standard. Overweight is commonly expressed as a percentage of the standard weight or as the relative weight.

Obesity and overweight are often used interchangeably. The very fat person is both obese and overweight. An individual who is moderately obese may or may not be overweight. Whether he is or not depends on the height-weight standard used and the percentage of excess weight at which overweight is defined. For example, a 47 year old man weighs 181 pounds. Referring to a table of desirable weights, his desirable weight is found to be 150 pounds. If a 20 per cent excess defines the lower limit of overweight, then this man is just included in the overweight category. If a standard weight table is used, in which weights increase with age, his "normal" weight for age 47 is 161 pounds and he would have to weigh 193 pounds before he would be classified as more than 20 per cent overweight. A person

294

may be overweight and not obese, as exemplified by professional football players. A person may be obese and not overweight, as a sedentary individual with poorly developed muscles and an excess of fat. Again, simply looking at the nude body or pinching a skin fold are practical ways of making the diagnosis. Skin fold calipers and underwater weighing are more precise.[1]

Significance

The experience of life insurance companies is limited to overweight, and thus involves obesity only indirectly. A man who is 30 per cent overweight is in all likelihood too fat, but he is not necessarily 30 per cent fatter than the man whose weight is at the standard. The relationship between excess fatness and relative body weight may be nonexistent in a plus or minus 20 per cent deviation from the standard weight. The Build and Blood Pressure Study of the Society of Actuaries,[2] was a long-term follow-up of 5,000,000 insured persons. It showed that there was a one-third greater mortality among males between the ages of 15 and 69 years who were 20 per cent or more overweight compared to persons insured as standard risks. This excess mortality was one-fifth greater for men 10 per cent or more overweight. Women had a somewhat better experience, but, for both sexes, the penalty increased with advance in overweight and age.

New tables of average weights resulted from this study.[2] The new average weights for men are about 5 pounds higher than the earlier averages,[3] with the new averages increasing 11 pounds between the ages of 25 and 40. In contrast, the average weight standards of women under 40 have decreased by about 3 pounds.

According to these new tables, 20 per cent of men and 25 per cent of women over age 20 are 10 per cent overweight, and 5 per cent of men and 11 per cent of women over age 20 are 20 per cent overweight.

Persons who are considered standard risks are not necessarily at the most desirable weight. When the mortality of the overweight is compared with that of the men in the weight range that has the best life experience, the excess mortality for those 20 per cent overweight is nearly one-half, and for those more than 10 per cent overweight it is increased to one-third.

The excess mortality of men 20 per cent or more overweight occurred from the following causes in the following order: diabetes, diseases of the digestive system, cerebral hemorrhage, heart disease, and malignant neoplasms. For women, the same order occurred, with heart disease displacing diseases of the digestive tract as the second most frequent cause of death among women 20 per cent or more overweight.

New tables of desirable weight were also constructed from the weights of persons associated with lowest mortality. When the frequency of overweight is measured by comparing actual weights with these more desirable weights, half of the men between 30 and 39 are at least 10 per cent above these standards and a fourth exceed them by 20 per cent. The maximum frequency is attained at ages 50 to 59 where the percentages are about 60 per cent and 33 per cent, respectively. For women under 40 years of age, the percentages of excess weight are a little less than for men; at ages 40 to 49 they are about the same; and, for those over 49, they are greater than for men of that age. As the total population increases and the proportion of older people becomes greater, the prevalence of overweight is increasing.[4]

Data on the prevalence of obesity in childhood are still meager[5] because there is no general agreement, even in the United States, on satisfactory standards.[6] One investigator states that 10 per cent of the "child" population can be classed as definitely overweight.[7] There is essentially no information on the relationship of obesity in childhood to the eventual height and weight in adult life. However, Heald[8] has noted that obese adolescents were heavier at one year of life than were nonobese adolescents. There is some suggestion that greater gains in weight are being made by children in good socioeconomic areas than by children in other areas.[4]

The cosmetic and other ill effects of great overweight are both physical and psychological. Many overweight children and adults are rather sedentary, which adds to their problems. Some forms of chronic illness are more likely to be present in the overweight adult, such as arthritis, heart disease, hypertensive vascular disease and gallbladder disease, and weight reduction often benefits patients with these conditions. Persons who are overweight and have one form of chronic illness are likely to have other chronic illnesses as well. The technical difficulties in surgery of the obese are well known. Overweight people tend to be accident prone. The fact that mortality rates from certain diseases are higher in the obese does not mean that obesity is the sole or primary cause. One must discriminate between the benefit of reducing for persons with certain diseases and the benefit of keeping an optimum weight to prevent disease.

Etiology

Some persons of all ages with overweight or obesity do reduce with advantage to themselves and maintain their lower weights with dietary restrictions. Physicians know there are many exceptions where nutritional knowledge and calorie counting are woefully inadequate as the only measures employed. This discussion does not include the relatively rare conditions of obesity with demonstrable organic causes. The discussion is limited to ordinary obesity which is commonly associated with eating too much and exercising too little.

To say that overeating causes obesity grossly oversimplifies the problem. It is no more logical than saying fever causes illness or the use of intoxicating beverages causes alcoholism. The obese person may consume more calories than he needs; he may spend fewer calories by being less active physically. It is possible that lesser amounts of physical activity and obesity may have common roots.

When psychological problems are evident in the obese, they are often considered to be the result of the obesity. Loss of weight is expected to solve them. The individual's life situation may help to create psychological problems, and obesity is, in many instances, a result rather than a cause. Obesity may offer the individual his best chance of "success" in coping with his troubles.[9]

Genetic factors can play a role in the development of obesity, even though their influence in humans is obscure. The science of animal husbandry is replete with examples of genetic influences on the development of obesity. There is no evidence to support the concept that humans are exceptions to this type of genetic influence. The potential for excess weight is not enough;

food has to be available in sufficient quantities to produce gross overweight. Some strains of obese animals have an excess of fat, even when their weight is the same as their normal litter mates.[10] They, like some humans, are obese without being overweight.

Persons whose weight is "normal" include the great majority to whom weight control is no problem, and those to whom insufficient food is available for becoming obese. Included also are those who make a conscious, continuing effort to remain at "normal" weight in spite of the hunger and other discomforts of dieting.

Present evidence indicates a multiple etiology for obesity. Hereditary, traumatic and environmental causes comprise the classification used by Mayer.[10] "Developmental" obesity and "reactive" obesity are described by Bruch.[9] These types in humans appear comparable to the "hereditary" and "traumatic" classification in animals. In both animals and humans, environment plays a permissive role, as it influences the availability of food. Environment plays a varied role with hereditary and traumatic factors in permitting or modifying the development of overweight and obesity. The nature of the diet, environmental temperature and physical activity are of importance in both humans and animals. Social, economic and familial factors are important in humans.

Obesity can be induced by hereditary or traumatic factors (involving injury to such areas as the hypothalamus) in experimental animals. The resultant obesity is attained by varying metabolic mechanisms. The components of the positive energy balance and the characteristics of fat metabolism differ in each instance.

Developmental obesity in humans occurs early in life and is characterized by overeating, inactivity and personality disorders. Reactive obesity follows some traumatic emotional experience and typically occurs later in life. In both instances research is needed to discover the metabolic mechanisms for the increased appetite and laying down of fat.

"Considerable advance has been made in the study of basic lipid metabolism. Simultaneously, research on the biochemistry of human obesity is developing. The following lines of evidence suggest that certain types of obesities in man may be metabolic in origin: the rapid rate of adipose tissue metabolism, experiments with genetically obese mice, lipid tolerance tests with human subjects, the concentration of plasma free fatty acids, and the apparent carry-over of a metabolic obesity from childhood to adult life. It is suggested that although these studies attempt to classify all types of obesity in human beings as either hyperphagic or metabolic, various degrees of metabolic obesity may be apparent within a population. Present studies may soon . . . chemically differentiate these obese human subjects."[11]

As animals and men become middle-aged they may slowly become overweight. Energy needs decrease as activity lessens and as the basal metabolic rate declines,[12] but the habitual food intake is continued. This results in a gradual increase in weight.

Prevention

The consistent experience of therapeutic failure in the treatment of obesity has stimulated recommendations for prevention of occurrence. Some success is attained in reducing persons who have become obese as adults, but it has been found very difficult to reduce effectively adults who have been obese throughout adolescence or since childhood.[13] The major effort in prevention should be directed toward children and adolescents who will become obese unless their caloric intake is restricted and their physical activity increased. Unfortunately, there are no methods of actually distinguishing the child who is potentially obese from one whose overweight is a transient phenomenon. The former is more likely to appear in families where both the father and mother are fat than in families in which only one parent is overweight.[10] The obese child is least likely to be found in families where both parents are of "normal" weight. This does not by any means identify the individual child. Some children become fat and later outgrow it, and neither they nor their parents consider it a problem. However, a significant reservoir for obesity in adult life are obese children or adolescents.

Prevention of occurrence of obesity in childhood and adolescence is an individual matter in deciding whether or not active measures should be taken, in appropriately using diet and physical activity, and in assessing the influence of other factors.[14] It is of equal importance not to intensify present problems as it is not to create new problems.

Treatment

Treatment of the obese person is an art as well as a science. The history of the onset of excessive weight and its subsequent course and duration are very important. Changes in the amount of physical activity can provide evidence of a contributory cause. A family history of overweight, illness and the causes of death provides clues to the characteristics of the obesity and its probable course as it may be related to the patient's present and future health and longevity. Determination of the role of obesity in his life situation is helpful in deciding whether the patient should or should not reduce. This decision will vary with the individual patient. Continuance of obesity may be the best practical solution for the moment.[8]

When the decision is made to have the patient reduce, detailed information about customary food intake and energy expenditure should be obtained. Weight can always be lost through starvation and by work so great that energy expenditure exceeds the possible calorie intake. However, the practical objectives are to take off excess fat at such a rate and in such a manner that the body is not damaged and the patient is able to function adequately at his work and in his home and maintain his reduced weight. In the dietary aspect of treatment, there may be a daily caloric deficit of 500 or 1000 calories which permits a loss of one or two pounds of fat a week. The dietary modification may be rather simple, as by excluding some desserts of high calorie content and by using less table fat and sugar. It may need to be more complex, but it is always based on the individual's personal eating habits and is a regimen which is realistic for him and his family. For example, prescribing roast meat for dinner 7 days a week is unrealistic for most people.

The dietary modification should be approached by trial and error in a spirit of humility. A person who is progressively gaining weight might be consuming considerably more calories than one whose weight has reached a plateau. Long-standing obesity and a minimum of physical activity, as may occur in older people, may combine in a situation where it is not practicable to create a sufficient caloric deficit to attain consistent weight loss.

Losing weight may not be within the capabilities of the patient. It may be psychologically as well as physiologically impossible for him to follow the prescribed regimen and continue to do his work.

The recommendation for increasing physical activity should be based upon the patient's daily routine. If there are no contraindications, a regular and moderate increase in physical activity is worked out with him. In addition to the obvious benefits of moderate physical activity for a sedentary individual, this exercise may sufficiently increase caloric expenditure so that calorie intake may be increased. Increased exercise may mean the difference between being hungry and not being hungry most of the time. This can be a lifetime decision for some who wish to maintain a certain weight. It can have such results as making an obese diabetic adult symptom free, or lessening the effects of arthritis on weight-bearing joints. In developed countries it can make a person more pleasing in appearance. Weight reduction can relieve many physical discomforts and symptoms. It can lead to a happier and more enjoyable life if something other than obesity can be substituted as a solution to life's tensions and problems.

JOHN H. BROWE, M.D.

REFERENCES

1. Keys, A., and Brozek, J.: Body fat in adult man. Physiological Reviews, 33:245, July, 1953.
2. The Society of Actuaries: Build and Blood Pressure Study. Long Island City, New York, Peter F. Mallon, Inc., 1959.
3. Association of Life Insurance Medical Directors and the Actuarial Society of America: Medico-Actuarial Mortality Investigation. Vol. I. New York, 1912.
4. Weight Control—a Collection of Papers Presented at the Weight Control Colloquium, Iowa State College. Ames, Iowa, Iowa State College Press, 1955.
5. Johnson, M. L., Burke, B. S., and Mayer, J.: Relative importance of inactivity and overeating in the energy balance of obese high school girls. American Journal of Clinical Nutrition, 4:37, January-February, 1956.
6. Mayer, J.: Some aspects of obesity in children. Postgraduate Medicine, 32:83, July, 1963.
7. Johnson, M. L., Burke, B. S., and Mayer, J.: The prevalence and incidence of obesity in a cross-section of elementary and secondary school children. American Journal of Clinical Nutrition, 4:231, May-June, 1956.
8. Heald, F. J.: The prevention of obesity. Journal of the American Medical Association, 186:28, November 9, 1963.
9. Bruch, H.: The Importance of Overweight. New York, W. W. Norton and Co., Inc., 1957.
10. Mayer, J.: Genetic, traumatic and environmental factors in the etiology of obesity. Physiological Reviews, 33:472, October, 1953.
11. Gaylor, J. L.: Metabolic obesity. New York State Journal of Medicine, 62:3801, December 1, 1962.
12. Pollack, H., Consolazio, C. F., and Isaac, G. J.: Metabolic demands as a factor in weight control—report to the Council on Foods and Nutrition. Journal of the American Medical Association, 167:216, May 10, 1958.
13. Young, C. M., Moore, N. S., Berresford, K. K., and Einset, B. M.: What can be done for the obese patient? American Practitioner and Digest of Treatment, 6:685, May, 1955.
14. Gordon, H. H.: Obesity—a panel discussion. Pediatrics, 20:540, September, 1957.

24   The Maternity Cycle and the Newborn Period

Sound obstetric care, perhaps more clearly than any other field of clinical medicine, is essentially preventive in nature. While pregnancy has been described as a physiological process, it is a delicate balance which can readily be disturbed, to the detriment of the health of the pregnant woman and her offspring. The objectives of obstetric care are to carry the pregnancy to term whenever possible, followed by a nontraumatic delivery, with mother and offspring in the best possible physical condition and with the stage set for sound mother–child relationships.

Maternal mortality, or death from conditions related to pregnancy, childbirth and the puerperium, has fallen to low levels in the United States in recent years. The maternal mortality rate has dropped sharply from 58.2 deaths per 10,000 live births in 1935 to 3.0 deaths in 1962. As a result, emphasis has shifted increasingly from almost exclusive concern for the mother to the saving of the offspring and to the avoidance of anoxia and other traumatic circumstances in the fetus which may produce brain damage with subsequent development of such conditions as cerebral palsy, mental retardation and epilepsy. Federal legislation enacted in 1963 recognized the vital role of sound obstetrical services in protecting the health of children by making grants available to the states and local institutions for the extension and improvement of obstetrical care.

Premature birth is the greatest single hazard to the offspring, since small premature infants, when they survive, are more susceptible to brain damage from anoxia or hemorrhage during delivery. Good prenatal care reduces the chance of premature birth. Prolongation of pregnancy for even a few weeks closer to term, when this can be accomplished without undue hazard to the mother, is, therefore, an important preventive measure in itself.

Preconception Care

The physical condition and attitudes of the pregnant woman at the start of pregnancy are the result of her previous experiences and medical care. For this reason, preconception care is part of proper preparation for childbearing.

300

It should include an adequate medical evaluation, followed by treatment and correction of any remediable conditions discovered. Advice may be given regarding the postponement or avoidance of pregnancy in the presence of urgent medical contraindications.

Ideally, preconception care should start with a complete premarital examination. At the time of the examination, counseling may be given which may help to prevent marital maladjustments by clearing up misconceptions before they lead to serious misunderstandings during marriage. Most states mandate premarital serological tests for syphilis, and some require evidence that a physical examination has been performed. In practice, however, many women are not psychologically ready before marriage to think of preparation for pregnancy and are reluctant to undergo a complete medical evaluation at that time.

Women who have suffered the loss of a baby are subject to a severalfold increased risk of losing their offspring in subsequent pregnancies by still-birth or early neonatal death. A definite assessment of the woman's health, with particular emphasis on her endocrine status, followed by treatment of any abnormal conditions discovered, may help to prevent a recurrence of the adverse outcome. Special preconception clinics have been organized in several states to provide the complicated services required in these cases.

Prenatal Care

Regularly scheduled visits to a physician should be instituted as early in pregnancy as possible, preferably monthly for the first 6 or 7 months, and weekly thereafter until delivery.

If the physician has had the patient under his care previously, he has a useful point of departure from which to judge any possible changes in the patient's health status. If not, the initial visit should include a careful medical history to disclose possible adverse factors in the pregnant woman's background. Determinations of the patient's blood pressure and weight are performed as part of a routine physical examination.

Minimum laboratory examinations on the first or second prenatal visit should include hemoglobin determination, serological test for syphilis, routine urine analysis and blood grouping, including Rh status. These are all essential in disclosing any pathologic conditions needing early correction and in providing a base line against which to measure any deviations occurring later in pregnancy. Knowledge of the blood hemoglobin is important because any anemia present may be aggravated as a result of the need for iron by the developing fetus. The presence of albuminuria, along with undue increase in weight or rise in blood pressure, may indicate early toxemia of pregnancy. The finding of a reducing substance in the urine should lead to a definitive diagnostic study for diabetes, since this disease, although not of special hazard to the mother during pregnancy, often carries serious consequences for the offspring. When a diagnosis of syphilis is made, prompt treatment is indicated, since congenital syphilis does not occur in the offspring if the mother has been adequately treated prior to the fifth month of pregnancy. Among pregnant women who are Rh negative and whose husbands are Rh positive, early knowledge of the situation permits base-line Rh antibody determinations against which subsequent antibody titers can be compared.

A roentgenogram of the chest, but not fluoroscopy, is indicated early in pregnancy. Prompt and continued care of the pregnant woman with tuberculosis will greatly enhance the likelihood of carrying the pregnancy through to term without spread of the disease in the mother. Many of the reported poor outcomes among pregnant women with tuberculosis are traceable to inadequate medical treatment, rather than to the effect of pregnancy upon the disease process.

Internal pelvic measurements to determine the adequacy of the birth passage should be made early in pregnancy. Roentgen pelvimetry is contraindicated before the final trimester. The danger of producing congenital malformations from radiation exposure is great during the first 3 months of fetal development. Moreover, the chief value of roentgen pelvimetry is the determination of the size of the fetal head relative to the size and contours of the birth passage, and this value is absent before the fetal head approaches its expected size at term. In doubtful cases, roentgen pelvimetry is often the decisive factor in selecting the preferred method of delivery.

On the periodic prenatal visits, the medical examinations should routinely include urinalysis, the determination of the blood pressure and weight and other examinations as indicated. Special attention should be paid to the nutrition of the pregnant woman, not only from the viewpoint of weight control, but also to ensure the adequacy of the diet in all the essential nutritive elements needed by the pregnant woman and the rapidly developing fetus. The physician should also keep in mind the emotional status of the pregnant woman. Apart from the effect of undue anxiety and emotional conflicts during this period on the course of the pregnancy and delivery, the mental health of the mother plays an important role in the establishment of future family relationships and, particularly, of subsequent relationships between the mother and child.

Parents' classes, i.e., classes for expectant mothers and fathers, are available in many communities. These usually consist of a series of six to eight sessions of one hour each, in which such subjects as the physiology of pregnancy, the mother's nutritional needs and the care of the baby are discussed. One of the chief values of these classes to participants is the free discussion of their attitudes and feelings as members of a group facing similar problems and situations. Most physicians refer their patients to these community classes, but some physicians prefer to conduct parents' classes for groups of patients under their care. In such cases, public health nurses and nutritionists employed by local health departments or voluntary agencies may be available for help in setting up the classes or in conducting some of the sessions after the classes are started.

The pregnant woman should be protected as much as possible against all communicable diseases, but especially against German measles. When this occurs during the first trimester of pregnancy, the offspring has a 15 to 18 per cent chance of developing one or more serious congenital conditions, such as mongolism, cardiac malformations or deafness. The effectiveness of gamma globulin in preventing congenital malformations in the susceptible pregnant woman who has been exposed to German measles is a matter of controversy.

Congenital malformations have been induced in the offspring of experimental animals by a wide variety of agents administered in early pregnancy. Aminopterin and sex hormones were known to produce malformations in human infants. However, it was not until the devastating outbreak of phoco-melia and other serious malformations following the use of thalidomide in the first trimester of pregnancy that the extent of the potential hazard was appreciated. The thalidomide episode points to the need for the utmost con-servatism in the use of drugs in early pregnancy.

While all pregnant women should receive adequate prenatal care, more intensive attention should be given certain groups shown to be more likely to have unfavorable outcomes in their pregnancies. These include women with tuberculosis, Rh incompatibility, diabetes or cardiac disease. Apart from these identifiable clinical conditions, special attention is indicated for the following groups: women who have suffered serious complications or loss of their offspring in previous pregnancies, very young women, women in their first pregnancy who are approaching the end of the childbearing period and women bearing children out of wedlock, especially adolescent girls.

Management of Complications

In the absence of a significant hazard to the life or well-being of a preg-nant woman, every effort should be made for the sake of the offspring to maintain pregnancy as close to term as possible. During the first trimester, uterine cramps or vaginal bleeding as indications of threatening abortion are sufficient reason for putting the pregnant woman to bed and keeping her under close observation. If the threatened abortion does not occur, the preg-nancy usually progresses to term just as if the symptoms and signs had not occurred.

Since premature delivery tends to occur in successive pregnancies, women who have experienced such a delivery should be studied carefully prior to a new pregnancy and any pathologic conditions present should be corrected if possible. With the occurrence of a new pregnancy, the pregnant woman should be advised to avoid strain of any kind and to obtain extra rest. A woman who has had more than one previous premature delivery should be put to bed prior to the period of pregnancy at which the previous pre-mature deliveries occurred, and she should be kept in bed until the fetus is considered mature enough to survive without serious danger of subsequent abnormalities. Even when uterine cramps occur in the early part of the final trimester, especially when previous pregnancies have been normal, the preg-nancy may continue to term if the pregnant woman is placed on bedrest. Preventing complications from occurring is far more effective than trying to treat them after they arrive.

Expectant treatment, rather than immediate intervention, is often em-ployed in the management of more serious complications of pregnancy. When toxemia of pregnancy develops, either because the pregnant woman neglected to observe a sound prenatal regime or, occasionally, despite good prenatal care, the physician's main objective is the avoidance of eclamptic convulsions in the mother. Through the immediate use of bedrest, sedation and a salt-restricted diet, it is often possible to maintain pregnancy until survival of a healthy infant becomes a probability. Induced termination of pregnancy has to be considered only if these measures fail.

The presence of placenta previa is the first possibility when painless vaginal bleeding occurs in the third trimester. A precipitate premature labor may often be prevented by hospitalizing the patient; of course, one must prepare for immediate blood transfusion. Vaginal examination should be performed only if roentgenographic visualization of the placenta fails to rule out the diagnosis of placenta previa. When performed, the vaginal examination should be done with extreme care and in an operating room with the patient fully prepared for cesarean section in the event this proves necessary.

Management of Delivery

Second only to prenatal care, the management of delivery by the physician offers a major opportunity in the prevention of permanent disability in the offspring. General improvements in obstetric care have minimized the hazard of gross physical trauma to the child. The major remaining problem is the management of the premature delivery, because of the greater fragility of the premature infant and its resultant susceptibility to cerebral injury from anoxia or mechanical factors. In premature labors, analgesia and anesthesia should preferably not be used, or, if used, they should be held to a minimum. Episiotomy is universally recommended to prevent trauma to the fetal head against a relatively unyielding maternal floor. There is less agreement on the use of forceps, although most obstetricians employ forceps as a further protection to the head of the premature infant.

Neonatal Care

Following delivery, the newborn infant in a hospital nursery requires protection against diarrheal and other communicable diseases. This can best be accomplished through proper safeguards in the newborn nursery which will ensure unit care of each infant, i.e., avoidance of common bathing and dressing tables, having the nursing personnel wash their hands between attentions to different infants and keeping the individual infant's clothing and equipment in a rack in his crib. Adequate terminal heating of infant feedings should eliminate this particular source of infection. Newly developed techniques involving prepackaging of individual infant formulas may eliminate the need for terminal heating. Relatively small nurseries, with ample space between cribs, and the use of a special small nursery to which any infant having suspicious signs of communicable illness may be transferred immediately, help to isolate any infections that may occur.

The detection of any of a number of inborn errors of metabolism within a few days after birth may prove to be the first step in prevention of mental retardation or other serious handicap. A mass screening test for elevated blood levels of phenylalanine to detect phenylketonuria may be the prototype for multiple screening tests for these disorders.

Premature infants, defined as those weighing 2500 grams (or 5½ pounds) or less at birth, require special individualized care. This is particularly true of smaller premature infants. Skilled nursing care is needed for feeding the small premature infant, since gavage, or feeding through a tube directly into the stomach, is often necessary until the infant's swallowing reflexes are sufficiently developed to avoid the danger of aspiration. Temperature and humidity of the environment must be carefully controlled, since the premature infant's heat-regulating mechanism is highly labile. Rigid precautions should be observed against possible exposure to infection in view of the great susceptibility of premature infants. Oxygen should be administered to premature infants only as a lifesaving measure, and then for as short a period as possible at concentrations not exceeding 40 per cent. Retrolental fibroplasia, a condition occurring exclusively among premature infants, which caused an increasing number of cases of blindness during the decade preceding 1955, has been shown to result from the administration of excessive amounts of oxygen. New cases of retrolental fibroplasia have virtually disappeared where proper precautions in oxygen administration have been observed.

The infant born more than two weeks after term to a primiparous woman faces greater danger of death in the neonatal period and greater risk of subsequent sequelae than does the infant born at term. Nevertheless, because of the difficulty in accurate timing of the length of gestation, interruption of pregnancy is not recommended by most obstetricians when pregnancy continues beyond calculated term. The postmature infant requires special care, similar in many respects to that given the premature infant.

Erythroblastosis fetalis, or hemolytic disease of the newborn, is the result of Rh or A-B-O blood group incompatibility between a mother who is negative and a father who is positive for the factor concerned. About 5 per cent of fertile, incompatible matings produce affected offspring after the birth of a first unaffected child. Sensitization of the mother occurs as a result of an earlier pregnancy or, occasionally, following a transfusion with incompatible blood. Erythroblastosis fetalis may result in death of the fetus in utero or, if untreated, may produce a severe form of cerebral palsy or mental retardation as late sequelae.

The mother with Rh incompatibility should be tested for antibodies periodically during pregnancy, and pregnancy should be terminated about 2 weeks before calculated term in the presence of a rapidly rising antibody titer. By leaving the umbilical cord long at delivery, it will be simpler to give the infant an exchange transfusion, a truly preventive measure, if this should be needed. An exchange transfusion is indicated in the presence of clinical signs of erythroblastosis in the infant, an elevated bilirubin level or lowered hemoglobin level in the cord blood, or a significantly elevated antibody titer in the mother or a previous history of a seriously affected erythroblastotic infant. A second exchange transfusion may be needed in the presence of continuing signs.

Postpartum Care

The patient should be instructed to return for medical examination about 6 weeks after delivery. In addition to an interval history and a general medical examination, visual examination of the cervix through a vaginal speculum is an essential part of this visit. This permits early discovery and treatment of chronic infection and erosions which might otherwise predispose to subsequent development of cancer of the cervix. Cervical cancer has been shown to occur more frequently among women who have begun bearing children at an early age, even though the total number of pregnancies may not be greater than those of women with a lesser incidence of cervical cancer.

Perinatal Mortality Conferences

Perinatal deaths—those occurring after the twentieth week of gestation plus deaths of infants during the first week after birth—are greater in number than all deaths occurring between the first week after birth and the fortieth birthday. The physician bears the major responsibility for the prevention of perinatal deaths. Some of the measures helpful in prevention have been presented in this discussion. To bring these measures more clearly to the attention of the practicing physician, hospital staffs and local medical societies have organized regular conferences to discuss the results of special studies of maternal and perinatal deaths. A frank discussion of the possible preventable factors in each case has often led to the improved management of similar types of clinical problems occurring subsequently.

EDWARD R. SCHLESINGER, M.D.

REFERENCES

1. Clifford, S. H.: The problem of prematurity: obstetric, pediatric, and socieconomic factors. Journal of Pediatrics, 47:13, July, 1955.
2. Gold, E. M.: A broad view of maternity care. Children, 9:52, March-April, 1962.
3. Green, C. R.: The incidence of human maldevelopment. American Journal of Diseases of Children, 105:301, March, 1963.
4. Guthrie, R., and Susi, A.: A simple phenylalanine method for detecting phenylketonuria in large populations of newborn infants. Pediatrics, 32:338, September, 1963.
5. Lesser, A. J.: Accent on prevention through improved service. Children, 11:13, January-February, 1964.
6. Lilienfeld, A. M., Pasamanick, B., and Rogers, M.: Relationship between pregnancy experience and the development of certain neuropsychiatric disorders in childhood. American Journal of Public Health, 45:637, May, 1955.
7. Macklin, M. T.: Etiologic factors in carcinoma of the uterus, especially the cervix. Journal of the International College of Surgeons, 21:365, March, 1954.
8. Manual of Standards in Obstetric-Pediatric Practice. Chicago, American College of Obstetricians and Gynecologists. Second edition, April, 1965.
9. Perinatal mortality and morbidity programs in the United States. Editorial, Journal of the American Medical Association, 167:1122, June 28, 1958.
10. Schlesinger, E. R., and Allaway, N. C.: Use of child loss data in evolving priorities in maternal health services. American Journal of Public Health, 47:570, May, 1957.
11. Scholten, P.: The premarital examination. Journal of the American Medical Association, 168:1171, November 1, 1958.
12. Shapiro, S., and Moriyama, I. M.: International trends in infant mortality and their implications for the United States. American Journal of Public Health, 53:747, May, 1963.
13. Standards and Recommendations for Hospital Care of Newborn Infants—Full-Term and Premature. Evanston, Ill., American Academy of Pediatrics. Revised edition. 1964.
14. Taussig, H. B.: A study of the German outbreak of phocomelia—The thalidomide syndrome. Journal of the American Medical Association, 180:1106, June 30, 1962.
15. Tips, R. L., and Lynch, H. T.: The impact of genetic counseling upon the family milieu. Journal of the American Medical Association, 184:183, April 20, 1963.

25 Preventive Health Services in Childhood

Preventive Pediatrics

Numerous activities carried out by the practicing physician and by community agencies bear on the promotion of health and the prevention of illness in childhood. Some community activities, such as the pasteurization of milk and fluoridation of the water supply, were developed as preventive measures of primary benefit to children. The practicing physician is only indirectly concerned with these. The practicing physician is, however, directly involved in another group of activities which, while ostensibly for the adults in the family, are of the utmost importance to the children. For example, hospitalization of the adult with infectious tuberculosis is an immediate protection to the children in the household. Similarly, maintenance of the integrity of the family by the prevention of disabling chronic illness in the parents contributes immeasurably to the well-being of their children.

Beyond his broader contributions to the health of the whole family, the practicing physician has immediate responsibilities for the care of children as individuals. The role of the physician in preventing long-term illnesses and disabilities by early and adequate care of the sick child is discussed in relation to the specific problems involved. His role in health supervision, or continued care of the presumably well child to promote the best possible state of health and to detect early evidences of ill health, is an equally important part of complete preventive pediatrics. Proper assumption of this continuing responsibility by the physician who treats the child during bouts of illness is more effective than delegating to another physician or to a community agency the care of the child between overt illnesses. First, knowledge of the child's usual physical status and personality provides an invaluable base line against which the physician may judge the extent of any deviations from the child's previous state of health. Second, seeing the child in the intervals between acute illnesses gives the physician an opportunity for early detection of any disabilities resulting from the illness.

Health supervision, through periodic visits of the child to the physician,

307

is a mechanism for channeling a variety of available preventive medical techniques to the individual child. It provides an opportunity for a complete medical examination, for routine immunizations, for counseling of the parents regarding the child's physical, social and emotional development and for advising on the child's nutritional needs and on measures for the avoidance of accidents. A continuing medical history may disclose symptoms suggestive of early physical or emotional ill health. Physical examination may reveal abnormalities, such as strabismus or congenital dislocation of the hip, at a stage when conservative treatment may be more effective in preventing permanent disturbances of vision or gait than a surgical approach to these conditions might be when the child is older. As part of regular health supervision, a schedule of initial and booster immunizations against diphtheria, whooping cough, smallpox, tetanus and poliomyelitis can be maintained. Above all, through periodic visits, guidance of the parents is possible in anticipation of the progressive stages of infant and child development. This may help to prevent the development of those behavior problems which occur characteristically at certain stages of development. Feeding problems occurring about the time of the second birthday may often be avoided by advising mothers to be particularly careful about not urging food at this time. The more general understanding by parents that the child's rate of growth, food needs and apparent appetite often decrease after 1 year of age may be an important factor in the decline in feeding problems in early childhood noted during the past decade. The potential benefit of the health supervisory visit is greatly enhanced if the mother is encouraged to express her feelings about her problems. This can be accomplished most readily by phrasing questions so as to avoid direct yes or no answers. Any implication of criticism or judgment of the mother should also be avoided.

During visits for health supervision, counseling of parents on the hazards against which to safeguard the child at each stage of development offers a valuable tool for preventing accidents in childhood. For example, poisonings reach a peak at 2 to 3 years of age; parents should be made aware of the danger of leaving potentially dangerous detergents or medications on the floor or table or in unlocked cabinets within reach of young children who have begun to move about the home by themselves. As the child grows older, the balance between protection of the child and education of the child in self-protection gradually moves toward education.

Infancy and the Preschool Years

Regular health supervision during infancy is almost universally accepted as desirable and is widely practiced. After infancy, however, visits for well-child care fall off rapidly, leaving an unfortunate gap in care before the start of the school years. The intervals between visits should increase in length as infancy and the preschool years progress. During the first 6 months after birth, visits are generally scheduled at monthly intervals because of the infant's rapid development and because of the number of initial immunizations that must be completed. Thereafter, quarterly visits are indicated on a routine basis until 2 years of age, and semiannual to annual visits should suffice during the remainder of the preschool period. To reduce the likelihood of cross infections in the physician's waiting room, it is desirable to use an appointment system and to set aside special days or hours for well-child care. The office nurse or receptionist should be alerted to watch for, and segregate, children with signs of infectious illness.

During infancy and the preschool period there is little division of responsibility for day-to-day health care of the child. The child is usually in or about the home most of the day under the immediate supervision of his parents. The family physician ordinarily needs to work only with the parents. Even so, community health services may be of considerable assistance to the practicing physician in improving his care of individual children. Through follow-up of birth certificates, families are visited by public health nurses, and parents whose children are not under regular health supervision are encouraged to take their children to their physicians for this purpose. A physician may himself request public health nurses or field physical therapists to visit families of children who have lapsed from his care or to help families implement his medical recommendations. There may be classes for parents of young children, similar in principle to those for expectant parents. In many communities, child health conferences (or well-child clinics) are conducted, usually by health departments or hospitals, for children who are not under the care of family physicians. The child health conferences do not provide treatment for sick children, and any child showing any deviation from good health is referred to the family physician or, when the parents cannot afford private care, to hospital clinics where these exist. Another community enterprise of help to physicians is the poison information and control center often operated jointly by a hospital and a health department. These centers have information readily available to physicians on the content and possible toxicity of substances swallowed by their young patients, as well as on the currently accepted treatment.

Infants and young children may suffer gross neglect or physical injury at the hands of some parents. The "battered child" syndrome, characterized by repeated bone and soft tissue injuries which may result in permanent damage or even death, is only the extreme manifestation of mistreatment of the child and disordered family functioning. Child-protective social agencies may be called upon for assistance in handling these difficult family situations.

Elementary School Years

With the advent of school age, the child spends the greater part of his waking day away from home. Although this divides the responsibility for supervision of the child's health, primary responsibility for continued care of the child still remains with the child's family and the family's own physician. Maintenance of a safe and healthful physical and emotional environment in the schools is the basic responsibility of the educational authorities. Health supervision of the school child through health services in the schools is being increasingly recognized as a supplement and support of family-centered health care, rather than the major source of health services during the school years. Community health services should serve as vital a role for school-age children as during infancy and the preschool period.

Maintenance of close working relationships between the family physician and health services in the school is essential to the interests of the child. School health services are abandoning the policy of having each child undergo a cursory medical inspection every year by the school physician, to the exclusion of more productive aspects of the health program in the schools. Emphasis is now placed on medical examinations by the family's own physician performed in the light of his knowledge of the child's health background. Serious attention is given by the school authorities to the recommendations of the family physician regarding modifications of the child's school program or his participation in competitive athletics, although final decision regarding these recommendations still rests with the school authorities. When this is the approach to health supervision in the school health program, it is incumbent on the family physician to use care in summarizing the results of his examination and in preparing his recommendations to the school. Special forms are usually provided by the school for this purpose. Any disagreements that may occur are most effectively cleared through informal discussion on a professional level directly between the family physician and the school physician, rather than simply through correspondence or second hand through the family. Reaching a common viewpoint is important for the child and his parents, since the school physician, aided by the school nurse, must share the task of counseling on health matters during the school years.

In place of the relatively wasteful annual inspections, schools have been substituting more thorough medical examinations spaced at longer intervals during the child's school career. Other techniques are used for detecting deviations from good health during the periods between these examinations. A widely accepted pattern is the scheduling of medical examinations on the child's entrance into school, in the fourth and seventh grades and prior to the child's graduation. When more intensive interim health services are provided, a single examination in the sixth grade may be substituted for those otherwise scheduled in the fourth and seventh grades. These examinations are performed by the school physician, preferably with parents present, only when efforts to have the child examined by a family physician are unsuccessful. Screening tests for vision and hearing (Chapter 31) are still recommended on an annual or biennial basis.

Various techniques are being used increasingly in the schools to detect deviations from good health in the intervals between periodic medical examinations. Among these techniques are routine follow-up of children with more than the average amount of school absences and the day-to-day observation of children by their teachers. The bulk of school absences in most schools is due to illness. Special attention to children with frequent short absences, as well as to those with one or more prolonged absences, should disclose many neglected health conditions which will require follow-up services to insure adequate care. Day-to-day teacher observation brings suspected health problems to attention, especially those of a subacute or chronic nature not severe enough to require the child to remain at home. Children with suspected health problems are discussed at conferences between the school nurse and teacher, which should be held several times during each school year. The school nurse may work directly with the teacher, without referral to the school physician, to help children whose complaints or signs are due to some obvious cause such as grossly inadequate diet or insufficient rest. The nurse selects the more difficult problems for discussion at a conference with the school physician. The school physician performs a screening examination on the children whose history appears to warrant further investigation. On the basis of this screening examination, the school physician decides whether or not referral to the family physician is indicated for diagnostic study and possible treatment. Under such a program, referral for trivial reasons is reduced to a minimum, and the family physician and the child's family tend to place greater reliance on the school's referral for medical care.

High School Years

Health services during the high school years tend to be less well developed than for the younger school-age children. Yet the health needs of the adolescent, especially in the emotional area, are in some ways quite acute. The role of the school physician as counselor to the adolescent school child himself stands out more sharply, and the direct relationship between the school physician and the student may result in cooperation on the student's part in measures recommended by the family physician. The special health needs of the adolescent are receiving new attention outside of the school setting. A recent development has been the organization of inpatient and outpatient units for adolescents in hospitals.

EDWARD R. SCHLESINGER, M.D.

REFERENCES

1. Adelson, L.: Homicide by starvation—The nutritional variant of the "battered child." Journal of the American Medical Association, *186*:458, November 2, 1963.
2. Colonna, P. E.: Care of the infant with congenital subluxation of the hip. Journal of the American Medical Association, *166*:715, February 15, 1958.
3. Farnsworth, D. L.: School and the adolescent. Pediatrics, *18*:809, November, 1956.
4. Health Supervision of Young Children. New York, The American Public Health Association, 1790 Broadway. Revised edition. 1960.
5. Hilleboe, H. E., and Schlesinger, E. R.: Pediatrics, preventive pediatrics, and public health. The Journal-Lancet, *75*:173, May, 1955.
6. Mattison, B. F.: Working together for school health. Journal of School Health, *33*:158, April, 1963.
7. Roth, A., Weissman, A., and Linden, C.: A plan for medical care for adolescents. Pediatrics, *18*:86, July, 1956.
8. Schlesinger, E. R.: Health Services for the Child. New York, McGraw-Hill Book Company, 1953.
9. School health policies, report of the Committee on School Health, American Academy of Pediatrics, Inc. Pediatrics, *13*:74, January, 1954.
10. Shultz, C. S.: Trends in school health services. American Journal of Public Health, *53*:1284, August, 1963.
11. The Pediatrician's Role in Preventing Delinquency. Evanston, Ill., American Academy of Pediatrics, 1960.
12. Wheatley, G. M.: Pediatrics in transition. Journal of the American Medical Association, *168*:856, October 17, 1958.
13. Wishik, S. M.: The effective pediatric interview. Pediatrics, *21*:143, January, 1958.
14. Yankauer, A., Lawrence, R. A., and Ballou, L.: A study of periodic school medical examinations. III. The remediability of certain categories of "defects." American Journal of Public Health, *47*:1421, November, 1957.

26   Dental Health

Dental health is considered an integral part of general health. Sir William Osler called the oral cavity a mirror of the rest of the body.

An adequate and healthy set of teeth and their investing tissues may play an important role in general growth and development and in the preservation of health in maturity and old age. An inadequate and nutritionally deficient intake of foods at all ages, except in early infancy, may be caused by teeth that are badly decayed, missing or in poor occlusion. Persons with such dental problems tend to neglect foods that require chewing, and their soft, liquid diet over an extended period may be inadequate.

The physician should be aware of the symptoms of dental diseases and their potential hazards. It is also highly desirable for the physician and the dentist to cooperate with one another in meeting the health needs of the patient.

Among the areas of dental health with which the physician should be concerned are dental caries, oral cancer, dental care in congenital heart disease, periodontal diseases of the investing tissues of the teeth, and malocclusion.

DENTAL CARIES

Dental caries is a disease of the calcified tissues of the teeth, characterized by acid decalcification of the inorganic portion and accompanied or followed by a disintegration of the organic substance of the tooth. It is one of the most prevalent diseases in man.

Etiology

Elimination or alteration of any one of several factors may influence the etiology of dental caries.[1] This disease occurs when the following factors are present:

1. Caries-susceptible individuals. It is well established that dental caries

312

is widespread. However, there is a small percentage of the population which is apparently caries immune.

2. Presence of acidogenic and aciduric bacteria on the surface of the tooth for the initial lesion of decalcification, and proteolytic bacteria to act on the organic tooth substance. Animal studies made in a sterile environment have demonstrated that even with a high cariogenic diet it was not possible to produce caries in these animals.[2]

3. Presence of readily fermentable carbohydrate in the mouth.

4. Presence of an appropriate bacterial enzyme system which is necessary for the oral degradation of the carbohydrates.

5. Presence of the bacterial plaque, which is a film adhering tenaciously to the surface of the tooth and is made up of food debris and microorganisms.

Incidence and Prevalence

This disease starts early in life and the annual increments of more than one carious lesion per person occur at a more rapid rate than the corrections made by dentists. This soon leads to an accumulated problem, so that between the ages of 20 to 35, the average man presents more than seven carious surfaces requiring filling, one tooth to be extracted and more than four teeth already lost. Nine out of 10 men in this age bracket require restorations such as partial or full dentures.[3] During the selective service examinations from 1941 to 1942, almost 10 per cent of the men examined did not have 12 sound teeth in good position out of a possible complement of 32 teeth.[4]

Prevention

Restriction of Fermentable Carbohydrate in the Diet. The complete restriction of these foods is obviously impossible. But there have been a sufficient number of studies among both animals and humans which demonstrate that a reduction of the carbohydrate intake to a minimum could effectively reduce the hazard of dental caries. While this may be an effective technique, the difficulty of changing the eating habits of the American people, especially where sweetened foods are concerned, makes this an impractical method, except in isolated cases.

Inhibition of Enzyme Activity. This has been done effectively in in vitro studies but has not proved effective in in vivo studies.[5] However, these studies are continuing and it is hoped an effective enzyme inhibitor will be found that will be efficacious in the mouth.

Elimination of Acidogenic and Aciduric Bacteria from the Mouth. This is obviously impossible to accomplish.

Observance of Good Mouth Hygiene. The use of the toothbrush with a neutral dentifrice immediately after eating or drinking any food, solid or liquid, has been demonstrated to reduce new dental caries by about 50 per cent.[6] This mechanical cleansing of the teeth removes any fermentable food-stuff from the teeth before degradation can take place in the mouth. This is of limited value for general use because of its impracticality.

The use of therapeutic dentifrices has been tried without any appreciable success. Actually the term "therapeutic dentifrices," commonly used by the dental profession, is a misnomer. Even the strongest proponents for dentifrice benefits do not claim it will correct existing caries. Perhaps a better term might be preventive dentifrices. The purposes of these are (a) to neutralize the acids formed in the mouth which are believed to decalcify the enamel of the tooth, (b) to reduce acidogenic and aciduric oral bacteria or inactivate bacterial enzymes, and (c) by the process of adsorption of the fluoride ion to make the enamel of the tooth more resistant to acid decalcification. The American Dental Association (ADA) through its Council on Dental Therapeutics (1964) has reviewed reported tests of commercially manufactured stannous fluoride dentifrices. These include both laboratory and clinical data. Each commercial dentifrice is evaluated on its effectiveness in controlled studies. One of these products has now satisfied the requirements for ADA approval and another for provisional approval pending additional clinical testing.[7]

Prophylactic Techniques

Topical Application of Fluoride Solutions. There have been numerous studies reported which show that the topical application of aqueous solutions of fluorides will reduce the onset of dental caries. The first studies were made with a 2 per cent solution of sodium fluoride. After cleansing the teeth with a revolving brush in the dental engine, four applications of the sodium fluoride solution were applied to the crowns of the teeth at intervals of 2 to 7 days. Such treatment reduced the hazard of dental caries by about 40 per cent.[8]

The use of stannous fluoride has also been reported as an effective agent for topical application. A single annual application of a freshly prepared 8 per cent aqueous solution, following a thorough prophylaxis, has been reported to be equally or more effective than four applications of sodium fluoride applied every 3 years.[9]

The stannous fluoride presents two possible disadvantages, taste and temporary staining of the teeth. The 8 per cent solution of stannous fluoride is quite bitter and it is difficult to keep some of the solution from dripping onto the tongue. This may be a disadvantage, especially with preschool and early school-age children whose introduction to dental services is frequently for dental prophylaxis and topical fluoride applications. The sodium fluoride does not present this problem. The staining which sometimes results from the stannous fluoride is not serious. Staining will occur in the presence of decalcified enamel or defective fillings. Some may regard this as an advantage since it may serve as a disclosing solution and lead to the correction of existing defects.

More recently, an acidulated fluoride solution has been tested and appears to be more effective than either the sodium fluoride or stannous fluoride. The in vitro studies showed a considerable fluoride uptake by powdered enamel. There was also an appreciable penetration of the fluoride into intact enamel after a 20-minute exposure to a phosphate-fluoride solution at pH 3. An in vivo study showed highly significant differences between study and control groups of children.[23, 24]

From a public health viewpoint topical applications of fluoride solutions have a limited but significant value as a caries preventive. They require trained personnel, either the dentist or dental hygienist, to make the applications. They are not so effective or so economical as a community water fluoridation program.

Fluoridation of Public Water Supplies. The ingestion of water fluorides at a concentration of approximately one part of the fluoride ion in a million parts of water (by weight) during the years of tooth development is the most effective caries prophylactic available. This involves adjusting the fluoride content of the public water supply.

The history of water fluoridation is one of the most curious paradoxes in medical science. It began with the search for the cause of disfiguring mottled enamel. This led to the finding of the cause, the fluoride ion in drinking water, and also to the use of this etiologic factor in mottled enamel as a prophylactic against dental caries, a totally different dental lesion from the mottling. A series of observations led to the caries-fluoride hypothesis that dental caries occurs in inverse relationship to the fluoride content of the potable water consumed. These observations were (a) the characteristics of a dental enamel defect called mottled enamel which varied from light, white chalky flecks to a dark brown stain and pitting of the enamel, noted about the beginning of this century;[10] (b) the direct relationship of ingested water fluorides to these defects;[11] and (c) the inverse relationship of dental caries to mottled enamel.[12]

The study of human populations living in areas with differing fluoride content of their community water supplies conclusively demonstrated that where the drinking water contained approximately one part of the fluoride ion per million parts of water there was about 60 per cent less dental caries than in areas where the water supply was fluoride free or contained only barely measurable quantities of fluoride. These epidemiologic studies also showed that 1.0 ppm of fluoride ion caused no disfiguring mottled enamel nor any adverse systemic effect.

While fluorides are found naturally in most water supplies, the vast majority of water supplies in this country do not have the optimum concentration. Studies begun in 1944 and 1945 to determine the benefits and safety of supplementing fluoride-deficient water supplies with fluoride compounds to bring the fluoride content up to the optimum show that the dental benefits are of the same order as found in areas which naturally have the optimum fluoride content in their water supplies.[13] The maximum benefits accrue when children ingest water-borne fluorides from early childhood. These benefits continue into adolescence and adult life.[14, 15]

Comprehensive pediatric studies over a period of 10 years in Newburgh and Kingston, New York, showed that ingested water fluorides at 1.0 to 1.2 ppm produced no health differences of significance among the Newburgh children who received fluoridated water from birth, as compared to the Kingston children of the same ages who used fluoride-deficient water.[16] However, the children receiving fluoridated water had much less dental caries.

Studies among adults who ingested high concentrations of water-borne fluorides (8.0 ppm) for periods of 30 years and more likewise showed no adverse systemic effects other than mottled enamel.[17]

The American Medical Association made a comprehensive study of the scientific literature and held hearings on the subject in 1957, and by resolution endorsed the benefits and safety of water fluoridation as a public health practice. Practically every recognized health organization and agency in this country, and many abroad, have endorsed water fluoridation.

As of January, 1964, more than 54 million people in the United States were drinking fluoridated water. There were 2612 communities serving a population of approximately 47 million people using fluoride supplemented water supplies, and 2321 communities serving 7 million people using naturally fluoridated water.

Among the 21 largest cities in the United States, all with populations over 500,000, there were 11 using fluoridated water and two more, New York City and Detroit have recently approved water fluoridation.

Fluoride Dietary Supplements. Another suggested method of using fluorides for dental caries prevention is the ingestion of a fluoride compound as a tablet or in a vitamin preparation. Theoretically, fluorides ingested in this manner should be effective providing one could depend on the family to ensure daily consumption by their children, at least during the period of tooth calcification. Some studies would indicate that such dependence on the family is unreliable.[18, 19] Furthermore, the cost per capita is greater than water fluoridation. As a communitywide program this method is neither effective nor practicable.

ORAL CANCER

Neoplasms of the head and neck account for about 10 per cent of all malignancies. Yet precancerous lesions and early cancer in these sites lend themselves most readily to detection. Physicians and dentists look into hundreds of thousands of mouths and should be alert to early signs of this killing disease. It is unfortunate that all too frequently the physician sees the mouth only as a passage through which he can observe the tonsils and the throat. The dentist, all too often, considers only the teeth and their investing tissues and not the whole mouth and tongue. It is the responsibility of the physician and the dentist to make complete oral examinations of their patients.

Considerable attention is being given today to alerting the dentist to his responsibility in detecting signs of precancerous lesions and early cancer in the mouth and on the face and lips. The use of the Papanicolaou cytology test to screen oral lesions promises to add a useful tool to the detection of early oral cancer. The technique is simple and lends itself readily to use by the dentist.[20]

Dentists are also being advised to refer suspicious cases to the physician for confirmation of diagnosis. Here is a fertile field for the close cooperation between the physician and the dentist in prevention of progression of cancerous lesions.

DENTAL CARE IN CONGENITAL HEART DISEASE

Subacute bacterial endocarditis has been reported following dental operations. While it is difficult to determine conclusively where the bacteria originate in these cases, there is reason to believe that the oral cavity, which is host to the alpha hemolytic streptococcus, may serve as the focus of infection. The extraction of teeth or the curettage of periodontal pockets may introduce a transient bacteremia. This may have little or no significance in the normal person, but in patients with rheumatic valvular lesions and congenital cardiovascular defects, the bacteremia may result in a subacute bacterial endocarditis.

The dentist does not, as a rule, take a comprehensive history of his patient and is unaware of these heart defects. It is therefore the responsibility of the physician to advise his patient to inform the dentist so that appropriate steps can be taken prior to dental treatment. The dentist may then call upon the physician to provide necessary prophylactic procedures for the patient's protection.

PERIODONTAL DISEASE

Periodontal disease is characterized by pathology of the investing tissues of the teeth. It is widespread, especially in adult life, although children may also be affected. Pathology of the investing tissues, i.e., the gingiva, peridental membrane and maxillary and mandibular alveolar structures, is responsible for a greater loss of teeth among adults than any other cause.

We do not, however, have any firm epidemiologic data upon which to base specific prevalence rates. This lack of prevalence data is due principally to the inability of dentists thus far to agree on an index for classifying the disease.

As with most diseases, palliative and corrective treatment is practiced long before control or preventive measures are developed. Yet the development of suitable indexes is essential before preventive or control measures can be applied. Considerable research is being done today to develop effective epidemiologic tools which may be generally accepted, so that this first step in the effort to control these diseases on a public health basis can be established.

Students of periodontal disease are generally agreed that both local and systemic factors may be involved in the etiology. Local factors such as irritants, traumatic occlusion, malposed teeth permitting food impaction between the teeth and poor mouth hygiene may be involved. Systemic factors such as blood dyscrasias, endocrine imbalance, nutritional deficiencies and the accumulation of heavy metals may also serve as etiologic factors. Complete examination of the patient is important to evaluate the possible role of these systemic conditions, if present.

There is some presumptive evidence that periodontal lesions may serve as foci of infection and this lends further emphasis to the importance of eradicating these lesions.

The dentist who treats periodontal disease should get a complete physical and laboratory work-up on his patient. The physician should be alert during an oral examination for signs of inflammation and exudation around the teeth and refer such patients to the dentist. This is another promising field for cooperative prevention by the physician and the dentist.

MALOCCLUSION

Malocclusion is a disharmony in the occlusal relationship of the maxillary to the mandibular teeth and may be responsible for many abnormal sequelae. Lack of masticatory function, traumatic occlusion leading to periodontal disease, speech defects and psychological trauma due to disfigurement are among the more serious results of malocclusion. As with periodontal disease there are no valid prevalence data available, but clinical examinations indicate that malocclusion in varying degrees is widespread.

While in general there is little that can be done to prevent its occurrence, the prevention of progression is most important. Severe malocclusions can be as great a handicap as other generally recognized physical defects such as, for example, a clubfoot. Most states have programs which provide needed financial assistance for the correction of physically handicapping defects, and some states include severe malocclusions as such.

In New York state the correction of severe malocclusions has been part of the state's medical rehabilitation plan since 1945. The medical rehabilitation program provides for financial assistance through the state-aid-to-county funds for diagnosis and the correction of physically handicapping defects.

Malocclusions associated with cleft palate, cleft lip or ankylosis of the temporomandibular articulation are considered handicapping. Other types which are so classified include malocclusions resulting from severe structural deformities involving growth and development of the maxilla or mandible. The most commonly noted handicapping malocclusions are those causing disfigurements or speech defects which may present a serious obstacle to normal development, education and employment of the person later in life.[21]

Frequently, the physician, especially the school physician, may be able to detect these severe malocclusions early. He should refer the child to the family dentist or local health officer who should be able to assist the family in obtaining care and, if necessary, help to arrange financial assistance to meet the high cost of orthodontic care.

CLEFT LIP AND CLEFT PALATE

The child with a cleft palate or cleft lip almost invariably presents a malocclusion along with the many other problems associated with these defects. In the past the usual procedure was for the plastic surgeon to repair the cleft; at a later date the orthodontist attempted to correct the occlusion. The speech therapist worked independently and rarely, if ever, was the psychologist or psychiatrist called in to help the family understand the problem and how to cope with it.

Within recent years the team approach is being recognized as a better way to meet the multiple problems of rehabilitating the child with a facial cleft. The team approach provides for the coordinated evaluation of the needs of this type of patient and sets a time schedule for corrective services by the several disciplines involved. Cleft Palate Evaluation and Rehabilitation Centers are in operation or are being developed in many urban centers.[22]

Among the specialties needed for the coordinated evaluation and treatment of these children are the following:

Pediatrics

A complete initial physical examination will determine the state of health and fitness of the patient to undergo surgical and other prolonged treatment. The pediatrician also assumes direction and responsibility for the correction of intercurrent ailments and feeding problems.

Psychological and Psychiatric

The shock and disappointment to parents when they learn that their child has a congenital cleft palate and/or cleft lip are very severe. In many instances the parents must be helped to understand that the defect is no fault of theirs and that correction is possible. Some parents feel a sense of shame and endeavor to keep the child from the outside world. Also, in some instances, parents reject the child with these defects. The psychologist or the psychiatrist has the important role of preparing both the parents and the patient for the acceptance of the rehabilitation, resolving emotional conflicts and aiding the child in personality development.

Surgery

The question as to when surgery should be initiated is one which requires the coordinated consideration of the surgeon, the pediatrician and the orthodontist. For correction of the cleft lip there is agreement that surgery should be done shortly after birth. Satisfactory closure of the cleft lip does much to boost the morale of the parents. The improvement in the outward appearance of the child often encourages the parents to help the child to live a normal life. There is, however, some difference of opinion as to when closure of the palate should be done. There is increasing belief today that surgery of the palate, if done too early, may destroy the bone growth centers, resulting in underdevelopment of the jaw bones and the face.

Orthodontics

Since the child with a cleft palate or lip almost invariably presents a severe malocclusion, it is the orthodontist who assumes responsibility for determining when orthodontic care should be started. This determination is based on periodic evaluation with diagnostic aids which include roentgen films of the teeth, lateral jaw and cephalostatic profile plates, photographs and casts of the jaws and teeth. Active orthodontic care may be necessary at different periods of the child's development, with periods of rest and observation in between.

Speech Therapy

One of the most serious sequelae resulting from the cleft palate is a speech defect. This contributes greatly to the problem of emotional instability and to interference with proper educational development. It is preferable to begin speech therapy during the preschool years rather than to wait until the child gets to school and must learn to overcome established incorrect habits. Instructing parents how to train the child during the early formative years proves helpful.

Otolaryngology

Children with cleft palates frequently suffer from colds and not infrequently the eustachian tubes are involved, which may affect hearing. Early treatment prevents later complications.

Prosthesis

In early infancy, before surgery of the palate may be indicated, the child may present a feeding problem which can be corrected by a prosthetic appliance. Before surgery has been instituted an obturator may also help to reduce speech problems. After surgery, if either the functional or anatomic result is not satisfactory, it may be necessary to construct an obturator to correct the defect. In these instances it may be advisable for the prosthodontist to confer with the speech therapist to achieve the maximum results.

Dental Care

Cleft palate patients, as a rule, show a high prevalence of dental caries. Operative and restorative dentistry present special problems in these cases.

Social Service

Socioeconomic problems are frequently encountered in the homes of these patients. The social service worker may assist in finding solutions to these problems, arrange for the transportation of the patient to the treatment center and stimulate interest and cooperation of parents and patient.

In New York state, through the state-aid-to-county program, fees have provided for diagnostic and consultation services by a team made up of the several specialties concerned. Financial assistance is also available through the state-aid-to-county funds for the correction services for those children whose parents cannot pay the high cost of these services. Similar programs are in operation in other parts of the country, and the physician faced with this kind of problem should confer with his local or state health agency concerning facilities that can be made available to the handicapped child.

These diagnostic and consultation services can lead to adequate closure of the cleft, proper occlusion of the teeth, good speech, preservation of hearing, normal breathing and a balanced emotional outlook. Thus the rehabilitated child may take his place in society with the same opportunities for a productive and satisfying life as other children. We do not know how to prevent the occurrence of these congenital defects, but the alert physician and dentist, with the help of their expert colleagues, can certainly prevent continuing disability by taking action soon after diagnosis is made.

DAVID B. AST, D.D.S.

REFERENCES

1. The Michigan Workshop on the evaluation of dental caries control technics. Journal of the American Dental Association, 36:3-22, January, 1948.
2. Orland, F. J., et al.: Use of germfree animal technic in the study of experimental dental caries. I. Basic observations on rats reared free of all microorganisms. Journal of Dental Research, 33:147-174, April, 1954.
3. Klein, Henry: The dental status and dental needs of young adult males, rejectable or acceptable for military service, according to selective service dental requirements. Public Health Reports, 56:1369-1387, July, 1941.
4. Rowntree, L. G.: Medical aspects of selective service. New York Journal of Dentistry, 12:100-106, March, 1942.
5. Fosdick, L. S.: Enzyme inhibitors as a factor in control of dental caries. Journal of the American Dental Association, 52:9-13, January, 1956.
6. Fosdick, L. S.: Reduction of incidence of dental caries. I. Immediate toothbrushing with neutral dentifrice. Journal of the American Dental Association, 40:133-143, February, 1950.
7. Report of Council on Dental Therapeutics. Journal of the American Dental Association, 69:115-118, 1964.
8. Knutson, J. W., and Scholz, G. C.: Effect of topically applied fluorides on dental caries experience. VII. Consolidated report of findings for four study groups, showing reduction in new decay by individual tooth and by tooth surface, and

frequency distribution of newly decayed teeth in treated and untreated mouth halves. Public Health Reports, *64*:1403-1410, 1949.

9. Gish, C. W., Muhler, J. C., and Howell, C. L.: A new approach to the topical application of fluorides for the reduction of dental caries in children: results at the end of five years. Journal of Dentistry for Children, *29*:65-71, 1962.

10. McKay, F. S.: Mottled enamel; a fundamental problem in dentistry. Dental Cosmos, *67*:847-860, September, 1925.

11. Churchill, H. V.: Occurrence of fluorides in some waters of the United States. Journal of the American Water Works Association, *23*:1399-1407, September, 1931.

12. Dean, H. T.: Domestic water and dental caries. Journal of the American Water Works Association, *35*:1161-1183, September, 1943.

13. Ast, D. B., and Fitzgerald, B.: Effectiveness of water fluoridation. Journal of the American Dental Association, *65*:581-587, November, 1962.

14. Russell, A. L., and Elvove, E.: Domestic water and dental caries. VII. A study of fluoride caries relationship in an adult population. Public Health Reports, *66*:1389-1401, October, 1951.

15. Englander, H. R., and Wallace, D. A.: Effects of naturally fluoridated water on dental caries in adults. Public Health Reports, *77*:887-893, October, 1962.

16. Schlesinger, E. R., et al.: Newburgh-Kingston caries fluorine study. XIII. Pediatric findings after ten years. Journal of the American Dental Association, *52*:296-306, March, 1956.

17. Leone, N. C., et al.: Medical aspects of excessive fluoride in a water supply. Public Health Reports, *69*:925-936, October, 1954.

18. Arnold, F. A., McClure, F. J., and White, C. L.: Sodium fluoride tablets for children. Dental Progress, *1*:8, 1960.

19. Lendrum, B. L., and Kobrin, C.: Prevention of recurrent attacks of rheumatic fever. Journal of the American Medical Association, *162*:13, September, 1956.

20. Sandler, H. C., et al.: Exfoliative cytology for detection of early mouth cancer. Oral Surgery, *13*:994, 1960.

21. Bushel, Arthur, and Ast, D. B.: A rehabilitation program for the dentally physically handicapped child. American Journal of Public Health, *43*:1156-1161, September, 1953.

22. Mosher, W. E.: Rehabilitation of the cleft palate child. Health News, New York State Department of Health, *33*:4-19, April, 1956.

23. Brudevold, F., et al.: A study of acidulated fluoride solutions—I. In vitro effects on enamel. Archives of Oral Biology, *8*:179-182, 1963.

24. Wellock, W. D., and Brudevold, F.: A study of acidulated fluoride solution—II. The caries inhibiting effect of single annual topical applications of an acidic fluoride and phosphate solution. A two year experience. Archives of Oral Biology, *8*:167-177, 1963.

PART TWO

PREVENTION OF PROGRESSION

27   Periodic Health Inventories

ROLE IN THE TOTAL DISEASE PROGRAM

There is general agreement that one of the most important steps a person can take to safeguard his health is to have periodic physical examinations by a competent physician. When such examinations are regularly and conscientiously done, it is frequently possible to detect disease or deviations from the norm early enough to institute corrective measures that will prevent, or at least postpone and minimize, subsequent disability.

Unfortunately, too few people make use of this important health safeguard. In some instances, this is the fault of the person himself. He may have the attitude that one goes to a physician only when sick; or he may have an "it can't happen to me" point of view. It may be that he is reluctant to spend the time and the money for such examinations. In other instances, periodic examinations may not be made because the physician does not appreciate the value of these examinations, or because he is so busy and so preoccupied with curative medicine that he has neither the time nor the inclination for them.

Nevertheless, a periodic health-maintenance examination should be provided for every patient by each physician who considers himself the family doctor. Otherwise, the physician is not fulfilling his obligation to his patient in preserving and maintaining health at the highest possible level.

At what age should a person begin having periodic health inventories? Most often these should begin at age 40. Prior to age 40, there are frequent opportunities for a physical examination—for life insurance, for induction into the Armed Forces, for employment and for many other reasons. Moreover, before the age of 40, most disease conditions produce symptoms sufficiently severe to persuade the patient to seek medical advice. In later life, many chronic conditions are insidious in onset and asymptomatic in nature, at least in the early stages.

325

How often should periodic health-maintenance examinations be done? Most physicians agree that once a year is the most desirable frequency.

Is it necessary to go to a hospital for such examinations? Most physicians feel that it is not, but in some centers that do many health-maintenance examinations it has been found convenient to hospitalize the person being examined.

OBJECTIVES OF PERIODIC EXAMINATIONS

To detect incipient chronic disease processes.
To discern correctable deviations from the norm.
To identify and advise on poor health habits and practices.
To establish base lines for future reference.
To increase the consciousness of the value of good health.
To provide reassurance regarding known disease.
To establish good physician-patient relationships.

METHODS OF ACHIEVING OBJECTIVES

Description

A proper health-maintenance examination consists of a medical history, a complete physical examination and the performance of certain laboratory tests and procedures, followed by a counseling session for the health guidance of the patient.

Many recommendations have been made as to what should constitute an adequate health inventory. In 1940 the American Medical Association published a *Manual for Physicians* on this important subject. At the National Conference on the Preventive Aspects of Chronic Disease held in 1951, the Committee on Early Detection and Screening in Private Practice recommended that office examinations for the detection of chronic disease include a history, a physical examination, tests for visual and auditory acuity, ocular tonometry to detect glaucoma, a hemoglobin test, blood sugar test, serologic test for syphilis, urinalysis and chest roentgenogram.

White and Geschickter have stated that 200 diseases are responsible for 98 per cent of all illnesses and that 18 common symptoms, 28 physical abnormalities and 6 laboratory procedures will suffice to detect these 200 most common diseases (Table 10).

There have been many suggestions for "streamlining" health-maintenance examinations. One of the most commonly used devices is a history form which the patient fills out himself. This is reviewed by the physician, who questions the patient in detail regarding any special point in the medical history. One of the most useful health questionnaires is the Cornell Medical Index,* which has undergone several revisions and has stood the test of time.

The use of health questionnaires can be justified because, among apparently well persons, the history is the least productive part of the health evaluation, accounting for only about 10 per cent of the information leading to the eventual diagnosis of newly discovered disease (whereas the physical

---

* Available from the Cornell University Medical College, Box 88, 1300 York Avenue, New York 21, New York. The index is available for men or for women, in packages of 50 copies at $3.00 per package.

Table 10. *Symptoms, Physical Abnormalities and Laboratory Tests to Detect 200 Common Diseases*

SYMPTOMS	PHYSICAL ABNORMALITIES	LABORATORY TESTS
	(*General*)	
Weakness: gain or loss of weight	Discolored or altered complexion	Urinalysis
Discharge of blood or pus	Cutaneous sores or blemishes	Hemoglobin
Fever, chills, or sweats	Stiffness, impaired motion or posture	Sedimentation rate
Uneasiness or worry	Hoarseness	Serologic test for syphilis
Inability to get along	Unsteadines, ataxia, tremors or twitches	Occult blood in feces
Headache	Vasomotor instability	Roentgenogram of chest
Fainting, coma or convulsions	(*Implemented examination*)	
Earache or tinnitus	Fever	
Sneezing, nasal drip or sore throat	Loss or gain of weight	
Cough or shortness of breath	Pulse or blood pressure variations	
Chest or precordial pain	Cardiac murmurs	
Dyspepsia or indigestion	Dental abnormalities	
Change of bowel habits	Inflamed or abnormal oral mucous membrane	
Cramps or abdominal soreness	Rales, rubs or squeaks in chest	
Menstrual disturbances	(*Palpation of neck, abdomen and limbs*)	
Frequency or nocturia	Masses or tenderness	
Lameness or backache	Edema	
Itching or rash	Vascular abnormalities	
	(*Pelvic and rectal examination*)	
	Inflamed or abnormal mucous membrane	
	Masses or tenderness	
	Displaced or relaxed structures	
	(*Neurological examinations*)	
	Hyperreflexia or hyporeflexia	
	Paralysis	
	Defective vision	
	Defective hearing	
	(*Psychiatric examination*)	
	Retarded, accelerated or bizarre animation	
	Abnormal emotional response	
	Fixed ideas	
	Suspiciousness or spread of meaning	
	Forgetfulness or disorientation	

examination discloses approximately 60 per cent, and laboratory tests approximately 30 per cent of such diagnoses).

Data such as these also enhance the importance of the physical examination itself, if the maximum yield is to be obtained from health-maintenance examinations. The tendency for physicians to omit such important examinations as ocular fundoscopy or palpation of the arterial pulses in the leg is, therefore, greatly to be decried.

Considerable time can be saved if the physician delegates the laboratory work and certain simple parts of the physical examination (e.g., tests for visual and auditory acuity) to a competent office nurse or technical assistant.

Probably the most difficult problem the physician faces in making periodic health-maintenance examinations is deciding which laboratory tests and procedures to include. This decision should be based largely on the yield that is to be expected from each procedure. Obviously, the yield will vary with the patient's age, sex, symptoms and many other factors. Nevertheless, there are some procedures that have a high yield regardless of these factors. These productive procedures are shown in Table 11.

Table 11. *Laboratory Tests and Procedures with High Yield in Periodic Health-Maintenance Examinations*[5]

PROCEDURE	NUMBER OF TESTS MADE	PERCENTAGE POSITIVE OR ABNORMAL
Electrocardiogram	15,619	11.91%
Proctosigmoidoscopy	26,186	8.23%
Hemoglobin	241,474	6.74%
Blood sugar	507,383	4.11%
Chest roentgenogram	18,839,473	2.88%
Urine sugar	396,800	2.56%
Urine albumin	119,756	2.23%
Cytology of cervix	138,233	0.49%

The yield from the tests shown in Table 11 is that from apparently healthy persons on whom the tests were done routinely. In the presence of suspicious symptoms, these and other tests that may be done on indication will give positive results in a much higher proportion of those tested.

Other factors that enter into the decision as to what procedures should be carried out include the sensitivity and specificity of the test, its cost, and the significance of the condition for which the procedure tests. Many procedures need be carried out only once, as for example, the determination of the blood grouping; others, because of the expense and the relatively low yield, should be done only when there is some indication from the history or physical examination, such as an x-ray of the upper gastrointestinal tract or gallbladder.

One of the important parts of the periodic health-maintenance examination, and the part most frequently neglected, is the physician's summation of the results of his examination and the opportunity it provides for health education. During this session the patient should receive specific instructions regarding what he should do about any abnormalities that have been found. He should be given general advice about good health habits, including diet, rest and exercise, posture, the use of medications available without prescription, smoking, drinking and the basic tenets of good mental hygiene.

If the health counseling is conscientiously carried out, the majority of patients will follow through on specific advice they receive. A few, perhaps 10 to 15 per cent, will not accept the advice they receive and will ultimately suffer as a result.

Validity and Reliability

The validity and reliability of periodic health inventories will be directly proportionate to the skill of the examining physician and the thoroughness of the examinations that are made.

Cost

The cost of a complete health-maintenance examination will depend upon a number of factors, but most of all upon the number and type of laboratory studies that are made and whether or not the patient is hospitalized for the examination. In general, a complete check-up, outside the hospital, will cost the patient approximately $50 to $150. For many people, this is a sizable amount of money, but the patient should note that, if budgeted, the cost of an annual health-maintenance examination actually amounts to $1 to $3 per week.

Results Anticipated

For the person actively interested in protecting his health, there is no better way than to have periodic health-maintenance examinations. The results, of course, will vary with the professional competence of the examining physician and the thoroughness of the examination, but as a case-finding device, the health inventory is more effective than any short-cut, such as multiple screening.

The results in terms of yield of significant abnormalities are appreciably higher. The experience of those who specialize in making health-maintenance examinations has been that at least one significant abnormality requiring correction can be found in approximately 80 to 90 per cent of adults examined over the age of 40. At the Greenbrier Clinic,[3] for example, among a group of 2178 business executives, 2181 significant abnormalities were found, a significant abnormality being defined as one producing symptoms or one with a bearing on the person's health now or in the future. The most frequent diagnoses were: obesity (29.1 per cent), hypertensive cardiovascular disease (13.9 per cent), rectosigmoidal polyps (7.7 per cent), anemia (6.9 per cent), cholelithiasis (4.6 per cent) and diabetes mellitus (2.4 per cent).

APPLICATION IN THE COMMUNITY

Physicians

Only a physician can make health-maintenance examinations and interpret the results to the patient. The need is to persuade busy practitioners of medicine that they have an obligation to their apparently well patients to give these periodic examinations. Such examinations are time consuming and are of lesser interest to the physician than curative medicine. Nevertheless, health-maintenance examinations are vital to preventive medical practice. The patient has a right to demand them and the physician has an obligation to do them thoroughly.

Health Departments

Periodic health-maintenance examinations are primarily the responsibility of the private practitioners of medicine. In a few instances, health departments have assumed the cost of physical examinations for selected population groups, e.g., Old Age Assistance recipients and migratory laborers. No doubt the greater role for health departments lies in the operation of tumor clinics and cancer detection centers, where the examination given may be sufficiently thorough as to justify use of the term health-maintenance examination. Health departments also can, through health education, promote public recognition that periodic health examinations are desirable.

Industry

Private industry is becoming more aware of the value of periodic health inventories, especially for executive personnel. Most industries now provide pre-employment examinations for all their workers, and more and more companies are making provision for periodic health-maintenance examinations at company expense.

FRANK W. REYNOLDS, M.D.

REFERENCES

1. Barsky, P. N., and Sagen, O. K.: Motivation toward health examinations. American Journal of Public Health, 49:514, April, 1959.
2. Clark, T. W., Schor, S. S., Elsom, K. O., Hubbard, J. P., and Elsom, K. A.: The periodic health examination: Evaluation of routine tests and procedures. Annals of Internal Medicine, 54:1209, June, 1961.
3. Elsom, K. A., and Elsom, K. O.: The periodic health examination—A study of the private practitioner's attitudes. Archives of Environmental Health, 3:217, August, 1961.
4. Franco, S. C., Gerl, H. J., and Murphy, G. T.: Periodic health examinations: A long term study. 1949-59. Journal of Occupational Medicine, 3:13, January, 1961.
5. Roberts, N. J.: The value and limitations of periodic health examinations. Journal of Chronic Diseases, 9:95, February, 1959.
6. Siegel, G. S.: Periodic health examinations: Abstracts from the literature. Public Health Service Publication No. 1010, 1963.
7. Bolt, R. J., Tupper, C. J., and Mallery, O. T.: An appraisal of periodic health examinations. Archives of Industrial Health, 12:420, October, 1955.
8. Brodman, K., Erdmann, A. J., Jr., Lorge I., and Wolff, H. G.: The Cornell Medical Index: An adjunct to medical interview. Journal of the American Medical Association, 140:530, June 11, 1949.
9. Fremont-Smith, M.: Periodic examination of supposedly well persons. New England Journal of Medicine, 248:170, January 29, 1953.
10. Franco, S. C.: Periodic health examination of executives. Industrial Medicine, 19:213, May, 1950.
11. Getting, V. A., and Lombard, H. L.: The mass screening or health protection program. New England Journal of Medicine, 247:460, 1952.
12. Lenson, N.: Analysis of a series of periodic physical examinations. New England Journal of Medicine, 248:943, March 28, 1953.
13. McCombs, R. P., and Finn, J. J., Jr.: Group health surveys in a diagnostic clinic. New England Journal of Medicine, 248:165, January 29, 1953.
14. Morhouse, E. J., Baker J. P., Ballou, H. C., and Crumpacker, E. L.: Periodic health examinations. Annals of Internal Medicine, 46:744, April, 1957.
15. Periodic Health Examinations: A Manual for Physicians. 1940. American Medical Association.
16. Saunders, G. M.: Executive health programs. Archives of Industrial Hygiene, 9:133, February, 1954.
17. Shillito, F. H.: Periodic health examinations. Annals of Internal Medicine, 39:7, July, 1953.
18. Steele, H. H., and Brown, C. H.: Analysis of 1500 "routine" proctosigmoidoscopic examinations. Gastroenterology, 12:419, March, 1949.
19. Miller, C. J., Emerson, D., and L'Esperance, E. S.: The value of proctoscopy as a routine examination in preventing death from cancer of the large bowel. New York State Journal of Medicine, 50:2023, September 1, 1950.

28 Cancer Detection and Screening

DEFINITIONS

The term "detection of disease" refers to the diagnosis of preclinical disease. The chief purpose of detection is identification of disease at an early stage of pathogenesis. Hence, theoretically, detection is best carried out among a population which is clinically well or at least free from symptoms which would ordinarily motivate the seeking of medical care. However, in practice some of the most extensive and successful detection procedures have been carried out among hospital admissions, as, for example, the routine examination of blood serum for evidence of syphilis and the photofluorographic examination of the chest for evidence of tuberculosis.

The terms "detection" and "screening" are sometimes used interchangeably, but I prefer to make a distinction between them in this discussion. Screening refers to procedures which can be applied rapidly to large numbers of persons, preferably by nonmedical personnel, and which can distinguish, within practicable limits of accuracy, between persons with a high probability that a given disease is present and those with a low probability. The purpose of screening is to confine the need for definitive diagnostic procedures to as small a group as possible. Hence, ideally, detection is best preceded by screening, which must be followed by the definitive diagnostic portion of the detection procedure. If a suitable screening method is not available, detection can still be carried out, though usually not on a mass scale.

Although the chief purpose of cancer detection is early diagnosis, i.e., diagnosis at an early pathologic stage, these two terms also are not synonymous. The term "early diagnosis" may refer either to diagnosis early in time, after the onset of symptoms, or early in pathogenesis, which, though highly associated with the former, is not necessarily the same and may occur at any

331

period. Early diagnosis is still possible after the onset of symptoms referable to the disease (after the detectable period). On the other hand, not all detected presymptomatic disease is necessarily early pathologically.

THEORETIC BASIS OF CANCER DETECTION

The value of cancer detection is postulated on two hypotheses: that the development of malignant neoplasia is a chronic process, and that, in general, the effectiveness of therapy decreases as the pathogenetic process develops.

Observations of experimental carcinogenesis in animals, as well as the natural history of occupationally induced cancer in man, support the view that the development of cancer is a chronic process extending for many years before the clinical signs are evident.[1] In experimental carcinogenesis at least two major phases are recognized: an *initiating* phase, which requires a specific carcinogen and is not considered reversible; and a *promoting* phase which may be induced by agents usually not capable of initiation and is considered reversible. Since the initiating phase is not accompanied by morphologic changes now identifiable, it cannot be detected directly. Its presence can only be inferred from information that there has been exposure to a known carcinogenic agent. Apparently, most initiating and promoting agents "have some degree of the other action as well, but the effect of their successive application is very much more than additive."[2]

The promoting phase is accompanied by hyperplasia. Although histologic features distinguishing this from noncarcinogenic hyperplasia have been described, these have not yet found clinical application in cancer detection.

At present, the objectives of cancer detection are to discover three types of lesions: precancerous, carcinoma in situ and cancer localized to the tissue of origin. There is much uncertainty regarding the definition, significance and prognosis of the first two of these lesions. The consensus is that, other things being equal, the adequate treatment of all three types of lesions prolongs life and prevents or postpones the development of metastatic, fatal cancer.

CANCER DETECTION CLINICS

A cancer detection clinic is an outpatient facility to discover asymptomatic cancer or precancerous lesions in presumably well persons by physical examination and various auxiliary examinations.

The first general cancer detection clinic was organized in 1937 at the New York Infirmary by Dr. Elise L'Esperance. A clinic for the detection of breast and pelvic cancer in women was established the following year in Philadelphia by Dr. Catherine MacFarlane.

By 1949 it was estimated there were over 250 detection clinics operating in the United States, examining about 3000 persons per week. However, it soon became evident that it was impracticable to aim, by this method, at examining more than a small proportion of the adult population. The role of the cancer detection clinic was then conceived as primarily that of a demonstration and training unit, rather than a means of providing cancer detection examinations to a significant portion of the adult population.

In 1957 it was estimated[3] there were about 200 detection centers in the

United States. Analysis of the experience of 21 of these clinics by E. Day[4] revealed wide variations in their scope and procedures. The number of sessions per week ranged from 1 to 10; persons examined per session ranged from 3 to 50. These centers examined from 220 to 22,500 persons per year. Of a total of 82,018 examinations, 46,042 were first examinations and 70.5 per cent of the examinees were women.

Extent of Examination

In addition to a general physical examination, all the clinics provided a blood hemoglobin determination, urinalysis and vaginal cytologic smear examination. Most clinics also included a chest roentgenogram, proctosigmoidoscopy and a white blood cell and differential count. These procedures should detect most lesions of the skin, blood, lymphatic system, lung, rectosigmoid, kidney, bladder and uterus.

Detailed procedures and methods for cancer detection are described in the excellent monograph by O'Donnell, Day and Venet.[5]

FINDINGS OF CANCER DETECTION CLINIC

Cancer

The number and types of malignant tumors discovered by detection clinic examinations are influenced not only by the thoroughness and competence of the examinations but also by various characteristics of the examined population, such as age, sex and the proportion of persons with symptoms which may be due to cancer. The rate of positive findings should be greater also for first examination than for re-examinations, since the former approximates the prevalence* of cancer, and the latter its incidence.

Data reported by Day et al. (Table 12) indicate a range of cancers detected from 3.3 to 22.2 per 1000 examinations, with no consistent relation between the sex and age distribution of the examinees and the magnitude of the rate. This suggests that the variations may be due chiefly to the extent of examination and the clinical characteristics of the examined population. The experience of the University of Minnesota Center (Table 13) is in accord with the expected finding of a greater rate of detected cancer for first examinations than in subsequent examinations of the same individuals.

At the Strang Memorial Clinic (1954-1956) the number of cancers detected at first examination were 7.8 per 1000 among females and 6.8 per 1000 among males; at subsequent annual visits the rates averaged 4.9 per 1000 for females and 4.0 per 1000 for males.[6]

Precancerous Lesions

A precancerous lesion may be defined operationally as one which indicates there is an increased (above normal) risk of cancer developing in the same tissue at some future time. However, there is some uncertainty both as to the definition and as to what lesions should be considered precancerous. In data from nine clinics reported by Day,[4] the percentage of "precancerous"

---

* Prevalence of disease may be defined as the ratio of *all* cases to the population at a given time. Incidence is the ratio of *new* cases to the population over a period of time, usually one year.

Table 12.   *Cancers Reported by 9 Detection Centers[4]*

| | | | CANCERS | | EXAMINEES | |
| | | | | RATE PER 1000 | PER CENT AGE 50 | PER CENT |
YEAR	CLINIC	NUMBER EXAMINED	NUMBER	EXAMINED	AND OVER	FEMALES
1955	Ca. Prev. Soc., Los Angeles	15,955	354	22.2	43	78
1956	Ca. Prev. Soc., Chicago	7187	104	14.5	n.d.*	74
1948-57	Univ. of Minn.	8229	104†	12.6	90	52
1955-56	Amer. Ca. Soc., Conn.	2439	25	10.3	25	75
1947-53	N.Y.C. Dept. of Health[7]	5687	58	10.2	19‡	70
1955-56	E. J. Meyer Mem. Hosp., Buffalo	1503	10	6.7	33	66
1954	Strang Clinic, Mem. Ctr., N.Y.C.	21,871	119	5.4	29	67
1956	Strang Clinic, N.Y. Infirmary, N.Y.C.	8000	32	4.0	40	98
1956	Amer. Ca. Soc., Rhode Island	2432	8	3.3	27	79

* No data.
† Initial examinations only.
‡ Age 55 and over.

Table 13.   *Cancers Detected at First and Re-examinations, University of Minnesota[8] 1948-1957*

| | | CANCER DETECTED | |
	NUMBER OF EXAMINATIONS	NUMBER	RATE PER 1000
First examination	8229	104	12.6
Re-examinations (second or more)	16,929	121	7.1

lesions reported varied from 1.6 to 64.7. In the University of Minnesota experience, a total of 4279 precancerous lesions were found among 8229 first examinations and 16,929 re-examinations, over a six and one-half year period. These were classified as follows:[8]

	NO.	PER CENT	RATE PER 1000 EXAMINATIONS
Polyps of rectum and colon	2386	55.8	94.8
Leukoplakia	589	13.7	23.4
Senile keratoses	573	13.4	22.8
Pigmented nevi, irritated	394	9.2	15.7
Thyroid adenomas	240	5.6	9.5
Kraurosis vulvae	57	1.3	2.3
Gastric polyps	39	0.9	1.6
Vocal cord polyps	1	—	—
Total	4279	99.9	168.1

Most noteworthy is the finding of rectal or colonic polyps in almost 10 per cent of the examinations. Rosenthal and Oppenheim reported finding polyps of the rectum and the colon in 7.6 per cent of men and 6.5 per cent of women on initial examination at three cancer prevention-detection centers in New York City.[7] The Minnesota clinic reported finding precancerous skin lesions in 6 per cent and thyroid adenomas in almost 1 per cent of examinations. The finding of precancerous conditions in almost 17 per cent of examinations indicates that from this standpoint alone the detection examination procedure is worthwhile. However, it must be remembered that these findings are the result of extensive examination procedures.

EVALUATION OF CANCER DETECTION

The experience of the University of Minnesota Detection Center group indicates that of a total of 225 cancers discovered by extensive examination procedures, 137, or 60 per cent, were discovered by a history, physical examination (including breast examination, pelvic examination and vaginal smear cytology), proctoscopy and examination of the blood for hemoglobin, cell count and morphology. An even larger proportion of precancerous lesions were discovered by these procedures. An examination of this scope would make cancer detection seem practicable for administration by individual physicians in their own offices, with provision for outside laboratory examination of the vaginal smear and, possibly, the blood examination.

Although such an examination is time consuming, one such examination a week by 100,000 physicians would provide over 5 million examinations each year. To a considerable extent, then, cancer detection by private physicians would seem feasible and worthwhile. For maximum usefulness, it should be associated with outside laboratory procedures. The practical limiting factor in cancer detection is the fact that it must be carried out by a physician.

CANCER SCREENING

Two essential features of a practical cancer screening method are that it be applicable by nonmedical personnel and that it have high validity, particularly when positive. These features are necessary so that the screening procedure can be applied to large numbers of people with a minimum use of physicians' time.

The chief types of cancer screening tests which have been proposed or tried thus far are various general tests applied to blood serum or blood cells, examination of exfoliated epithelial cells (cytology) and roentgenograms.

Blood Serum Tests

A number of such tests have been proposed but none has been considered sufficiently accurate for practical use. Among those described in recent years are the Penn-Hall, Zuccala, Fuchs, Parfentjer (plasma protein pattern), serum lactic dehydrogenase, chromate serum precipitation, hexokinase activity and lactic acid production (glycolysis) tests, the carotene effect on hemolysates of washed erythrocytes, urine fluorescence and infrared spectroscopy of serum albumin. All these tests have low reliability (reproducibility) and low validity, being characterized by high percentages of false positive and false negative reactions.[9-20]

Since the report by Fishman and Lerner[21] that the L-tartrate sensitive portion of total serum acid phosphatase was derived from the prostate (prostatic acid phosphatase), it appeared likely that tests for increase in this form of acid phosphatase might prove useful in screening for prostatic carcinoma before metastasis has occurred. Several encouraging studies have been published.[22-24] The value of this procedure has not, however, been established.[5]

Examination of Exfoliated Cancer Cells (Cytology)

Cytologic screening for cancer depends on the fact that the surfaces of malignant tumors or tissues bearing carcinoma in situ are continually desquamating epithelial cells and that these malignant cells can be identified with a high degree of accuracy by suitably trained pathologists and technicians. That exfoliated cancer cells could be recognized microscopically has long been known in pathology, but the practicability of this method, first proposed by Papanicolaou in 1928,[25] was firmly established for uterine cancer by Papanicolaou and Traut in 1943.[26] The practicability of the method as a diagnostic aid and potential screening method has been explored by cytologic examination of vaginal, cervical and endometrial aspirates or scrapings, sputum, gastric contents, colon washings, urine, breast secretions, prostate secretions, pleural and peritoneal transudates, nose and throat secretions, accessory nasal sinus washings, lymph node smears and skin smears.

Cytologic screening proceeds in the following steps: (a) obtaining the specimen, (b) staining the specimen, (c) microscopic examination to eliminate definite negatives and (d) microscopic examination of the remainder for definite classification of the specimen as positive, doubtful or negative. The fact that steps b and c can be performed by trained technicians makes this a screening procedure, since only d requires the services of a physician (pathologist). Validation of a positive cytologic diagnosis may be by biopsy, surgery, roentgenogram and the course of disease. Validation of negatives in screening is usually not attempted; however, a false negative would be revealed by subsequent clinical course of the disease.

As a mass screening procedure, only the vaginal smear has developed sufficiently for wide-scale testing. It has been used routinely or in patients presenting gynecologic symptoms by physicians in their office practice, by outpatient clinics and by hospitals as a screening procedure for female inpatients. Preliminary results of the most extensive single mass screening experience for uterine cancer, begun in 1952 by the Public Health Service in Memphis-Shelby County, Tennessee, are given in Table 14, as reported by Dunn.[27] They show a prevalence at first screening of cervical cancer (invasive and in situ) of 5.9 per 1000 white women and 8.8 per 1000 Negro women. The rates on subsequent screening are considerably lower. It should be noted that over 60 per cent of these women were under 40 years of age and that considerably higher rates were found among women aged 40 years and older.

Even with well-trained technicians available, the widespread use of vaginal cytology for screening is limited by the number of slides which a technician can examine accurately per day. This has been estimated as being from 25 to 35. To overcome this bottleneck, a microfluorometric

Table 14. *Results of Repeated Vaginal Cytology Screening*[27]

A. White Women

| | NUMBER SCREENED | CERVICAL CANCERS | | | | |
| | | NUMBER OF CASES | | RATE PER 1000 | | |
		INVASIVE	IN SITU	INVASIVE	IN SITU	TOTAL
First screening	53,585	120	198	2.2	3.7	5.9
Second screening*	15,929	4	6	0.3	0.4	0.6
Third screening*	4185	2	4	0.5	1.0	1.4

B. Negro Women

| | NUMBER SCREENED | CERVICAL CANCERS | | | | |
| | | NUMBER OF CASES | | RATE PER 1000 | | |
		INVASIVE	IN SITU	INVASIVE	IN SITU	TOTAL
First screening	29,372	106	152	3.6	5.2	8.8
Second screening*	10,076	8	29	0.8	2.9	3.7
Third screening*	2517	3	6	1.2	2.4	3.6

* Persons found "negative" in previous screening.

scanner is being developed. This instrument, named the cytoanalyzer, would, if perfected, automatically detect presumptive cancer cells by identifying cells with abnormal configuration and pigmentation characteristic of malignancy. In spite of continued experimentation, the cytoanalyzer has not yet reached practicability. The chief problem is the large number of false positives due to superimposition of cells. Since each positive smear requires examination by a pathologist, a large number of false positives makes the screening procedure impracticable. Work on the cytoanalyzer is continuing, chiefly in the preparation of suitable monolayer smears so as to minimize the number of false positive results.

Another instrument, the cytoviewer, is a scanning microscope that automatically throws a sharp image of successive fields of a slide on a screen, permitting more rapid examination of slides. This instrument has now been modified (Leitz & Co., New York City) so that the mirror system is replaced by closed-circuit television which does not require a special light source and facilitates cytometric studies. Although not as yet widely employed because of its high cost, the cytoviewer is being used as a research instrument in cytological laboratories in this country.[28, 40]

Roentgen Examination

Roentgen Screening for Lung Cancer. Microfilm chest roentgenograms taken primarily for tuberculosis case finding can also be utilized as a screening procedure for lung tumors, as well as for cardiovascular disease. In Los Angeles County, experience with 1,725,766 microfilm chest roentgenograms taken over a 6-year period showed a positive lung neoplasm screening rate of 203 per 100,000 persons,[29] or 3500 neoplasm suspects. Follow-up of this group resulted in the discovery of 213 cases of bronchogenic cancer, 79 cases of benign chest tumors and 47 chest neoplasms of extrapulmonary origin (Table 15)—a total chest neoplasm rate of 20 per 100,000, or about one-tenth of the positive screening rate. Of the 213 patients with bronchogenic cancer, 100 could not be operated upon. Of the 113 treated surgically, 70 received

Table 15. *Chest Neoplasms: Findings in 1,725,766 Chest Roentgenograms, Los Angeles County*[29]

CHEST NEOPLASMS		NUMBER
Bronchogenic cancers		213
Benign chest tumors		79
Neurofibromas	25	
Bone tumors	15	
Lipomas	11	
Hamartomas	5	
Bronchogenic cysts	5	
Thymomas	4	
Others	14	
Extrapulmonary malignant chest neoplasms		47
Lymphosarcoma (mediastinum)	20	
Hodgkin's disease (mediastinum)	10	
Other mediastinal tumors	9	
Esophageal carcinomas	5	
Others	3	
Total		339

surgery potentially curative (20 lobectomies and 50 pneumonectomies). The per cent of patients operated on is similar to that of many clinical series; the per cent of operated cases receiving curative resection is somewhat greater. Of the 70 patients receiving "curative" surgery, 24 (34 per cent) were alive and free from cancer 3 years later; 5 of the other 143 patients were alive with cancer. This represents an over-all 3-year cure rate of 11 per cent, a survival rate of 14 per cent.

For comparison, two clinical series report over-all 5-year survival rates of 10 per cent[30] and 8 per cent.[31]

There has not as yet been reported a trial of lung cancer screening by chest roentgenogram utilizing the known higher incidence in males at older ages and in cigarette smokers, in whom the incidence of lung cancer is approximately 10 times that in nonsmokers.[32] Screening and detection directed toward these groups would probably yield a much greater positive detection rate and possibly a greater 5-year survival rate.

Roentgen Screening for Gastric Cancer. In 1949 Morgan and his associates,[33] utilizing a high speed Schmidt camera, reported that photofluorograms of the stomach, comparable in detail to conventional roentgenograms, could be obtained by a suitably trained technician without excessive radiation exposure of the patient and sufficiently rapid for practical outpatient screening. In the procedure, six films were taken (one anteroposterior, one posteroanterior and four right anterior oblique exposures). Although taken by a technician, the films were read by a roentgenologist.

From 1948 to 1952 Morgan and his staff routinely performed this examination on all new dispensary patients aged 40 years or over at Johns Hopkins Hospital. Out of a total of over 10,000 such examinations, there were 33 patients with minimal or no gastric symptoms in whom roentgen changes interpreted as indicating gastric cancer were found.[34] However, only 12 of these submitted to surgery, and among these there were found

5 patients with gastric carcinomas, 2 with gastric polyps, 1 with leiomyoma, 1 with neurofibroma and 2 patients with no demonstrable pathologic lesion. In these last 2 patients, the roentgen findings were attributed to extensive adhesions or hypertrophied rugal folds. At the time of reporting, one of the approximately 10,000 patients with normal photofluorograms had returned to the hospital with a gastric cancer.

A serious limiting factor in the use of photofluorography for gastric cancer screening is the necessity for having a physician read the films. This means, in the experience reported by Morgan, that about 2400 films had to be read to find one suspected case of gastric cancer. Morgan believes this feature makes the method impractical as a mass screening procedure. The possibility of training technicians to screen out definite negatives so as to reduce greatly the number of films which must be viewed by the roentgenologist has not as yet been considered feasible.

MORTON L. LEVIN, M.D.

REFERENCES

1. Foulds, Leslie: The natural history of cancer. Journal of Chronic Diseases, 8:2, July, 1958.
2. Salaman, M. H.: Co-carcinogenesis in causation of cancer. British Medical Bulletin, 14:116, May, 1958.
3. American Cancer Society. Annual Report. 1956.
4. Day, Emerson: A Report on Cancer Detection in the United States, 1937-1957. Prepared for the Subcommittee on Cancer Detection of the International Union Against Cancer. July, 1957. (Mimeographed.)
5. O'Donnell, Walter E., Day, Emerson, and Venet, Louis: Early Detection and Diagnosis of Cancer. St. Louis, The C. V. Mosby Co., 1962.
6. Day, Emerson: Cancer screening and detection: medical aspects. Journal of Chronic Diseases, 16:397, May, 1963.
7. Rosenthal, T., and Oppenheim, A.: Evaluation of cancer prevention-detection centers. Journal of the American Medical Association, 155:538, June 5, 1954.
8. Data from Sullivan, W. A., Jr., and Lunseth, J. B.: The cancer detection center: nine-year report. University of Minnesota Medical Bulletin, 28:439, June 1, 1957.
9. Maver, M. E.: Review of sero-diagnostic tests for cancer. Journal of the National Cancer Institute, 4:571, June, 1944.
10. Dunn, J. E., Jr., and Greenhouse, S. W.: Cancer Diagnostic Tests. Principles and Criteria for Development and Evaluation. Public Health Service Publication No. 9. Washington, D.C., U. S. Government Printing Office, 1950.
11. Fong, Conrad T. O., Lippincott, Stuart W., and Eriksen, Nils: Infrared spectroscopy of crystalline albumin in human neoplasm. Journal of the National Cancer Institute, 18:271, February, 1957.
12. Peacock, Andrew C., and Williams, George Z.: A study of the Penn-Hall serofloccu-lation reaction for cancer. Journal of the National Cancer Institute, 18:277, February, 1957.
13. Peacock, Andrew C., and Highsmith, Eleanor M.: On the Fuchs cancer test: species-specific proteolysis of fibrin by serum. Journal of the National Cancer Institute, 18:285, February, 1957.
14. Hill, J. H., and Greenhouse, S. W.: Analysis of plasma proteins by turbidimetry: an unsuccessful aid in cancer diagnosis. Journal of the National Cancer Institute, 18:291, February, 1957.
15. Hill, J. H.: An evaluation of the Zuccala cancer tests. Journal of the National Cancer Institute, 18:301, February, 1957.
16. Hill, J. H.: Serum lactic dehydrogenase in cancer patients. Journal of the National Cancer Institute, 18:307, February, 1957.
17. Hill, J. H.: An evaluation of the chromate-serum precipitation reaction in the diag-

nosis of cancer. Journal of the National Cancer Institute, 18:315, February, 1957.

18. Hill, J. H.: The effect of carotene on the lactic acid production and hexokinase activity of hemolysates from cancerous and noncancerous persons. Journal of the National Cancer Institute, 18:323, February, 1957.

19. Hill, J. H.: Urine fluorescence in cancer diagnosis. Journal of the National Cancer Institute, 18:335, February, 1957.

20. Hall, G. C., Dowdy, A. H., Penn, H. S., and Bellamy, A. W.: The role of bile acid derivatives in the sero-flocculation reaction. II, Clinical evaluation. Journal of the National Cancer Institute, 16:237, August, 1955.

21. Fishman, W. H., and Lerner, F.: Method for estimating serum acid phosphatase of prostatic origin. Journal of Biological Chemistry, 200:89, 1953.

22. Fishman, W. H., Bonner, C. D., and Homburger, F.: Serum "prostatic" acid phosphatase and cancer of the prostate. New England Journal of Medicine, 255:925, 1956.

23. Baurys, W., and Wentzell, R. D.: Prostatic serum acid phosphatase as an aid in the diagnosis of prostatic carcinoma. Preliminary report. Guthrie Clinic Bulletin, 26:72, 1956.

24. Day, E., Ying, Sai Hou, Schwartz, M. K., Whitmore, W. F., Jr., and Bodansky, O.: Serum prostatic acid phosphatase levels in the male patients of a cancer prevention clinic. Cancer, 9:222, March-April, 1956.

25. Papanicolaou, G. N.: New Cancer Diagnosis. Proceedings of the Third Race Betterment Conference, 1928, p. 528.

26. Papanicolaou, G. N., and Traut, H.: Diagnosis of Uterine Cancer by the Vaginal Smear. New York, The Commonwealth Fund, 1943.

27. Data rearranged from Dunn, J. E., Jr.: Preliminary findings of Memphis-Shelby County uterine cancer study and their interpretation. American Journal of Public Health, 48:861, July, 1958.

28. Nieburgs, H. E.: The cytoviewer: a new automatic scanning microscope. Annals of the New York Academy of Sciences, 63:1321, March 30, 1956.

29. Guiss, L. W.: Mass roentgenographic screening as a lung cancer control measure. Cancer, 8:219, March-April, 1955.

30. Gibbon, J. H., Jr., Templeton, J. Y., III, and Nealen, N. F.: Factors which influence the long term survival patients with cancer of the lung. Annals of Surgery, 145:637, May, 1957.

31. Ochsner, A., Ray, C. J., and Acree, P. W.: Cancer of the lung. American Review of Tuberculosis, 70:763, November, 1954.

32. Dorn, H. F.: Tobacco Consumption and Mortality from Cancer and Other Diseases. Presented at the Seventh International Cancer Congress, London, July 8, 1958.

33. Roach, J. F., Sloan, R. D., and Morgan, R. H.: Detection of gastric carcinoma by photofluorographic methods. American Journal of Roentgenology, 61:183, 188, 1949.

34. Morgan, R. H.: The detection of gastric carcinoma by photofluorography. Journal of Chronic Diseases, 2:461, October, 1955.

35. Levin, Morton L.: Screening for asymptomatic disease. Journal of Chronic Diseases, 2:367-374, October, 1955.

36. Dunn, J. E., Jr.: Screening for cancer. Journal of Chronic Diseases, 2:450, October, 1955.

37. Graham, Ruth M.: Diagnosis of cancer of internal organs by Papanicolaou technic. In Advances in Internal Medicine. Vol. VI. Chicago, Year Book Publishers, 1954.

38. Urbach, F., Burke, E. M., and Traenkle, H. L.: Cytodiagnosis of cutaneous malignancy. New York State Journal of Medicine, 56:3481, November 15, 1956.

39. Breslow, L.: Multiphasic screening in California. Journal of Chronic Diseases, 2:375, October, 1955.

40. Nieburgs, H. E.: Modern cancer cell screening technique. International Record of Medicine, 170:103, 1957.

29 Screening Methods for Heart Disease

Diseases of the heart and blood vessels killed only 2 out of 10 Americans in 1900; over half a century later, the most recent figures[1] (1960) show that over 5 out of 10 persons die from these causes. The cardiovascular renal deaths in 1960 were broken down by categories as follows: arteriosclerotic heart disease, including coronary artery disease, 52.8 per cent; cerebral vascular lesions, 20.7 per cent; hypertension, 8.4 per cent; rheumatic fever and rheumatic heart disease, 2.0 per cent; all others, 16.1 per cent. Nearly one-third of the total cardiovascular renal deaths were coronary artery disease; from all indications the incidence of this type of heart disease appears to be rising steadily. The underlying pathologic finding in the majority of cardiovascular renal deaths is atherosclerosis, which seems to be ubiquitous from early life onward. It has been estimated that 40 per cent of the men over 40 years of age in the United States have significant atherosclerosis in their coronary arteries.

It might be assumed, as Rutstein[2] points out, that a health inventory with a complete history and physical examination, performed at annual or other suitable intervals, would discover heart disease at an early stage and assure maximum benefits of prevention and therapy. This sounds ideal but is impractical for many reasons, such as a lack of physicians, expense or unwillingness of lay people to have the examination done. If we had a simple and inexpensive screening test for the many types of heart disease our task would be much easier. Unfortunately, there are no easily applied mass survey techniques to supplement the physician's day-by-day case-finding activities among the patients, both sick and healthy, who come to him.[3-5]

According to the definition of the Committee on Early Detection and Screening of the National Conference on Chronic Diseases,[6] a screening test must be (1) *reliable*, so that reproducible results can be obtained by ordinary technicians or persons trained to perform and interpret the tests, and (2) *valid*, to separate diseased persons from normal ones in a high

341

proportion of the tests, as confirmed by diagnostic studies following the screening tests. Furthermore, those persons falsely labeled diseased or normal by the test should be minimal in relation to the total number of persons examined.

When a screening test is found to be satisfactory as to reliability and validity by diagnostic work-up, its effectiveness as a screening device needs to be evaluated further by yield, cost and acceptance. The cost includes follow-up, diagnostic study and referral of persons for treatment when indicated. Obviously, there is no point in screening a population group unless one plans to follow-up the persons suspected of having disease.

One of the communitywide surveys for heart disease that meets the above requirements is the mass roentgen survey of the chest, using 70 mm. or 4 × 5 inch photofluorographic film or rapid paper film. This screening test is limited to the kinds of heart disease detected by changes in the size, shape and position of the cardiac silhouette on the flat film of the chest in the posterior-anterior or lateral position. Rutstein et al.[7] reported optimistic results in finding heart disease in the reading of 31,091 films taken in a survey in Boston using 70 mm. photofluorographs. Films were read twice, once by public health officers looking for all abnormalities, secondly by radiologists reading films only for abnormalities of the heart and blood vessels. Of the total films, 3.54 per cent (1101) were read as abnormal and 76.7 per cent (845) of the persons filmed returned for further study. Heart disease was verified in 59.6 per cent (504) of the 1101 suspicious films. Nearly one-half (280) had no previous knowledge of their disease; clinicians who made the x-ray diagnosis gave the opinion that 45.7 per cent (128) of these 280 were benefited by this early detection.

As mass chest roentgen screening is usually limited to persons over 15 or 20 years of age (because of the low yield of abnormal shadows and unnecessary radiation of children), congenital defects are, of course, not discovered early in life by this means.

Mass roentgen screening for heart disease is reasonable in cost, because tuberculosis and other pulmonary diseases are detected on the same film. It is essential, however, to provide for interpretation of the roentgen films by experts in heart disease; otherwise, the yield will be considerably lowered.

A multiple screening program is more efficient than a series of individual mass screening tests,[8] yet the component parts should meet the same criteria mentioned above. As a part of such a program, the determination of blood pressure serves as a simple and inexpensive screen for hypertension. Arbitrary standards are set by different groups of physicians because there is no universal agreement on critical levels. In the Cardiovascular Health Center at the Albany Medical School, a single blood pressure reading of 150/100 mm. mercury is used as the screening level.[9] When 100 mm. of mercury was used as the diastolic level of hypertension, among the initial 1065 men 40 to 55 years old who were examined, one-tenth of those aged 40 to 45, one-seventh of those 45 to 49 and one-quarter of those 50 to 54 were labeled hypertensive.[10]

It is worth the additional effort involved to include heart disease case finding in mass roentgen screening for tuberculosis. Blood pressure determinations should also be done regularly at periodic health examinations, multiple screening programs in group practice, clinic programs and when patients are admitted to a hospital. Because of the potential disease detected and referred for diagnostic confirmation, physicians stand to benefit by encouraging and participating in such programs in their communities.

CORONARY ARTERY DISEASE

There is no simple, efficient and economical screening test for coronary artery disease. Routine electrocardiograms on adults, using single or multiple leads, do not possess validity or reliability and are not inexpensive to perform. This means that the best screener for this disease is the physician who routinely makes a careful and complete medical examination on all his new patients. Exercise tests, sufficient to place the circulation under stress, are useful adjuncts in doubtful diagnoses. The Master two-step test is most commonly used for this type of screening.

In addition to the history and physical examination, a battery of tests including electrocardiogram, roentgen studies and laboratory examinations of the blood are necessary to diagnose coronary artery disease, especially its early stages. A carefully taken history yields a diagnosis of coronary artery disease more often than any other diagnostic procedure, but it takes time and requires the interpretation of a physician.

For certain classes of persons, such as executives, comprehensive health insurance participants, recipients of employee's health services and individuals who can afford to go to group clinics where specialists' services are available, it is possible to streamline examinations for early coronary artery disease. Under optimum conditions, nevertheless, this is expensive (from $50 to $150) and takes a minimum of 1 to 2 hours for the first visit. The minimum examination includes history and physical, 6 or 12 lead electrocardiograms, chest roentgenogram, urinalysis and hemoglobin determination. Exercise tests are desirable. Studies of blood cholesterol or lipoproteins are also desirable.

From studies at the Cardiovascular Health Center at Albany[9] among male state civil service employees, ages 40 to 54 years and of a variety of occupations, it appears that gross obesity, marked elevation of blood pressure and a serum total cholesterol of 275 mg./100 ml. or more are associated in the group with a greatly increased risk of developing clinical evidence of myocardial ischemia. Recent studies have shown that heavy cigarette smoking also increases the risk of coronary artery disease.

The American Heart Association recommended in June, 1964, that the general public begin reducing the amount of fat eaten and begin "reasonable substitution" of vegetable oils for animal fats. The change is urged as a means of reducing the risks of a "heart attack or a stroke." Yet the Association emphasized that there is not yet proof that changes in diet will prevent heart attacks or strokes. The recommendation is based only on the belief that reduction of animal fats in the diet by reducing the blood cholesterol level may lessen the development of atherosclerosis, which appears to be related to coronary artery disease.

Morris, the English epidemiologist, states that there is no evidence that lowering the cholesterol level is worthwhile.[11] The Gofman levels of lipoprotein as indicators of coronary artery disease have not been corroborated.[12]

The American Medical Association has not concurred in the recommendation of the American Heart Association.

With the limited state of our knowledge in 1964 of the relationship between fat in the diet, the blood and the coronary arteries and ischemic heart disease, blood cholesterol determinations are not acceptable as a mass screening method for coronary artery disease or cerebral vascular diseases.

The transaminase test has been used as a screening aid in persons with angina with the hope that early positive tests might indicate preinfarction stages.[18] But the test is more of a diagnostic aid than a screening method and accordingly has limited usefulness.

HYPERTENSION

The etiology of essential hypertension remains unknown, although a variety of factors has been implicated. As pointed out, there is a simple and rapid method for determining blood pressure, but lack of agreement continues on the dividing line between abnormal and normal pressures by age and sex. There is a frequent association between overweight and high blood pressure, and weight reduction has often favorably influenced blood pressure levels. Determining the weight of an individual is a useful screening test that adds further information to the health profile of the person suspected of having cardiovascular disease. Every multiple screening examination, accordingly, should include blood pressure and weight determination; they are rapid, easy and economical tests that are also valid and reliable.

Screening of persons as potentially hypertensive by one or two blood pressure determinations is only the first step in a series of clinical and laboratory studies that require skillful interpretation by the clinician. There are few things in medicine more tragic than falsely labeling a patient as seriously hypertensive on the basis of a casual blood pressure reading or two. The careful physician does not confuse a screening test with a comprehensive diagnostic study.

If the increased blood pressure is accompanied by eyeground changes or other evidence of brain or kidney involvement, then one considers a diagnosis of hypertensive cardiovascular disease. In the hands of experts the ophthalmoscope is useful as a screening tool for early signs of cardiovascular disease.[14] The physician must have skills and experience to do this type of screening, which could become a part of every routine health status inventory. If a patient with persistent diastolic hypertension in a compensated stage also shows evidence of left ventricular hypertrophy by roentgenogram or electrocardiography, the doctor naturally thinks of hypertensive heart disease. The discovery of such serious diseases after initial detection of increased blood pressure is of great importance to the well-being of the patient.

RHEUMATIC FEVER AND RHEUMATIC HEART DISEASE

Present knowledge and modern antibiotic therapy have made it possible for rheumatic fever to become a preventable disease. The physician can prevent first attacks of rheumatic fever when the initiating streptococcal infection is diagnosed and promptly treated with adequate amounts of penicillin.[15] The big problem is the detection of children with streptococcal throat infections prior to the first attack of rheumatic fever. In schools and institutions when infections do occur, screening of children can be done by throat cultures and typing of organisms. Physicians, particularly those associated with elementary schools, can help to prevent rheumatic fever by alerting themselves to detection opportunities.

For those youngsters who have had their first attack of rheumatic fever, the chances of a recurrence may be as high as 50 per cent if a new streptococcal infection develops.[16] It appears that persons with a history of rheumatic fever should be placed on a prophylactic regimen for a period of at least 5 years from the last attack and preferably for the rest of the person's life. Recommendations for dosage have been formulated by the Council on Rheumatic Fever and Congenital Heart Disease of the American Heart Association.[17]

Here again, the only screening test feasible on an economic and reasonably rapid basis is a history taken in schools or institutions where large numbers of children are gathered. This can be done by nurses or teacher assistants and reviewed by the physician as he makes his periodic medical examinations of the children. It may be done also by the family physician as he examines the schoolchild privately prior to entrance to school each year. Physicians working in concert with health department and school authorities can reduce rheumatic fever by as much as 85 per cent if early detection, diagnosis and prophylaxis are assiduously followed.[18]

Tape recordings of heart sounds have been used on schoolchildren on a mass scale for early detection of heart disease.[19] The results have not been too encouraging because of the difficulty of picking up early, remediable lesions and the added problem of the significance of certain heart sounds.

Rheumatic heart disease is a crucial medical problem, not only in the western hemisphere but in many European countries as well. Mass roentgen examination is an easily applied method of detection of later stages of this disease, but only when changes have occurred in the size, shape or position of the heart shadow on the film. Unfortunately, many persons with rheumatic heart disease in its early stages do not show roentgenographic changes.

PERIPHERAL VASCULAR DISEASE

Estimates from cardiovascular clinics indicate that the disability and economic loss from peripheral vascular disease are considerable. Arteriosclerotic peripheral vascular disease, varicose veins, thrombophlebitis, Raynaud's disease, thromboangiitis obliterans, frostbite and immersion foot are some of the more common examples. Early recognition of the disease and medical supervision are prerequisites in preventing complications in patients with these diseases.

Screening for diabetes leads to early diagnosis and dietary regulation. Optimal health habits help to avoid mechanical, thermal and chemical trauma to the extremities of diabetics. Educational material on foot care for diabetics, easily distributed by health workers, is also useful for patients with other peripheral vascular diseases. Public health nurses on the lookout for peripheral vascular disease signs and symptoms can serve as effective screeners who refer potential patients to physicians for prevention of progression of disability.

CONGESTIVE HEART FAILURE

A survey of cardiac patients admitted to general hospitals often reveals many persons with recurrent episodes of congestive heart failure. Most of these patients have lapsed from their prescribed regimens of digitalis, diuretics, sodium restriction and avoidance of stress. Repeaters can be detected by an alert admitting officer and kept out of unnecessary trouble by experienced physicians who take the time to make certain that patients understand and carry out their prescribed regimens. It has been estimated that more than half of the people with organic heart disease develop congestive failure.[20] A program of detection of recurrent bouts followed by optimum long-term treatment would bring economic savings and prevent disability.

CEREBRAL VASCULAR LESIONS

Unfortunately, there are no practical screening methods that will detect the presence of incipient cerebral vascular lesions.

Realistic estimates place the number of persons disabled by cerebral vascular lesions in the United States at nearly 2 million. The hemiplegia and associated disabilities resulting from this disease, particularly among older persons, lead to disability and dependence that annually waste millions of dollars of public and private funds. Usually atherosclerosis and thrombosis and, to a lesser extent, embolism, are the underlying factors in surviving hemiplegics. Hemorrhage alone is usually not the primary factor. Screening for generalized atherosclerosis alerts the physician to possible cerebral vascular lesions.

In persons prone to recurrences of thromboembolism in rheumatic heart disease (with auricular fibrillation and a history of previous emboli), long-term anticoagulant therapy has reduced recurrences.[21] Similar studies are in progress on persons with cerebral thrombosis. The major approach to the hemiplegic is the provision of rehabilitation services early after the causal lesions show their presence.

CONGENITAL HEART DISEASE

Congenital heart defects continue to be an important cause of death and disability in our population, especially among infants and young children.

Richards et al. in a study of 6053 unselected births found 0.83 per cent (50) infants with congenital heart defects, of whom 29 survived for one year.[22] In a school survey of a representative sample of schoolchildren in an urban area, Mattison and associates found that congenital heart defects were as prevalent as rheumatic heart disease.[23]

If the physician makes the diagnosis early, surgery done at the optimal age corrects the defect or halts progression of the disability in a considerable proportion of patients.

There is no simple screening method for the detection of congenital heart defects. But there are several coarse screens available for sifting out some of the suspects. One of these is routine examinations of babies immediately after birth, a careful scanning of the mother's history for German measles, for roentgen examination of the pelvis and for information on the use of drugs early in pregnancy.

Public health nurses and school nurses who are alerted to the signs and symptoms of heart defects can search for early suspects as they make home visits to newborns. School physicians alert to the diagnostic signs of heart defects can use the periodic health inventory in the first grades as a screening opportunity. Health officers in states which report congenital defects on birth certificates can check these reports as they come in and make certain through visits of public health nurses that suspects are referred for clinical study. Until further research reveals causative factors in congenital heart disease that may lead to prevention of occurrences, we have no choice but to use constant vigilance to detect early heart defects by the means at our command.

HERMAN E. HILLEBOE, M.D.

REFERENCES

1. Vital Statistics, 1960, United States Census.
2. Rutstein, David D.: Screening tests in mass surveys and their use in heart disease case finding. Circulation, 4:659-665, November, 1951.
3. California State Department of Public Health: Bibliography on disease detection, health maintenance, periodic health examination and multiple screening. Prepared by the Chronic Illness and Aging Unit, Bureau of Chronic Diseases. Berkley, 1962, 20 p.
4. Kurlander, A. B., and Carroll, H. E.: Case finding through multiple screening. Public Health Reports, 68:11, November, 1963.
5. Thorner, R. M., and Remein, Q. R.: Principles and proceedings in the evaluation of screening for disease. U. S. Public Health Service, Division of Chronic Diseases, P.H.S. Monograph 67, P.H.S. Publication No. 846. Washington, U. S. Government Printing Office, 1961, 24 p.
6. National Conference on Chronic Disease: Preventive aspects, Chicago, 1951. Report of the Commission on Chronic Illness, Raleigh, North Carolina, Health Publications Institute, 1952, pp. 184-201.
7. Rutstein, David D., Williamson, Charles R., and Moore, Felix E.: Heart disease case findings by means of 70 millimeter photofluorographic films. Circulation, 4:641-651, November, 1951.
8. Canelo, C. K., Bissell, D. M., Abrams, H., and Breslow, L.: A multiphasic screening survey in San Jose. California Medicine, 71:409, 1949.
9. Doyle, Joseph T., Heslin, S., Hilleboe, H. E., and Formel, P. F.: Early diagnosis of ischemic heart disease. New England Journal of Medicine, 261:1096-1101, November 26, 1959.
10. James, George, Hilleboe, Herman E., Filippone, John F., and Doyle, Joseph T.: Cardiovascular health center. A. General observations and hypertension. New York State Journal of Medicine, 55:754, March 15, 1955.
11. Morris, J. N.: Some current trends in public health. Proceedings of the Royal Society, sB, 159:65-80, 1963.
12. Gofman, John W., et al.: Dietary Prevention and Treatment of Heart Disease. New York, G. P. Putnam Sons, 1958.
13. Resnik, William H.: Preinfarction angina—Parts I & II: The transaminase test—a diagnostic aid. Modern Concepts of Cardiovascular Disease, 31(No. 10):751-761, October, 1962.

14. Marr, William G.: Ophthalmoscopic signs of cardiovascular disease. Modern Concepts of Cardiovascular Disease, *31*(No. 12):763-767, December, 1962.

15. Rammelkamp, C. H., Jr., Houser, H. B., Hahn, E. O., Wannamaker, L. W., Denny, F. W., and Eckhardt, G. C.: The prevention of rheumatic fever. In Rheumatic Fever—A Symposium. Edited by L. Thomas. Minneapolis, University of Minnesota Press, 1952, pp. 304-315.

16. Bland, E. F., and Jones, T. D.: Rheumatic fever and rheumatic heart disease: a twenty-year report on 1,000 patients followed since childhood. Circulation, *4*:836, 843, December, 1951.

17. Prevention of rheumatic fever and bacterial endocarditis through control of streptococcal infections. American Heart Association, New York City, 1956. Circulation, *15*:154-158, January, 1957.

18. Stollerman, G. H.: Potentialities for and limitations in the control of chronic rheumatic fever by prophylactic measures. Journal of Chronic Disease, *1*:216-221, February, 1955.

19. Abrams, I.: Evaluation of tape recording of heart sounds on a mass scale in school children. The Journal of School Health, *33*:62-69, No. 2, February, 1963.

20. White, P. D.: Heart Disease. Ed. 4. New York, The Macmillan Co., 1951, p. 803.

21. Millikan, C. H., Siekert, R. G., and Shick, R. M.: Studies in cerebrovascular disease. III. Use of anticoagulant drugs in the treatment of insufficiency or thrombosis within the basilar arterial system. Proceedings of the Staff Meetings of the Mayo Clinic, *30*:116-126, March 23, 1955.

22. Richards, M. R., Merritt, K. K., Samuels, M. H., and Langman, A. C.: Congenital malformations of the cardiovascular system in a series of 6,053 infants. Pediatrics, *15*:12-32, January, 1955.

23. Mattison, B. F., Lambert, E. C., and Mosher, W. E.: Cardiac screening in a school health program. New York State Journal of Medicine, *53*:2966-2970, December 15, 1953.

30 Screening Methods for Diabetes Mellitus

Diabetes mellitus is a genetically determined disease of metabolism, characterized by a deficiency or defective utilization of the pancreatic hormone insulin and by abnormally high concentrations of glucose in the blood and urine. Diabetes is a common disease, since at least 2 per cent of American adults over the age of 40 are afflicted. It is a serious disease, particularly because it predisposes to atherosclerosis and the development of arterial thrombi in the coronary, cerebral, renal and peripheral vessels. It is also a common cause of blindness.

In children, diabetes is usually a severe and almost invariably symptom-producing disease. Classically manifested by polyuria, polydipsia, polyphagia, loss of strength, weight loss, postprandial drowsiness, and genital pruritus, "juvenile" diabetes is seldom detected during the presymptomatic phase. In contrast, diabetes first manifested in adult life is insidious and frequently asymptomatic in onset and may often be detected before symptoms or complications develop.

It is assumed, although not as yet conclusively demonstrated, that the early detection of diabetes and adequate control of the abnormal carbohydrate metabolism through diet and the use of insulin postpones or minimizes the many complications of the disease.

It has been estimated that there are over 1¼ million known diabetics in the United States today and that the disease exists unknown in another group equally as large. In seeking to find cases of unsuspected diabetes, the most productive groups to test are: relatives of known diabetics, those overweight, and those over the age of 40. The mothers of babies born with a birth weight in excess of 8 pounds should be considered potential diabetics and followed by periodic blood sugar determinations.

DETECTION

Screening tests for the detection of diabetes mellitus depend upon analyses of the blood and urine for glucose content. These tests can and should be done routinely by physicians in their private offices, and by clinics, and hospitals as a part of the routine patient work-up. They also may be done on a mass basis, either as a short-term "drive" or as a continuing year-round detection program.

Urine Testing

For the determination of glucose in the urine, there are many simple and inexpensive procedures. Best known is the test employing Benedict's solution and heat. Unfortunately, this test is difficult to use in large scale detection programs because of the need to collect urine specimens in a central location. This difficulty has been overcome by the use of the St. Louis Dreypak in which a piece of blotting paper is dipped into the urine specimen, allowed to dry and mailed to a laboratory where testing with Benedict's reagent is carried out. More recently tests have been developed for glucosuria that depend upon the presence in test paper of a specific enzyme, glucose oxidase (Clinistix and Tes-Tape). With these tests, the test paper is dipped into the urine specimen and if glucose is present in the specimen, a color change develops within a minute.

Mass urine testing through the use of St. Louis Dreypaks has been widely and successfully used during Diabetes Week (in November). These short-term drives are sponsored by the American Diabetes Association in collaboration with local medical societies.

In spite of its simplicity, diabetes detection through urine examinations for the presence of glucose leaves much to be desired. Compared to blood glucose determinations, urinalyses for sugar are relatively low both in sensitivity and in specificity (Table 16).

Blood Sugar Testing

Diabetes screening methods that depend upon analyses of blood for glucose content are more sensitive and more specific than are urinalyses,

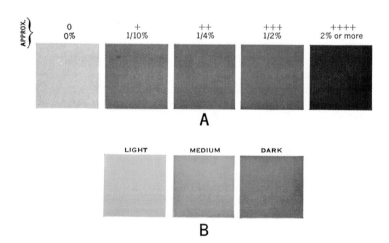

Figure 34.   Color changes with glucose oxidase tests for the presence of glucose in the urine: *A*, Tes-Tape (Lilly); *B*, Clinistix (Ames). Read the strips of Clinistix one minute after dipping. Usually a light color corresponds to a small amount (less than ½ per cent) of glucose, and a dark color to a larger amount (more than ½ per cent). A medium color may be produced by either a large or small amount of glucose.

Table 16. *The Superiority of Blood Sugar Tests over Urine Testing in Diabetes Detection Programs*

In any diabetes detection activity, a decision has to be made as to whether the program should be based on blood sugar determinations or on urinalyses for sugar content. A recent study by Wilkerson and his colleagues[*] clearly illustrates the superiority of blood tests.

Shown below is a comparison between blood tests made with the Clinitron using the Wilkerson-Heftman method, taking blood one hour after a meal and using 160 mg. per cent as the screening level; and urine tests, using the St. Louis Dreypak, taking specimens one hour after a meal and using 1+ as the screening level.

	SENSITIVITY	SPECIFICITY
Blood test	63.2%	98.9%
Urine test	53.1%	90.4%

Applying these figures to a population of 10,000 people with a prevalence of diabetes of 2 per cent, there would actually be:

200 diabetics
9800 nondiabetics

(1) The urine test would produce:

106 true positives
941 false positives   (nondiabetics)
8859 true negatives
94 false negatives   (missed diabetics)

It would be necessary to recheck all positive screening tests, in this case 1047 persons, in order to confirm the diagnosis of diabetes in 106 persons. *Thus, it would be necessary to recheck about 10 persons to confirm the diagnosis of diabetes in 1 person.*

(2) The blood test would produce:

126 true positives
108 false positives   (nondiabetics)
9692 true negatives
74 false negatives   (missed diabetics)

It would be necessary to recheck 234 persons to confirm the diagnosis of diabetes in 126 persons. *Thus, it would be necessary to recheck only about 2 persons to confirm the diagnosis in 1 person.*

It is apparent, therefore, that in addition to finding more of the diabetics, the blood sugar method will greatly reduce the number of persons who would be referred to their physicians for time-consuming and expensive recheck examinations.

[*] Unpublished data.

the results depending on when the specimen is taken in relation to meals and on the predetermined height of the blood sugar that is used as the screening level.

In the past, blood sugar determinations have seldom been used for mass screening projects because of the technical difficulties inherent in the chemical analysis for glucose and the necessity of obtaining specimens of venous blood. However, a method (Wilkerson-Heftman) for analyzing capillary blood for glucose content has been developed. When performed with tablet reagents and with the use of a mechanical device (the Clinitron) for performing many tests quickly, this method makes mass diabetes detection based on blood sugar determinations highly feasible. Only about 0.1 ml. of capillary blood is required, and the result of the test can be available

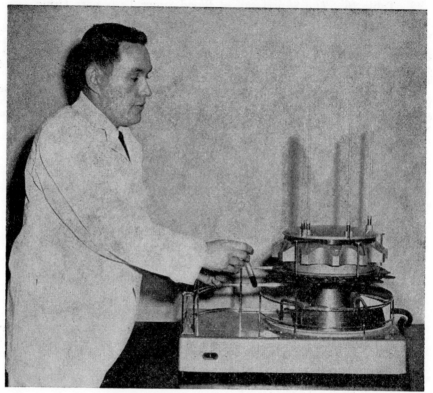

Figure 35. The Clinitron used for performing capillary blood sugar screening tests.

within 5 minutes and while the patient is still present at the testing station.

The Clinitron greatly facilitates mass screening surveys for diabetes. In a recent survey, 4300 analyses were made with the machine in operation for only 40 hours. If desired, water-diluted specimens of blood can be kept up to 48 hours under refrigeration, provided sodium fluoride is added as a preservative. This means that blood specimens can be drawn anywhere, diluted with 5 ml. of distilled water and sent to a fairly remote center for analysis.

For many years, great credibility was placed on the height of the *fasting* blood sugar in the diagnosis of diabetes mellitus. Recent studies have shown, however, that fasting blood sugars are definitely lacking in sensitivity, and that the optimal time to draw blood for diabetes detection is 1 to 1½ hours after a meal. During this period, a blood sugar in excess of 160 mg. per cent constitutes presumptive evidence of diabetes.

The Wilkerson-Heftman method for blood sugar determinations can readily be used in the physician's office through the use of convenient kits available from the manufacturer of the tablet reagents (Eli Lilly).

The Clinitron also has been employed satisfactorily as a presumptive screening procedure. In this technique, the screening level is purposely lowered, usually to 135 mg. per cent glucose, and all positives are rechecked quantitatively with a device such as the autoanalyzer.

Another recent development has been a blood sugar test involving "Dextrostix" (Ames Company). These are glucose oxydase impregnated filter papers on which a drop of whole blood is placed for 60 seconds, washed off and the resultant color compared to a standard. This test is roughly quantitative, and the results are highly accurate.

NOTIFICATION

All persons who have participated in a diabetes screening project should be apprised of their test result as soon as possible. Those whose tests are normal can be sent a simple postcard, and it is suggested that cards mailed to persons who are relatives of known diabetics, or who are obese or over the age of 50, contain a paragraph suggesting that an annual recheck is desirable. Persons whose test is suspicious of diabetes should be so informed by sealed letter, and a report also should be sent to the person's physician, informing him of the result of the test.

FOLLOW-UP

The detection process is completed only when patients with suspicious screening tests have been fully evaluated by their physicians, and either a definitive diagnosis of diabetes established or evidence obtained whereby the patient can be reassured that the disease is not present.

Experience has shown that many patients who have been notified of a suspicious screening test fail to report to their doctor for diagnosis. This situation can largely be obviated by having visiting public health nurses make follow-up visits to the patient. The usual procedure is for the nurse to phone the practicing physician to inquire, first, whether his patient has reported to him, and second, if not, whether the physician would wish to have the nurse make a home visit to persuade the patient to seek medical advice.

DIAGNOSIS

Persons whose screening test for diabetes is positive must be rechecked by their own physicians, who have the responsibility of either establishing a diagnosis of the disease or excluding the possibility.

Most often the first step is to obtain a quantitative, 1- to 1½-hour postprandial blood sugar determination. This alone will suffice to establish the diagnosis or rule it out in the vast majority of cases. If the blood sugar result is between 160 and 180 mg. per cent, further tests may be taken and postprandial urine specimens examined for glucose content. In some cases, a glucose tolerance test may be required.

Even after all these examinations have been made, there will be an occasional patient in whom the diagnosis remains in doubt. These persons should be considered prediabetic and followed accordingly. If the suspected diabetic is pregnant, the best course is to treat her as if a diagnosis of diabetes were definitely established.

FRANK W. REYNOLDS, M.D.

REFERENCES

1. Fox, R. E., et al.: A report on diabetes detection. Journal of the American Medical Association, *183*:622, November 10, 1962.
2. Parks, L. L., et al.: Screening relatives of diabetics in five Florida counties. Public Health Reports, *75*:55, January, 1960.
3. Reynolds, F. W., et al.: Routine tests for diabetes mellitus among adult hospital patients. Geriatrics *14*:784, December, 1959.
4. Harting, D., and Glenn, B.: A comparison of blood sugar and urine sugar determinations for the detection of diabetes. New England Journal of Medicine, *245*:48, July 12, 1951.
5. Margolin, M., and Gentry, H. E., Jr.: Chemical usefulness of the Wilkerson-Heftman blood sugar test. Diabetes, *2*:285, July-August, 1953.
6. Olmstead, W. H.: St Louis Dreypak. Unpublished statement prepared for the Committee on Detection and Education of the American Diabetes Association, August, 1954.
7. Wilkerson, H. L. C.: Diabetes control in the public health program. New York State Journal of Medicine, *49*:2945, December 15, 1949.

31 Screening Methods for Hearing Defects and Visual Defects

HEARING DEFECTS

Early detection of hearing defects facilitates prompt diagnosis of the underlying causative factors, correction of these factors when possible and the early use of hearing aids and auditory and speech training when correction is not possible. Only the more profound degrees of hearing loss are usually suspected among children up to 3 years of age. Clues to severe hearing loss in early life are: lack of response to any but very loud sounds, the development of babbling at the expected age only to be followed by cessation of the babbling instead of progression into speech, and interest in motion to the exclusion of sound. Special attention should be paid to young children who have had conditions predisposing to impaired hearing or whose parents are deaf. Among the predisposing conditions are the occurrence of German measles in the mother during the first trimester of pregnancy; the occurrence of birth trauma or the presence of neurologic symptoms during the newborn period; erythroblastosis fetalis; meningitis and other diseases of the central nervous system; and recurrent ear infections.

For children of school age and for adults various screening tests for hearing may be used. With proper preparation and great care by the examiner, many children between 4 and 6 years of age can also be screened. Phonograph audiometry, using a phonograph record of the spoken voice in gradually decreasing volume transmitted through earphones to groups of children, was the most frequently used method of screening of school-children until recent years. The phonograph audiometer is being rapidly supplanted by the "sweep-check" pure-tone audiometer for screening purposes in the schools. The pure-tone test is used almost exclusively in multiple detection programs for adults. The individual being tested is exposed to selected frequencies of sound at various levels of intensity in quick succession. Thus early hearing loss outside the usual range of the spoken voice can be detected. The individual pure-tone tests, although more sensitive and accurate than the group phonograph methods, are also more time consuming and expensive. The availability of the Massachusetts Hearing Test for groups and the Johnston Group Pure-Tone Test has overcome even this objection. The incidence of hearing loss among younger schoolchildren is high enough to warrant screening tests for hearing at annual or biennial intervals.

The level of hearing loss for which the tested individual should be referred for diagnostic evaluation should be determined in advance of any testing program. In establishing such a level, the advice of the otologists and audiologists in the community should be sought. Individuals referred to practicing physicians following detection programs should not be dismissed on the basis of examinations with inadequate diagnostic tools, but should be assured a complete evaluation by a private qualified otologist with training in hearing disorders or in a community conservation of hearing center.

VISUAL DEFECTS

Detection and treatment of strabismus before the second or third birthday will almost always prevent the loss of vision that otherwise develops following suppression of the visual image in the unused eye. Monocular visual loss may be as severe in the less obvious untreated deviations as in the severe cases of strabismus. The cover test may be used to screen doubtful deviations. One eye at a time is covered with an occluder while the patient looks at an object, first at a distance of 20 feet and then at reading distance. The deviating eye shifts when the occluder is removed.

The most frequently used screening test for visual acuity among children over 3 years of age and among adults is the Snellen test, which employs a special chart with lines of letters of decreasing size. For children who are too young to read letters, a modification, using the letter E turned in various directions, is available. The Snellen test is of great value in detecting myopia and in disclosing differences in visual acuity between the two eyes. The test is reliable under standard conditions of light in the hands of nurses and teachers as well as physicians, and it is often carried out in the schools by volunteers trained in its use.

Several more complicated screening tests, such as the Massachusetts Vision Test and the Telebinocular and Ortho-Rater Tests, are also in use. These measure fusion, muscle imbalance and other visual functions, and are much more difficult and expensive to administer than the Snellen test. Even in the hands of well-trained testers they often result in gross overreferral for medical examination. The selection of the proper screening test for any community should be based on the availability of private ophthalmologic consultation supplemented by community diagnostic facilities.

When glaucoma is detected and treated early, useful vision can be retained for prolonged periods in about 85 per cent of the cases. Screening of patients over 40 years of age by measurement of ocular tension through simple tonometry discloses that 2 to 3 per cent have an ocular tension of 30 mm. or more of mercury, which is considered to be above the normal level. Following installation of an anesthetic into the conjunctival sac, the foot plate of a tonometer is placed lightly on the center of the cornea and the approximate tension read. Persons whose corneas have been anesthetized should be cautioned not to rub their eyes and to stay away from dusty environments until the effects of the anesthetic wear off, lest they unwittingly get a foreign body in the eye that might lead to corneal ulceration.

It is well to test visual acuity before doing tonometry, since there is the possibility that a person who develops visual difficulty subsequently may try to relate this causally with the examination. There is a slight risk of damaging the cornea if the tonometer is not applied properly, but the risk is very small and in no way should obviate routine tonometry.

Routine tonometry should be performed in the general practitioner's office as part of the periodic medical examination. It is being used increasingly in community testing programs, either singly or in combination with other screening tests. The Harrington-Flocks screening test, using a multiple pattern method of visual field testing rather than direct tonometry, is still in the experimental stage. No reliance should be placed on the use of tactile tension in detecting glaucoma. The patient should not be told that he has glaucoma on the basis of a single reading. The screening tests should simply lead to referral to an ophthalmologist for complete evaluation.

EDWARD R. SCHLESINGER, M.D.

REFERENCES

Hearing Defects
1. Geyer, M. L., and Yankauer, A.: Detection of hearing loss in preschool children. Public Health Reports, 72:723, August, 1957.
2. Robinson, G. C., Kendall, D. C., and Cambon, K. G.: Hearing loss in infants and preschool children. Pediatrics, 32:103, 115, July, 1963.
3. Harrington, D. A.: Services for the child who is hard of hearing. Washington, D.C., Children's Bureau, U. S. Department of Health, Education, and Welfare, 1963.
4. Wishik, S. M., and Kramm, E. R.: Audiometric testing of hearing of school children. Journal of Speech and Hearing Disorders, 18:360, December, 1953.

Visual Defects
5. de Roetth, A., and Dorman, P.: Role of the general practitioner in prevention of blindness. Journal of the American Medical Association, 164:1525, August 3, 1957.
6. Foote, F. M.: Screening for eye disease. American Medical Association Archives of Industrial Health, 16:254, September, 1957.
7. Harrington, D. O., and Flocks, M.: Multiple pattern method of visual field examination. Journal of the American Medical Association, 157:645, February 19, 1955.
8. Packer, H., Deutsch, A. R., Deweese, M. W., Kashgarian, M., and Lewis, P. M.: Frequency of glaucoma in three population groups. Journal of the American Medical Association, 188:123, April 13, 1964.
9. Rychener, R. O.: Vision tests in infants and young children. Pediatric Clinics of North America, February, 1958, p. 231.
10. Taubenhaus, L. J.: Patterns of ocular care in a New England community—A comparison of the use of ophthalmologists and optometrists by an adult population. New England Journal of Medicine, 268:818, April 11, 1963.

32 Follow-up of Screening and Diagnostic Examinations

In sections A and B of Part Two, emphasis has been given to the methods for preventing the progression of disease through early detection by periodic physical examinations and screening techniques. It is obvious that these are not objectives in themselves. The best organized screening program is of little value unless it leads to a correct diagnosis of individuals for whom positive findings are reported. In turn, a correct diagnosis is meaningless unless it is followed promptly by therapy that corrects or cures a disease or disorder, prevents or arrests the progression of a chronic illness or compensates for residual disabilities by rehabilitation procedures.

Unfortunately, adherence to these seemingly fundamental principles is too often neglected, both in the planning and operation of community programs and in the private practice of medicine. In this section, we shall examine various methods which might be utilized so that the ends may be gained after the means have been accomplished.

CONFIRMATION OF POSITIVE SCREENING TESTS

As emphasized previously, the screening examination, whether carried out on a mass or an individual basis, is intended to detect the possibility rather than the certainty of disease and to screen out those who, because of a negative reaction, may need no further work-up for the disease or diseases covered by the tests. Every person with a positive screening reaction must thereafter undergo a complete diagnostic examination which will utilize all necessary clinical and laboratory techniques to either establish or rule out the existence of a disease. Numerous examples of the extent to which positive screening examinations lead to the identification of treatable disease appear in the analysis of 33 multiple screening projects conducted by the Council on

Medical Service of the American Medical Association.[1] To choose but one example, the Boston Multiple Screening Survey (Massachusetts Pilot Clinic Number 2) screened 4536 persons and reported positive findings in 62.06 per cent, or approximately 2815 individuals. Of the 1399 persons on whom the family physician reported, 1252 were found to have 2065 conditions. Table 17 shows the extent to which the presence of disease was confirmed by the examinations of family physicians for a group of selected diseases.

Table 17. *Confirmation of Disease by Family Physicians Following Positive Screening Tests*

FINDINGS	TOTAL POSITIVE SCREENING TESTS	SCREENING TESTS CON-FIRMED BY FAMILY PHYSICIANS	PER CENT OF CONFIRMATIONS
Anemia	108	70	64.8
Heart disease	106	41	38.7
Hypertension	324	176	54.3
Diabetes	66	40	60.6
Respiratory infection	32	10	31.2
Tuberculosis	3	1	33.3
Syphilis	7	5	71.4
Rectal hematest	29	11	37.9
Visual defect	202	65	32.2
Overweight	554	347	62.6

Some controversy exists as to: (a) whether a screening program for a given disease should also include laboratory or roentgenologic examinations of those showing positive screening results, referring to the personal physician only those individuals in whom abnormal findings have been confirmed; or (b) whether such confirming examinations should be the responsibility of the personal physician to whom any person with a positive screening reaction should be immediately referred.

Confirmation by the Screening Agency

Several arguments favor the same agency carrying out both the screening examinations and the confirming tests. First, the personal physician may not be equipped with the complete laboratory and roentgen facilities required to confirm or to rule out the suggestive findings of the screening test. His office may not be able to give a complete glucose tolerance test when the screening examination reports a positive urine or blood test for sugar. He may also not be equipped to take a standard 14 × 17 inch chest film after a miniature film of the screening test shows suspicious findings. He must refer such patients to other physicians or laboratories to have these tests done. Also, for certain conditions, such as hearing defects and orthopedic disorders, a qualified specialist may be necessary. In either case, the patient must first go to the personal physician, then to the necessary clinical or laboratory referrals and finally back to the personal physician before the diagnostic examination is completed. If the diagnostic tests were offered by the screening agency, it might be possible to have clinical specialists and necessary laboratory facilities at the same place, with considerably more convenience to the patient and more speed.

The economic factor is the second major argument for placing responsibility for confirmatory testing upon the screening agency. By definition, screening is offered only to persons who are completely asymptomatic. If a person with a positive screening test goes to his personal physician and is then referred for a series of specialist consultations, laboratory tests and roentgen examinations, he will be subjected to a considerable expense. If all clinical and laboratory findings point to a positive diagnosis, the patient should feel that the screening examination has been worthwhile and he is fortunate in having had his disease identified at the earliest possible time so that prompt treatment may be instituted. On the other hand, if no abnormality is ultimately found, the person, while reassured about his health status, may resent the considerable personal expense which he would have been spared if he had not gone through the screening procedure in the first place. Because false positive tests are a necessary concomitant of any screening procedure, a high frequency of such individual reactions may have an adverse effect upon the public relations of the screening program and interfere with its success in the community.

Confirmation by Personal Physician

A major argument in favor of referring persons with positive screening tests directly to their personal physicians is the desirability of maintaining the physician-patient relationship. Physicians may accept and actually help to promote screening programs because they recognize that such programs are best established on a community basis; they are less expensive to operate than screening tests in a private office; and they reach people who would not otherwise submit to such tests on an individual basis. However, it may be well argued that all subsequent examinations, including confirmatory laboratory tests and roentgenograms, history taking and physical examinations, definitely lie within the bounds of private practice and should not be duplicated in a community program.

A second major argument in favor of direct referral to the personal physician is that it is desirable to keep the screening tests as simple and inexpensive as possible. This is best accomplished by not encumbering the program with the addition of personnel and facilities for confirming positive screenings.

All of these considerations must be carefully evaluated in establishing the proper responsibilities and relationships in any screening program. The important thing is that diagnostic examinations follow the screening examinations. The personal physician can be brought into the program, either immediately upon the finding of a positive screening test, or after completion of confirmatory tests by the screening unit. The choice is a community decision, to be made after conferences with representative groups of practicing physicians, public health personnel, voluntary health agencies and other civic groups concerned.

If time and care are taken to assure that each interested person and group is thoroughly informed as to the purposes, objectives and methods of disease detection, there is little doubt that an effective program can be developed to meet the needs of the community. The methods finally adopted will be determined not only by the interest of the various persons and agencies concerned, but by the time each group can devote and the availability and the location of the necessary testing apparatus.

It is of particular interest that physicians, despite the heavy pressures brought upon them for diagnostic and treatment services, are devoting more and more of their time to preventive medicine and health education in the office. This has long been well established in pediatric practice, but there is evidence that it is becoming more and more true of practice with adults. In a study of the time spent by internists on adult health education and preventive medicine, questionnaires were returned by 41 internists.[2] It was noted that 55 per cent of the time spent with patients during a test week was utilized specifically for diagnosis and treatment, 19 per cent on education of patients in health matters, and 26 per cent for various preventive measures, including health examinations, immunizations and counseling.

FOLLOW-UP OF POSITIVE SCREENING TESTS

Follow-up of positive screening tests may be accomplished in the following ways.

1. A public educational campaign regarding the disease or diseases in question is of the utmost importance. Most often this will be carried out in connection with the establishment of a screening procedure. The important thing to remember is that the education should be directed not only at the need to participate in the screening program, but at establishing an understanding of the disease in question and of the importance of carrying through to diagnosis if screening tests are positive. When screening tests are performed the year around, health education must be continuous. When a screening program is periodic, education should be carried over into the postcampaign period to help promote the follow-up for diagnosis.

2. Obviously, all patients should be told the results and significance of their screening examination, whether positive or negative. Persons with positive findings should be advised to see their physicians, or otherwise place themselves under medical care for the establishment or ruling out of diagnosis. The recommendation to seek medical advice should be firmly made, but the person must not be unduly alarmed.

It is important that the screening agency follow through to assure that this necessary medical work-up is completed. The actual findings of the screening examination should be referred to the examining physician and he should receive a return card to be filled out and mailed when the patient reports to him. After a reasonable period of time, follow-ups may be done with the physician's office to determine whether the diagnostic examination was completed and what the findings were. This is important in determining the efficiency of any screening procedure. If the card is not returned, calls to the physician may also be made to determine whether he simply failed to return the card when the patient reported or whether the patient actually did not report. Follow-up with the physician seems to be the most direct way to determine information about whether the patient pursues the necessary course required to establish or to rule out a diagnosis.

Follow-up may also be achieved through the patients themselves by inquiring what they have done. However, this is not so reliable.

In the case of reportable diseases, such as tuberculosis and, in some states, cancer, follow-up can be done through health departments to see whether positive diagnostic findings were reported subsequent to the screening tests.

3. Follow-up is much easier to carry out for persons participating in industrial group-screening programs. Whether the confirmatory and diagnostic examinations are to be done in the medical clinic of the industrial plant, or in the office of the patient's personal physician, it is important to industry that the worker follow through. This can be ascertained through the industrial nurse, the personnel office or possibly through the shop foreman, without, of course, violating the confidentiality of specific information regarding the worker's condition. It may also be done through those labor unions that have active health programs.

4. When a person with a positive screening test fails to follow through to receive a confirmatory or diagnostic examination, especially after a second or third letter has been sent to him, the public health nurse may be employed. This will depend, of course, upon the availability of public health nurses and other demands upon their time. However, the detection of existing disease which can be cured or arrested, or for which rehabilitation procedures are indicated, is of sufficient importance to the community to warrant some allocation of public health nurses' time for this purpose. Such nurses should call when the individual is most likely to be at home and discuss the importance of follow-up examinations. Talking to other members of the family when the individual cannot be reached or proves to be obstinate must be left to the discretion of the public health nurse.

5. For children found to have suggestive evidence of disease or defects during the course of adequate school examinations (which may often be considered as screening examinations), follow-through by school nurses is definitely indicated. Here it may often be found that the mothers have failed to understand the importance of the communications received from the schools in reference to the examination. The nurse should explain the significance of the findings and the necessity for further tests.

6. Other means of follow-through are available when persons are clients of social agencies. The largest group here are those on public assistance who are regularly visited by the caseworkers of the public welfare department. Another group are the children who are under the child welfare program of either the public welfare department or the voluntary family or case agency. The screening agency often requests these caseworkers to interpret positive screening findings and to encourage follow-up of the individuals concerned.

DIAGNOSTIC EXAMINATION AND FOLLOW-UP FOR TREATMENT

Accurate diagnosis depends upon a complete examination by the attending physician, including a detailed history, physical examination and appropriate laboratory and roentgenologic tests. Diagnosis may be made during the asymptomatic stage of a disease, when a person reports to the physician for a periodic physical examination or is referred as a result of a positive screening test. This is actually preferable to waiting until symptoms have already appeared. In either instance, if progression of the disorder is to be prevented and irreversible changes avoided, it is important that persons found to have a treatable disease be placed under treatment at the earliest possible time.

Often screening programs result in diagnostic examination of persons who already know they have a disease but have quit therapy. The return of such patients to treatment is obviously an important contribution of a screening program.

The frequent and dangerous delays in establishing diagnoses of serious diseases among positively screened persons or those with early symptoms are well known. Of 223 patients seen at the Syracuse Medical Center Tumor Clinic between 1948 and 1950, Wiggins, Hilfinger and Berman found that only 13 per cent were promptly diagnosed.[3] In 43 per cent of the cases, the patient was considered to be at fault because he either had not consulted his physician within 1 month of the onset of symptoms, or he refused to accept his physician's advice aimed at establishing a correct diagnosis. The physician was considered to be at fault in 22 per cent of the cases because correct diagnosis had not been established within 1 month after the patient first sought medical advice for symptoms, or improper advice or treatment was given to the patient and not corrected within 1 month of the patient's initial visit. An additional 22 per cent of delayed diagnoses were attributed to joint delay by both physician and patient.

When 3 months was used as a critical period rather than 1 month, the study showed no delay in 26 per cent of the cases, patient delay in 30 per cent, physician delay in 27 per cent and patient-physician delay in 17 per cent. Utilizing the 3-month critical period, Wiggins et al. were able to compare their results with those of other studies done in 1948, 1947 and 1938. Such comparisons showed more patient promptness in recent years, but an increase in the number of times physicians alone were responsible for delay in diagnosis.

In a study related to patient delay in seeking medical care for symptoms associated with cancer, Kutner and Gordan observed that: delay is a function of decreasing socioeconomic status; it is clearly associated with minimal educational attainment; and those possessing least knowledge of cancer tend to greatest delay in responding to important signals of danger.[4] However, fear is also a significant contributing factor, as long delays were observed more frequently in the presence of cancer symptoms than in the presence of general medical symptoms. These findings were corroborated by Goldsen, who observed that "a cancer symptom has to wait somewhat longer to be brought in for diagnosis than does another symptom or syndrome not involving the danger signals of cancer."[5]

The importance of prompt treatment upon the diagnosis of disease needs little emphasis. In a report summarizing the first 9 years of operation at the Cancer Detection Center of the University of Minnesota, Sullivan and Lunseth reported the finding of 225 cancers occurring among 8229 persons who received an average of three examinations, the range being from one to nine.[6] The 5-year survival rate among the truly asymptomatic group was 76.9 per cent while that in the group with minor though related symptoms was 53.2 per cent. This is contrasted with the over-all survival for the country of 25 to 30 per cent. With lesions of the lower gastrointestinal tract, the differences were more striking. The survival rates for asymptomatic colon and rectal cancer were 85 and 81 per cent, and for symptomatic cancer 20 and 33 per cent, respectively.

Joslin[7] repeatedly stressed the potentialities of avoiding serious complications through adequate treatment and control of diabetes. Although complications of diabetes have at times been observed to occur early in the course of the disease and despite apparently adequate treatment, Root,[8] utilizing the experiences of the Joslin Clinic, observes that the prognosis for diabetes is steadily improving and that this "will continue as long as better methods of public information are energetically applied, and as long as early diagnosis and more aggressive treatment are carried out."

These studies, among many others, point up the importance of a sound program of public health education directed at the development of: (a) understanding of the nature of medical problems, and (b) motivation to secure proper advice and treatment at the earliest possible time, when disease is suggested by a positive screening test or through early symptoms. There must likewise be a well-planned professional educational program maintained on a continuing basis among physicians and related personnel. A well-informed and motivated public and a prevention-oriented medical profession, combined with a functioning follow-up and referral system, plus adequate facilities, will assure that any person with a suspicion of disease is properly diagnosed and promptly treated if necessary. The method of referral and follow-up for treatment depends upon which physician or agency established the diagnosis.

Methods of Follow-up for Treatment

1. When the diagnosis has been confirmed by the screening agency, the procedures for getting the patient to go to the personal physician for treatment are the same as those described above for referral for confirmation.

2. When the diagnostic examination is done in the physician's office, the ordinary procedure is to give a patient an appointment to return for treatment as soon as possible. However, if the patient fails to return for treatment, the physician is faced with an ethical consideration. Some believe that physicians should not call patients to return to their offices as such action might give the appearance that they are trying to build up their practices. However, it would seem that such follow-up, where the patient's welfare is at stake, can be carried out in a dignified fashion which meets ethical standards. If the patient is well known to the physician, a call by the doctor's secretary may be the only necessary reminder. If the relationship is very close and informal, the physician may wish to speak to another member of the family about the importance of early treatment. On the other hand, if the relationship is more formal, there are still a few courses open to him. First, he may send a letter to the patient or to a member of the family pointing out the importance of early treatment and suggesting that the patient arrange for an appointment either at his office or at some other facility where treatment might be obtained. Second, he might refer the matter to the public health department, requesting that a public health nurse visit the patient and persuade him to place himself under treatment, either with his own physician or with some other physician or clinic. Third, if the physician is aware that the patient is known to a welfare agency, such as the public welfare department or a voluntary family or child welfare agency, he may refer the matter there.

3. When patients have gone to clinics or to outpatient departments of hospitals for the diagnostic examination, the problem of follow-up is probably not so difficult. This may take the form of one or two letters, a visit by

the social worker attached to the clinic or hospital, or referral to the public health nursing service.

4. When the patient has had a diagnosis established by an industrial examination, whether periodic or pre-employment, management has a specific responsibility. Skilled workers are important to industry and thus it is to industry's benefit to see that the patient receives necessary treatment. Obviously, people cannot be compelled to act, but in some cases management might find it necessary to do so; a worker with infectious tuberculosis would certainly be taken off the job. In most cases an active educational and persuasive approach can be utilized.

When positive findings are obtained by a pre-employment examination, and the patient is not hired for medical or other reasons, the industrial clinic should refer its findings to the person's personal physician or to the patient himself if no physician has been indicated.

FOLLOW-UP AFTER TREATMENT

Although this book is concerned with the prevention of occurrence or progression of disease, this discussion would be incomplete without some reference to the importance of following up after a series of treatments have been given to see that the benefits of that therapy are maintained and the possibilities of relapse are minimized. The same applies to the follow-up of patients discharged from rehabilitation facilities. This assures that the achievements from rehabilitation during a hospital stay are utilized to their maximum extent on the outside. It also encourages any follow-up therapy required for maintaining such gains.

I. JAY BRIGHTMAN, M.D.

REFERENCES

1. Brochure, Council on Medical Service: A study of multiple screening—descriptive data on 33 screening surveys. Chicago, American Medical Association, 1955.
2. Dowling, H. F., and Shakow, D.: Time spent by internists on adult health education and preventive medicine. Journal of the American Medical Association, 149:628, June 14, 1952.
3. Wiggins, W. S., Hilfinger, M. F., and Berman, L. G.: Delay in cancer diagnosis. New York State Journal of Medicine, 51:626, March 1, 1951.
4. Kutner, B., and Gordan, G.: Seeking care for cancer. Journal of Health and Human Behavior, 2:171, 1961.
5. Goldsen, R. K.: Patient delay in seeking cancer diagnosis: behavioral aspects. Journal of Chronic Diseases, 16:427, 1963.
6. Sullivan, W. A., and Lunseth, J. B.: The cancer detection center: nine year report. University of Minnesota Medical Bulletin, 28, June 1, 1957.
7. Joslin, E. P.: Renaissance of the control of diabetes. Journal of the American Medical Association, 156:1584, December 25, 1954.
8. Root, H. F.: The aging diabetic patient. Geriatrics, 17:317, May, 1962.

33   Rehabilitation

Rehabilitation has frequently been called the "third phase of medicine" following preventive medicine and acute medicine and surgery.[1] Such classification is, of course, an oversimplification and should not be interpreted as meaning each classification is mutually exclusive. In fact, just the reverse is true. There are elements of rehabilitation always present in preventive medicine just as there are always elements of preventive medicine in rehabilitation.

In this book the reader will come across two phrases frequently, "prevention of occurrence" and "prevention of progression." Although rehabilitation is not concerned with the prevention of specific disease, it is greatly concerned with the prevention of the physical, emotional, social and vocational sequelae of specific pathological processes upon the individual, his family and the community. It is true that many of our chronic diseases are still pathologically irreversible. This, however, does not mean that the development of undesirable effects of the disease upon the individual cannot be prevented.

The first objective of rehabilitation is to eliminate the physical disability if that is possible; the second, to reduce or alleviate the disability to the greatest extent possible; and the third, to retrain the person with a residual physical disability to live and to work within the limits of his disability but to the utmost of his capabilities.

In contrast to "convalescence" in which the patient is left alone to let nature and time take their course, rehabilitation is a dynamic concept in which the skills of the rehabilitation team consisting of the physician, physical therapists, occupational therapists, nurses, social workers, counselors and other trained personnel are integrated as a single force to assist the patient in reaching the maximum of his physical, emotional, social and vocational potentials.

One of the most significant medical and social advances of the past decade is the growing interest, both professional and lay, in the development of rehabilitation services for the physically handicapped. Undoubtedly, much of this interest in expanding rehabilitation opportunities and services for the handicapped has resulted both directly and indirectly from World War II when attention was focused on the problems of disabled servicemen.

Such advances, however, are not entirely due to this impetus, as the growth of rehabilitation services for the handicapped is a part of a total pattern of an expanding community, national and global consciousness of social welfare, which is reflected in similar advances in all educational, health, and social services. As in all great social movements, this increased interest in rehabilitation has been a result of the impact and recognition of increased needs: in this instance, the rapid increase in the developed parts of the world of the incidence of chronic disability as a result of the increasing age of the population.

Although some nations of the world still have pressing problems of communicable disease, life expectancy varies from nation to nation, depending upon the availability of medical care, public health measures, food supply, the general standard of living, and other factors. The trend in all nations, however, is towards a greatly increased life expectancy, with the result that throughout the world the population is gradually becoming older.

At the same time that the average age is advancing in the developed parts of the world, a new concept of the dignity of man and the worth of the individual is beginning to emerge in those nations of the world which do not yet have the benefits of modern programs of public health and medical care. This new concept of the worth of the individual has been symbolized, and is finding its expression in many instances, in the desire of these nations to institute programs of services for their physically handicapped.

Rehabilitation has been defined as the ultimate restoration of the disabled person to his maximum capacity—physical, emotional, social and vocational. Implicit in this definition is the need for a team whose members can bring together a wide variety of skills and understanding. No one profession can furnish all the services needed; rehabilitation is an area of specialized activity within a number of professional disciplines.

Based on data collected by the U.S. National Health Survey during July, 1959, to June, 1961, the leading single cause of disability in the United States is hearing impairment, with a rate of 35.3 per 1000 population. About 93 per cent of persons with hearing impairments, however, reported they had no limitation of any kind in their usual activities because of their hearing.

Ranking second behind hearing impairment was visual impairment with a total rate of 19.8 per 1000. The rate for those with severe visual impairment was 5.6, and among these 32 per cent were unable to engage in the usual activity of their population group (work, keep house, or go to school) because of their vision and 27 per cent were partially limited.

Other disability rates per 1000 population were speech defects, 5.9; paralysis, complete or partial, 5.4; and absence of major extremities, 1.5. About 63 per cent of the cases of paralysis occurred among persons over the age of 45, with vascular lesions of the central nervous system as the outstanding cause. Paralysis caused a major limitation of activity in 52 per cent of the cases at ages over 45 and 20 per cent among persons 45 years and under.

Absence of a major extremity was due to injury in 76 per cent of such cases. About four-fifths of the amputees were males, whose losses were caused by injury in 85 per cent of the cases.

In general, there are two kinds of medical rehabilitation: physical rehabilitation for musculoskeletal defects or disabilities, and adaptive rehabilitation for other handicaps associated with diseases such as tuberculosis, heart disease and mental illness. Medical rehabilitation is eminently practical. The emphasis is on training the disabled to carry out the essential activities of daily living, such as getting up, getting dressed, eating or going to the toilet. Whether the patient is temporarily disabled by a fractured hip or permanently disabled by poliomyelitis, similar rehabilitation services are required to restore function in the shortest possible time. Since rehabilitation helps to avoid further disability and economic dependency, it is prevention of progression of disease or disability.

Successful medical rehabilitation of a disabled person depends on many factors: the skill of his physician and his use of rehabilitation resources, the motivation of the patient to improve, the age of the patient, the presence of concomitant disease and social and economic factors.

The three principal killers and disablers—heart disease, cancer and cerebral vascular lesions—require specific rehabilitation sooner or later in the majority of individuals. If it is started soon after diagnosis, rehabilitation can play an effective role in preventing progression of disability in these chronic diseases. It can also help the disabled to learn to live with their handicaps. This is also true of other chronic ailments that plague our population from middle age on, such as arthritis and neuromuscular disorders. Because of the high prevalence of these disorders and their tendency to resist ordinary treatment, medical rehabilitation has much to offer the patient if the physician will only insist on its application.

Rehabilitation pays rich dividends when invested in those presumably permanently disabled persons who can be transformed into temporarily and only partially disabled persons through the skills of rehabilitation workers. The disabled person can be made independent enough to perform the ordinary chores of life and perhaps productive in employment if conditions permit.

PROCEDURES AND DEVICES

Essential to successful rehabilitation are the coordinated services of qualified professional workers. The team is usually headed by a specialist in physical medicine, but many other trained persons are needed. These include the internist, the orthopedist, the neurologist and the psychiatrist, to name a few. Supporting these is a formidable array of other workers: physical, occupational and speech therapists, nurses, social workers, brace makers and prosthetists. Rehabilitation is more than medical skill applied to the handicapped; it includes the services of educational and psychological experts in prevocational and vocational testing, guidance, training and in actual job placement.

For some persons, rehabilitation begins soon after surgery, most often orthopedic or plastic. Occasionally other types of surgery are indicated for various disabilities.

The procedures used in medical rehabilitation are the modalities of physical therapy: heat (moist or dry), massage, electrotherapy and ultra-sonics. Their total purpose is to prepare the patient for therapeutic exercises designed to strengthen muscles, to improve the range of joint movement and to reduce pain on activity.

Assistive devices are important tools. These include canes, crutches, braces, splints and wheel chairs. For those who have lost an arm or a leg, prosthetic devices must be provided and their use taught. Not infrequently an action that is difficult or impossible for a handicapped person can be carried out with self-help devices. A number of such "gadgets" have been developed, such as one-handed egg beaters, holders for a deck of cards, and many others. The Institute of Physical Medicine and Rehabilitation of New York University Medical Center has compiled a long list of available devices helpful to disabled persons.

Rehabilitation services of some types are provided in approximately 8 per cent of the nonfederal, short-term general hospitals and allied special hospitals. Most of these services are located in larger sized hospitals in metro-politan areas and concentrate their efforts on the physically disabled. Only about one-third of such services in general hospitals are prepared to serve psychiatric patients.

THE PHYSICIAN'S RESPONSIBILITY

Until recent years, the great majority of the medical profession looked upon rehabilitation as an extracurricular activity of medicine: something dealing with social work and vocational training, but something which had little concern and which held but few implications for medicine. Today, how-ever, that trend is being reversed. Although there are still many physicians who are unfamiliar with the aims and procedures of rehabilitation, medicine more and more is beginning to recognize that medical care cannot be con-sidered complete until the patient with a residual physical disability has been trained "to live and work with what he has left." Except in a few isolated instances, the physically handicapped person must be retrained to walk and travel, to care for his daily needs, to use normal methods of transportation, to use ordinary toilet facilities, to apply and remove his own prosthetic devices and to communicate either orally or in writing. These are such simple things that they are often overlooked, but the personal, vocational and social success of the handicapped person is dependent upon them.

The practice of rehabilitation for the general practitioner, or for any doctor, begins with belief in the basic philosophy that the doctor's responsi-bility does not end when the acute illness is ended or surgery is completed. It ends only when the individual is retrained to live and work with what is left. This basic concept of the doctor's responsibility can be achieved only if rehabilitation is considered an integral part of medical services. Any program of rehabilitation is only as sound as the basic medical service of which it is a part. The diagnosis and prognosis must be accurate, for it is upon them that the feasibility of retraining is determined.

Every physician should learn to know the rehabilitation resources in his community. In addition to the general hospitals and medical centers there are nursing homes, infirmaries and some homes for older people which provide rehabilitation services to their clients. The state and local health departments in the larger states often maintain hospitals to serve handicapped children. They also provide hospitals for the tuberculous where rehabilitation is available. Some of these health departments administer hospitals for the chronically ill. The local health officer can advise practicing physicians on the details of these programs and how to bring such services to individual patients.

REHABILITATION RESOURCES

Rehabilitation resources fall into these categories: (1) comprehensive centers providing a full range of services either as independent institutions or as parts of general or specialized hospitals; (2) physical medicine units including physical therapy and to a lesser degree occupational therapy in short-term general and allied special hospitals; and (3) small, independent centers offering some but not a full range of services.

As of January 1, 1962, some 1730 facilities in the United States offered rehabilitation services in one or more areas which included medical, psychological, social and vocational services. Of the group, however, only 221 offered comprehensive programs with services in all four areas, and approximately 20 per cent of these limited their services to a single disability or disease entity, such as cerebral palsy or epilepsy.

Since 1954, there has been a marked expansion of vocational rehabilitation services in the United States. The number of disabled persons rehabilitated into employment rose from 55,825 in 1954 to 110,136 in 1963.

In most communities of any size there are voluntary health agencies that usually provide some type of assistance to disabled persons. These include, among others, local units of the American Cancer Society, the American Heart Association, the Arthritis and Rheumatism Foundation, the Association for Crippled Children and Adults, the United Cerebral Palsy Associations, the National Foundation and the National Tuberculosis Association. Physicians should seek out and use these resources in their own communities.

Many communities operate speech and hearing centers. In New York state, for example, the state department of health provides sizeable grants to such centers over a developmental period of 5 years, and also matches local health department funds that are used for patient services.

PUBLIC AID FOR REHABILITATION

As can readily be appreciated, rehabilitation usually requires a prolonged period. Some of the more difficult conditions, such as paraplegia, frequently require expensive hospitalization for more than a year. Since so few people can afford such prolonged hospitalization, payment is often made by third parties, such as the state division of vocational rehabilitation, local welfare departments, the state medical rehabilitation or workmen's compensation programs, or health and welfare funds of labor unions. In June, 1962, for example, approximately 417,000 persons in the United States were receiving public assistance because of total and permanent disability other than blindness, and 100,000 blind persons were receiving public assistance.

A major resource for comprehensive services is the vocational rehabilitation agency in each of the states and the Commonwealth of Puerto Rico.

In these state-operated programs, which are partially financed by federal funds, disabled persons may receive evaluation, medical and physical restoration, counseling, vocational training and placement services if such services may make the disabled client employable or improve his employability.

The type and degree of rehabilitation services provided by local and state health departments varies from community to community and state to state. For example, in addition to services for crippled children, the New York State Department of Health operates a large specialized rehabilitation hospital at West Haverstraw. It also administers a program of state grants to nonprofit rehabilitation centers to aid them in expanding and sustaining their services.

Most patients who return home after treatment require maintenance therapy to prevent "back-sliding." Assistance in follow-up services is available from local health and welfare departments through public health nurses, physical therapists and social workers.

Because of the extent and nature of the problems of providing rehabilitation to persons with physical handicaps, health departments play an important part in this field. Their role may be providing rehabilitation facilities and services, giving financial assistance, stimulating the development of services or making studies of new rehabilitation techniques.

Industry also has considerable interest in medical rehabilitation because of the effect of disability on productivity and the losses associated with work-connected disabilities. It has been repeatedly demonstrated that an industrial worker with a corrected disability can make a good employee. Absenteeism is lower among the disabled than among other workers, there is less "job shopping," and the output of the properly placed handicapped workers compares favorably with that of the nonhandicapped.

RESULTS OF REHABILITATION

It is often surprising what intensive rehabilitation can accomplish, even among the severely disabled and at all ages. In a pilot study at the New York State Rehabilitation Hospital,[2] in which a group of presumably totally and permanently disabled recipients of public assistance were treated, the following results were obtained on the first 100 persons in this category admitted to the hospital (Table 18).

Table 18. *Diagnosis and Status of Disabled Recipients of Rehabilitation Services on Their Discharge*

DIAGNOSIS	MARKED IMPROVE-MENT	MODERATE IMPROVE-MENT	SLIGHT IMPROVE-MENT	NO CHANGE	DIED	TOTAL
Arthritis	8	8	1	3	0	20
Hemiplegia	5	7	4	4	0	20
Paraplegia or quadriplegia	4	6	1	4	2	17
Malunited fracture	3	4	3	3	0	13
Multiple sclerosis	0	5	2	4	0	11
Amputation	1	1	0	1	0	3
Miscellaneous	2	5	3	6	0	16
Total	23	36	14	25	2	100

Follow-up studies of these patients made 6 months after their discharge showed that adequate social services were absolutely essential when these patients returned to their homes, so that the gains made in the hospital would not be lost. It was equally important that vocational guidance and training be pursued to make the most of the vocational potential of persons who had been given hospital care. From this study it is reasonable to conclude that there exists an unknown but sizeable number of welfare recipients now totally disabled who could benefit substantially from intensive rehabilitation. The results of rehabilitation in the general population would be better than that suggested by the data from Table 18, since this was from a group of severely disabled people with multiple disabilities, many of whom were over 60 years of age.

The tuberculous patient presents special problems in rehabilitation because he does not give the outward appearance of disability, and yet impairment of lung function may be severe. In such individuals it is essential to do cardiopulmonary function studies to determine the capacity of each to carry on useful activities. It is not enough to determine vital capacity by one of the common "blowing" tests; one must have access to a laboratory where cardiopulmonary function measurements are done and evaluation of the rehabilitation potential is determined by persons with experience in this field.

The practicing physician can usually call upon a nearby tuberculosis hospital for consultation in the care and supervision of his ambulatory tuberculosis patient after the patient leaves the hospital. Rehabilitation is not an auxiliary service for the tuberculous; it is fundamental. It should begin with the initial diagnosis, extend through the entire period of isolation and hospital care and end only with maximum social and economic security. When one considers the millions of dollars spent annually on basic services for early case finding, hospitalization and other medical care, the provision of rehabilitation services for tuberculous patients is one of the simplest ways of preserving this great investment. The job of tuberculosis control is accomplished only when maximum rehabilitation of the tuberculous individual has been achieved.

SPECIAL PROBLEMS IN REHABILITATION

Although many people are familiar with the effects of chronic disease upon our older population, most people are less familiar with the crippling disorders of childhood. Because of improvements in obstetrics and pediatrics, many more children survive today than previously, even after premature birth. Among those who survive there are a number who have auditory and visual defects and cardiovascular, orthopedic and mental disorders that interfere with normal growth and development. These conditions may be either congenital or acquired. Unfortunately, we do not know how to prevent the occurrence of most of these congenital conditions, so we must use rehabilitation in an effort to enable those afflicted to lead happy and useful lives.

Recent surgical advances make it possible to correct many congenital and rheumatic heart lesions. Improved hearing devices and speech-training techniques can assist children with auditory defects to live virtually normal lives. New rehabilitation and surgical procedures have helped orthopedically handicapped children to attend school and to become self-supporting, aided by vocational education and training. Modern techniques of physical and occupational therapy have aided children with cerebral palsy; new drugs control the vast majority of epileptic seizures in children. Early care for children born with cleft lips and palates, including plastic surgery, skillful prosthodontia and speech therapy, achieves cosmetic and functional miracles.

An important part of the physician's task in pediatric rehabilitation is to be on the lookout for disabilities of every type, beginning with a careful examination of the newborn child for congenital deformities or abnormalities. The physician can then arrange for correction of these disabilities at the earliest possible time. If the family does not follow his advice, the physician should ask a representative of the health or welfare agencies in the community to explain to the parents the great importance of early treatment and rehabilitation. It is easier for the physician to do nothing when families are uncooperative but the physician has a responsibility to follow through on the provision of rehabilitation.

Adequate nutrition is an important adjunct to rehabilitation. Often nutritional deficiencies and inadequacies are common among the aged disabled, more so than any other group. Inactivity, diminished taste acuity, long-standing habits of poor food selection and a growing tendency to take up food fads, are characteristic of this group. The general physician in his daily practice can help to guide the eating habits and food intake of older people, particularly those with chronic diseases. One cannot take for granted that these older persons know what to eat or that they receive adequate amounts of food (Chapter 22).

Older people do not require as many calories per day as they did when they were working and more vigorous. However, it is essential to maintain protein requirements and to give consideration to special diets necessary as part of the treatment for patients with multiple chronic illnesses. Local or state health departments usually have nutrition services which make available the help of experts on the nutrition of older people with chronic disease.

Rehabilitation of the physically and mentally handicapped calls upon all the resources of the medical and allied professions. The family physician of the future will spend a large share of his time on the rehabilitation of the chronically ill of all ages. The many different needs of the disabled individual will demand a variety of skills and resources in the community.

The physician who is oriented in modern rehabilitation services uses all the resources available in the community to help him in the treatment of his patients. There is no greater satisfaction for the family physician than to see the completed rehabilitation of one of his more seriously disabled patients, even though the net results in the severe cases are simply the ability of the patient to get out of bed, to make his toilet, to dress and to feed himself.

Rehabilitation involves one of the fundamental elements of our culture, to help a person who is unable to help himself. Conservation of resources, especially the productivity and dignity of handicapped individuals in the community, requires full participation of private physicians and of their colleagues in the official and voluntary health agencies and in all government units concerned with human resources. Rehabilitation brings profit to the individual in the form of health and happiness, professional satisfaction to the practicing physician and social and economic benefits to the community.

HOWARD A. RUSK, M.D.
HERMAN E. HILLEBOE, M.D.

REFERENCES

1. Rusk, Howard A., et al.: Rehabilitation Medicine. St. Louis, The C. V. Mosby Co., 1958.
2. Hilleboe, H. E., and Levin M., et al.: A pilot program for the rehabilitation of disabled welfare recipients. A preliminary report. New York State Journal of Medicine, 57:1737, May 15, 1957.
3. Areawide planning of facilities for rehabilitation services. Report of a joint committee of the Public Health Service and the Vocational Rehabilitation Administration. P.H.S. publication 930-B-2. Washington, D.C., U. S. Government Printing Office, 1963.
4. Hilleboe, H. E.: Teamwork in rehabilitation—From fancy to fact. American Journal of Public Health, 54 (No. 5): 751-757, May, 1964.

34   Alcoholism

DEFINITION

Alcoholism has been defined in many ways but, from the viewpoint of the practicing physician, the most helpful definition appears to be the following:

"Alcoholism is a chronic illness, psychic or somatic or psychosomatic, which manifests itself as a disorder of behavior. It is characterized by the repeated drinking of alcoholic beverages, to an extent that exceeds customary dietary use or compliance with the social customs of the community and that interferes with the drinker's health or his social or economic functioning. Many special categories of alcoholics have been identified, including 'alcohol addicts,' who cannot control their drinking, and 'alcoholics with complications.' The latter are those whose excessive drinking has led to recognizable physical or mental sequels."[1]

This definition does not include those persons who have occasional bouts of excessive drinking but who do not drink habitually. Their periods of intoxication may too frequently involve them in disorderly conduct or in motor vehicle accidents. After medical evaluation excludes them as alcoholics, their problem is essentially the concern of moral and legal authorities rather than of medical or public health personnel.

PREVALENCE

The prevalence of excessive drinking and alcoholism is difficult to determine because of the general secretiveness about the disorder on the part of both patient and family, the frequent refusal by physicians and hospitals to treat such patients, the lack of comparable and reliable data on arraignments for intoxication, the difficulty in making a correct diagnosis without detailed and prolonged study, and, undoubtedly, many other factors.

Some time ago, Jellinek estimated alcoholism prevalence rates by a formula based upon the presumption of a constant relationship between deaths from cirrhosis of the liver and the occurrence of recognizable physical or mental sequels to excessive drinking.[2] This formula was utilized for many years for studies of trends and for comparison of rates among different countries.

Utilizing data available for the years 1954 through 1956, it has been estimated that there are 5,000,000 alcoholics in the United States and that of these, 1,250,000 are suffering from the complications of alcoholism.[3] These figures give the United States a rate of 4760 cases of alcoholism per 100,000 adults 20 years and older in the population. This would be the highest rate among all major countries. If alcoholism with complications only is considered, then the United States figure of 1098 is surpassed by the prevalence rates of Switzerland (1590), Chile (1497) and France (1420).

It would also be expected that the alcoholism rate would vary from state to state. California ranked highest in 1955 with a rate of 6600 alcoholics per 100,000 adults 20 years and older, with and without complications, followed by New Jersey with 6060, New Hampshire with 6030 and New York with 5850.

However, the reliability of the Jellinek formula is questionable both because of its statistical complexity and because of the possible differences in diagnostic criteria, in completeness of reporting as well as in clinical acumen among the countries studied. Other approaches are now being investigated.

An index to alcohol intake in different countries may be obtained by analyzing information dealing with liquor taxes, deliveries to distributors and other indirect data.[4] In the United States, the estimated consumption of alcohol (as contained in distilled spirits, wine and beer) by the population 15 years of age and older in 1962 was 7.99 liters per capita. France had by far the largest intake per capita, 25.72 liters, although much of this is taken as wine. Other countries exceeding the United States figure were Italy 13.26 liters, Switzerland 10.85, Australia 9.6, New Zealand 9.03, West Germany 8.84 and Belgium 8.48. The ratio of male to female alcoholics is 5.8 to 1, a figure which has been essentially unchanged in this country for nearly 50 years.

In reference to age, it has been noted that alcoholism appears most frequently during the most productive decade of life, between the ages of 40 and 50 in men and approximately 5 years younger in women. However, there is usually a long prior period of excessive drinking before a person reaches that stage of alcoholism in which recognizable signs of mental or physical illness may be seen. This period averages about 10 years in men and somewhat less in women. This sequence is of practical importance as it emphasizes the need to institute preventive measures early in adult life, preferably before the first signs of excessive drinking.

PHASES OF ALCOHOLISM

As with other chronic disorders, preventive measures, whether aimed at prevention of occurrence or progression, may be applied at several stages. These measures will vary depending upon the stage which the patient has reached and the various social, economic and legal aspects which may be involved. Therefore, before presenting the preventive aspects of alcoholism, it would seem best to review briefly the natural history of alcoholism as it has been determined to date.

The question has repeatedly arisen as to whether there is an individual personality type or constellation of frequently predominate characteristics which might identify a person as being a "prealcoholic." Many studies utilizing both projective and nonprojective techniques have been published since 1949. The alcoholic is frequently described as a person who has always shown evidences of dependence and emotional immaturity or instability; he is in some way related to the socially acceptable obese person who utilizes his excess food intake as an escape mechanism, as well as to the user of narcotic drugs who resorts to narcotics as a crutch. Actually, there has been a failure to produce data supporting a consistent theme relative to the alcoholic personality.[5] Also, there is always the question of whether any personality characteristics of the alcoholic are the cause or the result of the disease.

As indicated, excessive drinking may be continued for many years before recognizable signs of mental or physical illness may be seen. Persons who have reached this stage of alcoholism have been divided into two categories, namely "alcoholic addicts" and "habitual symptomatic excessive drinkers." The latter are often referred to as nonaddictive alcoholics. In both groups, the excessive drinking is symptomatic of underlying psychological or social pathology. However in the former group, after several years of excessive drinking, loss of control over alcohol occurs. As soon as a very small quantity of alcohol enters the body a demand for more alcohol is set up which is felt as a physical demand by the drinker. This demand lasts until the drinker is too intoxicated or too sick to drink more alcohol. The loss of control may be manifested whether the drink is taken because of an assumed personal need of the moment, or as a social gesture.

The loss of control phenomena does not occur among the habitual symptomatic excessive drinkers, even though they may drink even more than the addict for 30 or 40 years.

PHASES OF ALCOHOL ADDICTION

The course of alcohol addiction develops in phases varying in duration according to individual characteristics and environmental factors.[6]

Prealcoholic Symptomatic Phase

This phase, characterized at the beginning by socially motivated drinking, shows a gradual change as the individual begins to experience a rewarding relief from tensions in a drinking situation and his tolerance for tension decreases to such a degree that he takes recourse to alcoholic relief practically daily. Overt intoxication may not occur and drinking may not be conspicuous either to his family or to his business associates. An increase in tolerance may gradually occur whereby the drinker requires a larger amount of alcohol than formerly in order to achieve the desired state of relief. This period may last from several months to 2 years.

Prodromal Phase

This phase is characterized by the sudden onset of blackouts, which may not be related to the amount of alcohol consumed and may be followed by an amnesia covering the period of the event. The signs of this phase include surreptitious drinking, a marked preoccupation with alcohol and the development of guilt feelings and fears about it. While drinking in this stage may not be heavy, it is beyond ordinary usage and on a level which may interfere with ordinary metabolic and nervous processes.

Crucial Phase

This is the phase at which loss of control appears. Although the drinker has lost the ability to control quantity once he has started to drink, he can still control whether or not he will drink on any given occasion. Thus through his own efforts or with outside encouragement, he may go through a period of voluntary abstinence. However, he often returns to drinking either to test himself or to demonstrate to others his ability to handle alcohol. He does not accept the fact that he cannot stop drinking and begins to rationalize about his drinking behavior. Other characteristics of this phase include marked aggressive behavior, persistent remorse, dropping friends, quitting jobs, loss of all outside interests, deeper concentration on alcohol, resentment toward family attitudes and geographic escape. There is also neglect of proper nutrition, decrease in the sexual drive and the beginning of drinking in the early hours of the day, although more intensive drinking may not start before 5 P.M.

Chronic Phase

This is the beginning of prolonged intoxications, with continuous drinking for days or weeks. This is followed by marked ethical deterioration, impairment of thinking and possibly by a true alcoholic psychosis.

PHASES OF HABITUAL SYMPTOMATIC EXCESSIVE DRINKING (NONADDICTIVE)

The prealcoholic phase is the same for the nonaddictive alcoholic as for the alcoholic addict; that is, he progresses from occasional to constant relief of individual symptoms through alcohol.[6] The absence of loss of control has important significance for his future course. He does have the ability to stop drinking within a given situation. Thus, there is no need to rationalize such behavior, although he may develop rationalizations for justifying the excessive use of alcohol and some neglect of his family. However, the course of heavy and habitual drinking over a period of 10 to 12 years may result in several, though usually not all, of the late manifestations of addictive drinking. In the presence of serious underlying psychopathies, the deteriorative process is speeded up by the habitual alcohol excess.

Jellinek describes four so-called "species" of alcoholism.[7] His Alpha, Beta and Gamma types correspond generally with the first three phases described above. His Delta Alcoholism is a form in which both psychological and physical dependence are observed, but the latter is characterized by an "inability to abstain" from alcohol rather than by a "loss of control." The Delta type is considered characteristic of the heavy wine drinking countries, particularly France, whereas Gamma Alcoholism (the Crucial Phase) predominates in the United States.

The nonsymbolic terminology used here seems preferable. It is more descriptive and is suggestive of the progressive nature of alcoholism. However, it must be recognized that the phases may be of varying duration in different individuals. The earlier phases may not be identifiable in persons observed for the first time in the later phases. The disease may appear to be nonprogressive in some patients.

PREVENTIVE ASPECTS

This discussion has emphasized the general high prevalence of alcoholism, thus indicating the frequency with which physicians will encounter this disorder in private practice, as well as in community or industrial health work. The natural course of the disease points up the importance of either preventing its occurrence or arresting its course at the earliest possible phase. In only rare instances is this a simple matter. Thus, each addicted alcoholic patient will present a serious challenge to the physician, and in many instances efforts to treat will be frustrating. However, there will be a strong sense of gratification for each patient who is helped and for each family that may thereby be maintained.

PREVENTION OF OCCURRENCE

As indicated earlier in this book, prevention of occurrence implies the avoidance of a disease through some action taken upon the causative agent, the environment or the host.

Alcohol cannot be considered as the causative agent in alcoholism. Neither can the social acceptability of moderate alcohol drinking and the general availability of alcohol beverages, except in certain "dry" areas, be blamed. Alcohol is consumed by a very high percentage of the adult population in accord with social or religious customs, with no unfortunate consequences. Of course, alcoholism could not occur without alcohol, but it is likely that some other toxic agent might be substituted by excessive users if alcohol were withdrawn from both legal and illegal markets. The problem of illegal markets under the prohibition era is too well remembered at this time. It must also be recalled that alcohol is a frequently used agent for medicinal and industrial purposes, and, despite denaturing, this type is often utilized in dilute form by addicted alcoholics for drinking purposes.

Therefore, efforts for prevention of occurrence must be directed at the host and the family and community in which he lives. The ill effects of alcohol on the body should be taught in courses on health in elementary and secondary schools.

As one cannot recognize any true prealcoholic personality type, there is no way of detecting which persons have greater potentialities for developing alcoholism.

However, a definite lead for prevention occurs in the prealcoholic symptomatic stage. Here, there may be a definite change in the drinking pattern of the individual. Such a change may be detected during a careful medical history and emphasizes the need to include questions about alcoholic intake in the physician's questioning.

PREVENTION OF PROGRESSION

This refers to care for the alcoholic during the prodromal and the crucial phases. Here, the behavior of the alcoholic patient is beginning to result in threats to domestic and vocational situations, or breaks in these relationships may have already occurred. It is important to bring to bear all that medicine and the related services can offer the alcoholic to prevent him from deteriorating into the chronic phase.

The personal physician has a key role to play in working with the patient and his family at this stage of alcoholism. It is important for him to make a diagnosis of the patient's condition, including a determination of whether addiction is present, the rapidity with which the alcoholic pattern is changing, the relationship of the drinking to underlying mental and physical disorders and the importance of various social or environmental factors. The personal physician must develop an intimate confidential relationship with the patient so that the patient will look upon him as a friend and a professional counselor, rather than as a disciplinarian. The nature of the disease must be explained to the patient, and this may have to be repeated several times before the patient may be ready to extend his cooperation in an attempt to reverse or at least arrest the course of the disease. The physician's relationship to the family may be very important in the successful handling of the alcoholic. A sympathetic understanding on the part of parents, wife or children are important concomitants of treatment. There is need for an enlistment of their cooperation in aiding the patient to make a satisfactory approach to his disease and in readjusting any situations in the home which are prejudicial to the patient's recovery.

Physicians have had an understandable reluctance in accepting addicted alcoholics as patients. In a study undertaken by the Committee on Public Health Relations of the New York Academy of Medicine it was found that only 13 per cent of the physicians included in a questionnaire survey returned the forms, and of these approximately 60 per cent stated that they treat neither alcohol addiction nor alcoholic intoxication.[8] Only a few physicians reported that alcoholism comprised a really significant portion of their practice.

The past decade has seen the development of many new techniques which have added significantly to the therapy of alcoholism. These include the introduction of steroid drugs, disulfiram and the tranquilizers, all of which have led to increased effectiveness in the management of the alcoholic. Thus, while alcoholism is still a very difficult disease to treat and requires much patience and detailed planning on the part of the physician, there is now a greater possibility of obtaining gratifying results than existed 10 or 15 years ago. Also, the handling of the patient is less objectionable because he is more readily quieted and placed in a position to respond to therapy.

Organized medicine has recognized the importance of alcoholism in several ways. The American Medical Association has appointed a committee on alcoholism as a unit of its council on mental health. This committee has prepared a *Manual on Alcoholism*,[9] dealing with the treatment of the disease, and also has prepared an exhibit for use at state medical society meetings. Both of these have been in very great demand. Many state medical societies have appointed committees on alcoholism which have directed their efforts at studying the problems in local communities and encouraging physicians to accept their responsibilities in this field.

Regardless of the personal physician's interest in providing medical care for his addicted alcoholic patient, he will most often require assistance from community agencies of various types. The more important of these are the following:

Clinics

Many communities provide medical care for addicted alcoholic patients through the organization of clinics in the outpatient departments of general hospitals, or in other community facilities. In some areas these alcoholics are offered care in general mental health clinics, whereas other communities have established specialized alcoholism clinics.[10]

The clinics vary in the type of service offered. Some offer simply psychiatric consultation. Others have a complete multidisciplinary, diagnostic evaluation and treatment program, including the services of a psychiatrist, internist, psychologist, psychiatric social worker and nurse.

While some of these clinics may be limited to low income groups or to persons referred by courts, the majority accept patients of all economic levels, with fees based on ability to pay. A private physician managing a patient with alcoholism may find it desirable to refer his patient to a clinic for a complete diagnostic work-up, with the patient to be returned to him for continued therapy.

Industrial Plants

It will be expected that many addicted alcoholic patients will come under the care of the industrial physicians of some of the larger manufacturing plants in the community. Industry has concerned itself deeply with the problem of alcoholism. The prevalence has been estimated at 2 to 3 per cent of employees, with an annual incidence of new cases at about 1½ to 2 cases per 1000.[11] Many companies have developed educational programs informing the medical departments and the supervisors of the importance of the disease and the means of recognition. Some have arranged for in-plant treatment while others have provided for referral of the worker to his personal physician or to specialized clinics. The object is to keep the patient on the job, a very important item to industry, especially for skilled employees or where there is a shortage of workers.

In some instances, the workers are put on probation whereby they are told that the continuation of their jobs is dependent upon their maintaining treatment. This motivational factor appears to have a corrective effect. The Consultation Clinic for Alcoholism, which is operated by the University Hospital of the New York University-Bellevue Medical Center, receives only patients referred by certain industrial plants.[12] This clinic has been able to report good results in about 70 per cent of its patients, with a reduction in absenteeism from 13.5 days per year prior to clinic treatment to 4 days per year in the rehabilitated cases. These results are far more favorable than those reported by alcoholism clinics serving the general public. It would be expected that private physicians might, likewise, have more effective results among patients referred by industry.

General Hospitals

The management of an alcoholic will frequently call for general hospital services. This may be for care during a period of acute intoxication, management of delirium tremens or for a diagnostic evaluation during a sober period to determine underlying mental and physical disorders.

Unfortunately, the majority of general hospitals have not accepted patients with alcoholism. In a study done in 1958 in New York state, it was found that alcoholic patients were accepted by only 18 per cent of voluntary hospitals and 35 per cent of public hospitals.[13] About 50 per cent of the nonaccepting hospitals had regulations against the admission of these patients. On the other hand, about 40 per cent of the hospitals admitting alcoholic patients found that they were not particularly troublesome. Practically all hospitals found that the tranquilizing drugs were very helpful in quieting disturbed alcoholics. Thus, it would seem that these favorable experiences could be readily transferred to a sufficient number of general hospitals to take care of community needs.

The American Medical Association has passed a resolution calling upon general hospitals to accept alcoholics in any instances where there is medical need.[14] The resolution stressed the importance of recognizing and treating acute alcoholic intoxication as a possible medical emergency, and also the need to offer training in treating the illness to house officers, who will eventually come in contact with this type of patient in practice.

Social Agencies

In many instances, the physician will find it important to explore the social background of the individual and his family and to determine the extent to which background factors are responsible for tensions relating to the alcoholism syndrome. It is not always possible for the physician to do this alone. Here he may find the various family agencies in his community to be helpful, or, with hospitalized patients, he may call upon the social service section of the hospital.[15]

For patients on public assistance, the caseworkers of the public agency will often be in a position to provide the physician with the social information he requires and also to assist him in helping to arrange for improvement of the home situation.

Vocational Assistance

For the addicted alcoholic patient who has lost his job or whose job is obviously unsuitable for him and a source of tensions, vocational retraining may be an essential part of his total treatment. If the physician recognizes this possibility early, he may be able to remove one of the irritants which is interfering with the satisfactory response of the patient. Here expert assistance from vocational counselors may be required and the physician may call upon the services of the official vocational rehabilitation agency of his state. Likewise, the selective placement unit of the state employment service may be helpful in obtaining a position for the individual which is compatible with his mental and physical condition.

Alcoholics Anonymous

This unique organization is made up of persons who have been alcoholics but have achieved control over their drinking and are dedicated to assisting other alcoholics to achieve this favorable stage.[16] Alcoholics Anonymous groups are organized in the majority of communities throughout the nation. While some individual alcoholic patients may be refractory to working with groups of persons who have gone through the same disease, it does appear that a significant percentage obtain considerable benefit by associating with persons who have also been sufferers. The acceptance of this assistance seems to create a better understanding of the disease and aids in effecting control. Many of the alcoholism clinics have developed close working relationships with Alcoholics Anonymous groups. Private physicians may find this organization an excellent source of assistance.

Half-way Houses

In many instances the alcoholic patient is found to have lost his home or to have an intolerable home situation. Such a patient does not necessarily need the highly technical services available in a general hospital.

Therefore, many communities have established facilities which may be known as half-way houses or rehabilitation centers, which provide for group living under supervision. These facilities will care for 10 to 30 patients. The men most often take care of the maintenance chores themselves, thus keeping down costs.

Services of psychiatrists and internists are provided as necessary and there is generally a full-time supervisor who may or may not be a controlled alcoholic. After about 2 weeks of initial convalescence, the patients are encouraged to accept jobs on the outside and return to the facility for evenings and weekends. After a satisfactory period of adjustment, an attempt is made to return the patient to his own home or to arrange for other independent living.

State Hospitals

While some states have provided for the acceptance of patients with all forms of alcoholism at state mental hygiene hospitals, the majority restrict such admissions to alcoholics with psychoses. Thus a physician can refer a patient to a state hospital only when the patient has an underlying psychosis or has developed a psychosis as a complication of his alcoholism. Recently, many state mental hygiene agencies have been adopting a more liberal and progressive policy. For example, New York State has recently established new units for nonpsychotic alcoholics in two of its institutions and plans additional units in the near future.

In New York state, alcoholics with psychoses have made up about 8 per cent of all first admissions to state hospitals.[17] More than half of these patients are discharged within the first 2 years and return to the community. Obviously, nonpsychotic alcoholics are discharged much earlier, usually within 2 or 3 months. Thus the physician or clinic referring such a patient should prepare for his return and provide the necessary follow-up during the posthospital period.

COMMUNITY RESPONSIBILITIES FOR ALCOHOLISM

In addition to the care of addicted alcoholic patients in private practice, in the office, hospitals and clinics, the physician may expect to be called upon as a consultant in community efforts relating to either alcohol or alcoholism. As a professional person it is important for him to cooperate with other community groups and serve as a consultant in the fields in which he is best qualified. A few of the more important community efforts in this area are briefly outlined.

Public Health Movement

There has been increasing acceptance of alcoholism as a public health problem, on the basis of its prevalence, seriousness, costliness and need for community services. In several areas health departments have accepted responsibility for educational, clinical and rehabilitation services for the alcoholic patient, and often the family as a whole. Services for alcoholism may be operated as a special program, developed as part of the mental health functions, or integrated with the general public health activities.

Regardless of the pattern, the health department can make several important contributions: (a) through the health officer who is experienced in detecting the epidemiological features of the disease in his community and in evaluating services to assure that results are consistent with objectives; (b) through the public health nurses who may play a role in case finding, hospital and clinic referral and follow-up, and family counseling, and (c) through the health educator who is familiar with community organization and the development and evaluation of educational tools. The potential of the health department will depend upon its general strength as a public health agency, the desire of the community that it engage in such a program, and the special training of its staff to cope with this special problem.[18, 19, 20]

The importance of mental health in the prevention of alcoholism should be stressed here. The observation and treatment of children with emotional disorders may be a step in preventing their later reliance on alcohol as emotionally immature adults. The early detection of abnormal signs of behavior and changes in the drinking patterns of adolescents and young adults, and the prompt referral of such persons to treatment resources are important phases of prevention.

Health Education in Schools

Most states require reference to alcohol and narcotic drugs in the curriculum for health education. The nature of this teaching varies from state to state and from community to community. It is important for physicians, as well as for other members of society, to determine just what is being taught to the schoolchildren and whether this is acceptable in the light of modern professional knowledge. It is necessary to know whether adequate distinctions are made between alcohol and alcoholism. It is important to determine whether the teaching in the school is consistent with the pattern of drinking in the community or whether such teaching may be confusing and frustrating to children who find it difficult to relate these teachings with their observations at home and in the community.

The Homeless Man

The homeless man presents a problem to every urban community. It is not likely that the physician will see many such persons in the course of private practice. Not all homeless men are addicted alcoholics, although the majority do use alcohol to an excessive degree. Their problem is primarily a social one. However, their disposition requires medical consultation because among them may be found persons from upper and middle social classes who have progressed to the chronic stage of alcoholism and slipped to skid row. Any program for the management of alcoholism should provide means of detecting such persons for rehabilitation purposes.

The National Council on Alcoholism

This is a voluntary health agency in which many physicians have become interested. Its objectives are the education of the community regarding the nature of alcoholism, arousing its sympathy and gaining support for an adequate control program.

I. JAY BRIGHTMAN, M.D.

REFERENCES

1. Keller, M., and Efron, V.: The prevalence of alcoholism. Quarterly Journal of Studies on Alcohol, *16*:619, December, 1955.
2. WHO Technical Report Series No. 42. Expert Committee on Mental Health, Alcoholism Subcommittee, Geneva, 1951.
3. Keller, M., and Efron, V.: The rate of alcoholism in the U.S.A. Quarterly Journal of Studies on Alcohol, *19*:316, June, 1958.
4. Efron, V., and Keller, M.: Selected Statistical Tables on the Consumption of Alcohol, 1850-1962, and on Alcoholism 1930-1960. New Brunswick, N. J., Rutgers Center of Alcohol Studies, 1963, page 10.
5. Syme, L.: Personality characteristics and the alcoholic—A critique of current studies. Quarterly Journal of Studies on Alcohol, *18*:288, June, 1957.
6. WHO Technical Report Series No. 48, 1952, and No. 94, 1955. Expert Committees on Mental Health and on Alcohol and Alcoholism, respectively, Geneva.
7. Jellinek, E. M.: The Disease Concept of Alcoholism. New Haven, Connecticut, Hillhouse Press, 1963, pages 35-41.
8. Committee on Public Health Relations of the New York Academy of Medicine: A survey of facilities for the care and treatment of alcoholism in New York City. Quarterly Journal of Studies on Alcohol, 7:405, December, 1946.
9. Manual on Alcoholism. Committee on Alcoholism of the Council on Mental Health, American Medical Association, Chicago, 1962.
10. Bahn, A. K., Anderson, C. L., and Norman, V. B.: Outpatient psychiatric clinic services to alcoholics, 1959. Quarterly Journal of Studies on Alcohol, *24*:213, June, 1963.
11. Franco, S. C.: The alcoholic in industry. New York State Journal of Medicine, *57*:3511, November 1, 1957.
12. Pfeffer, A. Z., Feldman, D. J., Feibel, C., Frank, J. A., Cohen, M., Berger, S., Fleetwood, M. F., and Greenberg, S. S.: A treatment program for the alcoholic in industry. Journal of the American Medical Association, *161*:827, June 30, 1956.
13. Brightman, I. J., Royle, C. M., Ferber, B., Robinson, P. F., and Robinson, W. T.: The admission of patients with alcoholism to general hospitals in New York State. New York State Journal of Medicine, *59*:237, January 15, 1959.
14. Report of Board of Trustees to Members of House of Delegates of American Medical Association. Journal of the American Medical Association, *162*:750, October 20, 1956.
15. Bailey, M. B., and Fuchs, E.: Alcoholism and the social worker. Social Work, *5*:14, October, 1960.
16. Berger, H.: Alcoholics Anonymous and the medical profession. New York State Journal of Medicine, *58*:108, January 1, 1958.
17. Malzberg, B.: Cohort Studies of Mental Disease in New York State, 1943-1949, 1958. National Association for Mental Health, New York.

18. Brown, B. S., Esquibel, A., Grant, M., and Pickford, E. M.: Health Department
    Alcoholism Program in Prince Georges County, Maryland. Public Health Re-
    ports, 77:480, June, 1962.
19. Freund, J., Gleidman, L. H., Thomas, R. E., Imber, S. D., and Stone, A. R.: Role of
    the public health nurse in alcoholic rehabilitation. Public Health Reports,
    76:378, May, 1961.
20. Brightman, I. J.: The future of alcoholism programs. Public Health Reports, 75:775,
    September, 1960.

35   Narcotic Addiction

INTRODUCTION

Addiction to narcotics undoubtedly springs from a universal human propensity for taking substances in order to enjoy the ensuing psychic effects. The preparations which are used range from harmless ones such as tea and coffee to drugs such as morphine and heroin which produce severe and rather specific syndromes of disability. It is primarily with these last that this chapter deals since in the United States at the present time the problem is essentially that of addiction to heroin or combinations of heroin and barbiturates (especially pentobarbital).

HISTORICAL NOTE

The virtues of the narcotic poppy are among the first recorded facts in medicine and references to the use of its various preparations have always abounded in the literature. However, it is a curious fact that though addiction itself was recognized from ancient times, there was no clear medical account of this state as we know it today until the last century, although widespread abuse of opium has existed in the Far Eastern and Arabic countries for well over a thousand years. It was not until the latter part of the 19th century that a true medical literature on opium addiction finally emerged.[1] Morphine was widely used by injection in military medicine in the American Civil War, but morphine addiction was not clearly described until almost 10 years after that war. Since then, the scientific literature has become voluminous and, in addition, addiction has become a favorite topic for a very large number of purely literary efforts of various types. Some of them were very excellent and followed after the style of DeQuincy[2] whose Confessions date to the early 1800's, but a great deal of sensational writing has been done, and has contributed heavily to the present state of public

387

misinformation on the subject, and perhaps even to some professional confusion.[3]

Currently this country, as well as a number of other nations are concerned about a cycle of marked increase in addiction which began after World War II and probably reached a peak several years ago in the United States, although scientific evidence is lacking on this question.

EXTENT OF THE PROBLEM

No one knows how many drug addicts there are in the United States. About 48,000 are known to government authorities,[4] a figure far higher than that reported from any other Western nation to the World Health Organization. Of these an estimated 20,000 to 30,000 are in New York State. The bulk of the remainder are judged to be in Illinois, California, Michigan, the District of Columbia, Ohio, and Texas. In these areas, as well as in others, addiction is concentrated in large urban centers. In New York State the problem is at its worst in New York City. There it is localized to a considerable extent in certain socioeconomically depressed multiple problem areas such as Harlem and is currently most prevalent among Negroes and those of Puerto Rican descent.

It is difficult to evaluate not only the present extent of the problem but also, to a lesser degree, its long-term trend. The United States Commissioner of Narcotics estimated that before the passage of the Harrison Anti-Narcotic Act in 1914 there was one addict for every 400 persons in the population, and that since that time the number has dropped to less than 1 in 3000. However, it must be admitted that since addicts do not become known to law enforcement officials unless they are apprehended in some illegal activity, many may never be listed by such agencies, and the problem may indeed be far larger than indicated by the figure of 48,000. On the other hand, there is also the possibility of duplication in these lists, and the likelihood that persons may continue to be counted after they have recovered or died. Finally, many addicts have alternate periods of being "clean" and being addicted, so a simple total cannot tell us how many persons are actively addicted at any given time.

Other indices of the narcotic problem, such as those based on arrests related to addiction must be interpreted with the reservation that there is wide variation in the level of local police activity from one time to another, and from one locality to another, according to the current level of local interest in the problem. Thus, narcotic addiction might remain relatively constant in a given community while the arrest figures could vary considerably. However, in spite of the general uncertainty of such statistics, it is apparent that the narcotic problem in this country reached an all-time low during the years 1939 to 1945 when the war disrupted travel and channels of trade, cutting off the source of illicit supplies. Subsequent peace-time controls were far less effective and a sharp postwar increase in addiction took place.

In New York State, arrests for illegal possession, distribution, procurement, dispensing and sale showed an increase from 813 in 1947 to 6605 in 1957 and 9003 in 1963.[5] Addiction itself is not a crime in New York and thus not directly measured in arrest figures. It is the opinion of those concerned with the problem that the rise was due not only to greater police activity but to a true increase in addiction as well. However, during the past few years, it has been noted that the intensity of the withdrawal syndromes in arrested persons has markedly decreased and severe cases are now relatively rare. This indicates what has been confirmed from other sources, namely that heroin is far more difficult to obtain and that the peak of the postwar upswing may now be past.

Of particular concern in recent years has been the question of juvenile addiction, and much has been written about "pushers" lurking near grammar schools, and enticing children with free drugs as a part of a far-sighted policy of creating new customers. This idea is not supported by available evidence, which indicates that drug addiction is spread by a form of social contagion in which the victim is driven by curiosity, his own psychic needs, and the example of his associates, and takes the initiative in experimentation. This begins mostly in the late teens and early twenties and the President's Interdepartmental Committee, in tabulating the results of arrests on narcotics charges in 1953 and 1954, found that only 13 per cent of those apprehended were under 21 and 1.1 per cent under 18. The use of narcotics by juveniles is even more tragic than at other ages but it is far less extensive than has been depicted, and this has been confirmed again by experience in the treatment units opened by New York State since 1959. Such addiction as does occur among juveniles must be considered within the framework of the increase of juvenile antisocial behavior of all types.

THE EPIDEMIOLOGIC APPROACH

Narcotic addiction is a medical, social, and legal problem, and while the emphasis historically has been upon the role of law enforcement, in recent years sociologists have shown an encouraging interest in certain aspects of the narcotics problem, and organized medicine, too, has affirmed that "Physicians have a fundamental responsibility to treat narcotic addiction because it is recognized as a medical syndrome based on an underlying emotional disorder."[6]

While medical treatment results only in a prevention of the catastrophic effects of uncontrolled and untreated addiction, nevertheless, the reduction of morbidity and mortality is of significance and the mitigation of human suffering is no less a medical responsibility in addiction than it is in other chronic relapsing conditions where cure may be limited to a minority of cases. The fact is that favorable results in narcotic addiction appear to be cumulative and the decrease of addiction after age 35 is thought to be due to a true "maturing out" phenomenon. Statistics on this issue are open to multiple interpretations, but this point of view is strongly supported by the experience of law enforcement agents and physicians who have had the opportunity to follow individuals for many years. Time appears to be working on the side of the physician in this matter, and palliative treatment may accomplish far more than merely delaying an inevitable outcome.

Interest in narcotic addiction has increased, both among individual physicians and local, state and national medical societies. Medicine has much to contribute, and among the elements of promise is that of the skills of the epidemiologist whose techniques, so successful in coping with the problems of communicable diseases, offer much in this area also. The narcotic problem can, in fact, be reduced to the same elements of host-agent-environment that are fundamental to any disease process. Since the preventive aspects of the problem can be brought into sharper focus by such a treatment of the problem, this presentation will follow such a framework.[7]

Host

Susceptibility to true narcotic addiction is apparently confined to individuals with definite personality aberrations. "Physicial dependence without underlying emotional disorder is easily terminated and does not constitute an addiction problem."[6] However, it should not be thought that all types of psychiatric disorder have this propensity, because opium and even morphine were widely used for treatment of serious depressions during the late 1800's and opium continues to have some vogue in Germany, but addiction problems have never been encountered in this work.[8] In general, one finds associated with addiction a special group of psychiatric problems, including character disorders and various inadequate and neurotic personalities, sometimes in pure form but usually in various mixtures. These disorders are thought to precede and predispose to addiction and are not merely the effects of drug abuse.

This premise is borne out by the experience of medical practice. Of the hundreds of thousands of patients to whom narcotics are administered daily in the United States, only a minute fraction ever becomes addicted. Similarly, those who have studied narcotic addiction among juvenile gangs in large cities have found that by no means all of those who are introduced to narcotics by a friend or by a peer in the gang ever become addicted to the drugs. Of the many who, in gang parlance, "joy-pop" (i.e., use narcotics occasionally for the "thrill'), only a comparatively few decide that it's for them and become "hooked" or addicted. In each case it would appear that a relatively specific susceptibility is involved. Addicts appear to be naturally of low frustration tolerance and poor reliability, and the drug use aggravates the expression of the personality disorder, but opiates are not a cause of full-blown psychoses, though toxic psychoses may be precipitated by simultaneous use of other drugs, or by their withdrawal.[6]

Whether there is difference in susceptibility on the basis of race or nationality has not been determined. The English, for example, are frequently cited in this country as having satisfactorily dealt with the narcotic addiction problem and in 1959 only about 350 narcotic addicts were reported in England.[9] Since then the known number has increased somewhat and there is concern about addiction in metropolitan areas, but the cases still number in the hundreds and the total is miniscule compared to ours. As has already been noted, the problem in New York City is concentrated among the Negro and Puerto Rican population. However, it seems certain that any association with race or nationality is quite fortuitous since these same persons were quite free of addiction in their home areas before their recent migration into the socioeconomically deprived areas of the city which are now so heavily infected. It must be admitted that as long as 1 to 2 per cent of all physicians in the United States are addicted to opiates at some time in their lives we must give more weight to availability of drugs than to some other factors.

Male addicts outnumber females by three or four to one and the 1962 reports of the United States Bureau of Narcotics list 38,654 male and 8835 female addicts. An even greater disproportion is seen in the number of male and female addicts coming for treatment to the New York State narcotic units. Yet early in the twentieth century the number of female addicts was at least equal to that of the males and it would appear that factors other than sex play a role in the present findings.

Of the various possible factors that may be related to susceptibility, the environment and its stresses appear most clearly implicated, especially the slum conditions in large cities. Addiction may occur in any individual under any social conditions, but environmental stress seems to be a necessary condition for heavy infection to occur. The fact that it is not a sufficient cause is to be seen from the fact that some areas of this type in other cities in the country are far less involved, and this may even be true of similar areas in the same city. These differences may be traced to historical accident, the availability of drugs to establish a market, and the effect of cultural patterns on the establishment and social toleration of addiction. Differences on these points may account in large part for the low incidence of narcotic addiction in England.

England's low incidence of narcotic addiction has been attributed by some to the existence of a "British Narcotic Control System." Actually, there is no "British System" but rather a collection of administrative practices, which the English themselves prefer not to refer to as a "system." Further, there is no demonstrable cause and effect relationship between the English narcotic administrative practices and the fortunate situation that exists in England with respect to narcotic addiction. The English have never had a serious narcotic problem and the present "system" is the result of the absence of a problem rather than the cause of it.[7]

Susceptibility to narcotic addiction appears to vary with age, and the bulk of addiction is concentrated among young adults. The reduction of addiction rates with advance of age has been demonstrated statistically by Chapman[10] and by the studies of Brill and others.[11] It may be noted that other types of antisocial behavior also decrease after age 30 to 35.

Within limits, abuse of alcohol indicates increased susceptibility to opiates. From the point of view of prevention it should be noted that alcoholics and those who abuse other drugs should be given opiates only with the greatest caution. Conversely, narcotic addicts should not be given barbiturates or minor tranquilizers except for specific reasons under well controlled conditions; likelihood of substituted addiction and abuse is high.

Psychiatric treatment of the personality disorders associated with addiction is arduous and the results have so far been unsatisfactory, but there appears to be clear indication that the effects of addiction can be mitigated by such an approach.

Agent

In this country the chief, and in point of numbers the only, important drug of addiction is heroin (diacetylmorphine). Cocaine is not important and marijuana is of concern chiefly as a steppingstone toward heroin addiction. Heroin by intravenous injection is generally preferred by addicts in the United States because of the rapid onset and greater intensity of effect.

It also has advantages to those in the illicit narcotic traffic since it is easy to manufacture from opium or morphine and is easier to smuggle, being less bulky. It is called "H" in the argot of the addict, and those who use the intravenous route are "mainliners." In spite of statements by pharmacologists who find little difference between the effects of morphine and heroin, the latter has gained ground rapidly in the Eastern countries and its use is also increasing in Europe. However, heroin is not the drug of choice for physician addicts and others in like professional positions, perhaps because of the nature of their source of supply.

As noted in the 1957 Report on Narcotic Addiction by the American Medical Association's Council on Mental Health, addiction to heroin and other opiates embraces two related phenomena; tolerance and dependence.[12] Dependence is further subdivided into physical dependence and emotional or psychological dependence (habituation). The mechanism of tolerance is still unknown, but the degree of tolerance that can be developed to the opiates seems almost boundless. Addicts have been known to take as much as 5 gm. (75 grains) of morphine intravenously in less than 24 hours without untoward effect.[13] Tolerance follows inevitably on repeated administration and develops most rapidly and to the highest degree when drugs are given on a regular schedule. What the final upper limit of tolerance would be is unknown. Contrary to popular opinion and in contrast to alcohol these substances in and of themselves are not known to leave any demonstrable somatic pathology; whatever does occur seems to be the result of the atrociously poor hygiene of the addict.

Emotional or psychological dependence is related to the effects of the opiates on the psychic life, but the mechanism is quite unknown. Psychic dependence persists long after physical dependence has been overcome just as it does in the case of tobacco, and it is the only known basis for the use of cocaine and marijuana which do not produce physical dependence. Psychic and not physical dependence is clearly the cause of the persistence of addiction, although there is much popular opinion to the effect that drug bondage is due chiefly to the pains of withdrawal. It is in the psychic area, too, where one may seek the reasons for preference among various drugs of addiction and habituation, but relatively little work has been done on this question to date.

Emotional or psychological dependence is probably related to the fact that the opiates depress primary drives, diminishing hunger, thirst, fear or pain, and sexual urges, and the drug experience seems to replace all other satisfactions, allaying anxiety, creating a sense of pleasant relaxation and freedom from worry. The stimulation of phantasy is prominent in literary accounts of addiction but it seems to play little role in the type of addict ordinarily seen in treatment centers. The emotional experience rather than the intellectual one is important and it is the "bang" that is sought, an orgasm-like burst of euphoria which is also called the "high."

Under the full influence of opiates the addict abandons the usual methods of adaptation to life situations; instead, taking the drug becomes the answer for all of life's problems. This tends to reduce him to an indolent parasitic existence. The psychological effect of allaying anxiety provides a courage or abandon of a sort that predisposes to minor types of crime such as prostitution and petty thievery. Occasionally, an addict who is pressed to obtain funds to support his addiction commits a violent crime but, in general, initiative is vitiated for crime as for other activities since in and of themselves the drugs create a passive dreamy state with depression of hostile urges as well as sexual ones. In small to moderate doses mental ability and manual dexterity do not deteriorate, but large doses approaching the level of 20 grains per day reduce the addict to a largely vegetative level where he leaves his bed only for limited meals and to secure additional supplies of the drug. It is to be noted that, when free, the addict follows a cyclic course with respect to the amount of drugs used, sometimes increasing and sometimes cutting back or even stopping for a while altogether. Many periodically withdraw from drugs completely, "cold turkey" (abruptly) and without outside help.

Physical dependence results from the altered physiological state induced by the opiates. When the drug is withdrawn from a physically dependent person, or the addict "kicks" the habit, a chain of unpleasant physiologic effects is set in motion, the intensity depending on the "size" of the habit (the amount of drugs taken daily). These range from minor symptoms resembling that of a cold with rhinorrhea, lacrimation, perspiration, and malaise, to more serious ones with vomiting, diarrhea, rise of temperature and blood pressure, rapid pulse and respiratory disturbances. In the most severe cases, especially when there is a complicating physical condition, death may occur. It is now generally acknowledged that it is a medical responsibility to provide a humane withdrawal for addicts.[6]

Efforts at narcotics control have in the main thus far been directed toward limiting the availability of the drug, largely through law enforcement activities. These efforts are essential and should in some areas be further amplified, but by themselves they have serious limitations as a complete solution to the problem. It is virtually impossible to limit the illicit flow of narcotic drugs in this country to the point at which narcotic addiction would disappear. The extensive seacoasts of the United States with their numerous ports and the country's north and south borders offer almost unlimited opportunities for smuggling. To close these borders and ports to the point where narcotics would be effectively shut out would virtually strangle travel and commerce. Even if this were possible there is the additional problem of the narcotic drugs essential to medical practice being diverted to illicit channels. This in practice is relatively minor and there is now encouraging research experience with a whole range of new drugs which promise to provide morphine-like analgesia free of addiction danger. More serious is the fact that if all supplies were shut off and diversion of legal stocks were controlled there would still be the problem of synthetic narcotic drugs, some of which can be manufactured with relative ease. There also remain, of course, a vast array of other substances which can be used for addictive purposes, not the least important being alcohol. Finally, punishment of those arrested is by no means a completely effective deterrent, especially for the small "pusher" addict who sells to support his own habit.

Thus, important though it may be to achieve control of the agent, and limit its availability, the degree of control which appears to be practicable does not in itself offer a total solution. Future research in the chemical and biochemical field promises much both for the understanding of the physical basis of addiction and for possible methods of treatment but, in addition, the environmental aspects will have to be further explored and understood.

Environment

It is readily evident in studying the narcotic addiction problem in this country that environmental factors play an important part. As has been noted, narcotic addiction is concentrated in certain large urban centers and in these centers it is localized largely in the so-called socioeconomically depressed multiproblem areas. In addition to narcotic addiction, these same areas have higher than average rates of delinquency, dependency, mental illness, and venereal disease as well as poorer health levels generally. These same areas also have the poorest housing and the most unstable family structures.[14] The contribution of the environment, particularly its socioeconomic factors, is further emphasized by the fact that addiction involves groups among whom narcotic addiction was virtually unknown in their previous setting as in the case of rural southern Negroes and Puerto Ricans.

The influence of associates in initiating the habit is apparently very important, though there is no substantial evidence of deliberate recruiting by "pushers" seeking to create markets. It would appear that if a person, who possesses psychological traits which make him susceptible to narcotic addiction, is placed in an environment where he is subjected to stress and at the same time falls in with a group of associates already using narcotics he is likely to become addicted, especially if the cultural patterns in the area are favorable to the use of addictive drugs. It is noteworthy that only a minority of persons so exposed actually become addicted, even under the most serious conditions, although the total proportion of persons with psychiatric disabilities is of course much higher. Susceptibility appears to be limited to a relatively restricted subgroup within the total field of psychiatric disorder. Indeed, it has been found that when a person with schizophrenia does become addicted the treatment of the addiction is likely to be quite successful.

The elimination or reduction of environmental factors which may contribute to narcotic addiction thus offers promise as one facet of a control program. This approach is admittedly not easy and requires a total social effort rather than a purely medical one. Nevertheless, it is important to recognize that better housing, increased social services, better law enforcement, greater preventive health services, education and vocational training all can mitigate the environmental factors which not only contribute to narcotic addiction but to higher than average illness rates, as well as delinquency and the other unfavorable health and social conditions of the multiple problem areas.

TREATMENT

Treatment of addiction is, of course, far less satisfactory than prevention of occurrence, and unless the goals of treatment are realistic, one is likely to be overwhelmed with a sense of futility in approaching the problem. If one expects to prevent relapse, and considers all other results as failures, treatment will be disappointing. If, however, one views this condition as a chronic relapsing disorder where the goal of treatment is to prevent as much mortality, morbidity and human suffering as possible and to reduce social disability to a minimum, one can see a value in the application of even the limited treatment methods now available.[11]

Physical withdrawal is relatively easy, although withdrawal on an ambulatory basis "is generally medically unsound"[6] and with certain rare exceptions institutional care is required. There is greater danger from an associated barbiturate addiction than from the opiate during withdrawal, and barbiturate withdrawal must be done slowly and cautiously because of possible convulsions and deleria with all the accompanying dangers. Physicians will ordinarily wish to refer patients for withdrawal to established narcotic treatment units such as have been established by New York State and New York City, by the state of California, and a number of other states and cities, during the last few years. Information as to such facilities is available from local medical societies, mental health groups, or from the local or state mental health authority. In addition, the United States Public Health Hospitals at Lexington and Fort Worth accept patients from anywhere in the country; information regarding admission procedures may be obtained by writing or telephoning the medical officer in charge at either institution or from the Public Health Service in Washington.

Records of the federal hospitals indicate that less than 15 per cent of the addict patients who have been treated there have remained free of drugs following treatment and 60 per cent of the cases admitted for treatment are "repeaters." However, no attempt has been made to compare the results of treatment with those of neglect, either as to mortality, morbidity or extent and degree of disability. Furthermore, it would seem medically wrong to refuse even palliative treatment to the patient who wishes to have it regardless of prognosis, since palliative treatment has a well-established place in medicine. History shows clearly that many of our most effective treatments had their beginnings in experience gained in the course of such efforts. It is to be expected that better and more effective methods will develop with further medical experience in narcotics, a field which has long been relatively neglected by physicians.

It is to be hoped that even with present techniques results will improve, with better aftercare facilities, more social services, more effective vocational rehabilitation, and a more active follow-up for the addict who has been withdrawn from opiates. It still remains to be demonstrated what can be accomplished by an effort which will provide all these services and bring to bear on a sample group of cases the best talents of specially trained physicians including psychiatrists and internists as well as social workers, vocational rehabilitation specialists and others who can apply in full measure all the present knowledge and skill in their respective fields.

RESPONSIBILITIES OF PHYSICIANS

While the bulk of black market opiates comes through nonmedical channels, there is always a danger of diversion of drugs, and the addicting effects of narcotics impose certain responsibilities on physicians. To prevent the abuse of such drugs, they should not be prescribed carelessly or in the absence of a definite need, and amounts should be limited to the minimum needed in each case. Except for patients suffering from a terminal illness, one must be ever mindful of the hazards of addiction in the administration of narcotics, providing them only as long as they are essential to treatment.

Physicians should become familiar with the provisions of the Harrison Anti-Narcotic Act and with state laws regarding the use of narcotic drugs and should observe them carefully.[6] Stocks of these drugs and even prescription blanks which can be easily forged have high value for the trafficker in illicit narcotics and offer a tempting target for the addict who needs a supply of drugs. Adequate precautions should be taken to protect both the drugs and prescription blanks.

The federal Harrison Anti-Narcotic Act and many state laws do not permit the prescribing or dispensing of narcotic drugs solely for the gratification of addiction. Such drugs may be prescribed only for bona fide medical needs in the course of professional medical practice. The American Medical Association's Council on Mental Health and the National Academy of Sciences–National Research Council have issued a statement on proper ethical medical practice in the use of narcotics, defining this area in the light of current medical opinion; their statement,[6] which appears to be quite acceptable to the Federal Bureau of Narcotics, provides a description of such practice in detail. Physicians need have no fear of difficulty with narcotic laws or regulations if they exercise due care in handling of narcotic drugs, act on good faith and follow these two principles: (a) Ambulatory treatment of addiction should not be attempted since institutional treatment is virtually always required. (See Appendix A.) (b) Narcotic drugs may not be given to an addict for self-administration. (See Appendix B.)

Physicians need to be on guard against being tricked by narcotic addicts who can be most glib and persuasive in their efforts to obtain drugs. Some addicts will admit frankly that they are addicted and claim that doctors have been supplying them with narcotics because of the condition. Others will feign a physical illness, such as angina pectoris, kidney stone or migraine, and will suggest that physicians have found that they can best be treated through prescription of narcotic drugs. If the physician is in doubt, a physical examination will often reveal evidence of addiction. A most important finding is the presence of needle marks, old or new, or both. These needle marks should be sought over the veins in the antecubital spaces, although small veins on the dorsum of the hands and over the forearm and even on the feet or the lower leg may be used. In addition, there may be scars of new and old abscesses resulting from subcutaneous injections over the deltoid, the anterior surfaces of the thighs, the abdomen, or indeed over any of the large body surfaces which are readily accessible for self-injection.

Nalline (nalorphine hydrochloride) is also used for diagnosis since it can precipitate withdrawal symptoms in an actively addicted person, but this is a procedure which requires specific precautions. It must be done only by a physician with experience in this field.

Once a diagnosis of active drug addiction is made, the patient should be advised that institutional withdrawal is necessary and then recommended to the nearest available location. Ambulatory treatment is not considered good medical practice (see Appendix A) and should not be undertaken. If the presence of concurrent physical disease makes the administration of narcotic drugs medically necessary, the physician should seek consultation before prescribing them. The conditions are outlined in Appendix C.

It will be noted from a reading of the total AMA-NRC statement that the present trend is to emphasize the positive aspects of medical responsibility with respect to addiction and addicts.[6] While the normal caution that is required in this field cannot be abandoned by the physician, he must try to do more than merely comply with the rules and regulations. Addiction is not a crime nor is it so regarded by the Federal Bureau of Narcotics or by the medical profession. The addict must be considered as suffering from an illness, and it is a medical responsibility to make treatment available to him as far as circumstances permit and as far as the patient will cooperate.

HENRY BRILL, M.D.
GRANVILLE W. LARIMORE, M.D.

Appendix A*

Ambulatory. Withdrawal on an ambulatory basis is generally medically unsound and not recommended on the basis of present knowledge. Only under exceptional circumstances is it proper to attempt withdrawal on an ambulatory basis and then it must be done only by a physician with special skill and experience in the management of addicted patients. In such cases there should always be consultation with a psychiatrist, if one is available, or with another physician experienced in this field, or with another physician who will substantiate the fact that ambulatory withdrawal is, in fact, indicated.

Appendix B

Interim Treatment of Addict on Waiting List for Admission to Narcotic Facility. When the diagnosis of addiction has been established and the patient is awaiting admission to a treatment facility and the fact of his acceptance and the date of admission have been confirmed by the attending physician, oral dosages of methadone, preferably in liquid form, may be given on daily visits by the physician for not more than 10 days to 2 weeks. Needed dosage will be established by observation of response to medication. No more than one day's medication should be dispensed to the addict at one time.

Appendix C

Administration of Narcotics to Persons with Intractable Pain. There is general recognition of the belief that it is proper ethical practice to administer narcotics over a prolonged period in the treatment of patients with chronic incurable and painful conditions, when all reasonable alternate procedures have failed. This is especially true in cases of terminal disorders but, in certain unusual instances, may apply also to nonfatal diseases with intractable pain in which no relief or cure is possible or none has been found after reasonable efforts.

In such cases the physician should obtain consultation and is required to maintain adequate records of the drugs administered and the indications for such administration. He must also maintain adequate safeguards against diversion of drugs into illicit channels.

---

* Appendices are excerpts from joint AMA-NRC statement.[6]

REFERENCES

1. Adams, E. W.: Drug Addiction. London, Oxford Medical Publications, 1937.
2. DeQuincey, Thomas: Confessions of an English Opium Eater. New York, Three Sirens Press, 1932.
3. Brill, H.: Misapprehensions about Drug Addiction. Comprehensive Psychiatry, Vol. 4, No. 3, June, 1963.
4. Traffic in Opium and Other Dangerous Drugs for Year ending December 31, 1962. Prepared by United States Treasury Department, Bureau of Narcotics.
5. Total Narcotic Arrests, New York State, 1963. Albany, New York, Annual Report, New York State Department of Correction, 1963.
6. Narcotics and Medical Practice. Journal of the American Medical Association, 185 (No. 12):976-982, September 21, 1963.
7. Larimore, G. W., and Brill, H.: Epidemiologic Factors in Drug Addiction in England and the United States. Public Health Reports, 77:555-560, July, 1962.
8. Personal communications from a number of German psychiatrists.
9. Larimore, G. W., and Brill, H.: The British Narcotic System. New York State Journal of Medicine, 60:1, 1960.
10. Chapman, K. W.: Personal communication.
11. Brill, Leon, et al.: Rehabilitation in Drug Addiction. Mental Health Monograph 3, United States Dept. of Health, Education, and Welfare, Washington 25, D.C. U. S. Government Printing Office, Supt. of Documents, 1963.
12. Council on Mental Health of the American Medical Association: Report on Narcotic Addiction. Journal of the American Medical Association, 166: November 30, December 7, December 14, 1957.
13. Nyswander, Marie: The Drug Addict as a Patient. New York, Grune & Stratton, 1956.
14. U. S. News and World Report: New York City in Trouble. June 8, 1964, p. 72-77.

PART THREE

SUPPORTING SERVICES FOR PREVENTIVE MEDICINE

SECTION **A**
THE ROLE OF EDUCATION
IN PREVENTIVE MEDICINE

SECTION **B**
SERVICES AIDING THE PRACTICE
OF PREVENTIVE MEDICINE

THE ROLE OF EDUCATION
IN PREVENTIVE MEDICINE

36 Health Education and the Social Sciences

INTRODUCTION

The aim of health education is to help people to achieve health by their own actions and efforts. Health education begins, therefore, with the interest of people in improving their conditions of living and aims at developing a sense of responsibility for their own health betterment as individuals, and as members of families, communities or governments.[1] Involved in health education are the imparting of information and the processes concerned with aiding in the utilization of that information for the protection or advancement of the individual's own, his family's or his community's health. Grout[2] has characterized health education as a procedure which involves the translation of what is known about health into desirable individual and community behavior patterns by means of the educational process. Turner[3] describes community health education as a learning process through which people in a community inform or orient themselves for more intelligent health action. Public health education, a term commonly used by health agencies, refers to that part of health education which takes place in the home or community, as opposed, for example, to school health education carried on as a part of the curriculum of an educational institution.

Health education is fundamentally a learning process, which aims at favorably changing attitudes and influencing behavior with respect to health practices. The same principles which govern any learning situation are inherent in the process. The aim of this chapter is to present to the physician amplification of these principles in the form of guide lines, so that he can be most effective not only in the education of his individual patient but also in fulfilling his responsibilities in community health education.[4]

In the early days of the public health movement in this country, health agencies were concerned primarily with such problems as typhoid fever, smallpox, dysentery and other epidemic conditions. These were, in a sense, mass diseases, the control of which could be achieved by such mass means as the chlorination of water, provision of adequate waste disposal facilities, pure food and milk supplies and the enforcement of regulations relating to mass immunization. Even then, of course, health education in its broadest sense was necessary, although its concern was with such limited groups as the community leaders or government officials whose actions made possible the safe water supply, who provided through tax laws the funds for waste disposal facilities and who enacted vaccination regulations. The individual citizen's part, other than helping to pay the cost, was often a passive one. Merely by turning on the kitchen tap, for example, he obtained for himself and his family the health protection against typhoid fever provided by the safe water supply. As he used the water, drank the safe milk or made use of the new waste disposal facilities he often did so without ever having participated actively in the process which made these health-protective measures available.

With the elimination of the mass diseases as major threats to the health of the developed nations, we have entered into a period in which both health agencies and practicing physicians are concerned with such individual disease problems as cancer, heart disease, diabetes and mental illness. These do not lend themselves to the same type of solution as do the problems of typhoid fever, dysentery and smallpox. There is, for example, nothing that can be put in the community water supply which will protect against cancer, no community facility, such as a sewage disposal plant, which is effective against diabetes and no mass vaccination procedure which will control heart disease or mental illness. In short, the mass approach to health problems, in which the individual was only passively involved, is of necessity yielding in many countries to an individual approach in which it is essential that each citizen be accurately informed about health matters and, most important, be motivated to use that information for the protection of his own health and that of the community.

FACTORS IN INDIVIDUAL HEALTH EDUCATION

Workers in preventive medicine are increasingly coming to recognize the fact that what people do to prevent illness and how they behave when they actually experience illness is determined by a combination of personal, social and cultural factors as well as by the disease itself. The body of relevant literature is already large and increasing constantly. Recent bibliographies by Polgar[5] and Pearsall[6] contain literally thousands of references to research on various aspects of health behavior.

What a person will learn and use is a function of the kinds of relevant beliefs and motives he has. Whether a message directed toward an individual will even register on him depends on his beliefs and motives. On the basis of considerable evidence, it is fair to conclude that people unconcerned with a particular aspect of their health will often fail to "receive" any material that bears on that aspect of their health; even if, through accidental circumstances, they do receive it, they will fail to learn, accept, or use the information. For example, an educational program in the area of nutrition was carried out among members of a low income group.[7] Since the diets of the group were deficient in both protein and calcium it was agreed that the addition of dried skim milk to the diet would provide an inexpensive and effective solution to the deficiency. The group was exposed to intensive educational efforts employing visual aids, printed materials, demonstrations and other techniques all aimed at informing the group about the advantages of dried milk and attempting to persuade them to use it. A check at the end of the educational program revealed that the group had indeed assimilated all of the facts about dried skim milk and its economic and nutritional advantages. The check also revealed that not a single one of the group was using dried skim milk. The reason for this situation turned out to be the fact that this group strongly believed that milk in any form had no place in the diet of adults.

No matter how intensely we try to persuade a person to protect his health, his interpretation of the message will be partly determined by the nature and extent of his prior motivations. *If we wish to increase the person's acceptance of our message, we must first learn the nature and extent of his relevant motives and then plan and direct our appeals to him in a way that serves and satisfies his motives.* While it is frequently difficult to determine the nature of an individual's motives, much information is now available on how selected publics are motivated in specified health areas. We know, for example, that an individual's decision to prevent or to seek diagnosis of a disease depends on at least three crucial beliefs: his beliefs about the extent to which he is susceptible to a particular illness, his beliefs about how serious it would be if he contracted that illness, and his beliefs about the extent to which taking some prescribed action will be beneficial in reducing his susceptibility to the illness or the severity of the illness should it occur.[8, 9] Many studies have shown the interplay and importance of these factors in influencing behavior in connection with screening for tuberculosis[8] and cancer,[10] and for the prevention of polio,[11] influenza,[12] dental decay[13] and recurrences of rheumatic fever.[14] Doctor-patient communications as well as program planning for community health could be improved if we could identify early those individuals who do not believe they are susceptible to a disease, or those who do not believe that contracting the disease would be serious, or those who are not sold on the efficacy of recommended health resources. Such data would make it possible to reduce our traditional reliance on mass communication efforts which attempt to say all things to all people and to concentrate rather on pin-pointed education to increase the intensity of an insufficient motive.

It might be thought that these beliefs, concerning susceptibility, severity and benefits of remedial action could be simply taught by providing appropriate medical information. We know this is not realistic. It has been shown that people may have, and be able to repeat, correct health knowledge without applying that knowledge to their own situations and behavior. In an interview study, a large group of people correctly reported that one could have tuberculosis in the absence of all symptoms. However, in a subsequent section of the interview many of those who were correctly informed gave evidence that *in their own cases* they would probably feel free of disease as long as they were without symptoms of disease.[8] Cassel[15] and many others have shown that it is difficult—sometimes impossible—to change beliefs relative to health if those beliefs reflect important elements of the culture.

In short, the mere possession of health information is no guarantee that it will be used for maintenance or improvement of the individual's health. This statement is supported by a number of studies which suggest that while people do have misconceptions about health, they also have much sound information, which, if properly used, would go a long way toward raising their level of health. One such study, conducted by Larimore and Leiby,[16] of the Army's venereal disease education program during World War II, tested the level of information possessed by troops both about the venereal diseases and the techniques of prophylaxis. When an attempt was made to correlate the information level with the incidence of venereal disease it was found that there was no significant difference between the information level of those troops who had avoided venereal disease and those who had acquired it. In other words, the mere possession of adequate information was not the critical factor in influencing behavior with respect to acquiring or not acquiring venereal disease.

Physicians themselves sometimes offer excellent examples of the fact that possession of knowledge about health practices does not ensure its utilization. Even in medical school, good health practices are at times made subservient to the goal of becoming a physician. Most physicians can recall when the demands of the medical school curriculum prevented their getting the hours of sleep recommended for healthful living, and there were undoubtedly days when these same demands interfered with getting the "basic four" of sound nutrition or otherwise contributed in a negative way toward good health practices, all in the interest of achieving the goal of becoming a physician.

In general, as Galdston[17] states, people are primarily concerned with the everyday business of living and are likely to be interested in health per se only insofar as it affects their achieving the goals they have set for themselves. Paradoxically, while people are generally not interested in health per se, they are avid readers of material on health published in newspapers, magazines and books. One readership survey carried out by the Department of Journalism of New York University[18] showed that 66 per cent of the persons polled were willing to give up some other kind of news to provide space for more coverage of public health and medical science.

Even though such material is widely read, it does not, as has been previously noted, ensure that it will be acted upon. Many physicians have among their patients obese persons who read every available column and article on reducing but continue on their way without losing a pound. Their resistance to change, based on their own personal sense of values, may be greater than the motivation necessary to improve existing habits of eating and exercise.

Facilitating Health Education

Health education can be facilitated by the desire to achieve individual goals. For example, if the obese teen-age girl has set for herself the goal of popularity among the community's teen-age boys and finds that her overweight interferes with attaining that goal, a strong motivation exists for her to reduce. This force may well be sufficient to induce her to keep to a prescribed regimen of diet and exercise, something she might not do in the absence of such a goal.

In addition to the motivation to achieve individual goals, there are other factors which directly or indirectly influence behavior in health matters. Prominent among these is the desire to do the accepted thing, which is represented by the behavior, or what the individual considers to be the behavior, of his own socioeconomic group. In fact, health beliefs and motives are frequently interrelated with other social motives. A person's decisions about whether to take a particular health action is guided not only by health concerns but also by other concerns of life. Economic, social, sexual and other concerns all impinge on the individual to increase or decrease the chances that he will follow a given health recommendation. Some of the most powerful motives for taking action, even health action, are not health related motives at all. It is well known from work on social pressures that groups exert powerful influences on their members to conform to group standards.[19, 20] This pressure may be so great as occasionally to lead the individual to deny his own senses.[21] Probably, we initially learn to brush our teeth, to wash our hands regularly, and perhaps to visit our physicians and dentists periodically, not primarily because of a direct concern with health but as an expression of the need to conform to social standards set by our families and our friends.

The implications of the foregoing are clear. Health practices will be more effectively taught if they are seen as related not exclusively to a health context but if they are related as well to a variety of other contexts. The most effective learning that takes place is that of learning one's culture through the process of socialization. In that process, the acts to be learned are embedded within the very fabric of society itself. One obtains many types of rewards and not just a single reward for becoming socialized. The child who takes one step closer to his parents' civilization (as they define it) is rewarded with love and affection not only by his parents but also by other members of his family, by other adults, by playmates and by the school system, and pressures to socialize or to conform emanate from all these sources.

There are many illustrations of the impact of social pressures on practices in the health field. Having babies in hospitals, for example, is now so much a part of the social mores in most parts of the nation that home deliveries are almost a thing of the past, except among the lower socioeconomic groups. This practice, which has positive values medically, has become the accepted thing to do for most, so that it may be practiced in some instances without reference to its medical merit. Similarly, "shots" for the baby have become so identified with social custom that it is the uncommon mother who would think of denying her baby the benefits of immunization procedures. Social factors influence diet as well, sometimes favorably. The consumption of citrus fruit juices at breakfast has become for some an accepted part of the diet, not in every instance because fruit juice is an excellent way to provide needed vitamin C, but because serving it for breakfast has become an accepted part of the dietary pattern for certain socioeconomic groups. Social customs or social pressures may at times work to the detriment of sound health practices.

One may well ask why different social and cultural groups vary in the extent to which they tend to hold the beliefs described earlier that are necessary to taking health protective action. Little is known about *why* social groups vary but a considerable body of information is available about *how* they vary. It is known, for example, that the preventive orientation described above is more often found in upper socioeconomic groups (as measured principally by income and education) than in lower socioeconomic groups and that it is found more frequently in relatively young adults than older adults, and more often in females than in males.[8, 22]

When we consider cultural variations in health matters, studies by Saunders[23] or those reported by Paul[24] clearly demonstrate how different social, cultural or subcultural groups may vary widely in their health beliefs and behavior.

The practicing physician has a position of unique potential importance in influencing the beliefs and behavior of his patients, especially those from the lower social and educational groups who are not likely to be influenced by impersonal methods. There is much he can do to influence the extent to which his patients believe they are susceptible to various conditions, that the occurrence of these conditions can have serious effects on their lives, and that there exist effective means for preventing or controlling these conditions if recommended advice is followed.

The physician who would have the maximum impact in educating his patients on these matters will have to become sensitive not only to the patient's medical condition but as well to the patient's social background and to his beliefs about relevant medical matters. He will have to work not only with the patient's symptoms but also with the patient's beliefs.

Some psychologists put this fact in another way when they say that behavior is overdetermined. By this they mean that there may be several operative motives and beliefs simultaneously reinforcing each other to increase the probability of a particular response. Thus, if a communicator, e.g., a physician, can show a patient that a particular recommendation will serve two, three, or four motives, it is more likely that the persuasion will be successful than if he merely relates the recommended act to some *one* of the motives, however powerful that one motive may be.

The physician also has an advantage in influencing his patients' health behavior since he often sees them at the "teachable moment." The most opportune time, for example, to teach a mother proper infant care may well be either late in her pregnancy or during the first days and weeks after the birth of her baby. At no other time is the interest of the new mother apt to be greater; at no other time is she more eager to learn and so likely to put to use the information given her. Illness also represents an opportune moment for health education. There is probably no time at which people are more interested in their health than when it is replaced by illness, nor any time when good health practices are more teachable.

Involvement in the dynamics of a group also provides motivation in changing attitudes and influencing behavior with respect to health. In many instances, an individual participating as a member of a group finds himself influenced to carry out the group decision which he participated in making.[20] If, for example, the group discussing the subject of immunization against poliomyelitis arrives at a collective decision that immunization is desirable, that group decision will assist in motivating the members of the group to be immunized.

Health education programs also need to be carefully considered in terms of the action desired by the group or the individual. The action should be as simple and as direct as possible, with a minimum number of choices for the individual to make. For example, a health education program directed toward tuberculosis control should emphasize one facet of the problem at a time, such as having a chest roentgenogram. The program should not add the burden of expecting the individual to decide whether he should have a chest roentgenogram instead of a tuberculin test. Having to make a choice will pose a psychological barrier for some individuals and the goal of the program may not be achieved.

Possibly one of the best examples of the problem presented by multiple choice is the army's venereal disease education program of World War II.[25] In this program the army, in order to appease the moralists, staunchly advocated sexual continence at all times, i.e., it said to the soldier "Don't do it!" Then, in order to go along with the more practical among the military chain of command, the use of venereal disease prophylaxis was vigorously promoted, and the army said: "Don't do it, but if you *do* do it, *do* it this way!" To complicate the situation even further, in an effort to satisfy the clinicians of the medical department who were worried about untreated venereal disease in prepenicillin days, the army finally said to the soldier: "Don't do it, but if you *do* do it, do it this way, but if you *do* do it and *don't* do it this way and you get venereal disease then come see your medical officer, he'll take good care of you!"

Hindrances to Health Education

In addition to the conflict that may exist between good health practices and the achievement of individual goals, there are also other factors which may interfere with health education. Pain, discomfort, inconvenience, expense or personal distaste all may deter a person from following a recommended procedure or practice. Health agencies find, for example, that people are more easily persuaded to have a chest roentgenogram at a mobile roentgen unit than to have a cancer detection examination. In the former procedure there is no discomfort, the roentgen unit is usually in a convenient location, it is often free and no undressing or other invasion of privacy is required. The cancer detection examination, on the other hand, presents the negative side of many of the points listed.

Another block to health education is the strong basic drive to protect the ego. This drive enables people to perceive only what they want to perceive, to read or listen only to such material as confirms or can be misinterpreted to confirm their existing views, to deliberately or unconsciously avoid anything which runs counter to pre-existing beliefs, or to refuse to perceive that the information refers to them.[9] The individual is rare who really thinks that he is ever going to get cancer or tuberculosis, so that health information on such subjects usually runs head on into a disbelieving "it can't happen to me" attitude. Even when it has happened, the individual may not be willing to accept the fact. Obese persons may not recognize or accept the fact that they are overweight even when they are markedly so; therefore, efforts to induce them to lose weight fall on deaf ears since they don't look upon themselves as obese or in need of reducing. This problem is recognized by the Alcoholics Anonymous group, one of whose tenets is that the alcoholic must recognize himself as such before he can be helped.

Thus, for an individual to take some constructive course of action relative to a real or potential health problem, he must not only feel threatened by the health problem but he must also see one or more courses of action open to him which he believes would either reduce the likelihood of occurrence or the seriousness of the problem. In selecting a course of action, the individual's motives and beliefs are often in conflict and the course of action that emerges represents a resolution of such conflicts.[11] The woman who detects a lump in her breast must resolve the conflict that may exist between the possibility of an unfortunate outcome from cancer if she takes no action and the possibility of the loss of a breast, a strong feminine symbol, if she seeks medical care.

Social customs and pressures may hinder as well as facilitate education for health by creating negative motivation for sound health practices. Women's fashions may dictate a slim figure which may be achieved by sacrificing the principles of sound nutrition. The ubiquitous automobile, so much a part of American mores, discourages walking, which could provide badly needed exercise for what is becoming an all too sedentary population. Many other examples could also be cited.

Much has been said about fear as a motivation in changing health behavior. It seems to be the consensus that fear is a powerful motivating force which will initiate changes in behavior under certain circumstances. It also appears that, beyond a certain point, fear may actually prove a deterrent to constructive action, particularly where the individual perceives no clear solution that he can follow to overcome the feared condition. For example, fear of cancer can reach the stage where the individual developing symptoms due to cancer is so gripped with panic and so imbued with the hopelessness of the situation that instead of seeking prompt medical care, he pursues a course of hopeful inaction until pain or some other circumstance drives him to his physician, possibly too late for definitive treatment. Fear of a sort may also deter diagnostic or screening procedures. Health agency staffs engaged in screening projects, such as mass chest roentgen services, are accustomed to hearing these reasons for declining to participate: "If there is something wrong, I don't want to know," or "I'm afraid to find out."[8]

In summary, it is noted that a person's behavior in regard to his health is affected by his motivations and beliefs just as all behavior is so affected. What he learns and does, indeed, *whether* he learns, is in part determined by the extent and kind of prior motives and beliefs he possesses.

Communication

If it is true that the health professions will need to work with people to increase their motives for taking health action, then it is appropriate to ask how one may most effectively communicate health educational messages.

Enough has been written about the relative strengths and weaknesses of the mass media of communication, and personal face-to-face approaches, to permit some summary statements in the form of principles.

1. Groups of differing educational and social status show different patterns of use of the mass media. Even when exposed to the same medium, there are differences related to education in how much and what kind of material is learned. For example, in a review of studies on response to polio vaccination campaigns, it has been shown that better educated groups rely on certain mass media to a greater extent than groups with lesser education. Moreover, even within the same medium the two groups tend to learn differ-

ent things. Groups of high social and educational status tend to obtain more of their health and science information from impersonal communication media, while those of lower social and educational status obtain more of their health information from personal face-to-face contacts.[11]

2. Mass communication methods are more effective in providing information and a favorable background climate than in stimulating a desired behavior. Personal solicitation is a more effective method for obtaining a desired response.[28]

3. The power of communications to influence behavior is limited. Griffiths and Knutson[29] have recently called attention to the limitations of mass media and Hovland[30] has shown how even the kinds of opinion changes achieved with modest success in the laboratory cannot readily be duplicated in natural settings. In the light of the facts presented earlier on motivation, this is not surprising. One would hardly expect unmotivated people to perceive, let alone be influenced by, outside communications. One would hardly expect strongly motivated people to be moved by information that conflicts with their beliefs.

4. Communications often flow through a two-phase process. Occasionally, communications intended for a target audience do not reach them directly.[31] Rather the information is received by a middleman who may be called "influential" or an "opinion leader" who, in turn, transmits selected aspects of the message to the ultimate audience. Thus, while health information transmitted through the mass media may not reach the target group for which it is intended, it may reach a group of opinion leaders to whom the target group looks for advice. However, the opinion leader transmits what he wishes to transmit and only what he wishes to transmit.

5. A corollary to these points is that individuals and groups differ in their acceptance of and reliance on various communications and the degree of acceptance may vary from situation to situation. In the studies of the 1957 influenza epidemic, it became clear that the general public relied on newspapers and radio for information about the abstraction-*epidemic* but they relied on their physicians for *personal* information on the threat to themselves and their families.[12]

Three conclusions may be drawn from the major findings on communication:

a. All media of communication should be used when appropriate; no one is appropriate in all situations. Where the target group is dis-covered to be well motivated in a particular health area, mass media methods may effectively provide needed additional details on how and when to obtain a particular health service.

b. Communication channels should be selected to accord with the known social-communication channels of the audiences. When the intended audience cannot be presumed to be well motivated or when the audience comprises groups that use unique individual channels of communication, education must be more personalized, using face-to-face approaches and working with and through opinion leaders, such as physicians. Even in such situations, mass communication methods may be useful in setting a favorable climate for the recommended health action.

c. Finally, when a specific health action is recommended, personal solicitation has been found to be effective in stimulating desired behavior.

FACTORS IN COMMUNITY HEALTH EDUCATION

Community health education, just as individual health education, is fundamentally a learning process. The objective of the process is to influence favorably, as they pertain to health, the attitudes and behavior of the groups making up the community. There are many health problems that can be solved only through the organized action of the people in the community. Public health nursing services, sufficient number and kind of hospital beds, organized case-finding facilities for tuberculosis, cancer, diabetes and glaucoma, and many more facilities or services can only be provided by the joint action of citizens. The successful operation of mass immunization programs, such as those against poliomyelitis or influenza, can also only be accomplished through the cooperation of the community as a whole.

The goal of community health education is to secure that cooperation which comes from the understanding and acceptance of health protection programs. In many communities there is a tendency on the part of the medical profession to leave community health education almost entirely to the voluntary or official health agencies. It is true that there may be some question of propriety in physicians taking an overly active part in such health education programs as one urging "see your doctor for your annual check-up," where the physician might be charged with seeking personal benefit. However, many other community health education efforts badly need the assistance of physicians, and this can be provided without fear of a charge of self interest.

It is hoped that physicians will participate increasingly in community health education activities. As one of the community's major health resources, the medical profession has an undeniable obligation to take part actively in educational programs which aim at improving the community's health. Many of the principles involved in patient education are equally applicable to community health education, such as using simple terms, explaining the reasons for community health education, using the teachable moment and recognizing the importance of motivation in translating health information into positive action.

In addition, a number of other principles are involved which stem from the peculiar problems arising from working with groups instead of individuals. In fact, whole volumes have been written on the principles and techniques of community health education. While such extensive treatment of the subject is beyond the scope of this book, certain fundamental points should command the attention of physicians participating in programs of community health education.

In community health education, smoother working relationships will exist between physicians and voluntary and official health agencies if physicians are accepted as the source for medical guidance and give leadership in medical affairs. Similarly physicians could well leave to others such decisions as who should serve as volunteers, where the clinic or screening facility should be located, when the campaign should be conducted and similar nonmedical matters.

Joint Planning

In the planning stage of community health education programs, care must be exercised to involve all community agencies and groups which have a major interest in the specific problem under consideration. Only through such joint planning will all of the community's interests and resources be brought to bear on the problem. Many community health education programs have failed because of the omission during the planning stage of some group whose presence, it later turned out, was essential to success.

It is most important that all community groups be informed about the health education program and its objectives. The communication process necessarily begins with the staff and members of the group or groups initiating the program. If the primary sponsor is a health agency, either voluntary or official, it must see that all of its personnel are informed. If the program is being initiated by the county medical society, earnest efforts should be made to see that all members of the society are familiarized with the program.

Not only must all groups concerned be informed, they should be informed in a proper sequence. Unfortunate is the health agency which, in launching a health education effort, does not inform the medical society of its plans and elicit the society's cooperation *before* it presents the project to other community groups. Similarly, the medical society in launching a community health education program should first seek out and inform the health agencies. There is scarcely anything more disconcerting either to physicians or to officials of health agencies than to learn first from the newspapers about programs or projects in which they have a vital interest or responsibility.

Community Perception of Need for a Program

A health program is unlikely to be accepted by a community group unless the program is seen as an effective way of accomplishing some goal that is important to the group.[26] By an extension of this principle, a group's decision to accept a program will more likely occur when the proposal for the program emanates from the group itself rather than from some professional outsider. It has already been indicated that individuals will not accept a particular proposed health action unless that health action is seen by them as likely to reduce a health threat that they experience. On the community level, it has been shown that community leaders will reject a proposed program, however sympathetic they may be generally to its aims, if they fail to see the program as satisfying community needs of which they are currently aware.[26] The health agency that merely distributes information to its clientele on proper ways to act and on proper procedures to apply is thus failing to make use of the social psychology of decision making. Lack of appreciation of this principle—the importance of communicating to and through local influence leaders—may, for example, account for some failures to promote fluoridation. Green has suggested that as far as the leaders of the antifluoridation movement are concerned the principal concern seems to be with the symbolism of fluoridation as a potential encroachment upon personal freedoms.[27] Any attempts to promote fluoridation or any other community health program without effective involvement of appropriate community leaders will reduce its likelihood of success.

Community Involvement

In the development of this phase, two points need to be borne in mind. The first of these involves the myth of the "general public," about which many talk glibly. From a health education standpoint, there really is no such thing as the *general* public; there are instead a great number of specific or *individual* publics. These individual publics are made up of people who live in a particular neighborhood, or belong to the same church, lodge, professional, business or civic organization, or patronize the same school, or have the same ethnic origin or are grouped together in one of countless other ways. By a careful study of the community's structure we are able to search out these individual groups and extend our information process from mass media to a personalized approach to each group, making major use of the spoken word supplemented by visual aids. By the same study of the community we are also able to ascertain its power structure and identify those members of the community whose approval is often essential for the success of any community project. These individuals may be civic leaders, top business men, political, religious or labor leaders or outstanding members of professional groups.

Community Power Structure

Many reasonable and many unreasonable claims have been made regarding community power structure. It has become fashionable in public health, and more generally in social work, to conceive of community power structure as a permanent, monolithic hierarchy composed principally of a pyramid of businessmen. (See, for example, Floyd Hunter.[32]) At the top of this structure is a mysterious and wealthy Mr. X who has it in his power to veto nearly any community proposal he does not prefer or to guarantee the success of any he chooses to support. Below Mr. X are a number of somewhat less wealthy persons who serve functionally as his lieutenants. Below them, indeed far below them, are the professionals in the community. The official governmental structure appears to have virtually no influence. The man on the street is generally persuaded to accept the advice and values that emanate ultimately from Mr. X and his lieutenants since the monolithic power structure supposedly controls all or most of the channels of communication. In any case, even if the man on the street does not accept Mr. X's values, there is virtually nothing he can do about it.

It has become increasingly apparent to social scientists that the kind of power structure described by Floyd Hunter in his "Community Power Structure" at best reflects a pattern of power distribution which may be applicable to some communities but not at all applicable to others. Many recent studies and reviews[33] demonstrate that different kinds of power structures may exist in different communities as a function of local conditions.

Not only does the kind of power structure that will be identified depend on the methods used, it also depends on the kind of community investigated and the kind of issue being considered. It has been suggested, for example, that in large, urban areas, governmental agency officials are likely to be among the most powerful decision makers since they often tend to be full-time, elected public officials, without principal loyalties to private interests. In smaller areas where public officials serve part-time, their major values and interests may be principally related to their private roles. Obviously, the power structure will differ in urban and rural areas.

In areas governed by nonpartisan election rules, permanent political alignments are discouraged. It is possible in such places for a small, well-knit minority to obtain representation out of all proportion to their numbers. Such nonpartisan rules may encourage demagoguery and monolithic power structure. In places governed by partisan politics, political and party officials are likely to exert the greater power.

The power structure will also vary in accordance with the type of issue considered. If a private or voluntary activity is under question, the nongovernmental powers will be dominant; if the issue is one requiring legislation or other governmental action for approval, the official power structure will tend to be dominant.

This brief description should show that the monolithic Mr. X may or may not exist in many communities; power structure is just not that simple.

While the variations in community power arrangements have been stressed here, all studies of power distribution agree on at least two items.

1. In any community, there are persons who are more influential than others in making community decisions or in stimulating public opinion in a desired direction.

2. All studies of the community power influences at the local level show that the upper levels of the occupational hierarchy hold prominent roles, which they may occasionally have to share or yield, as a result of democratic process.

In short, then, the studies that have been performed demonstrate that there are influential individuals in communities, differing from place to place or from issue to issue, who play important roles in determining what the community will do and how residents will behave.

There are no widely accepted methods for correctly identifying all the influential groups in any specific public issue. However, local physicians and public health officers may be able to obtain needed information on power structures by taking time to find out informally which individuals and groups have been prominent in the past in getting the community to adopt or reject a particular health or welfare proposal. For example, it should be feasible in any given community for a physician to identify through informal, intermittent contacts those persons and groups who played an important role in past decisions, say, to build a community hospital, to develop a voluntary agency, or to promote or defeat a particular health or welfare proposal. It is a reasonable hypothesis, though not entirely validated, that those who have been influential in the past are likely to be influential in the future. The health officer or practitioner who obtains such information can store it away for future use in subsequent attempts to develop community health services. Similarly, it would be instructive to health agencies for the public health nurses and other members of the staff to inquire more or less systematically of their clients:

"Who are the people you usually talk to for advice about health, or medicine, or money?"

"Whose advice is usually good on such matters?"

"Where do you usually get information about health and sickness?"

In summary of the principle concerning community decision making, it is suggested that the physician and the health agency identify those individuals and groups who have been influential in determining community health and welfare policy and decisions in the past as well as the informal community leadership to which the public turns for advice. In promoting any health campaign, the key persons and groups from this list should be chosen as the initial points of contact. The health worker should assess initial attitudes and enthusiasm among these groups for a proposed program and, where necessary, carry on educational activities in advance of actually proposing the program. Finally, it is suggested that insofar as possible, the attempt be made to stimulate the community leadership to take responsibility for initiating the decision to adopt the proposed program as a means for solving or preventing important health problems.

Dynamics of Group Action

As people become involved in the health education effort, the process of learning, which is essential to changing attitudes and influencing behavior, is strengthened. The involvement of members of organizations may take a number of forms. Among these is the group meeting itself, when the organization devotes meeting time to a presentation and discussion of the proposed project. As each member becomes involved in the group discussion and the group decision-making, a motivational force is developed which influences each individual to carry out the decision of the group. Social scientists have found[34] that better results in terms of influencing behavior have been achieved by one nutritionist meeting with a group of mothers to discuss a nutritional problem, than by individual instruction by nutritionists at which the same problem was discussed on an individual basis with an equivalent number of mothers. The mother participating in a group discussion and a group decision was more likely to carry out the recommended course of action than if she had the same information presented to her on an individual basis. The opportunity to participate in the making of a group decision provided a motivating force not present when the approach was personal.

In addition to the group discussion, the involvement of the members of a community organization may take other forms. Contributing money, providing volunteer service or participating in other ways may also contribute toward the learning process and toward changing attitudes and behavior. In fact, there is no doubt that the voluntary health agency movement, unique to America, has been a positive force in the health education of those who actively support and participate in the work of each agency.

Timing is of importance. The need for timing in communications has already been mentioned. Timing is just as critical in community involvement. First, the community must be ready for the project. Communities have teachable moments just as do individuals. For example, polio vaccination programs that languish in December often come to life when the polio season approaches. Second, there is a definite incubation period involved in health education just as there is with communicable diseases. This incubation period manifests itself as a time lag between the point at which the community is informed and the point at which it acts. Health agencies and the medical profession may sometimes move too rapidly in attempting to carry out programs which require active citizen participation. Just as the incubation period varies with individual diseases so does it vary with different health programs or projects. The period may be quite short. In a real health emergency where the community may be faced with an epidemic or some other major hazard, the community can become informed and respond with definitive action in an amazingly short time. In other instances, such as those where changes in diet or personal health habits are involved, the lag between information and action may be quite long indeed. In general, the incubation period may be measured in terms of weeks or months and an allowance should be made for it in planning the various phases of the program.

GRANVILLE W. LARIMORE, M.D.
IRWIN M. ROSENSTOCK, Ph.D.

REFERENCES

1. Expert Committee on Health Education of the Public: World Health Organization Technical Report Series No. 89. Geneva, World Health Organization, October, 1954.
2. Grout, Ruth E.: Health Teaching in Schools. Philadelphia, W. B. Saunders Company, 1948.
3. Turner, Clair E.: Community Health Educator's Compendium of Knowledge. St. Louis, The C. V. Mosby Company, 1956.
4. Derryberry, Mayhew: Some Problems Faced in Educating for Health. Address given at 29th annual meeting of the American Academy of Physical Education, March 29, 1958, Kansas City, Missouri.
5. Polgar, S.: Health and Human Behavior: Areas of Interest Common to the Social and Medical Sciences. Current Anthropology, 3(No. 2): 159-179, April, 1962.
6. Pearsall, M.: Medical Behavioral Science: A Selected Bibliography of Cultural Anthropology, Social Psychology and Sociology in Medicine. Lexington, University of Kentucky Press, 1963.
7. Shimberg, B., and Harris, J. S.: Evaluation of a nutrition education program through follow-up interviews (abstract). American Psychologist, 6:7, 385, July, 1951.
8. Hochbaum, G. M.: Public Participation in Medical Screening Programs: A Socio-Psychological Study. U. S. Public Health Service Publication 572. 1958.
9. Rosenstock, I. M.: What Research in Motivation Suggests for Public Health. American Journal of Public Health, 50(No. 3):295-302, March, 1960.
10. Flach, E. G.: Participation in Case Finding Program for Cervical Cancer. Administrative Report, Cancer Control Program, U. S. Public Health Service, Washington, D.C.
11. Rosenstock, I. M., Derryberry, M., and Carriger, B. K.: Why People Fail to Seek Poliomyelitis Vaccination. Public Health Reports, 74(No. 2):98-103, February, 1959.
12. Rosenstock, I. M., Hochbaum, G. M., Leventhal, H., et al.: The Impact of Asian Influenza on Community Life: A Study in Five Cities. U. S. Public Health Service Publication 776. 1960.
13. Kegeles, S. S.: Some Motives for Seeking Preventive Dental Care. The Journal of the American Dental Association, 67:111-118, July, 1963.
14. Heinzelmann, F.: Determinants of Prophylaxis Behavior with Respect to Rheumatic Fever. Journal of Health and Human Behavior, III(No. 2):73, 1962.
15. Cassel, J.: A Comprehensive Health Program Among South African Zulus. In Paul, B. (ed.): Health Culture and Community. New York, Russell Sage Foundation, 1955, pp. 15-41.
16. Larimore, Granville W., and Leiby, George: Study of Factors in VD Control. Third Service Command, United States Army, 1945. (Unpublished data.)
17. Galdston, Iago: Motivation in health education. American Journal of Public Health, 39:1276-1283, October, 1949.
18. Krieghbaum, Hillier: Readers Crave News of Health and Science. Editor and Publisher, August 30, 1958.

19. Festinger, L., et al.: Theory and Experiment in Social Communications. Ann Arbor, Research Center for Group Dynamics, Institute for Social Research, University of Michigan, 1950.

20. Lewin, K.: Group Decision and Social Change. *In* Newcomb, T. M., and Hartley, E. L. (ed.): Readings in Social Psychology. New York, Henry Holt & Co., 1947, pp. 330-344.

21. Asch, S. E.: Effects of Group Pressure Upon the Modification and Distortion of Judgments. *In* Guetskow, H. (ed.): Groups, Leadership, and Men. Pittsburgh, Carnegie Press, 1951, pp. 177-190.

22. Koos, E. L.: The Health of Regionville. New York, Columbia University Press, 1954.

23. Saunders, L.: Cultural Differences and Medical Care. New York, Russell Sage Foundation, 1954.

24. Paul, B. D.: Social Science in Public Health. American Journal of Public Health, 46(No. 11):1390-1396, 1956.

25. Larimore, Granville W.: Behavior-centered health education; its potential contribution to the epidemiology of health. The Epidemiology of Health. New York, Health Education Council, 1953.

26. Meltzer, M. S.: A Psychological Approach to Developing Principles of Community Organization. American Journal of Public Health, 43(No. 2):198-203, February, 1953.

27. Green, A. L.: The Ideology of Anti-Fluoridation Leaders. Journal of Social Issues, XVII(No. 4):13-25, 1961.

28. Cartwright, D.: Some Principles of Mass Persuasion. Human Relations, 2:253-267, 1949.

29. Griffiths, W., and Knutson, A. L.: The Role of the Mass Media in Public Health. American Journal of Public Health, 50(No. 4):515-523, April, 1960.

30. Hovland, C. I.: Reconciling Conflicting Results Derived From Experimental and Survey Studies of Attitude Change. The American Psychologist, 14(No. 1): 8-17, 1959.

31. Katz, E., and Lazarsfeld, P. F.: Personal Influence. Chicago, The Free Press of Glencoe, 1955.

32. Hunter, F. A.: Community Power Structure. Chapel Hill, University of North Carolina Press, 1952.

33. Rossi, P. H.: Theory and Method in the Study of Power in the Local Community, presented at the 1960 Annual Meeting of the American Sociological Association, New York, August, 1960.

34. Radke, Marian, and Klisurich, Dayna: Experiments in changing food habits. Journal of the American Dietetic Association, 23:5, May, 1947.

37 Patient Education and Communication

Effective doctor-patient communication was never more important than in today's "scientific" medicine, often practiced by a "team," each of whose members possesses specialized skills but no one of whom may assume the old-time "family doctor" relationship to the patient. The lay press and patients themselves are frequently critical of what they term the cold impersonal approach of modern medicine. Though patients would not accept the old time physician's level of medical care, they still want the warm, friendly, personal touch, characteristic of the horse and buggy doctor of years gone by. Particularly, they want an attentive listener who will provide the personal attention each patient feels he wants, and correctly so since doctor-patient communication must be a two-way process if it is to be effective.

Patients want to be made to feel that their problems are important to the physician and that he has time to listen to them regardless of how rushed he may be. They want explanations of their illnesses and what is to be done for them and they want their questions answered. In spite of the fact that today's patient is considerably more sophisticated medically than his counterpart of a generation ago, he wants the explanations and the answers in simple understandable terms.

This latter is not always easy for the physician, particularly one just beginning practice, for during his four years of medical school and the training period that follows, the physician acquires a whole new vocabulary. Practically a new language is built around the activities and fundamentals of his profession. He is constantly encouraged to extend his medical vocabulary and along with it he picks up a considerable amount of pseudoscientific medical jargon. All of this is indispensable in conversing with his medical colleagues, in preparing records and reports; and in giving orders to nurses and others who aid in caring for his patients.

As far as suitability for communication to patients, however, this hard-won medical vocabulary is just so much Sanskrit. Nephrolithiasis is eminently correct terminology for medical discussions and for the patient's record. Yet it is pretty useless as a language symbol to the patient suffering from a kidney

417

stone. Retrolental fibroplasia, accurately descriptive to the medical mind, is likely to be incomprehensible to the parents of a baby who has become blind. Even such a relatively simple term as reduction of a fracture is better understood by the layman as setting the fracture or setting the broken bone.

To communicate satisfactorily with his patient, the physician must learn early in his practice to translate into everyday language the medical terminology he spent so many years mastering. The translation, that is, the degree of simplification employed, will depend on the educational background, experience and intellectual capacity of the patient.[1] The experienced physician has learned that it is better to err on the side of oversimplicity, in the interest of being certain that important information is understood. Effective communication may also be impeded by misconceptions the patient may have which influence his interpretation of the information given him. He will tend to fit the new information into his own pattern of thinking. This makes it important that the physician ascertain whether the information being given is understood by encouraging the patient to repeat it. Unfortunately, the physician must approach this subtly, since many patients would be insulted if he said, "Now tell me in your own words what I have told you." On the other hand, if the physician asks, "Do you understand," he is likely to get "Yes," the easiest answer, even though the patient, not wishing to appear ignorant, may not understand at all. The physician alert to this problem can find many ways of meeting it tactfully; for example, he may repeat the information given and leave gaps for the patient to fill in, or he may encourage the patient to talk freely about the instructions.

An effective job of patient education is admittedly not easy. There are several factors involved, in addition to the need to translate the technical terms and jargon of medicine into everyday, simple language. The physician must arrange the information which he wants to give his patient in a logical, forthright manner. Instructions,[2] to be meaningful, should be in terms of the patient's own pattern of behavior and can best be prepared from having a thorough knowledge of the patient's living and working habits. The physician should also bear in mind that, since his objective is usually not only to inform but also to influence the patient's behavior, he needs to give reasons why the prescribed course of action should be followed. Finally, he must be prepared to answer the patient's questions in an equally forthright and understandable manner. The simplest question should be carefully answered and even the seemingly ridiculous query should not be scoffed at or treated with derision. Care must also be taken to ensure that even the physician's facial expression or voice inflection does not create the impression of lack of sympathy or unwillingness to invite patient queries. Effective patient education requires the physician to combine successfully the art of the teacher, the persuasiveness of the salesman and the patience of Job.

In patient education, the physician does, however, have certain innate advantages—after all "doctor" does mean "teacher." First, he has the benefit of the cloak of authority that his knowledge and professional status provide him, although too heavy a reliance on the authoritarian approach will limit his effectiveness. Second, there are few more "teachable" moments healthwise than at the time of illness. When an individual is sick, he and often his family are usually eager both to learn and to practice those things which will help rid him of his misery. This period of "teachability" may, however, be relatively short. Sullivan[3] found, for example, that parents of children with rheumatic fever began to seek all of the information they could about the disease immediately following the diagnosis, not only from physicians, but from the lay press and other sources as well. After the first two weeks, however, they were less interested in information that was given to them. They had "learned," even though some of the information which they had obtained from nonmedical sources might not have been correct. Third, the physician's advice benefits from the tremendous faith of the American people in the "miracles of modern science," which gives a special credence to what the doctor says.

Some physicians have had unhappy experiences with their efforts at patient education. Possibly they have found that what they have told patients is sometimes misunderstood, with unfortunate results. They may have found, too, that to do a good job of patient education requires time, so that when days become too crowded patient education loses out. The time factor can be considerably offset by intelligently using office assistants, printed materials and visual aids (p. 421). Some physicians, possibly because of what they feel are inadequacies in their educational backgrounds, or because of language difficulties or for reasons of personality, tend to skimp on their educational responsibilities. The result is the complaint that practically every physician has heard from patients who have come to him from a colleague: "He never tells me anything," or "He won't ever answer my questions," or "He is always in such a hurry, I never find out anything." No matter how it is expressed, it represents a valid criticism of any physician's professional conduct, since adequate patient education is essential to effective medical practice. Further, patient education, good or bad, planned or fortuitous, takes place at every contact between physician and patient, except, of course, when the patient is anesthetized or unconscious. Thus, the physician really cannot decide that he will or will not be responsive to his patient's need for education about his condition, even though he may not think of himself as a teacher in the usual sense.

Physicians must recognize that the patient's visit to the doctor is often a highly charged emotional experience. The patient may be full of anxieties and fears about the possible consequences of his illness and its effect on his home, family or job. In such an emotional state the patient's anxiety may feed on such extraneous items as the physician's facial expression during the physical examination. The patient may interpret, for example, a frown or a pursing of the lips as suggestive of a disastrous course for his illness. A lingering of the stethoscope over the precordium may similarly suggest to the nervous patient that something is amiss. In these and in countless other ways, patient fears may be engendered that will require repeated reassurance to erase. Particularly with an anxious patient communication may occur by other means than words alone.

This same emotional tension that may exist during the visit to the doctor may also make it difficult for the patient to remember all of the information or instructions that the physician gives. Thus it is wise to reinforce the important points by giving the patient written instructions or some other type of educational aid. It is all too easy for the anxious patient, particularly the elderly, to confuse even simple instructions so that, for example, "one pill twice a day," becomes "two pills once a day."

Successful physicians find in patient education a basis for establishing the rapport with patients which is fundamental to an effective doctor-patient relationship. The physician who does an effective job of patient education also finds that he is spared many of the day-to-day vexations and frustrations of medical practice. These include needless calls from patients who didn't understand his instructions, problems with patients who didn't carry out directions because they failed to grasp them, or patients who became discouraged or discontinued treatment because they didn't comprehend fully either the nature of their illness or the reasons for the course of treatment prescribed.

Instruction of the patient should include, in addition to the essential information about his condition, a definite plan for action outlined in sequential steps and so specific that the patient has a firm grasp of what he is to do until he sees his physician again. Whenever possible, the patient should be given the reasons for the course of action recommended. There is probably no better motivating force in getting the physician's recommendations carried out than the patient's clear understanding of the reasons for them.

WHAT TO TELL THE PATIENT

What to tell the patient? The decision must, of course, be made at the outset of any patient education program. In general, it poses no major problem if the patient is simply given the facts about his condition accurately and forthrightly. However, there are times when the decision is not an easy one. For example, when it has been determined that the patient is suffering from a malignancy which has reached the point where palliation is the best that can be hoped for, should the physician tell the patient the whole story? Or, should he tell the patient little, but describe the situation in detail to the relatives or to the patient's key business associates? The experience of many physicians clearly indicates that there is no categorical answer to these questions that fits all circumstances.

Interestingly enough, physicians tend to differ from cancer patients themselves as to whether the patient should be told. In a study of 100 cancer patients, Kelly and Friesen[4] found that 89 favored knowing their diagnosis. Samp and Curreri[5] surveyed 560 cancer patients and their families and found that 87 per cent felt that the cancer patient should be told of the diagnosis. However, in a study of 193 staff-members of Michael Reese Hospital in Chicago, Oken[6] reported that 88 per cent of the physicians said that they did not tell cancer patients their diagnosis. In this and other studies of physicians the reasons given for not telling are centered around the fear of causing profoundly disturbing psychological effects on the patient. It has been asserted that disclosure is followed by fear and despondency which may culminate in suicide. However, such instances are rare, and physicians in the Oken study could also recall many instances in which the patient was told and seemed to do well.

The answer to this admittedly perplexing question, which also applies to other serious illnesses in which a fatal outcome is a very real possibility, is, of course, not an easy one. It must of necessity lie within the physician's best judgment arrived at only after carefully and sympathetically weighing all of the factors.

If, for example, the patient holds a top spot in a big business upon which many people depend for their livelihood, the answer is more likely to be that he should be told all of the facts about his condition so he can put the firm's affairs in order before his death. If, however, the patient is emotionally unstable and likely to react badly when told of the seriousness of his condition, the physician might judge that the situation warrants giving the minimum of information to the patient, while discussing the condition in considerable detail with relatives. Only in exceptional circumstances would the physician withhold information from both the patient and relatives or business associates. In virtually every instance, there is someone who should be prepared in advance for the possible fatal course of a gravely ill patient. When it has been decided not to tell the patient about his condition, the physician needs to be extremely cautious in answering specific inquiries from the patient. Withholding of information is one thing; actual lying to a patient about his condition is yet another. Here again the physician must approach the problem with all the judgment he possesses and resolve the question solely in the best interest of the patient.

When it is necessary to impart bad news to the patient or his family, the physician must accomplish the task with the least possible psychic trauma to the patient or his relatives. At no time in the physician's professional career are kindliness, gentleness and a sympathetic understanding more important. Many physicians have endeared themselves to the patient and his family by the way in which they have revealed the existence of a serious or terminal illness.

AIDS TO PATIENT EDUCATION

Effective patient education is of necessity time consuming, a fact accepted by the conscientious physician who sees the education of his patient as an integral and important part of the doctor-patient relationship and, in the final analysis, an important part of treatment. For example, the life of the diabetic may well depend on how good an educational job his physician does. Insulin and the oral agents, important though they are, are of little help unless the diabetic understands the why, how and when of their use. Many such examples can be cited from everyday medical practice.[7] All point to the essential part that patient education plays in the work of the physician who treats not only the disease but the patient as well.

Conscious efforts at improvement, augmented by practice, will enable the physician to do an increasingly better job of patient education in a shorter period of time. The physician can increase his effectiveness while at the same time decreasing the time involved by the use of carefully prepared, printed instructions and other aids.[8] Printed instruction sheets which may be in mimeograph form have been found to be especially helpful for obstetric patients as well as those with diabetes, and for all those who must follow special diets. Such printed instructions not only save the physician's time but reinforce the patient's memory of any verbal instructions he receives. However, instruction sheets, no matter how well written or carefully prepared, are not a satisfactory substitute for the physician's personal efforts. They must be regarded solely as supplementary.

Another aid to patient education that some physicians, particularly obstetricians and pediatricians, have found helpful is to encourage patients to write down their questions beforehand so that all points which the patient considers important are covered during the visit. It is well to give the patient a chance to ask questions before a formal history taking is begun. Letting the patient ask questions first may present diagnostic leads which might otherwise be missed, since the patient in answering the physician's questions may overlook his own.

The physician's office nurse or assistant can be trained to take over certain patient education responsibilities. Professional nurses often make excellent instructors because of their background and experience. Here again, as with printed instruction sheets, the efforts of the physician's assistants can only be supplementary. The physician should make himself available for patient's questions or, at least, lend authority to the efforts of his assistants.

In addition to printed instructions, various other types of visual aids, such as charts, diagrams, pictures, a chalk board, photographic slides and anatomical models, when properly used, can increase the effectiveness of the physician's health education job.[9] Gay[10] recommends that every physician set aside space within his office for the education of patients. Whenever possible, a separate instruction room should be provided where printed materials and visual aids are assembled for use in patient teaching. Gay notes that, ideally, the patient progresses from the reception area to the consultation and examining rooms and finally arrives at the room which has been specially equipped and planned for educational purposes. While instructional equipment and materials cannot be provided for every conceivable condition, certain problems are encountered frequently enough so that it is practical to prepare educational aids for them. Possible sources for ready-made instructional aids are: medical societies, both state and national, voluntary health agencies and local health departments, U. S. Public Health Service and other federal agencies, drug houses and commercial firms specializing in this field.

Whenever the patient's treatment requires him to learn a skill, such as the administration of insulin or the wearing or adjustment of an appliance or prosthesis, the physician should provide the patient with an opportunity to demonstrate the skill in his presence. This is the only way to make sure that the instructions given have been understood and can be carried out. The physician should make greater use of physiotherapists in teaching the use of appliances and artificial limbs and in helping to speed up recovery from fractures.

Medical schools can contribute significantly to the development of skills in patient education through a period of observation and demonstration during clinical clerkships. In the course of clerkships students should be encouraged to interview patients repeatedly to find out what they know about their conditions or the reasons why they think certain types of treatment are being given. Comparisons between what the patients say and what they have been told will often sharpen the students' skills in communicating with patients. Another teaching technique especially applicable to training in patient education is the use of role playing in which students alternately play the role of the physician or patient.[11] Students thus have an opportunity to observe the patient education process in action. Such a technique encourages the development of empathy on the part of the student.

One development which has merit is the employment of specially trained health educators by large clinics, hospitals and other medical institutions. These paramedical specialists are equipped to organize and administer patient education in such a setting. Their training, usually acquired at the graduate level in a school of public health, embraces both educational and health knowledge and skills.

GRANVILLE W. LARIMORE, M.D.

REFERENCES

1. Bateson, Gregory: Social Planning and the Concept of "Deutero-Learning." Readings in Social Psychology. New York, Henry Holt and Company, 1947.
2. Skinner, Mary Lou, and Derryberry, Mayhew: Some aspects of health education for medical students. Journal of Medical Education, 34, No. 4, April, 1959.
3. Sullivan, Daniel: Sedgwick County's Exploratory Program in Chronic Disease Education. (Unpublished data.)
4. Kelly, W. D., and Friesen, S. R.: Do cancer patients want to be told? Surgery, 27:822-826, June, 1950.
5. Samp, R. J., and Curreri, A. R.: Questionnaire survey on public cancer education obtained from cancer patients and their families. Cancer, 10:382-384, March-April, 1957.
6. Oken, Donald: What to tell cancer patients. Journal of the American Medical Association, 175:1120-1128, April 1, 1961.
7. Skinner, Mary Lou, and Derryberry, Mayhew: Health education for outpatients. Public Health Reports, 69:1107-1114, November, 1954.
8. Schwartz, D.: Health promotional literature for clinic patients; and experiment by the Nursing Service of the New York Hospital, Cornell Medical Center, Out-Patient Department. American Journal of Public Health, 43:1318-1323, October, 1953.
9. Dale, Edgar: Audio-Visual Methods in Teaching. New York, The Dryden Press, 1954.
10. Gay, James R.: Education and instruction of patients in private practice. Journal of the American Medical Association, 167:1616, July 26, 1958.
11. Bradford, Leland P., and Lippitt, Ronald: Role-playing in supervision training. Personnel, 22:358-369, 1946.

38 Continuing Education for Physicians

Every practicing physician should be aware of the need to continue his education beyond medical school for as long as he practices medicine. Only thus can he give the best service to his patients whether his field be preventive or therapeutic medicine.

This idea is not new. Eight centuries ago Maimonides stated in his Daily Prayer of a Physician: "May there never develop in me the notion that my education is complete, but give me strength and leisure and zeal continually to enlarge my knowledge." In 1892 William Henry Welch observed, "Medical education is not completed in medical school: it is only begun."[1]

Need

At the beginning of the twentieth century, thousands of children died from diphtheria. Diphtheria antitoxin had just been developed and its use in treatment prevented many deaths. Valuable as this was, it was only partially effective. Soon diphtheria toxin-antitoxin was developed. Physicians now had a means of preventing their patients from getting diphtheria. General practitioners and specialists, working with the public health authorities, administered this agent, and later toxoid, in such an effective manner that today diphtheria is a rare disease in the United States.

The classic studies on diabetes of Banting and Best in 1921 led to the development of insulin for the control of the disease. Physicians were thus given another tool in the prevention of the progress of a disease, even though the means of preventing diabetes have not yet been established.

More recently, the contributions of Salk and Sabin have been hailed throughout the world because their vaccines would actually prevent the dreaded poliomyelitis. Millions of children and young adults have been vaccinated in the United States. Every up-to-date physician now administers these vaccines as a part of modern preventive care. There is every reason to believe that in developed countries poliomyelitis will soon become as rare as diphtheria.

These are but a few of the advances in the field of preventive medicine in the last half century. Millions of dollars are being spent each year in medical research. It is reasonable to expect that the next decade will bring forth scientific information concerning the prevention of cardiovascular diseases and cancer—the two major causes of death in the United States today. Because of our aging population, new rehabilitation techniques are being developed. Physicians must be skilled in the rehabilitation techniques to prevent the progress of debilitating diseases in their geriatric patients.

This rapidly changing picture of the practice of medicine requires the physician to keep abreast of new knowledge in the field of preventive medicine. He is morally and legally responsible to give his patients the care which is consistent with the best medical practice in his community. This includes the prevention of disease where possible, the early diagnosis of illness, adequate care and treatment, prevention of progression of illness, and rehabilitation when necessary.

A pamphlet on Continuing Medical Education Programs prepared by the Council on Medical Education of the American Medical Association[2] states: "Vital new discoveries are of little immediate use against human disease until physicians in practice learn about them. Regardless of how well prepared a physician may be at the time of entering practice, the adequate knowledge of yesterday is not fully adequate today." A professor of medicine recently stated that "eighty per cent of the drugs used today were not yet discovered twelve years ago."

Responsibility of Physicians

Each physician must want to continue his education beyond his formal training. He must want to use in his practice all of the newer medical knowledge that is constantly becoming available. Dryer[3] says he should be dedicated to a lifetime of learning.

The responsibility for continuing education rests on the individual physician. The educational incentives of the twenty or more years of study prior to licensure are lacking. He has reached his goal. He is no longer studying to get a degree. His license to practice is his for a lifetime. Now the incentive is only the reward of a job well done.

The fact that a large majority of physicians do not formally continue their education is evidence that the incentive is not enough. Should there be a penalty, other than out-of-date medical practice, attached to a failure of the physician to continue his education?

Methods

How is new knowledge learned? Miller[4, 5] and co-workers emphasize that a teacher teaches but a student learns. The student must be an active participant in the learning process. The material presented must have an immediate practical application. Student involvement is important in choice of method of continuing education.

The physician may continue his medical education throughout his active practice in many ways. Here are some good examples.

Reading Scientific Articles. A physician should subscribe to at least one general medical journal, and others which may be of special interest to him. The medical literature is voluminous but by subscribing to one or more of the services which abstract articles, the field can be fairly well covered. Cultivating the habit of setting aside a portion of each day for reading medical literature is desirable. This is a habit which can be carried out systematically, as for example, immediately after lunch or just before retiring. In this way the physician may combine relaxation with education.

Membership on a Hospital Staff. Frequent informal discussions with other physicians in the hospital will assist the physician in continuing his medical education. He should attend and participate in staff meetings—learning from the experience of others. This will expose him to a broader review of the medical literature as well.

Journal Clubs. Several physicians can meet regularly once a month for a few hours. Each can review and summarize some of the literature at the meeting. This practice permits the group to take advantage of a wide variety of medical information. Interesting cases in a physician's practice can be considered by the group as a whole and serve as illustrations of the subject under consideration.

Medical Organizations. One of the primary objectives of most medical societies is the continuing education of the members. Scientific meetings of medical organizations offer new knowledge to each physician in attendance. The physician will find it educational to accept some responsibility for planning his society's meetings, including securing a speaker, introducing a subject or discussing a paper. It will require him to review material on the subject at a time when he has an intense interest in it and will assist him in the formation of regular study habits.

Refresher Courses. The formal, short refresher course provides an excellent means of reaching busy doctors. The Academy of General Practice requires all of its members to take not less than 50 hours of short courses every 3 years in order to continue membership. A survey by the American Medical Association in 1953 of a representative sample of practicing physicians in the United States indicated that each physician should have approximately 60 hours of formal instruction each year. Other estimates vary, but it is agreed that each physician does need formal instruction at least annually. Many such courses are provided, the most common of which are the following:

1. Continuing education programs of medical schools or medical centers. These have the advantage of accessibility for faculty, teaching facilities, clinical material for demonstrations and a location accessible to a large population of physicians.

2. Scientific assemblies. These are usually conducted once a year by special interest groups. Among those of particular interest to the general practitioner are the courses provided by the American College of Physicians.

3. Circuit riding type of instruction is useful in areas far removed from medical teaching facilities. In this approach a group of three or four faculty from a medical center give a course in one area and immediately move on to a second area and repeat the course. The lecturers repeat this procedure in several locations before returning to the medical center. This is usually part of a statewide plan for providing continuing education to physicians.

Regular Teaching Days in a Locality. The plan of the School of Medicine of the State University of New York at Buffalo for continuing education of the physicians in the western part of the state provides for this type of teaching. Each month the local physicians choose a topic of current interest to them. The Director of Postgraduate Education obtains two faculty members of the medical school who meet with the physicians in the local hospital, first for ward rounds conducted by the visiting faculty and later for a formal scientific meeting. The local physicians participate actively in this instruction through the presentation and discussion of cases in their practices.

Observation Experience. Attendance at a teaching hospital and participation in ward rounds with the teaching staff are advantageous in keeping the physician up to date. This practice should be continued regularly because the topics under discussion at any given time will be limited to the material currently available on the wards. Periodic observation at a medical center for a week or more annually will also be valuable.

Radio. This is a particularly useful medium in areas where transportation presents a problem. It also serves to reach a large number of physicians with a minimum of disruption of their daily activities. The Albany Medical College in New York[6] first developed the use of the two-way radio for teaching. An educational FM broadcast station was established in 1958, with the main studio at the Medical College. Fifty-four "remote broadcast units," located in hospitals up to 100 miles away, can receive and transmit questions and discussions. At the same time, any FM receiver within range can pick up the broadcast. The presentation by the faculty of the Albany Medical College usually takes about half an hour; physicians listening to the broadcast during the lunch hour in their hospitals then have the opportunity to ask questions of the faculty via the two-way radio system. This method of continuing education has the advantage of saving time, inasmuch as practically no travel is involved on the part of either the faculty or the participating physicians. There is exceptionally high attendance and lively participation by the practicing physicians in the rural areas. It has the disadvantage of being fairly expensive, requiring special installations at each receiving and broadcasting point, and there is a minimum of student participation.

Radio, and particularly two-way radio, has played an increasingly important part in continuing medical education in recent years.

Television. To be most useful this should be a closed circuit. It has been used to advantage locally with large audiences, and nationwide also for rapid dissemination of new medical knowledge, such as the use of the poliomyelitis vaccine. It is used for teaching days where techniques such as operative procedures need to be visible to a large group. It is a useful adjunct to the formal short course. Experiments with commercial television broadcasts in continuing medical education are being tried.

Tape-Recorded Lectures. This is similar to reading medical articles. It is easier for some physicians to listen to a tape recorder than it is to read an article in a journal. Some practicing physicians in rural areas have portable tape recorders in their cars and listen to recorded medical lectures while traveling.

Joint Responsibility

Private practitioners, medical societies and public health authorities have joint responsibilities for the continuation of education in the prevention of illness and the prevention of progression of illness.[7] It is the professional responsibility of each physician to give a specific amount of time regularly to continuing his education.

The medical society should (a) determine the relative needs for continuing education and make provision for satisfying these needs; (b) encourage its members to take advantage of opportunities provided; (c) keep its membership informed of courses, seminars and scientific meetings; (d) assume leadership in coordinating all groups concerned with continuing medical education.

Public health authorities have the responsibility for prevention of occurrence and of progression of disease in the community as a whole. They should work with the private practitioners and the medical societies in determining the need for continuing medical education and providing for the satisfaction of these needs, including financial assistance as required. Continuing medical education of physicians is a large component of many of the preventive medicine programs described elsewhere in this book. Health department interests may be carried out jointly with the medical societies, by providing teaching days, formal short courses or speakers for scientific meetings, or by continuing support for individual continuing education programs.

Results

The value of continuing education to the individual physician can be as great as his medical school training. A physician today cannot practice modern preventive medicine without adequate, continuing education. Continuing medical education should assist each physician to achieve, within his own natural limitations, his optimum level of practice of medicine.

FRANKLYN B. AMOS, M.D.

REFERENCES

1. Welch, W. H.: The Advancement of Medical Education: Remarks made at the annual dinner of the Harvard Medical School Association, June, 1892. Bulletin of the Harvard Medical School Association, 1892, pp. 55-64.
2. A Guide Regarding Objectives and Basic Principles of Continuing Medical Education Programs. Council on Medical Education and Hospitals of the American Medical Association, 1960.
3. Dryer, B. V.: Lifetime learning for physicians: Principles, practices and proposals. Journal of Medical Education, 37(6):1-134, June, 1962, Part 2.
4. Miller, G. E., Abrahamson, S., Cohen, I. S., Graser, H. P., Harnach, R. S., and Land, S.: Teaching and Learning in Medical School. Cambridge, Harvard University Press, 1961.
5. Miller, G. E.: Medical care: Its social and organization aspects. The continuing education of physicians. New England Journal of Medicine, 269:295-299, August 8, 1963.
6. Ebbert, A., Jr.: Two-way radio in medical education. The Journal of Medical Education, 38(4):319-328, April, 1963.
7. Promotion of Medical Practitioners' Interest in Preventive Medicine. WHO Technical Report Series, No. 269, March, 1964.

SERVICES AIDING THE PRACTICE OF PREVENTIVE MEDICINE

39   Social Work

Physical, social and psychological factors in health and illness are closely interwoven. A person overwhelmed with personal adjustment problems is not well equipped to withstand disease. A patient's treatment may be delayed, interrupted or fragmented because of adverse social circumstances. A patient's will to recover may be sapped if he has to cope unaided with an array of personal, family and social problems. Early identification and prompt, sympathetic management of such problems are essential to insure that maximum benefits are derived from medical treatment, to minimize the effects of illness and disability and to prevent progression or recurrence of disease.

Frequently, the physician first exposes the existing problems and, depending on his interest and skill, may be in a position to effect a satisfactory solution. When the situation is more complex, one of several social work facilities may assist the physician in the management of the social problem.

INTERRELATIONSHIPS BETWEEN PHYSICAL AND SOCIAL WELL-BEING

The human organism must constantly adjust to environmental conditions to maintain equilibrium. This involves not only physiologic adaptation to factors such as climate, biological agents or chemical substances, but also continuous adjustment to ever-shifting circumstances in the social environment, such as economic conditions, moral value systems, family and interpersonal relationships. Just as individuals differ in their ability to maintain physiologic equilibrium and to resist or overcome disease, so they vary in their ability to maintain or regain equilibrium in their social adjustment. In two identical cases of leg amputation, one patient may readily accept his physical limitations, adapt his family life to his conditions, enter a new occupation and find new recreational outlets. The second patient may solve these problems only with considerable assistance, if at all. A wide range of factors accounts for such individual differences—the person's physical, intellectual and psychological endowment, the kind and magnitude of social adaptation problems he has encountered throughout his life, and his successes and failures in meeting such problems. Although each person's problem-solving capacity is a highly individual matter, certain general observations can be made regarding typical social problems confronting individuals and families in our society.

In our era of industrialization, urbanization, mobility and high living standards, the average small family unit is more vulnerable to economic, political and other vicissitudes beyond its control than was the larger family in the less complex and more rural American society of 50 or 75 years ago. Being socially and economically less self-sufficient, today's family depends on an intricate network of supporting services and technical experts in all areas of living. It must exercise considerable planning and organizational skill if it is to maintain some measure of control over its own destiny. Modern day families are preoccupied with ever-changing opportunities and risks; they are frequently not deeply rooted in any one community; they are often lacking in consistent affectional support from relatives and neighbors. They face complicated problems in maintaining cohesion and in performing family functions such as rearing children or making a living. Some traditional functions such as care for elderly relatives frequently cannot be undertaken at all. When the attention of families and individuals is riveted on social problems, health needs are easily neglected. When their energies are depleted in a search for new social solutions, their resistance to disease may be lowered and accidents are more likely. When a social breakdown has occurred, a physical breakdown may ensue.

Certain social adjustment problems are a by-product of the spectacular advances of medicine during the last half century. Treatment in a modern hospital, staffed by a team of specialists, often makes it necessary for the patient to adapt to a cold world of science without the sustenance and protection afforded by the continuous relationship with one trusted family physician. Many lives are saved by early diagnosis and prompt medical or surgical intervention, but patients often must make rapid decisions to undergo necessary treatment, often lacking time to plan wisely for their absence from home. Early ambulation shortens the duration of hospitalization, but resultant extended convalescence at home presents new problems to the small family unit. If such social stresses, as well as complex financing problems, cannot be absorbed by the patient or family or be cushioned through other resources, an unfortunate cycle of new social and medical problems may follow.

Probably the most fundamental change brought about by medical science is the vast increase in the number of chronically ill and disabled people in all age groups. Millions of people can now be restored to partial functioning but yet are not completely equipped to solve their daily problems of living in a complex society. In order to meet their combined medical and social needs, society has had to invent many new devices and facilities. These include rehabilitation centers and home care programs; foster home programs and half-way houses to facilitate readjustment of persons discharged from mental hospitals; various special aids such as public health nursing services, mechanisms of financial assistance, schools for the handicapped, sheltered workshops, homemaker services and specialized housing facilities for the elderly. These and many other kinds of medical-social devices are effective but their development has not kept pace with the mounting need. Few communities have a master plan for the systematic development of such resources. Individuals and families often face perplexing and overwhelming problems due to gaps in services, deficiencies in coordination, or lack of knowledge about what is available.

SOCIAL PROBLEMS ENCOUNTERED IN PRIVATE MEDICAL PRACTICE

It is apparent from this discussion that personal and social problems occur in all population and income groups and that people seeking medical help cannot separate medical from social problems when these are so closely interrelated. These facts are underscored by the results of a study by this author in 1955 in which one hundred general practitioners, internists and pediatricians in Minneapolis, Minnesota, were asked to estimate how frequently during one year they encountered each of nine selected social problems among their private office patients (see Table 19). For example, mounting financial difficulties as a result of illness were estimated to occur on an average of more than twenty-five times a year in each medical practice; serious marital difficulties twenty-four times a year; family problems arising from the presence of an elderly ambulatory patient in the household, twenty-two times a year. Most of the physicians indicated that they encountered

Table 19. *Number of Selected Social Problems Encountered in Private Medical Practice During One Year**

PROBLEMS	MEAN NUMBER OF PROBLEMS PER PHYSICIAN
Patients who as a result of illness have mounting difficulties in meeting financial responsibilities for their families.	25.6
Patients unhappy in their marriage to a point where this causes considerable strain.	23.8
Elderly ambulatory patients whose presence in their children's household contributes significantly to family problems.	21.9
Chronically ill housewives and mothers whose duties at home prevent them from getting the amount of rest recommended by the physician.	21.3
Patients worried about their teen-age girls or boys "running wild" and getting out of control.	12.4
Couples whom the physician has found physically unable to have children and who are eager to adopt a child.	6.6
Children whose physical handicaps or long-term illnesses seriously affect relations with siblings and friends.	6.4
Girls pregnant out of wedlock who are bewildered about their and the child's futures.	5.4
Young men with recent physical handicaps which cause radical changes in their personal and family lives.	3.8

* From Reichert.[1] Based on estimates by 100 general practitioners, internists and pediatricians in Minneapolis, Minnesota, in 1955.

many other types of social difficulties among their patients which were not included in this list.

THE ROLE, OBJECTIVES AND METHODS OF SOCIAL WORK

Professional social work has developed during the last 50 years to help prevent, ameliorate or solve some of the recurrent and persistent personal and social problems, including those associated with illness. A wide range of social work services for individuals and for groups have arisen, which from the viewpoint of the physician may be classified as follows:

Medical or psychiatric social work departments in health and medical care programs, such as hospitals, clinics, rehabilitation facilities, public health departments and voluntary health agencies. These departments exist for the purpose of dealing with social factors incident to health maintenance, illness and rehabilitation. They are the physician's primary social work resources.

Social work agencies or departments set up to deal with specific social problems which often have health implications. Although these agencies do not operate under medical auspices, they cooperate closely with physicians and should be used when medical or psychiatric social work departments are not available. Family service agencies offer marital counseling and a wide range of other services designed to aid with personal and family adjustment problems. Child welfare agencies are concerned with foster home placements, adoptions and services to unmarried mothers. Public assistance agencies, employing professional social workers usually only in supervisory or consultant positions, are responsible for financial aid to persons in need, including certain expenses for medical care. There are social work departments in many public schools, in neighborhood centers, in facilities concerned with adjustment of special groups such as veterans, immigrants, minority groups, juvenile offenders, and in various other types of specialized facilities.

Whatever the major function of a social work department or agency, social work has two basic objectives which are often pursued simultaneously: the remedial objective of helping a person to overcome an existing difficulty or crisis and the preventive objective of strengthening the person's ability to cope with future personal or social problems. Because of this double emphasis, professional social workers try to enable people to utilize their own psychological and tangible resources in the solution of a problem—to "help people help themselves"—while at the same time guarding against unnecessary depletion of these resources.

The social work method usually consists of the following components: (a) a careful study of the person, his family and inter-personal relationships, the history and nature of his problem, and ways in which he or others have tried to meet it; (b) development of a helping relationship with the person which will enable him to feel understood but not judged, accepted but not falsely reassured, encouraged but not pushed, thus freeing him to look calmly at the realities of his problem and various ways of meeting it; (c) application of a variety of techniques designed to strengthen the patient's ability to deal with his problem, to create a favorable social and psychological environment, or to assist him in the use of community resources, depending on the circumstances in each case.

It should be noted that this method of working with individuals is usually referred to as "social casework." Another method is "social group-work" in which similar techniques are applied to groups of individuals.

PHYSICIANS' USE OF SOCIAL WORK DEPARTMENTS AND AGENCIES

The following examples of ways in which physicians use social work resources were selected to illustrate the major techniques used by professional social workers.

Strengthening the Patient's Ability to Deal with His Problems

Assistance in Planning. A person usually able to plan for the future may flounder in working out unusual or complex social problems. He may require assistance in carefully considering his current situation, in concentrating on the most urgent matters, in obtaining information necessary to plan for the future. For example, a 45 year old minister, after a coronary occlusion, is advised by his physician to reduce his extensive workload. His restlessness and anxiety about remaining at his church lead to referral to the hospital's medical social work department. As he discusses his situation in a series of interviews, he is able to evolve a plan of action which includes the use of his wife, whose mother can help with the children, as an assistant; better use of layman's committees; and an over-all schedule for daily rest with its attendant release from tension.

Emotional Support. As a result of physical and emotional exhaustion some people find it difficult to come to grips with the inevitable daily demands of living; they develop a rather pessimistic outlook and are increasingly beset with unresolved difficulties. A social worker may be able to prevent or ameliorate situations of this kind by giving the person sympathetic understanding and encouragement over a period of time.

A freshman college student in a large university, frequently depressed, unable to mobilize himself for his course work and feeling he is thereby letting down his distant family, seeks help in the mental hygiene unit of the Student Health Center. After a complete workup he is referred to the psychiatric social worker who encourages and supports him in temporarily reducing his classwork, in seeking some social contacts, and in withstanding the unrealistically high expectations of his family. By focusing the student's energies on limited attainable goals and by supportive counseling over a period of time, the social worker helps the student to gain self-confidence through a series of additive successes.

Development of Improved Self-understanding. A person's feelings or attitudes about himself, other people, or about his difficulties may interfere with adequate solution of his problems. Intensive social work counseling may help him to gain new insight and perspective. For example, a 21 year old woman in her eighth month of pregnancy comes to an obstetrician's office in a panic and confides that she is not married, has lived anonymously for several months in the city, but has not been able to bring herself to obtain earlier prenatal care. He finds her in reasonably good physical condition with no complications, assures her of his continued medical care, and at the same time refers her to a child welfare agency. The social worker helps her to gain insight into her flight from her total situation, to consider her relationship with her own family, her feelings about the desertion by the child's father, and her anxiety that she could not go on with her plans to become a fashion designer. She is helped gradually to overcome her deep sense of rejection and isolation and to use her family to help her to make constructive future plans for herself and the child.

Strengthening the Patient's Social and Psychological Environment

Helping the Family to Help the Patient. Mutual understanding, support and help among family members are often the key resources in prevention and resolution of social problems. Social workers are concerned with the whole matrix of family relationships and may assist the individual through working with members of his family. In this approach it is a basic principle that family members cannot be manipulated for the sake of the individual. Rather, their own needs and interests must be carefully considered.

The overly anxious mother of a 3 year old child with moderately severe palsy who is slow in walking tends to protect him to a point where he cannot spontaneously exercise his abilities. She has never been able to allow someone else to care for the boy and is convinced that it is he who does not want her out of his sight. She cannot accept the recommendations of the psychiatrist in the cerebral palsy clinic that the child be enrolled in a specialized nursery school. The medical social worker in the clinic enables her to gain some perspective and reassurance by having her participate in informal group discussions with other parents of children with cerebral palsy and by suggesting she observe other children at play in the nursery school. More relaxed in discussing her anxieties with the social worker, she accepts nursery placement on a trial basis. In the course of this experiment she is helped to become aware that her overconcern with the patient has led to some emotional neglect of her 5 year old daughter. Eventually she is able to meet the needs of both children more happily and realistically.

Helping the Individual through Group Experiences. People under stress often look for support to others experiencing the same difficulties. Increasingly, social workers bring together people confronted with similar problems, carefully guiding discussion and group activities so that they can constructively share one another's failures and successes. In some instances this is done to supplement individual counseling, as in the situation described above of the mother of the cerebral palsy patient meeting with other mothers. In other instances, group techniques are being used by social workers with expectant parent groups to anticipate changes in family relationships, with young people's groups to consider questions of premarital behavior and with a variety of medical or psychiatric patients who have been referred by their physicians.

Use of Community Resources. Various community resources may be required to help a family or individual solve a social problem or to obtain medical care. Social workers know what resources are available and how they can best be used. For example, the hospitalization of a 30 year old mechanic suffering from tuberculosis leaves his wife ill equipped financially and emotionally to care for their two small children. Referred by her physician to a family service agency, she is repeatedly given an opportunity for unhurried consideration of her situation and concurrently is helped in the following ways: by referral to the local welfare department from which she receives a monthly financial assistance grant pending her husband's return; by provision of one of the agency's homemakers to care for the children and to maintain the household while she herself is temporarily ill; by referral to a child guidance clinic recommended by the private physician when the oldest child develops reading problems in school; and by effecting close liaison among the physician, the public health nurse, and the several agencies concerned.

SUGGESTIONS REGARDING PHYSICIAN'S USE OF SOCIAL WORK SERVICES

The Social Work Yearbook is the best single reference for describing services and major trends in social work.[6] Information regarding social work agencies and other community resources in a particular community may be obtained through medical or psychiatric social workers, through community referral centers located in councils of social agencies or health and welfare councils, through local health departments or welfare departments.

Physicians should familiarize themselves with the specific functions and eligibility requirements of local social work departments and agencies. Individual social workers render services within the framework of these policies.

Whenever feasible, physicians should ascertain whether a given social work department or social agency employs professionally qualified personnel, educated in graduate schools of social work and eligible for membership in the National Association of Social Workers. Nonprofessional personnel may render useful service but cannot be expected to function at the level of professionally trained social workers.

In making a referral to a social work facility, the physician does not thereby give up his case. Social work services can and should be used concurrently as an adjunct to medical treatment.

Social difficulties are best managed in their early stages. Referrals should be made as soon as the physician becomes aware of the patient's problem.

The effectiveness of social work is greatly enhanced if the physician himself is interested in and informed about the patient's social problems. Close cooperation and communication between physician and social worker are essential.

KURT REICHERT, Ph.D.

REFERENCES

1. Reichert, K.: Some Aspects of the Relationship between Private Physicians and Social Agencies. Unpublished doctorate thesis, University of Minnesota, 1955.
2. Bartlett, H. M.: Social Work Practice in the Health Field. New York, National Association of Social Workers, 1961.
3. Beck, H. L.: Short-term case work service in a preadmission-admission unit of a mental patient. Mental Hygiene, 42:51, January, 1958.
4. Ekdahl, M. C., Rice, E. P., and Schmidt, N. D.: Children of parents hospitalized for mental illness. American Journal of Public Health, 52:428, March, 1962.
5. Hemmy, M. L. (ed.): Family-Centered Social Work in Illness and Disability. New York, National Association of Social Workers, 1961.

6. Kurtz, R. H. (ed.): Social Work Yearbook. New York, National Association of Social Workers, 1960.
7. Monahan, H. B., and Spencer, E. C.: Deterrents to prenatal care. Children, 9:114, May-June, 1962.
8. Moncure, C. H.: Clinical social work planning with 5000 general medical and surgical patients for their hospital discharge. Journal of Chronic Diseases, 11:176, February, 1960.
9. Rice, E. L.: Concepts of prevention as applied to the practice of social work. American Journal of Public Health, 52:266, February, 1962.
10. Wilensky, H. L., and Lebeaux, C. N.: Industrial Society and Social Welfare. New York, Russell Sage Foundation, 1958.

40   Public Health Nursing

The purpose of this chapter is to acquaint the physician with public health nursing services designed to assist in the prevention of the occurrence and progression of disease and disability.

The forerunner of modern public health nursing was nursing service to the sick poor at home. As medical science discovered ways of preventing disease, more emphasis was placed on teaching prevention to all members of the community and less on service to the sick. As public health practice has changed in the United States, so has public health nursing. The pendulum has now swung to include not only prevention of occurrence but also care of the sick and disabled so as to prevent progression of disease and to assist in rehabilitation. Service remains available to all people regardless of race, color, creed and economic status.

NURSING CARE OF THE SICK AT HOME

Although public health nursing now has wide scope and responsibilities in nearly all aspects of public health, care of the sick at home remains important. In the last few years it has grown in importance because of the change in medical practice. Many people who would once have been hospitalized are now treated at home; hospitalized patients are discharged earlier than formerly to continue treatment at home. The population now includes a large group of elderly people who live to develop chronic diseases and who need care for a long period following hospitalization.

People sick at home usually need nursing in varying amounts over a 24-hour period. The plan will vary according to the family situation and the patient's condition. Whenever possible, the nurse attempts to teach the patient or some member of the family to give the necessary care and then supervises to see that the care is adequate. If the care needed cannot be given by a lay person or if there is no one in the home to give it, the nurse may continue to give it herself.

The following case will illustrate how the nurse works with families to provide the necessary care.

437

A man called the health department requesting a home visit because his mother had been discharged from the hospital and needed care. The public health nurse found a 77 year old woman who had had a partial left hip resection. Other members of the household were her husband, 80 years old, and her son, 40 years old. All were obviously upset. On instruction from the family physician, the patient was given an enema, was catheterized, her dressing was changed and a bath given. It was apparent that the son was mentally disturbed. He paced constantly, never looked at anyone but kept his hands over his eyes. During the later part of the visit, a married daughter arrived. The father asked her to go home. She began jumping up and down, waving her arms, and refused to leave. Further questioning revealed that both the son and daughter had been in mental hospitals at one time. It was obvious that the mother needed care over a 24-hour period and the question was who should be taught to give it. The nurse consulted with the family physician who agreed that the father was perhaps the one most capable. The public health nurse began teaching the father, and later the son. They learned to irrigate the Foley catheter, get the mother in and out of bed and position her in bed properly. The son, under direction, built an apparatus to keep her affected leg in alignment and worked out a plan for nursing care. Aided by periodic visits by the nurse, the family came to manage the patient to the satisfaction of the physician.

FAMILY HEALTH SERVICE

A public health nurse generally visits a home in response to a call for nursing service needed by a particular person in the family. However, as a public health worker she is responsible for assessing the health needs of the whole family and for helping the family to solve any health problems which may exist. Sometimes the person or the family may be unaware of existing health problems or, being aware, has not taken action because of ignorance or fear. In any case, the nurse is responsible for motivating a responsible family member to seek medical care. A family health service contains certain basic services in addition to the specific ones for the individual or the family. These include instruction in desirable health habits, such as instruction in good nutrition, in correcting environmental health hazards conducive to disease or accidents and in the importance of immunization.

AID FROM COMMUNITY HEALTH WORKERS

Although this chapter necessarily emphasizes nursing service and the relation of the nurses to the physician and the family, there are other community health workers the nurse calls upon to provide specialized assistance. These include nutritionists, physical therapists and social workers, to mention only a few. These specialists may be purely consultative to the nurse or they may render direct services to the patient or family. For example, a physician may order a low sodium diet for a cardiac patient. To assure selection of a variety of foods low in sodium and to prepare attractive menus, the nurse may call upon a nutritionist to assist her, even though the nutritionist never sees the patient. Patients sometimes have social and emotional problems with which the nurse cannot deal effectively. These are always discussed with the physician, who will plan with the nurse for help which may be provided by social workers or a social agency.

MEDICAL DIRECTION

The public health nurse is administratively responsible to the agency which employs her. There are certain activities which she carries out at the request of and under the direction of the health officer, such as epidemiologic investigations and other measures involving community health. However, when providing service to a family she is professionally responsible to the family physician. She seeks his direction before giving anything except emergency care. Most agencies require the physician to provide the diagnosis for which the nursing care is given and written orders for specific treatment with periodic review and renewal. The nurse will also report to the physician regularly on the progress of the patient, or immediately if she observes any unusual development. The physician may make an arrangement with the nurse for periodic review of needs of his patients receiving nursing service.

POLICIES ON NURSING SERVICE

Most agencies have policies under which nursing service will be given. These usually include standing orders for the nurse to follow in emergencies when a physician cannot be reached. They may also include such items as: the number of visits a nurse may make to urge medical supervision when a physician is not in attendance, the hours service is available, the kind of treatment procedures which may be given and the kind of medications and the circumstances under which they may be given. For example, some agencies will not permit the nurse to give injections for allergy while others will permit the nurse to take blood and in rare instances to give intravenous therapy.

EMPLOYING AGENCIES

The most common agencies employing public health nurses for direct service are local health departments, visiting nurse associations, and boards of education.

Local Health Departments

Public health nurses employed by local health departments assist the health officer by carrying out the nursing phases of the department's basic services, such as maternal and child health and communicable disease control. Care to people ill at home is a service fairly new to health departments, although it is rapidly expanding in many communities. The amount of such care available will depend upon the number of nurses and the availability of other community nursing service. In addition, public health nurses help at health department clinics, teach classes and provide service in schools which do not employ their own nurses.

Visiting Nurse Associations

Visiting nurse associations are voluntary agencies supported by private donations and fees for service paid by patients, insurance companies or other agencies such as welfare departments. The nurses so employed provide health guidance and, by agreement, may perform some preventive service for the health department, for example, the follow-up of tuberculosis patients. A large part of their work is care of the sick at home. When a charge is made for service the fee is adjusted to the family income and will vary from full payment to no charge at all. Most large communities have visiting nurse associations; rural and semirural communities depend largely upon official health agencies.

Boards of Education

Nurses are employed by boards of education to provide service to schoolchildren. These nurses work closely with the school faculty in promoting optimum health habits and provide first aid and home follow-up of children found to need dental and medical supervision.

SPECIFIC PUBLIC HEALTH NURSING SERVICES

Prenatal Care

Often the nurse learns about a pregnancy before the woman seeks medical care. The first step the nurse takes is to emphasize to the patient the need for early medical supervision by her physician. After a patient has been to her physician, the public health nurse may be asked to provide general health supervision or to carry out specific recommendations, such as taking blood pressure or urine specimens.

General health instruction is sometimes given in parents' classes conducted by the public health nurse. The subjects covered usually include the physiology of pregnancy, nutrition, care of the baby and preparation of other children in the family for the new baby. Emphasis is placed on group discussion to allow parents to bring out their questions or anxieties, which are usually common to the whole group. When the nurse becomes aware of what appear to be unduly exaggerated anxieties, she advises the patient to talk these over with her physician and also reports them to the physician herself.

If it is not feasible to conduct parents' classes or if the classes do not meet the needs of an individual patient, the public health nurse will make visits to the patient at home. She is constantly alert for unfavorable symptoms and reports them to the physician promptly.

In some communities, classes are available for teaching the exercises that help prepare for the process of natural childbirth. These are taught by nurses with special training. Physicians who are interested in such classes can find out about them from the local health officer.

Delivery Service

In most communities in developed countries, very few women are delivered at home so that assistance by public health nurses has been largely discontinued. Wherever home deliveries continue, the public health nurse teaches home preparation which will be needed at the time of delivery. She may also assist the physician at the delivery.

Neonatal and Postpartum Care

In most communities there are not enough nurses to visit every newborn baby at home, nor is such a visit indicated for every child. Sometimes mothers, especially those with a first child, need reassurance and help in caring for the baby. The public health nurse is prepared to demonstrate the bathing of the baby, the preparation of formula, and to discuss feeding and some kind of a schedule. At this time she also stresses the importance of returning to the physician for the scheduled postpartum examination. She will look for any abnormal signs in the infant and symptoms in the mother and report them promptly to the physician. Sometimes abnormalities in the infant may not be apparent at the time of discharge from the hospital and the nurse, during her home visits, will be on the alert for them.

It is not uncommon for parents to be apprehensive about the care of a premature infant. If the hospital staff notifies the public health nurse of the birth of a premature baby she can visit the home, talk with the parents and report back to the hospital on the home situation. This information will assist the staff in making plans for discharge. If the nurse is notified of the date of discharge, she can again visit and help in the preparation for the return of the baby. When the baby is home, she can assist the mother in bathing, preparing the formula, feeding and proper clothing. Failure to gain, feeding difficulty and skin eruptions can be reported immediately to the physician.

Parents of congenitally defective babies frequently can benefit from the support the nurses can give them in meeting their emotional problems. Here, too, the nurse can help the family to carry out instructions for special care advised by the physician.

Care of the Older Infant and Preschool Child

During this period, parents may become lax about continued and periodic medical examinations and the nurse can stress continued medical health supervision. This is a time when children may develop emotional problems, exhibited in a variety of behavioral patterns upsetting to parents. The nurse can augment the advice of the physician in helping parents to understand these problems and how to handle them.

In some communities, public health nurses skilled in leading discussion groups may conduct child study groups for parents of preschool children. In these classes emphasis is placed on normal growth and development.

Care of the School-age Child

School health programs are designed to educate students in desirable health attitudes and to insure adequate health supervision. The public health nurse is responsible for working with the school personnel in the educational programs and for working with the parents as they follow out the health recommendations made at school. Frequently, these involve the need for medical care by the family physician. When the family does not take action, the public health nurse talks with the parents to help them to see the need for such care and to aid them in obtaining it.

CONTROL OF COMMUNICABLE DISEASE

In many communities public health nurses were first employed primarily to assist in the control of communicable disease. Although the volume of work has diminished, it still remains an important field. Her functions are to teach prevention, find suspicious cases as early as possible, help secure medical care, and assist in carrying out medical recommendations for further care.

Prevention

In all visits for any purpose the public health nurse takes every opportunity to stress the importance of early immunization as well as booster doses at the indicated time. If there are clinics for this purpose in the community, the physician should indicate to the nurse if he wishes particular patients referred. The nurse always urges care by the family physician since immunization is part of general health supervision.

Case Finding

The public health nurse is ever alert to signs suspicious of any kind of disease so that patients may obtain medical care as soon as possible. In communicable disease this is particularly important, not only for the patient's sake but to break contact with the susceptible population. The nurse does not attempt to diagnose, but merely calls attention to symptoms, such as a fever and a red throat, for which medical care should be sought.

Nursing Care

The nurse can also help the family by instructing the mother in the care needed in a communicable disease, particularly in procedures designed to prevent spread in the home or to protect the patient from those who may carry other communicable diseases.

TUBERCULOSIS CONTROL

It is generally agreed that any screening program for finding cases of tuberculosis and other lung diseases should be undertaken only with adequate facilities for follow-up. Not the least important of these is public health nursing service. When a person is suspected of having lung disease, the family physician is notified and the suspect is advised to see his physician for diagnosis. Sometimes the patient does not accept such advice. In these instances the public health nurse can seek out the person either at home or at his place of work to explain the reason why a physician should be consulted as soon as possible. Sometimes more than one visit is needed to get the patient or family to take action.

When a diagnosis of tuberculosis is made, the public health nurse can assist in getting family contacts examined. Many people will not respond to a letter but will respond to the personal urging of the public health nurse. Experience has shown that the sooner contacts are visited after being informed of exposure to tuberculosis the better are the results in terms of the number examined.

In the care of a patient with tuberculosis, the nurse must first consult the physician about the care he recommends, whether it be hospitalization or home care. A diagnosis of tuberculosis almost invariably requires some adjustment in family living. Hospitalization usually means separation from the family for a period of several months. If the mother is the one affected, it may mean a temporary break-up of the family. If it is the father, it may mean severe economic loss. The worry and fear aroused may result in refusal to accept hospitalization. The nurse can supplement the physician's advice and, with her knowledge of community facilities, help the family in meeting the social, emotional and economic problems they face.

If the patient needs care at home pending admission to the hospital, the nurse can instruct the patient and family on isolation techniques, disposal of sputum, diet, rest and medication.

Patients who reach the maximum benefit from hospitalization may continue drugs and rest at home and may need nursing care. The nurse can supervise the regimen recommended and see that the patient returns for medical supervision regularly.

VENEREAL DISEASE CONTROL

When a patient is diagnosed as having gonorrhea or syphilis in the infectious stage, the physician may request the health department for assistance in contact investigations. Frequently it is the public health nurse who is assigned this task. Great skill and tact in interviewing the patient is needed to obtain the names of contacts. It takes sleuthing to track down contacts, for sometimes the nurse gets only a first name, a nickname, a description of the person or a vague address. The nurse makes every effort to arrange the time and place of the interviews so as not to embarrass the persons concerned. She can be especially effective when infections occur in the teen-age group, for often these young people are frightened and need guidance in getting help.

MENTAL HEALTH SERVICES

Community interest in mental health and the growing practice of discharging patients from mental hospitals to their homes while still on drug therapy has focused attention on the need for follow-up of people who are suffering from mental illness of various types.

The public health nurse through her visits to families often observes and identifies behavior which indicates the need for psychiatric supervision. Sometimes a relative or a neighbor will call the nurse because a person is exhibiting strange behavior. The nurse's first responsibility is to motivate the person or the family to consult the family physician. Whether the family physician provides the supervision or refers the patient to a psychiatrist, the nurse, because of her opportunity to observe the family members and their relationships to each other, can impart information to the practitioner which will be valuable to him in the management of the patient.

When the patient's illness is serious enough to require hospitalization, the public health nurse can help to persuade the patient and the family to accept institutional care and the benefits to be derived from it.

The step from institutional to community living is sometimes very difficult for the patient and for the family, and the nurse can help in this adjustment. The public health nurse does not enter into the therapy. Her function is the same as in the care of a person with physical illness, namely to assist in carrying out the regimen recommended by the physician, to be alert to symptoms which indicate relapse and to lend support and encouragement to the patient and family.

CARE IN CHRONIC DISEASES

Public health nurses contribute invaluable services to the chronically ill. Although chronic diseases affect people of all ages, the nursing care need is greatest in the older age groups where the problems are multiple and complex. In addition to physical ailments, the problems are social, emotional and economic. Many old people are lonely because they cannot get out to meet others. Sometimes true nursing care is needed less than homemaker service. Someone must help, for example, with the daily activities the well person ordinarily does for himself, such as bathing, eating, walking and performing simple tasks. Homemaker services may be provided by a health department or some other community agency. These services together with nursing care may meet a need which will allow a person to remain at home instead of being admitted to a nursing home or a convalescent institution.

Public health nurses can help the family to carry out specific treatments, such as dressings, caring for colostomy after operation, general bed care or parenteral medications. Their main role is to see that the patient continues treatment and does not regress. Many patients are taught to undertake certain activities in the hospital but on return home will not continue with them unless they receive help and encouragement. For example, the diabetic patient may fail to follow his diet because the family does not know how to make it attractive and appetizing. Or the patient who has had a cerebral vascular accident may fail to continue exercises either because he becomes discouraged at his slow progress or finds them too difficult to do in the home. Public health nurses are prepared to assist in such problems. It has been observed that many patients enter institutions again and again for the same disease or condition. Some of these readmissions could have been prevented if the patient had been helped to carry out the recommendations of the physician.

The nurse's knowledge of community resources can be truly supportive in providing recreational and occupational therapy that add to the comfort and contentment of the chronically ill.

SUMMARY

Public health nurses, as the largest single group of workers in public health, contribute greatly to the prevention of occurrence and progression of disease and disability. They are in the unique position of doing what the practicing physician and others cannot do. They can seek out persons needing medical supervision and direct them to the physician of the individual's choice. They can help families to carry out the physician's recommendations and to obtain the community assistance available to prevent progression of disease and disability. They help to teach people how to stay well and give skilled care and comfort to those who develop illness.

MARY E. PARKER, R.N.

REFERENCES

1. Anderson, Gaylord W., Arnstein, Margaret G., and Lester, Mary R.: Communicable Disease Control. Ed. 4. New York, The Macmillan Company, 1962.
2. Freeman, Ruth B.: Public Health Nursing Practice. Ed. 3. Philadelphia, W. B. Saunders Company, 1963.
3. Home Care. Hospital Monograph Series 9. Chicago, American Hospital Association, 1961.
4. Lemkau, Paul V.: Follow-up services for psychiatric patients. Nursing Outlook, 6:149, March, 1958.
5. McIver, Pearl: Trends in public health. Nursing Outlook, 2:353, July, 1954.
6. Parker, Mary E.: Home care programs for New Yorkers. Nursing Outlook, 11:No. 6, June, 1963.
7. Public Health Nursing Care of the Sick at Home. New York, Department of Public Health Nursing, National League for Nursing, April, 1953.
8. Schwartz, Doris, Ullmann, Alice, and Reader, George: The nurse, social worker and medical student in a comprehensive care program. Nursing Outlook, 6:39, January, 1958.

41 The Role of the Hospital in Preventive Medicine

The modern hospital, the result of advances in medical science and the age of specialization in medical practice, is rapidly becoming a center for community health. Its aggregate of special medical and paramedical skills, together with a wide diversity of special diagnostic, curative and rehabilitative equipment, presents a setting for a teamwork approach for the diagnosis, cure and alleviation of human disease and disability. The well-staffed, well-equipped community hospital of today is in direct contrast to earlier hospitals which were inclined to be dreary places offering little more than custodial care and routine treatment.

A factor that is significant in any discussion of preventive medicine is the generally changed attitude of the public toward hospitals. With the development of scientific medicine, starting in the last half of the nineteenth century, and the improvement of hospital facilities and services, the public has gradually lost its fear of hospitals. The hospital is no longer a place of suffering and death but has become a community center, representing a focal point of what is considered best in medicine. The so-called charitable institution of the past has evolved into a social institution serving all economic groups of the community.

The modern hospital system has developed upon the premise of adequate diagnosis, care and treatment of specific pathologic conditions. The recent concept of the study and care of the individual as a complete being living in a complex society with its many economic, social and geographical factors, is relatively new. This concept is not yet universally accepted in hospital practice. The specialization developed in medical care during the past half century has been responsible for many of the remarkable improvements in medical diagnosis and treatment which have rapidly changed the public attitude toward hospital services. In this process, however, many of the desirable attributes of the family physician (appraising his patient's physical and emotional life in relation to his family and environment) have been lost or have assumed a position of secondary importance.

The hospital of the future will align its services and its goals to a broader concept of community health. It may well provide or participate in services aimed at keeping human beings at their best throughout a normal life span. Hospitals will place greater emphasis on the prevention of the occurrence or the progression of disease and disability in situations for which medical science has not yet developed specific preventive procedures. The community hospital of tomorrow will concern itself with avoiding unnecessary institutionalization. With its staff of general and specialized medical practitioners, it will work cooperatively with other hospitals and a variety of health and social forces in the community toward a goal of optimum health for all of the people.

THE GENERAL HOSPITAL

Shortly after the end of the last century many hospitals were devoted to particular specialties in medicine. Some of these limited their care to mental or psychiatric disorders; others to the isolation and treatment of communicable diseases; and, later still, others to the care of maternity patients and to various specific diseases.

Gradually this trend toward specialized hospitals has changed and the general community hospital has widened its scope to provide treatment for a broad scale of disease conditions and for the care of all age groups. This branching-out process has not yet reached its full growth.

Proposals for making the general hospital a community facility include the development of units for psychiatric care, rehabilitation services for the chronically ill and for long-term home-type nursing care. These expanded services of the general community hospital assure better preventive medicine practices. Such arrangements, in contrast to the establishment of separate, isolated units, permit savings in capital construction costs for these facilities. Certain central services, such as the heating plant, dietary department, x-ray and laboratory facilities and departments of physical medicine and rehabilitation—essential parts of the modern hospital—can also be utilized in caring for patients requiring chronic disease hospital care or nursing home care. Moreover, this type of planning would allow greater flexibility as disease patterns change in the future. Of perhaps greater benefit to the public would be the assurance of proper continuity of care so that the patient could easily be transferred to the medical and nursing settings best suited to his needs at various stages of his illness. Such arrangements have economic as well as medical importance.

Much remains to be done in providing psychiatric services, though many of the better general hospitals, and particularly the medical teaching hospitals, have established such units. Many general hospitals provide a variety of services for long-term care of disease and disability, yet many of our so-called specialized chronic disease institutions and nursing homes are still relatively isolated from the desirable medical assets which the well-organized community general hospital makes available.

REGIONALIZATION

Mountin, Pennell and Hoge,[1] recognizing the inequitable distribution of specialized skills and services in the field of hospital care, recommended a coordinated hospital service which would encourage working relationships among hospitals of varying size and capacity for comprehensive medical care. The 1947 report of the Commission on Hospital Care pointed out the need for bringing about a better distribution of special skills among rural and small urban hospitals and of the medical teaching centers. The World Health Organization endorsed this principle.

Under the program of the United States Hospital and Medical Facilities Survey and Construction Act (Hill-Burton), states are required to plan for an integrated hospital service. The vital role of the medical school and its teaching hospitals was specified under these proposals. The hub of regional hospital planning is the medical teaching center. Such a center is well suited for this role with its full range of medical and related skills, diagnostic laboratories and research facilities, and its potential for bringing new techniques and procedures to rural and small urban hospitals. The proposals are designed to provide smaller hospitals with consultation and supporting services for expert diagnosis and therapy and to ensure transfer of patients requiring complicated investigation and treatment to the medical teaching hospital (Fig. 36). Successful regional programs have been carried on for a number of years. One of these is the program of the Bingham Associates in Boston carried on in cooperation with Tufts Medical School. The Rochester Regional Hospital Plan, of New York, also includes consulting services in hospital administration, hospital records, medical audits, postgraduate education and referral services.

Improvement in hospital and medical care in rural and small urban hospitals will result in more prompt and accurate diagnoses. The development of an effective referral system will increase the chances of early, accurate and comprehensive treatment. Regional hospital planning councils, composed of representatives of the medical and nursing professions, hospitals, voluntary and public health and welfare agencies, industry and others, have had notable success in developing needed hospital facilities and services.

The strategic position of the modern community general hospital is pointed up by the suggestion that chronic disease hospital facilities and nursing home services become part of the community general hospital. If these resources are located some distance from the hospital, suitable affiliations should be developed. Such arrangements would encourage better care and provide quicker rehabilitation by guaranteeing greater attention to such problems as nutrition, emotional balance and patient motivation. Preventive medicine requires these necessary elements. Moreover, such arrangements encourage better relationships between the patient, the hospital and the home during the treatment phases.

HOSPITAL OUTPATIENT SERVICES

Historically, the hospital dispensary or outpatient department was developed mostly in metropolitan areas as a charitable enterprise whose staff diagnosed and treated indigents. The outpatient departments of our better hospitals later became important clinical training centers for undergraduate and graduate medical students. However, the potential of outpatient hospital service for improving medical diagnosis and care and for preventive medicine has not been widely appreciated.

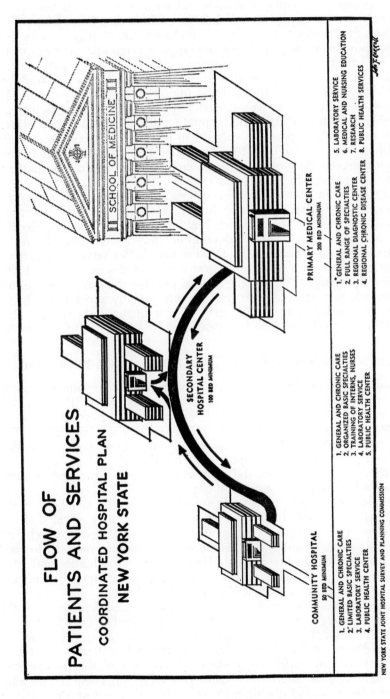

Figure 36. (From Blueprint to Reality. Legislative Document No. 47, March, 1949. New York State Joint Hospital Survey and Planning Commission, Albany.)

The importance of these facilities to the private physician took on new meaning as modern medical diagnosis and treatment dictated the use of increasingly complex equipment and skills, such as diagnostic laboratories and radiological services. For economic and professional reasons, very few practicing physicians can provide the full range of diagnostic and therapeutic equipment and services in their own private offices. The community general hospital, with its organized medical staff, has accepted the responsibility for providing these services to the practicing physician for his patients who may either be ambulatory or hospitalized. Physicians are referring an increasing number of their patients to the hospital for special tests and procedures.

The extent of this practice is shown in reports from many community general hospitals. As much as 65 per cent of the clinical laboratory and radiological procedures performed by general hospitals are done for patients referred as outpatients by their physicians.

Outpatient clinics at hospitals have been slow to develop. If preventive medicine of the future is to have the advantage of early and thorough diagnostic appraisal with emphasis on health maintenance, then the medical staffs of our hospitals will have to develop organized ambulatory diagnostic programs for private practitioners. Doctors may better serve their patients by placing greater emphasis on the prevention of disease and disability. The recent trend toward developing general practice sections in our hospital medical staffs may stimulate progress in this field by providing a better working relationship between the general practitioner and the specialist. This will narrow existing gaps between preventive and curative medicine.

MEDICAL SOCIAL SERVICE AND HOME CARE PROGRAMS

Good medical practice embraces a consideration of the human being in all his aspects—physical, psychological, economic and social. The hospital's administrative and medical staffs need to understand the physical and social settings of the patients. As responsible public servants, the hospital's staff of doctors, nurses and other technical personnel should encourage and participate in community efforts to improve the health and medical care of the people they serve. They should be concerned about living and working conditions affecting disease and disability.

This does not imply training as sociologists for the members of the medical staff of a hospital. However, the hospital and its medical staff can benefit from the development of good medical social service which will provide the personal, family, social and economic attention essential to good medical care. Social data are invaluable in providing rehabilitation and other preventive services, particularly those pertaining to the prevention of progression or recurrence of existing diseases.

The public health nursing service of the local health department or the community visiting nursing service can make valuable contributions in supplying information to the physician and the hospital about the home and family conditions of the patient. Likewise, the public health or visiting nursing services can contribute to the early recovery of the patient after hospital discharge by care in the home. This follow-up home service aims at avoiding recurrence of disabling illness. In fact, the local nursing services should be part of any home care programs developed in the community.

The monograph, Medical Care of the Discharged Hospital Patient, by Jensen and associates,[2] gives important data on the advisability of developing satisfactory programs for complete medical care of the public, regardless of financial status. The monograph reports on the experiment carried out in Syracuse, New York, as a cooperative enterprise of the medical school, the hospital, the outpatient department and the social service agencies. It provides an excellent example of a cooperative working relationship among the community's medical and social agencies in the care and follow-up of discharged hospital patients.

Similar medical social service and home care programs in New York City and elsewhere have revealed the importance of a cooperative approach to preventive services. Operating within a framework of community service, the hospital and its staff can avoid hospitalizing patients unnecessarily and can provide continuity of service for patients at various stages of disease or disability.

If our hospitals are to meet their basic responsibilities, they should concern themselves with factors involving the admission of patients and the health needs of patients following their discharge. Better communication between the hospital and the various segments of community life is essential for good preventive medicine, including a satisfactory rehabilitation program.

A number of medical schools and their teaching hospitals recognize the need for their medical students, interns and residents to know how to deal with the social and psychological aspects of health and illness. These institutions have developed programs which allow the medical student to study the patient in his family and community setting and to recognize nonmedical factors which influence results. This is preventive medical service at its visual best for the students. We may expect that all community hospitals eventually will be called upon to provide well-staffed medical social service departments. The young physician of tomorrow may look to his community hospital to provide home care services to assist him in maintaining a high quality of medical practice.

COOPERATION BETWEEN LOCAL PUBLIC HEALTH SERVICES AND HOSPITALS

Both public health services and community hospitals have specific assets which can complement each other in attaining a desirable level of community health. Public health workers have the decided advantage of broad experience in using communitywide disease control techniques. In fact, hospitals of today would be burdened with an insurmountable patient load of institutional care were it not for the success of preventive health services.

Mass methods for the control of disease and the promotion of health undertaken by our official and voluntary health agencies have yielded results that can be measured statistically in lives saved and in illness and disability prevented. These achievements happened within a relatively short period of time and have brought about changes in our community health needs.

The major unsolved problems of public health and preventive medicine concentrate now in health protection for adults and those in the older age periods. Public health and preventive medicine are becoming increasingly concerned with many of the degenerative diseases and conditions for which medical science has yet to find specific methods for prevention or cure. This shift in emphasis is evidenced by the increasing number of special clinic and case-finding services, even in hospitals. They include such health problems as diseases of the heart and blood vessels, cancer, diabetes and emotional disorders.

Until recently, public health agencies have carried on their activities largely in cooperation with the privately practicing physicians. There has been relatively minor reliance upon the community general hospital. Considerable epidemiologic work has been done on mortality from certain diseases and morbidity in a limited number of disease conditions. Much more epidemiologic emphasis needs to be placed on many additional disease conditions, primarily those of a chronic nature and those which are concerned primarily with the individual patient and his family.

In recent years public health physicians have been increasingly concerned with the promotion of individual health. The earliest public health activities in this field centered about protection of the health of the individual child and the welfare of mothers. Great help was given to this phase of public health by the physicians in the specialties of pediatrics and obstetrics. Historically, accomplishments in this field are an excellent example of cooperative effort between private physician and public health agencies in preventive medicine for the private patients of physicians.

As these developments progress, the hospital assumes additional responsibilities for early diagnosis and adequate therapy, including rehabilitation. For a successful attack upon these problems, the community hospital will work more closely with official and voluntary public health agencies. Nationwide studies recommend closer physical and operational arrangements between community hospitals and the public health agencies. To develop a more effective and economical community health service and to avoid the undesirable isolation that has existed between these two important community health groups, it will be necessary to develop a closer working relationship between them. Each can contribute those community health services it is best able to provide. Under this arrangement, the community general hospital may become truly a center for health and, working with the public health agencies, concern itself with the preventive aspects of medical care and disease control rather than merely continuing its traditional role in the treatment of disease.

Many analyses of hospital records in specific diseases and disabilities have been made, but the full effectiveness of the epidemiologist has not been realized by our community general hospitals. If the epidemiologist had hospital data as well as data from other health and social agencies in the community, he might well point the way to effective prevention and control of diseases which demand expensive hospital and related care. These same diseases are also significant morbidity and mortality factors in our national life. The present lack of sufficient epidemiologic research in this field hinders over-all health and medical care economy. This lack should be of great concern to the Blue Cross, Blue Shield and other voluntary health insurance programs as well as to public and voluntary agencies which contribute to the support of the indigent and medically indigent sick and disabled.

The modern hospital is well staffed and well equipped to carry out programs for periodic health appraisal in cooperation with public health agencies. It can also develop programs for the early diagnosis of disease and for full rehabilitation services.

Public health education has always been recognized as an effective technique for improving the public health. This becomes more evident as greater emphasis is placed upon preventive medicine, in which the attitude and will of the individual are so important in seeking and utilizing services for health promotion. The hospital is in a good position to help public health agencies carry out health education activities.

Recommendations for a closer working relationship between public agencies and hospitals include the suggestion that the facilities of health and welfare agencies be located in wings or in buildings adjoining community hospitals. Such an arrangement should benefit working relationships and alleviate communication problems which exist between the hospitals and health agencies in many communities.

THE PRACTICING PHYSICIANS AND THE CHANGE IN HOSPITAL CARE

The medical student and the practitioner of medicine in developed countries find themselves in a period of rapid change in both medicine and community health. Economic, social and scientific factors are accelerating these changes. The physician who used to give individual care to the sick, utilizing only his own knowledge, skills and equipment, now enters into a world of medical practice which is quite different. The well-equipped and staffed hospital is essential to the modern care of his patients. He finds within his community a multiplicity of voluntary and public agencies and individuals who are interested in his patients' well-being. They are also necessary to him in carrying out his responsibilities to his patients. The welfare of his patients no longer consists only of the accurate diagnosis of specific disease conditions and effective therapy. His responsibility also is to prevent disease and disability, to employ every means and to use every local resource for better health for his patients and their families. It is his responsibility to keep human beings at optimum health throughout a normal life span. In order to do this, he must acquaint himself with his patient's physical, emotional and social life as well as the family genetic factors. To do this, he needs to appraise personal and family habits and be aware of the physical and psychological stresses in the total environment.

The hospital is a prime necessity for the general practitioner and for his colleagues in specialized fields of medicine. In order to assist them in securing a more effective and satisfying medical practice experience in the field of preventive medicine, the hospital should expand its role. It can supply an organized method for securing complete diagnostic and consultation services for ambulatory patients. It can initiate or support proper medical social services and home care and follow-up programs. It can participate in a system of coordinated hospital services so that the assets of the medical school and the teaching hospital are made available. The hospital should provide an opportunity for continuing medical education in new and accepted diagnostic methods and preventive, therapeutic and rehabilitative procedures. In turn, hospital and local public health agencies may ask physicians to participate actively in community disease prevention and disease control programs.

The medical practitioner's responsibilities to his individual patients become more meaningful if he receives the benefits of public health education from his community health agencies. He seldom has an opportunity to seek out patients and offer them preventive services. The community hospital and other health agencies can do this through programs designed to direct the public to the proper type of medical care and to advise them about desirable health practices.

The role of the hospital in preventive medicine is ever expanding. If the boards of trustees and the medical staffs of our community hospitals will give enlightened consideration to the principles of modern public health and preventive medicine, they will serve their communities well, advancing the stature and achievements of medical practice.

To the modern practicing physician, the local community hospital is essential for comprehensive medical care for his patients. It has been noted that the practicing physician is referring an increasing proportion of his patients to the hospital on an ambulatory basis for a wide range of special laboratory and other diagnostic and therapeutic procedures. Studies by Rorem[3] show that a substantial number of community general hospitals are leasing office space to physicians serving on their staffs. Usually, this office space is made available within the hospital. In other instances, either the hospitals or the doctors provide "medical arts" buildings near the hospitals.

Where there is local medical support for such a program, these arrangements would appear to have advantages for both the patient and his practicing physician. The proximity of the doctor's practice to the hospital should result in closer working relationships with his medical colleagues in the various specialties in the day-to-day handling of private patients. Such an arrangement might conserve the travel time of the physician and offer economic and other advantages to his patients. There should be savings to the individual physician through the utilization of the equipment and technical personnel of the hospital, in contrast to the maintenance of expensive equipment and personnel in his private office. Such arrangements need not disrupt the patient-physician relationship. Furthermore, they would permit the physician to use the organized clinics, medical social services, and home care and follow-up programs of the hospital.

Much of the medical work in the modern community hospital is actually performed under a group arrangement. If financial and other obstacles can be surmounted, the hospital is a logical setting for the development of group practice. Under such arrangements, the preventive medical aspects of patient care might receive considerably more emphasis than is now possible under the prevalent system of the solo practice of medicine. There is room for both types of practice.

As medical science provides more specific and complex procedures for diagnosis and treatment of disease and disability, the hospital will take on increasing importance and expand its community health activities and responsibilities. The hospital can contribute significantly to the public and to the practicing medical profession both in prevention of occurrence and of progression of disease and disability. Working closely with voluntary and public health agencies, the community hospital will take its rightful place in maintaining and improving the health of our people.

JOHN J. BOURKE, M.D.

REFERENCES

1. Mountin, Joseph W., Pennell, Elliott H., and Hoge, Vane M.: Health Service Areas. Public Health Bulletin No. 292. Washington, D.C., Government Printing Office.
2. Jensen, F., Weiskotten, H. G., and Thomas, M. A.: Medical Care of the Discharged Hospital Patient. New York, The Commonwealth Fund, 1944.
3. Rorem, C. Rufus: Physicians' Private Offices at Hospitals. American Hospital Association Monograph Series #5. Chicago, 1959.
4. American Hospital Association: Background Statement on Role of Hospitals in Long-term Care. Chicago, 1962.
5. American Hospital Association: Essentials of a Social Service Department in Hospitals and Related Institutions. Chicago, 1961.
6. American Hospital Association: The Guide to the Development of Effective Regional Planning for Hospital Facilities. Chicago, 1962.
7. American Hospital Association: The Nursing Home—A Health Care Resource. Chicago, 1962.
8. American Hospital Association: Principles of Administration of Hospital-based Co-ordinated Home Care Programs. Chicago, 1961.
9. American Hospital Association: Psychiatric Services in General Hospitals. Chicago, 1961.
10. Areawide Planning for Hospitals and Related Health Facilities. Report of the Joint Committee of the American Hospital Association and Public Health Service. Public Health Service Publication No. 855. Washington, D.C., Government Printing Office, 1961.
11. Areawide Planning of Facilities for Long-Term Treatment and Care. Report of the Joint Committee of the American Hospital Association and Public Health Service. Public Health Service Publication No. 930-B-1. Washington, D.C., Government Printing Office, 1963.
12. Bayne-Jones, S.: The hospital as a center of preventive medicine. The Diplomate, 22:1, January, 1950.
13. Commission on Chronic Illness: Chronic Illness in the United States. Volume 1: Prevention of Chronic Illness. Cambridge, Harvard University Press, 1957.
14. Commission on Hospital Care: Hospital Care in the U. S. New York, The Commonwealth Fund, 1947.
15. Galdston, I.: The Meaning of Social Medicine. Cambridge, Harvard University Press, 1954.
16. Hess, Irene, Reidel, Donald C., and Fitzpatrick, Thomas B.: Probability Sampling of Hospitals and Patients. Bureau of Hospital Administration, Research Series No. 1. Ann Arbor, The University of Michigan, 1961.
17. Littauer, David, et al.: Home Care. American Hospital Association Monograph Series No. 9. Chicago, 1961.
18. McNerney, Walter J., and Reidel, Donald C.: Regionalization and Rural Health Care. An Experiment in Three Communities. Ann Arbor, The University of Michigan, 1962.
19. Medicine in the Changing Order. Report of the New York Academy of Medicine Committee on Medicine and the Changing Order. New York, The Commonwealth Fund, 1947.
20. Nicholson, E.: Planning New Institutional Facilities for Long Term Care. New York, G. P. Putnam's Sons, 1954.
21. Organized Home Medical Care in New York City. A Study of Nineteen Programs by the Hospital Council of Greater New York. Cambridge, Harvard University Press, 1956.
22. Planning of Facilities for Mental Health Services. Report of the Surgeon General's Ad Hoc Committee on Planning for Mental Health Facilities. Public Health

Service Publication No. 808. Washington, D.C., Government Printing Office, 1961.

23. Role of Hospitals in Programmes of Community Health Protection, Technical Report Series No. 122. Geneva, World Health Organization, 1957.

24. Rosenfeld, L. S., and Makover, H. B.: The Rochester Regional Hospital Council. Cambridge, Harvard University Press, 1956.

25. Simmons, L. W., and Wolff, H. G.: Social Science in Medicine. New York, Russell Sage Foundation, 1954.

42   Vital Statistics

In the practice of medicine, the physician constantly makes biological measurements. He measures blood pressure, he measures temperature, he measures pulse rate. Many measurements are done routinely; others are done only under special circumstances. In simplest terms, he measures life, death, and the extent of health.

These measurements relate to the individual and would, of themselves, have limited value except that norms based on similar measurements in large populations are available for evaluation of the individual measurement.

These data based on the aggregate of the population rather than the individual are the elements of *vital statistics*. Vital statistics, in turn, are biologic measures of the total population which can be valuable if used correctly. To do this, it is necessary to understand them.

It is the purpose of this chapter to provide an introduction to vital statistics and their uses so that physicians may use them correctly and understand their use by others. Such knowledge is important because (a) the physician is the primary source of information concerning the health of the population, (b) measurements of health are obtained from large populations, (c) an understanding of medical reports necessitates such knowledge, and (d) community health programs are based on vital statistics. Every physician should understand these vital statistics if he is to carry out his responsibility in community activities.

Vital statistics are expressed generally in two ways:

1. Frequency of occurrence or a count of events. For example, 37 people dying of cancer in a given community; or the occurrence of a case of poliomyelitis; or 35,000 people killed in automobile accidents in the United States.

2. Rates, which relate the number of counted events to the population from which they arise. The simple recording of numbers of occurrences has limited usefulness in itself. It has meaning when we relate it to the population at risk. Thirty-seven deaths from cancer in a community of 3000 people has a much different significance than 37 deaths in a population of 300,000. To make comparisons and draw inferences, it is necessary to use rates rather than just counts.

RATES

A rate is the number of occurrences of an event per specified unit of population per specified unit of time. The numerical value of a rate is obtained by counting (or occasionally estimating) the number of occurrences during a specified time period, dividing this by the total population at risk during the period of time and multiplying by an accepted unit of population such as one hundred, one thousand, ten thousand or one hundred thousand.

A rate (R) in a statistical sense is expressed by the formula

$$R = K\left(\frac{E}{P}\right)$$

in which: K is a constant (the accepted population unit), which is some power of 10, and is selected conventionally to eliminate excessive zeros, e.g., 10,000 so that .00175 would be expressed as 17.5

E = the number of times the event occurs

P = the population exposed to risk of the event

A rate is generally limited to a particular length of time specified in the original definition. This is usually a year.

Sometimes a ratio is used instead of a rate. A ratio expresses the frequency of one event relative to another but need not involve a time period. The rates and ratios most commonly used in vital statistics follow:

Death (Mortality) Rates

Crude Death Rate. The number of deaths reported (or registered) in the calendar year per 1000 actual or estimated total population at the middle of that year.

Specific Death Rates

1. Cause specific. The number of deaths from a specific cause (e.g., arteriosclerotic heart disease) in the calendar year per 100,000 persons in the total population at the middle of that year.
2. Age specific. The number of deaths in a selected age group (e.g., 60 to 69) in the calendar year per 1000 persons in the same age group in the population at the middle of that year.

Infant Mortality Rate. The number of deaths occurring under one year of age during a calendar year per 1000 live births during that year. Live births are used rather than the census population because of the known underenumeration of the population under one.

Neonatal Mortality Rate. The number of deaths occurring under 28 days of age during a calendar year per 1000 live births during that year.

Stillbirth Rate. The number of stillbirths during a calendar year per 1000 total births (live births plus stillbirths) during the year.

Perinatal Mortality Rate. The number of stillbirths plus neonatal deaths during a calendar year per 1000 total births during that year.

Maternal Mortality Rate. The number of deaths attributed to puerperal causes occurring during a calendar year per either (a) 10,000 live births or (b) 10,000 total births. The former is generally preferred because of the unreliability and variability in stillbirth reporting.

Proportionate Mortality Rate (Ratio). The number of deaths from a specific cause (e.g., arteriosclerotic heart disease) per 100 (or 1000) total deaths.

Case Fatality Rate (Ratio). The number of deaths from a specific cause (e.g., tuberculosis) per 100 (or 1000) reported cases of the same condition.

Birth (Natality) Rates

Crude Birth Rate. The number of live births reported (or registered) in the calendar year per 1000 actual or estimated total population at the middle of that year.

Age Specific Birth Rate. The number of live births to women in selected age group (e.g., 30 to 39) during a calendar year per 1000 women in the same age group in the population at the middle of that year.

Morbidity Rates

Prevalence Rate. The number of cases of a given illness in a population at a particular time per 100,000 population at the same time. In other words, this is the prevailing rate.

Incidence Rate. The total number of cases of a given disease occurring during a calendar year per 100,000 population at the middle of that year.

Prevalence rates and incidence rates are frequently misunderstood and misused. Each measures a different facet of population health. The prevalence rate shows the proportion of persons in the population with the condition at a particular time. This is static.

The incidence rate on the other hand is dynamic. It is a measure of the occurrence of a condition over time. It expresses the number of new events that occur in persons previously free of the condition.

The incidence rate tends to be relatively higher than the prevalence rate in diseases of short duration such as acute infectious diseases. A disease occurs, is reported and the patient quickly recovers or dies. Therefore, the cumulative count increases while the number ill at any one time is constantly and rapidly decreased by the deaths and recoveries. The incidence rate expresses the proportion of the population who have or have had the disease over a specified period of time.

Conversely, the prevalence rate tends to be relatively higher in diseases of long duration. The number ill with a chronic disease, such as diabetes or arteriosclerosis, is increased by those acquiring it during a given unit of time (incidence) which are added to the number who have acquired the disease in all previous units of time and who are still alive and have the disease.

Thus, in a chronic disease, the prevalence rate may be several times the incidence rate, whereas in an acute infectious disease, the reverse may be true.

Adjusted Rates

Standardized or adjusted rates are special theoretical rates developed for use in vital statistics. They should be used when one wishes to compare rates such as death rates for two populations whose age compositions are different. As an alternative to comparing a series of age-specific rates, the crude rate for each population can be adjusted. To do this, age-specific rates from each population are applied to the same selected standard population.

As a result, the number of deaths that would occur in each population, if the age distributions were similar, is obtained. The expected number of deaths in each population divided by the total number in the standard population results in comparable rates.

SOURCES OF INFORMATION

To determine a rate, it is necessary to have a denominator and a numerator. The denominator is the population at risk. The numerator is the number of occurrences of the event with which we are concerned.

DENOMINATOR

To obtain the denominator, the population at risk must be counted. The usual source of the denominator in the United States is the census taken by the federal government.

This federal census is a complete count of all individuals living in the United States at the time of the population survey. Each person is counted at his usual place of abode, "which is generally construed to mean the place where he lives and sleeps most of the time."

A population census is not a recent innovation. The Bible and reports of medieval cities mention censuses. The earliest modern census appears to have occurred in Sweden in 1750. In the United States there has been a population census every ten years since 1790 as required by the Constitution for purposes of Congressional representation. The Population Division of the Census Bureau administers the census. Information provided by the census has usefulness in so many areas that the original, and still primary, reason for its existence (i.e., determining Congressional districts) is quite often forgotten and in many instances unknown.

Although the census is intended to be a complete enumeration of the total population, there are some segments that tend generally to be under-reported. These are the very young—children under one year of age—who for some unknown reason are frequently omitted when data on a family are supplied; and those members of the population who live alone, or who remain only a short time at any one address.

The information collected in the 1960 census was of two kinds:

1. Personal data which included age, race, sex, marital status, country of origin if not born in the United States, relationship to the head of the household, school enrollment, years of school completed, place of residence in 1955, employment status, occupation group, industry group, place of work, means of transportation to work, and income.

2. Information concerning housing such as tenure, color of head of household, vacancy status, condition of plumbing facilities, number of rooms, number of bathrooms, number of housing units in the structure, the year the structure was built, whether or not there is a basement, type of heating equipment, number of persons in the housing unit, number of persons per room, the year the household head moved into the unit, automobiles available, value of property, gross and contract rent as well as certain additional information in selected tracts relating to housing and peculiar to the area.

TABULATION OF CENSUS INFORMATION

The information obtained from the census enumerators is tabulated by the Bureau of Census. Total populations are tabulated by political subdivisions. This gives the populations for each town, village, city, county and state.

The population used as the denominator in determining rates for any community is based on the last reported federal census.

The population figures are adjusted for intercensal years to obtain a more accurate estimate of the "population at risk" on which to base a rate.

The composition of populations is constantly changing. It is increased by births and in-migration and decreased by deaths and out-migration. An intercensal estimate made by adding the births and in-migration to and subtracting the deaths and out-migration from the census population is the most accurate. However, all these data are not readily available on other than a national level. Therefore, this method can seldom be used locally.

There are a variety of other methods of estimation. The most commonly used are:

Arithmetic Estimate. This assumes that population growth between two time periods has been by a constant yearly increment. To obtain an estimate of the population for a particular intercensal year, the average annual increase or decrease is obtained by subtracting the population at the earlier census from that at the later census and dividing this by the number of years between the censuses. The average annual increase or decrease is multiplied by the number of years which have elapsed between the earlier census and the date at which the estimate is being made. The result is added to the population at the earlier census to obtain the estimate.

$$P_t = (t\text{-}a) \left(\frac{P_b\text{-}P_a}{b\text{-}a} \right) + (P_a)$$

in which P_t = population to be estimated for time t
      P_a = population at earlier census
      P_b = population at later census
    $b\text{-}a$ = number of years between censuses
    $t\text{-}a$ = number of years between earlier census and date for which population is desired

Example: P_a = New York State as of April 1, 1950: Census, 14,830,192
          P_b = New York State as of April 1, 1960: Census, 16,782,304
    $P_b\text{-}P_a$ = 1,952,112
     $b\text{-}a$ = 10
     $t\text{-}a$ = 6

$$P_{1956} = 6 \left(\frac{1,952,112}{10} \right) + 14,830,192 = 16,001,459$$

An alternative to this computational procedure is a straight line graphic estimate which is obtained by plotting the two populations on an arithmetic grid and connecting them by a straight line. Then for any intervening point on the time scale (abscissa) the population can be read from the population scale (ordinate).

Geometric Estimate. This assumes that population growth between two time periods has been at a constant yearly rate rather than a constant yearly amount. Population for any intercensal year can be estimated according to the formula:

$$P_t = P_a \left(\frac{P_b}{P_a} \right)^{\frac{t-a}{b-a}}$$

where P_t = population to be estimated for time t
P_a = population at the earlier census
P_b = population at the later census
t-a = number of years between earlier census and date for which population is desired
b-a = number of years between censuses

This formula can be expressed as $P_t = P_a (1 + r)^t$ which is the familiar formula for compound interest.

Example: $P_{1956} = 14,830,192 \left(\frac{16,782,304}{14,830,192} \right)^{6/10}$ which is evaluated using logarithms and gives the result
$P_{1956} = 15,975,000$

A graphic alternative to this method of estimation is to plot both populations on an arithlog grid. This grid has an arithmetic scale on the abscissa, and a logarithmic scale on the ordinate. Connect the two points with a straight line and the population at any point in time can be read from the ordinate.

Either the arithmetic or geometric method can be used in postcensal estimation. The increment or decrement is computed as previously but is added to the population at the later census. For example, to make an estimate for 1965, the increment or decrement is applied to the 1960 rather than to the 1950 population.

The census enumeration then gives us an instantaneous view of a population—that is to say, a population at a point in time.

Data similar to those from the census are often obtained on a more limited scale through a survey. Surveys are, in general, executed as a part of a particular investigation and are designed to provide information necessary to that investigation.

NUMERATOR

Reporting and Recording of Vital Events

Kinds of Reports.   In general, the numerator of a vital rate is obtained from one of two kinds of reports.

1. Routine reports. Legal requirements (state or local) provide for the reporting of certain types of vital events to an official agency, usually the health department.

a. Birth reports. In all states in the United States, every birth is required to be reported. The usual definition of a reportable birth is the product of conception of 20 weeks or more gestation. There is some variation from state to state in this definition.

b. Death reports. There is a requirement in every state that all deaths regardless of the cause must be reported to an official agency.

c. Morbidity reports. Every state requires the reporting of certain diseases. These diseases are identified in the laws of the state or municipality and vary slightly from state to state. In nearly every state the major communicable diseases are reportable and certain noncommunicable diseases such as cancer, heart disease, cerebral palsy or diabetes may also be reportable.

2. Special reports. Special reports may be either mandatory or voluntary. A temporary regulation may require the reporting of certain diseases or conditions either for special study or because an emergency exists. Such special reports may also be on a voluntary basis for study purposes, for surveillance, or for control of a communicable disease.

Source of Reports. Reports of births, deaths and occurrences of disease originate with the physician. Information obtained from tabulations of these vital events is only as valid as the reports which come from each physician.

It is quite common for the physician's office assistant, the record clerk in the hospital or some other person to complete many of the details of the reports for the physician. It is the legal responsibility of the physician to sign the report attesting to the medical facts contained therein. He should discharge this responsibility conscientiously and accurately. Only if this is done can vital statistics be accurate and comprehensive.

Routing of Reports. Reports of vital events (births, deaths, morbidity information) are sent by the physician to the local health department. (We are assuming that the office of registrar of vital statistics to which births and deaths are reported is a part of the local health department, although this is not always so.) The local health department makes a record of the information received from the physician and uses it as necessary for public health purposes.

The local health department then sends the original report to the state health department for its information, use and permanent recording. The local health department also uses this information to determine the public health problems of its community and to report to the medical profession and to citizens in the community. The health department thus takes the individual reports received from the several physicians in the community, collates them, and reports them in numbers or rates as vital data of the community.

The state health department receiving these reports similarly makes tabulations for purposes of determining statewide public health problems, to take appropriate public health action and to report to the localities and the physicians in the state. The state health department, in turn, transmits summary or duplicate reports to the federal health authority, the Public Health Service of the United States Department of Health, Education, and Welfare.

The United States Public Health Service, which receives information currently from all 50 states (as well as directly from certain major cities) tabulates, correlates and collates this information and reports it back to the several states at periodic intervals. For acute communicable diseases, this reporting is usually on a weekly basis. Other information is submitted on a less frequent cycle. The Public Health Service also passes the information on to the international health authority, the World Health Organization, which similarly tabulates information and reports it to all of its member countries.

This system of reporting is described graphically in Figure 37.

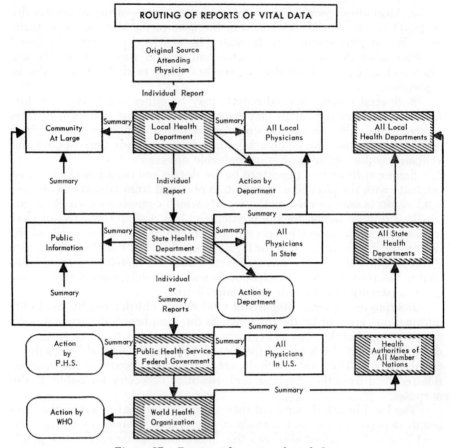

Figure 37. Routing of reports of vital data

This system of reporting, routing and recording is a complex one and each individual or unit plays an important part. The basic and most important element in this system is the report of the individual physician who records the original data. The reports made by the physician are confidential. As such, the privilege of examining these records is limited to the local registrar, the health officer and other authorized persons when this is required in connection with their official duties. Copies of a birth record may be issued to the person named in it, if he is of age; to his parents or other lawful representative; or upon court order. Copies of a death certificate, or information from such a certificate, may be issued to an applicant who requires it for a judicial or other proper purpose.

REGISTRATION OF VITAL DATA

Births and deaths were registered by some English parishes as early as 1538. In England registration was made a civil function in 1837. In the United States the registration of births, marriages, deaths, and fetal deaths (stillbirths) is provided for by each state. State laws relating to registration and vital data are now quite consistent. Although the Massachusetts Bay Colony required the registration of births and deaths as early as 1639, it was not until 1902 that registration of deaths became a federal responsibility. In that year, the Death Registration Area was established with the District of Columbia, ten states and some large cities in other states. A Birth Registration Area was established in 1915. By 1933 the entire United States was included in both Birth and Death Registration Areas.

The administration of the registration areas resides in the National Vital Statistics Division of the United States Public Health Service. Standard certificates are available and are revised periodically by the National Division in consultation with other interested groups. The certificates of most of the states conform closely in content and arrangement, although they may have been modified to meet the particular needs of a state, or because of special provisions in a state's vital statistics law. Copies of original birth and death certificates are sent by the states to the National Vital Statistics Division. From these, annual natality and mortality reports for the entire country are published.

Each state is subdivided into registration districts, each with a local registrar. The district is usually a political subdivision—county, town, village or city. Birth and death certificates are filed with the local registrar of the district in which the events occur. The local registrar is required to check each certificate for completeness and accuracy. He keeps a local record of each event certified and then sends the original certificate to the state health department.

When the certificates are received at the state health department, they are again checked for accuracy and completeness and the informant queried when necessary. They are numbered, indexed, bound, coded, and the data finally transferred to punch cards and possibly magnetic tape for processing, analysis, and the publication of reports.

Birth Registration

Births are reported on a standard birth certificate. The World Health Assembly has adopted the following definition of a live birth which has been recommended by federal authorities for use in the United States: "A live birth is the complete expulsion or extraction from its mother of a product of conception, irrespective of the duration of pregnancy, which after separation breathes or shows any other evidence of life such as beating of the heart, pulsation of the umbilical cord or definite movement of the voluntary muscles whether or not the umbilical cord has been cut or the placenta is attached: each product of such a birth is considered live born."

The certificate of birth should be filed immediately (usually within 5 days after the birth) by the physician or other person who delivered the child.

Figure 38 illustrates a standard birth certificate. All items must be completed. The writing must be legible. No erasures are allowed, since this is a permanent legal record.

Birth certificates in use in most states have a separate health and medical section which contains data related to race, complications of pregnancy, birth injuries, congenital malformations and other such items. This material

This is a permanent document. Type or use permanent black ink.
Do not use ball-type pen.

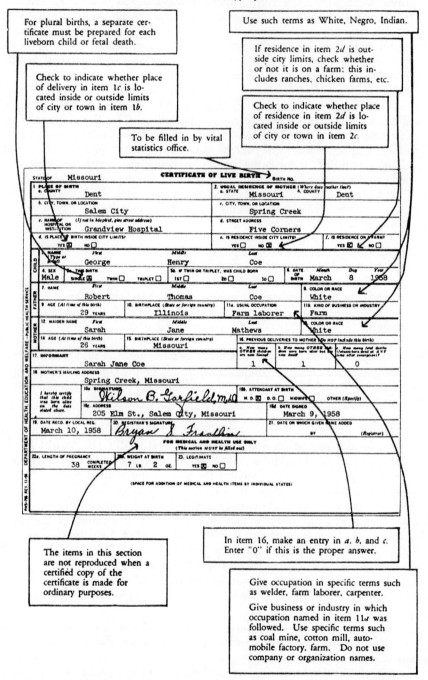

For plural births, a separate certificate must be prepared for each liveborn child or fetal death.

Use such terms as White, Negro, Indian.

Check to indicate whether place of delivery in item 1c is located inside or outside limits of city or town in item 1b.

If residence in item 2d is outside city limits, check whether or not it is on a farm: this includes ranches, chicken farms, etc.

Check to indicate whether place of residence in item 2d is located inside or outside limits of city or town in item 2c.

To be filled in by vital statistics office.

The items in this section are not reproduced when a certified copy of the certificate is made for ordinary purposes.

In item 16, make an entry in a, b, and c. Enter "0" if this is the proper answer.

Give occupation in specific terms such as welder, farm laborer, carpenter.

Give business or industry in which occupation named in item 11a was followed. Use specific terms such as coal mine, cotton mill, automobile factory, farm. Do not use company or organization names.

Figure 38. The standard certificate of live birth. (From Physicians' Handbook on Death and Birth Registration, 11th edition, National Vital Statistics Division, Public Health Service, **1963.**)

is considered confidential and does not appear on copies of the certificate. It provides much useful information for research purposes.

Common uses of birth records and the information derived from them are:

1. Establishing the date of birth for such purposes as:
   Entering school
   Obtaining licenses
   Proving age of capacity or incapacity in court cases
   Qualifying for pensions or social security benefits
   Obtaining work permits
   Voting
   Entering military service
2. Establishing birthplace to prove citizenship for such purposes as:
   Obtaining a passport
   Entering employment limited to citizens
   Obtaining licenses limited to citizens
3. Establishing family relationship for such purposes as:
   Proving legal dependency
   Obtaining inheritance benefits
   Receiving insurance payments
   Tracing lineal descent
4. Providing information on which health departments base their plans for:
   Immunization of children
   Care of crippled children
   Evaluation of the need for health services and facilities
   Evaluation of the effectiveness of infant care

Death Registration

Figure 39 is an example of a standard death certificate. The filing of the certificate is the responsibility of the person who is in charge of interment, usually the funeral director. The death certificate must be filed before a burial permit can be issued, usually within 72 hours. The funeral director completes all of the nonmedical items on the certificate, while the physician's responsibility is for the medical certification.

The medical certification is designed to identify the underlying cause of death as determined by the attending physician. It was the 1948 recommendation of the World Health Organization that the underlying cause of death be used in basic mortality tabulations.

In Part I of the medical certificate, the underlying cause of death and conditions leading to this are entered. The first condition entered is generally the immediate cause of death, while the last is the underlying cause. Space is provided in Part II for reporting other important diseases or conditions present but not directly related to the chain of events in Part I.

In completing the medical portion of the certificate, the disease or condition should be described in the most specific terms possible. For example, terms that describe only symptoms such as "high blood pressure" should be avoided. In reporting accidents, it is not sufficient to report merely "automobile accident"; the place of occurrence and the nature and means of injury

This is a permanent document.   Type or use permanent black ink.
Do not use ball-type pen.

THE FUNERAL DIRECTOR COMPLETES ITEMS 1-3, 5-17, 23, 24

To be filled in by vital statistics office.

Check to indicate whether place of death in item 1d is located inside or outside limits of city or town named in item 1b.

Use such terms as White, Negro, Indian.

Complete items 10a and 10b for all persons 14 years and over even though they were disabled, retired, unemployed, or institutionalized.

Give occupation followed during most of working life.   Use specific terms such as welder, farm laborer, carpenter.

Give business or industry in which occupation named in item 10a was followed.   Use specific terms such as coal mine, cotton mill, automobile factory, farm.   Do not use company or organization names.

Check to indicate whether place of residence in item 2d is located inside or outside limits of city or town in item 2c.

If residence in item 2d is outside city limits, check whether or not it is on a farm; this includes ranches, chicken farms, etc.

CERTIFICATE OF DEATH

| BIRTH NO | STATE OF Michigan | STATE FILE NO |

1 PLACE OF DEATH a. COUNTY Crawford	2. USUAL RESIDENCE a. STATE Michigan	b. COUNTY Crawford
b. CITY, TOWN, OR LOCATION Grayling Twp.	c. LENGTH OF STAY IN 2 months	c. CITY, TOWN, OR LOCATION Beaver Creek Twp.
d. NAME OF HOSPITAL OR INSTITUTION (If not in hospital, give street address) Mercy Hospital	d. STREET ADDRESS RR 1 Roscommon
e. IS PLACE OF DEATH INSIDE CITY LIMITS? YES ☐ NO ☒	e. IS RESIDENCE INSIDE CITY LIMITS? YES ☐ NO ☒	f. IS RESIDENCE ON A FARM? YES ☐ NO ☒

3 NAME OF DECEASED (Type or print)	First Rufus	Middle Henry	Last Smith	4 DATE OF DEATH Month June Day 21 Year 1957
5. SEX Male	6 COLOR OR RACE Negro	7 MARRIED ☒ NEVER MARRIED ☐ WIDOWED ☐ DIVORCED ☐	8. DATE OF BIRTH April 10, 1912	9 AGE (In years last birthday) 45	IF UNDER 1 YEAR / IF UNDER 24 HRS.
10a. USUAL OCCUPATION (Give kind of work done during most of working life, even if retired) Truck Driver	10b. KIND OF BUSINESS OR INDUSTRY Retail coal	11 BIRTHPLACE (State or foreign country) South Carolina	12. CITIZEN OF WHAT COUNTRY? U. S. A.
13. FATHER'S NAME James Smith	14. MOTHER'S MAIDEN NAME Maud Richardson
15 WAS DECEASED EVER IN U. S. ARMED FORCES? Yes World War II	16 SOCIAL SECURITY NO. 232-02-5678	17 INFORMANT Mary Alice Smith	Address Grayling, Mich.

18. CAUSE OF DEATH [Enter only one cause per line for (a), (b), and (c).]	INTERVAL BETWEEN ONSET AND DEATH
PART I. DEATH WAS CAUSED BY: IMMEDIATE CAUSE (a) Tuberculous meningitis	3 weeks
Conditions, if any, which gave rise to above cause (a), stating the underlying cause last. DUE TO (b) Pulmonary tuberculosis	6 months
DUE TO (c)	
PART II. OTHER SIGNIFICANT CONDITIONS CONTRIBUTING TO DEATH BUT NOT RELATED TO THE TERMINAL DISEASE CONDITION GIVEN IN PART I(a)	19. WAS AUTOPSY PERFORMED? YES ☐ NO ☒

20a ACCIDENT ☐ SUICIDE ☐ HOMICIDE ☐	20b. DESCRIBE HOW INJURY OCCURRED. (Enter nature of injury in Part I or Part II of item 18.)
20c TIME OF INJURY Hour ___ a.m. p.m. Month, Day, Year	
20d INJURY OCCURRED WHILE AT ☐ NOT WHILE WORK ☐ AT WORK	20e. PLACE OF INJURY (e. g., in or about home, farm, factory, street, office bldg., etc.)	20f. CITY, TOWN, OR LOCATION	COUNTY	STATE

| 21 I attended the deceased from February 4, 1957, to June 21, 1957, and last saw him alive on June 21, 1957. Death occurred at 4:25 ☐ m on the date stated above; and to the best of my knowledge, from the causes stated. |
22a SIGNATURE Walter M. Blais, M. D.	22b ADDRESS (Degree or title) Grayling, Michigan	22c. DATE SIGNED June 21, 1957
23a. BURIAL, CREMATION, REMOVAL (Specify) Burial	23b. DATE June 24, 1957	23c. NAME OF CEMETERY OR CREMATORY Chambers Cemetary	23d. LOCATION (City, town, or county) (State) Geneva Twp. Van Buren Co. Mich.
24 FUNERAL DIRECTOR Robert D. Bliss, Grayling, Mich.	ADDRESS	25. DATE RECD. BY LOCAL REG. June 22, 1957	26. REGISTRAR'S SIGNATURE John D. Jones

THE PHYSICIAN, MEDICAL EXAMINER, OR CORONER COMPLETES ITEMS 4, 18-22

In part I, give the sequence of events that led to death, specifying the last underlying cause which initiated the train of events.   Do not report symptoms or mode of dying.

In part II, report other important diseases or conditions, if any, that contributed to the death but were not related to the causes given in part I

Complete items 20 a-f if death was due to violence or external causes.

Figure 39. The standard certificate of death. (From Physicians' Handbook on Death and Birth Registration, 11th edition, National Vital Statistics Division, Public Health Service, 1963.)

should be reported. When reporting a death from cancer, the histological type and primary site should be reported. Acceptable terms are listed in the Standard Nomenclature of Diseases and Operations.[1]

When the certificates are received in the State Office of Vital Statistics, the underlying cause of death as certified by the physician is codified according to the World Health Organization's International Classification of Diseases.[2] This is a list which provides code numbers for proper terminology for causes of death. It is the outgrowth of a series of international conferences and is in wide usage. The more exact the certification, the more accurate the coding and tabulation.

Some specific uses of death certificates are:
1. Establishing the fact and date of death for such purposes as:
   Claiming life insurance carried by the decedent
   Claiming pensions
   Settling estates
2. Providing certain facts about the deceased such as:
   Circumstances of death and cause
   Date or place of interment
   Evidence as to age, sex, or race
   Genealogical information
3. Providing data for public health uses, such as:
   Determining the incidence of specific causes of death
   Planning disease control programs
   Investigating the nature and place of occurrence of fatal accidents
   Establishing the need for health services and facilities
   Measuring the effectiveness of health programs

Fetal Death (or Stillbirth) Registration. Fetal deaths (or stillbirths) are reported on a standard fetal death (or stillbirth) certificate. Federal authorities have recommended the use in the United States of the definition of a fetal death adopted by the World Health Assembly.

"Fetal death is death prior to the complete expulsion or extraction from its mother of a product of conception, irrespective of the duration of pregnancy; the death is indicated by the fact that after such separation, the fetus does not breathe or show any other evidence of life such as beating of the heart, pulsation of the umbilical cord or definite movement of the voluntary muscles."

If the twentieth week of gestation has been reached before the death of the fetus occurs, the term stillbirth is usually used. The requirements for the registration of fetal death vary from state to state. Some states require that all fetal deaths be registered while others require only the registration of stillbirths.

USE OF VITAL STATISTICS

Rates and the statistical methods applied to vital statistics provide data which can be used:
1. As simple numerical assessments of the state of public health and to make comparisons for different periods of time or for different places. These

can point out problems in preventive medicine and when and where remedial action may be needed.

2. To attempt to determine basic reasons for contrasts observed. Cross tabulation of the data can provide useful leads.

3. To attempt to determine etiology of disease.

4. To evaluate the efficacy of disease control programs.

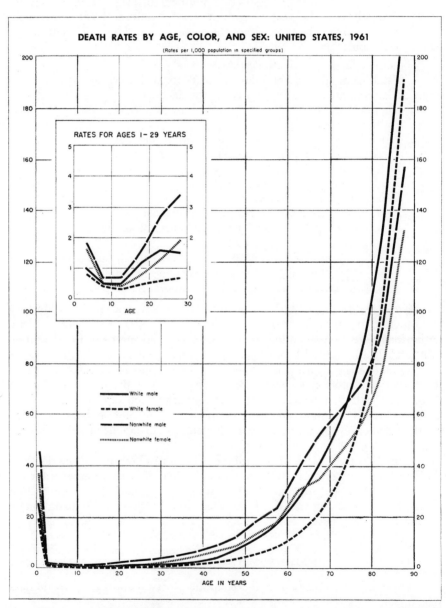

Figure 40. Vital Statistics of the United States, 1961. Mortality Analysis and Summary. U. S. Department of Health, Education, and Welfare, Public Health Service, National Vital Statistics Division, Vol. II.

Presentation of Vital Statistics

Once the rates have been obtained, they are tabulated and combined in an orderly sequence so that they can be presented concisely in a readily comprehensible manner. The two most frequently used modes of presentation are tables and graphs.

The purposes of a table are (a) to facilitate comparison and (b) to permit rapid comprehension of the material. There are essentially two types of tables:

1. The general purpose table, which is a reference table and contains very extensive information (for example, a table of deaths for a given year by cause, age and sex).

2. The specific purpose table, which contains selected data and is used for the presentation of significant and characteristic relationships.

A table should be completely labeled and understood without reference to the text. (See examples of tables on pages 476 to 478 and elsewhere in this book.)

A graph is often used to express the data more simply. It is generally preferred by the reader. The graph should be as simple as possible and completely labeled. Improper graphic presentation may result in a distorted impression of the data. A graph, as well as a table, should be understood without reference to the text. A graph does not necessarily replace a table and, in general, the tabular material should be available for anyone who wants to go over the data in detail.

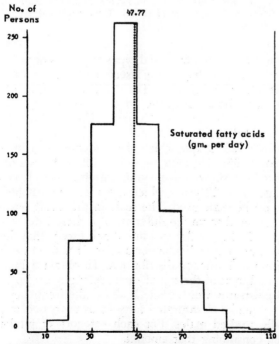

Figure 41. Distribution of usual dietary intake of saturated fatty acids expressed in grams per day in 250 men. (From Health News, New York State Department of Health, Albany, New York, 1961, Vol. 38, No. 1, p. 8.)

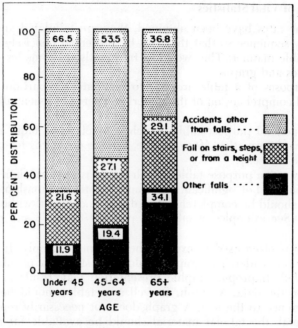

Figure 42. Per cent distribution of impairment due to injury in the home attributed to falls, by age. (From Impairments due to injury by class and type of accident, United States, July, 1959, to June 1961. Vital and Health Statistics, National Health Survey. Washington, D. C., U. S. Department of Health, Education, and Welfare, Public Health Service, Series 10, No. 6, 1964, p. 4.)

Some of the more commonly used types of graphs are:

Line Graph.　This is frequently used in plotting a variable such as a death rate over a time or age span. The death rate, or the frequency of the occurrence no matter how it is expressed, is plotted on the ordinate (Y axis) and the time span on the abscissa (X axis). The points so plotted are connected by a straight line.

Figure 40 is a line graph which shows death rates by age, color and sex: United States, 1961. Through the use of different types of lines, the four sets of rates have been shown on one graph. An insert has been used to clarify the rates for ages 1 to 29 years which are indistinguishable on the larger graph because of the scale used. The scale in the insert has been stretched out to enable one to observe the differences in these rates.

Histogram.　This is similar to a line graph except that the points on the line are replaced by perpendicular rectangles. It is used most often in presenting data from a frequency distribution. To obtain a line graph from a histogram, the midpoint of the top of each rectangle can be connected.

Figure 41 illustrates a histogram. It shows the frequency distribution of the usual dietary intake of saturated fatty acids expressed in grams per day for 250 specially studied males. For each category of intake it shows the number of men consuming that amount.

Bar Diagram.　A bar diagram is similar to a histogram in that parallel rectangles are used in each, but the thickness of the bars or the areas have no meaning in the bar diagram. It does not have to contain an element of time.

Figure 42, which shows the per cent distribution of impairments due to injury in the home attributed to falls by age, is an example of a bar diagram. By cross hatching of the bars, it is possible to show for each age group the relative importance of more than one type of accident.

Scatter Diagram. A scatter diagram is frequently used to determine the degree of correlation between two variables. It relates pairs of measurements on each item in the sample and enables one to make a visual assessment of the relationship between the two measures.

Figure 43 shows a scatter diagram relating cigarette consumption to

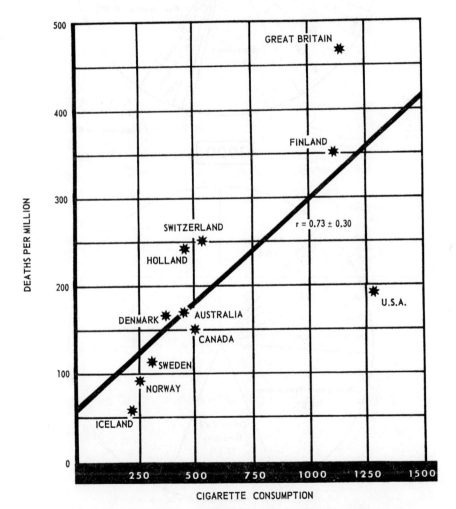

Figure 43. Crude male death rate for lung cancer in 1950 and per capita consumption of cigarettes in 1930 in various countries. (From Smoking and Health, Report of the Advisory Committee to the Surgeon General of the Public Health Service, U. S. Department of Health, Education, and Welfare, Public Health Service, U. S. Government Printing Office, 1964, p. 176.)

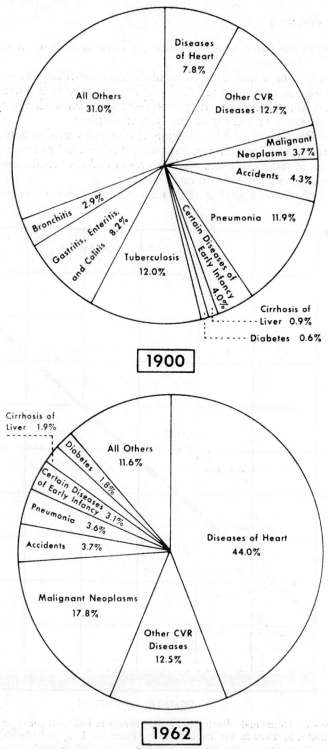

Figure 44. Distribution of recorded deaths due to chronic and other diseases, New York State, 1900 and 1962. (From New York's Health, State of New York, Revised January, 1964.)

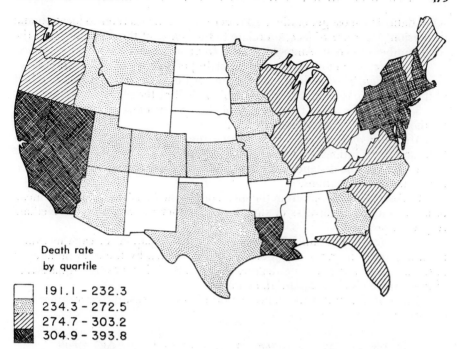

Death rate by quartile

	191.1 – 232.3
	234.3 – 272.5
	274.7 – 303.2
	304.9 – 393.8

Figure 45. Age-adjusted death rates for coronary heart disease in white males, 1950. (From Enterline, P. E., Stewart, W. H.: Geographic Patterns in Deaths from Coronary Heart Disease. Public Health Reports, 1956, Vol. 71, No. 9.)

lung cancer death rates and also shows the line which mathematically assesses the relationship.

Pie Chart. A pie chart is a graphic presentation in which a circle is divided into pie-shaped pieces whose areas and circumferences are proportional to the quantities to be represented.

Figure 44 is an illustration of two pie charts which show the distribution of recorded deaths due to chronic and other diseases, New York State, 1900 and 1962. Although they enjoy some favor, they are difficult to construct and to interpret and, in general, some other mode of presentation is preferable.

Spot maps and shaded maps are useful in attempting to picture the geographic pattern in the variable being examined.

Figure 45 is an example of a shaded map which shows coronary heart disease mortality for white males for each state in 1950.

There are a number of other graphic techniques in common usage, including some for portraying three dimensional data.

Statistical Terms

Frequency Distribution. This is a device for organizing and summarizing data. It is a simple statistical table which shows the number of observations for a set of classification groups. For example, the number of deaths occurring each month is a frequency distribution.

Although a frequency distribution achieves a reduction from the original data, a still greater reduction can be accomplished through the use of a descriptive statistic, that is, a single number describing some feature of a set of data. The most generally used descriptive statistics refer to location and dispersion. *Measures of location* relate to the center of the distribution of the total number of events. Among the most frequently used are:

1. *Mode.* The most commonly occurring of a series of observations.

2. *Median.* The "middle" observation, or the value above which one-half of the observations lie and below which one-half of the observations lie.

3. *Mean.* The sum of the values of the observations in a series divided by the number of observations in the series.

Measures of Dispersion. These tell the degree to which the observations and distributions are spread from the center:

1. *Range.* The distance between the highest and lowest values recorded in a series of observations.

2. *Average deviation* from the mean or the median. The arithmetic mean of all deviations, regardless of sign, around either the mean or the median, respectively.

3. *Variance.* The sum of the squares of the deviations of each measurement in a series from the mean of the series, divided by the total number of observations minus one (the degrees of freedom). The positive square root of the variance is the *standard deviation.*

Table 20 illustrates the computation of these measures of location and dispersion.

Table 20. *Systolic Blood Pressure in 10 Males, Age 40-49*

READING (mm. Hg)	DEVIATION FROM		(DEVIATION FROM MEAN)^2
	MEAN	MEDIAN	
130	−22	−15	484
130	−22	−15	484
140	−12	−5	144
140	−12	−5	144
140	−12	−5	144
150	−2	+5	4
150	−2	+5	4
160	+8	+15	64
170	+18	+25	324
210	+58	+65	3364

Sum of measurements	1520
Sum of deviations from mean, disregarding sign	168
Sum of deviations from median, disregarding sign	160
Sum of squared deviations from mean	5160

Mean	152 mm. Hg
Median	145 mm. Hg
Mode	140 mm. Hg
Range	130 mm. Hg to 210 mm. Hg
Average deviation from mean	16.8 mm. Hg
Average deviation from median	16.0 mm. Hg
Variance	573.33
Standard deviation	24 mm. Hg

TESTS OF STATISTICAL SIGNIFICANCE

The physician has frequent occasion to question whether observed differences between methods of treatment, or treatment under different sets of circumstances, are greater than might be attributed to chance variation; that is, are the differences significant?

Tests of significance are techniques which enable one to determine whether observed events are different in the statistical sense; that is, whether the observation is sufficiently different from the expected to be probably due to some factor other than chance. Some commonly used tests are the t-test, the F-test and Chi square (χ^2).

Table 21 illustrates the use of the χ^2 test which is a test commonly encountered by the medical student or the physician.

Table 21. *Mortality under 28 Days among Premature Births in Three Different Hospitals*

| HOSPITAL | TOTAL | PREMATURE BIRTHS | | |
		DIED UNDER 28 DAYS	SURVIVED 28 DAYS OR MORE	DEATH RATE UNDER 28 DAYS PER 1000 PREMATURE BIRTHS
A	622	124	498	199
B	831	182	649	219
C	499	137	362	275
Totals	1952	443	1509	227

A χ^2 test can be used to answer the question, "Are death rates under 28 days among prematures in the three hospitals different from what one would expect on the basis of sampling variation?"

One proceeds as follows:

1. Obtain the expected value for the under 28 day mortality rate by computing the rate for all three hospitals combined by dividing total deaths under 28 days by total premature births:

Expected death rate under 28 days = 443/1952 = 227/1000

2. Obtain the expected survival rate by subtracting the death rate from 1000:

Expected survival rate = 1.000 − 0.227 = 0.773 or 773/1000

3. For each hospital get the expected number of deaths and survivors by multiplying the total premature births in each hospital by the expected under 28 day death rate (227/1000) and by the expected survival rate (773/1000), respectively. The results are shown below:

Table 22. *Expected Mortality under 28 Days among Premature Births in Three Different Hospitals*

| HOSPITAL | TOTAL | PREMATURE BIRTHS | |
		DIED UNDER 28 DAYS (EXPECTED)	SURVIVED 28 DAYS OR MORE (EXPECTED)
A	622	(a) 141	(d) 481
B	831	(b) 189	(e) 642
C	499	(c) 113	(f) 386
Total	1952	443	1509

4. For each cell (a) through (f) obtain the difference between the actual number of events, Table 21, and the expected number of events, Table 22, ignore the sign of the difference.

For example: cell (a) 124-141 = 17
cell (b) 182-189 = 7
cell (c) 137-113 = 24
and so on through cells (d) to (f)
5. Square each difference.
For example: cell (a) $(17)^2 = 289$
cell (b) $(7)^2 = 49$
and so on through cells (c) to (f)
6. Divide each squared difference by the number in the corresponding cell in the expected table (Table 22).
For example: cell (a) 289/141 = 2.05
cell (b) 49/189 = 0.26
and so on through cells (c) to (f)
7. Add the values obtained for all 6 cells. In this example, this adds up to 9.58.
8. To determine the significance of this value, consult a table of χ^2 probability (Table 23).

Table 23. *Table of Chi Square Probability*

n	.99	.98	.	.	.	.	.05	.02	.01	.001
1	0.0157	0.0628					3.841	5.412	6.635	10.837
→ 2	0.0201	0.0404					5.991	7.824	*9.210*	*13.815*
.										
.										
.										
30	14.953	16.306					43.773	47.962	50.892	59.703

*The calculated value of $\chi^2 = 9.58$ and lies between the 0.01 (9.210) and the 0.001 (13.815) probability levels.

9. The difference in rates among these three hospitals would occur less than one time in a hundred if the only factor affecting these differences were chance. On this basis, one would assume that the differences were due to some influence other than chance alone.

Interpretation of Vital Statistics

A *statistic* may be defined as an observation, made on any element of a population, which can be expressed numerically. If an attribute is being observed, it can be counted as either absent or present (and accordingly it is a zero or a one); if it is some characteristic such as height or weight, it can be measured directly.

In both instances, the actual usefulness of the statistic is completely dependent on the accuracy with which it is measured.

Statistics is the body of mathematical technique which has evolved for the analysis and interpretation of data obtained from the observational procedure. Statistics are either descriptive and help to classify, summarize, and present results in forms which are comprehensible and likely to suggest fruitful hypotheses, or they are analytic and concerned with the testing of hypotheses.

Vital statistics arise in and are collected from a population living and dying in the everyday course of events. As such, they provide useful information on the biologic experience of the population.

It is well, however, to observe some cautions in using vital statistics data so that the inferences drawn are valid. One should keep in mind first that, in dealing with a rate, we are concerned with a numerator and a denominator, and errors in either influence the result. Second, in making comparisons between areas or times, we must insure that we are comparing like characteristics and populations. Conclusions should not be drawn from noncomparable data.

Errors in the denominators of our rates may include:
1. Underenumeration of population segments such as persons under one year of age.
2. Misstatement of age.
3. Invalid assumptions in population estimation.
4. Errors made by census enumerator.

Some possible sources of errors in the numerators are:
1. Incorrect information on the report due to:
   a. Inadequate data.
   b. Error in judgment.
2. Under- or overreporting of conditions.

An illustration of the effect of one of these (the incorrect certification of cause of death) is provided by a study by James, et al.[3] For the period 1950 to 1951 data were obtained on over 1800 persons from 12 different hospitals and were used to compare the cause of death as entered on the death certificate with the cause of death as determined at autopsy. There was disagreement on the classification of cause of death in 48 per cent of the certificates, and in 25 per cent of the certificates the disagreement was such that the death did not even fall into the same major cause group.

It was of interest that, in general, the total cause-specific death rates were not influenced greatly because of compensatory errors. For example, there were 57 pneumonia deaths according to the death certificates and 57 according to the autopsies, so that the crude pneumonia rate was unchanged. However, only 25 of the 57 certificates agreed on both, and the age-sex distribution of the death certificate group was different from that of the autopsy group.

In making comparisons of rates there are a number of factors which may invalidate the comparisons. Among these are:

Differences in Definition of Events Being Compared. If one is comparing the fetal death rates for two areas, one must be sure that the definition of a fetal death is the same. One locality may consider a fetal death to be any product of conception which is not living at birth, while another may consider only events which occur after the twentieth week of gestation. Using these different definitions, one will obtain different results.

Method of Selecting Cases. A series of hospitalized cases is apt to contain more seriously ill individuals than a series of nonhospitalized cases, and so a comparison of case fatality ratios would not be valid. Comparisons must be made between series with the same characteristics.

Inaccurate Measurement or Classification of Cases. If the fashion in certification of cause of death varies from place to place or from time to time, this will be reflected in mortality data. If underreporting of disease exists, morbidity rates will reflect this bias.

Inappropriate Comparisons. A comparison of crude death rates in two populations known to have different age compositions may result in an invalid conclusion.

Misinterpretation of Association and Causation.   Two sets of data may show a relationship in time such as the sales of refrigerators and the incidence of cancer of the liver. However, this does not mean that one caused the other. Causation requires that a plausible, biologically sound relationship, suggested by scientific methods of analysis, be verified through further carefully designed studies.

Disregard of Dispersion.   It is natural in all biological observations to note differences. The basic question is whether these are outside the range of expected variation. Analysis using the proper statistical techniques will indicate whether the observed differences would probably have occurred by chance alone.

SANDRA KINCH, M.S.
FRANKLYN B. AMOS, M.D.

REFERENCES

1. Plunkett, Richard J., and Hayden, Adaline C. (ed.): American Medical Association Standard Nomenclature of Diseases and Operations. New York, Blakiston Division, McGraw-Hill Book Co., 1952.
2. International Classification of Diseases. Geneva, World Health Organization, 1959.
3. James, G., Patton, R. E., and Heslin, A. S.: Accuracy of Cause-of-Death Statements on Death Certificates. Public Health Reports, 70:No. 1, January, 1955.
4. Physicians' Handbook on Birth and Death Registration. National Vital Statistics Division, U. S. Public Health Service, Government Printing Office, Washington, D.C., ed. 11, 1958, reprinted 1963.
5. Walker, H. M., and Durost, W. N.: Statistical Tables, Their Structure and Use. New York, Bureau of Publications, Teachers College, Columbia University, 1936.
6. Arkin, H., and Colton, R. R.: Graphs: How to Make and Use Them. New York, Harper & Brothers, 1936.
7. Hill, Bradford A.: Principles of Medical Statistics. Ed. 6. New York, Oxford University Press, 1956.
8. Mainland, Donald: Elementary Medical Statistics. Ed. 2. Philadelphia, W. B. Saunders Company, 1963.
9. Mosteller, F., Rourke, R. E. K., and Thomas, G. B., Jr.: Probability and Statistics. Reading, Mass., Addison-Wesley Publishing Company, Inc., 1961.

43 Epidemiologic Methods and Inferences

Since the time of Hippocrates, epidemiologic methods have been used in an attempt to elucidate the etiologic factors of human disease. These methods have contributed to the control of many infectious diseases, one of the major accomplishments of preventive medicine and public health. Recently, increasing research interest in determining the etiologic factors of such diseases as cancer and heart disease has correspondingly increased interest in the epidemiologic approach to these major current public health problems.[1] We shall attempt to review briefly some of the general methods used by the epidemiologist, with particular emphasis on the reasoning involved in the elucidation of etiologic factors. Most illustrations will concern noninfectious diseases, although a few infectious diseases will be considered. Before proceeding to our main discussion, it would be well to define epidemiology, indicate its practical uses and discuss some of the sources of epidemiologic data.

DEFINITION AND USES

Epidemiology may be defined as the study of the distribution of a disease or condition in a population, and of the factors that influence this distribution. Thus, the epidemiologist is interested in the variation in frequency of diseases or conditions by such characteristics as age, sex, race, social class and occupation. This knowledge is useful for the following reasons.

1. It permits the development of hypotheses concerning etiologic factors. Thus, if the disease is observed to be more frequent in one particular population segment than in others, hypotheses are developed to explain this increased frequency. An example occurs in a study by Epstein, et al., of the prevalence of coronary artery disease among clothing workers in New York City.[2] It was found that the prevalence of coronary disease was higher among Jewish than Italian men (Table 24). Such a difference requires an explana-

481

Table 24. *Prevalence of Coronary Heart Disease among Men by Ethnic Group*[2]

AGE	ITALIAN MEN (Total, 232)		JEWISH MEN (Total, 372)	
	NUMBER WITH CORONARY DISEASE	PER CENT OF TOTAL	NUMBER WITH CORONARY DISEASE	PER CENT OF TOTAL
40-49	2	4.2	2	2.9
50-59	5	5.0	17	13.9
60-69	9	11.7	32	20.6
70-79	1	16.7	10	38.4
Total	17	7.3	61	16.4
Adjusted to age, distribution of Italians and Jews		7.9		15.8

tion, and hypotheses which may be related to factors of etiologic importance are developed.

2. The knowledge of variations in frequency can be used to test hypotheses developed in the laboratory or clinic. It is important to determine if an etiologic hypothesis, based on laboratory or clinical observations, is consistent with the distribution of the disease in human populations, and, to the extent that it is not consistent, the hypothesis will have to be modified. An illustration is Holsti and Ermala's production in 1955 of bladder cancer in mice by the application of tobacco tar to the buccal mucous membrane.[3] To determine if such a relation existed in humans, Lilienfeld, et al., analyzed the smoking histories of patients with bladder cancer and other types of cancer who were admitted to a cancer hospital.[4] The results presented in Table 25

Table 25. *Percentage of Men Aged 45 Years and Over with History of Tobacco Use, by Class of Patient*[4]

CLASS OF PATIENT	NUMBER OF PATIENTS	PER CENT TOBACCO USERS			
		ANY TYPE OF TOBACCO	CIGARETTES ONLY	CIGARETTES ALONE AND IN COMBINATION WITH OTHER TYPES OF TOBACCO	ANY TYPE OTHER THAN CIGARETTES
		Unadjusted Percentage			
Bladder cancer	321	84.1	47.0	59.8	24.3
Benign bladder conditions	39	76.9	30.8	38.4	38.5
No disease	337	70.9	40.0	46.3	24.6
Prostate cancer	287	74.6	28.2	37.2	37.3
Lung cancer	306	91.8	67.3	84.3	7.5
		Age-adjusted Percentages			
Bladder cancer	321	84.7	48.7	61.4	23.2
Benign bladder conditions	39	77.9	32.8	37.1	40.8
No disease	337	70.8	35.8	44.1	26.7
Prostate cancer	287	77.8	32.6	42.3	36.1
Lung cancer	306	92.0	64.9	82.9	9.1

show that there is an association between bladder cancer and cigarette smoking. Thus, a relationship determined by experiment was confirmed in a human group.

3. These data provide the scientific basis for measures to control the disease. Even if knowledge of etiology is erroneous, epidemiologic data may still be used for such control measures as case finding and the early detection of affected individuals. This is illustrated by a study of Steinberg and Wilder.[5] From a group of diabetic patients admitted to the Mayo Clinic, they obtained a history of the presence or absence of diabetes among parents and siblings (Table 26). The authors interpreted these data as indicating the genetic basis

Table 26. *Frequency of Diabetes among Siblings and Parents of Diabetic Patients*[5]

	PARENTS		SIBLINGS		
				DIABETES	
DIABETES STATUS	NUMBER	TOTAL	NUMBER	PER CENT	
Both parents diabetic	22	100	16	16.0	
One parent diabetic	370	1,620	185	11.4	
Neither parent diabetic	1,589	6,664	311	4.7	
Total	1,981	9,384	512	5.5	

of diabetes. Whether one agrees with a genetic etiologic hypothesis or thinks that such familial aggregation could result from environmental factors common to family members, the observations are useful to the physician as indicating a method for the early detection of diabetes. It emphasizes the need for the examination of the parents and siblings of diabetic patients to determine if they have diabetes. Such early detection and treatment will prevent the development of complications.

METHODS

An epidemiologic study provides data for the derivation of a series of statistical associations between a disease and various characteristics of the population. From this pattern of associations, biological inferences may be drawn. The totality of the associations and the inferences constitutes what may be termed the epidemiology of a disease. Thus, the epidemiologic method consists of two stages: first, the determination of one or more statistical associations and, second, the derivation of biological inferences from these associations. Two types of studies are used to determine statistical associations: studies of the distribution of the disease in the general population and studies of data based on individual histories. These two types are not mutually exclusive. However, it is helpful to consider them separately since, in general, each presents different methodological and inferential problems.

GENERAL POPULATION STUDIES

Two principal sources for studies of the over-all distribution of disease in the general population are statistics of mortality and morbidity and special surveys of samples of the population. Such studies provide information concerning the distribution of disease by time, age, sex, race, social class and other characteristics. These data may differ from data based on individual histories in several respects. For example, they may show an association between two events in time, which may not be directly related to each other. On the other hand, individual history data may show that an individual with a certain characteristic also has another characteristic, which type of association is more likely to reflect a biological relationship. To illustrate these differences, we can observe the trend of mortality from lung cancer in the United States for the period from 1930 to 1950, and the trend of cigarette consumption from 1905 to 1950 (Fig. 46). We note that these two trends are similar and therefore associated in time, which might suggest that they are causally related. However, such an interpretation can only be considered as being slightly suggestive, since others factors can be shown to have similar trends (Fig. 47). Associating similar time trends may be very misleading.

In contradistinction to this type of association, the relationship of lung cancer to cigarette smoking was presented by Levin, et al.,[8] who studied the smoking habits of lung cancer patients and patients with other types of cancer. The frequency of cigarette smoking was found to be higher among the lung cancer patients than the other groups, indicating an association between lung cancer and cigarette smoking. The likelihood of such an association in individuals reflecting a biological relationship is obviously greater than the similarity of time trends.

Certain data, such as the distribution of mortality or morbidity by social class, may deal with average characteristics of groups rather than with the characteristics of each individual. Again, such a relationship may reflect other factors that are independently related to the variables being studied and would be less likely to be indicative of a causal relationship.

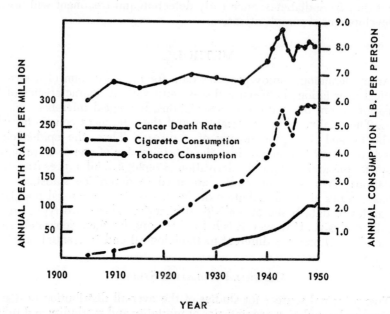

Figure 46. Trends in death rates from lung cancer, and consumption of cigarettes and tobacco in the United States from 1905 to 1950. (Doll, R.: Bronchial carcinoma: incidence and etiology. British Medical Journal, 2:585, 1953.)

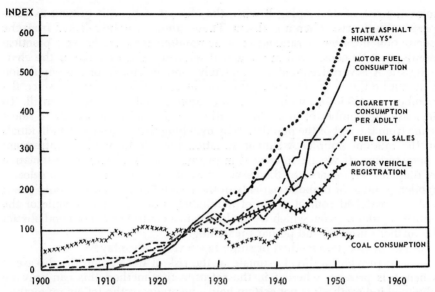

Figure 47. Trends in selected environmental factors in the United States from 1900 to 1953. (Hammond, E. C.: Lung cancer and common inhalants. Cancer, 7:1100, 1954.)

STUDIES OF INDIVIDUAL HISTORIES

When a lead develops from an analysis of data obtained from the general population or from the laboratory or from a clinical impression, the statistical association should be further investigated by a study of individual histories. In general, we can consider three different kinds of such studies, retrospective, prospective and experimental.

Retrospective Studies

The retrospective approach consists of obtaining a group of individuals with the disease, which we shall call B, and determining the percentage of these individuals who have the characteristic A, which is considered a possible etiologic factor. The frequency of A is then compared with a similar frequency in a so-called control or comparative group of individuals without the disease. If the frequency of A is higher among those with B than among those without B, an association is said to exist between A and B. In such studies, the cases (with B) and the controls (without B) can be selected in several ways.

Frequently, both the cases and the controls are obtained from hospital patient populations. Practically all retrospective studies indicating an association between lung cancer and cigarette smoking have been of this type.[9] Control groups usually consist of patients with other diseases admitted to the same hospitals. This method is popular because data can be obtained easily and inexpensively.

Prospective Studies

In prospective studies, groups of individuals with and without the characteristic A are obtained and followed for a definite period of time to determine the risk of developing B when the characteristic A is present as compared with the risk when it is absent. These groups may be selected from the population in either a random or a nonrandom manner. Several practical points must be considered in the actual selection. For example, if the characteristic A is very frequent, a completely random sample of the population may not be the most efficient method of selecting the two groups, since the number of individuals without A in a random sample may be too small. To increase the number of individuals without A, it may be necessary to select some from the rest of the population by matching them with the A individuals in the random sample. A similar situation may occur with an infrequent characteristic. If we are interested in prospectively studying the association of diabetes with cancer of the cervix, it would probably be best to select a random sample of diabetic patients in the community. Then we could select either a matched control group of nondiabetics or a random sample of the entire population from which we could obtain a control group of nondiabetics by further sampling and perhaps matching.

The prospective method of study has several advantages:

1. It provides a direct estimate of the risk of developing the disease B when A is present, whereas in the retrospective method this can only be obtained indirectly. It is not certain how advantageous the follow-up method really is when the major objective is to determine possible etiologic factors. Nevertheless, some investigators prefer direct rather than indirect estimates.

2. It decreases the risk of subjective bias, provided that the criteria and procedures are established in advance.

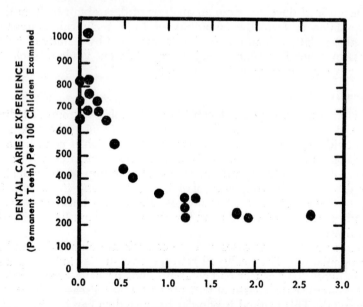

Fluoride (F) Content of the Public Water Supply in P.P.M.

Figure 48.   Relation between dental caries and the amount of fluoride in the water supply. (Dean, H. T., Arnold, F. A., Jr. and Elvove, E.: Domestic water and dental caries. Additional studies of the relation of fluorides in domestic waters to dental caries experience in 4425 white children aged 12 to 14 years of 13 cities in 4 states. Public Health Reports, 57:1155, 1942.)

3. It decreases the likelihood of misclassifying individuals with and without the characteristic. For example, in determining the relationship of artificial menopause to female breast cancer retrospectively, we are dependent on a history of artificial menopause. In a certain proportion of cases the history would be erroneous. However, in a prospective study we would start with individuals who currently have an artificial menopause, and, therefore, could not misclassify them.

Experimental Studies

Both retrospective and prospective studies deal with naturally occurring phenomena, in the sense that the investigator has no direct control over factors that may influence the associations he observes. Obviously, properly designed experiments are a more certain way of establishing an association. A classic illustration of the role of experimentation is afforded by the study of the relationship of fluoride in the water supply and dental caries.[14] Many studies had indicated the relationship between a high concentration of fluorides in the water supply and the absence of dental caries. One set of data indicating this relationship is presented in Figure 48, suggesting that the addition of fluorides to the water supply would result in a decrease in the dental caries risk. The only way this could be determined would be to add fluorides to the water supply of one community and to select a comparable community whose water supply, lacking natural supplies, would be untouched. Several such studies were initiated, one of which was carried out in New York state in the two communities of Kingston and Newburgh.[15] The results are presented in Table 27. We note that in the community with fluorides in the water supply, the index of dental caries (DMF) is less than in the community without fluorides. Admittedly, this kind of an experiment is not ideal in that random procedures were not used; obviously this would

Table 27. *DMF* Teeth per 100 Children, Ages 6 to 16, Based on Clinical and Roentgenographic Examinations—Newburgh† and Kingston, New York, 1954 to 1955*[15]

Age‡	NUMBER OF CHILDREN WITH PERMANENT TEETH		NUMBER OF DMF TEETH		DMF TEETH PER 100 CHILDREN WITH PERMANENT TEETH§		
	NEW-BURGH	KINGS-TON	NEW-BURGH	KINGS-TON	NEW-BURGH	KINGS-TON	PER CENT OF DIFFERENCE
6-9‖	708	913	672	2134	98.4	233.7	−57.9
10-12	521	640	1711	4471	328.1	698.6	−53.0
13-14	263	441	1579	5161	610.1	1170.3	−47.9
15-16	109	119	1063	1962	975.2	1648.7	−40.9

* DMF includes permanent teeth decayed, missing (lost subsequent to eruption) or filled.
† Sodium fluoride was added to Newburgh's water supply beginning May 2, 1945.
‡ Age at last birthday at time of examination.
§ Adjusted to age distribution of children examined in Kingston who had permanent teeth in the 1954 to 1955 examination.
‖ Newburgh children of this age group were exposed to fluoridated water from the time of birth.

be impossible in this type of situation. However, the results of such an experiment measurably increase the confidence in the observed associations.

CAUSAL INFERENCES FROM EPIDEMIOLOGIC STUDIES

Causality in Biological Phenomena

After a statistical association has been ascertained, we would like to make some inference as to whether a cause and effect relationship exists between the disease and the associated characteristic. Before discussing factors that influence this type of inference, we need to consider the concept of causality.

In medicine and public health, it is reasonable to adopt a pragmatic concept of causality. One major reason for determining the etiologic factors of human disease is to use this knowledge to prevent the disease. Therefore, a factor may be defined as a cause of a disease if the incidence of the disease is diminished when exposure to this factor is likewise diminished.

This concept is not so logically rigorous as the more formalistic one held by some investigators, which requires evidence indicating that a factor is both a necessary and a sufficient condition for a disease before it is incriminated as a cause. In biological phenomena, both these requirements do not have to be met because of the existence of multiple causative factors. For example, in tuberculosis the tubercle bacillus is a necessary but not a sufficient condition for tuberculosis. Other additional factors included under the term susceptibility are important. Also, in other infectious diseases, the microorganism is a necessary factor but not always a sufficient one. In diseases generally considered noninfectious, such as cancer, the concept of causation may have to be broadened further, since one particular etiologic factor may not even be a necessary one because of the probable existence of multiple causative agents.

Actually, in both infectious and noninfectious diseases, the differences in these two concepts depend upon the frame of reference. To illustrate, the cause and effect relationships with multiple etiologic factors, labeled A_1, A_2, A_3, and so forth, each acting independently, are presented in Figure 49. These factors can be looked on as producing a change in B at a cellular level.

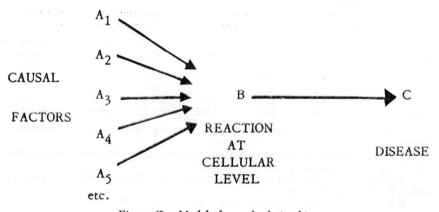

Figure 49. Model of causal relationship.

The changed cell B could then develop into C, the disease. Clearly, the cellular change in B can be considered as the necessary and sufficient condition for the disease C. Therefore, to meet the more rigorous definition of causality, the biological mechanisms relating A to B and B to C must be determined. Pragmatically, however, the determination of each of the A factors is important, since attention must be focused on these to enable us to apply preventive measures.

To derive causal inferences from observed statistical associations is difficult, because one cannot eliminate the possible effect of other variables that may influence both the characteristic A and the disease B. For example, in the cigarette smoking–lung cancer relationship, one may postulate the existence of another factor that causes a person to smoke and also causes lung cancer. Or, perhaps there is some constitutional factor among non-smokers that decreases their risk of developing lung cancer. The latter viewpoint is not unreasonable since there may be a tendency for persons participating in athletics not to start smoking at that time of life when smoking habits are developed. Such individuals may be constitutionally hardier as shown by their participation in athletics, and perhaps this constitutional factor decreases their risk of developing lung cancer. If such relationships exist, they would result in a statistical association without a causal relationship. This situation may be termed biological selection, since individuals are selected for both the characteristic and the disease by a third mutually related factor. Similar problems are encountered in many fields, such as genetics and sociology.[16, 17]

Biological Considerations

One important biological consideration that may influence the derivation of causal inferences concerns the ability to experiment. If one can select samples of individuals from a population and randomly allocate them to two groups, one with and the other without the characteristic, and the statistical association continues to exist, the random procedure has taken into account most, if not all, of the other related variables. However, experimentation is not usually feasible in most human diseases.

Another influential factor is the degree of the observed association. If the statistical association is very strong, it is less reasonable to suppose that a mutually-correlated third factor was involved. Admittedly, a 100 per cent association does not completely eliminate the possible existence of a third factor, but it does make such a possibility less likely. However, such a situation is rarely encountered.

Probably the most important consideration is whether or not the association is consistent with the existing biological theory. If a statistical association makes biological sense, it is more readily accepted than one that is at the moment not capable of biological explanation. By biological sense we mean that the mechanisms leading from the characteristic A to the disease B fit into some physiological or pathological framework. If this framework exists, it was probably derived from other kinds of observations; therefore, it is felt that the association has been verified by other, independent observations.

This type of reasoning can be illustrated from studies of pregnancy experience and neuropsychiatric disorders of childhood.[18] In these studies,

Table 28. *Summary of the Association of Maternal and Fetal Factors with Certain Neuropsychiatric Disorders of Childhood*[18]

| TYPE OF NEUROPSYCHIATRIC DISORDER | ONE OR MORE COMPLICATIONS (PER CENT) | FREQUENCY OF | | | MATERNAL AGE AND BIRTH ORDER | MATERNAL HISTORY OF PREVIOUS INFANT LOSS | OPERATIVE PROCEDURES |
		PREMATURITY (PER CENT)	ABNORMAL NEONATAL CONDITIONS (PER CENT)	TOTAL ABNORMALITIES (PER CENT)			
Cerebral palsy							
cases	38	22	Not studied		+?	+	—
controls	21	5					
Epilepsy							
White { cases	27	13	17	34	—	+	—
controls	19	4	6	25			
Nonwhite { cases	47	15	14	55	—	+	—
controls	43	12	3	50			
Mental deficiency							
White { cases	35	12	16	46	+	—	—
controls	25	7	8	31			
Nonwhite { cases	59	18	7	65	+	—	—
controls	55	12	6	60			
Behavior disorders							
White { cases	33	6	10	39	—	—	—
controls	25	2	7	31			
Nonwhite { cases	64	17	14	73	—	—	—
controls	51	5	15	54			
Speech defects							
White only { cases	25	5	9	29	+?	—	—
controls	19	8	11	26			

+ Definite association;   +? suggestive association;   — no association.

which are summarized in Table 28, an association was demonstrated between certain maternal factors during pregnancy and the development of such disorders as cerebral palsy, epilepsy and mental deficiency in the offspring. This association fits into a reasonable biological framework since the mechanisms of such relationships are readily conceived. These same factors have been shown to produce anoxia in the fetus, and anoxia may result in damage to the brain, which, in turn, is logically related to the disorders mentioned. Consequently, the statistical association is readily aceptable as a causal hypothesis.

On the other hand, in the association of cigarette smoking and lung cancer, no direct links between cigarette smoking and cancer have been worked out. There is evidence indicating that environmental agents are important in the etiology of cancer, which does strengthen the hypothesis that cigarette smoking and lung cancer are causally related.[13] It has been shown recently that a relationship exists between cigarette smoking and cellular changes in the bronchial mucosa which are interpreted as being precancerous. It also seems more reasonable to accept cigarette smoking as a causal factor than the application of a certain ointment to one's feet or the ingestion of alcohol, since cigarette smoke does come into contact with the site where lung cancer develops. But the biological plausibility of this causal hypothesis is not of the same order as in the example of pregnancy factors and neuropsychiatric disorders.

There are historical instances in which a statistical association did not originally conform to existing biological concepts. As advances in knowledge changed the biological concepts, they were then found to be consistent with the previously observed association. The classic example of this is afforded by Snow's investigation of cholera in London in 1854.[19] Snow noted that two-thirds of the population living south of the Thames was served by both the Southwark and Vauxhall and the Lambeth water companies. The former company had its water intake in a grossly polluted part of the Thames, whereas the latter's intake was in a far less polluted section. As each company had its water mains laid throughout this area, some of the houses on the same street took their water from one and some from the other company. By a house-to-house investigation, Snow determined the source of the water supplied to each house in which a death from cholera had occurred during the first seven weeks of the epidemic. He then ascertained the total number of houses supplied by each water company and tabulated the rates, as shown in Table 29. Thus, Snow was able to show that in one area, one population group using a grossly polluted water supply had a cholera mortality about nine times that of the other, though they were the same kinds of people, living in the same area and often in adjacent houses.

Table 29. *Deaths from Cholera, per 10,000 Houses, by Source of Water Supply, London, 1859*[20]

WATER SUPPLY	NUMBER OF HOUSES	DEATHS FROM CHOLERA	DEATHS PER 10,000 HOUSES
Southwark and Vauxhall Company	40,046	1263	315
Lambeth Company	26,107	98	37
Other districts in London	256,423	1422	59

At that time, prior to the establishment of the germ theory of disease, the accepted etiologic hypothesis for cholera was the miasmatic theory. Snow's observations were not generally accepted since they did not conform to this theory. After the germ theory of disease was established, Snow's statistical association was accepted as consistent with the germ theory. Thus, the prevailing opinion was erroneous, whereas the inference made from the statistical association was not.

There also have been instances in which the statistical association was interpreted as consistent with existing biological concepts, but later the interpretation of the association was found to have been erroneous. This is exemplified by Farr's observation of an association between elevation of residence above sea level and cholera mortality in London[20]; his data for 1848 to 1849 are shown in Table 30. Farr noted that with increased elevation,

Table 30. *Deaths from Cholera in 10,000 Inhabitants, by Elevation of Residence above Sea Level, London, 1848 to 1849*[20]

ELEVATION ABOVE SEA LEVEL, IN FEET	DEATHS IN 10,000 INHABITANTS
Under 20	102
20-40	65
40-60	34
60-80	27
80-100	22
100-120	17
340-360	7

cholera mortality declined. This association was consistent with the miasmatic theory and was interpreted as confirmatory evidence. When the miasmatic theory was replaced by the germ theory, this association was still reasonable since elevation was, in turn, inversely associated with the etiologic factor, polluted water.

One other biological consideration is the role of animal experimentation. There is a widespread feeling that, if a statistical association is confirmed by an animal experiment, definite proof of a cause and effect relationship in humans is established. It is important to realize that extension of the results of animal experiments to human situations may be dangerous. If we are concerned with such disturbing influences as sampling and biological selection in human studies, we should be even more careful in drawing inferences from animal experiments. Admittedly, confirmation by animal experimentation increases the biological reasonableness of a causal inference. It also provides a model by which possible biological mechanisms may be elucidated, thereby indicating how and where such mechanisms might be investigated in humans. But, in interpreting results from animal experiments, it is important to distinguish between definitive proof and increased plausibility.

NONBIOLOGICAL CONSIDERATIONS

Certain nonbiological considerations may influence an individual's attitude toward acceptance of a causal inference. These concern the course of action to be taken when an inference is accepted. They reflect the outlook, background and administrative responsibilities of the individual. For example, a research scientist, without direct responsibility for the health of a population, might require a very high degree of plausibility before accepting a causal inference and recommending definite action. On the other hand, a health officer, directly responsible for the health of a population, may accept a lower degree of plausibility as sufficient to warrant preventive action. He may, therefore, accept a causal inference before it is proved when he thinks that it has a good chance of being correct.

Such considerations usually arise after the statistical association is established and before a causal relationship is proved. During this period, causal inferences are regarded with varying degrees of plausibility. It is helpful to consider the possible relationships between courses of action and degrees of plausibility, as follows. At the first level, the evidence is considered sufficiently suggestive to warrant further investigation. At the second level, the evidence is considered sufficient for recommending attempted preventive action. At the third level, the evidence is considered sufficient to state that a causal inference has been proved, and is included in our body of scientific knowledge.

In evaluating decision levels, it is important to keep in mind that action based on a statistical association could be successful even though it is interpreted incorrectly from a biological viewpoint. To illustrate this, we recall Farr's observation of decreasing cholera mortality with increasing elevation of residence above sea level.[21] If the health officer had recommended that people living in the lower-lying districts of London move to the higher districts, a decline in cholera mortality would probably have resulted, although the action would have been based on the erroneous miasmatic theory.

SUMMARY

Epidemiology is concerned with the study of the distribution of a disease or condition in a population and of the factors that influence this distribution. Such knowledge is useful for the following reasons:

1. It leads to the development of hypotheses concerning possible etiologic factors.

2. It permits testing of hypotheses developed in the clinic or laboratory.

3. It provides the scientific bases for measures to control the disease.

Epidemiologic studies provide data for deriving a series of statistical associations between a disease and various characteristics of the population. Such data are obtained from studies of the general population and of individual history data. From the pattern of these associations, biological inferences with respect to such items as etiology and modes of transmission of infectious diseases are derived.

Clearly, a large part of the epidemiologic method consists in determining statistical associations. This has led to the misconception that epidemiologic evidence is "merely statistical" in nature and qualitatively different from "biological evidence." Such a distinction is patently artificial. Our discussion has indicated that the strength of epidemiologic concepts and methods lies in their ability to integrate various sources of data into a biological concept of a specific disease as it occurs in humans. It is only by such an integration of clinical, laboratory and epidemiologic evidence that we can arrive at an understanding of human disease.

A. M. LILIENFELD, M.D.

REFERENCES

1. Parran, T.: Nationwide need—epidemiologists. Journal of the American Medical Association, *163*:742, March 2, 1957.
2. Epstein, F. H., Boas, E. P., and Simpson, R.: The epidemiology of atherosclerosis among a random sample of clothing workers of different ethnic origins in New York City. I. Prevalence of atherosclerosis and some associated characteristics. Journal of Chronic Diseases, *5*:300, March, 1957.
3. Holsti, L. R., and Ermala, P.: Papillary carcinoma of the bladder in mice obtained after peroral administration of tobacco tar. Cancer, *8*:679, July to August, 1955.
4. Lilienfeld, A. M., Levin, M. L., and Moore, G. E.: The association of smoking with cancer of the urinary bladder in humans. Archives of Internal Medicine, *98*:129, August, 1956.
5. Steinberg, A. G., and Wilder, R. M.: A study of the genetics of diabetes mellitus. American Journal of Human Genetics, *4*:113, June, 1952.
6. Doll, R.: Bronchial carcinoma: incidence and etiology. British Medical Journal, *2*:585, September 12, 1953.
7. Hammond, E. C.: Lung cancer and common inhalants. Cancer, *7*:1100, 1954.
8. Levin, M. L., Goldstein, H., and Gerhardt, P.: Cancer and tobacco smoking. A preliminary report. Journal of the American Medical Association, *143*:336, May 27, 1950.
9. Cutler, S. J.: A review of the statistical evidence on the association between smoking and lung cancer. Journal of the American Statistical Association, *50*:267, June, 1955.
10. Berkson, J.: Limitations of the application of fourfold table analysis to hospital data. Biometrics Bulletin, *2*:47, June, 1946.
11. Kraus, A. S.: The use of hospital data in studying the association between a characteristic and a disease. Public Health Reports, *69*:1211, December, 1954.
12. Morris, J. N.: Uses of Epidemiology. London, E. and S. Livingston, Ltd., 1957.
13. Smoking and Health, Report of the Advisory Committee to the Surgeon General of the U.S. Public Health Service. Washington 25, D.C., U.S. Public Health Service, 1964.
14. Dean, H. T., Arnold, F. A., Jr., and Elvove, E.: Domestic water and dental caries. V. Additional studies of the relation of fluoride in domestic waters to dental caries experience in 4,425 white children, aged 12 to 14 years, of 13 cities in four states. Public Health Reports, *57*:1155, August 7, 1942.
15. Ast, D. B., and Schlesinger, E. R.: The conclusion of a ten year study of water fluoridation. American Journal of Public Health, *46*:265, March, 1956.
16. Lilienfeld, A. M.: Selection of probands and controls. American Journal of Human Genetics, *6*:100, March, 1954.
17. Yates, F.: Sampling Methods for Censuses and Surveys. Ed. 2. New York, Hafner Publishing Company, 1953, pp. 327-332.
18. Lilienfeld, A. M., Pasamanick, B., and Roger, M.: Relationship between pregnancy experience and the development of certain neuropsychiatric disorders in childhood. American Journal of Public Health, *45*:637, May, 1955.
19. Snow, J.: On the Mode of Communication of Cholera. London, J. and A. Churchill, 1855.
20. Farr, W.: Vital Statistics. London, Office of the Sanitary Institute, 1885, pp. 341-351.

44   Voluntary Health Agencies

GENESIS AND GROWTH

With the blossoming of the bacteriological era during the last two decades of the ninetenth century an impatience developed at the delays in applying new scientific knowledge to the improvement of the health of people. This impatience was shared by lay and professional leaders, and one outcome was the development of voluntary health agencies. Thus, mechanisms grew up by which community resources could be mobilized to supplement individual and governmental efforts aimed at the conquest or amelioration of disease.

Few taxpayers really welcome their opportunity to provide health (or other) services; but many people happily give money, time, and effort to attack an illness which has directly touched them or their families. Such special concern has been translated by nonofficial health organizations into enthusiastic support for massive programs against specific diseases on local, state, and national dimensions.

The earliest voluntary health agency to be formed in the United States of America was not aimed at a single disease but at any emergency affecting people; it was the American Red Cross, established in 1881. It was the first to weld professional and other groups together in a national effort based on contributed funds.

In 1892 the Pennsylvania Society for Prevention of Tuberculosis blazed the trail for many single disease-centered agencies to follow. Its objectives established a pattern to be repeated over and over: public education, special services to the poor, support of official health departments and stimulation of appropriate disease control statutes. By 1904 several states had antituberculosis societies which later merged to form the National Tuberculosis Association.

Other early voluntary agencies in the health field included the American Cancer Society, the American Social Health Association, the National Society for Crippled Children and Adults, and the National Society for the Prevention of Blindness.

By the end of the fourth decade of the twentieth century only a dozen voluntary health organizations existed nationally. But this number was more than doubled during the forties (another thirteen), and during the fifties sixteen more were organized. Usually they start as local or state groups, later expanding and merging into nationwide associations. One notable exception was the National Foundation for Infantile Paralysis, later renamed the National Foundation, which was inspired at the national level with subsequent organization of local and state units.

The recent phenomenal rate of appearance of new agencies has caused a wave of criticism because of the difficulties arising from nearly continuous campaigns of one kind or another to seek out the philanthropic dollars. However, it cannot be denied that appealing to the special interests of individuals has resulted in much more substantial support for health services than could have been expected from state or federal taxes alone.

TYPES OF AGENCIES

A study of voluntary health and welfare agencies published in 1961 reported that more than 100,000 national, regional, and local agencies were soliciting contributions from the general public. Most of them fall into two types: the disease- or problem-centered and the health service-centered. Obviously, the categories are not mutually exclusive.

In the first group fall the majority of nonofficial health organizations. In addition to those already mentioned against tuberculosis, venereal disease, cancer, crippling conditions and blindness there are now societies concerned with alcoholism, allergy, arthritis, cerebral palsy, deafness, diabetes, epilepsy, heart disease, kidney disease, maternal health, mental health, multiple sclerosis, family planning, mental retardation, virus diseases and many others. Some of the less well known include organizations interested in Parkinson's disease, myasthenia gravis, muscular dystrophy, hemophilia and cystic fibrosis.

Nearly all of these agencies, in one degree or another, support research in their own fields, demonstrations of new approaches, education of the public and the professions as well as direct services to patients and their families.

In the second, more generalized service group fall health agencies like the Red Cross with its disaster-oriented services and blood bank resources; the Visiting Nursing Associations, which are usually local or regional in coverage; and some aspects of the programs of the United Service Organizations. Here the scope of helpful activities may be much broader than the disease-centered agencies. Frequently, too, more economic levels are served and both contributed and service fees are utilized.

There is also a third category of voluntary or nonofficial health agencies which is quite different from the other two. It is the professional organizations like the American Medical Association, American Nurses Association, American Dental Association, American Public Health Association and others. These groups do not rely on or seek funds from solicitation of the general public, although monies from foundations and private individuals may be used for special service projects having an impact on the public's health. In some instances, such as the National League for Nursing, these gifts may represent a major element of total expenditures. The public service element of these professional association programs may represent a significant force in determining community health practice.

Among the functions of these organizations made possible by mobilizing the resources of a profession are included the following: stimulation of improved preparation of workers within a particular discipline through scientific journals, by local and national meetings, by continuing education for their members; establishment of acceptable standards of practice and of personnel training; encouragement of modern legislation at local, state, and federal levels as public health knowledge and resources improve. In addition, efforts are made to gain more recognition for the profession, better understanding of its contributions and appropriate rewards for its accomplishments.

Major financial support for the professional societies in the health field comes from individual membership dues and fees from agencies that benefit directly (as in the American Hospital Association).

FUNCTIONS

Several major objectives have been mentioned in discussing the genesis and growth of voluntary health agencies. As they have developed, as health problems have changed and resources to meet them have improved, the health agencies have also changed their roles. Hamlin[4] suggests the following functions:

1. Determine new methods to improve the health and welfare of the American people.

2. Demonstrate practical means by which these improvements may be made by both governmental and voluntary agencies.

3. Inform the general public and the professions.

4. Supplement government programs with personnel, facilities and service.

5. Protect the public interest by working for effective government agencies.

6. Develop comprehensive, balanced community health and welfare programs.

7. Promote and maintain legislation in the public interest.

8. Support research into the causes of disease, deprivation, and inadequate services.

Another way of describing voluntary agencies in the health field is suggested by the National Health Council[6] under five headings: humanizing, balancing, sustaining, stimulating and initiating. These agencies also provide an outlet for expressing personal concern by participants who give their help.

Perhaps the most important function of voluntary health agencies is to provide a communications link between practicing members of the health professions and the laity. Working together on committees or boards on community-centered problems creates an atmosphere of understanding and common interest which frequently leads to much more sympathetic interpersonal relations.

Similarly, community lay leaders and professional leaders are brought together with official health department workers through the medium of voluntary health agency activities; here, too, better understanding and relationships result.

Since 1921 the National Health Council has brought together most of the health agencies: official and voluntary, disease centered, service and professional. In 1941 it sponsored, and the Rockefeller Foundation financed, a nationwide study of the effectiveness of voluntary health work, which is summarized in the Gunn-Platt report.[2] This deplored a lack of central direction and planning as well as considerable duplication and overlapping of effort.

With the pronounced upswing of numbers of agencies since that time, a second study was found necessary in 1960. It was carried out by Hamlin under the direction of an ad hoc advisory committee, with financing again from the Rockefeller Foundation. Five recommendations resulted:[4]

1. Stronger voluntary agency leadership.
2. Higher standards for local affiliates.
3. Increased participation in organized planning.
4. Better reporting of programs and accomplishments.
5. Greater emphasis on research and the application of new knowledge.

The National Health Council, aware of the criticism of ever-increasing numbers of agencies, has suggested a number of criteria for consideration before a new national health organization is established:[6]

1. Is the problem national in scope?
2. Is it likely to be affected by community action apart from governmental action?
3. Is the required action sufficiently intensive and widespread to justify national action?
4. Can the action not be achieved as well by an existing agency?
5. Is necessary professional direction available?
6. Is the need a long term one?
7. Is the proposed organizational structure sound?

When all of these questions can be answered satisfactorily, a reasonable base exists for considering a new agency.

Some years ago Homer Folks, in discussing Democracy and Welfare, said,[3] ". . . it is self evident that democratic government will be as safe, as permanent, as effective, as the majority of its sovereign citizens are intelligent, informed, resourceful, patient, but not too patient, alive to the interests of others as well as of themselves." In the field of public health greater participation by citizens in the voluntary health agencies will greatly enhance their preparation for community leadership.

FINANCING

Contributed funds for voluntary agencies (other than professional societies) having a primary interest in health increased nearly tenfold during the decade 1940 to 1950, from $38 million to $360 million. In the succeeding decade these funds passed the half billion mark, and it has been estimated that by 1970 the billion dollar level may be reached.

About 85 per cent of this money comes from individual contributors by way of door-to-door canvassing, special "benefit" events, mail solicitation or in-plant collections; the remaining 15 per cent comes from bequests and corporate gifts.

The multiplicity of fund raising campaigns in local communities has given rise to attempts at consolidation through Community Chest or Federated or United Fund drives. Although having the advantage of simplicity and lowered costs of solicitation, these combined efforts lose some of the impact of personal interest, enthusiasm and emotional involvement. In 1960 there were more than 2000 combined drives raising funds for over 26,000 local and national agencies; in 1939 there were only 549 such joint appeals.

Since 1961 a new source of support has been made available to all health agencies for demonstration projects serving the aged and chronically ill. The Community Health Services and Facilities Act provides federal funds for this purpose to voluntary as well as official health agencies.

There has been a reversal of the pattern of support for medical and health related research. In 1940 the federal government provided only 7 per cent and 38 per cent came from philanthropic sources; in 1960 over 53 per cent came from federal agencies and only 12 per cent from private donors.

The influence of special pleading by groups like the American Cancer Society, the American Heart Association and the National Association for Mental Health on federal research and service programs in those fields is great. Much of the rapid growth of the National Institutes of Health can be directly related to organized support for increased appropriations by their counterpart nonofficial agencies.

In 1960 the five leading health fund drives netted over $200 million, distributed as follows:

American Red Cross	$95.97 million
American Cancer Society	$34.47 "
National Foundation	$32.69 "
National Tuberculosis Association	$29.80 "
American Heart Association	$27.76 "

Distribution and dispensing of these funds vary considerably. From 6 to 75 per cent may flow from local collection points into a national program. The Hamlin study of 56 national health agencies' expenditures patterns showed 31.6 per cent going to services to patients, professionals and the public; 16.6 per cent to organizational expenses and fund raising; 16.1 per cent to professional training and research; 7.7 per cent to public and professional information; and the remaining 28 per cent to all other purposes.

There is growing acceptance of the concept that use of voluntarily contributed monies solicited from the public merits the same degree of accountability as do tax expenditures. In New York State the Charities Registration Bureau of the State Department of Social Welfare annually collects information from over 3000 organizations soliciting funds within the state. The National Information Bureau provides a similar central clearing house for income and expenditure data among voluntary agencies on a nationwide basis.

ORGANIZATION

The typical organization of a national voluntary health agency consists of a governing body, usually called a board of directors; an executive committee; and an executive director and professional staff. The board of directors is quite frequently adorned with well-known personalities from industry, the arts or professions. Other agencies prefer their boards to be represented by leading persons in the medical specialty concerned and with persons who represent geographic areas. The board usually meets once or twice a year to determine major policies, while its smaller executive committee meets more frequently and conducts most of the organization's business by itself or through an executive. Many such boards are advised by special committees on matters of finance, public relations and technical problems.

The relationship between the national and local units may be cumbersome as several have more than 3000 state, regional and local components. Usually standards of local program performance are established by the national organization with contractual arrangements with local chapters. These are reviewed and revised annually.

The Visiting Nursing Associations are exceptions, with more local autonomy preserved under a local board and professional advisory committee.

Some national health agencies, like the American Diabetes Association, are almost entirely professional in composition. Others have a preponderance of lay members, e.g., the National Foundation. Others, like the National Tuberculosis Association have a separate, closely related professional organization (the American Thoracic Society) apart from its lay and volunteer membership.

In general, the greater the agency's emphasis on personal service, the more money is retained at the local level, with relatively greater local determination of how it is to be spent; where the emphasis is on research and national programs of education or legislation the reverse is usually true.

The maximum impact of voluntary health agencies on community health problems is achieved when inspired medical leadership from well-informed physicians is coupled with extensive and enthusiastic volunteer participation by interested laymen. The latter group becomes informed about one aspect of health work in terms of local problems and resources to meet them. This provides a nucleus of understanding and sympathy among community leaders which may favorably affect other health programs as well.

Trained leaders from the medical and allied health professions are vital to the community's well-being. Second only to this is the need for well-trained professional staff in the voluntary agencies themselves. Both recruitment into the voluntary health field and adequate training programs are far behind present demands. Opportunities for productive and satisfying careers are many and varied.

BERWYN F. MATTISON, M.D.

REFERENCES

1. Carter, Richard: The Gentle Legions. Garden City, New York, Doubleday and Co., Inc., 1961.
2. Gunn, S. M., and Platt, P. S.: Voluntary Agencies: An Interpretative Study. New York, The Ronald Press, 1945.
3. Folks, Homer: Public Health and Welfare. Selected Papers. New York, The Macmillan Co., 1958.
4. Hamlin, Robert H.: Voluntary Health and Welfare Agencies in the United States. New York, Schoolmaster's Press, 1961.
5. Rosen, George: A History of Public Health. New York, M. D. Publications, Inc., 1958.
6. The National Health Council: Voluntaryism and Health. 1790 Broadway, New York, 1962.

45 Official Health Agencies

The health of the citizens is recognized in the United States as a proper concern of government. This concept is based on historical tradition that has been strengthened over the years by the accomplishments of official health units. It parallels government attitudes in almost all developed nations and an increasing number of the developing nations. It is reflected in the existence of a vast network of public health organizations, ranging from small departments in rural areas to the extensive concerns of the World Health Organization of the United Nations.

The growing need for competent personnel to serve in public health organizations is recognized throughout the medical profession. There is great demand, and equal opportunity, for physicians trained in full-time work in preventive medicine, and for specially trained engineers, nurses, social workers, radiation experts and others. The public health requirements of an increasingly complex world have assumed a breadth and diversity that continues to extend in scope.

Public health work attracts the physician who finds personal reward in ministering to the health requirements of persons on a group basis. In a sense, he is a specialized practitioner with the total community as a patient. He is paced to the dynamics of medical science, for each preventive weapon forged by medical research is quickly seized and committed to use in the war against disease and debility.

Financial rewards for health workers have kept pace, in the main, with the increasing value that modern society places on optimum health and the esthetic worth of a favorable environment. The public has demanded more and better health services, and has gotten them. Few legislators choose to go against this strong current of public interest; elected officials quickly sense the will of their constituents and take appropriate action.

A broadening concept has changed the character of public health work so its identity today differs from that of only a few decades ago. Earlier, the founding units dealt primarily with epidemic control through quarantine and other forms of isolation. As medical knowledge expanded, public health activities launched into new directions—immunization, public health nursing, health education, maternal and child health, and others. This growth continues and the end of public health activity is far from sight, for each new medical advance finds its unique application within the framework of public health.

This growth-in-function has extended public health into the environment of its collective patient, the citizenry. As knowledge about the sources and modes of infection increased, public health workers acted to control all known environmental conditions that bred disease or encouraged debilitation. Today this public health philosophy embraces human life from preconception to death; it considers the total environment of land, water and air; it includes all ways of life—urban, suburban and rural; it ignores no disease or condition antithetical to human welfare; its area of concern embraces the entire world. Space medicine now is tearing down the final boundary for the specialist in preventive medicine. This extension of public health activity offers unique opportunities to physicians interested in every medical specialty, as part-time or full-time participants in the continuing battle to improve the health of all people.

The public health responsibility is pursued by both official and voluntary organizations. Official organizations, which will be discussed in this chapter, are a part of government, either at the international, federal, state or local levels, and they are supported by tax funds. Voluntary agencies are operated by citizens groups, and they are supported by money from fund-raising and other private sources. (See Chapter 44.)

INTERNATIONAL HEALTH ORGANIZATIONS

The World Health Organization

The functions and goal of the World Health Organization (WHO) are far more inclusive than were those of the international health groups that preceded it. The recognition that disease is no respecter of man-made boundary lines was manifested from ancient times when lepers were shunned and isolated wherever they traveled. Some beginnings in organized cooperation in meeting health problems were made in 1831 when the Egyptian Quarantine Board was established at Alexandria to prevent the spread of the "plague diseases" by mercantile contacts between nations. Various nations were represented on this board and its successor, which was dissolved in 1923 when the League of Nations' Health Commission was founded. The League's Health Commission, even with its small staff, accomplished good work in maintaining worldwide epidemiologic intelligence and helping national health services. WHO was born on April 7, 1948, as a specialized agency of the United Nations (UN). A nation may retain membership in WHO without being a member of the UN. WHO's organization includes the following:

The World Health Assembly. This is comprised of delegates from 124 member nations (December, 1964) and meets once a year. Each member nation may have three delegates but has only one vote.

The Executive Board. This consists of 24 persons designated by as many members. The Health Assembly, taking into account an equitable geographical distribution, elects the members entitled to designate a person to serve on the Board. It meets twice a year to give effect to the decisions and policies of the Health Assembly and acts as the executive organ of the Health Assembly.

The Secretariat. This carries out the administrative job under the direction of a director general who is nominated by the Executive Board and appointed by the Assembly.

In addition, there are various panel groups which investigate special health problems from time to time. Headquarters of WHO is in Geneva, Switzerland, and various sectors of the world are served by six regional offices at Copenhagen, Denmark; Washington, D.C.; Alexandria, United Arab Republic; New Delhi, India; Brazzaville, Congo; and Manila, Philippines.

The purposes of WHO are:

1. To assist governments, upon request, in strengthening health services.

2. To furnish appropriate technical assistance and, in emergencies, necessary aid upon the request or acceptance of governments.

3. To promote, in cooperation with other specialized agencies when necessary, the improvement of nutrition, housing, sanitation, recreation, economic or working conditions and other aspects of environmental hygiene.

4. To establish and revise as necessary international nomenclatures of diseases, of causes of death and of public health practices.

5. To standardize diagnostic procedures as necessary.

6. To develop, establish and promote international standards with respect to food, biological, pharmaceutical and similar products.

7. To promote and conduct research in the field of health.

8. To promote improved standards of teaching and training in the health, medical and related professions.

9. To study and report on, in cooperation with other specialized agencies when necessary, administrative and social techniques affecting public health and medical care from preventive and curative points of view, including hospital services and social security.

The United Nations International Children's Fund (UNICEF)

The United Nations International Children's Fund (UNICEF) was established by the United Nations General Assembly on December 11, 1946. Its purpose is to help developing countries improve the living conditions of their children and youth. UNICEF aids country projects, preferably forming part of the national program of development. In its broad approach to the health and welfare problems of children, UNICEF works closely with the United Nations FAO, ILO, UNESCO, WHO and the UN Department of Economic and Social Affairs. UNICEF assists a country only on request of the government.

UNICEF provides assistance in such fields as health, nutrition, social welfare, education and vocational training. It also helps governments to assess the principal needs of their children and plan comprehensive programs to meet them. UNICEF is helping projects for children in over 110 countries of Africa, Asia, Europe, the Americas and the Eastern Mediterranean area.

A large part of UNICEF aid takes the form of equipment and supplies; for example, health center equipment, drugs, well drilling rigs, dairy plant equipment, school garden supplies, prototype equipment for day care centers, equipment for production of textbooks, workshop equipment for vocational training, vehicles and bicycles. UNICEF provides assistance for all levels of training, from the simplest form of practical training for auxiliary workers in disease control campaigns to postgraduate studies.

Pan American Sanitary Bureau

The Pan American Sanitary Bureau, with headquarters in Washington, D.C., is the oldest international health body in the world and was organized by the Republics of America in 1902. It is the operating arm of the Pan American Health Organization, whose membership includes the 23 American governments, and France, The Netherlands and the United Kingdom on behalf of their American departments and territories. The Pan American Sanitary Bureau serves as the regional office of the World Health Organization in the Americas.

The Bureau coordinates international health programs in the Americas and assists national health administrations in eradicating communicable diseases, strengthening national public health services and training vitally needed physicians, nurses, engineers and other health personnel.

In the treaty ratified by the then existing 21 republics in 1924, the functions of the Bureau are as follows:

It appoints representatives to confer with the health authorities of the various signatory governments; receives, publishes and distributes information on vital statistics, public health organization, preventive medicine and other pertinent information; undertakes cooperative epidemiologic studies; stimulates and facilitates scientific research; brings about exchanges of professors, medical and health officers, experts and advisers in public health; and provides technical information relative to the actual status of communicable diseases, the progress effected in the control or eradication of such diseases and new methods for combating them.

In carrying out its tasks, the Pan American Sanitary Bureau works in close harmony with and receives funds from a number of other organizations, including the United Nations International Children's Fund (UNICEF), the Agency for International Development (A.I.D.) and the Organization of American States (OAS).

The Agency for International Development

Since 1949 a succession of federal agencies have been concerned with furnishing foreign aid from the United States to free countries. This aid has taken the form of economic, military, and technical assistance, and has included medical services in public health. In 1961 the Agency for International Development (A.I.D.) was established in the Department of State, as a semiautonomous combined agency to distribute funds under the Foreign Assistance Act.

A.I.D.'s appropriation for health and sanitation activities, totaling approximately 59 million dollars in 1965, will cover a wide range of public health activity. A staff of some 279 professionals, including 36 physicians, will carry on studies, training and demonstrations in 53 countries. Special emphasis of the A.I.D health program is placed on malaria eradication, sanitation, water supply, training programs, population dynamics, research. U. S. universities contract for health services in overseas medical schools and hospitals under A.I.D. auspices. Over half the positions in the A.I.D. health program are occupied by U.S. Public Health Service officers. This is a For-

eign Service operation of magnitude and importance in the broad field of
preventive medicine in public health.

HEALTH AGENCIES OF THE UNITED STATES GOVERNMENT

The primary public health activities of the federal government are
conducted by the Department of Health, Education, and Welfare, which
was established in 1953. Below is the organization of the Department, including the units that have direct concern for public health:

1. Public Health Service
     Office of the Surgeon General
         National Center for Health Statistics
     Bureau of Medical Services
         Freedman's Hospital
     Bureau of State Services
     National Institutes of Health
     National Library of Medicine
2. Welfare Administration
     Children's Bureau
     Office of Aging
     Office of Juvenile Delinquency and Youth Development
     Bureau of Family Services
3. Office of Education
4. Vocational Rehabilitation Administration
5. Saint Elizabeth's Hospital (for mentally ill)
6. Food and Drug Administration
7. Social Security Administration

The United States Public Health Service

The United States Public Health Service was established in 1798 and
serves as the principal public health agency of the federal government. Its
main subdivisions divide the public health role in the following manner:

Office of the Surgeon General. This bureau is comprised mainly of
staff services for the three operating bureaus. Its various offices assist in
(1) providing leadership in the development of policies for the management
of the Services; (2) making studies of national health problems and planning health programs; (3) planning civil defense and other health emergency
activities; (4) advising mobilization agencies on estimated civilian needs
of medical supplies, equipment and facilities; (5) providing health statistics
and studying the needs of health professions; (6) coordinating the international aspects of Service programs; (7) directing and coordinating the
Service's information, publications and public inquiry programs; and (8)
providing certain administrative services on a centralized basis.

Bureau of Medical Services. This bureau administers hospital and
outpatient care to federal beneficiaries. It operates 15 hospitals, 25 outpatient
clinics and 117 outpatient offices where seamen employed on vessels of
United States registry, Coast Guard personnel and other legal beneficiaries
receive treatment and preventive care for their medical and dental needs.
This bureau administers medical and related facilities and services for
Indians, including 50 hospitals. The bureau enforces foreign quarantine regu-

lations covering sea, land and air traffic. It conducts medical examinations abroad of prospective immigrants to this country. It maintains surveillance of crews and passengers arriving at seaports, airports and border stations in the United States through 51 major domestic and 16 medical examination units overseas. Finally, it furnishes technical advice and assigns personnel to other federal agencies that provide medical care for their employees and other beneficiaries.

Bureau of State Services. Through grants-in-aid, consultation services and technical assistance, this bureau assists states in the application of knowledge to prevent and control disease, maintain a healthful environment and develop community health services. The bureau has programs in the following areas: accident prevention, chronic disease, communicable disease, community health services, dental public health and resources, hospital and medical facilities, nursing, air pollution, environmental engineering and food protection, occupational health, radiological health, and water supply and pollution control.

National Institutes of Health. This bureau is the principal research arm of the Public Health Service. It is concerned primarily with the extension of basic knowledge regarding health problems and how to cope with them. Its various institutes conduct fundamental research in causes, prevention and methods of diagnosis in the fields of cancer, heart and circulatory diseases, allergy and infectious diseases, arthritis and metabolic diseases, dental diseases and conditions, mental illness, neurological diseases and blindness, child health and human development, and general medical sciences. Other functions include the regulation of biologic products and interstate sale of serums, toxins, vaccines and human blood products used in treating disease, support for the construction or renovation of research facilities, and research, fellowship and training grants to private researchers and institutions. The Service provides grants-in-aid for research to individuals and institutions throughout the United States. It currently supports about 40 per cent of the total medical research in this country.

The Children's Bureau

This bureau, an arm of the Welfare Administration, investigates and reports on all matters related to child life, and works to promote the physical, social, economic and mental well-being of children. Under the provisions of the Social Security Act, it administers grants-in-aid to states for maternal and child health and crippled children's services, and it provides grants directly to localities and institutions for special projects in maternity and infant care, for training in maternal and child health and for program oriented research. It cooperates with other American republics in scientific and cultural matters. The bureau also gives special attention to four groups of children: juvenile delinquents, children of migratory workers, mentally retarded children and children in unprotected adoptions.

Other Federal Agencies in Health Work

A number of other federal agencies also minister to the health needs of citizens, either directly or indirectly. The Medical Corps of the Army, Navy and Air Force and the Veteran's Administration primarily are concerned with the health needs of present or past members of the armed services. Significant contributions are made to public health by the Food and Drug Administration and the Vocational Rehabilitation Administration, both in the Department of Health, Education, and Welfare, and the Bureau of Census in the Department of Commerce.

STATE AND TERRITORIAL HEALTH DEPARTMENTS

The safeguarding of public health is an official responsibility in every state in the United States and in the commonwealth of Puerto Rico, and the territories of the Virgin Islands and Guam. This responsibility is established in the state or territorial constitution, or through enabling legislation. It is translated to intent by codes and regulations governing the health department. It is propelled to action by the department's system of health services and enforcement.

The state is sovereign in its relationship to its municipalities; local governments and their health departments have only powers that have been granted by the state. Except in interstate matters, such as quarantine, the federal government's municipal powers also are limited to those granted by the state.

A state health department normally has the power to move into a municipality and administer any or all health activities when it judges local action to be inadequate. This sovereign option is rarely exercised, but it is a determinant in shaping the state-municipal relationship.

The state health department generally provides indirect services to the public by assisting and advising local health units in districts, counties, cities or townships. In many states, the department also gives a variety of direct services.

The organization of a state health department usually includes:

State Board of Health

Many boards have from 5 to 7 members who serve part-time, generally without pay. They are appointed by the governor, and at least some are physicians. They determine general health policies and advise the state health department.

State Health Officer

He is a physician with administrative skills and special training who serves as a full-time salaried leader of the state health department. He usually is appointed by the governor, and his period of appointment often differs from the gubernatorial term. This is designed to free the post from possible political intervention.

Administrative Divisions or Bureaus

The operating units of a state health department usually include:
1. Communicable disease control.
2. Maternal and child health.
3. Public health laboratories.
4. Environmental control.
5. Vital statistics.
6. Public health nursing.

7. Health education.

8. Local health services.

Many state health departments also maintain units for dental hygiene, mental hygiene, industrial hygiene and research. The rising problem of chronic disease, and its relationship to an aging population, is leading to the more frequent establishment of units for chronic disease and medical care services.

The activities of a state health department's units are (1) to advise local health departments, (2) to provide direct services in local communities, and (3) to cooperate with the federal government, other states, other state departments, medical organizations and voluntary health agencies.

Its advisory services to local health departments may include assistance in selecting qualified personnel, long and short term planning, epidemiological studies, supervision of field services and similar activities.

Direct services may include vital statistics, laboratory tests, sanitary engineering services, health education, professional training, epidemic control, and the operation of hospitals for tuberculosis, crippled children, mental health or cancer.

An increasing number of state health departments conduct research programs related to the various diseases for which they bear responsibility for control.

The state health department joins with other states and the federal government in promoting health programs that require cooperative action. These activities range from federal grants-in-aid to a variety of interstate conferences on public health matters.

The size of a state health department is determined largely by the population and wealth of a state. As an example, the New York State Health Department in 1964 operated on a $101 million budget, employed 4400 persons, maintained 3 tuberculosis hospitals and a medical rehabilitation hospital, and conducted an extensive research program, including the operation of a cancer research hospital.

LOCAL HEALTH DEPARTMENTS

The local health department carries the front-line responsibility for protecting the health of the community. The department can be a branch of the county, city, town or village government, or of some combination of these governments. In many respects, the department's organization parallels that of a state health department. It usually has a board of health (nonsalaried, advisory and policy setting), a health officer (usually appointed by the chief electoral executive in local government), and administrative divisions (with civil service or non-civil service staffs, or combinations).

Functions

The activities of a local health department are determined largely by the socioeconomic pattern of the area and by the balance of its rural, industrial, urban or suburban elements. These activities may include:

1. Prevention and control of communicable disease.

2. Supervision of water supply and waste disposal systems.

3. Inspection of milk production and processing.

4. Supervision of food preparation for the public.

5. Inspection of health conditions in industry and commerce.

6. Public health education.

7. School health services, including health supervision and physical examinations.

8. Vital statistics.

9. Public health nursing.

10. Operation of disease-detection clinics; conduct of immunization campaigns.

11. Laboratory services to aid private physicians in diagnosis.

12. Investigation of health-hazard complaints.

13. Advice on local legislation related to health matters.

14. Control of air pollution sources.

15. Inspection of radiation hazards.

16. Consultation on health matters with other units of government.

RESPONSIBILITIES OF PHYSICIANS IN HEALTH AGENCIES

The physician with interest in preventive medicine can find an important place in the work of an official or voluntary health organization.

If he is in private practice, he can serve as a consultant on a medical advisory committee or as a part-time clinician. His knowledge can make him a valuable member of a voluntary association's board of directors or of an official agency's board of health. Time given to such activities benefits the community, brings credit to the medical profession and increases respect for the individual.

Official and voluntary health organizations offer broad opportunities for physicians with interest in the full-time practice of preventive medicine. The World Health Organization and our State Department's Agency for International Development need physicians in all parts of the world. State and local health departments and voluntary health associations offer a variety of opportunities in preventive medicine, clinical practice and public health.

The problems of preventive medicine become public health problems when their solution calls for organized community action. The public health physician understands this. He recognizes the importance of the family doctor in preventive medicine. He knows that his own job is to supplement and enhance the work of the private physician.

A major responsibility of official and voluntary health organizations is to heighten public awareness of the preventive services offered by private physicians. An example is the annual physical examination. Private practitioners, working through their medical societies, in turn support the public health aspects of preventive medicine. This is accomplished through the endorsement of pending legislation, the conduct of joint studies and other activities. The broadening area of shared responsibility in protecting community health is increasingly recognized by official and voluntary health agencies and professional organizations.

HOLLIS S. INGRAHAM, M.D.
HERMAN E. HILLEBOE, M.D.

INDEX